Propaganda and Culture in Mao's China

Studies on Contemporary China

The Contemporary China Institute at the School of Oriental and African Studies (University of London) has, since its establishment in 1968, been an international centre for research and publications on twentieth-century China. *Studies on Contemporary China*, which is sponsored by the Institute, seeks to maintain and extend that tradition by making available the best work of scholars and China specialists throughout the world. It embraces a wide variety of subjects relating to Nationalist and Communist China, including social, political, and economic change, intellectual and cultural developments, foreign relations, and national security.

Editorial Advisory Board
Dr R. F. Ash
Mr B. G. Hook
Professor C. B. Howe
Professor Bonnie S. McDougall
Dr David Shambaugh
Professor Lynn T. White III
Dr Jonathan Unger

Volumes in the Series
Art and Ideology in Revolutionary China, *David Holm*
Economic Trends in Chinese Agriculture, *Y. Y. Kueh and R. F. Ash*
In Praise of Maoist Economic Planning, *Chris Bramall*
Chinese Foreign Policy: Theory and Practice, *edited by Thomas W. Robinson and David Shambaugh*
Economic Reform and State-Owned Enterprises in China 1979–1987, *Donald A. Hay, Derek J. Morris, Guy Liu, and Shujie Yao*
Rural China in Transition, *Samuel P. S. Ho*
Agricultural Instability in China 1931–1990, *Y. Y. Kueh*
Deng Xiaoping: Portrait of a Chinese Statesman, *edited by David Shambaugh*
Greater China: The Next Superpower?, *edited by David Shambaugh*
The Chinese Economy under Deng Xiaoping, *edited by R. F. Ash and Y. Y. Kueh*
China and Japan, *edited by Christopher Howe*
The Individual and the State in China, *edited by Brian Hook*
China's Legal Reforms, *edited by Stanley Lubman*
China's Economic Transition, *edited by Andrew Walder*

Propaganda and Culture in Mao's China

Deng Tuo and the Intelligentsia

by

TIMOTHY CHEEK

CLARENDON PRESS · OXFORD

This book has been printed digitally and produced in a standard specification in order to ensure its continuing availability

OXFORD
UNIVERSITY PRESS

Great Clarendon Street, Oxford OX2 6DP

Oxford University Press is a department of the University of Oxford.
It furthers the University's objective of excellence in research, scholarship,
and education by publishing world-wide in

Oxford New York

Auckland Bangkok Buenos Aires Cape Town Chennai
Dar es Salaam Delhi Hong Kong Istanbul Karachi Kolkata
Kuala Lumpur Madrid Melbourne Mexico City Mumbai Nairobi
São Paulo Shanghai Taipei Tokyo Toronto

Oxford is a registered trade mark of Oxford University Press
in the UK and in certain other countries

Published in the United States
by Oxford University Press Inc., New York

© Timothy Cheek 1997

The moral rights of the author have been asserted
Database right Oxford University Press (maker)

Reprinted 2004

All rights reserved. No part of this publication may be reproduced,
stored in a retrieval system, or transmitted, in any form or by any means,
without the prior permission in writing of Oxford University Press,
or as expressly permitted by law, or under terms agreed with the appropriate
reprographics rights organization. Enquiries concerning reproduction
outside the scope of the above should be sent to the Rights Department,
Oxford University Press, at the address above

You must not circulate this book in any other binding or cover
And you must impose this same condition on any acquirer

ISBN 978-0-19-829066-7

Cover photography:

Deng Tuo, 1956 (informal photo, courtesy of Ding Yilan).

Preface

A greying man sat at the table beneath the portrait of the honoured scholar-official. He read a poem, intoning it emotionally. The congregation of friends, colleagues, and relatives gathered in the courtyard of a traditional Chinese family compound nestled in the foothills of Fuzhou listened intently. It was May 1986. The meeting was a poetry conclave following an academic forum. Poems in local dialect, in the *shi* style of the Tang dynasty, the *ci* style of the Song, and freer modern verse echoed over the PA system and around the walls. There sheets of calligraphy honoured the departed literatus. The ageing official finished his memorial poem:

> *Injustice so deep, Resentment so profound,*
> *These stains of Blood and Tears have brought green again*
>   *to our Divine Land;*
> *Generations beyond number will revere you—a martyr and a sage.*[1]

'Thank you, Hu Jiwei,' the master of ceremonies said.

Hu Jiwei. Observers of contemporary China do not think of Mr Hu as a classical-style poet. Hu Jiwei is a former editor of *People's Daily*, better known during the 1980s for his courageous campaign for press and propaganda liberalization.[2] As a leading delegate to China's National People's Congress Hu became an active reformer around the popular protests of 1989. What link is there between Hu Jiwei, propaganda, reform, and this strikingly traditional style of scholarly display? The link is represented by the subject of Hu's poem and of this biography: Deng Tuo.

The 1986 symposium and poetry meeting commemorated Deng Tuo, who died under criticism in 1966 at the start of the Cultural Revolution. The poetry meeting serves to show that the elements that made up Deng's life are still at play in the People's Republic of China (PRC) today. Intellectual service occurs mainly through service to the Chinese Communist Party (CCP). Propaganda is a principal avenue of that service. The intellectuals who serve the Party-State maintain a strong group identity, and for some that identity is bound to the expression of a scholarly style that appears surprisingly traditional. How these variables will mix in the future is not the topic of this book.[3] Where they came from is. Deng Tuo's life illustrates an experience of intellectual service in Mao's China that not only contributes to our understanding of the rise, successes, and major crises of Chinese Marxism in the twentieth century but also introduces us to the world that produced Hu Jiwei and the current generation of intellectual leaders in China.[4]

That experience of intellectual service in Mao's China revolved around propaganda and culture. To Western readers 'propaganda' may not sound like an honourable vocation for the intelligentsia. In Mao's China, for a time, it was. Nevertheless, many Chinese intellectuals in the CCP continued to define themselves culturally—by their command of the written language, China's aesthetic and literary heritage, and the defining skills of literary composition, criticism, and calligraphy or painting. Propaganda and culture capture the central themes of this biography as the central tension between the *social roles* of the intelligentsia as Party functionaries and as political theorists and the *ideological stances* of faith Maoism and bureaucratic Maoism. Propaganda was the core of Deng Tuo's intellectual service, and culture defined his intellectual identity. He was both servant and savant. These naturally incompatible elements worked for China's intelligentsia in the 1940s and did not in the 1960s. Deng Tuo's story traces the rise and fall of this remarkable form of intellectual participation in public affairs under Mao—a trajectory that parallels the rise and fall of Maoism itself.

Deng Tuo's life ended in tragedy. Both he and his surviving colleagues have used traditional images from Chinese culture to make sense of his career. Deng served Mao and was dismissed by Mao. Tension between minister and ruler has existed since the Han dynasty (3rd c. BCE); it has been enshrined in the earlier ritual suicide of the spurned minister, Qu Yuan (338–278 BCE). Deng Tuo was a loyal Communist; he was driven to ritual suicide by those he served. Deng's story fits the Confucian trope of Qu Yuan, the tragic rejection of a loyal minister by a foolish ruler.[5] Hu Jiwei's poem invokes that identity.

From a broader view, which this biography seeks to inform, Deng's life and death contribute to our understanding of the changing role of the intelligentsia in China and the reasons for the self-destruction of Maoism. Deng Tuo served as a generalist savant in a cosmocratic state that claimed to divine the movements of history. He was a veritable priest to his proletarian flock. That charismatic role in the public arena shattered in the Cultural Revolution and with it the priestly calling of the Maoist cadre. The honourable vocation Deng Tuo discovered in the hills of Shanxi as a Party propagandist in the 1940s is now in pieces; today the intelligentsia eschew Maoist rhetoric and seek employment in a distinctly uncharismatic bureaucracy or an emerging commercial sector. We shall see, in the pages to follow, how that vocation collapsed and what resources it has left for China's intelligentsia today.

Preface vii

Equally, the world-mastering ideology, Maoism, that brought China together at mid-century and led her to the beginnings of wealth and power in the 1950s has shattered. Most people familiar with China in the 1990s know that Maoism, or Chinese Communist ideology, holds little prestige among the intelligentsia or general public. Maoism, however, was precious to Deng Tuo, and to many who served with him. It was science, it was profound political philosophy, it was the answer to China's problems. We shall see what this vision of Maoism to which Deng Tuo dedicated his life was like and why it failed in its promises. Recalling this historical reality is a useful reminder as we view China today, rudderless, without a public moral code. For it is from the pieces of Deng Tuo's vocation and beliefs that a new social role and ideological stance for China's intelligentsia will have to be constructed.

In his poem Hu Jiwei was seeking to revive something of that vision, trying to inherit critically, through the example of Deng Tuo, the positive aspects of Maoism that might serve the politically secular society in China today. By the end of this story we should be able to understand more fully the meaning Hu Jiwei was giving to Deng Tuo's life and the help he was seeking from his spirit for China in the twenty-first century.

NOTES

1. Hu Jiwei (1986). The translation is of the last line of the poem, 'Chang xiang si: "Yi Deng Tuo"' (Long-Held Thoughts: Commemorating Deng Tuo), found on p. 50. In a fashion usual for such commemorative poetry, Hu's poem evokes language from one of Deng Tuo's most famous poems on a similar theme. 'These stains of Blood and Tears' (*xue lei banban*) echoes the 'When blood stains where . . .' (*xue banban*) from Deng's 1960 paean to Gao Panlong, the martyr of the late Ming Eastern Wood party. This is discussed in detail below in Ch. 4. I have translated *xianshi* (the honourific reference to one's late teacher and standard reference to Confucius himself) as 'martyr and sage' in the context of the full poem by Hu.
2. See Goldman (1994), esp. 298–9, and Polumbaum (1994). Polumbaum is preparing a study of Hu Jiwei's life and work based on extended interviews with him.
3. For thoughtful considerations of current developments, see Goldman (1994), Brugger and Kelly (1990), and McCormick and Kelly (1994).
4. In fact, Deng Tuo was Hu's mentor at *People's Daily* in the 1950s. Other notables of the post-Mao period who figured centrally in Deng Tuo's life are Peng Zhen, Liu Binyan, and Wang Ruoshui.
5. See the excellent study by Laurence A. Schneider (1980).

Acknowledgements

This book has been many years in the making. I have accumulated debts to my colleagues and friends beyond count. Most recently, I am indebted to those who took the time to read the revised manuscript carefully and to offer specific suggestions, not all of which, alas, I have followed: the two anonymous reviewers for SOAS, Paul Cohen, Philip Kuhn, David Ownby, Tony Saich, Patricia Stranahan, Frederick Teiwes, James Wilkerson, and James Williams. I am particularly grateful to my dissertation advisers for their guidance: Roderick MacFarquhar, Merle Goldman, and particularly my senior adviser, Philip Kuhn, who challenged me 'to relate thought to social experience'. I have benefited from the opportunity to submit portions of this work for scrutiny at China seminars at Harvard, the University of Michigan, the University of Chicago, the University of Washington, and the University of California at Berkeley. I am grateful to colleagues who participated in these meetings and offered suggestions. Over the years a number of colleagues have read chapters or conference papers based on the book, or otherwise materially influenced the results you have before you. My greatest debt is to my friend and collaborator, Carol Hamrin. I am grateful, also, to: Lucien Bianco, Tim Brook, Tom Fisher, Howard Goldblatt, Nina Halpern, Kathleen Hartford, John Israel, David Kelly, Paul Kroll, Gregory Lee, Bonnie McDougall, Pitman Potter, Judy Polumbaum, Sidney Rittenberg, Kyna Rubin, Pierre Ryckmans, David Shambaugh, Lawrence Sullivan, Hans van de Ven, Lyman Van Slyke, Jeffrey Wasserstrom, Philip Williams, Molly Wingate, Yeh Wen-hsin, and Joseph K. S. Yick. Thanks are especially due to Robert Ash for guiding this manuscript with care and good humour through the editorial process at CCI.

    This book relies in part on interviews I carried out in China and especially on documentary materials I collected there. Without the help of my Chinese colleagues this book would have been impossible. I owe a great deal to Ding Yilan, Deng Tuo's widow, for her generosity since we met in 1981. The kindheartedness of her and her family to a foreign scholar of admittedly different persuasions has been a model of Chinese hospitality. I thank her for permission to use the first twelve photographs in this book from her private library collection in Beijing. She, of course, bears no responsibility for the interpretations I adopt. Other friends and colleagues of Deng Tuo's gave generously: Gu Xing, Liu

Acknowledgements

Yongcheng, Su Shuangbi, and others not forgotten but best not mentioned. Chinese friends introduced me to the realities and practicalities of life and research in China and challenged my assumptions: Mei Jing, Zuo Taihang, Ding Xueliang, Jiang Hong, Cheng Mei, Zhang Lei, Su Shaozhi, Wang Ruoshui, Li Zehou, and Deng Tuo's young biographer, Wang Bisheng. I am grateful to each and hope they will forgive the limitations in my scholarship.

I have benefited from the resources of the Harvard-Yenching Library, the Beijing University Library, the People's University Library, and the Hoover Institution. I am grateful to the librarians at each institution for their professional help. I am disproportionately indebted to Nancy Hearst of the Fairbank Center Library, Harvard. She maintains the single best library on CCP history in the West and shares these resources cheerfully.

Research for this book was supported by a post-doctoral fellowship from the American Council of Learned Societies and by a Benezet Prize and annual Research and Development awards at The Colorado College. I am grateful to former Dean David Finley and the History Department here for their support over the years, especially Dennis Showalter and Carol Neel. My wife, Tricia, and young daughter, Tessa, have endured years of anxious revisions. They, as I, look forward to the day Deng Tuo is in your hands rather than mine.

T. C.
Colorado Springs
August 1997

Contents

List of Illustrations	xii
List of Figures	xiii
List of Tables	xiv
List of Abbreviations	xv
Introduction: *Intellectuals, Propaganda, and Culture in China's Party-State*	1
1. A Provincial Scholar Turns to National Revolution	25
2. The Revolutionary Propagandist: Life in the Jin Cha Ji Border Region	65
3. Life in the Establishment	123
4. Maoism in Crisis: The Price of Engagement	167
5. Theory Worker and Culture Bearer: Beijing after the Great Leap	215
6. Death and Afterlife as Villain and Hero	279
Conclusion: Broken Jade	307
Appendix: Evening Chats *and* Three Family Village *Essays by Date*	319
Bibliography	331
Glossary	371
Index	377

List of Illustrations

1.1 Deng Tuo (2nd from left) and middle school classmates at Fengchi Hill, Fuzhou, 1928	25
1.2 Deng Tuo, Shanghai, 1934	33
2.1 Deng Tuo, Fuping county, Hebei, April 1943	65
2.2 Nie Rongzhen, Deng Tuo (behind), and Norman Bethune, Jin Cha Ji Military Hospital, Wutai, September 1938	83
2.3 Deng Tuo's 1940 poem on Mao's 'New Democracy'	102
3.1 Deng Tuo's official portrait, 1956	123
3.2 Deng Tuo and wife, Ding Yilan, Beihai Park, Beiping, 1949	134
3.3 Deng Tuo, 1956 (informal photo)	154
4.1 Deng Tuo's calligraphy for 'Taking Leave of Friends at *People's Daily*', February 1959	168
5.1 Deng Tuo penning calligraphy for hosts in Inner Mongolia, 1964	215
5.2 Calligraphic frontispiece to *Evening Chats at Yanshan*, 1963	245
6.1 Deng Tuo's memorial portrait, 1982	278
6.2 Poetry meeting commemorating Deng Tuo, Fuzhou, May 1986	297

List of Figures

2.1 Organization of the *Jin Cha Ji Daily*, 1940–1942 77
3.1 A simplified map of Deng Tuo's social circles 126

List of Tables

2.1 Staff and print runs of *Resistance News* and *Jin Cha Ji Daily*, 1938–1948   75
5.1 Political nature of Deng Tuo's essays   249
5.2 Pattern of Deng Tuo's 'contentious' essays   251

List of Abbreviations

CAS	Chinese Academy of Sciences
CB	*Current Background*
CC	Central Committee of the Chinese Communist Party
CCP	Chinese Communist Party
DTWJ	*Deng Tuo wenji* (Beijing, Beijing chubanshe, 1983–6)
ECMM	*Extracts from China Mainland Magazines*
FBIS-CHI	*Foreign Broadcast Information Service-China*
JPRS	*Joint Publications Research Service*
KMT	Kuomintang (Nationalist Party)
NCNA	New China News Agency (Xinhua She)
NPC	National People's Congress
PRC	People's Republic of China
SCMM	*Selections from China Mainland Magazines*
SCMP	*Survey of China Mainland Press*
SEM	Socialist Education Movement
YDT	Liao Mosha *et al.*, *Yi Deng Tuo* (Fuzhou, Fujian renmin chubanshe, 1980)

Introduction
Intellectuals, Propaganda, and Culture in China's Party-State

> Over the years, Deng Tuo also trained a great number of propaganda cadres. This is one of his great contributions.
>
> (Nie Rongzhen, May 1979[1])
>
> It is perhaps no exaggeration to say that to future historians who approach this period of bureaucratic tyranny, people such as Wu Han and above all Teng T'o will appear as those who, throughout these shameful years, really saved the honour and dignity of the Chinese intellectual.
>
> (Simon Leys, 1971[2])

Deng Tuo is known in China largely in the terms suggested by Marshal Nie Rongzhen, as a journalist and propagandist, a loyal Party man victimized in the Cultural Revolution. In the West he is known, as in Simon Leys' depiction, as a fighting intellectual who dared to make public criticisms of Mao's capricious leadership. In both China and the West Deng Tuo is seen as a notable and significant Chinese intellectual, but for apparently different reasons. Was he, then, a propagandist? A dissident? Both? Or neither?

Deng Tuo's life and death link the past and present of Chinese intellectuals. The Chinese Communist Party could not have taken over China or governed it without a coalition of social forces, including the intellectuals who articulated its goals and administered its complex bureaucracy. How did this work in Mao's China? What did intellectuals do in the Communist revolution? Why did Mao turn on his intellectuals and bureaucrats in the Cultural Revolution? Is there a role for intellectuals similar to Deng Tuo's in China today?

Deng Tuo's life provides a window into life in the Party establishment from the 1930s to the 1960s, putting a human face on the anonymous bureaucracy of socialist China. It also demonstrates in particular the workings of the 'propaganda state' which Deng Tuo served as a journalist, editor, and theorist. Deng's career illustrates the daily operation of the Party propaganda apparat from the wartime base areas to the Great Leap Forward. Because of Deng's importance as a leading figure in that establishment, his life also sheds light on several major political events, particularly the Hundred Flowers movement in 1956–7 when Mao tried to enlist intellectuals to keep an eye on the Party and again in 1966 when Deng Tuo became one of the first 'capitalist roaders' denounced in the Cultural Revolution. In particular, he spoke eloquently for the values of his bureaucratic colleagues in the post-Leap recovery in the early 1960s. Deng not only had a long and tumultuous career in central institutions in Beijing, he was also a prolific, clear, and opinionated writer.

What was the nature of Deng Tuo's service to the Party? His long service as a propagandist put him at the centre of the new Maoist orthodoxy. Deng Tuo edited the first *Selected Works of Mao Zedong* in 1944, and the second in 1947. He became the founding editor of the CCP's flagship newspaper, the *People's Daily*. He penned dozens of major articles on ideology, journalism, agriculture, and literature on behalf of the orthodoxy.

That orthodoxy fell apart. Two trends within Yan'an Maoism emerge in Deng Tuo's story: faith Maoism and bureaucratic Maoism. Deng Tuo always leaned toward the latter, but like all Party faithful from the anti-Japanese War period, he embraced both aspects of this 'sinified' Leninist ideology. Through his career we will be able to trace the dissolution of the powerful mix of charismatic and routine authority patterns within Maoism. In the end, and only in the 1960s after the debacle of the Great Leap, these two aspects of Maoism would split into competing versions of Maoism. Deng Tuo as a chief propagandist was at the heart of this split, and his life at this time provides a trenchant explanation of how the great divorce between Mao and his Party took place. Deng Tuo's famous essay columns, *Evening Chats at Yanshan* and *Notes from a Three Family Village*, along with his less-noted Party theory articles, made him one of the most articulate spokesmen for bureaucratic Maoism. When the conflict broke out into political warfare, with tragic consequences for all of China, the system Deng Tuo served blew up in his face and cost him his life.

If, as has often been the case in popular accounts of 'Communist China', we have thought that intellectuals and Communists are mutually exclusive categories, Deng Tuo's life puts that misconception to rest. He was a quintessential Chinese intellectual, a literatus (*wenren*) competent in China's traditional three arts—poetry, calligraphy, and painting. He was a serious historian and a noted art collector. He wrote humanist essays based on China's long history to inspire China's youth.

At the same time Deng Tuo was a top Communist Party propagandist, a Marxist-Leninist theorist, and a firm believer in historical materialism. He penned elegant calligraphy to show his respect for Chairman Mao. How did this spectrum of ideas and activities make sense to him? Deng Tuo conceived of his service to China and the Party in twin roles: as both servant (cog and screw in the revolutionary machine, to use the Soviet metaphor adopted by Mao) and as savant or culture-bearing cadre. These roles appear contradictory and parallel the internal tensions between the charismatic authority of faith and the rule-based authority of method in Maoism. Deng Tuo lived the dual roles of servant and savant harmoniously for over twenty years under CCP administration.

Mao himself acknowledged the Leninist distinction between cadre and 'masses'. The tragedy for Deng Tuo and for other intellectuals serving the Party was that Mao could unilaterally change the rules. Mao came to reject the bureaucratic side of his namesake orthodoxy, and the culture-bearing role of his more educated cadres, because his bureaucrats frustrated his will and stood in the way of his utopian vision. In the end, Deng Tuo was for Mao an irritating and representative example of the Chinese bureaucracy: elite, unresponsive to charismatic appeals from the top leader, fussy, rule-bound, cautious, proud; in short, a pack of pedants. For the Deng Tuos of China, Mao in his turn became dangerous, unpredictable, inconsistent, and capable of creating much damage. Deng Tuo tried to 'handle' his quixotic and cruel supreme leader; Mao largely succeeded in crushing his incorrigible bondservants.

If the relationship between Mao and his bureaucracy is so reminiscent of that between the Emperor's inner court and the Confucian's outer court in Imperial China, this is less due to some immutable Chinese political culture than to the structural similarities between the Leninist and Confucian-Legalist state. Both were highly centralized administrations with cosmocratic claims to legitimacy and staffed by a morally trained cadre of scholar-officials adept in an esoteric ideology. Equally, it is no surprise that Marxism-Leninism shares some structural similarities with Imperial Confucianism as a state system. The very 'neo-traditional' aspects of Maoism and the PRC Party-State are the *mechanism* for a massive socio-historical evolution of Chinese culture and polity. There were both structural and overt aspects to Deng Tuo's life and the system he served which were neo-traditional. This was not a case of changeless continuity or of 'China's resistance to change'. Just the reverse. These points of contact, we can say 'fit', between Chinese political culture and Marxism-Leninism have been the channels of change. The result was more one of synthesis. For intellectuals, the role of scholar-official made the role of Leninist cadre somewhat familiar. Over half a century's experience, both have transformed the political role of the educated elite in China. In such social change, to ignore the traditional tool is to miss a key component of the equation. To dismiss the novel use to which an old tool is put is equally to miss the point.

Culture, however, did not simply define the parameters of Deng Tuo's actions. It was a set of tools which he actively employed. But it was so much more. Chinese culture was his identity, his *raison d'être*. It was the storehouse of human artifice (*wen*) which defined him as a literatus (*wenren*). In particular he loved the lessons of classical history and the beauty of literati arts. His job was to keep that culture alive, develop it, and pass it on to the next generation. Deng Tuo felt socialism, and particularly Marxian historical materialism, could add to China's heritage. Earlier in his career he emphasized the new contributions of Marxism-Leninism; later in life he dwelt on the enduring contributions of tradition. 'Tradition' for him was not a single thing to be contrasted with 'modernity'. It was a set of examples, potent symbols, living lessons. It was natural for Deng Tuo to cast his troubles with Mao in traditional terms of Confucian loyalists from the Song and Ming. These symbols enabled Deng to articulate an ideological space for loyal criticism after Mao had withdrawn that privilege from the Leninist discourse of the Party. When Leninist minority rights went by the board, Deng Tuo revived the remonstrating official from China's still-living cultural tropes. The loyal minister and other such symbols spoke authentically to Deng Tuo, to his colleagues, and to their superiors; they speak to Hu Jiwei and many surviving Party intellectuals in China today.

This story pursues these broader issues by following three concrete questions. For Chinese intellectuals in general these are: Why was Maoism attractive to some intellectuals? What was service to Maoism like when it worked? What went wrong in that service to bring its demise? In Deng Tuo's life these questions become, first, *how was Deng Tuo conditioned to think about service to the state?* Why did this educated Chinese choose to serve the CCP and its administration over alternative strategies to save China in the 1930s? Why Marxism and the CCP instead of the 'Three People's Principles' and the Nationalist Party (Kuomintang, KMT), or 'liberalism' and 'Darwinism' with the Third Parties, or withdrawal from politics into Christianity, Buddhism, or academe? Each of these alternatives was chosen by members of Deng's family.

Second, *how did the relationship between scholarly integrity and political service work out in practice for Deng Tuo during the two decades of productive service between 1937 and 1957?* What did he do and what was life like in the CCP for him? Although Deng Tuo had joined the CCP in 1930, his effective service to the Party really began as a journalist in North China during the anti-Japanese War and the Civil War. In 1949 he moved to Beijing and the *People's Daily*. Through his propaganda work Deng Tuo implemented the social revolutionary goals of the CCP. How did he see his role in that revolutionary project?

Finally, *what went wrong? What made it impossible for Deng Tuo to balance the roles of savant and functionary in the CCP during the late 1950s and early 1960s?* Why did this loyal servant—and thousands like him—fall foul of the Party he had served for three and a half decades? What on earth did he do to be excoriated by his own Party in 1966? What does this reveal of the nature and functioning of state socialism in China? Deng Tuo and his colleagues have been 'rehabilitated' since 1979. What does this tell us of the resolution or the continuation of the tensions in intellectual service to the CCP that 'broke the jade' in 1966?

Biography, Social History, and Theory

A single life, such as Deng Tuo's, is of no more interest or significance than the goings-on in a single village, the life of a particular factory, or the price of eggs on a given day. Disciplined study of communities, social structure, and economic systems has generated significant studies of a Chen village, the neo-traditionalism of Chinese factory life, and *getihu* entrepreneurship.[3] This book seeks to bring general questions of significance in intellectual, cultural, and social history to the study of Deng Tuo's life. Deng Tuo's service in Mao's China involves three significant issues: political ideology, the public sphere, and the role of culture. We need to have a better sense of each in order to make sense of our story. I have drawn from studies and theorists in political science, anthropology, and related social sciences where I feel their concepts help me explain the material of Deng Tuo's life or present it in a manner that promotes comparison with other cases. Our goal remains historical: to recover something of the truth of past experience in a form that has some meaning and significance for us now.

Previous biographies of Chinese intellectuals in the twentieth century provide excellent models of research and examples of the contribution of biographical knowledge to our understanding of the Chinese revolution. Most of these studies embrace what Paul Cohen has called the 'China-centred approach' to Chinese history, which treats 'even exogenous sources of change from a more interior perspective'.⁴ Yet there is a gap in this field of study. There have been few analyses of the role of the educated elite in the socialist revolution. Certainly Chen Duxiu, Li Dazhao, and Mao himself were intellectuals, but studies of their lives have focused on their roles as thinkers and individual political leaders.⁵ There have been excellent studies on the roles of social elites in the late Qing and Republican periods.⁶ There are as well an increasing number of fine studies of intellectuals in the broader Chinese revolution, to which the present study can hope to contribute. Deng Tuo's life is best read in the context of the broader range of intellectual participation: Charlotte Furth's study of Ding Wenjiang and science in the New Culture Movement, Guy Alitto's account of Liang Shuming and neo-traditional responses to revolutionary change, and Charles Hayford's example of James Yen and the transpacific ties of liberalism.⁷ Deng Tuo's famous predecessors in journalism show the continuity of vocation, as well as the changes in circumstances, from Wang Tao's efforts in the 1860s to Liang Qichao's famous essays at the turn of the century.⁸ There have also been initial steps to look at intellectuals *per se* as agents in the CCP's revolutionary activities, particularly in the realm of philosophy and ideology. Raymond Wylie has demonstrated the central role of Chen Boda in the emergence of Maoism, Joshua Fogel has revealed Ai Siqi's contributions to the CCP's state orthodoxy, and Lars Ragvald has opened our view to the role of Yao Wenyuan among the left wing of Maoism.⁹ Kamel Sheel has attempted to describe intellectual participation in the CCP's rural revolution in Jiangxi province.¹⁰ Mary Mazur has chronicled the participation of a leading academic, Wu Han, in the United Front strategy of the CCP.¹¹

The present work was begun as part of a series of shorter studies by several colleagues that appeared in 1986 in the volume *China's Establishment Intellectuals*.¹² Carol Hamrin undertook a reconsideration of Party theorist Yang Xianzhen in the mid-1970s which introduced me to the idea of 'alternatives within Chinese Marxism'.¹³ By the early 1980s, Tom Fisher had brought out a revisionist interpretation to Wu Han's play *Hai Rui Dismissed from Office*, that stressed Wu's loyalty to Mao, Clifford Edmunds had reassessed Jian Bozan's historiographic critique of the Great Leap, and I had suggested Deng Tuo was not the anti-Maoist dissident we had thought.¹⁴

Nevertheless, down to the present day we still need *social histories* of intellectuals as agents in China's socialist revolution. Jeffrey Wasserstrom in his review of recent works on the social history of the broader Chinese revolution notes the many gaps in our understanding of China's revolutionary political parties. He concludes, 'we still know much less about the *mentalités* of the members of either political party than we know about the formal ideologies the groups espoused, and we have a much hazier understanding of the social dynamics of actual Communist or Nationalist working groups than we do of high level factional cliques.'[15] Indeed, this gap exists more broadly in the field of modern China studies. Harry Harding in his comprehensive review of recent American scholarship notes topics which have not received adequate attention in studies published in the 1980s, including 'the composition of the new party and government elites, [and] the content and attractiveness of official ideology . . .'[16] To get at what Maoism meant to actors in the CCP and to the life of Party intellectuals we need to connect their thought to their social experience, to their social roles and activities. We need to ask why they liked Maoism. Such an approach should not only help us better understand the lives and ideas of these intellectuals but also cast light on the social history of the Chinese revolution. This biography seeks to do just that.

Some of the key variables of this analysis are likely to cause us trouble, because they meant very different things to Deng Tuo and in China than they do, generally, in most Western societies. Four in particular need comment: intellectuals, Maoism, propaganda, and ideology. Intellectuals for Deng Tuo were engaged in the government or supportive of its goals, not independent and certainly not alienated. His picture of intellectual life contrasts with Western notions of intellectuals and with the experience of many non-Communist Chinese intellectuals. Maoism here is not the extreme left-wing form of Chinese-style Leninism. It was the whole system under the CCP, its ideology and organization. Propaganda was good. Deng Tuo found in it a noble vocation bringing to life the goals of the Party among its cadre and the public. Propaganda was also an institutional system at the heart of the Chinese Party-State, comprising not only the media but cadre training, universities, research institutes, and cultural organs. Finally, ideology is used here in Geertz's sense of a cultural system of symbols that describes our thinking as much as that of our subjects. This parallels to some degree the CCP usage of '*sixiang*' which we usually translate as 'ideology' but also means 'thinking' or 'thought'. This will enable us to see the 'fit' of Maoist ideology into Chinese culture more clearly.

Intellectuals

Chinese administrations have long made use of the services of the educated elite. Over the centuries many educated people have answered the call to civil service and have been well rewarded for their services. During Deng Tuo's youth, intellectuals as a social group were poorly integrated into republican and warlord regimes.[17] These regimes suffered a corresponding dearth of educated talent to staff their administrations because they could not sustain the political ideals and career security to draw intellectuals into service, and this contributed to their failure. In 1930 the CCP was hardly a promising career path for Chinese intellectuals. Despite its attractive claim to a non-Western (i.e., non-imperialist) road to wealth and power, the Party was in organizational disarray following its violent split with the KMT in 1927 and a series of utter failures to foment urban revolution.[18] Nonetheless, the CCP remained popular with university students and took off again after 1936 as increased Japanese assaults on China, continuing KMT mismanagement, and renewed organizational reform made the Party a viable alternative for intellectuals wishing to serve China and find a vocation.[19] By 1950 the CCP had become the first political organization after the Empire which, *in practice*, offered an attractive opportunity for intellectuals to serve in a state administration. This was an opportunity that numerous intellectuals accepted. Revolutionary nationalism, military success, and a reputation for administration free from corruption drew many intellectuals to the CCP from the late 1940s who were disillusioned with the Kuomintang.[20] The ideals of rectification developed by the CCP in the 1940s, including democratic centralism, reasonable rules for political criticism, and the goal of building a new and equitable society under a United Front which welcomed non-Communists, furnished the vision to inspire intellectuals. They also provided the channels for intellectual participation in government and the vague promise that their views on public affairs were welcome.[21]

Different intellectuals served the CCP at different levels of responsibility and commitment. Some stayed on the mainland after the Communist victory only with grave misgivings. Some served with great enthusiasm based on extensive experience as CCP cadres. Deng Tuo was one of those intellectuals who had firmly embraced Marxism-Leninism, joined the CCP in the 1930s' and served in the CCP base areas during World War II and the Chinese Civil War. He stands in contrast to the great majority of intellectuals in China who never joined the CCP, or who were less wholeheartedly committed to Marxism or Maoism.

Deng Tuo was among the founding generation of establishment intellectuals in the People's Republic of China. As such, he was both a high-level intellectual (*gaoji zhishifenzi*) and a high-level cadre (*gaoji ganbu*). However, there were great differences within this group based on individual experiences during late adolescence (ages 17 to 25), the period many scholars define as the formative stage of a political generation.[22] Some radical students studied abroad—particularly the elder ones who studied in Europe or Japan in the 1910s and 1920s and the younger ones who studied in the Soviet Union in the 1920s and 1930s. Some received their higher intellectual training at Chinese or foreign universities in China. The latter group, to which Deng Tuo belonged, was far better trained in traditional Chinese skills such as poetry and calligraphy. They relied more heavily on Chinese history in their thinking and writing. The overseas students were often better trained in the classics of Marxism-Leninism and many felt a strong commitment to the international socialist movement. A good example of the latter from Deng's generation is Sun Yefang, a leading economist in the People's Republic, who studied in the Soviet Union and who did not reflect Deng Tuo's preoccupation with Chinese history in his writings.[23]

Wartime experiences strongly influenced these future establishment intellectuals, whatever their university backgrounds. Deng Tuo served in the Jin Cha Ji (Shanxi-Chahar-Hebei) Border Region under leaders such as Nie Rongzhen and Peng Zhen. This was the first and largest of the CCP base areas which, unlike the Yan'an area, were behind the Japanese lines and subject to continual and brutal military assaults. In addition, the local society in Hebei and Shanxi was a complex mix of rich and poor, requiring a delicate balancing act on the part of the Party as it sought to gain and consolidate its rule in those areas.[24] Intellectuals in Yan'an and Chongqing had far different experiences. Yan'an was situated in the provinces of Shaanxi, Gansu, and Ningxia, the Shaan Gan Ning border region. It offers two stark contrasts with Jin Cha Ji. First, in Yan'an there were no Japanese attacks. Second, the mix of rich and poor was far less complex and much more polarized than in Jin Cha Ji. These conditions contributed to a more radical and extreme application of CCP social policies than in Jin Cha Ji, where the Party developed pragmatic techniques to cope with a more complex local society under constant threat of Japanese military assault.

Deng Tuo's background differs from that of another important group of intellectuals, the left-wing writers of the 1920s and 1930s who joined the Communist movement. Yan'an welcomed a number of left-wing writers who fled Shanghai and other major metropolitan centres in 1937 at the start of the anti-Japanese War. They came into bitter conflict with Mao's group in 1942, leading to the notorious literary rectification of that spring and summer. Mao's pronouncement on the proper role of creative writing given at that time, the 'Talks at the Yan'an Forum on Art and Literature', became a major component of the CCP orthodoxy for intellectuals. Many of the left-wing writers experienced this as a brutal attack on themselves and their right to speak out.[25] Deng Tuo and intellectuals in Jin Cha Ji and other base areas did not suffer the same fate. First, there were clearly left-wing writers in the base areas behind the Japanese lines who shared the same romantic vision of literature as a political weapon to be wielded by the individual writer, but they were not subject to the same degree of repression.[26] Second, Party intellectuals like Deng Tuo shared little with May Fourth writers like Ding Ling, Xiao Jun, or Wang Shiwei. Deng Tuo did not stress the independent insight of the artist. Rather, he put his literary skills—including classical poetry—comfortably in the service of his local Party organization. Deng was no simple minion of the Party, and his elite ways would bring him grief in the long run. Before the Cultural Revolution, however, Deng's elite cultural style posed no conflict to his Party service.

Neither 'the Party' nor 'the intellectuals' were monolithic groups. Nor were they separate groups; they were intermingled. Deng Tuo was part of the revolutionary elite of Chinese Communism. Whatever their differences in background, literary temperament, and wartime experience, all the intellectuals who served in the Party were part of the broader revolutionary elite which led the CCP to victory. Even among the military elite many, such as Nie Rongzhen and Chen Yi, continued something of the traditional intellectual model of the scholar-official, whether they wrote poetry in the Tang style, novels in the realist style, or Marxist treatises in the Soviet style. Meanwhile, intellectuals like Deng Tuo who joined the Party accepted the elite status within Marxism-Leninism of the 'Party cadre' along with the relative power and wealth it afforded them.[27]

Deng was more classically grounded than most, with his well-known accomplishments in traditional-style poetry, calligraphy, and historiography, but he is representative of the entire group in his paternalistic approach to politics and enthusiastic embrace of Maoism. Deng Tuo continued an elite and classically oriented life of private art, but this did not lessen his commitment to Marxism-Leninism. Rather, it reflects a compatibility between aspects of inherited models of public service by the educated elite and the role of the cadre in Leninism. Deng Tuo was not alone in this. The figure of Mao's secret police chief Kang Sheng, with his quasi-legendary cultural attainments, shows just how far the classically trained literatus could follow the Party line in Mao's China.[28]

Maoism: The Leninist Response in China

Deng Tuo embraced Maoism, yet he was driven to death by Mao. How do we make sense of this? I have found the analysis of non-Chinese Leninist parties by Kenneth Jowitt helpful in understanding both the original success of Yan'an Maoism in helping the Chinese leadership unite and found a nation and the later dissolution of this ideology into conflicting charismatic and bureaucratic tendencies. Jowitt accepts Max Weber's analytical distinction between status (or traditional) society and class (or modern) society. He posits that when traditional societies have faced threatened or actual domination by a powerful, modern society, resulting in political, cultural, and economic 'national dependency', Leninism has often been more successful than alternative ideologies for organizing the efforts of traditional societies to throw off intruders and to begin to modernize. The key to the 'Leninist response' is the 'enmeshment of class and status' in the 'charismatic impersonal Party'—a peculiar organization that combines attributes of charismatic rule, which can speak to and mobilize traditional elements (particularly the peasantry), and attributes of modern rule based on norms of achievement, which can promote the modernization of industry and the rationalization of the bureaucracy. The key legitimizing principle of the Leninist response is not the views of a single leader, but the 'correct line' determined by a collective leadership, which, theoretically, transcends individual failings, including mortality.[29]

Applying Jowitt's model to China, it would seem that the mix of charismatic and rational-bureaucratic modes of operation in Maoism did indeed suit the needs of the Party's constituency then—a status society of peasants and kinship groups in rural China. We shall see in Chapter 2 that this mix of charisma and rationality served intellectuals as well as the rural inhabitants in the Jin Cha Ji border region even before the model was fully developed in Yan'an. However, in the face of massive, chronic problems inhibiting Chinese economic development, the assumptions and attendant methods of this ideology fell short in the PRC. Perceiving the reappearance of traditional elite bureaucratism and social class differentiation, the charismatic leader, Mao, pushed for a revival of the mass movement approach of Yan'an in 1958 and 1966. Perceiving in turn the re-creation of traditional emperor worship and what they thought to be dysfunctional populism, Party leaders and Party intellectuals deeply involved in the administration naturally turned to the more rational-bureaucratic side of the Yan'an amalgam. Both approaches aimed to modernize China; both failed inasmuch as their pre-modern roots emerged to block their aspirations. As Carol Hamrin concludes, 'in response to the crisis of the Great Leap Forward, "one divided into two"'.[30]

The finer details of Jowitt's analysis of the Leninist phenomenon helpfully articulate the forces at work in Deng Tuo's public life. Maoism, despite the efforts of post-Mao Party theorists, is inseparable from Mao the charismatic leader. Yet such a leader helps create a special organization, the Leninist Party, which represents a novel, contradictory, and extremely powerful social force: *charismatic impersonalism*. This is 'an institutional amalgam of charismatic and modern orientations...'[31] Jowitt's description of this peculiar organization, its leader, and its historical context fits Deng Tuo's world of the 1940s quite well:

> A charismatic leader dramatically reconciles incompatible commitments and orientations. It is in this sense that the charismatic is a revolutionary agent—someone who is able in certain social circumstances institutionally to combine (with varying degrees of success for varying degrees of time) orientations and commitments that until then were seen as mutually exclusive. It is the extraordinary and inspirational quality of such a leader that makes possible the recasting of previously incompatible elements into a new unit of personal identity and organizational membership...[32]

That organization is, of course, the Party. It is both charismatic as the representative of the forces of history and heroic struggle and rational and materialist as the organization that directs empirical, cool-headed examination of social change and the collective discussion of social issues. The charismatic impersonal features of the Party constrain and shape the behaviour of its members. Individualism is expressed in the neo-corporate unit of the collective such as Party cells or work units. Achievement as a standard of success stands in continual tension with Party membership itself as a heroic quality. Scientific socialism, equally, carries contradictory meanings as a critical orientation and as an unquestionable grasp of unilinear historical laws. In sum, says Jowitt, 'The Leninist Party and regime constitute a novel package of charismatic, traditional, and modern elements. ... in such a way that the Party combines impersonal and affective elements and appeals effectively, if not logically, to some persons and groups in a turbulent society who themselves are a composite of heroic, status, and secular orientations.'[33]

Jowitt raises two other points particularly useful in understanding Deng Tuo's service to Maoism. First, he suggests that the charismatic aspects of Leninism appear traditional to members of a status society, especially peasants, and thus provide a way of entry for a revolutionary organization into that society. Without these neo-traditional trappings (which Jowitt calls 'more formal than substantive') local society would reject such alien ideas and goals as are found in Marxism.[34] Deng Tuo's case shows that a similar package of traditional aspects of Leninism, from the elite status of the cadre to the role of the intellectual as historical agent of cultural renewal, was attractive to highly educated

Chinese as well. Second, Jowitt raises a significant distinction between social and cultural mobilization of actors in revolution.[35] Many participants in the CCP, and this will include Deng Tuo, were socially mobilized in the pre-1949 period. That is, they lost or had no jobs, had no economic or social security, and thus were 'free' to join a new movement. This should not be conflated with cultural mobilization based on a profound doubt or rejection of one's inherited culture. As we will see, Deng Tuo was socially but not culturally mobilized.

David Apter and Tony Saich in their study of Yan'an rectification confirm aspects of Jowitt's picture of the Leninist phenomenon from a different tack. They focus on language and the power of 'discourse communities'.[36] Their detailed study of the experience of rectification in Yan'an during the 1940s provides the details of the 'certain social circumstance' and 'varying degrees of time' raised in Jowitt's more general definition of the Leninist phenomenon. Apter and Saich show how the ideological study movement under Mao was a process of 'exegetical bonding' that moved heart as well as mind among its participants. The results were a 'symbolic capital'—an élan, an *esprit de corps*, a sense of heroic mission—that made ordinary people do extraordinary things. They remind us of the affective aspects of Maoism that were real to Deng Tuo but muted in his writings. Deng Tuo's work in the 1940s and 1950s (Chapters 2 and 3) gives us a view of this symbolic capital at work in the bureaucracy.

Apter and Saich, along with a number of recent studies, also alert us to the dark side of the Yan'an model: the inquisitions of cadre purges. Dai Qing and Chen Yung-fa have detailed the ghastly costs of the purge of Wang Shiwei in the literary rectification and the purge of literally thousands of ordinary CCP cadres in the 1943–4 'rescue campaign'.[37] At the time Mao acted quickly to put a lid on such witch-hunts. Coming into the new PRC most Party leaders acted as if that unfortunate episode was behind them.[38] Deng's troubles in the last decade of his life (Chapters 4, 5, and 6) show that the shadow self of the Yan'an rectification movement would not stay buried. His fall gives us a detailed account of the dissolution of Yan'an's symbolic capital, the decline and fall of Yan'an Maoism.

Propaganda State and the 'Public Sphere'

Deng Tuo was, as his survivors proudly recall, first and foremost a propagandist.[39] To the Western ear a 'propagandist' does not sound like a promising candidate for intellectual biography. However, in China 'propaganda' is not a pejorative term, at least among the members of

China's establishment. The original meaning of 'propaganda' in early modern Europe more closely corresponds to the meaning of *xuanchuan* in Chinese: to propagate what one believes to be true, with overtones of propagating an orthodoxy.[40] In addition, most modern readers value independence and, most of all, originality and creativity. These are not similarly valued goals in China's intellectual establishment, nor were they always so prized by our predecessors. Medieval intellectual life in Europe accepted a body of knowledge and tested the individual by one's ability and preparation for joining the ranks of the select few who could 'converse' with Aristotle or the Church Fathers.[41] Deng Tuo saw himself as a *doctor* to society. His pride was his mastery of Chinese culture and Marxism-Leninism and his ability to apply both well in practical administration. Deng Tuo viewed himself both as a literatus (*wenren*) and as a cadre (*ganbu*), and he felt both roles were needed for a good propagandist.

Deng Tuo's journalism was a sub-set of his propaganda work. The press and propaganda has had a broad social function in socialist China:

The newspaper network was the blood-circulation system of the body politic: it carried essential information everywhere rapidly.... The average citizen learned what were the legitimate public issues as defined by the leaders and learned the verbiage of political discourse. For the activist and for the Party functionary, reading the newspaper diligently was even more important. They found out how they had to act in small and large matters and learned how to discuss political and even nonpolitical issues with their fellow citizens.[42]

This quote actually describes the operation of the Soviet press in the 1920s. However, the 'practical ideology' and mass media in Mao's China parallels this picture.[43] The CCP borrowed more than a media system from the Soviets. They created their own version of the Bolsheviks' 'propaganda state'. Peter Kenez calls this a state-dominated polity that co-ordinates the education of cadres, the development of a political language, the politicization of ever-larger segments of life, and the substitution of 'voluntary' state-controlled societies for independent organizations.[44]

Propaganda was not only a total media system; it was a project. For Deng Tuo propaganda work was the concrete application of Maoist leadership methods. Party journalism was meant to be a major example of the 'from the masses, to the masses' function of Party leadership in which Party representatives go down among the common folk, discover their problems and needs, go back and synthesize those particular problems with the insights of Marxism-Leninism (hence the need for proper ideology), and finally return to the masses to publicize the Party's synthesis among the people in such a way as to make them take on such formulations as their own values. Deng Tuo did not intend to lead the brute masses, he intended to transform them through education (*jiaohua*). He claimed his goal was to raise their cultural and political level to the heights of the traditional literati. The results in practice were somewhat less egalitarian. Nonetheless, Deng Tuo believed in the dynamic Maoist leadership cycle. He thought it was scientific, practical, and liberating. Propaganda was the key link in this transformational process which empowered the masses and reconnected China's educated elite with China's heart and soul, its people. Such mutual transformations, Deng believed, would address China's economic wants and security worries, and most importantly would preserve China's civilization more surely by broadly cultivating it among her masses. This is why Deng Tuo felt propaganda work was an honourable vocation.

Propaganda was also part of the elite training and monitoring of leaders, part of the 'rectification' (*zhengdun zuofeng*) of cadres. Study sessions (*xuexi xiaozu*) are part of both cadre training and policy implementation. Propaganda writings, as well as official Party publications, are read and discussed in these orchestrated study sessions.[45] Rectification, when it works, is the organizational system to back up the ideological pronouncements the Chinese Communists produce.[46] Frederick Teiwes has analysed that system in its broadest aspects as the leadership system of Maoist China. His model of politics in China, which stresses the centrality of rectification norms in tension with a charismatic Mao, accurately describes the political world of Deng Tuo. Propaganda, then, is a part of a system that underwrites CCP legitimacy, provides practical political feedback on current policy, and informs their cadre training and discipline system. In fact, it is called a system, the *xuanjiao xitong*.[47] That system includes the current newspaper and media system, as well as internal reporting systems and even the Chinese Academy of Sciences. It was born in the revolutionary base areas run by the CCP during World War II. Deng Tuo 'grew up' with that system. His life and work there in the 1940s and 1950s helps us to see how this system evolved and how 'thought reform' of intellectuals worked and how it served to train propagandists. The picture we see of rectification there is considerably less extreme and dogmatic than the literary rectification in Yan'an which has set the tone of Western understanding of CCP rectification.

The information system that comprises the Chinese propaganda state in which Deng Tuo operated seems to correspond to what Jürgen Habermas conceptualizes as the 'public sphere' in European polities. The functions of the propaganda *xitong* appear to parallel those of the 'civil society' Habermas sees operating in the public sphere.[48] This comparison is of central importance not only for making Deng Tuo's experience more comparable with other examples but for highlighting the social role of intellectual service. The key difference is, of course, that Habermas sees the public sphere as *independent* of the State. In China's propaganda state the propaganda *xitong* has functioned as a sort of 'directed' version of the 'civil society'. The concept of 'directed culture' comes from Victor Serge's depiction of the Stalin period, in which the state controls art, ethics, and ideas 'for the good of the people'. Miklós Haraszti has shown the appeal of directed culture for intellectuals under state socialism in Hungary. In his ironic novel, *The Velvet Prison*, Haraszti's cynical censor concludes, 'Socialism, contrary to appearances, does not suppress artists' Nietzschean desires but satisfies them. . . . The state prevents my art from becoming a commodity, and it guarantees my status as a teacher of the nation.'[49] The propaganda *xitong* in China includes the arts and universities. Writers, professors, researchers, as well as journalists, belong to that web which is under the direct control of the Propaganda Department of the CCP. In Mao's China there was no other 'space' in which to speak. The better we understand the assumptions and functions of this 'directed public sphere', the more we will appreciate Deng Tuo's (and the system's) intolerance of democracy in the Western sense.

The better also we will be able to appreciate the great distance between Deng Tuo's world and our own. Although Habermas's terms are offered as historically specific to eighteenth-century European experience, they have come to carry much more general weight in scholarly debate. Indeed, they really stand as disguises for our own values of liberal democracy.[50] Over time, for Habermas himself, the public sphere has garnered a more general meaning as the core of what makes liberal democratic society:

By 'public sphere' we mean first of all a domain of our social life in which such a thing as public opinion can be formed. Access to the public sphere is open in principle to all citizens. A portion of the public sphere is constituted in every conversation in which private persons come together to form a public. They are then acting neither as business or professional people conducting their private affairs, nor as legal consociates subject to the legal regulations of a state bureaucracy and obligated to obedience. Citizens act as a public when they deal with the guarantee that they may assemble and unite freely, and express and publicize their opinions freely.[51]

These are the values we commonly carry in the back of our minds when considering the role of intellectuals in public affairs. These values utterly contradict the assumptions of Deng Tuo's service to the Chinese revolution in all but one respect: he, too, was looking for a just, prosperous, and cultured society.

The assumptions and social practices behind propaganda in contemporary China can be seen in the *xuanjiang*, the lectures propagandizing the sacred edicts of the Kangxi Emperor which were to be given in villages all around China in the Qing period, and in the 'community compact' (*xiangyue*) tradition in Neo-Confucian writings from which they drew.[52] Central to this tradition was the injunction from the ancient *Rites of Zhou* 'to transform the common people through ritual' (*yi li jiao min*). The audience for these Confucian propaganda lectures is passive and in need of moral reformation (sometimes simply to survive the vicissitudes of rural life, sometimes to avoid and turn back from banditry or litigiousness—as in Wang Yangming's sixteenth-century *xiangyue*). The audience is both literate (overlapping with potential and actual practitioners) and illiterate (the farmer majority). They are also homogeneous, at least in their role as recipients of the cultural education the propaganda lectures provided. In Li Laizhang's *Explanations of the Sacred Edict Lectures* of 1705 the audience is divided between commoners and local scholars.[53] This distinction between the commoner and the highly educated audience extends into CCP documents on propaganda in the internal (*neibu*) materials for cadre study and the public (*gongkai*) materials for general and foreign readers.[54]

The main form of propaganda for the CCP has been journalism. The rise of journalism and newspapers in China at the turn of the century reinforced the polemical and 'educational' nature of the *xuanjiang* experience of scholar-officials in the Qing. Following the defeat of Qing forces in the Sino-Japanese War in 1895 and the failure of the 1898 reform, Liang Qichao's journalism, particularly Liang's *Current Affairs* (*Shiwu bao*), became the model for China's new journalism. Two key characteristics of journalism of this period were: first, Liang's use of journalism to get the ear of the monarch and his imitators' focus on the same 'audience'; and second, the times—China's dire straits and economic upheaval—which led Chinese journalism to be much more serious than Western journalism. 'Editors', says James Pusey, 'were interested not in "all the news that's fit to print" but only in that news pertinent to their main concern, China's welfare.'[55] The strengths of such journalism lay in polemical essays and educational articles in the cause of China's salvation. They also gave voice to dedicated patriots, a public forum for frustrated reformers. The famous official reformer, Zhang Zhidong, an early supporter of *Current Affairs*, had this to say of early efforts at journalism:

After 1895, literary men of patriotic spirit began to publish journals. . . . Internal politics, foreign affairs, academic knowledge—all were within their scope . . . they shared a common aim: to spread information, arouse unselfish spirit, wash clean the poisonous apathy. . . . One cannot say that this was not an aid in the education of men who wanted to help their country.[56]

Propaganda was a project well grounded in the experience and assumptions of Chinese statecraft, as well as a system of methods and media outlets borrowed from Soviet experience and refined during the war years, in which the aspiring socialist literati cadre could serve the people of China while obtaining rewards and recognition which they felt appropriate for such intellectual service.

Culture: Symbols and Habits

Culture was central to Deng Tuo's service. By culture he meant Chinese culture and especially the practice of its refined arts—painting, calligraphy, and poetry. He also meant the storehouse of human experience and wisdom in Chinese history. It was the scholarly culture of his personal pastimes that contributed to his sense of mission and role as culture-bearing cadre. The symbol of Deng's elite status and the representative example for us of the power of this culture in Mao's China is Deng Tuo's art collection. His artistic connoisseurship had meanings both public and private beyond art itself. For the public the art collection contributed to Party goals of national pride and confirmed Deng's status as a member of China's cultural elite. Amongst his fellow devotees Deng's particular selection of art provided an esoteric commentary on China's cultural heart. At different times this scholarly style would play different roles. In the 1940s it supported the CCP's legitimacy. In the early 1950s it was private. In the late 1950s it was solace to a dismissed official. And, in the early 1960s it was a critique of faith Maoism and a vantage point of intellectual autonomy for a loyal critic.

Culture in another sense will appear in this story: organizational culture. That is the set of habits and practices, assumptions and often unexamined beliefs that shape behaviour on a daily basis. Organizational culture comes out of social experience. The details of Deng Tuo's work in Jin Cha Ji and the offices of *People's Daily* give us a sense of that experience. It was the organizational culture of the PRC bureaucracy that contributed to Deng Tuo's bureaucratic interpretation of Maoism.

Culture is important to us in one further way, as a way to understand 'ideology'. As a propagandist, Deng Tuo was passionately concerned about ideology. He felt it was central to productive work and rational administration. Ideology, however, is still a dirty word in general Western usage. This does violence to Deng Tuo's understanding of ideology; he thought ideology was, and should be, extremely rational and empirically based. Clifford Geertz put it well when he said that ideology is a cultural system of symbols that is particularly good for motivating actors.[57] We all have ideology, though for most of us it is almost unconsciously assumed unless sharply challenged. When the dominant ideology of a society is sharply challenged, as the Confucian world-view was after the mid-nineteenth century, ideology becomes explicit, and explicit ideologies compete for the public mind. We must keep sight of the obvious difference between the informal, politically unsanctioned ideology (for example, 'civil society' assumptions) that guides the editor of the *New York Times* and the formal, politically sanctioned ideology (Maoism) which guides the editor of *People's Daily*.[58]

Deng Tuo began with formal ideology in the 1930s but his social experience as a senior propagandist in the CCP bureaucracy wore down the central elements of 'ideological thinking' of the sort Jerome Grieder describes for revolutionary movements.[59] The totalism, the 'we versus they', the dogmatic assurance of Right, and unquestioning faith in the charismatic leader were first softened and then eroded by the requirements of predictable administration and the tasks of economic development. This was not the end of ideology and the propaganda state nor was it the birth of liberalism and civil society. For example, ideology for Deng Tuo was first and foremost *method*. He believed in dialectical materialism in 1933 and he believed in it in 1966. The transformation we see in Deng Tuo's life is not from ideology to something else, but of Yan'an millenarianism into another variant of Maoism. We see in Deng Tuo's career and writings a *process* of ideological change, but not the simple routinization of charisma. Deng Tuo tried to shift the awful power of charisma more fully to the institution, the Party, and to its priesthood, establishment intellectuals.

The key difference between Deng Tuo and Mao, and Deng's colleagues and radical Maoists, was their understanding of ideology. For Deng Tuo ideology was very real, but it was a largely cerebral exercise, a conversion based on incremental study and a method made manifest only through planned, rational, and repeated application. It was a method that well suited the socialist bureaucracy in which Deng Tuo served. In this sense, Deng's ideology was a civil service ethos which domesticated the wild populism in some of Mao's utterances to the predictable categories of a job description. Such a wonderful method needed competent practitioners; it did not work of itself. Thus, Deng valued training, discipline, and education. After his troubles with Mao began in the late 1950s, Deng Tuo more emphatically stressed this need for a culture-bearing literati-cadre to ensure proper propagation of correct ideology.

Sources and Perspectives

Deng Tuo was invisible to Western scholars until he was denounced in the Cultural Revolution. Most studies include Deng Tuo as an example of CCP politics of the late 1950s and early 1960s. There have been no other extensive studies of the man outside China, aside from H. C. Chuang's insightful terminological study of *Evening Chats*.[60] Since Deng came to the fore as a victim in the Cultural Revolution, he has, for the most part, been presented in terms of liberalism, humanism, and anti-totalitarianism.[61] It was natural at the time to assume that Deng Tuo was 'anti-Party' because in 1966 the Party itself said so. Furthermore, Western approaches of the 1960s were dominated by totalitarian models which inclined scholars to assume that if one was not fully with the CCP then one was against it.[62] With the Party's own renunciation of the Cultural Revolution, the release of considerably more material on Deng's life and times, and a shift in American scholarship toward the disaggregation of the CCP's parts and an appreciation for institutional constraints on political behaviour, the old picture no longer holds.

New sources and new perspectives emerging from the 1980s influence any study of China and the CCP. The tragic events of 1989 in China add poignancy to any study of the role of students and intellectuals. In addition, the revival amongst Western academics of the study of 'political culture'—stripped of its Freudian reductionism and cultural totalism—directs our attention back to ideology, to signs, symbols, meanings of words, and to the specialists who craft those words, intellectuals.[63] Approaching Deng Tuo's life in this manner, particularly reading his many writings with an eye to the symbols he chose to employ, greatly influenced the interpretations I offer in this book.

The greatest influence on research on the CCP in the past fifteen years is the 'new historiographical period' occasioned by the post-Mao reforms and opening by China to the outside world.[64] Central to this has been the appearance of new source materials and access to Chinese scholars, even to some of the subjects of our studies. Three major categories of new sources inform this research: (1) newly published or newly available documentary sources, particularly from *neibu* (internal circulation) publications, such as the three-volume *Compilation of CCP Documents on Journalism* (*Zhongguo gongchan dang xinwen gongzuo wenjian huibian*, 1980), as well as first-time access to other documents, such as full runs of *Jin Cha Ji Daily* and the Beijing theory journal, *Frontline*. The core documents, of course, are Deng Tuo's own publications. I have benefited from the massive republication of his writings, including a four-volume *Works* (1983–6), but have always used original documents when available; (2) newly compiled almanacs and chronologies that organize vast arrays of data unavailable to us before, such as the *Chronology of* Jin Cha Ji Daily and the *Press Yearbooks*; and (3) personal reminiscences of key actors, such as those of Marshal Nie Rongzhen and Deng Tuo's colleagues.[65] All of these sources, particularly the hagiographies of Deng Tuo, have their limitations (explored case by case in the chapters below), but in general, careful comparison between inner Party documents, public (*gongkai*, or 'openly published') documents, chronologies and almanacs, and reminiscences in conjunction with interviews with surviving colleagues can open new vistas on all topics in CCP history. Nonetheless, there are limits to these developments. Although I benefited greatly from the generosity of Deng Tuo's family and friends, I was never allowed to see two critical documents: his remaining diary entries and his long suicide letter. This is generally the case: research on CCP history by those outside of China has not been able to make use of archival resources in a fashion similar to developments in Qing historical studies in the past decades: we can read original notes from the Qing's Grand Council but not from the Politburo.

Equally important in influencing new perspectives on the CCP has been our personal access to Chinese scholars and surviving participants of the events we study. In the realm of intellectual history such contact has been especially influential, since discussions with these Chinese confronts us with their concerns in a visceral and fundamental way that documents almost never can transmit. In short, such contact changes the way we read documents by sensitizing us to the agenda of their creators. In my case, the opportunity to meet frequently with Deng Tuo's remaining family and colleagues and to attend a conference that included most of his surviving colleagues in 1986 (in Fuzhou) had such an impact.[66] Throughout the story that follows I raise and assess the interpretations of current Chinese biographers of Deng Tuo. I consider this part of the conversation that has graced China studies in recent years in which Chinese and Western scholars have taken each other seriously by applying critical standards to each other's work.

NOTES

1. Nie Rongzhen (YDT: 6).
2. Leys (1977: 33). The original French edn. was published in Paris in 1971.
3. Chan et al. (1984); Walder (1986); Gold (1988).
4. Cohen (1984). Cohen places this latest phase of American studies of China in the broader context of American 'other-centred historiography' of the 1970s and 1980s. See Cohen (1984: 7).
5. Feigon (1983); Meisner (1967); Schram (1967).
6. Esherick and Rankin (1990).
7. Furth (1970); Alitto (1979); Hayford (1990).
8. Cohen (1974/1987); Levenson (1953); and Huang (1972).
9. Wylie (1980); Fogel (1987); and Ragvald (1978).
10. Sheel (1989). Readers should consider Stephen Averill's (1991) trenchant criticism of this book.
11. Mazur (1994).
12. Hamrin and Cheek (1986), and Goldman, Cheek, and Hamrin (1987).
13. Hamrin (1975). A portion of this analysis is readily available in Hamrin's chapter, 'Yang Xianzhen: Upholding Orthodox Leninist Theory', in Hamrin and Cheek (1986: 51–91).
14. Fisher (1982, 1986); Edmunds (1987); and Cheek (1981).
15. Wasserstrom (1992), quotation from 312.
16. Harding (1993: 30). Harding is referring specifically to aspects of the post-Mao reforms, but I take his point (which is given in a cumulative assessment of trends over the past thirty years on 34) to apply to our understanding of the Maoist period as well.
17. The best general account of this question is found in Grieder (1981), esp. 326–50.
18. See, for example, Hartford (1995) and Stranahan (forthcoming).
19. Stranahan (forthcoming: ch. 5); Israel (1966); Wasserstrom (1991).
20. Grieder (1981) and Pepper (1973). We should not forget that the KMT, too, was a revolutionary organization of great attractiveness, particularly in the 1920s. The CC Clique's 'rectification' within the KMT of 1930 is seen as the end of that revolutionary reputation; see Geisert (1986).
21. The ideal and practical aspects of rectification theory are clear in the original rectification documents of 1942, translated in Compton (1952), and they are analysed in their historical context both in Compton's introduction and in Teiwes (1979: 15–101).
22. Definition from Yahuda (1979). Generations of revolutionary intellectuals are identified by Li Zehou (1979: 470–1); this is helpfully expanded in English in Li Zehou and Schwarcz (1983–4). Deng Tuo falls into Yahuda's 'Older Intellectuals' category and crosses Li and Schwarcz's third 'Generation of the 1920s' and fourth 'Anti-Japanese War Generation'.
23. Naughton (1986: 125–31).
24. This is the thesis of Kathleen J. Hartford's doctoral dissertation (1980). These issues and Hartford's work are discussed further in Ch. 2.
25. Goldman (1967: 18–50); Lee (1973); and Wylie (1980: 162–95 and 261–80).
26. For instance, in the Taihang region just south of Jin Cha Ji such writers remained in control of the editorial boards of the local publishing houses well into the 1940s. See

Introduction 23

the complaint of Yang Xianzhen (1983), a more orthodox Marxist, who was there in the 1940s.
27. Thus the experience of Deng Tuo and his cohort of establishment intellectuals parallels the experience of Eastern European intellectuals as analysed by Konrád and Szelényi (1979).
28. See Zhong Kan (1982).
29. Kenneth Jowitt (1978: 34–62). This essay has been reprinted in revised form as 'The Leninist Phenomenon', in Jowitt (1992: 1–49).
30. This is her phrasing, drawing from her case study of Yang Xianzhen, whose fall in the 1960s was in part over the philosophical concepts of 'one divides into two' and 'two combines into one'; see Cheek and Hamrin (1986: 19).
31. Jowitt (1992: 4).
32. Jowitt (1992: 2).
33. Jowitt (1992: 18–19).
34. Jowitt (1992: 16).
35. Jowitt (1992: 15, n. 24).
36. Apter and Saich (1994). For example, they too note the 'collective individualism' produced among believers in the CCP.
37. Dai Qing (1994); Chen Yung-fa (1991); and Seybolt (1986).
38. Teiwes and Sun (1995), esp. 370–5.
39. Nie Rongzhen (YDT: 6).
40. The archetype, of course, comes from the Jesuits, the Society of Jesus, set up by the Pope in the 16th century to 'propagandize' the Catholic faith in the Counter-Reformation.
41. Panofsky (1976).
42. Kenez (1985: 224).
43. Schurmann (1968: 58–68).
44. Kenez (1985: 12–13 and ch. 10).
45. These are the weekly *xuexi* sessions visitors to Chinese work units have all observed. Before American scholars could visit China, Schurmann described the role of these study sessions in political communication (1968: 60–1). The classic study of *xuexi xiaozu* is Whyte (1974).
46. Teiwes (1979: 30–57), and chart on 45. Lest this picture appear too 'perfect,' the reader should note Teiwes's subtitle—his book is a study of the declining effectiveness of rectification.
47. *Xuanjiao xitong*, literally 'the propaganda and education system'. This is one of the six major integrated administrative systems of the PRC which are common knowledge to Chinese officials but little studied, so far, outside China. See Yan (1995). A useful chart of the range of activities covered in the propaganda *xitong* in the 1950s appears in Chang (1997). See also Liu (1975: 36–8). The best summary account of *xitong* is in Lieberthal (1995: 192–208).
48. Habermas (1989: 23).
49. Haraszti (1987: 54–79).
50. For the great influence of Habermas's concepts in recent American China studies see Wakeman (1993), which is part of a special issue of *Modern China* devoted to the question. Huang (1991) puts the question in broader context. Rowe (1990) sounded a clarion call to use the concept. I suggest we own up to our value orientations in Cheek (forthcoming).
51. Habermas, in Seidman (1989: 231).
52. Hsiao (1960: 184–5); Kuhn (1975: 261), which gives the most succinct review of Zhu

Xi's and Lü Kun's models; Victor Mair's chapter on 'Sacred Edict Lectures' (1985); and Übelhör (1989). A general survey of these propaganda systems can be found in Cheek (1984a).

53. *Li Shanyuan quanji*, 'Shengyu xuanjiang xiang-bao tiaoyue' (Regulations for Community Security [Xiang and Bao] Sacred Edict Lectures). Marvellous illustrations for the set-up of these lectures appear in this collection.
54. See Hsiao and Cheek (1995: 76–90).
55. Pusey (1983: 84–5).
56. Quoted in Ge Gongzhen (1964: 162), tr. Pusey (1983: 85–6).
57. Geertz, 'Ideology as a Cultural System', in Geertz (1973). He sets up ideology in contrast to 'science' as a cultural system good for obtaining and organizing knowledge.
58. It would appear, as Geertz suggested, that such Ideology is a temporary response to the social dislocation of modernization and that it is short-lived and will return to a more assumed small 'i' ideology or set of ideologies such as that which characterizes people and societies not under acute transformational stress. For his views on ideology, see his introduction and the essay 'Ideology as a Cultural System' in Geertz (1973).
59. Grieder (1981: 284–7).
60. Chuang (1970).
61. For an exhaustive literature review, see Cheek (1986: 14–26). Representative studies include Leys (1977); MacFarquhar (1974); Ahn Byung-joon (1976); Moody (1977); Lee (1978); Teiwes (1979); and Goldman (1981). Two studies are worthy of note for their early recognition of Deng's role *inside* the CCP: Maitan (1976: 198–200) and McDougall (1984: 271).

Deng Tuo's works have been translated into Japanese in To Taku, De Gan, and Ryo Umatsusa (1966). The translations from *Three Family Village* also include selections by Wu Han and Liao Mosha. This volume was updated by the same publisher in 1979 with a new essay by Nakano Kenji on 325–30. A German version, largely based on the Japanese versions, appears in Glaubitz (1969). I have translated a dozen *Evening Chats* essays and related texts in Cheek (1983–4).
62. See for example the reviews of American scholarship on China in Perry (1992: 1–3) and Harding (1993).
63. See Perry (1992), esp. 4–6; Wasserstrom (1991).
64. Titles mentioned below in this paragraph can be found in the Bibliography; their strengths and weaknesses are assessed individually in the text when they are used. For a review of pre-1987 Chinese materials, see Cheek (1986: 26–30).
65. For an assessment of these new kinds of sources on Party history, see Hearst and Saich (1997) and Zhang Zhuhong (1987).
66. The impact of such contacts on interpretation of documents is discussed in Cheek (1990). This is part of a series of different case studies on the topic in *Republican China*.

1

A Provincial Scholar Turns to National Revolution

During an abortive rebellion in his home town of Fuzhou in 1933 the subject of this biography changed his name to Deng Tuozhou. He is now known by the shortened version, Deng Tuo. The personal name means 'open up the continent'. At the time, Deng told a friend that he thought Fujian was too restricted a place and that they ought to go out into the raging storms beyond the province.[1] The name change symbolizes Deng Tuo's move from the life of a member of the provincial scholar-official elite in south-east China with local interests and universal cultural concerns rooted in the Chinese tradition to a career as a cadre in a revolutionary party with national political and economic concerns. Why did

1.1 Deng Tuo (2nd from left) and middle school classmates at Fengchi Hill, Fuzhou, 1928

he do this? Why did Deng Tuo join the Communist Party? What assumptions did he bring to that service? Why did he choose one particular set of ideas and institutions to serve rather than others available to him at the time?

Deng Tuo's life from childhood to the summer of 1937, when he went to the rural areas controlled by the CCP, traces the genesis of a young revolutionary. We see how the son of a former Qing dynasty district magistrate experienced the turmoil of the 1920s and 1930s and how he came to choose Marxism-Leninism and the CCP as the object of his service. There was both continuity and change in the attitudes Deng Tuo brought to his political activities. In fact, a synthesis or combination may best describe the traits which developed in him over these years and which formed the basis for his service to the CCP. His elite scholastic heritage was inculcated into him as a child, and he combined it with his own choice of a revolutionary ideology and organization. His intellectual work in history and the arts combined traditional concerns of classical Chinese historiography and aesthetics with the ideas and methods of Marxist historical materialism and the goals of the CCP to carry out political revolution and to popularize culture to the masses. Equally, Deng Tuo's service to his new organization, the CCP, reflects a neo-traditional mix of ancient scholar-official attitudes of loyalty and personal superiority of the educated elite and new ideas of nationalism, revolution, and obedience by cadres to Leninist democratic centralism. It was an unstable mix that came apart in the 1960s, but during the turmoil of the 1930s and 1940s this version of the Communist movement provided a successful way for the educated elite to participate in an emerging national government. It gave people like Deng Tuo a transitional role in Chinese history between Confucian scholar-officials and modern professionals and elected officials.

Family and Schooling

Deng Tuo was born in Fuzhou, Fujian province on the south-east coast of China. By the 1920s, when Deng Tuo was a teenager, Fuzhou was a moderately active port of some 600,000 people. The house in which Deng Tuo was born and raised still survives. It is a traditional-style complex in an extended U shape within courtyard walls. It lies on the north-eastern lower slopes of Wushi Hill (*Wushi Shan*), one of the major hills and parks in the south-western corner of this hilly city. The Deng household was not wealthy, but enjoyed space and beauty. The household courtyard, even today, is overwhelmingly verdant, with a steep slope rising behind the house, home of a thicket of plants and trees, mainly bamboo.[2] In Deng's youth the garden slope inside the compound also contained banyan, willow, banana, and other trees, lotus and other flowers. Behind the house is an old pagoda with yet more flowers in the springtime. During his childhood Deng Tuo often studied and played there.[3]

This was a traditional scholar-official's family; gentry of the south-east China coast. The household was run by Deng Tuo's mother and his maternal grandmother, who made sure the children knew all the stories of their clan history. Deng's father, Deng Ouyu, was a Qing dynasty scholar-official turned schoolteacher during the Republic.[4] The family survived on his teacher's salary and thus were not wealthy. However, descriptions of the Dengs as outright poor in the reminiscence literature rather overlook the rich cultural life and large house the family enjoyed.[5]

Deng Tuo was the fifth son and seventh child of the family and the youngest. His birthday is recorded as 26 February 1912, which was the traditional New Year's dating of a birth. Thus, he was born some time during the twelve months before. He was formally named Zijian. Like many of his social class, Deng had a battery of childhood and family pet names. At school he was known to his friends as Deng Zijian.[6]

The lives and careers of Deng's three surviving elder brothers reflect the changes confronting Confucian gentry in the early twentieth century.[7] The eldest of the three surviving older brothers was Deng Boyu. He was eighteen years older than Deng Tuo and had graduated from school and moved away before Deng could remember. In fact, Boyu had joined the KMT and was instrumental in bringing Deng Tuo to Kaifeng and Henan University in 1934. The next-to-eldest brother, Deng Zhongzhou, became a teacher in the arts and handicrafts, and owned his own workshop. He died at age thirty, late in Deng's adolescence. The third eldest brother, Deng Shuqun, was nine years older than Deng and closest to him. Shuqun graduated from Qinghua University in Beiping and received a government scholarship to study in the United States, where he received a Ph.D. in entomology. By the time Deng Tuo left home in 1929 to attend university, Shuqun had become a successful scientist and was at the Academy of Sciences in Nanjing. He encouraged his younger brother to follow in his footsteps.[8]

Deng Tuo also grew up with a strong awareness of his clan history, which claimed notable heroes such as Deng Su, a model of Confucian rectitude from the *Standard History of the Song*, and Deng Mouqi, the famous leader of a peasant rebellion in Fujian in the fifteenth century.[9] Deng Tuo's sense of heritage extended to his social group—the literati elite of traditional China and the emerging intelligentsia of the New Culture Movement of his day. In traditional style the school-aged Deng Tuo would sit in the courtyard studying under the great banyan tree with his brother Deng Zhongzhou. A large rock there was carved with the calligraphy of Chu Lucai, a literatus of the late eighteenth century.[10] Chu's poem, which Deng memorized, ran in part: 'Flowers and birds become in the end friends of the wind and the moon; | Poetry and books written for posterity serve as fields for children and grandchildren.' Brother Zhongzhou told him about poets, ancient worthies, and calligraphers. Such literary monuments as this inscribed boulder were common in Fuzhou and were an active part of Deng Tuo's youth. He and schoolmates would visit the many historic parks and Buddhist temples of Fuzhou. Gu Hill park in particular has boulders inscribed with poems by famous scholar-officials, monks, and literati in their own calligraphy. Among them are those of Wen Tianxiang, who made a heroic stand against invading Mongol forces in Fuzhou in the thirteenth century,[11] Qi Jiguang (1528–87), who battled the 'Japanese pirates' off the Fujian coast on behalf of the Ming, and Lin Zexu, the famous Fuzhou native who confronted the British at Canton in 1840 over the opium trade. In later life Deng Tuo honoured this heritage by his choice of the pen name under which he wrote poetry, Zuo Hai (Left of the Ocean); this alludes to these and other 'great men from left of the ocean' (*zuo hai wei ren*).[12]

Deng's affiliation with traditional scholar-officials was more than a matter of admiration. Deng Tuo was raised in the manner of the traditional Chinese literati elite—memorizing poetry and practising calligraphy. Deng Ouyu paid great attention to his children's education and monitored their 'morning classes' at home before he went to teach at school. Long before he was school age, Deng Tuo participated in these classes. The children had to memorize traditional poems and practise calligraphy daily. They practised calligraphy by the '*xuan wan*' method, in which the student writes large versions of each character over and over without letting the arm or wrist touch the writing surface. Once mastered, this technique enables one to write exceptionally smooth and powerful strokes, for which Deng Tuo achieved some renown later in life.[13]

Deng Tuo's early family life provided a model of a scholarly, if somewhat impoverished, life based largely on the Neo-Confucian model of practical public service.[14] Poetry was the soul of a scholar and calligraphy his refinement. Although evidence is scant, family relations seemed to conform to traditional patterns of authority and organization: a busy corporate life built around grooming the children for future success in their studies, along with a rich sense of literati heritage. The house was full of books. Of the four traditional categories, 'Classics', 'History', 'Philosophers', and 'Poetry', the latter two dominated among the string-bound traditional editions in Deng Ouyu's library. Deng Tuo was an avid reader and is said to have made his way through the entire library before ranging farther afield to local libraries and friends' collections. *The Four Books* and *The Five Classics*, the philosophers, poetry, traditional novels, and writings by modern literati were among his fare. He was particularly interested in poetry and his friends recall that he preferred the poetry of Qu Yuan, Du Fu, Su Dongpo, and Lu You.

Deng Ouyu's library was not antiquarian nor was his outlook conservative. It included modern texts such as those of the late Qing reformer Liang Qichao and books and periodicals from the New Culture Movement, including translations of European works and even revolutionary texts that had been proscribed.[15] Deng Tuo later remarked that he was especially influenced by Liang Qichao's essay, 'On Inspiration'.[16] Thus Deng Tuo was raised to believe, from his childhood experience, that new and revolutionary ideas such as those found in *The Communist Manifesto* and the journal *New Youth* were not incompatible with his literati heritage but were part of that with which his father expected him to deal. Unlike others of his generation, Deng Tuo did not have to reject his father's ideas in order to entertain the radical alternatives that were to confront them all in later adolescence.[17]

The schools Deng Tuo attended, however, marked a break with the traditional heritage of his upbringing. They were new schools set up by the provincial authorities, no longer the private tutors for the rich or the *shuyuan* which primed gentry boys for Imperial Exams. In this school system Deng Tuo emerged as a bookish but outspoken lad, self-confident, an acknowledged leader among his peers, convivial and earnest, and most definitely opinionated. He broadened his reading, particularly in modern political texts, polished his poetry, and tested the waters in political organization. Most importantly Deng was confronted personally with the political turmoil of his time during the critical period of life (ages 17 to 25) by which most scholars define a political generation.

Deng probably entered 'early middle school' in 1923 at age 11 and was promoted to the 'upper middle school' in 1926, graduating in 1929 at age 17.[18] During these years, 1923–9, the impact of China's military unrest and social revolution reached Fuzhou. In 1924, in the second year of lower middle school, Deng and his school friend, Fu Jialin (Fu Yiling), saw their hometown become the centre of the New Culture Movement in their province. As they walked home from school, they could not have missed the boycott of Japanese products that had swept the city. The boys also witnessed the arrest of several students from their school by the forces of the local militarists. The scene was repeated more violently during Deng's more impressionable years in upper middle school when he was around 16. Then warlord troops surrounded Deng's school and arrested several students on the pretext that a copy of the proscribed 'revolutionary' journal, *New Youth*, had been found on campus. It takes little schooling in psychology to imagine the effect direct military intervention in one's high school would have on a teenager, particularly on a thoughtful and outspoken young man such as Deng Tuo.[19]

Ever since their later years at lower middle school, Deng Tuo and Fu Yiling had been constant companions, often reading together in the Wushi Hill library or at Deng's house. Like many of their generation, they enjoyed the writings of Guo Moruo and Lu Xun. Fu particularly recalls their favorite readings: Liang Qichao's famous reformist writings in *Essays from the Ice Drinker's Studio*, the romantic poem-novel, *The Lone Swan*, by the Buddhist writer Su Manshu (The Reverend Mandju), and the rather sappy 'anti-feudal' romantic novels of Jiang Guangchi.[20] Deng Tuo's first love, however, was poetry and the two traditional pastimes associated with it: wandering through historic gardens and participating in refined poetry gatherings. The central area of Fuzhou is dotted with beautiful parks and gardens, many on the slopes of its hills along which small paths wind between boulders inscribed with elegant calligraphy of famous literati. Deng Tuo and his friends wandered through these sites savouring the beauty and the *haute culture* of the remaining literary and religious artefacts that dotted the gardens.

One of the most powerful images of Deng Tuo's youth is a photograph of him taken in 1928 with some classmates in just such a scene at Fengchi park. Carved on the rocks of Fengchi are poems by the traditional heroes Wen Tianxiang and Li Gang, in various styles of calligraphy—great seal, small seal, standard, and grass style. The photo (reproduced at the beginning of this chapter) shows a dozen boys, some in traditional scholar's robes and some in trousers and school tunics, standing in front of rounded boulders inscribed with ancient calligraphy. Second from the left is Deng Tuo, aged 16. He is in scholar's robes, but his arms are crossed before him outside the broad sleeves, and he stands with his weight on one leg in a pose of casual self-confidence. The photo reflects his classmates' reminiscences of Deng as a leader among his school peers.[21]

Deng also accompanied his father to extracurricular poetry gatherings held by local literati. These 'Poetry Competitions' were held in a large temple with a table set on a platform and a candle or incense burner on it. Each poet would rise to give his reading and the group would select and honour the best. Deng was so taken with the idea that he set up similar poetry gatherings with his classmates in his father's house. His interest in poetry was intense. Li Tuozhi, another schoolmate, recalls finding Deng Tuo reclining on his bed reciting Liu Yong's poem, 'Yu lin ling' (Rain-Drenched Bells). Li was impressed that Deng did not parse ancient poems according to a rigid grammatical formula, but rather memorized so many that he developed a 'feel' for the proper intonation.[22]

Deng's special love for Liu Yong's poem reflects Deng's mix of traditional and contemporary concerns. He read revolutionary articles in *New Youth*, explored Marxist interpretations of Chinese economic history, enjoyed low-brow romantic fiction, and identified with classical poets. In Liu Yong's case, the poem is associated with the scholarly tradition of laments for imperilled dynasties, clearly relevant to China in the 1920s.[23] Fu Yiling recalls that Deng not only excelled at poetry and calligraphy, but that he could sing beautifully and paint as well. Educated in all the skills a gentleman should have, Deng Tuo's response to the invasion of his school by warlord government soldiers was to paint a scene of pine trees on a fan and compose a colophon to go with it: 'Lingering to Console the Lonely Pine'. The classical poetic image is one of unbending character in the face of adversity.[24]

Naturally, we should be mindful of the selectivity of memory among Deng's high school friends. In addition to the usual vagaries of memory over half a century, this selectivity is heightened by the politicized nature of the exoneration literature in post-Mao China.[25] Here that extra selectivity serves as notice of the continuing relevance of Deng Tuo's example. The same mix of classical poetry and revolutionary commitments continues among a part of the intellectual establishment in the PRC, as we have seen in the striking poetry meeting to commemorate Deng in Fuzhou in 1986.

Aside from politics, Deng Tuo was exposed to an amazing array of lifestyles, each of which he investigated. One of Deng's uncles was a Buddhist monk, and Deng read sutras with him. They even went to hear Fuzhou's renowned scholar-monk, Yuan Ying (1879–1953), expound the dharma. One of Deng's brothers was a Christian,[26] and Deng accompanied him to church to hear sermons and even glanced through the New Testament. Deng also took an interest in martial arts, spending some time practicing Shaolin-style Kungfu.[27] Thus Deng Tuo was aware of and had both the opportunity and the family model to choose from two powerful but very different religious traditions. He did not choose one over the other, but he seemed able to integrate an appreciation for them into his intellectual world. These childhood experiences seem to have left Deng comfortable with difference and accepting of diversity, an attitude he carried throughout his life and one which did not interfere with his primary commitment to his chosen orthodoxy. His ire was reserved for more direct and flagrant injustices.[28]

During his last years of middle school Deng began to read the current debates of the day as they appeared in the new journals. He followed the debate over 'Science and the Outlook on Life' between Carson Chang (Zhang Junmai) and Ding Wenjiang from 1923. Later it was the debate on 'Socialist Ideology'. Finally, he studied the 'Debates on China's Social History' published in *Dushu zazhi* (Reader's Magazine) beginning in 1928. Deng himself was to contribute to the continuation of this debate in the mid-1930s.[29] During this time, Marxist analyses of China's social and economic problems were popular in the intellectual magazines of Shanghai and Beiping. The social history controversy of 1928–33 centred around the Chinese revolution and why, by 1927 when Chiang Kai-shek turned against the Communists, it had failed. Wang Lixi (1899–1934), the editor of *Reader's Magazine* (*Dushu zazhi*), launched a special double issue on social history by explicitly announcing that the concern for revolutionary strategy underlay the study of history.[30] Participants in this debate were not professional historians or Party propagandists, but young intellectuals carrying on the ideas from the New Culture Movement. Although they differed in interpretation, all embraced a faith that historical materialism was a truer mirror than any other, reflecting the dynamics of the contemporary world and thus providing vital information for those who wished to shape society.[31] Indeed, Wang Lixi's introduction to the debate announces the goals which were to shape Deng's historical writings between 1934 and 1937:

> The present is the time when blind and undirected revolutions have reached a blind alley.... therefore there is dire need of *correct* revolutionary theories to guide *correct* revolutions on their new path.... In order to search for the correct future revolution, we must first decide on the solution to a foremost problem: 'Upon what stage has Chinese society already embarked?'[32]

Deng Tuo's first sustained study of the application of Marxism to Chinese problems thus came through the pages of a public debate over the periodization of Chinese history that claimed to explain the roots of China's problems and the road to her salvation. When he wrote, Deng Tuo predominantly wrote on history. It was not until late 1933, though, that Deng published his first sustained scholarly article, and that was on the philosophical importance of dialectical materialism, which is the

1.2 Deng Tuo, Shanghai, 1934

root of the Marxist view of history. He had much to say and do before then.

Student Activism in Shanghai

Deng Tuo graduated from upper middle school in the early summer of 1929.[33] Together with a group of friends he took the boat to Shanghai to sit the entrance exams which were offered there for various universities. At this critical juncture in his life a very human mistake determined much of his future life. Deng Tuo went to the Academy of Sciences in Nanjing to visit his elder brother, Deng Shuqun, who insisted that Deng sit the Qinghua University exam and work toward obtaining a government scholarship to study in America, as he had done. A caring elder brother, Shuqun offered to pay for Deng Tuo's college expenses. An obedient younger brother, Deng Tuo agreed. However, upon his return to Shanghai, the young Fuzhou literatus succumbed to the lures of the city and accompanied a group of fellow provincials to the movies. They stayed out late and Deng slept through the first half of the Qinghua entrance exam. He did manage, in the end, to sit the exams for the less prestigious Guanghua University in Shanghai, which he passed. His elder brother was incensed when he failed to find young Deng's name in the newspaper lists of entrants to Qinghua. A fraternal squabble ensued when Shuqun dressed down his errant younger brother. Deng Tuo retorted, 'Do you think Qinghua and studying in America will save our country? Under the corrupt bureaucrats of the Kuomintang all contributions of science and literature, all experiments, all are empty talk.'[34] These may have been words borrowed from politics to defend the blunders of a teenager, but they were sadly accurate. The decades ahead failed to provide a liberal alternative to the KMT and CCP.[35] Instead of turning his eyes to science and America and going to Beiping, where the Communist Party was in complete disarray,[36] Deng Tuo returned to Shanghai, the home of the CCP, and became involved in local politics.

Deng Tuo entered the Socio-Economics Department (*shehui jingji xi*) of Guanghua University in Shanghai in the fall of 1929, where he also specialized in English.[37] Shanghai was a different world from Fuzhou, and Guanghua University was a scene of patriotic fervour. As soon as Deng Tuo arrived he heard the school slogan, 'Don't forget saving the country when studying; don't forget studying when saving the country.'[38] Deng made good use of the new opportunities to expand his reading into the wide range of progressive and revolutionary literature available then in Shanghai, particularly the numerous translations of foreign literature and political theory. Guanghua University's underground Party organization was quite active and Deng was eventually recruited into the CCP through a front organization. After the famous League of Left-Wing Writers was set up in Shanghai in March 1930, the Party set up another group that June known as 'The Alliance of Chinese Social Scientists' (*Zhongguo shehui kexuejia lianmeng*). There may have been a branch of these organizations or individual members active on the Guanghua campus in the spring of 1930, and Deng Tuo was drawn into them.[39]

The purpose of the 'Alliance', and particularly of its front organization—'The Social Scientist Research Association' (*Shehui kexuejia yanjiu hui*)—was to prepare university students and factory workers for

Party membership.⁴⁰ It was a recruiting organization. A number of future CCP establishment intellectuals were active in the parent organization, the 'Alliance': Ai Siqi, the orthodox theoretician; Hu Qiaomu, later a secretary for Mao and a dominant Party leader in the post-Mao period; and Xu Dixin, later to become one of the PRC's leading economists.⁴¹ From March 1930 to his arrest in December 1932 Deng Tuo studied Marxism-Leninism in this group. It clearly shaped his future work, particularly his many historical writings in the 1930s. The Alliance's guiding principles proclaimed: 'On the basis of the Marxist viewpoint to analyse the political economy of China and the world in order to promote the Chinese revolution [and] . . . vigorously to join in the practical revolution of the Chinese proletarian revolutionary movement.'⁴² The 'Alliance' was under the direct control of the CCP underground (Wang Xuewen, former editor of *New Thought Tides*, was Party secretary) and organized demonstrations and marches on a nearly weekly basis from the spring of 1930.⁴³ Here Deng learned how to be a student agitator.

Deng Tuo joined the Communist Party in December 1930, taking the revolutionary name of Ding Binggen.⁴⁴ In the Party Deng served as the secretary (*mishu*) of both his alliance group at Guanghua and the 'Shanghai Anti-Imperialist Great Alliance' (*Shanghai fandi da tongmeng*) of the district Party organization. He also handled day-to-day liaison with various Party cells (*zhibu*) of the French Concession District Party Committee, which was in the southern districts of the city and thus known as 'Fa'nan': French South.⁴⁵ At this time his work seemed mostly administrative and surely included a period of probation. In any event, he took part in Party study sessions where he learned more about Marxism-Leninism and particularly the complex debates over historical materialism.

All was not revolution, however. In the summer of 1930, Deng returned home for the school holidays. Back in Fuzhou he continued his interests in classical studies, though his topics were not of antiquarian interest, but rather were ancient patriots and Fujian worthies. Fu Yiling, who was up from Xiamen University on the same holidays, recalls discussing ancient poetry with Deng that summer in Fuzhou.⁴⁶ Again, in the spring of 1931, Deng returned to Fuzhou, this time to prepare for entrance exams to another university. At home for the summer, he took the opportunity to spend time back at the library at Wushi Hill and to continue his literary studies.⁴⁷ During the summer and early fall, Deng caught up with his old classmate Li Tuozhi, who soon published an essay by Deng in Fuzhou's *Nanhua Daily*.⁴⁸ Deng Tuo's piece, 'Beneath Violet Gold Mountain' (*Zijin shan xia*), appeared under the pen-name of Xiao Jing. The original text is not available, but Li's memory of it is enough to indicate that Deng's satirical style, for which he would later be famous in the 1960s, was already effective.

When Deng Tuo returned to Shanghai for the new school year in September 1931 he had transferred to the Shanghai Academy of Law and Politics (*Shanghai fazheng xueyuan*), where he enrolled in the Economics Department. At that time the leading Communists Li Da and Zhou Xinmin were teaching there, presumably passing on more of the academic and activist Marxist currents in the Party.[49] Deng's academic interests certainly continued, for Fu Yiling recalls that in the fall of 1931 Deng sent him the translation of a foreign social science text, *Shehui kexue yu lishi fangfa* (Social Science and Historical Method).[50] Fu says the book both reflected the scientific nature of Deng's approach to history and deeply influenced Fu himself.[51] Although the translation of the book's title and the tone of Fu Yiling's comments stress 'social science', which after all was the popular thing for aspiring progressive Chinese intellectuals in the 1930s, the book turns out to be a translation of **La Méthode historique** *appliquée aux sciences sociales* (**The Historical Method** Applied to the Social Sciences) by Charles Seignobos (1854–1942).[52]

As with Yan Fu two generations earlier, Deng Tuo's and Fu Yiling's use of a major European text did not conform to the spirit of the author's intention even though, in this case, they adopted much of his critical methodology. A detailed content analysis is not necessary to see how this book was used by these young historians. In this case the books may be judged by their covers. The French original emphasizes *history*, as the bold face in the title above accurately reflects. It is, in fact, a book on historiography and the ways in which the social sciences may be improved by the historical method. The Chinese translation places '*Social Sciences*' in front, and while the body of the text appears to be an accurate translation, the Chinese prefaces emphasize the social sciences, sociology, and Durkheim. Seignobos, though not well known to English readers, is considered one of the founding fathers, along with Ferdinand Lot, of modern historical methods.[53] While the rules of documentary evidence which Seignobos favoured (criticism of sources, philological analysis, and sympathetic interpretation of texts) are all to be found in Deng's and Fu's historical writings in the 1930s, what Seignobos is remembered for in the West—that history is an autonomous branch of learning which should not try to formulate general laws but rather should aim at explaining reality—is not found in their work.[54] Deng's and Fu's commitment to Marxism and the general laws of dialectics contradicted Seignobos's views. Since the translation which the young historians had in hand was basically accurate, the failure was less in the transmission than in the reception: it did not serve their needs for an explanation of China's ills that was directly relevant to revolutionary change. As with much of Western culture, these young Chinese radicals took only what they could use.[55]

The autumn of 1931 was not a time of quiet academic pursuit for Deng Tuo. Shortly after the Mukden Incident of 18 September, there was an upsurge of student activity in protest at the 'selling out' of the north-eastern provinces to Japan.[56] At this time Deng Tuo and his colleague Tao Bai joined in the propaganda work of the CCP underground as full Party members. Deng served as head of the Propaganda Department for the decimated French South District Committee from the fall of 1931 until December 1932.[57] They made banners, wrote wall newspapers, and printed tracts.[58] In line with the policies of the Internationalists in the Party leadership, Deng added public speaking. Not only did he march down Nanjing Road with other demonstrators, but he took to giving public speeches at busy intersections.[59] Such work was extremely dangerous. Deng Tuo was critical of the Party rules which required organizers to announce the place and time of their demonstrations in advance, since this only helped the KMT police. He took this up with his superior, Zhang Jiafu, but the higher-ups did not respond.[60] As Patricia Stranahan has shown, it was precisely this policy of public demonstrations that contributed to the murderous number of arrests and executions of Shanghai CCP members in the early 1930s.[61]

Deng Tuo was arrested on 11 December 1932 during a public march commemorating the Canton Uprising. He had been arrested before and briefly held by the authorities, but as often happened at the time was soon released. This time, however, the KMT military police remembered 'Ding Binggen' and sent him to the Suzhou Reformatory.[62] It was a ghastly experience, and understandably a turning point in the young student's life. Two important things happened in prison: Deng suffered bitterly, and he lost organizational contact with the Party for some five years.

Deng Tuo was in prison in Nanjing and Suzhou for approximately eight months, from December 1932 until the summer of 1933.[63] He was tortured though he maintained that he 'didn't talk'. In addition, he contracted tuberculosis, which plagued him for the rest of his life.[64] Deng also confronted the death of his comrades. He memorized poignant 'Wall Poems' left by an inmate executed for political crimes.[65] He collected them in a volume under the title of his own poem, 'Southern Crown Weeds' (*Nan Guan Cao*), which borrowed the title of a poetry collection by the noted late Ming loyalist, Xia Wanshun.[66] Wall poems were common in prison, since the inmates did not have paper. This would indicate that most political inmates were fairly well educated—intellectuals active enough in the Communist movement to get arrested. Deng's own prison poems are written in the form of classical seven-character-line quatrains and express his sense of sacrifice and mission both in the traditional natural imagery that literati before him used and by reference, as in the title borrowed from Xia Wanshun, to previous literati who opposed governments they thought wrong. One significant aspect of Deng's prison poems is this combination of quite elegant traditional forms of poetry with revolutionary verve.[67] These poems, like his history essays a few years later, are examples of the ease with which he sought to combine traditional literary and scholarly skills with the new revolutionary movement.[68]

Current Chinese biographies of Deng Tuo say that he was released from jail through the efforts of his father, who came up to Suzhou from Fuzhou to 'arrange' his bail.[69] However, unpublished accounts maintain that in order to secure his release from gaol, Deng Tuo signed a formal recantation of communism. This was hardly an unusual practice in the 1930s, as demonstrated by the case of Bo Yibo, An Ziwen, Yang Xianzhen, and others, who later obtained their release from Beiping's Caolanzi Prison in this fashion.[70] The important difference between Deng and the others was that the Bo Yibo group received Central Committee approval for this deception, while Deng Tuo did *not*. As such, Deng's 'confession' has been seen as weakness in the face of the enemy, and this 'historical error' was to haunt him in later years.[71] Nonetheless, if one keeps in mind that the KMT secret police under Dai Li in the 1930s operated in a fashion similar to security units in Chile and Argentina in the 1970s, then Deng Tuo's desire not to be written off as 'missing' is more than understandable.

Prison was not only a traumatic experience; it separated Deng Tuo from the Communist Party. Current Chinese biographies maintain that he tried several times to re-contact his cell or some authority, but searched in Shanghai in vain.[72] It may seem strange that Deng could not establish connections, especially since he worked with active Party members such as Ji Bufei in the Fujian rebellion later that year. However, it was not unusual for Party members to lose organizational contact with their Party cell. The CCP underground was extremely clandestine in the early 1930s. And for good reason. One after another Party cell was being rolled up by Dai Li's KMT secret police.[73] Nonetheless, Deng's inability to reconnect with the Party organization after working with CCP cadres in Fuzhou the next year and spending a further six months in Shanghai in similar circles in 1934 is notable. One cannot but wonder if the lad was not trying very hard. Given the disarray of the Shanghai CCP, particularly in 1934, reconnecting probably would have led to his untimely death.

Fuzhou: A Cadre Without a Party

From the history of Deng Tuo's life between 1933 and 1937 we can see that his adherence to Marxism-Leninism was integral to his idea of himself. Deng's communism was based on intellectual appreciation of some complexity and free choice and was not based on a vague sense of patriotism or compulsion. He thought Marxism and a Leninist Party were the best vehicles to serve China. The real question is, given the organizational disarray of the Party in the 1930s what possessed the young man to serve it? The short-term answer is that he didn't, or at least he could not find a Party contact during these years. The long-term answer for his faith in dialectical materialism and the Party emerges from his activities and writings during the next five years.

On Dialectical Materialism

Deng Tuo returned to Fuzhou in the autumn of 1933.[74] There, amid the ruins of his war-torn home town, Deng spent his days with his old schoolmate, Fu Yiling, in the Wushi Hill library. There they caught up on current events, particularly by reading the contemporary affairs journal, *New China*. In this journal he encountered the raging debate over the philosophical bases of Marxism, the ontology and epistemology underlying the historical materialism of Marx and Engels.[75] In particular Deng reacted to Zhang Dongsun's essay, 'Is a Logic of Motion Possible?', published in the same journal three months earlier.[76] Deng sent his reply from Fuzhou in an article dated 12 October entitled 'Formal Logic or Dialectical Materialism?' and published in the December issue of Shanghai's *New China*. This is the earliest contemporary piece of Deng's writings available today.[77] The article is a review and rebuttal of Zhang's, which had championed formal logic. In his article Deng sets out to demonstrate the weakness of logic in explaining motion and development in the material world.[78] He argues that the only scientific method of analysis is dialectical materialism.

Deng Tuo's Chinese biographers have justifiably emphasized this historical document.[79] In it, the 23-year-old Deng Tuo voices his beliefs, and they show him to be a committed Communist. One biographer, Zuo Lu, quotes several sentences to represent what Deng said. Since this is the first event in this early period for which there is independent evidence (the journal is available in the West) we can get some sense of the 'editorial bias' of his Chinese biographers. In the main they come out quite well; whatever distortions or omissions they make seem to be due more to the genre, that of the exemplary biography, than to any political censorship that would require wholesale denial or twisting of important facts. Nonetheless, they differ significantly in interpretation from a Western view.

Zuo Lu says that after his release from jail, Deng Tuo continued 'to fight against the reactionary KMT "encirclement campaign" in literature'. Thus, Deng took on one of Chiang Kai-shek's 'lackeys', the philosopher Zhang Dongsun, who was denouncing dialectical materialism and Marxism. Zhang is quoted as saying, 'In human thought, dialectical materialism is an obsolete curio, best put on display in a museum.' Deng Tuo's article, says Zuo Lu, refutes Zhang's view and upholds the Marxist philosophical viewpoint. Zuo quotes from Deng's essay several times to the effect that there are objective laws in the material world whether we choose to recognize them or not; further, if the laws people perceive (subjective laws) correspond accurately with these objective laws, we then have in our hands a powerful scientific tool. Deng Tuo goes on to say that all things carry within themselves contradictions that develop through an accumulation of quantity that turns into qualitative transformation, and, through the sublation (*aufheben*) of these internal contradictions, things progress to higher stages. This summary of the article concludes with Deng's claim that 'Dialectical materialism, then, is the universal law of the existence, motion, and development of nature, human society, and thought.'[80]

This summary conforms to orthodox dialectical materialism in the PRC, and would easily please the leading CCP dialecticians on whom Deng was likely relying—Li Da and Ai Siqi.[81] As well, it places Deng squarely on the side of the angels according to Mao's later description of the early 1930s as the time of KMT 'military and cultural encirclement campaigns'. The biographers thus imply that Deng was doing his bit for some imagined coherent Party line on the cultural front while the Red Army was doing its bit on the military front.[82] The implication that Deng worked in concert with the Party at this time is inaccurate, as he was out of touch with the organization. While this claim remains unproved, the account is still an accurate reflection of what Deng wrote.

Deng's essay is far richer than simply an example of a precocious Party pundit. First of all, it is a pleasingly clear and direct article, no mean feat for a discussion on dialectics. While the prose is clear, the vocabulary is not. One is reminded of Deng's high school chum's dismay at his command of technical terms as he peppers the article with a cloud of foreign terms and names, many printed vertically in English, producing an effect similar to printing Chinese characters or Arabic script in *The Economist*. It is a 'May Fourth' article of the sort Qu Qiubai decried as 'the new classical language (*xin wenyanwen*)' with confusing neologisms and foreign words throughout. This text was thus addressed to a very elite group, and indeed, Deng early on complains of ill-educated writers' abuse of dialectics. It also conforms to the combative tone of the period. Deng addresses his object of criticism always as 'Mr Zhang Dongsun' or, irreverently, as 'Mr Dongsun', and announces at the start that academics is impartial and everyone may politely state their views. Yet, Deng proceeds to ridicule Zhang and his ideas for the rest of the article, saying, for instance, that 'Chinese-style' (i.e., traditional Confucian) scholars have always pursued 'jumbled scholarship', conflating the ideas of obviously different thinkers, such as Zhu Xi and Cheng Yi, into the 'Cheng–Zhu' school, and that Zhang Dongsun is no better in his identification of Marx with Hegel.[83]

This article on philosophy from 1933 reflects Deng's show of scholarship and clear line of argumentation which characterize his famous essays from the 1960s, *Evening Chats at Yanshan*. Deng does not suffer fools gladly, and in the academic argument he gives no quarter. Yet he is not totalistic. After demonstrating to his own satisfaction that Zhang's formal logic is the same as Bertrand Russell's—hopelessly unable to perceive and analyse motion in the material world (as Bogdanov said) and therefore, to quote Engels (twice), not worthy of the name 'science'—Deng cautions the over-enthusiastic supporter not to discard formal logic entirely. Formal logic has considerable merit in studying isolated problems (as Plekhanov has said); it is simply useless for grasping the big picture.[84] Deng is more successful in rebutting Zhang's assertions than in laying out a clear defence of his view. Deng's faith in dialectical materialism is unequivocal, but rests, weakly, on two appeals to authority (Engels and Plekhanov) and a patently question-begging passage in which he says the components of dialectical materialism—internal contradictions as the motive force of change in things, sublation, etc.—accurately reflect reality, because reality *is* that way.[85]

This essay confirms Deng Tuo's positivist faith in the 'science' of Marxism. He believes there is a way to know the world and 'to take it in hand' and that way is dialectical materialism. 'Therefore, subjective laws are only objective laws which people have recognized. The only question is whether or not the subjective laws which people have recognized accord with the laws of motion and change among the material things of the outside world (objectively existing laws), and so whether or not they are able to grasp the truth of material things. If they can, this is the unity of subjectivity and objectivity. This is scientific truth.'[86] Deng follows this with a statement of faith in the Communist future, made in passing in a list of self-evident truths to which Zhang and his logic are hopelessly blind. Here we may return to the idealism of a 23-year-old student radical:

> he [Mr Zhang] does not see that the society of the future will be entirely different from the present, that humanity will be able to control the natural world and moreover eliminate the natural character of society, that the development of history will be completely subject to human prescription, that people's will shall be completely free. Then human society will make unprecedented advances, developing humanity to the highest level of culture, and will be able to control nature in order to provide humanity with universal happiness.[87]

The Fujian Rebellion

Fuzhou in the autumn of 1933 was a scene of seething political intrigue, warlord posturing, and confused patriotic and revolutionary hopes in which Deng Tuo actively participated.[88] As was the case for most of south China, Fujian was only nominally under control of the central government in Nanjing. The provincial governor, Jiang Guangnai, was not connected with important factional circles in Nanjing and soon led the uprising against Nanjing. Fujian was ostensibly well integrated with the KMT administration through the famous 19th Route Army, which had valiantly battled the Japanese during fighting in Shanghai in January 1932. They had fought so well that the battle convinced the Japanese to review their military policy toward China.[89] The 19th Route Army had then been transferred to Fujian later in 1932 to serve as the eastern flank of the Nationalist Government's fifth encirclement campaign against the CCP's Red Army in neighbouring Jiangxi province. Yet the army bristled at being forced to fight fellow Chinese instead of the Japanese, and it suffered humiliating defeats at the hands of the Communists in August and September of 1933.[90] Like Zhang Xueliang's Manchurian troops in Xi'an three years later, these soldiers were willing to risk rebellion in order to stop fighting other Chinese and to start fighting the Japanese. Their leader, Cai Tingkai, was the Nanjing-appointed commander of the 19th Route Army, and he quickly became 'the military power behind the Fukien regime'.[91]

The rebellion was spearheaded by another dissatisfied KMT leader, Chen Mingshu, a former governor of Guangdong province who had made a tour of Europe following his retirement from the post of Minister of Communications in Nanjing due to his involvement in a corruption scandal.[92] Thus the rebellion in Fujian was led by the nominal KMT governor, the commander of the central government's army and a standing member of the government's Military Affairs Commission. This serves to remind us how tenuous Nanjing's hold on outlying provinces was. It also indicates, contrary to contemporary claims made in Nanjing and later Communist historiography, that the 'People's Revolutionary Government' formed in Fuzhou on 2 November 1933 was not a Marxist regime, but rather a 'motley assortment of dissident KMT elements, left-wing politicians and military officers'.[93]

Deng Tuo worked for this motley assortment as the propaganda liaison officer for the People's Government in the Cultural Affairs Committee.[94] Deng temporarily resumed contact with some CCP members when his associate, Ji Bufei, asked him to participate in the rebel government. However, unlike Ji, Deng Tuo was not officially assigned to this task by a CCP organization.[95] Together with others, such as Liu Xiangwen, Ji and Deng worked to propagate the radical goals proclaimed by the revolutionary leadership. When the revolutionary government fell less than two months later, Deng lost contact with Ji and, once again, the Party.[96] Given the poor track record of the Fujian regime,[97] not to mention its questionable leaders, one may wonder why Deng participated at all.

We do not know why Deng Tuo participated. In the brief time during which the Fujian People's Government operated (mostly in Fuzhou, Quanzhou, and Xiamen, it seems), all we know of Deng Tuo's personal activities is that he changed his name to Deng Tuozhou.[98] In line with CCP historiography, his biographers simply state the revolutionary and anti-KMT goals of the rebellion, implying that these were compelling to Deng.[99] We know, however, that it was not really revolutionary at all. Deng Tuo was no fool. He knew who Li Jishen was and what he had done in Canton. There are several likely reasons why Deng participated in the Fujian rebellion, but the most probable reason was CCP policy—which was confused. Deng, naturally, may have felt the need to do what he could for his home province and may have felt that these warlords had at least proclaimed a 'revolutionary' set of goals, while Nanjing had not. There is further indication that popular resentment against the fascist Blue Shirt organization, the secret police of the KMT under the notorious Dai Li, was an important cause of discontent leading to rebellion in Fuzhou.[100] As a recent subject of KMT police suppression, it is not difficult to imagine that Deng shared this resentment. CCP policy toward the rebellion was a part of its emerging second United Front policy. This may well have convinced Deng that he should participate, no matter how flawed the Fujian regime's leadership might be. Since 1932, the Comintern had been stepping up its call for a new 'United Front from below' between the CCP and any group willing to resist Japan.[101] The CCP leadership in Ruijin had been negotiating with representatives from Fuzhou since April 1933, and on 26 October the two sides signed a preliminary agreement.[102] With CCP emissaries going in and out of Fuzhou in late 1933 it is entirely possible that Deng Tuo was contacted or heard about the CCP policy, the gist of which was published in Communist journals.

Despite the quick and complete defeat of the Fujian rebels by KMT forces, Deng Tuo was able to stay at home safely and publicly, even after having participated in the rebellion. His biographers report that he was wanted by the KMT, but this did not seem to drive him away or make him avoid public places such as the Wushi Hill library. This lack of thoroughness on the part of the victors is reflected in the strange 'surrender' negotiated by the KMT and rebel forces at the end of the rebellion at Quanzhou, some 100 miles south of Fuzhou, on 23 January. The terms reported in the KMT press are astonishingly lenient: the retirement of all officers of the 19th Route Army over the rank of major, reorganization (i.e. dispersal) of the army itself, and the promise that all officers and their families would be given safe passage to Guangdong.[103] These are not the terms of unconditional surrender, nor are they as stringent as the terms handed down to dynastic rebels, where at least the leaders were brought back to the capital for execution. Clearly, it was either against Chiang Kai-shek's interests or beyond his ability to enforce a thorough punishment of the rebel forces.[104] Such leniency provided the 'space' for people like Deng Tuo to survive and fight again another day.

By the summer of 1934 Deng Tuo had returned to Shanghai, where he roomed with his schoolmate, Li Tuozhi, at his dormitory at Pudong Middle School and taught some classes through the summer.[105] Deng also joined the Chinese Rural Economy Research Society (*Zhongguo nongcun jingji yanjiuhui*),[106] an organization formed in 1933 by the American-trained Chen Hanseng which was 'the most effective front group the Communist Party was to establish in intellectual circles' and included men destined to be among the most influential economists in the PRC, such as Xue Muqiao, Sun Yefang, and Luo Gengmo.[107]

Deng soon received an invitation from his eldest brother in Kaifeng to come and stay with him and to attend Henan University. Deng accepted. His brother, who was a KMT official in the Military Supply department of General Shang Zhen, had a large house which would easily include Deng Tuo, and he promised Deng that he could find him both employment as a teacher and entrance into the university.[108] Deng left Shanghai in the fall of 1934 in time to enter Henan University's fall classes.

Why Deng left a prestigious group like the Rural Economy Research Society after at most six months, why participation in this CCP front organization did not facilitate a reconnection with the Party, and why he would leave Shanghai for the far more remote Kaifeng are all troubling questions. His Chinese biographers note the unsettled times that hindered Party organization (alluding, as mentioned above, to the often successful suppression of Party cells by the government) and to the noisy and crowded living conditions Deng had to endure in Shanghai. Thus, Deng took the opportunity to join his brother's affluent household in Henan province. It is reasonable to suspect, as well, that Deng was somewhat chastened by the utter failure of precipitous political action and wanted both personal security and the opportunity to study China's history as a guide to future action.[109]

Historical Studies in Kaifeng

Deng's three years in Kaifeng were a period of intense study. He was formally enrolled in a degree programme at Henan University in the Economics Department from which he graduated in June 1937, having written a thesis for the degree entitled 'Research on the History of Natural Disaster in China'. Again he went by his old name, Deng Zijian.[110] During this period he published all the major history works he was to write before 1955. He lived in his brother's home and taught English in local high schools to make extra money. He was involved in the rising National Salvation student movement, but less so until 1936–7, and it was for this student activism that he was once again arrested.

Through his brother, Deng was introduced to the chairman of the Economics Department, Luo Zhanglong, who personally handled Deng's transfer to Henan University.[111] Luo Zhanglong was a veteran revolutionary, currently in disfavour with the CCP, but nonetheless a specialist (who could read German) on Marx and socialism. He had a considerable influence on Deng, who took Luo's course, 'Socialism and Social Movements', and under his direction read deeply in the Marxist classics. For the first year in Kaifeng, all Deng did was read.[112] Henan University was established under the Boxer Indemnity and by the early 1930s could boast of a few famous professors in philosophy and history, such as Fan Wenlan, Xiang Lida, and Deng Chumin. One reason Deng was less involved in politics is that the local CCP organization was in disarray and had been crushed after the December 9th Movement in 1935. It did not reorganize until late in the summer of 1936.[113]

Meanwhile, Deng Tuo became part of the household of his brother, Deng Boyu. The elder Deng worked in the Provincial Government offices and his wife was an obstetrician at a local hospital. The family was well connected in KMT social circles in Kaifeng.[114] In addition to attending classes, Deng taught history and English at two local middle schools, the Ji-Bian Middle School and the Liang-Yuan Girls' Middle School.[115] Deng's command of English was considerable, for he not only earned his keep by teaching it, but later served as an interpreter in the Jin Cha Ji Border region. Deng made use of English-language sources in his history writing, and in fact, his first publication from this period was a translation.[116]

From this safe haven Deng Tuo published at least seven lengthy studies of China's social and economic history, and he published his university thesis as a 500-page historical monograph.[117] All these works were published in Shanghai, and he communicated with the publishers there by regular mail. They knew him as Deng Yunte, the name under which he published, and by all accounts they were unaware of his personal background, particularly his junior status.[118] His greatest association was with the Sun Yat-sen Institute for Advancement of Culture and Education, through which he published four articles and some translations. It had been established in 1933 and published two journals, *The Quarterly Review of the Sun Yat-sen Institute for the Advancement of Culture and Education* and *Collectanea of Current Events*. The *Quarterly* published scholarly articles, ostensibly on the thought of Sun Yat-sen but in fact on Marxist interpretations of Chinese history. The Institute was patronized by Dr Sun's son, Sun Fo, who was a leading official in Nanjing, and was supported by Cai Yuanpei, the famous president of Peking University. In light of its prominence and association with establishment leaders it is fascinating to note the prominence of historical materialism in many of the journal's articles.[119] While left-wing parties suffered from official censure during the Republic, Marxist academic approaches occasionally flourished.

Deng Tuo's history essays, written between 1935 and 1937, reveal a faith in a reasoned, scholarly, Marxist approach to social problems and their solutions, an approach he maintained throughout his life. He published these in scholarly journals while out of contact with the Party, so they can serve as good sources for his personal beliefs, uncontaminated by the need to adhere to the Party line. His motivation behind these articles is clear: to find out what has made China stagnate. His first article published in the *Quarterly*, 'A Study of China's Social-Economic "Long-Term Stagnation"', was published in October 1935.[120] His other topics read like a checklist of China's difficulties in 1935: stagnation in China's society and economy, the collapse of the Chinese handicraft industry, problems in the development of modern Chinese capitalism, the history of agricultural production relations in traditional China, and most of all, famine relief.[121] With these concerns, Deng was continuing his interest in the 'Social History Controversy' that had started in 1928, but with his training at Henan University and finally with his long monograph on famine relief, Deng moved beyond many of the original contributors, who were non-professionals, into the ranks of professional historians.[122]

Deng's recent biographers emphasize his contribution in these studies to the refutation of 'bourgeois' and Trotskyist theories of China's social development—particularly Tao Xisheng's and Li Yafeng's—and the consequent implications of these theories for correct revolutionary policy. The 'bourgeois' scholars argued that Chinese society was still in a feudal stage and therefore needed a bourgeois revolution under the KMT; the Trotskyist writers argued that Chinese society was already capitalist and thus needed a proletarian and internationalist revolution. Deng Tuo argued, in line with later CCP orthodoxy, that China was semi-feudal and semi-colonial and so needed a nationalist peasant revolution under the leadership of the CCP.[123] Equally, as Timothy Brook has observed, the materialist conception of history provided scholars like Deng Tuo with 'a comprehensive and programmatic programme for dealing with the chaos at hand, an approach that would cut through the tangle of problems that seemed to get more knotted the more one tried to untangle it.'[124]

A fair example of Deng Tuo's historical essays from this period is 'The Process and Characteristics of the Development of China's Modern Capitalism', published in early 1937.[125] This fifteen-page article clearly assumes that the study of Chinese history is directly relevant to the formulation of successful government policy. Deng opens the essay by asking why China has been unable to adopt capitalist methods of production and has, instead, become a semi-colony of Western Europe. His thesis is that it was the failure of China's long-term social and economic development to prepare the material base for the independent development or positive acceptance of capitalism, and not Qing diplomacy, a lack of overseas markets, or insufficient steam engines that caused this failure.[126] Deng then details just what material conditions China lacked, and how she failed to develop, or even successfully borrow, newer capitalist methods of production. He covers cottage industries, landholding patterns, the role of official industry, the military-industrial complex of Li Hongzhang, and the problematic rise of machine industry in China—all with detailed examples.

Although detailed, Deng's articles were not designed to reconstruct the past beyond a few salient examples to support his political ideas. For instance, he took pains to demonstrate that whatever industry did develop in the nineteenth century, especially mining and munitions, 'did not rise up from below out of self-developing demand, but was based on the bureaucratic government's need for self-preservation.' He then quotes Li Hongzhang's memorials on defence against the Taipings as proof, and follows with examples of merchant indifference to industrialization. The Kaiping Mining Service Bureau fell over 500,000 taels short of its private investment goals and Zuo Zongtang's well-planned Kansu Wool-Spinning Headquarters of 1878 met an early demise.[127] All these were intended to support the thesis that China was not yet a capitalist society.

In the essay Deng makes thirty-five citations, mostly from Western studies, Qing palace memorials, and Marxist histories,[128] particularly the one by the Soviet sinologist, Georgii Ivanovich Safarov (1891–1937?), the former Comintern Far Eastern Specialist who was purged by Stalin in the late 1930s. Deng relies heavily on the last two chapters on modern China from Safarov's *Class and Class Struggle in Chinese History*, which was translated into Chinese, perhaps prudently, as *A History of Chinese Social Development* in 1933.[129]

Deng concludes that the industrialization of China in the late nineteenth century was as useless to the real (i.e. rural) Chinese economy as it was minuscule in size. This paltry industrialization, however, combined with foreign imports, was sufficient to destroy the market for peasant handicrafts and thus to undermine the delicate peasant economic system and to drive rural China into economic depression.[130] Deng finishes by proclaiming that imperialist oppression had injected into Chinese society a new militancy that would reject capitalism and choose a socialist industrial revolution.[131]

There is an obscured history to Deng's participation in the polemics over China's social history, one that points to the limitations of PRC publications and reprints on this topic. Deng Tuo carried on a lengthy and pointed debate over 'protracted stagnation' (*changqi tingzhi*) in China's social and economic development with a younger left-wing historian, He Ganzhi.[132] The debate took place largely in the Shanghai intellectual journal *Contemporary Forum* (*Shidai luntan*), which He helped to edit, and began with He Ganzhi's detailed rebuttal of Deng's

October 1935 article on 'protracted stagnation'.[133] He Ganzhi devotes the last section of his essay to a detailed consideration of Deng's previous article. He questions Deng's focus on 'small-scale production', social anomie, and government corruption as key roots to the stoppage and suggests in contrast the Japanese scholarly idea of *kyodotai* (community) as a social, as well as economic, nexus in Chinese society which blocked contributions from outside the hermetically sealed village community. He Ganzhi turns to the theories of the 'Asiatic Mode of Production' (AMP), which emphasize the smothering effects of despotic control.[134] The two young historians continued to debate these issues through the summer.[135] The essence of the argument was that Deng saw Chinese society squarely in the sequence of five universal stages of society as adopted by the Comintern in 1930. He Ganzhi, on the other hand, reflected the minority view supporting the idea that China was a version of the Asiatic Mode. Historiographically, these two approaches can both be supported by the scattered writings of Marx on the topic and reflect a difference of emphasis on economic (China is 'feudal') and political (China is 'Asiatic') aspects of property relations in pre-modern Chinese society. Each view has its merits. Politically, however, He Ganzhi was on the losing side because the Comintern supported the view that the AMP perspective was 'the wet-nurse for the theoretical position of Trotskyism'.[136] Nonetheless, the lines were not so clearly drawn in these articles, and He's and Deng's debate reads more like a heated scholarly disagreement among colleagues. He's use of AMP was not consistently applied and, as one observer notes, He was younger and less experienced.[137] These debates entirely disappear in the 1950s PRC reprints of He's and Deng's essays. This later papering over reflects not only the embarrassment that He must have felt, but the collegial status of the two men, which began when he joined Deng on the editorial board of *Northern Literature* in 1946.[138] Deng's view that China was semi-feudal and semi-colonial simply happened to become Party dogma.

Deng Tuo's major contribution as an historian was a 500-page Marxist analysis of famines. *A History of Famine Relief in China* was published in July 1937 by the prestigious Commercial Press in Shanghai as part of the series *Collectanea of Chinese Culture and History* edited by Wang Yunwu and Fu Weiping, and it was based on his Henan University thesis.[139] This book marks Deng Tuo as a professional historian.[140] It was translated into Japanese and published in Tokyo in 1939, and since then has been republished several times in both the People's Republic and Taiwan.[141]

The book is divided into three sections: *facts* of famine relief, *thought* on famine relief, and *government policy* on famine relief, presented chronologically over all the dynasties and the Republic. Deng's general thesis is that famine is caused by bad government—poor administration, poor distribution, and poor planning—which undermines human control of natural conditions. Thus famine is a social and not a natural problem.[142] Deng seems to quote every conceivable Chinese history or chronicle and dozens of Western texts. He writes in a clipped condensed style, relying heavily on cut-and-paste quotations. This, of course, is the traditional Chinese 'proof'—ancient documents carry far more weight than the analyses of contemporary historians. This style of presentation seems to have been dictated, as well, by force of circumstance. Deng reportedly wrote the book in something under three months, using four scribes from his brother's family and friends to get it done in time.[143] None the less, Deng's union of the classical Chinese historiographical approach with European (Marxist) economic systems analysis is a promising example of the sort of hybrid that can emerge from the mixing of these two cultural streams. *Famine Relief* stands in marked contrast to the many formulaic histories written in the People's Republic. It appears that it is CCP control over editing, specifically during radical Maoist phases in Party policy, rather than a commitment to Marxist theory that makes for sterile and simplistic history. Deng's book and his debate with He Ganzhi show that Marxist theory in China, when not subjected to rigid political control, can take a range of different forms and be a flexible instrument of historical analysis. Another aspect that distinguishes the Marxist theory in *Famine Relief* and Deng's other writings in the 1930s from later orthodox Party-approved histories is its lack of emphasis on class struggle. Rather, in line with Safarov and with most Chinese writers during the 1930s, Deng focused upon social and economic forces as the key factors in history.[144]

The purpose of Deng's histories is well within the bounds of traditional Chinese historiography. Like Sima Guang's famous eleventh-century work, Deng's writings constitute a 'Comprehensive Mirror for Aid in Government'.[145] However, his advice is for a modern government, not the Emperor. Like the Qing dynasty school of realistic statecraft (*jingshi*) writings, Deng seeks solutions to famine relief, to foreign encroachment on China, and to the plight of an underemployed peasantry. What is new is his methods. Marxist historical materialism, in particular its emphasis on organized categories of economic systems and their relations, and its de-emphasis on the morality or venality of individual historical actors, provided new and useful answers for Deng Tuo to long-standing questions in Chinese historiography.[146] Thus Deng makes a systematic quantitative comparison of the apparent causes of famine and the success rate of previous governments' relief programmes to prove that famine has social origins, and he constructs a model of rural handicraft marketing to demonstrate the destabilizing impact of mass-produced factory goods in rural China. The calls of Confucian historiography for this young scholar were thus answered by Marxist historical materialism.

Deng was a competent historian, but he chose not to follow the path of a professional historian. The career of his high school colleague, Fu Yiling, highlights the difference. After flirting with polemical writing in high school with Deng Tuo, Fu's biography shows a steady output of scholarly studies on late imperial Chinese social and economic history, particularly focusing on Fujian history. Fu's career traces a long list of teaching positions and, during times of unrest, unrelated jobs such as a banking clerk. This left him time to follow his vocation: academic history. Fu is now one of the most internationally respected historians of Ming-Qing China in the PRC. In contrast, Deng gave preference to his political work and in particular, propaganda.[147]

Deng's academic interests continued to be broad. He sent money in 1936 to Fu Yiling, who was then studying in Tokyo, to buy him the *Rowa jiten* (*Russian–Japanese Dictionary*) and other books to help him study Russian.[148] Deng also wrote a fair amount of poetry during this period. One of his poems gives a feel for what was on the 24-year-old student's mind. In the winter of 1935 he wrote a poem in the *jueju* style, 'From Kaifeng to Li Gongchuo':

> At day's end a terrifying gale rises,
> A visitor from the heartland dreams in winter.
> Tides of the heart rushing day to night,
> Sword spirit conceals winds and torrents.
> The great wilds tell the dragon's screams,
> In the empty vault the white crane wheels.
> When [shall I] follow and leave this scene,
> Taking to wing beyond the layered hills?[149]

The poverty and distress of the old imperial capital, and the news of suffering and defeat at the hands of the Japanese, clearly depressed Deng, and he longed to get out and do something. He was not the only one.

After the December 9th Movement of 1935 the Beiping Student Union organized the 'Chinese People's Vanguard in Resisting Japan' (*Zhonghua minzu kangRi xianfengdui*), which was brought to Kaifeng in the person of a Party activist, Liu Zihou, in the late summer of 1936. It was not a CCP organization, but had close contacts with the Party.[150]

Deng Tuo had been trying to organize student activities that summer and became the leader of the Kaifeng branch of the 'Vanguard'. The 'Vanguard' students competed with the local chapter of the KMT's fascist youth organization, the 'Blue Shirts'. Part of Deng's duties included acting as liaison for visiting Party organizers from Beiping. In the spring of 1937 Deng was impelled to shepherd one visitor back to Beiping after nearly being arrested at a Kaifeng meeting of the 'Vanguard'. In Beiping Deng Tuo not only drank in the sights of the old imperial capital, but received his marching orders from the Party. He was to transfer to the Party's base area in central China. However, shortly after his return to Kaifeng to pack he was arrested and imprisoned.[151] Clearly, Deng must have revived his organizational links with the Party, or at least the Beiping branch, though his Chinese biographer makes no mention of it.[152]

Deng's second incarceration was brief. It lasted only a month, due in part to the increasing tensions with Japan and in part to the connections his brother's family had. As an obstetrician, Deng Boyu's wife was well acquainted with the wives of the leading KMT officials in Kaifeng and was able to use those connections to get her brother-in-law out of jail.[153] Once again Deng had survived through the good offices of his family.

Before he got out of gaol, though, the galleys of his book, *Famine Relief*, came back from the publisher. His distraught brother travelled down to Shanghai—with page proofs and the original manuscript in hand—to ask Deng Tuo's old friend, Li Tuozhi, who was still teaching at Pudong Middle School, to proofread this technical book. He even paid for a quiet hotel room for Li to work in for the fortnight it took to do the job. Li was impressed but felt there ought to be a chronology at the end. Deng did in fact write the chronology after his release from gaol and before its publication in July.[154] This story again strikes one with its normality in a period of profound turmoil, and it directs our attention to the differences between public history, in which the CCP and the KMT are mortal enemies in the 1930s, and private experience. Within a month of the outbreak of the Sino–Japanese War, the KMT brother of a Communist prisoner takes the train to Shanghai and spends extra money to see that his radical sibling's book is properly prepared for publication. From this we can only conclude that family interests outweighed political differences—the brothers were close and the family deeply respected scholarship and the prestige of publishing a major work with a notable press.

In September 1937 the Japanese bombed Kaifeng's railway station, bringing the war to the city. The Deng household decided to go to Xi'an, further west. The family packed and Deng carefully boxed his library. Before he left he wrote his last letter to Fu Yiling, declaring his intention to 'go west' to the Communist areas:

Now our country's troubles have come to a head. We must perform feats of great strength. Not wrestle to the death with the enemy on the field of battle; we must contribute in the field of academics, write one or two great studies extolling the culture of the Motherland.[155]

Deng clearly felt that scholarship could maintain and promote China's culture and contribute to the war effort. During the war years he would make clear what he here assumes—cultural pride among the Chinese is a source of strength in adversity and a deep well of wisdom for practical policy.

Deng got on the train to Xi'an, on the Long-Hai Railway, with his brother's family, but made a hasty midnight exit at Fenglingdu station (on the Shaanxi–Shanxi–Henan border) to avoid the KMT secret police.[156] From there he headed north, and reached Taiyuan, probably before the end of September.[157] There he met the famous student movement leader Huang Jing, and together the two crossed into the Jin Cha Ji Border Region.[158]

Conclusion

Several key experiences helped determine Deng Zijian's choice to become Deng Tuo, the name of the CCP official he became for the next thirty years. The name change, in this case, is not only part of the rich texture of life among the Chinese scholar-elite. It reflects a change of identity: not the rejection of the earlier self, but a new integration based on an act of will. Deng's service to the CCP had been in fits and starts through the early 1930s. This was in part due to his own reticence and in part due to the disarray of the CCP then. When Deng jumped off the train and headed north into Shanxi he had made a final decision, a final declaration of vocation. From then on he would be an active and open CCP official. Deng Tuo chose Chinese Marxism-Leninism and the CCP because he felt Marxism provided the best scholarly and practical science of society to save China in his day. His choice of Marxism was based on considerable scholarship; his choice of the CCP was based more on some activist experience inside and outside the Party.

The experiences which contributed to that choice reflect the syncretic mix of inherited and contemporary attitudes among Deng Tuo's generation. Deng Tuo was raised as a *wenren*, a literatus. He always thought of himself as such. He saw no contradiction between that intellectual and aesthetic self and his bureaucratic self as a propagandist and *apparatchik* for the CCP. In fact, he felt they went together rather well. This sense that the *wenren* can be a *ganbu* is reflected in Deng's poetry of the 1930s (and later) as well as in his final letter to Fu Yiling in 1937. The tradition of loyalist literati from his home town, such as Wen Tianxiang and Lin Zexu, provided this provincial scholar-poet with reason to believe political activism did not negate scholarly commitments. He hoped to maintain China's rich culture *and* serve the revolution. The reported open-mindedness of Deng's father contributed to this. Deng's historical scholarship from the 1930s demonstrates not only his free choice of Soviet Marxism as his orthodoxy but his belief that scholarship had a key role to play in its promised revolution. Here we see a proper Confucian scholar choosing communism for understandable reasons.

Powerful personal experiences during the key decade of Deng's life as a young man from 1927–37 (the young adult years most sociologists see as the definition of a 'political generation') contributed to this choice.[159] The turmoil of China reached Deng in his provincial high school when warlord troops swept through his school looking for 'revolutionaries'. In Shanghai, Deng took to the streets as a Communist student agitator. The two most powerful experiences must have been his imprisonment and his participation in the abortive Fujian rebellion. Suffering torture and seeing the death of friends and colleagues in the name of the CCP added a fire, what psychologists call affect, to his intellectual commitments. We must assume, too, some amount of the unconscious guilt of the 'survivor syndrome' as a further motivating force (since, it appears, Deng temporarily caved in and signed a renunciation of the CCP to get out of gaol). The ludicrously organized and quickly suppressed uprising in Fujian less than a year after his release from gaol showed the danger of hasty action and the need for a deeper understanding of China's social order and place in the world.

Deng turned his scholarly gaze to the intellectual and historical claims of Soviet Marxism and, while involuntarily free from organizational supervision from the CCP, found the claims and promises of the creed persuasive. The *shi*, the traditional scholar, could serve China's new revolution. The CCP through its science of Marxism-Leninism provided the path. In neo-traditional fashion, Deng Tuo and other Party intellectuals took upon themselves the task of bringing society in line with the *dao* (the universal Way now revealed in the analytical methods of historical materialism) through fostering its *de* (proletarian virtues spread among the masses by propaganda) according to the dictates of the *jing* (authoritative classics, now written by Marx, Engels, Lenin, Stalin, and soon Mao as appropriated through careful study). Serving the Communist revolution was not a radical break for Deng Tuo; it was simply the current version of 'The Way and its Power'. The contents of historical materialism, proletarian virtues, and Party classics were radically different from the cosmological harmony, Confucian virtues, and Chinese classics Deng's father served as an imperial official, but the *form* of service as a veritable priest ministering to the public through the state was fundamentally similar. A new branch had been grafted onto the old trunk of literati service. The fruits would be different, but the graft had to be of the same family in order to take root and grow in the minds of Deng Tuo and his generation. The reformed CCP in the late 1930s offered just such a recognizable opportunity. When Deng Tuo finally obtained the opportunity to serve in the Jin Cha Ji Border Region, he literally leapt to the task.

NOTES

1. Li Tuozhi (1979: 240 or YDT: 224). Deng only used 'Deng Tuozhou' during the rebellion and reverted to using his high school name, Deng Zijian, or his other name, Deng Yunte, until 1937, when he revived and simplified his *nom de guerre* as Deng Tuo. Like most children of literati families, Deng had many different names at different times in his life and for different roles. For clarity's sake, however, 'Deng Tuo' will be used throughout, with notice as necessary of his other names.
2. Li Tuozhi (1979: 244 or YDT: 224). I visited the old house during the May 1986 conference.
3. Ding Yilan (1984a: 12). Ding's article is the first of a series of six under the general title of 'Deng's Life'. Others are by Zuo Lu, (Wang) Bisheng, and Gu Xing, which appeared consecutively in the three subsequent issues of the journal. The pagoda is still easily visible from the house today.
4. His *ming* was Yizhong, his *zi* Ouyu, by which he is best known. He had passed the last Imperial Exam of the Qing in 1903, received the *juren* degree, and was appointed a district magistrate in a county of Guangxi province in 1907. He retired from that office and brought his family back to Fuzhou around 1911. He became a teacher of Chinese language and literature at the Fuzhou Normal School.
5. Ding Yilan (1984a: 12); Li Tuozhi (1979: 241 or YDT: 224); Wang Bisheng (1981: 71); Fu Jialin [Fu Yiling] (1980: 221).
6. Because he was born at the break of day his father called him Xuchu (Dawn's Beginning), the name he was known by before he went to primary school (Wang Bisheng 1981: 71 and 1986: 2). Deng's birth date corresponds to the ninth day of the first month in the traditional agricultural calendar. He had another original name, Deng Yunte, which is remembered mostly as the name under which he published his historical studies in the 1930s. Both Deng Zijian and Deng Yunte are given as his oriinal names in the entry on Deng Tuo in *Zhongguo wenxuejia cidian* (1982:

110). His eldest son, Deng Yun, is the namesake of this other original name. One source, Zhang Shuzheng (1985: 17), notes that Deng was known as 'Deng Yunte' when he arrived in the Jin Cha Ji base area in autumn 1937.
7. Ding Yilan (1984a: 12); Ding Yilan interview with author, Beijing, 8 July 1981; Li Tuozhi (1979: 241 or YDT: 225). For further details on Deng's family and early life, see Cheek (1986: ch. 1). Li Tuozhi makes several minor errors in the names of family members; consult Ding Yilan (1984a) for correct personal names and birth order.
8. Li Tuozhi (1979: 246–7 or YDT: 229). Deng Shuqun (1902–70) was a famous biologist specializing in fungi. See *Ci Hai* (Shanghai, 1979: 1101), which says he taught at numerous universities before 1949 and became vice-director of the Shenyang Agricultural School, vice-director of the Fungi Research Institute and Bacteriological Research Institute of the Chinese Academy of Sciences in Beijing, etc. He joined the CCP in 1956; he died in the Cultural Revolution.
9. Li Tuozhi (1979: 241 or YDT: 224); Ding Yilan (1984a: 13). See *Ci Hai* (Shanghai, 1979: 1101).
10. Ding Yilan (1984a: 13) quotes the inscription and describes Chu as a 'literatus of the Jiaqing period'.
11. Frederick Mote cites Wen's futile resistance as an example of the irrational norms of Neo-Confucianism, which required absolute loyalty to one's dynasty, and he considers Wen's fame in traditional historiography among 'those who died maintaining their moral principles' as part of an unfortunate tradition which wasted good men. See Mote (1960: 232–5).
12. Ding Yilan (1984a: 13). Fujian natives consider their province to be on the left-hand side of the ocean. I visited Gushan and other parks in May 1986. Deng Tuo's pennames and many of their sources are given in Zhang Shuzheng (1985: 123–4).
13. Wang Bisheng (1981: 72); Ding Yilan (1984a: 13).
14. Deng Tuo most resembles the scholar elite of the 'school of realistic statecraft' (*jingshi*) which developed in the Qing and is represented in part by Lin Zexu and other objects of Deng's early studies. However, I have discovered no explicit link between Deng Tuo and *jingshi* ideas. He could just have easily been influenced by the metaphysical thinking of Wang Yangming, though in the 1960s Deng emphasized the practical political policies of the Dong Lin party, which reacted against those metaphysical ideas. The only direct link Deng Tuo has with a 'statecraft' figure is with Zhang Jiliang, a member of Lin Zexu's and Wei Yuan's circle in the late Qing. Deng prepared an article on Zhang in 1934, but it was never published. See YDT: 222 and Wang Bisheng (1981: 75).
15. Among the books listed as part of Deng Ouyu's library, particularly after 1917, were: *The Monism of History*, *From Ideal to Scientific Socialism*, and *The Communist Manifesto*. See Wang Bisheng (1981: 72); Ding Yilan (1984a: 13); Li Tuozhi (1979: 241 or YDT: 225). Zhang Shuzheng (1985: 4) says that the journal *New Youth*, edited by Yun Daiying, was in his father's library; by the mid-1920s that journal was illegal in Fujian.
16. 1979a: 387.
17. Indeed, the elder Deng Ouyu lived with his son, Deng Tuo, in Beijing during his last years after 1952. Among the urban intelligentsia, submission to family expectations was more the rule. For example, the great left-wing writer, Lu Xun, submitted to a marriage arranged by his mother. It was really only the writer Ba Jin who rebelled against his family. Such traditional subordination at home while pushing revolution in society is well analysed in Philip Williams's biography of the 1930s meliorist writer, Wu Zuxiang (1993).

18. He attended Fuzhou No. 1 Middle School, which survives to this day. See *Xiaoyou zhi sheng* (1982: 1-2; Ding Yilan's speech to the students on their famous alumnus is on pp. 2-7); Fu Jialin (YDT: 220); and Cheek (1986: ch. 1).
19. Wang Bisheng (1981: 73); Ding Yilan (1982*b*: 3); Fu Jialin (YDT: 220).
20. Fu Jialin (YDT: 220) simply lists the titles; Zhang Shuzheng (1985: 4) says they enjoyed Guo and Lu's works. Guo Moruo was known as a romantic poet as well as an iconoclastic historian. *Ice Drinker's Studio* is a collection of Liang's inspirational prose essays. Deng particularly read a text by Jiang Guangchi called *Duan ku tang* (The Short Pants Party). Jiang, better known as Jiang Guangci, was not an outstanding writer, but his novels combining revolution and love were popular among Chinese youth who wished at least to read about bucking the rigid Confucian family system. This novella appears in *Jiang Guangci xuanji* (1979: 85-192). See Lee (1973).
21. Wang Bisheng (1981: 72); the photo is printed on the second page of photos in *Wenwu tiandi* (The World of Cultural Artifacts), 1983:3 as part of Wang Bisheng (1983*d*).
22. Wang Bisheng (1981: 72); Li Tuozhi (1979: 242 or YDT: 225); Yuan Ying (1979: 162 or YDT: 177).
23. See Kroll (forthcoming), which analyses 'Yu lin ling'.
24. Wang Bisheng (1981: 72); Fu Jialin (YDT: 221).
25. See Fogel (1988).
26. Yuan Ying (1979: 162 or YDT: 177). Neither the brother nor the branch of Christianity are named. The author, Yuan Ying, writing on Deng Tuo is not the monk.
27. Yuan Ying (1979: 162 or YDT: 177).
28. Li Tuozhi (1979: 242 or YDT: 226); Wang Bisheng (1981: 73); Ding Yilan (1984*a*: 14); Zhang Shuzheng (1985: 4). Fu Yiling remembers Deng as a student activist, openly criticizing some unreasonable teaching practices, debating contemporary problems, even writing a play, 'Proclamation of Self-Evident Truth', and an article in Fuzhou's *Nationalist Daily*. See Fu Jialin (YDT: 221).
29. Li Tuozhi (1979: 242 or YDT: 225); Ding Yilan (1984*a*: 15). For a history of these debates, see Grieder (1981).
30. Dirlik (1974: 194).
31. Dirlik (1974: 195 and 174).
32. Quoted in Wong (1979: 25). This text provides an excellent overview of the historical as well as sociological debates of the day (24-36).
33. Wang Bisheng (1981: 71).
34. From Deng Tuo's own account to Li Tuozhi in 1934 and recalled by Li in 1979 (YDT: 229). This account is highly simplified and presented without the portion on how and why Deng Tuo missed his exam, thus giving the impression of greater revolutionary fervour on the part of Deng Tuo, in Zhang Shuzheng (1985: 4-5).
35. For the demise of liberalism in China, see Israel (forthcoming) and Yeh (1990).
36. The local Party cells were completely broken by the early 1930s and their members for the most part in Caolanzi Prison; see Yang Xianzhen and Guan Shan (1980: 17ff).
37. YDT: 221; Wang Bisheng (1981: 74).
38. Zuo Lu (1984*a*: 26). Note: since this 6-part series was given to me by Ding Yilan with parts 2-6 as tear-outs, I am presuming they appeared once each issue of this monthly magazine.
39. Chinese sources vary on this topic. Earlier works such as Zuo Lu (1984*a*: 26) and *Zhongguo wenxuejia cidian*: 110 maintain that the 'Chinese Left-Wing Literary

General Alliance' (*Zhongguo zuoyi zong tongmeng*) was set up in Guanghua in Mar. 1930, and that the 18-year-old Deng Tuo secretly joined then. A later, and more scholarly source, Wang Bisheng (1986: 24–5) makes no mention of this 'General Alliance', whose given dates lead me to believe that the other authors have confused it with the famous 'League'. I follow Wang's chronology.
40. Wang Bisheng (1986: 24–5). Wang explicitly presents the 'Research Association' as the 'front organization' (*waiwei zuzhi*) of the 'Alliance'. For the critical role such front organizations played in CCP recruitment in the 1930s, see Hartford (1995: 144–74).
41. Wang Bisheng (1981: 74 and 1986: 24–5); Zhang Shuzheng (1985: 4). Other members included Du Guoxiang, Zhu Jingwo, Liu Zhiming, and Ma Dungu. See Zhang Shuzheng (1985: 6 and 13–16).
42. Wang Bisheng (1981: 74); Zhang Shuzheng (1985: 13–14), which cites the original publication of the proclamation from *Shijie wenhua* (World Culture), inaugural issue, 7 Sept. 1930.
43. Wang Bisheng (1981: 74).
44. Zuo Lu (1984a: 26); Wang Bisheng (1981: 74 and 1986: 26). Ding Yilan (interview with author, Beijing, July 1981) is the only source specifying the month; other sources say 'the winter of 1930'. According to Ji Bufei, who was later active in the Fujian rebellion in 1933, someone surnamed Hao introduced Deng. See Ding Yilan, conversation with Ji Bufei as cited in Wang Bisheng (1986: 26). There remains confusion on who introduced whom and none can find out more about 'Mr Hao'. This underscores the secretiveness of the CCP in the early 1930s and adds credence to Deng's claim to have lost contact with the Party between 1933–7.
45. Deng would transfer to the Fa'nan Party branch the next fall, in 1931. Zuo Lu (1984a: 26); Wang Bisheng (1981: 74 and 1986: 26–7).
46. Fu Jialin (YDT: 221–2). Fu does not name the articles, nor do other sources. They may be hard to locate if Deng used yet more of his pen-names. Considering Li Tuozhi's account about 'Violet Gold Mountain' in 1931, it is possible that Fu mixed up his summers and that this portion of his reminiscence properly belongs to 1931. Fu makes at least one dating error in his article, placing Deng's 'Leaving Home' poem in 1931 while it is usually dated 1929. See Fu Jialin (YDT: 222), and (1979c: 1).
47. Wang Bisheng (1981: 74). It is unclear whether or not this essay was ever published. It is also unclear why he chose to change universities. Tao Bai, an active Communist, studied there, so we may presume Deng wished to join his fellow Party members.
48. Li says he edited the paper's 'Night Before' (*Qian ye*) supplement and the morning edition's 'The Morning After' (*Ming ri*) supplement. He published Deng's *zawen* in 'The Morning After'. Note: Li says Deng wrote it in 1930, but Ding Yilan (personal communication) corrected that to 1931. See (YDT: 226).
49. Wang Bisheng (1981: 74); Zuo Lu (1984a: 26).
50. Translated by Zhang Zongwen and published by Dadong Shuju in 1930. On the bibliography page it states that the original text was in French by 'Seignobos'.
51. Fu Jialin (YDT: 222); Fu Yiling (interview with author, Xiamen University, 5 May 1983).
52. The second edition, with corrections, was published in Paris by Félix Alcan in 1909.
53. Such is the opinion of the entry on 'History' in the *Encyclopedia Britannica* (1985: xx. 634). See also McNeil (1970).
54. Seignobos argued his case against general laws of history with Durkheim in 1908; see 'Debate on Explanation in History and Sociology' (Durkheim 1982 edn.:

211–28). Given Durkheim's desire to find universal sociological laws, we may presume that Durkheim's focus on consensus and social bonds and his lack of any revolutionary agenda lessened his appeal to Deng Tuo and Fu Yiling.
55. Seignobos also rejected the economic interpretation of history and was more a liberal than a radical; both views were dissimilar to Deng's and Fu's. See Deng Tuo's comments in his 1933 article on dialectical materialism, below. This small case study confirms this theme in Dirlik (1978).
56. Wasserstrom (1991: 155–64); Coble (1991: 39–50).
57. His predecessor in that post, Liu Duanlong, had served from February to 'fall' 1931. Stranahan notes that the multiple turnovers in Party staff reflect the huge number of arrests of CCP members. Deng's official appointment is listed in Shanghai Municipal Party Committee Organization Department, *et al.* (1991: 169). Interestingly, this valuable and authoritative reference lists Deng Tuo as 'Deng Tuo'— a name he did not even use until 1937. One presumes the editors have interpolated the better-known names of cadres rather than one of their plethora of *noms de guerre* for the convenience of researchers. But serious scholars should be aware of this practice.
58. Tao Bai (YDT: 234).
59. Tao Bai (YDT: 234); on CCP policy in Shanghai, see Stranahan (forthcoming).
60. His biographers consider this open policy to be one of the mistakes of early Party leader Li Lisan's 'leftist line'; Zuo Lu (1984*a*: 26–7). However, Li had already been deposed by this time; Wang Ming was in charge. See Stranahan (forthcoming).
61. Stranahan (forthcoming). This period of Party history is still the subject of controversy. Recently obtained inner-Party documents, however, detail the depth of bad management by ideological purists at this time. See two documents by Liu Shaoqi (1937, 1939). Both are translated in Saich (1996).
62. Zuo Lu (1984*a*: 27); Wang Bisheng (1981: 74 and 1986: 28). Wang does not comment on errors of Party policy.
63. Once again, the sources vary. Ding Yilan (1982*b*: 4) says he was out by September. Wang Bisheng (1981: 74 and 1986: 28), Fu Yiling (YDT: 222), Zuo Lu (1984*a*: 27), Li Tuozhi (YDT: 227) say spring or summer.
64. Li Tuozhi (YDT: 228); Ding Yilan (1982*b*: 4).
65. The young Communist was Yang Pao'an, and the text of the poem appears in YDT: 227.
66. Wang Bisheng (1981: 74–5). Xia Wanshun (1631–47) was the son of Xia Yunyi (d. 1645) and continued his father's anti-Qing chronicle, *Xingcun lu*; see Franke (1968: 66). This example again shows Deng's sense of continuity with the patriots of Chinese history. The volume may never have been published and is now lost, but the title poem and some other of Deng's prison verses appear in 1979*c*: 2–4 and YDT: 227–8.
67. Wang Bisheng (1986: 28–9) makes a particularly sensitive analysis of Deng's prison poetry. Wang is a promising amateur poet in the traditional style as well.
68. See further examples of this in Deng's poetry and calligraphy in the 1940s, discussed in Ch. 2.
69. Zuo Lu (1984*a*: 26–7); Wang Bisheng (1981: 74).
70. The famous '61 Prisoners' who shared Caolanzi Prison in Beiping from 1931–6— Bo Yibo, An Ziwen, Yang Xianzhen, and others. See Tai Huaiji (1982).
71. Chinese source, M1 (personal communication). Additionally, Sidney Rittenberg (personal communication, 4 Mar. 1985) recalls that when he travelled from Kalgan to Yan'an in September 1946 with Liu Lantao, Liu told him Deng had committed

'serious ideological errors'. Several people I interviewed in China confirmed that Deng declined nomination to the 8th Central Committee because of some 'historical mistake', but declined to elaborate.
72. Ding Yilan (interview with author, Beijing, July 1981); Zuo Lu (1984a: 27); and Wang Bisheng (1986: 30).
73. The plausibility of losing connection in the 1930s is echoed by Li Zehou, the Beijing historian and philosopher who has written on modern intellectual history. Li stresses that Party cells were organized by hierarchical chains of communication (*dan xian*) which, when broken, left the lower cell completely isolated. This, of course, was meant as a defence against confessions extracted by torture (Li Zehou, conversation with author, Colorado Springs, Oct. 1988). This picture is confirmed in Stranahan, (forthcoming: ch. 1). See also Tai Huaiji (1982). Yang Xianzhen and Guan Shan (1980: 6–22) give a vivid account of Yang's capture after the Beiping Party cell was busted. See also Hartford (1995).
74. Ding Yilan (interview with author, 8 July 1981); Wang Bisheng (1986: 31).
75. Wang Bisheng (1986: 31).
76. Zhang Dongsun (1933: 1–11). Actually, Deng's rebuttal in the December issue was the second of two articles devoted to Zhang's essay; Ye Qing, the noted Marxist apostate, devoted nearly 20 pages preceding Deng's on a much more detailed point-by-point consideration of Zhang's attack on *aufheben*, the role of 'time' in dialectics, etc. Deng's is a simpler and more direct article.
77. Published in 1933 under his alternative name, Deng Yunte.
78. On the core significance of 'motion' in dialectical materialism, see Williams (1994).
79. Wang Bisheng (1981: 75 and a long consideration in 1986: 32–5); Fu Yiling (YDT: 222); Zuo Lu (1984a: 27).
80. Zuo Lu (1984a: 27; although he does not give page citations, I did locate all quotes in the original text: Zhang's 'museum curio' comment is on p. 57 and Deng's remarks, in order, on pp. 55, 54, and [quoted in full] 57). Wang Bisheng's account gives longer quotations, but shares the same viewpoint.
81. See Meissner (1990). While I disagree with Meissner's instrumentalist depiction of dialectical materialism as 'merely' esoteric communication amongst elites (indeed, I see Deng Tuo as a counter-example showing the philosophical authenticity this system held for many young Chinese of the time), his sensitive analysis of language is a model worthy of emulation by all scholars. See also Fogel (1987).
82. For documentation of the disarray in Party leadership and policy in the early 1930s, see Saich (1996).
83. 1933: 52–3.
84. 1933: 57–8; Deng gives a careful four-point summary of Zhang's thesis and rebuts each point (53–6).
85. 1933: 57; Deng's thesis is stated at the end of sect. ii on p. 53.
86. 1933: 55.
87. 1933: 56. Interestingly, Wang Bisheng (1986: 34), also chose to quote this paragraph in full. Both Deng in the 1930s and his biographer, Mr Wang, today are the audience for dialectical materialist philosophy and hardly seem the cynical Party manipulators of 'esoteric communication' that Werner Meissner (1990) claims.
88. The best single review of the revolt is in Eastman (1974: 85–139). Further information and context is provided in Coble (1991).
89. Coble (1991); Elmquist (1951).
90. Indeed, it seems all that kept the 19th Route in line was money: it survived on a 900,000-yuan monthly subsidy from Nanjing and Canton. See 'The Future of the

Fukien Rebellion', *Chinese Affairs* (Nanking), 5:12 (30 Nov. 1933), 177–8; Dorrill (1969: 32–3).
91. Ch'en (1969: 28).
92. 'Generalissimo's (Chiang Kai-shek's) Momentous Manifestoes', *Chinese Affairs*, 5:12 (30 Nov. 1933), 185; Dorrill (1969: 32–3); Harrison (1972: 567, n. 51).
93. As says Dorrill in his review of CCP historiography (1969: 32 and 44ff.). For the KMT view at the time, including accusations that Fuzhou was following the line of the 'reds' in Jiangxi, see Wang Ching-wei (1933: 533–5).
    In fairness, as Parks Coble (1991) points out, the Fujian government's plan, compared to the other major effort at anti-Japanese mobilization by Feng Yuxiang, was much more credible.
94. Fu Jialin (YDT: 222); Li Tuozhi (1979: 244 or YDT: 227); Wang Bisheng (1981: 75 and (1986: 35); Zuo Lu (1984a: 27). A few authors suggest Deng was Secretary of Foreign Affairs, but this seems unlikely since it is not repeated in the newest biography, Wang Bisheng (1986).
95. Zhang Shuzheng (1985: 10) and Wang Bisheng (1986: 35) both clearly state that Ji was assigned by the Party but does not include Deng Tuo under this. In the context of giving the nature of Ji's Party assignment, the silence on Deng should be taken as an active statement: he was not so assigned. High-level CCP cadres were in contact with the rebels. Peng Dehuai says he negotiated with a representative from Fuzhou in western Fujian in August 1933 and wrote a letter to Cai and Jiang inviting them to Ruijin for further negotiations. See Peng Dehuai (1984: 340–1).
96. Ding Yilan (personal communication, Sept. 1985) says Ji Bufei drew Deng into the rebellion.
97. Dorrill (1969: 37–8), who quotes Harold Isaacs as shocked by the ineffectiveness of the left-wing leadership, which seemed unable to enforce the revolutionary slogans of the regime's manifesto.
98. Li Tuozhi (1979: 244); apparently Deng only used this name during the rebellion and reverted to using his high school name, Deng Zijian, or his other name, Deng Yunte, until 1937 when he went to the Communist base areas, where he simplified it to Deng Tuo.
99. For example, Wang Bisheng (1986: 35).
100. Eastman (1972: 25), repeated in Eastman (1974: 78).
101. For details, see Saich (1996).
102. Garavente (1965: 96); Harrison (1972: 232–3).
103. 'Fukien Revolt Completely Liquidated', *Chinese Affairs*, 5:16 (30 Jan. 1934), 252.
104. Parks Coble suggests such easy truces were a common practice—and problem—in the KMT's competition with and absorption of warlord armies. See Coble (1991: 136–48).
105. Ding Yilan (personal communication, Sept. 1985) says he taught classes in January; Fu Yiling says it was in the summer and recalls chatting with Deng in Fuzhou during the spring (YDT: 222); other sources say spring or are not specific.
106. Li Tuozhi (YDT: 229); Zuo Lu (1984a: 28).
107. Naughton (1986: 128).
108. Li Tuozhi (YDT: 229); Zuo Lu (1984a: 28); Ding Yilan (personal communication, Sept. 1985).
109. It is not out of the question that Deng may have entertained at least temporary doubts about the CCP for deserting the rebellion. In any event, the CCP was under deadly siege, as Chiang Kai-shek's 5th Encirclement Campaign began its successful invasion of the Central Soviet in 1934.

110. Fu Yiling (YDT: 222); Li Tuozhi (YDT: 230); Zuo Lu (1984a: 28); Ding Yilan (personal communication, Sept. 1985). Ding's views are based on interviews with the man who was chairman of the department at that time, Luo Zhanglong, and with a classmate from that time, Ding X X, and Zhou Zhenzhong.
111. Wang Bisheng (1986: 37), based on his 27 May 1984 conversations with the octogenarian. Luo Zhanglong (also Luo Zhongyan) was one of the founding members of the CCP who had joined the 'New People's Society' study group at Peking University with Mao Zedong. Luo was a specialist on Marx, holding to an orthodox version of Marxism which squarely placed the proletariat in the revolutionary vanguard. He had studied in Germany. He was purged from the CCP in the early 1930s for opposing the Wang Ming leadership. For details on Luo and a translation of his writings from the 1920s, see Saich (1992-3).
112. He also studied with Ma Feibai, a history professor about whom little else is known.
113. Wang Bisheng (1986: 38). In fact, in early 1936 the Beiping branch of the CCP's North China Bureau had been busted. See Hartford (1995).
114. Ding Yilan (personal communication, Sept. 1985).
115. Ding Yilan (personal communication, Sept. 1985); Zuo Lu (1984a: 28); and Wang Bisheng (1986: 37). 'Ji-Bian' stands for Ji'nan and Kaifeng, perhaps indicating that the school was an amalgamation of the local and Shandong schools. 'Liang' and 'Yuan' are Chinese family names.
116. 1935a. The full English bibliography and a brief introduction of Professor Grabau is given on p. 81 by 'the translator'. For more details, see Cheek (1986: ch. 1).
117. Six of the seven were collected in book form and slightly edited in 1959j. It appears that two 1930s articles on 'Long-Term Stoppage in China's Feudal Economy' were conflated by Deng in the 1959 edition, removing the debate Deng had with He Ganzhi (which I discuss below). By the 1950s they were colleagues in Beijing. See 1936b and 1936c for Deng's originals.
118. Zuo Lu (1984a: 28).
119. For details on *Sun Zhongshan wenhua jiaoyuguan jikan* and *Shishi leibian*, see Fairbank (1950: 515) and Teng and Biggerstaff (1971: 80 and 73). For examples of Marxist interpretations published in the *Quarterly* see selected translations in Tawney (1939: 35-42, 65-72, 224-9). Both Sun Fo and Cai Yuanpei wrote in the inaugural issue of the *Quarterly*, 1:1 (Autumn 1933), 1-7.
120. 1935b.
121. Essay topics by Deng in *Sun Zhongshan wenhua jiaoyuguan jikan* in order: 1935b, 1936a, 1937a, 1937b, and 1937c.
122. The best analytical review of the history debates of the 1920s and 1930s and their significance may be found in Brook (forthcoming).
123. Naturally, Deng could not explicitly endorse the CCP in these 1930s articles. See Liu Yongcheng's biographical entry on Deng Tuo (1980: 315-18) and Wong (1979: 24-7).
124. Brook (forthcoming, typescript p. 18). This political role for historical debates lies behind the significant 'Asiatic Mode of Production' debates raging at the same time: see Fogel (1988).
125. 1937a. A revised version of this text appears in 1979d: 148-66 as 'Jindai Zhongguo zibenzhuyi fazhan de quzhe' (The Twisted Path of Modern Chinese Capitalism's Development).
126. 1937a: 116.
127. 1937a: 110-11.
128. He cites Li Hongzhang's memorials frequently, the *Donghua Lu*, A. F. Sargent's

1907 text on Anglo–Chinese commerce and diplomacy, the Revd Arthur Smith's views, and Karl Marx, Lenin (as 'Wu-li-ya-luo-fu'), Radek, Madjar, and Safarov. I have made an annotated translation (unpub.) of this essay by Deng.
129. Safarov (1928). Translated by Li Liren as: Sha-fa-lou-fu, *Zhongguo shehui fazhan shi* (Shanghai: Xin shengming shuju, 1932; 2nd edn. 1933). It is an ambitious book. In 560 pages (in the Chinese translation) Safarov covers Chinese history from the ancient Zhou dynasty to the Republic. The last two chapters, on which Deng relies heavily, are ch. 24, 'The Invasion of Capitalism into China', and ch. 25, 'Impoverished Rule in the 20th Century' (pp. 491–560). Half a dozen of the foreign authors Deng quotes in his essay come from those cited in these chapters by Safarov, and some of the quotes Deng uses are identical to Safarov's. For more on Safarov and his book, see Harrison (1969: 36).
130. 1937*a*: 109.
131. 1937*a*: 117.
132. The relevant articles of the debate were re-edited before inclusion in each man's collection of historical essays in the 1950s. See 1959*j* and He Ganzhi (1989), which includes many of He's historical works of the mid-1930s on exactly these social history issues, including his review of the AMP issue in Japan from July 1937 (183–97), but does not include He's debate with Deng Tuo on blockages in feudal China from that June in the same journal, *Shidai luntan*. See the following two notes for details. Post-Mao literature on Deng and He has not remedied this alteration. See Chen Qingchuan *et al.* (1985): 'He Ganzhi', pp. 1622–66, esp. pp. 1628–31; 'Deng Tuo', pp. 1714–26.
133. He Ganzhi (1936*a*: 238–43). He Ganzhi (1906–69) had studied in Japan, was active in various CCP front organizations, such as the 'Social Scientists Alliance' in Shanghai, and joined the CCP in May 1934. See Chen Qingchuan *et al.* (1985: 1624–7).
134. He Ganzhi (1936*a*: 242–3). The actual term He uses for AMP is 'dongyang jueduizhuyi de quanwei' (The Authority of Eastern Pacific Absolutism). He developed his ideas on the AMP in a review of Japanese scholarship on the topic the next month (1936*b*). On this school of thought in Japanese sinology, see Fogel (1984).
135. In Issues 1:8, 1:9, and 1:11 (which was 1 Sept.).
136. Mikail Godes, quoted in Brook (1989: 13).
137. Liu Yongcheng (interview with author, Beijing, 1 April 1983).
138. Chen Qingchuan *et al.* (1985: 1640). He also became a senior historian at People's University in Beijing. Current literature maintains that He, in fact, opposed ideas associated with AMP, but never quite addresses He's view on AMP itself (Chen Qingchuan *et al.* 1985: 1631).
139. 1937*c*; Ding Yilan (personal communication, Sept. 1985).
140. Such is the opinion of H. C. Chuang, who made the first study in English of Deng's writings before 1957 (Chuang 1970: 13). Professor Lillian Li, who specializes on famine in Chinese history, regards Deng's books as the only major modern Chinese study on the topic, but faults him for his traditional 'cut and paste' style of stringing sources together and for his reliance on published, rather than archival, sources, which of course were not available to historians in the 1930s (personal communication, 1982).
141. 1939*a*; 1958*e* repr. June 1961; the Commercial Press in Taiwan made simple photolithographic reprints in 1970, date unknown, and 1978. All editions maintain the name 'Deng Yunte'. *Famine Relief* was published once again in 1986 as part of DTWJ (vol. 2).

142. 1937c: 2–3 and 81. This is Zuo Lu's assessment as well (1984a: 28).
143. Li Tuozhi (YDT: 231).
144. Harrison (1969: 36 and 95). Harrison says (95) that Deng sees peasant rebellions in Chinese history 'more as products of natural disasters than of class struggle.'
145. Such is the title of Sima Guang's 'universal history', *Zizhi tongjian*. If Deng has lost something of the traditional approach (and his *Famine Relief* is analytically organized rather than as the simple chronology Sima Guang gives) it is the weakening of the 'praise and blame' historiography—which emphasizes individuals, good or ill. See Gardner (1970: 13–14 and esp. n. 12).
146. Such an economic focus and statist faith were not new in Chinese scholarship. See examples of economic analyses of Qing problems by officials before the Opium War, which reflect a range of moral and economic, statist and laissez-faire positions, in Lin Man-houng (1991).
147. Fu Yiling, 'Fu Yiling zizhuan' (Fu Yiling's Autobiography), in *Zhongguo dangdai shehui Kexuejia*: 279–86.
148. Fu Yiling (YDT: 222–3).
149. 'Kaifeng ji Li Gongchuo', dated winter 1935 in 1979c: 5. I do not know who Li Gongchuo is. See also Zuo Lu (1984a: 28).
150. According to the sources interviewed by Ding Yilan in Kaifeng in 1985 (personal communication, Sept. 1985) and Wang Bisheng (1986: 38). Both Wang and Ding call the association by another name: 'Chinese People's Liberation (*jiefang*) Vanguard', which strikes me as anachronistic. Here I follow Zuo Lu (1984a: 28).
151. Wang Bisheng (1986: 40). Sources disagree as to where he was arrested: at a meeting of the 'Vanguard' or while trying to slip out the back door of the university.
152. Wang Bisheng (1986: 40). Deng was to go through another recertification later in the year by the new Jin Cha Ji Party committee.
153. Ding Yilan (personal communication, Sept. 1985), based on her interview with Zhou Zhenzhong, a classmate of Deng's at the time and now a professor at the International Relations Institute in Beijing.
154. Unless, of course, the Chinese publishers, like American publishers, were loose about the accuracy of the publishing date, in this case perhaps by a month. See Li Tuozhi (YDT: 231). The chronology of major famines from the Shang dynasty to 1935 appears in 1937c on pp. 495–509, and in 1958e on pp. 367–76.
155. Fu Yiling (YDT: 223); Wang Bisheng (1981: 75) quotes this, but misprints Fu's personal name.
156. Zuo Lu (1984a: 28); Ding Yilan, (personal communication, Aug. 1985). The family continued, eventually settling in Canton. Further information on them is not currently available.
157. Ding Yilan (personal communication, Sept. 1985); Zuo Lu (1984b: 27).
158. Ding Yilan (personal communication, Aug. 1985). She also notes that Deng did not go into Jin Cha Ji with the late former vice-president Wang Zhen; also, Deng never went to Yan'an before 1949.
159. See Introduction, Li Zehou and Schwarcz (1983–4), and Yahuda (1979).

2

The Revolutionary Propagandist: Life in the Jin Cha Ji Border Region (1937–1945)

Deng Tuo served the CCP as a journalist and a propaganda chief for a decade in the Jin Cha Ji Border Region which bridged Hebei, Shanxi, and Chahar provinces just west and south of Beiping. During most of these years, the Border Region, as a 'base behind enemy lines', was subject to repeated and brutal attacks by the Japanese army. Yet these were perhaps Deng Tuo's happiest years and certainly among his most

2.1 Deng Tuo, Fuping county, Hebei, April 1943

productive. There is a strange freedom in adversity, where goals are clear and a sense of historic purpose justifies effort and sacrifice. Deeper contradictions fade into insignificance; there is freedom from complicated choices. After years of marginal existence, warlord politics, and frustration, Deng expressed great relief in being confronted with a straightforward, if formidable, task. He went to it with gusto.

The Structure of Intellectual Service

Deng Tuo's decade of propaganda service in Jin Cha Ji throws light on three central aspects of intellectual service in Mao's China. First, he served in a system that worked and attracted metropolitan intellectuals to CCP service—the propaganda system of an emerging 'propaganda state' that would dominate China in the years ahead. Deng's work gives us a sense of what intellectual service was like in the propaganda system, as well as an example of the 'institutional culture' of a basic work unit (*jiceng danwei*). Second, Deng's approach to propaganda highlights the diversity of intellectual service in the CCP, particularly the contrast of Deng's work and cultural pastimes with those of Party intellectuals in Yan'an. Finally, Deng's writings reveal the content of this intellectual service—the emerging 'mass line' (*qunzhong luxian*) politics of the CCP made famous in Yan'an but begun earlier in Jin Cha Ji. The roles for intellectual service in the Jin Cha Ji mass line reveal the initial articulation of two styles of Maoism—faith Maoism and bureaucratic Maoism—that include conflicting ideological styles and social roles for intellectual participation within the single emerging orthodoxy of the CCP and China—Marxism-Leninism Mao Zedong Thought. We shall see why Deng Tuo's bureaucratic Maoist approach to propaganda worked well in the specific conditions of Jin Cha Ji and how that initial success left unaddressed fundamental tensions in the Party which would lead to disaster in the future.

The System

Deng Tuo's life in Jin Cha Ji demonstrates a factor which contributed to the growth and success of the Party, a factor which has been neglected in previous studies: its ability to attract and make use of the services of metropolitan intellectuals. Previous studies have put forward reasons for the Party's resilience under terrible wartime conditions and its increasing power thereafter—appeals to peasant interests or to anti-Japanese nationalism, moderate reforms and 'house-cleaning' of the

The Revolutionary Propagandist

Party, inspiring social revolutionary goals, and the ability to co-opt local elites.[1] These achievements relied not only on soldiers and line cadres, but also on metropolitan intellectuals. Such people are needed not only to staff higher levels of a modern administration, but also to articulate and propagate the ideology of its rulers. The first success of the CCP in Jin Cha Ji was to survive brutal Japanese attacks and maintain and organize a system that could possibly employ metropolitan intellectuals.

Deng's life in Jin Cha Ji shows what intellectual service to the Communist movement during World War II was like. Deng Tuo found an opportunity to serve an administration that promised an effective and morally uplifting rule of China. His job was propaganda. He edited the base area's chief newspapers and contributed to the increasingly organized official pronouncements on journalism and cultural matters. The case of the *Jin Cha Ji Daily* provides an example of the 'institutional culture'[2] of CCP propaganda organs in north China, of how politics and ideology worked out in daily practice inside a particular organization. As such, this is a study of political culture writ small, the political culture of a discrete subsection of the cultures that make up Chinese civilization. Deng Tuo's writings, particularly on ideology, show why, for Deng Tuo and his colleagues, propaganda was not a dirty word, but an honourable vocation.

The Agents

Who were the metropolitan intellectuals attracted to CCP service? By definition the term 'metropolitan intellectuals' is intended to describe people with both advanced education (some equivalent of university training) and an active interest in public affairs and values beyond strict professional concerns. This most closely resembles the current PRC term, 'high-level intellectuals' (*gaoji zhishifenzi*). In Jin Cha Ji during the war, several generations of such intellectuals were active—from older scholars (such as the poet Hao Qing), to older students or writers, to younger university or secondary school students in their teens and twenties (such as Deng Tuo). Most had been trained in China's capital or treaty ports and all but the eldest had received some of their training at new educational institutions—the Western-style universities (set up around the turn of the century) or various technical or military schools or academies. The generational differences among such intellectuals significantly influenced each one's response to conditions offered by the Party.

The cohort represented by Deng Tuo's life were in their teens and twenties during the war and became part of the founding generation of establishment intellectuals in the PRC. Thus, their political experience centred around anti-Japanese nationalism and the destructiveness of fragmented warlord governments.[3] They were also influenced by the New Culture Movement or May Fourth Movement, which popularized radical Western notions of anti-imperialism, democracy, science, and socialism. The intellectuals who came to the hills of western Hebei and Shanxi in the late 1930s thus carried the dual baggage of traditional scholar-officials (from their parents' generation) and contemporary social critics in search of new creeds (from their own political experiences). Most urgently, they carried the frustration of not being able to convince the Nationalist government to fight the Japanese.[4]

Deng's life during these years brings to the fore the diversity of intellectual participation within the CCP. His experiences in Jin Cha Ji contrast sharply with those of many left-wing intellectuals in Yan'an during the same time who suffered stricter Party control. Throughout these years Deng contentedly maintained his traditional scholar-elite interests in the arts. His job was journalism; his love was poetry. The ease with which his elite pastimes fit in with his revolutionary propaganda duties opens up a corner of intellectual life under the CCP not much viewed before. This was, of course, the continuation of Deng's own mix of traditional and contemporary concerns from the 1930s. His life in Jin Cha Ji shows that this mix was compatible with the branch of the CCP there. It would also find a niche in the new People's Republic.

The Mass Line

The project to which the propaganda system and Party intellectuals were committed in Jin Cha Ji was the Mass Line: the CCP's set of ideological pronouncements, policies, and administrative procedures designed to strengthen the CCP and its revolutionary goals in local society. Deng Tuo's propaganda work gives us a window into the content and operation of the Mass Line in Jin Cha Ji, from the promotion of the charismatic leader, to a new government organization, to new versions of cultural life, and most fundamentally, to the emerging Maoist ideology.

The propaganda system which the CCP developed and staffed was not an original creation or a repetition of earlier forms. It was largely an import from the Soviet Union. Bolshevik experience and assumptions were particularly amenable to Chinese conditions. The originators of Soviet propaganda systems viewed propaganda as part of education (indeed administering propaganda efforts for a time from the Department of Education). Lenin viewed propaganda as transformative, the needed consciousness to spur the working class on to revolution, and he acknowledged that this propaganda work was the domain of intellectuals. In all, the Bolsheviks created what Peter Kenez calls the 'propaganda state', a state-dominated polity which co-ordinates the education of cadres, the development of a political language, the politicization of ever-larger segments of life, and the substitution of 'voluntary' state-controlled societies for independent organizations.[5]

Deng Tuo's successful blend of revolutionary propagandist and traditional poet and aesthete, however, rested upon some fundamental tensions. Deng Tuo's work in Jin Cha Ji reflected his acceptance of dual and ultimately irreconcilable authority patterns. On the one hand, he stressed *rational administration*. He felt Marxism-Leninism (and soon, Mao Zedong Thought) was best applied in a rational, incremental fashion. Deng's experience of rectification and his explanations of Mao Zedong Thought reflected this managerial approach and mirrored his social experience as a bureaucrat. On the other hand, he lauded his own superior General Nie Rongzhen, and later Mao Zedong, as a *charismatic leader* of extraordinary wisdom and personal authority. Such praise reflected Deng's personal respect for these leaders as well as pragmatic propaganda for mobilizing a rural constituency. But what if the genius leader disagreed with the scientific conclusions of organized Party committees? Deng Tuo would have to face this nasty prospect later.

The related question left unresolved from these years was the precise nature of the role for the educated elite in propagating the new orthodoxy. Were they to maintain the literati role of 'culture bearers', sustaining and disseminating China's rich heritage as well as its developing new socialist culture? Could they retain their identity as individuals, trained and loyal surely, but largely autonomous moral actors due their measure of private preferences? Or were intellectuals to be 'cogs and screws' in the revolutionary machine, mechanically transmitting the precise contents of culture ('the will of the People') as determined by their organizational superiors? Was their contribution to be limited to adding their individual polish and elegance to a pre-determined message?

These pairs of authority patterns and social roles reflect two kinds of Maoism—*faith Maoism*, which turned ideology into faith in the charismatic authority of the leader and gave functionaries the role of 'cog and screw' to carry out the leader's wishes, and *bureaucratic Maoism*, which turned ideology into a method which highly educated 'culture bearer' savants applied rationally in order to make manifest the ideals provided by the leader. In faith Maoism, propaganda was a chiliastic bonding ritual;[6] in bureaucratic Maoism, propaganda was a process of revolutionary administration—praxis—research, training, public agitation, and policy feedback. The history of the CCP in the 1940s shows that these incompatible models of authority and participation emerged *together* in mid-century Chinese Marxism-Leninism. They formed a powerful but unstable amalgam that worked well under the specific conditions of the 1940s.[7] Maoism so conceived corresponds to the general model of the 'Leninist response' posited by Kenneth Jowitt. In this model elements of status (or traditional society) and class (or modern/rational) authority patterns combine in the 'charismatic impersonal Party'.[8] All Maoists—that is, all Party members in good standing by the 1945 Seventh Party Congress—maintained both faith and bureaucratic styles of Maoism. Only later, under the historical conditions of the new PRC, did the amalgam come apart. The two faces of Maoism remained canonically sanctioned tools available to actors in the CCP as the CCP then faced new and different challenges of administration and modernization. The result was a divorce between faith and bureaucratic Maoism, and neither was capable alone of sustaining the promise of the revolution.

In Jin Cha Ji, Deng Tuo found that his literati assumptions about political service, such as he had expressed in his summer 1937 letter to Fu Yiling, were congenial to the local Party leaders and intellectuals alike. His essentially bureaucratic Maoist approach to work did not collide with his faith Maoist respect for his ideological leaders. Yet there were no guarantees, and the leadership could, as Mao later would, change the rules. In fact, in one of the downturns in Deng's career glossed over by his hagiographers, these issues played a central role. The dark side of the Yan'an rectification movement, the notorious 'rescue campaign' purges of 1942–4 under secret police chief Kang Sheng, reached Jin Cha Ji and Deng Tuo in 1944. Deng's attitudes about service then became part of the 'ideological errors' which forced him out of the editorship of his paper and into local villages for re-education in 1945. However, in this case, the tensions were resolved and Deng Tuo was promoted again in 1946 and began a brilliant career leading to Beijing and the *People's Daily*.

The Jin Cha Ji Propaganda System: Survival

In 1937 obtaining the motivated services of metropolitan intellectuals was not simply a matter of providing an attractive and persuasive ideology for intellectual youth and displaced older intellectuals in Republican China.[9] It included the nasty business of surviving concerted

The Revolutionary Propagandist 71

attacks by the Imperial Japanese army and the effects of economic blockade. It further required the wearying task of creating viable organizations in a web of administrative order to make good use of intellectual talents.

Deng Tuo entered Shanxi at a time of turmoil. In September 1937, Taiyuan, the provincial capital, was in an uproar with anti-Japanese banners across every street. The Communist 8th Route Army took advantage of the public furore and the fears of the provincial governor, Yan Xishan, of imminent Japanese attack in order to organize openly. Deng Tuo easily contacted the local Party organization and soon joined a group of intellectual youth on a high-spirited march to Wutai, a county town some 70 miles up-country to the north-east.[10]

Military conflict with the Japanese dominated the history of the Jin Cha Ji Border Region from its beginning, which strongly influenced the way in which CCP goals of reform and revolution could proceed. When the fighting was intense not only the danger of complete chaos, but the need for support from the local elite, compelled the Communist authorities to seek moderate social reform rather than the radical change the Party had pursued in the earlier Jiangxi Soviet. Survival was the key concern. As Kathleen Hartford concludes, constant Japanese and local elite repression 'caused a tremendous loss of will among the general populace and brought the border region to the brink of disaster.'[11] Under these terrible conditions the CCP developed three progressive policies: first resisting Japan, then reforming local abuses, and finally implementing the CCP's social revolution.[12]

Throughout this period the Jin Cha Ji Border Region did more than survive. Under its real leader, General Nie Rongzhen, a veteran from the Jiangxi Soviet, Jin Cha Ji became the prototype for Mao Zedong's 'rural line' in revolution, in contrast to the 'urban line' espoused by Wang Ming. In 1939, Mao used the example of Jin Cha Ji to push his point of view in his support of Nie's account of the region, *A Model Anti-Japanese Base Area: The Jin Cha Ji Border Region*.[13] The Jin Cha Ji Border Region provided a model for the social basis of Communist success in the Civil War, and it propelled a cadre of leaders into prominence in the PRC: not only top officials like Nie Rongzhen and Peng Zhen, but the rank and file leaders of the establishment. Prominent among these were the propaganda cadres from Jin Cha Ji's press and propaganda corps. Deng Tuo grew with this group.

Deng Tuo was 25 years old when he left Taiyuan for Wutai on 25 September 1937, the day that news arrived of the Chinese victory—led by the Communist general, Lin Biao—over the Japanese at Pingxing Pass. Once in Wutai, Deng was assigned to the staff of the Propaganda

Department of the provincial committee of the 115th division of the 8th Route Army. As an educated youth and a Party member, Deng Tuo was needed. He soon met the commander, Nie Rongzhen, who recalls that Deng was a spirited and ardent young revolutionary, yet congenial and easy to chat with. Nie was particularly impressed that this university student had already studied how to spot and collect various local herbs—in preparation for hard times.[14] Deng Tuo joined Nie's retreat as the Japanese army chased the resistance troops eastward over the Taihang mountains into Fuping county, Hebei. There, on 7 November 1937, the Jin Cha Ji Military District was established in Fuping county, Hebei. The civil administration was the Jin Cha Ji Border Region, which held its official congress in Fuping in January 1938.[15] The 8th Route Army had survived the initial Japanese assault but realized it needed to communicate with its public and its often separated divisions. The CCP had always used the press to propagandize its policies and inform its cadres about them, so Nie's group set about founding a Party newspaper. On 11 December 1937, *Resistance News* (*Kangdi bao*), one of many informal broadsheets, was made the official publication of the Political Department of the Jin Cha Ji Military District and offices were set up in Fuping. It was upgraded from a mimeographed sheet to a lithographically printed two-page paper appearing once every three days. The first two editors were Sha Fei and Hong Shui.[16] By January 1938 they claimed to print over 1,000 copies per issue.[17] From the start Deng Tuo wrote frequently for the paper on topics such as the importance of spring plowing in the resistance effort.[18]

The paper lived on the run; in March 1938 its plant was bombed by the Japanese. Three weeks later, back in the Wutai area of Shanxi along with the resistance forces, the paper resumed publication.[19] There the Jin Cha Ji CCP Provincial Committee convened its first congress in April 1938. Peng Zhen was deputized from the Party's Northern Bureau to represent its interests and to chair the congress, beginning Peng's four years of Party leadership in Jin Cha Ji.[20] The Party congress was the natural forum in which to make *Resistance News* the official newspaper of the Jin Cha Ji Party committee and a young (26-year-old) metropolitan intellectual and party member, Deng Tuo, its director and editor-in-chief. The paper had a staff of about 40, including printers and labourers.[21] This was Deng Tuo's first leadership post in the CCP.[22]

In the summer of 1938 the paper was host to Chen Kehan, a CCP journalist and later a leading official in the PRC. The following year, Chen published his account of the visit for readers in Chongqing. *Resistance News* was housed in an old temple in which Chen found seven or eight young men drawing, editing, and organizing the layout of the paper. In the main room he saw the stereotype presses under the care of a dozen workers. Chen describes a wide network of correspondents and a chain of distributors for the paper. Deng's own June 1938 account of the paper reflects this pride, but tellingly omits discussion of distribution and focuses on the paper's punctual and continuous publication record.[23]

In the months that followed, the paper grew in size and scope, though distribution remained a problem.[24] The paper sought to be responsive to the needs of its readership, soliciting amateur contributions and rotating writers and editors from local government and public associations. Deng Tuo, as one of the few highly educated intellectuals in the area, put in long hours, writing most of the editorials for the paper, coaching his young and untrained staff, and coping with the practical problems of finding presses, type, and paper in the barren Taihang mountains.[25] The paper's topics and slant directly reflected the policies of the CCP commissars in the 8th Route Army, with whom Deng as editor had daily contact. Peng Zhen's fulsome praise of the paper's successor, *Jin Cha Ji Daily*, in May 1940 as the 'voice of the people' indicates it served his plans, which Pitman Potter has shown were to establish an organizational mechanism to create and ensure Party supremacy in the Border Region's government.[26]

The Japanese attacked the Wutaishan and Taihang area in earnest in late September 1938 with some 50,000 troops. It was a devastating attack, and though the Communist armies retreated and put guerrilla tactics to good use, it was a rude awakening for the populace lulled by the previous quiet months. At the end of the month, the paper took to the hills, producing a roaming version of the paper, *Kangdi waibao*, during the last three months of 1938.[27] The paper was on the run for several months, but when the dust settled in April 1939, Deng followed the administration back to Fuping county in western Hebei and set up the paper in a small village called Malancun.[28]

Nie Rongzhen reported on the state of the Border Region at a Party meeting in January 1939.[29] Nie reviewed the military situation, which was bleak. The Border Region had been badly cut up by Japanese attacks. Although he puts a positive interpretation on 'future tasks', it is clear that the Border Region was still fighting for its life. The goal, said Nie, was to reach a stalemate with the Japanese, but that objective had not yet been attained and plans for 1939 called for continued guerrilla warfare tactics. Nie particularly stressed the need to carry out United Front policies and castigated old revolutionary cadres for not supporting these moderate policies. It was essential that all classes and friendly armies co-ordinate under CCP guidance. This was not possible if the old 'leftist' methods (which attacked the rural elite) continued. Nie cites 'Comrade Mao Zedong' on the necessity to 'prepare the battlefield in advance', that is organize among the local population before battle.[30] As Nie mentions no other top Yan'an leader by name, this can be taken as an early sign of support for Mao and his policies well before Mao had consolidated his victory over Wang Ming.[31] Throughout the report, Nie emphasizes the need for administrative regularity and obedience to Party directives. He notes with pleasure that even under such difficult conditions, the Party has been able to publish over fifty periodicals.[32]

By the summer of 1939, all three major power groups of the Jin Cha Ji Border Region had their propaganda organs: the Border Region government (a United Front institution recognized by the KMT), the Military District, and the local branch of the CCP. After April 1938, *Resistance News* was 'publicly' published by the Border Region government (although in fact controlled by the regional branch of the CC). On 7 July 1939 Deng Tuo became the 'responsible person' for a new journal published by the Political Department of the Jin Cha Ji Military District. At first called *Resistance News Supplement*, it was later entitled *Resistance Weekly*.[33] At the end of July, Deng also became the leading 'responsible person' for a new monthly journal, *New Great Wall*, published by the Border Region Party Committee. Three other people were listed as 'responsible people' on the journal: Li Changqing, Yao Yilin, and Hu Xikui.[34]

In November 1939, *Resistance News* once again abandoned its home under Japanese attack, leaving Fuping's Malancun and crossing the Sha and Tang rivers to the desolate Langyashan (Wolf's Tooth mountain) region, some 50 miles to the north-east.[35] It was a time of particular hardship for the staff, with the onset of winter, the poverty of the region, and Japanese attacks. Things improved slightly in early 1940, until the Hundred Regiments offensive brought vicious Japanese counterattacks that autumn.

The paper's foremost responsibility was to continue to publish, particularly during the Japanese extermination campaigns. Clearly, the continued publication of the paper would embarrass the Japanese as well as encourage the dispersed guerrilla groups. Praise of *Resistance News* (and later, *Jin Cha Ji Daily*) has centred on its successful publication and distribution during the period of 'mopping up'.[36] This was no easy task, as the temporary demise of *Central Hebei Guide* (*Jizhong daobao*) in late 1938 and again from the winter of 1942 through the spring of 1945 in the face of such attacks testifies.[37] The Jin Cha Ji journalists took a practical approach, based on their limited resources. Together with the print-shop workers they devised a way to break the press down into portable sections that could be transported on three horses. Due to a shortage of type, they settled on a 3,000-word vocabulary limit for all stories, which was also in line with Party calls to make papers readily understandable to the newly literate. Finally, the paper had three foundries for type and paper factories for newsprint (all quite primitive) set up in mountain areas, where the 'guerrilla publishers' were likely to pass through. Slowly, the developing organizational strength of CCP mass organizations secured the distribution of *Resistance News*, as sympathetic villagers and militia members took on the task of hiding and passing on the paper.[38] The control of the *Resistance News* by the CC Branch Committee boiled down to the editor, Deng Tuo, personally keeping daily contact with the leadership in the military headquarters and the Party committee of the region. He regularly sent in his editorials for vetting or would literally ride over to discuss how best to publicize a policy.[39]

This picture of how the *Resistance News* survived up to 1940 gives us a sense of how the CCP maintained itself. A similar pattern continued during the harsh Japanese attacks on the Border Region in winter 1940, spring 1942, and 1943.[40] One measure of the survival of the paper, and the toll later attacks took on its operations, can be seen from the partial figures of its staff and copies of each issue printed (Table 2.1). While

TABLE 2.1 Staff and print runs of *Resistance News* and *Jin Cha Ji Daily*, 1938–1948

Date	Staff	Copies per issue
1938	40	1,100–1,600
1939	150–200	10,000
1940	300	21,000
Dec. 1940	—	3,600
May 1941	480–530	17,000
Sept. 1941	—	5,000
early 1942	530	—
late 1942	270	—
1943	—	c. 1,000
1944–7	—	—
14 June 1948 (last issue)	—	50,000

Note: a dash indicates figures are lacking for that period.
Source: *Jin Cha Ji ribao dashiji*: 20, 39, 60–1, 111, and 277. The paper changed names in Nov. 1940.

they show success, comparison with production figures at *Liberation Daily* in Yan'an in the 1940s indicate we should take figures like 21,000 copies for 1940 with a grain of salt.[41]

A further quantitative indication of survival and success is the number of other periodicals published in Jin Cha Ji. Preliminary data show an impressive number of titles. According to the *Jin Cha Ji Daily Chronology*, by August 1938 the new Jin Cha Ji Border Region boasted some 50 different papers and magazines. The cumulative count for periodicals for the 1937–48 period for publications from the Military District level (the highest in the region) to the divisional (*budui*) level and for municipal Party committee periodicals in enemy-occupied areas (such as Beiping and Tianjin) are 73 newspaper titles and 71 journal/magazine titles.[42] The *1984 Press Yearbook* lists 67 combined titles of newspapers and magazines for Jin Cha Ji during the war of resistance.[43] While the output of periodicals by the CCP in Jin Cha Ji was by no means as extensive as the impression the *Chronology* tries to put on the data, clearly, by the quantities of materials produced, the Party had made impressive use of the talents of metropolitan intellectuals to produce the vehicles for Party propaganda.

The Jin Cha Ji Daily: *Organization of a Work Unit*

Jin Cha Ji's propaganda periodicals were organized rationally to survive wartime conditions and to achieve the mobilizational goals of the CCP. Thus, the *Jin Cha Ji Daily* was under strict Party leadership but was 'held' in a web of other intellectual and cultural organizations sponsored by the Party, which attracted intellectuals and promoted and channelled their interests.

Following the Japanese counterattacks to the Hundred Regiments, conditions must have improved temporarily for the Jin Cha Ji administration by early November, for *Resistance News* was renamed and expanded on 7 November 1940 to become the *Jin Cha Ji Daily*.[44] Aside from increasing its publication from a once-in-three-days schedule, the paper increased its size from two to four pages.

The organization of *Jin Cha Ji Daily* was not significantly different from the recent organization of its predecessor. It was carefully arranged to achieve two major goals: (1) to unify leadership—that is, to ensure that the message delivered was both coherent and in line with the desires of the Party Centre and well grounded in local concerns of resistance, reform (for the public), and revolution (for Party cadres); and (2) survival of both repeated direct military attacks by the Japanese and puppet forces and the economic deprivations of Japanese 'burn all' policies and KMT blockade. Thus, the paper had a clear administrative hierarchy under the local branch of the Party Centre and had dispersed production and distribution networks.

An administrative chart of the paper's organization for December 1940 to June 1942 is given in Figure 2.1.[45] There are several observations to be made from viewing this organization. First, Party control is clear: a full-time Party branch secretary sits at the top of the organization, along with the Director (invariably also a Party member). The Party Branch Committee for the paper had been established with the paper itself in the fall of 1937 under the military government and under the Party at the first Jin Cha Ji Party Congress in April 1938. Hou Xin was the first branch secretary, followed by Liu Ping.[46]

The paper is a typical *jiceng danwei* (basic-level work unit) combining administrative, health, Party, and other functions inside the paper's organization—what Lowell Dittmer later calls 'frames' (and which the

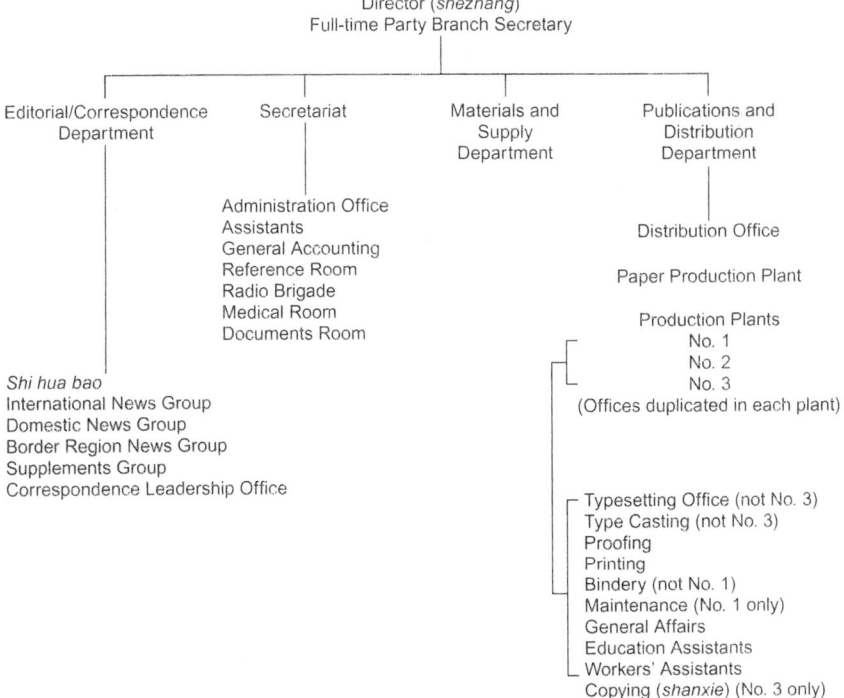

FIG. 2.1. Organization of the *Jin Cha Ji Daily*, 1940–1942

Source: *Jin Cha Ji ribao dashiji*: 111.

Chinese call *kuangkuang*).⁴⁷ Most of the subsections of the secretariat deal with non-professional concerns such as health, housing, and staff questions, although the radio room is responsible for links with Xinhua she, telegram traffic for the CCP leadership, and foreign radio monitoring. This is the social organization that would encourage people in the PRC to become so dependent on their *danwei* (work unit).

It was also a professionally minded organization with rational division of labour toward purely professional goals of producing a newspaper on a reliable schedule with reasonable sources of information and with a sensible distribution organization. Naturally, the Japanese attacks often wreaked havoc on these goals, but significantly, did not shut the paper down. The organization reflects the professionalism expressed by members of the *Daily* in their reminiscences. It also reflects sensible organization in the face of military assault by setting up its printing and production facilities in three separate spots.⁴⁸

The *Daily*'s staff association had published an in-house newsletter, *Life of the Paper* (*Baoshe shenghuo*), since March 1940 under Chen Chunsen and Li Xiaobai. In April 1941, the staff association was given new leaders, Zhang Fan and Kang Cunhuai. This was followed immediately by the paper's mini-rectification in May, so one presumes that the staff association served Party surveillance and education functions among the staff as well as providing a forum for social get-togethers.⁴⁹

The *Daily* also benefited from another important aspect of propaganda organization in Jin Cha Ji—radio links with other Party areas, particularly Yan'an, and the outside world. The vital role of radio communications for the Party during the war years is just beginning to emerge (and we can see why Nie Rongzhen and the Jin Cha Ji administration were so grateful to Englishman Michael Lindsay for his technical assistance in radio technology).⁵⁰ In May 1940, the paper (then *Resistance News*) took on the region's radio work and set up a radio group (*dianxun zu*) within the editorial board to handle radio broadcasts of Jin Cha Ji news.⁵¹ This also included a receiving and transcription station which by June 1941 was equipped to receive and transcribe English broadcasts from Radio Moscow.⁵²

The *Jin Cha Ji Daily* Publishing Society also produced a special paper for distribution in the occupied cities, *Straight Talk News*. This underground journal started publication on 20 December 1941, shortly after the Americans entered the Pacific War and the consequent confiscation of their areas in Japanese-held Beiping. Thus, the journal may have been intended to replace lost channels associated with these. In any event, the paper was available in Beiping, Shijiazhuang, Taiyuan, Datong, Kalgan, and other occupied cities. Deng Tuo was in charge of publishing this paper. It seems to have had an impact, for the collaborationist Chinese press in Beiping singled Deng Tuo out as one of the 'Two Guardian Temple Gods' of Peng Zhen.[53]

The paper was not only carefully organized for coherent control by the Jin Cha Ji Party leadership ('unified leadership') and for survival in the face of attack and blockade, it was also placed in a web of organizations and associations designed to attract and 'organize' educated elites in the Border Region. A careful study of each organization awaits further research, but a glance at the range of organizations gives a sense of the care that was taken to co-opt intellectuals (in a manner similar to the various other militias, peasant associations, etc.). The first and obvious political organization was the Border Region government under Song Shaowen. The linkage between meetings of the government and special meetings of intellectuals for artistic and literary purposes, seen in the case of Yenching professor Yu Li, who was elected to the leadership, is telling (discussed below). Several other organizations appear. As early as March 1940 the Jin Cha Ji Border Region Students' Anti-Japanese Alliance (*Jin Cha Ji bianqu xuesheng kangRi lianhehui*) and the Jin Cha Ji Branch of the China Youth Journalists Society (*Zhongguo qingnian xinwenjizhe xuehui*) were officially set up. At the journalism meeting, Liu Ping, An Gang, Deng Tuo, and six other Party intellectuals addressed the young journalists. The authorities even provided an inspirational drama, 'In Guerrilla War' (*Zai youji zhong*), whose theme was to explain how to publish a newspaper on the run.[54] The drama presentation is a telling indication of the likely low literacy among the Journalists' Society's members. The young journalists met again in September 1943 to hear talks on how to reform the Party press by the same cast of speakers.[55] This time, they apparently had no need for inspirational skits.

The first meeting of the Border Region Cultural Circles Anti-Japanese National Salvation Association (*Bianqu wenhua jie kangRi jiuguo hui*) convened on 10 October 1940 with such leading Party intellectuals as journalist Cheng Fangwu and historian He Ganzhi elected to its standing committee.[56] The *Daily*, naturally, produced a supporting editorial honouring the meeting on 18 October. In June 1942, four more related associations were officially established (and publicized by the *Daily*): the Border Region branch committees for the Philosophy Society, the Natural Science Research Society, the New Educational Research Society, and the New Script Association (*Xin wenzi xuehui*).[57] All were plausible foci for intellectual energy for less politically minded intellectuals, well under control of the CCP.

Institutional Culture

The *Jin Cha Ji Daily* had more to do than survive and print the news efficiently. It was part of an emerging 'propaganda state' which sought to transform not only the general public, but its leaders. What was propaganda work like in practice? What was daily life in it like, and how could service in it be seen as an honourable vocation? What might have attracted intellectuals to this project?

First of all, the Jin Cha Ji propaganda system needed inspired leadership, an appealing challenge to intellectuals such as Deng Tuo who had experienced little other than political marginality in the previous decade. Despite the impressive organizational system set up for the press in Jin Cha Ji, there was trouble with distribution—a problem Nie Rongzhen would still have to emphasize after three years of publication.[58] The paper also had had trouble being taken seriously by its most important audience: experienced Party cadres. This was a general problem. Over the years of secretive underground work during the 1930s when the CCP could not publish newspapers and magazines openly, cadres had grown accustomed to ignoring 'front organization' publications and developed the habit of only paying attention to secret internal Party communications. With the advent of the United Front, the CCP was legally entitled by the Nationalist government to publish openly. *Resistance News* was one such publication. On 2 April 1938 the Party's Central Committee (CC) issued a directive addressing the importance of 'open' (*gongkai*) Party periodicals in transmitting its wishes and co-ordinating its work. It set out regulations which required all Party branches to subscribe to its nationwide paper, *New China Daily* (*Xinhua ribao*), and to set up correspondents' offices to contribute to the paper. Additionally, it stipulated that branch meetings should read and study any articles in the open press by members of the CC Politburo.[59] Deng Tuo explained the directive's application to local cadres in a December 1938 issue of *Battlefront* (*Zhanxian*), the restricted circulation (*neibu*) bi-monthly journal edited by the Jin Cha Ji branch of the CCP CC.[60]

The article is a classic example of what we may call 'internal propaganda'—transmitting Party instructions to local cadres. Deng Tuo uses precise wording from the directive, even quoting a few lines directly. His prose is a good deal more lucid than the bureaucratic document and he fleshes out the directive's points with examples and numerous citations from Lenin. His theme is that the Party's openly published papers must, to cite Lenin, form the 'guide wire' (*yinxian*) along which the Party builds up the activities of the masses.[61] Therefore, in Jin Cha Ji all branches and, as far as possible, all Party members will subscribe to *Resistance News* and to *Battlefront*. Each branch will set up a sales agent for these publications, as well as organize local reporters for them. Equally, branch meetings will read aloud and study important articles by Jin Cha Ji leaders and the reprints from other Party papers. Deng especially emphasizes the organization of 'reading groups' in which these key articles are to be read by cadres to the citizens of remote villages and discussed. This will not only bind the Party more closely to the masses, says Deng, but will 'broadly raise the political and cultural level of the masses.'[62] Deng also asks local branches to help distribute copies of the periodicals in Jin Cha Ji. Finally, local Party members are to organize clandestine distribution networks to sell Party papers in Japanese-occupied areas to counteract enemy propaganda. Here we see the footwork that went behind the CCP's famous propaganda machine. Clearly, the propaganda network had not been well established in Jin Cha Ji by the end of 1938; it probably wasn't until well into 1940.[63]

We get a preliminary sense of the 'institutional culture' of the paper from its rectification efforts. In May 1941 the *Jin Cha Ji Daily* carried out what amounted to a mini-rectification campaign aimed to 'regularize' (*zhengguihua*) thought, rectify work, and increase the quality of the paper. The staff and workers met to commemorate May Day. They resolved to start a movement called the 'Red May Assault Programme'. The study movement was paralleled by authoritative editorials on how to study Marxism-Leninism.[64] For the paper's editor, Deng Tuo, this was ideological rectification. The goal, said Deng, was regularization of the paper, which meant 'no matter whether in times of relative stability or change to be able firmly to maintain a definite system, to uphold a definite order, and to raise the technology of production and the efficiency of work to the highest possible levels.' Deng saw the 'basic conditions' for this regularization in strengthening the *parti'nost* (party character or discipline; *dang xing*) of their work.[65] This version of rectification was a rather more systematic and professionally concerned version of the model later made famous in Yan'an. Records of other rectification 'study' for the paper's staff are not available, though the general picture of Jin Cha Ji is that rectification was not pursued with the same vigour as it was in Yan'an.[66] Furthermore, the area was under direct attack during spring 1942.[67] Although the paper published all the major rectification speeches by Mao and others in a timely fashion in 1942, space in the paper was shared by extensive reports on the campaigns of the spring and summer.[68]

The ideal picture of the rectified *Jin Cha Ji Daily* is given in the reminiscences of former workers at the paper. Zhang Fan, a junior editor in the transcription section, recalls life with his editor in the 1940s, when all the members of the paper's staff did a stint of reporting from the front, as well as working as copy-editors and printers. This was called the 'unity of reporting and editing'. Deng Tuo also insisted that every manuscript from outside writers had to be considered for publication, and if not published had to be returned with encouraging criticism on what needed to be improved. This extension of professional training is said to have included helping local people to print their own papers and setting up local branches of the paper. Certainly a number of other CCP papers were set up with the help of *Jin Cha Ji Daily* staff: the *Central Hebei Guide*, *Boldly Forward News* from the districts west of Beiping (Pingxi), and later the Hebei-Shanxi district's *Ji Jin Daily* and the *Shijiazhuang Daily*.[69]

Deng was the personal and paternalistic leader of this work unit. He is remembered much in the model that Deng painted of the ideal leader Nie Rongzhen in 1942 (on Nie, see below). For his editors and reporters, Deng Tuo was the Party, a role he played as a kind-hearted patriarch. At one point, Zhang Fan, a junior editor, failed to record a radio broadcast according to Deng's instruction. Deng did not castigate him, but rather played on his guilt—he reminded Zhang of his responsibilities and all those who were affected by his failure. Zhang felt horrible and searched until he found another copy of the missed broadcast.[70]

A sense of what Mass Line service by the intellectual elite meant to Deng Tuo in practice comes from his relations with the villagers of Malancun, where the *Daily* was housed at the time. The picture more resembles that of a good-hearted, if informal, Confucian gentleman than a Bolshevik agitator. When the paper moved in, Deng called the villagers to a meeting to explain why everyone should fight Japan. Deng chatted with villagers on his daily rounds and would put a peasant's load on his horse if he encountered a burdened soul on the road back to the village. The villagers called him by the informal appellation of respect, 'Old Deng' (*Lao Deng*). The village chief would regularly consult him on local problems and how to resolve them.[71] Though this is clearly an example of a rosy reminiscence, one can only imagine what satisfaction this respected mandarin role provided for a former frustrated student radical. Michael Lindsay was probably not deceived in his impression that the Communists in the early war period were much as follows: national patriots bringing hope, fair administration, and defence to a sorely underdeveloped area subject to brutal foreign attack.[72]

The new year in 1942 brought the US into the war and thus a small flood of European expatriates and Chinese academics fleeing from the lost haven of Yenching University in Beiping to Jin Cha Ji. For these

2.2 Nie Rongzhen, Deng Tuo (behind), and Norman Bethune, Jin Cha Ji Military Hospital, Wutai, September 1938

people Deng served another role for the Party—as English interpreter. Nie Rongzhen recalls the importance the Party attached to good relations with British and American visitors to the region, beginning with Evans Carlson's visit in December 1937. By the summer of 1938 if not before, Deng was translating for English-speaking visitors at mass rallies; in 1941 he was photographed with Michael Lindsay, who trained a generation of radio operators for the Communists (see Illus. 2.2); and Deng is remembered as Norman Bethune's interpreter.[73] Old friends from each period of his life remark on Deng Tuo's excellent command of English, yet Deng betrayed no influence of British or American works or ideas. Deng held his linguistic abilities as yet another mark of scholarship which was fundamentally Chinese.

Deng may have translated for foreign visitors to the Border Region, but he interacted with the Chinese scholars. Among the Chinese professors who came at that time was one Dong Lu'an, who was known by his pen-name, Yu Li. This specialist in classical Chinese and Buddhist sutras from Yenching University was a target of base area policy to provide cultural activities to keep such high-level intellectuals content in the countryside. In fact, he soon became a leading organizer of these activities in partnership with Deng Tuo. Yu Li was surprised and impressed by the scholarly erudition of the young Communist cadre—especially his ability to write classical verse—and the two traded poems in traditional literati fashion throughout the rectification years of 1942–4.[74]

Despite the harsh Japanese attacks in the spring of 1942, life went on. Deng Tuo married at this time. That May, Ding Yilan and her future husband strolled in the moonlight, courting by the banks of the Hutuo River in Pingshan county.[75] This was the first time they had met, though the editor of *Jin Cha Ji Daily* and the young activist from Tianjin in the local Women's Association had been corresponding for nearly a year. Ding had come to Jin Cha Ji from Yan'an in late 1938 and had gone to work in the Pingshan district. In February 1941, a young woman active in the resistance, one Chen Zhuni, was murdered by her husband and father-in-law. Ding wrote a long piece denouncing the pair and after a number of months the county government punished them. The county officials sent Ding's report to the *Jin Cha Ji Daily* for publication. After it was published on 24 June 1941, the editor, Deng Tuo, wrote to Ding and initiated a correspondence that eventually moved beyond editorial concerns. Soon after their moonlight stroll, Deng formalized his proposal in a poem, 'Xin meng' (Alliance of the Heart).[76] It was the first of a number of love poems Deng would write for her, and the next year, in the spring of 1943, the two made their pledges. These served as acceptable marriage vows, for the two were travelling together as husband and wife later that year.

Life also went on for the newspaper. During the spring ploughing, a portion of the paper's staff was sent off to help organize the ploughing and diversionary tactics designed to thwart Japanese attempts to halt the sowing. In the early summer of 1942, the offices of *Jin Cha Ji Daily* were moved from Gunlonggou to the village of Chenjiayuan, also in the Pingshan area of western Hebei. This was a change of scenery for the staff: a wide and green river flat. They set up shop next to a small stream. There they worked, played, and studied. After each military engagement, Deng would call a meeting to sum up the experiences and celebrate the 'victory' of their survival. At quiet times the staff would repair their huts, plant vegetables, set up basketball competitions or other sports, or sit and chat. Deng invariably turned to talking about poetry and would regularly recite poems to his staff.[77] Such scenes of domestic tranquillity seemed to have alternated regularly with the turmoil of guerrilla warfare.

It was at this riverside scene that Deng Tuo and the newspaper staff began their rectification study in 1942. Rectification officially came to Jin Cha Ji in 1942, but the Border Region had few of the leadership and ideological debates that churned in Yan'an.[78] This is not surprising since Nie's programmes had been lauded a few years earlier by Mao as part of his competition with Wang Ming and the Party 'internationalists'. Wang Ming's followers were not well represented in Jin Cha Ji, so the factional struggle underlying the Yan'an rectification was missing. In addition, Jin Cha Ji was not the scene of manoeuvring for supreme leadership of the Party. A number of Jin Cha Ji leaders including Nie were recalled after 1941 to Yan'an to accept promotions in the 'rectified' Party.[79] Deng Tuo reflected the Jin Cha Ji attitude in his July 1942 editorial, 'The Whole Party Studies and Grasps Mao Zedongism':

The Party's ability to lead the glorious revolutionary struggle to liberate the Chinese people and society in the twentieth century, to become a completely consolidated and powerful Party with a mass nature in politics, organization, and ideology is because it has Mao Zedongism [*Mao Zedong zhuyi*] . . . We must hold high the banner of Mao Zedongism . . . and carry it into every concrete problem and practical study.[80]

For Deng Tuo, the study of rectification documents was an established habit by 1943. Zhao Qingxue, who was transferred to the *Jin Cha Ji Daily* in the summer of 1943, was surprised that the editor was still reading the standard set of *Rectification Documents* (*Zhengfeng wenxian*).[81] Deng was most interested in using the rectification materials to improve the work of his paper. When Zhao had trouble writing an article, unable to decide what slant and particularly what vocabulary to use, Deng laughed. 'What terms?' he said. 'Local terms or foreign terms—so long as the common people understand them—are good terms.[82] Our paper carries out propaganda for the fighters, for the common people; so long as the literate can read the articles we publish and the illiterate can hear and understand them the goal of our propaganda will be achieved.' Deng lent Zhao his dog-eared copy of *Rectification Documents*, suggesting that in order to strengthen this approach the lad should read Mao's 'Reform our Study', 'Rectify the Party's Work Style', and 'Oppose Stereotyped Party Writing'.[83] While this story comes from the posthumous hagiography of Deng, the impression that Deng liked Mao's rectification writings from Yan'an is confirmed several times over Deng's career.

The Jin Cha Ji Image of Mass Line

The propaganda which Deng Tuo and the 'rectified' *Daily* produced was the content of the CCP's Mass Line and reflects the values that attracted some metropolitan intellectuals to propaganda service in Jin Cha Ji. For intellectual service there had to be not only administrative networks and organizational obedience but also an appealing goal and a unity of purpose. Such values are reflected in the Jin Cha Ji propaganda: ideals of public service, harmonious relations among new citizens, and the revival of Chinese culture. These images of the new society help to explain the success of the Communist movement in Jin Cha Ji, but they also outline the fault lines that would bring the establishment down two decades later: the tension between charismatic and rational bureaucratic authority styles and between the intellectual roles of 'culture bearer' and 'cog and screw' in the revolutionary machine.

Most fundamentally, the *medium* of propaganda, state-sponsored journalism, spoke powerfully to intellectual traditions of public service and propagating the orthodoxy among the common people with which Deng Tuo had grown up. Since at least the tenth century, various leading Confucian scholars and various Emperors supported the transformation of popular morals through literati-led propaganda efforts—community compacts (*xiangyue*) or readings of Sacred Edicts (*shengyu*) from the Emperor.[84] The Western idea of an independent and critical press, as opposed to an engaged one which promotes the orthodoxy, did not take root in CCP areas (though not without some dissent). In the early 1940s Mao Zedong laid down the function of the news media in the new Mass Line: propagating the party's policies, gathering information about the grass roots for the leadership, serving as a forum for individual grievances, and supervising the bureaucracy by exposing wrongdoing.[85] Deng Tuo's June 1938 review of the work of *Resistance News* already captured much of this spirit:

> Of course, the production of *Resistance News* has its mission. It must become the propagandizer and organizer of the Border Region's mass resistance and salvation movement, it must represent the needs of the broad masses, reflect and pass on the real conditions and experience of the broad masses' struggle, promote various aspects of work, and educate the masses themselves. At the same time, from the promotion and assistance of the broad masses, the paper itself progresses. It is the paper of the masses; it gives impetus to others, and at the same time it also gets impetus from others. It teaches others, and at the same time is taught by others. Only under this mutual promotion and education has it been able to come to today [its fiftieth issue].[86]

This is journalism in the 'propaganda state'. Deng Tuo later used Lenin's image of Party journalism as the 'guide wire' (*yinxian*) along which the

Party guides the people toward revolution.[87] Naturally, the mutual education which Deng mentions here was under the direction of Party policy. In an editorial from late 1938, Deng points out that the people get their directions for what to do in war from editorials, articles, and reports in Party newspapers and so these must be carefully written in consultation with the leadership.[88]

The idea of the 'propaganda state' directs us to an obvious aspect of the CCP: it is a revolutionary organization seeking not only power but to transform society. It has, as Lowell Dittmer has emphasized, a 'salvationary mission'.[89] Since it promotes radical change in order to 'save China', the Party must communicate its goals and motivate concerted action towards them. This is, once the hot rhetoric is stripped away, the social function of ideology—a set of cultural symbols which represent reality in a persuasive manner to motivate action.[90] Propaganda is applied ideology, and metropolitan intellectuals are needed for its organization and initial dissemination. They weave the 'fabric of hegemony' (that series of alliances among social classes which dominates state and society) which constitutes the consensual ideology that buttresses the constraining political power of a state.[91] The opportunity to help weave the fabric of China's new society proved to be compelling to many Chinese intellectuals at mid-century.

Thus, what would become Maoist dicta on the Party-controlled press—particularly its role as a conduit between state and society—was already for Deng Tuo and the Jin Cha Ji press corps both the standard operating procedure and a matter of painstaking work that included careful listening as well as authoritative goal-setting. Deng Tuo's ease with developing Maoist methods underscores a distinction that will be vital in understanding later troubles between Mao and some Party intellectuals in the PRC. These Mass Line methods were familiar and congenial to Deng Tuo—he simply could not abide the abuse of Mass Line methods, particularly the rules of inner-Party regulations, in the name of utopian schemes. The kind of Mass Line which did appeal to intellectuals in Jin Cha Ji in the 1940s can be seen in the images of the new leader, the new-style government, the new version of Chinese culture, and the new ideology—Maoism—given in its own propaganda.

The New-Style Leader: Nie Rongzhen

The clearest picture of Deng's ease with the goals and propaganda style of the rectified Party exists in Deng's paean not to Mao, but to Nie Rongzhen. In July 1942, Deng wrote a lengthy account of 'Jin Cha Ji's Helmsman, Nie Rongzhen', which fully embodies the new style of idealized leadership emerging out of Yan'an. Deng's article gives the impression that Nie is the 'Chairman Mao' of Jin Cha Ji. This was less a sign of competition between Mao and Nie for the title of 'helmsman' (the actual wording in Chinese was slightly different) and more an indication of Deng's adherence to the Leninist habit of personalizing the Party in propaganda in order to give his audience a single and charismatic figure to revere.[92] The very fact that the essay's topic is *not* Mao underscores the general use of such charismatic appeals within rectification propaganda and Deng's acceptance of them.

The *Jin Cha Ji Pictorial* itself is an interesting case in the history of CCP journalism. It was originally *Resistance Pictorial*, and like the newspaper changed over to the 'Jin Cha Ji' masthead. It looked like *Life* magazine. In fact, it was the first major pictorial ever published by the CCP or Red Army and was published by the Political Department of the Jin Cha Ji Military District.[93] Full-colour cover photographs introduce a professional layout of some 100 black-and-white photographs. With the exception of Deng's long tribute to Nie, most captions and articles in the journal appear in both English and Chinese. The editors' intent to influence European and American opinion is highlighted by the inclusion of letters praising Jin Cha Ji by Michael Lindsay and William Band, along with Lindsay's 'Reminiscences of Dr. Bethune', none of which appears in Chinese. Available during the first year of US involvement in the Pacific War, this was an impressive piece of international propaganda. The themes are resolutely nationalist and anti-Japanese, and focus on local self-defence and self-improvement. Naturally, there is no anti-imperialist rhetoric. This was not to be the case in later issues of the journal which gave up the use of English (other than on the back cover). These later issues had a different, more local audience in mind. That Deng's article on Nie was not translated indicates that it and its personification of the base area in a semi-deified image of Nie was intended to appeal to Chinese audiences, not foreigners.

Deng's glowing account of Jin Cha Ji and General Nie appeared as the lead article in the inaugural issues of *Jin Cha Ji Pictorial*, dated 7 July 1942. Using one of his more common pen-names, Xiao Si, Deng titled the piece: 'Jin Cha Ji's Helmsman Nie Rongzhen—A Model Anti-Japanese Base behind Enemy Lines and the Life of its Commander'.[94] Because of its significance, this article has been subject to serious editing, both in the mid-1940s and in a sobering example of documentary tampering in PRC reprints. In 1980 it was 'reprinted' as the 1942 text with a new title (minus the problematic 'helmsman' claim) and 20 per cent of the text excised *without notice*. Later PRC reprints, such as in

Deng Tuo's Works, are marginally better.⁹⁵ Naturally, for my purposes here I use the original 1942 text.

The piece is ostensibly a brief history of the Jin Cha Ji base area from the formation of the Military District in November 1937 to the spring of 1942, but the details of military campaigns and administrative programmes play second fiddle to descriptions of Nie hard at work and the emotions of his awed followers. Deng builds a picture of the sort of proletarian leader we normally associate with the cult of Mao. It was to provide a personification of the ideals of CCP policy on which the local, mostly peasant, readers (and listeners) could project their loyalty and from whom they could derive inspiration. That is, Nie stood for Jin Cha Ji.⁹⁶ This makes Deng's piece a typical example of rectification propaganda. Despite Deng's punishment later (in 1944) for his excessive praise of Nie, this inspirational hagiography continues in CCP biography. Much of the hagiography on Deng Tuo, and a host of other CCP cadres, written in the recent past follows the same model on the more humble level of how to be a good Party journalist, historian, administrator, or whatever.⁹⁷ Thus Deng's piece is also an archetypal example of propaganda that continues in post-Mao China.

Deng is clearly happy with the project. He starts with a poem he sent to Nie in 1937 (and which now appears in Deng's collections of poetry). The text itself flows easily, and sections of the dialogue and description make better reading than most popular short stories during the Mao period.⁹⁸ Deng produces a portrait worthy of revolutionary respect. Nie, a humble man of vision and military genius, leads his troops through the valley of death to victory. Nie has become the hope of millions of people, and though his shadow is cast over twenty years of revolutionary history he is not a loud or boastful man.⁹⁹ The cadre school Nie set up in Fuping in late 1938 reflects the educational methods and spirit of this great revolutionary leader, and however brief the courses, they are helping to train a new generation in his image. Furthermore, the school is not 'French style' or 'Soviet style' or any foreign model, but is the creation of Nie's own synthesis of his observations and experiences.¹⁰⁰

Nie is capable of that high Marxist-Leninist art of 'synthesis' in order to create a cadre school. He is pictured as equally capable of issuing military plans 'that everyone knows will work' based on his revolutionary experience. This talent, however, comes through his long hours of devoted work, late into the night, hearing reports, poring over maps, and consulting with his talented aides: Generals Zuo Quan, Liu Bocheng, He Long, Guan Xiangying, Cheng Zihua, and Party stalwart, Peng Zhen. He is the picture of the earthy genius, who after a night of planning will breakfast with the troops and crack jokes with them. This is all given in rich and easy detail, such as the picture of Nie, in raincoat and walking stick in hand, trudging off in the spring rain to consult with Peng Zhen 'his comrade in arms'. They walk, chat, and laugh along the banks of the Sha River.[101] Nie, we are reminded, has worked in factories in France, but loves to read and is a competent intellectual. A tough-minded general, Nie loves children. He gives candy to two Japanese girls and passes them on to local villagers with admonitions to care well for them. He cried at the death of Norman Bethune. Details of his life with his wife, Zhang Ruihua, round out the picture of the general at home.[102] All in all, Nie is so busy that 'he can do the work of five', and his staff officer, Tan Yanjie, is on the telephone all day.[103]

The accolade reaches a crescendo in the last three pages, all of which have been cut in the 1980 reprint, save three brief paragraphs on his love for literature. Here the need for *lie zhuan* exemplary biographies in the Confucian historiography which Deng Tuo imbibed as a student in Fuzhou provides another cultural point of contact for the 'fit' of Communist propaganda and Chinese political culture.[104] 'Jin Cha Ji's Helmsman Nie Rongzhen' is a Communist *lie zhuan* combining Chinese and socialist values and assumptions. Here, too, Deng's picture of Nie sounds astonishingly similar to the recent reminiscence literature on Deng Tuo himself. In spite of the hyperbole of this genre (role models in propaganda), it is hard not to imagine that Deng Tuo admired and sought to emulate the leadership qualities he described in Nie as a model for all. Nie was vigorous, well-educated, and a wonderful public speaker. His reports were always complete and clear. When he spoke he used only small note-cards with the main points listed out: A, B, C, ... The text was all in his head. He had a marvellous memory. He could remember something about every person he met—enemy or friend—a talent that Deng admires as useful in political work. Most of all, his leadership style was one of 'seeking truth from facts' (*shishi qiushi*). In all of this, says Deng, Nie is a worthy follower of Mao Zedong:

Jin Cha Ji is a vanguard among base areas and Nie Rongzhen is its talented guide (*xiandao*). This talented creator will have his glorious position in Marxist-Leninist military science, in the realm of Mao Zedongism military theory. This shows that comrade Nie Rongzhen is a Mao Zedongist proficient in creative Marxism.[105]

Nie is presented as both a highly trained Marxist and a bookish intellectual. However, at a literary conference the general defers to the specialists, reminding them only that 'the weapon of literature and art must complement the development of military struggle.'[106] The essay ends with the statement that the broadening of the Pacific War has opened a new historical stage in which Jin Cha Ji may grow. Only on the last page is Song Shaowen, putative head of the Jin Cha Ji Border Region civilian government, mentioned as Nie's right-hand man.

This essay on Nie Rongzhen stands as Deng's most vivid picture of the new ideal leader who embodies the goals of resistance and reform (revolution was glossed over in this piece). Deng's medium is his message as well. Deng was happy to paint such role models, and judging from the reminiscences of his colleagues from the newspaper, he sought to practice such ideals, excepting of course any overt claims to 'synthesize Marxism'. Nonetheless, one cannot but wonder if Deng Tuo had not insinuated a good deal of his own literati proclivities into his portrayal of the bookish, gentle, and intellectual Nie, creating, as it were, a helmsman in his own image.

For much of this time Deng Tuo was in poor health. He suffered from tuberculosis contracted during his time in prison, and he was always thin and frail. Yet this did not impair his work, which included long rides on horseback and the general privations of guerrilla war. Indeed, he is remembered much as he painted Nie Rongzhen—up all night, puffing away on his home-rolled cigarettes and poring over his work (he usually wrote his editorials in the early hours) while being modest and convivial.[107] Without doing injustice to his colleagues, it is reasonable to wonder if these reminiscences may not be somewhat rosy, as they so perfectly conform to the idealized image of the revolutionary hero that is part of the propaganda image Deng himself accepted and helped to shape. Indeed, there is a troubling woodblock print of Deng in a 1984 series on his life in *The Journalist* which pictures Deng being arrested in the 1930s—Deng Tuo is indistinguishable from numerous similar woodcuts of Lu Xun, save for the lack of a moustache.[108]

New-Style Organization: Peng Zhen's Machine

If Nie Rongzhen was the model of the revolutionary leader in Jin Cha Ji, Peng Zhen was an embodiment of its organizational approach, which was to influence many Party leaders and intellectuals, such as Liu Ren, Deng Tuo, and Fan Jin (*Central Hebei Guide* editor and later member of the Beijing Party Committee) through the rest of their careers. This was the organizational side of the emerging CCP orthodoxy, Maoism. Despite the image of a 'two-line struggle' given during the Cultural Revolution,[109] Maoism, particularly in its formative, or Yan'an, stage, included both charismatic and bureaucratic styles of authority. Peng Zhen's elaboration of CCP administration not only provided attractive roles for metropolitan intellectuals as 'transformational bureaucrats'—

an almost priestly function in the revolution—but also contributed to the success of Mao's policy package back in Yan'an.[110]

The Jin Cha Ji Border Region's internal organization was formalized in 1943. The fifth anniversary of the founding of Jin Cha Ji and its survival were celebrated by a major convocation of the Border Region Congress held between 15 and 21 January 1943, at Wentang village in Fuping county. It was actually the first convocation of representatives who had been elected in a 1940 plebiscite, according to the rules of what became known as the 'Three Thirds' system. Thus, Nie reports, the 288 representatives gathered for the Congress not only represented every geographical unit, but included 'representatives of the CCP, the KMT, non-party patriots, forward-looking gentry, scholars from literary circles, scientists and technologists, national minorities, as well as representatives of worker, peasant, women's, youth, and other mass organizations.'[111] The Congress marked a new stage for the Border Region, for it was finally able to pass laws in a parliamentary fashion on issues such as rent and tenant relations, taxation, and marriage, and it was able to follow these up with regulations promulgated by a duly elected administrative council. This replaced earlier decrees by the Party or military.[112] This also consolidated Party control over the institutions of power in the Border Region—a long-time interest of Peng Zhen, who was the architect of these laws.[113]

Peng Zhen's authoritarian but carefully pragmatic approach to Party administration was the version of Mass Line politics Deng Tuo and his colleagues experienced in the base area and praised in the *Jin Cha Ji Daily*.[114] The laws passed at the January 1943 Jin Cha Ji Congress were based on Peng Zhen's 'Double Ten Programme' of August 1940. Three aspects of the programme and these laws, as Pitman Potter has pointed out, are important not only for understanding Jin Cha Ji, but also the later history of the PRC. First, the laws were designed to provide the 'organizational means of ensuring the party's dominance over popular and governmental organizations.'[115] Second, the model of political life embodied in Peng's example is one where issues of personal liberties and statutory rights do not exist. Rather, legal constraints are limited to controlling the abuse of power by officials. This problem, which has become one of central concern in China after the Cultural Revolution, was not a problem in a time of war and moderate reform policies—all of which bred unity. Rather, Peng's model of political life was one of 'careful analysis of specific local conditions before introducing policy proposals, revealing a characteristically strong faith in the value of rational objective analysis in the preparation of policy.'[116] Third, this approach reveals Peng's view about Chinese society and change. For

Peng it was the control of political institutions, rather than engineering basic socio-economic change (as dictated by orthodox Marxism), which determined historical periods. Peng was closer to Lenin than to Marx when he concluded that Party dominance of politics in Jin Cha Ji constituted the overthrow of the feudal system of political power.[117] We must remember these were the ideals, not the realities. Kathleen Hartford's work has detailed the great difficulties the CCP had in carrying out even moderate reform in Jin Cha Ji.[118]

The core of the 'New Democratic Government' proclaimed at the Congress was detailed in a 12 February editorial in the *Jin Cha Ji Daily*.[119] The government was based on five principles: democratic elections, the 'Three Thirds' system of corporate representation of CCP and other major social groups, democratic centralism, the rule of law and regulations, and opposition to bureaucratism. Naturally, this was all under the effective control of the CCP. The result was an intricate web that guaranteed *participation* more than political *power* to various social groups in the Border Region.[120] This was natural, as the Party's goal was to neutralize competitors and mobilize the population. Here was a government which patriotic intellectuals could serve. And the government was interested in obtaining those services. As a part of this programme, the authorities took considerable efforts to organize and keep their elite intellectuals happy by addressing their cultural interests.

The New Culture

During these years Deng Tuo had been propagandizing the Party's evolving policies on literature. His writings on cultural and ideological matters provide us with one set of rationales for intellectual service to the CCP. As a journalist, he naturally focused on news, agitation, and what we would call magazine feature articles. However, he did speak on the role of fiction and creative literature, and his own literary activities in the realm of classical poetry in many ways served as propaganda for the Party's United Front policies (by attracting intellectuals and displaying the Party's cultivation of Chinese culture). Deng's approach to literature, however, reflected his work. News—current and ancient—was Deng's main focus, not the artistic spirit of creative writing.

Fundamental to his participation is, on the one hand, an acceptance of Party dominance as outlined by Mao in his infamous 'Yan'an Talks', while on the other hand assuming and inserting into that service a two-track model of intellectual and cultural life in which intellectuals could maintain a space for their elite pastimes. Both Deng's version of historical materialism and his reliance on the bureaucratic structure erected by Peng Zhen supported a role for intellectuals as 'culture bearers', as the select few with sufficient education to make manifest the transformational goals of the Party.[121] The attraction of this ministering role for metropolitan intellectuals is not limited to the sons of Confucius. Miklós Haraszti has made a devastating satire of the lure of 'directed culture' for intellectuals in the Hungarian state socialist regime and George Konrád and Ivan Szelényi include the temptation to reform society as one of the factors of East European intellectuals 'on the road to class power'.[122]

The Border Region administration and Deng had turned to the role of literature in a forum held in February and March 1939. Deng was clearly on what would become Mao's side in the famous 'Yan'an Talks' on art and literature later in 1942. Deng demanded that literature serve the masses and conform to Party policy needs. Yet he made clear that these requirements should pose no conflict with the equally important demands of authenticity and historical accuracy. He favoured typical models in literature, but saw this as a challenge to the writer, not as an encumbrance to artistic freedom. Deng makes his position in the development of China's new literature since the May Fourth movement clear. The new literature can only come out of a critical acceptance of the old national forms imbued with new revolutionary content. Ignoring popular interests or vulgarization won't do. The entryway into 'mass literature', says Deng, is *language*. The terms and expressions of the working people will allow writers to express their new revolutionary experiences among the masses. 'The combination of new content and old national forms is the most pressing question of the current literary movement and is the most important difference between the new enlightenment movement and the old enlightenment movement.'[123]

This hints at a very important part of Deng's views on literature, a part he leaves unsaid but about which his educated audience would be all too aware. By his use of the term 'new enlightenment movement' (*xin qimeng yundong*), Deng is aligning himself with the movement of the same name which Chen Boda proposed during the hot debates over literature and 'national forms' (*minzu xingshi*) in Shanghai in 1935–7.[124] Like Chen (Mao's secretary by the late 1930s), and former Party leader Qu Qiubai, Deng does not support the romantic and spiritual literature of enlightenment based on the individual authority of the artist. This stands in marked contrast to the heart of May Fourth literature and to the values expressed by their representatives in Yan'an.[125] In fact, Deng's speech ignores foreign literature aside from works in the Soviet canon, such as Gogol. Lenin is Deng's literary authority.

Deng, however, was not proposing that writers become docile 'cogs and screws' who merely advertise the policies of their Party superiors. His definition of national forms differed from that of Mao's disciples in Yan'an who, using the same language Deng Tuo employs here, supported a uni-track policy of popular culture that gave artists a subordinate 'cog and screw' role.[126] For instance, Deng concludes his consideration of the value of the language of the masses as a vehicle for writers to express new (revolutionary) content by saying:

Of course, massification cannot be carried out merely through words; it is not just a matter of simple words (at times new words can be part of massification, such as 'imperialism', 'traitors', etc. . . .). Also important are: massification of methods, thought, structure, and the representation of the direction and real materials of mass life. Best is to *raise the cultural level of the masses* in the midst of developing the real mass literary and artistic movement.[127]

The grounds for Deng's version of what soon became orthodox CCP literary policy become clear in his discussion of poetry. He accepts the leadership's view that poetry and popular songs should be, ultimately, the same thing. Indeed, Deng tried his hand at such popular art, including a revolutionary skit, an agitprop song, 'Walls of Iron', and articles aimed at drawing meaning and inspiration from the growing list of martyrs in Jin Cha Ji.[128] In his speech he derides scholars who look down on popular songs as people lacking in patriotic pride and appreciation of China's long culture (a sleight of hand unless one realizes his unnamed target: May Fourth cosmopolitans). Yet, Deng declares that under current historical conditions where class distinctions continue to exist, poetry and popular songs will each have their place. They will realize their basic unity in the future society, not now. Thus Deng allows for an arena of elite culture as a legitimate part of the 'New Democracy'. By also catering to the masses in other literary arenas, writers will naturally begin the long mutual transformation of elite and popular culture which will ultimately bring them into unity.[129] Mao would provide Deng with authoritative support for this two-track approach in his 'On New Democracy', which appeared some six months later.[130] However, Mao's opinions about elite writers would harden by the time of his 'Yan'an Talks' in 1942 and, although he acknowledged the need for 'higher level' literature for cadres, he would demand a more uni-track approach to art whenever literature threatened Party policy.[131] Deng Tuo maintained this two-track cultural approach throughout his life. Popular culture would always be for Deng Tuo an effort to popularize elite culture for the peasant and worker majority. This contrasts with the peasant-based literature, such as the *yang'ge* drama movement, favoured by leaders in

Yan'an. Deng's goal was to elevate popular culture, not to cut intellectual snobs down to size.

Yan-Zhao Poetry Society

The importance of poetry to Deng Tuo and to his relations with his superiors and direct subordinates becomes clear in his activities with a poetry society immediately following the January 1943 Border Region Congress. The 'Yan-Zhao Poetry Society' that Deng Tuo formed provides an instructive look at what is normally considered the negative side of the Party's cultural policies: constraints on the intellectual pastimes of high-level intellectuals.[132] Following the Congress meetings, a few of the intellectual and political elite of the Border Region organized a traditional-style poetry society for mutual enjoyment. It was unabashedly elitist. The ability to produce classical regulated verse (particularly *qilü*) was the requirement for membership, and it was peopled by the political elite—those administering the new 'Mass Line'. Furthermore, stories about this group and other elite poetry soirées are repeated with great reverence in the post-Mao literature on Deng, indicating continued approval of them among part of China's intellectual establishment today.

The apparent contradiction is this praise of elite cultural pastimes beyond the reach of workers and peasants in the populist culture of Mao's rectified Party. Were not writers, even revolutionary writers, suppressed in Yan'an? The answer lies in the traditional nature and content of the Yan-Zhao Poetry Society. The society's stated goals were literary enjoyment and support of the government. Deng's very traditional 'Record of the Society's Formation' abounds in traditional imagery and classical prose echoing dynastic loyalists with phrases such as 'To serve as a drummer for the three armies with the poetry and song of Yan and Zhao.'[133] The society's activities repeated those of the poetry societies to which Deng Tuo had belonged in Fuzhou in the 1920s. In this case the elder poet, Hao Qing, produced a set of four regulated verses 'to initiate the poetic fraternity'. Deng replied in metre and rhyme, and the group was on its way. Such elite cultural pastimes not only harked back to Deng's literati origins, but clearly were appropriate in Jin Cha Ji in 1943.

The Yan-Zhao Poetry Society is an example of Deng's two-track policy for poetry and popular songs. In Jin Cha Ji such activities were also considered part of the necessary services the administration should provide for high-level intellectuals to keep them content.[134] This is a simple application of Mao's dictum that literature must serve the people, an application made more along the lines of Peng Zhen's realistic assessments of current reality: intellectuals are people, much-needed people. They have their needs which, so long as they do not contradict urgent Party goals, should be met just as much as should the entertainment needs of the masses. This approach presaged Deng's continued rich variety of cultural life—in poetry, painting, antique collecting—in the People's Republic until his death.

The invidious political distinction between 'national forms' and elite literature (which bedevilled writers in Yan'an) disappears when the content of literature is, as in this case, not May Fourth European models but Chinese literati arts. The related division between intellectuals and the Party apparatus, often so distinct in the case of leftist literary intellectuals in China, does not appear among these devotees of traditional poetry. The founding members of the Yan-Zhao Poetry Society included Deng Tuo, Nie Rongzhen, Hao Qing, Ruan Muhan, Liu Dianji, Song Shaowen, Lu Zhengcao, and Yu Li.[135] Here the interests of high-level intellectuals overlapped with those of the leading military (Nie, Lu) and administrative (Song) figures of the Border Region. In fact, Deng and Yu Li were both leaders in the Jin Cha Ji establishment. The vitriolic debates over the evils of traditional literature and the poor discipline of left-wing writing that dominated Yan'an in 1942 are not apparent in the current record of Deng Tuo's life in Jin Cha Ji. He was never a left-wing writer like Lu Xun or Ding Ling. The problems of left-wing writers, which have served to set the impression for Western scholars on intellectual–Party relations under the CCP, are highlighted by this contrast with the Yan-Zhao Poetry Society. The left-wing writers were generally out of power, offered a competing strategy in the rectification movement, were unable to harmonize their elite pastimes with popularization work among the peasantry, and were small in number, even among the tiny class of the educated elite.[136] On the other hand, establishment intellectuals like Deng Tuo were in positions of influence, abided by the tenets of Yan'an rectification policy, were comfortable with the peasant population, were much larger in number, and maintained friendly relations with the military and political leadership. Equally, Deng Tuo's two-track approach to culture was unlike that of the 'cog and screw' artists in Yan'an who produced the *yang'ge* folk propaganda dramas. Establishment intellectuals like Deng Tuo carried considerable cultural authority and respect in the eyes of Party and military leaders for their artistic and scholarly skills. Deng Tuo used this authority to carve out a 'culture bearer' role that combined something of the *moral autonomy* of the left-wing critical writers and the *loyalty* of the *yang'ge* dramatists. It was a powerful and attractive role—an honourable vocation.

This is not to say Maoist cultural policy had no conflict with elite culture—cosmopolitan or traditional—or its role in the evolving political culture of the propaganda state. Rather, the version of Maoism at work in Jin Cha Ji, which was itself a vanguard of Maoist policies, was more comfortable with elite culture. The cadre and leaders who dominated the North China Bureau and later much of the central administration of the People's Republic in general shared this comfort. This comfort masked differences with Mao himself and those given to 'faith Maoism'. The establishment's acceptance of two tracks for elite and popular culture during the long transition to Communist society and their managerial approach to Party rectification, however, left begging the underlying contradictions between the roles of 'culture bearer' and 'cog and screw' for intellectuals and the political styles of charisma and routine for the leadership. Thus, when Mao turned on elite pastimes and managerial politics *en masse* in the Cultural Revolution, it was a case of one *part* of the wartime Communist tradition turning on another equally well-pedigreed part. Until that time, the model of intellectual–state relations under Chinese communism on a day-to-day level (leaving aside the very significant periodic campaigns Mao instigated to combat this quotidian accommodation) is better represented in the Yan-Zhao Poetry Society than in either Wang Shiwei's 'Wild Lilies' and the purges of the literary rectification in Yan'an in 1942 or the sterile literature of socialist realism.[137]

Deng's elite tastes in poetry did not alienate him from his constituency, nor from his subordinates. In this way Deng Tuo's work style continued the mind-set of traditional literati and did not reflect the romantic 'alienation' expressed by many left-wing writers of the period. Rather, his cultural pastimes were an opportunity for sharing through a paternalistic style of personal education. This dominated his professional relations with subordinates for the next twenty-five years. Deng's love of poetry is a constant theme among the reminiscences of his colleagues on the paper. He would recite poems and explain them to his staff, even when on the run. He struck his subordinates as the bookish type (*shusheng qi*). He was known in the base area as the author of a book on famine relief, and his poetic skills were admired and in demand. Chen Chunsen, an editor for the paper, recalls that Deng would often tell them stories from Chinese history, stressing to his listeners that a people with such a long history as the Chinese could not perish. He loved to collect gazetteers and historical artefacts, making a search in each town he travelled through. He seemed to know something about everything while maintaining the humble manners of a well-educated gentleman. His charges were keen to know how he did it. Deng replied:

'I came from a family that loved books; my father's way of thinking was new and original while he was a disciplined scholar proficient in history, calligraphy, and general knowledge; my elder brothers were studious and excelled in English. I learned the approach, if not all the details, at home.'

Deng's life as a scholar-cadre demonstrates that the new political organization and new goals of the CCP 'fit' traditional literati concerns. This blend of traditional and revolutionary goals formed his approach to work for the rest of his working life. It is what he passed on to the Jin Cha Ji propaganda corps. Not only did this form the basis behind his specific editorial corrections of article drafts for the *Daily*,[138] it informed the broad network of journalists and propagandists that developed under Deng's hand. The Jin Cha Ji propaganda corps published *Straight Talk*, the underground journal aimed at Beiping and other occupied cities. They also helped publish *The Border Region Government Guide* and another news sheet, *National Salvation News*. Increasingly the *Jin Cha Ji Daily* Society printed books, along with the local branch of the Xinhua Society, all of which were under Deng Tuo's management.[139] One colleague reflects that the *Jin Cha Ji Daily* under Deng and other leaders 'nurtured a militant group of journalists who . . . in the next twenty years fanned out over the whole country.'[140] Deng Tuo can justly be considered as one of the founders of socialist journalism in the People's Republic, and his approach to Mass Line journalism and propaganda provided one of the models for future CCP journalism in the People's Republic. Deng Tuo himself later employed this approach as editor-in-chief of the *People's Daily*.

Bureaucratic Maoism: Ideology of a Transformational Bureaucrat

Deng Tuo's writings on ideology reflect his role as 'culture bearer', bringing the good news of Marxism-Leninism and, soon, Mao Zedong Thought to the public. They also show why he felt the role of propagandist was an honourable vocation in which ideology was a method, a tool, to be used in a discriminating fashion by an educated elite. His exhortations and popularizations call to mind similar efforts by Confucian literati who tried to reform local society through community compacts (*xiangyue*) in the Song and Ming dynasties or propagandized the 'Sacred Edicts' of the Kangxi Emperor in the Qing dynasty.[141] Both believed they were bringing morality and civilized life to the untutored masses. Interestingly, Ming and Qing examples also reflect the two-track (popular and elite) approach to moral-cultural education which Deng Tuo applied in his service to the CCP.[142] Naturally, the *content* of these two propaganda efforts was profoundly different, with Deng Tuo's emphasizing radical change rather than the status quo and a new foreign ideology rather than the ideas of Neo-Confucianism. What we do see here is a structural continuity in Chinese political culture, a continuity in form—of the *role* of the educated elite as privileged propagators, social teachers, of a state ideology that claims to serve the people. Nonetheless, Deng's ideological writings reveal the bureaucratic strain in Maoism, what would over the next fifteen years disassociate with the faith aspects of Yan'an Maoism to become bureaucratic Maoism.

In early 1941, Deng Tuo penned a long series of articles popularizing dialectical materialism, his first sustained writing on the topic since his 1933 criticism of Zhang Dongsun. In the 2 March 1941 issue of the *Jin Cha Ji Daily*, he began his series 'A Short Course in Dialectical Materialism'.[143] It was the first of eight articles in the 'Cultural Ideology' (*wenhua sixiang*) page of the paper. Later topics included quantity and quality and the subjective and objective. Deng reiterates his themes from his 1933 defence of dialectical materialism, albeit in a far more readable form. His gurus are Marx, Engels, and Lenin. Stalin, naturally, is quoted, though Mao's philosophical essays from the late 1930s such as 'On Practice' and 'On Contradiction' are not. The bulk of Deng's citations, however, come from Engels. *Natural Dialectics* figures largely. Deng's 1941 essays on dialectics demonstrate that he had a detailed appreciation of dialectical materialism, the ideological basis of Marxism-Leninism, before Mao consolidated his version of the ideology. This is no surprise as works by Li Da and Ai Siqi popularizing the Soviet Stalinist version of dialectics had been broadly available by the mid-1930s. Nonetheless, Deng's version of dialectical materialism largely parallels Mao's.[144]

Two important conclusions come from this. First, Deng's acceptance of Mao's leadership must reflect a considered acceptance of the merits of Mao's ideas. That is, Deng arrived at broadly similar conclusions to those of Mao's essays, which were circulating in mimeograph drafts by the late 1930s.[145] Thus Deng's support of Mao was more on the basis of intellectual appreciation than hero worship or Party cant—since in 1941 Mao was still at least a year away from achieving his dominance in the rectification movement. Second, when Mao strayed in the late 1950s from the tenets of a rather materialistically determined version of dialectics, Deng had a pre-Mao basis in Marxism-Leninism (as did his colleagues like Yang Xianzhen at the Central Party School) from which to criticize Mao.

Why then did Deng *not* cite Mao? It is reasonable to conclude that as a senior propaganda official in Nie Rongzhen's administration Deng Tuo had access to Mao's various unpublished philosophical writings. Deng did not cite Mao's essays in the press, I suspect, for the same reasons he would not again in 1957: Party propaganda, and especially ideological education, must be based on published and certified texts. In 1941 Mao's essays on dialectical materialism were neither; by 1944 they were, and Deng lavished his praise on the Chairman as the editor of Mao's first *Selected Works*.

More importantly for our understanding of the man, Deng Tuo, like Nie Rongzhen, personally came to accept Mao's ideological leadership.[146] This is not surprising for Nie, who was a leader in the Jiangxi Soviet and on the Long March. Deng, on the other hand, had not met or worked with Mao. Thus, Deng's favourable reception to Mao's controversial outline of Party goals in 'On New Democracy' is a reflection of Deng's acceptance of the need for a charismatic leader, such as he would affirm for Nie in his own 1942 paean to the general.[147] While foreshadowing stern Party cultural policies that would become mandatory in the 1942 rectification, Mao's February 1940 essay was his bid, premature at that time, in his struggle with Wang Ming to map out a rival formulation for coalition government with the KMT under the United Front.[148] Deng, however, liked the essay and in what was a common practice for him during the war, he wrote a poem about it:[149]

> The myriad waters and thousand mountains are no difficulty,
> The Great Wall is like the points of the eyebrows to which
>   we turn our fingers.
>
> The battle formations[150] open the field without strong resistance,
> Brush and ink uplifted easily encompass the broadest view.
>
> In winds and rains the returning ships are being shaken,[151]
> Planning strategy from within the tent[152] he forgets the troubles.[153]
>
> We can bind the Black Dragon, the rope is in our hands,
> Let's ascend the mountain peaks, and take a view from the very top.[154]

It is an optimistic piece—resounding with the imagery of the semi-fictional hero, Zhuge Liang, of the popular novel, *Romance of the Three Kingdoms*. The second couplet praises both Mao's military strategy and his theoretical writings, while the third pictures Mao unperturbed as everything around him is in turmoil. The last couplet is borrowed from one of Mao's poems—and indeed the rhyme scheme of the whole poem imitates Mao's. It implies that 'On New Democracy' is one of the ropes in hand to overcome the Black Dragon. Deng uses classical imagery

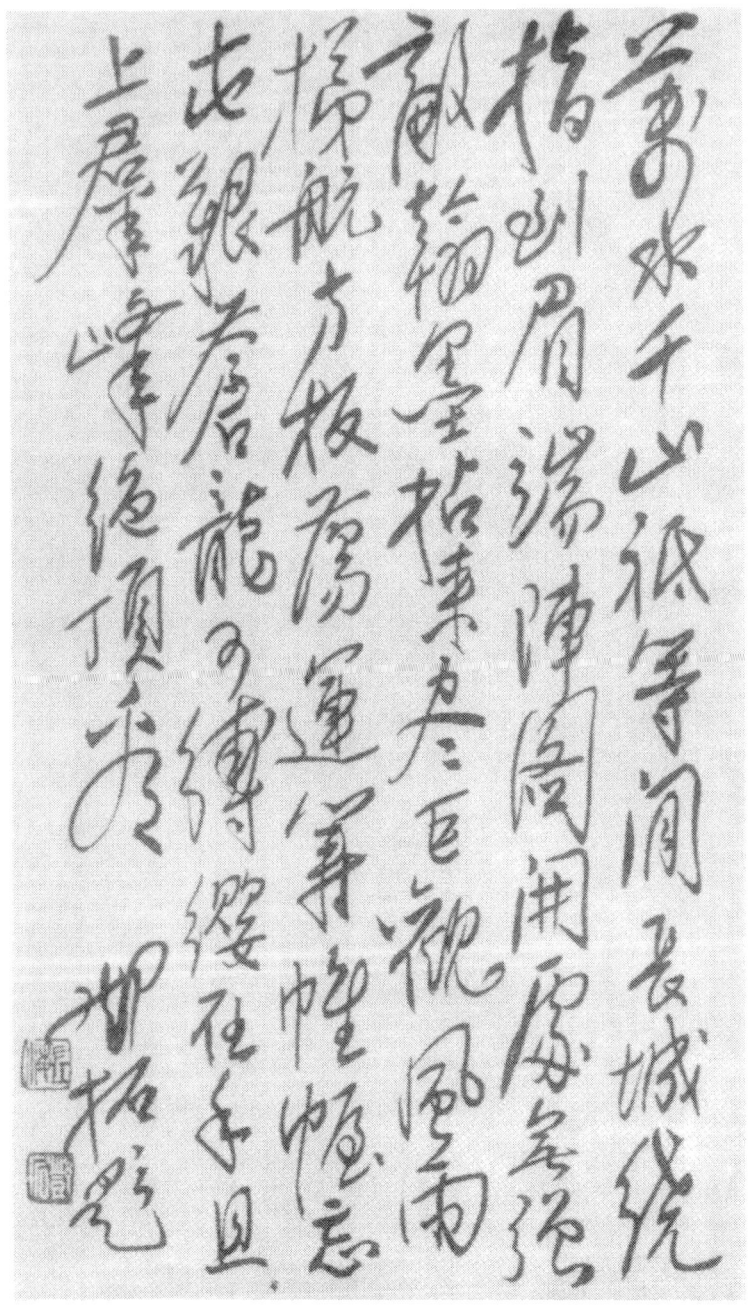

2.3 Deng Tuo's 1940 poem on Mao's 'New Democracy'

from the *Book of Songs* and the *Book of Changes* to highlight the turmoil of the times and Mao's ability to rise above it. The wealth of allusion in this 'regulated verse' (*qilü*) serves to show some of the literary qualities Deng Tuo felt appropriate to employ in his praise of Mao. Finally, the calligraphic style of the handwritten version of the poem completes the homage by imitating Mao's 'running style' calligraphy (see Illus. 2.3)—a style the classically trained Deng Tuo had used much less before then.[155]

This poem is our best window into Deng Tuo's personal attitude toward Mao and his leadership—ideological and military—of the CCP. Newspaper propaganda is one thing, and Deng Tuo was invariably observant of Leninist discipline in propaganda work. Tang-style poetry in an elegant hand is altogether another matter. For Deng Tuo this poem represented real admiration; poetry was his personal voice as much as journalism was his public persona. For the select audience of highly educated Chinese (and indirectly the general public which heeded the intellectual elite's views) this poem has to do with political hegemony. Such a marshalling of cultural symbols on behalf of Mao—linking him to the famed generalship of Zhuge Liang and the cosmic powers of the *Book of Changes*—was a powerful certification of Mao's leadership in Chinese political culture. Unlike the Taiping generals of the nineteenth century, Mao was able to attract literati compliance and positive support—a key to the success of any national administration in China.[156] In the model of Deng Tuo's two-track policy for literature, his calligraphic imitation of Mao's own hand (when Deng was clearly accomplished in several styles of calligraphy) was a signal to the elite (who could decipher the running script, not to mention appreciate the poem's allusions) declaring Mao's qualifications as supreme leader. The degree of Deng Tuo's mastery of these arcane symbols of Chinese culture proportionally increased the impact of his endorsement of Mao.[157] In this sense, the Party received its part of the bargain which provided in return an honourable vocation for Deng Tuo—it received cultural legitimation from some of the sons of Confucius.[158] Deng Tuo's endorsement for the general public appeared in his propaganda work and sometimes anonymously, as in his 'Editor's Preface' to Mao's *Selected Works*.

In May 1944 the *Jin Cha Ji Daily* Society published the first official *Selected Works of Mao Zedong*.[159] The Jin Cha Ji Branch of the Politburo took up Central Party directives that Mao Zedong's writings should be systematically published. Leaders in the Division Office, Nie Rongzhen, Cheng Zihua, and Liu Lantao, gave the responsibility to Deng Tuo.[160] Deng Tuo edited the volume and wrote 'A Word by the Editor'. The volume contains 29 articles by Mao, including his rectification period writings. Raymond Wylie has argued that by 1942 Mao needed to demonstrate his expertise in the four fields of theory that Mao himself had demanded of a true proletarian leader: economics, politics, military affairs, and culture. Mao lacked a comprehensive treatise on culture and economics as he entered the competition for chief Party theorist in 1942, but by the end of the year he had them in his 'Talks at the Yan'an Forum on Literature and Art' and his December 1942 'Economic and Financial Problems'.[161] The Jin Cha Ji edition of Mao's works was the first to include these and therefore to complete his claim as chief theorist of the Party.

In contrast to his 1941 essays on dialectical materialism, Deng Tuo now presented Mao as the ideological fount of the Party as well as its great leader. In his 'A Word by the Editor', Deng wrote:

> The thought of comrade Mao Zedong represents the Chinese proletariat and their political Party—it is the thought of the Communist Party. It is the Bolshevik thought in the Party.... Colonial, semi-colonial, and semi-feudal China have been the historical conditions in which Mao Zedongism[162] came to be. The revolution has already passed through these three periods, and in each one of them comrade Mao Zedong, and all those comrades who rallied around comrade Mao Zedong, struggled against enemy thought outside the Party and against so called 'Left' but in fact Rightist opportunism inside the Party. Historical practice has fully demonstrated that comrade Mao Zedong's thought is the only correct thought.[163]

Deng then called on cadres and Party members 'to study modestly and attentively the theories of comrade Mao Zedong.' Deng adopts Mao's periodization of China's recent history, indicating that the question of historical periodization, which Deng had declared in his 1930s historical essays was a key to understanding China's revolution, had now been settled in Mao's favour. Since the collection includes Mao's rectification pieces, particularly the 'Yan'an Talks', Deng's praise of Mao's work indicates his satisfaction with the orthodoxy that emerged from the rectification movement, including the dominance of the Party in all spheres of intellectual endeavour. Deng's official propagation of Mao's Thought combined with his 1940 calligraphic paean extolling Mao's virtues show that he accepted Yan'an Communism as the fulfilment of intellectual life, an orthodoxy that finally gave intellectuals a chance to participate in the political and cultural renewal of China.

Deng elaborated his praise for the Maoist approach, echoing the application of it that had developed in Jin Cha Ji, at a major propaganda work conference held by the Jin Cha Ji branch of the Central Propaganda Department in May 1944. Following the new policy of 'the entire Party shall run the press', the Jin Cha Ji conference set out to tell journalists how to do this. Deng's speech was later published in the 1946 *Guidelines on Journalism*.[164] What Deng said about journalism accorded with what the Yan'an *Liberation Daily* editorialized in August 1942 during the rectification campaign: 'We already know that newspapers do not only report the news; they are also sharp weapons in constructing our nation and Party and in reforming our work and our lives.'[165] Deng Tuo, too, thought journalism should be used as a form of public education, particularly to mobilize readers to act: 'Because real-life struggle is developing, our news reporting methods must be able to reflect and *lead* the whole process of that struggle's development.'[166]

The bulk of Deng's speech is on how to write better copy. He covers three aspects of correspondence work and four aspects of news reporting that need to be reformed according to the new Party Mass Line. He directs his listeners to eschew Western grammar and flowery classical Chinese expressions. Reporters are to live among the masses and encourage ordinary people to write for themselves. More important for the future of socialist journalism in China, Deng Tuo introduces the concept of 'key reporting' (*zhongdian baodao*) in which a key issue, usually an aspect of current policy, forms the guiding theme and central content of all forms of writing in a newspaper—news items, correspondents' reports, essays, and editorials. In this way, Deng says, all the most important aspects of a key issue will be concentrated on and therefore better understood by the readers.[167] This style of 'key reporting' continues in China today.

Deng Tuo's conclusion to his 1944 speech is an example of the bureaucratic Maoist approach to propaganda, and, indeed, to all work:

In order to reform the correspondence and reporting methods of our Party periodicals, every single correspondent and Party periodical worker must reform his own thought, and, on the basis of comrade Mao Zedong's speech at the Yan'an forum on literature and art, the Central Propaganda Department's resolutions on literary and art policy, and the directives on military propaganda by the General Political Department, each one of us must link our personal thought and work through deep personal self-examination and reflection.

The frustration one may experience reading this quotation from Deng Tuo well summarizes the nature of his Maoism. It begins and ends with Mao's dearest concepts—thought reform and reflection—and refers to his 'Yan'an Talks', yet it all gets lost in the middle. How a shred of enthusiasm could survive the labyrinth of bureaucracies Deng lists as guides to implementing Mao's ideas is beyond imagination. This list, though, is significant: it reflects the organizational approach to power employed by Peng Zhen to maintain the Party in Jin Cha Ji. Deng Tuo believed in the system and its institutions. Mao's genius is relegated to the realm of basic principles which the various departments will articulate in any given situation. This institutionalizing approach to implementing Mao Zedong Thought, rather than any grievance with the Party's claims to dominance or with Mao's ideas, lies at the root of future conflicts in Deng Tuo's career, and indeed within the CCP from the late 1950s, when Mao tried to rid himself of the bureaucracies represented in the middle section of the quotation above.

Investigation and Promotion

Conflicts about ideology, however, were not an unimaginable thing of the future for Deng Tuo in the 1940s. *Something* happened around this time, and it was a set-back for Deng Tuo. The reminiscence literature on Deng gives no hint of trouble in the 1940s. Other sources, however, do. The problem seems to have been an 'ideological error' by Deng, but one that he worked through, since he later ran the *People's Daily*.

The first indication of something amiss comes with a change among his official appointments. He was both promoted and demoted. In May 1944, just as his edition of Mao's *Selected Works* came out and he gave his speech on news reporting methods, Deng Tuo was demoted to vice-director and editor-in-chief of *Jin Cha Ji Daily*. Hu Xikui took over the top positions at the paper until late August 1945 (when the paper stopped briefly during fighting in Kalgan). It is unclear who ran the paper until 1947, when Deng became director (the leading post) with Hu Kaiming as vice-director and Wang Kangzhi, a veteran Jin Cha Ji journalist, as editor-in-chief. When the paper was transformed into the *People's Daily* on 15 June 1948, Deng Tuo held no leading position. In March 1949, when the paper moved from Fuping to Beiping, Fan Changjiang directed the paper, and only later did Deng Tuo come on board.[168] From 1945, however, Deng held many positions of responsibility. In September 1945 he was appointed vice-director of the Central Party Propaganda Department for Jin Cha Ji,[169] and by March 1946 he had joined the editorial board of *Northern Culture* in Kalgan under chief editors Cheng Fangwu (former chief of the 1943 Base Area Congress) and Zhang Ruxin (Mao's Yan'an ideologue).[170] Since Deng was still holding important positions at this time, his change of posts at *Jin Cha Ji Daily* may well have been a case of moving cadres around for reasons clear at the time but unexplained in retrospect.

Suspicion arises, however, from two sources. First, this shifting around of titles would also occur when Deng was clearly in trouble between

1957 and 1960 at the *People's Daily*. Then Mao wanted him out, and supporters responded by shifting him from editor-in-chief to general manager. This is not what happened in 1944. He was not kicked upstairs. Instead, someone else was put over him. Still, such a shifting of posts has often been associated with political ill fortune. Second, an American travelling in Jin Cha Ji in 1946, Sidney Rittenberg, recalls that Deng was a target for criticism at the time. He met Deng Tuo in Kalgan in the summer of 1946 and was deeply impressed by the man.[171] In September, Rittenberg travelled to Yan'an with Feng Wenbin, Deng's associate from Jin Cha Ji. Along the way Rittenberg sang Deng Tuo's praises to Feng, who replied ominously that comrade Deng Tuo had nonetheless committed 'serious ideological errors'.

Chinese colleagues report privately that Deng was investigated for these ideological errors in 1944–5, but was exonerated.[172] It now appears that Deng was under criticism for his paean to Nie Rongzhen, as well as undergoing scrutiny again for his 1933 prison activities. There is no documentation on this criticism, if it even occurred, but it may reflect the arrival of a more thorough rectification campaign and the ominous cadre-screening programme to Jin Cha Ji, following the end of the Japanese military threat.[173] One veteran recalls that rectification and cadre screening came to Jin Cha Ji in 1943 with the same tendencies toward inquisition as we now know for the Yan'an case.[174] Superficially, we can see that by 1944 Party leaders had decided that there would be only one 'helmsman' (and reserved such terms for Mao). However, below the surface it is most likely that the Yan'an cadres who brought the second wave of rectification (and the cadre investigation campaign) to Jin Cha Ji in 1944 also insisted on the reduced 'cog and screw' role for intellectuals and thus would attack the 'culture bearer' model Deng had created of Nie. At present, however, we cannot know what caused Deng Tuo's demotion, but the rumblings serve as a harbinger of the final showdown after 1957 between two trends of thought and social roles inside Maoism.

Although the post-Mao historiography tries to obscure these events, they should not be seen as a major calamity in Deng's life. In all likelihood this is an example of the rectification screening of cadres working, since Deng achieved his highest posts in the Party afterward. Before the 1957 anti-Rightist campaign, such investigation was not necessarily a witch-hunt.[175] Liu Binyan, a junior colleague of Deng's later in the *People's Daily*, was subject to a similar investigation in 1954. Because of it, he was unable to accompany Deng to the Soviet Union as planned. Liu's assessment of the experience may serve for Deng's: 'I felt the system worked.'[176] It is probable that Deng was similarly cleared by

1945. He was promoted up the Party's policy-making chain, leaving others to handle the detailed editorial work. The limited number of publications by Deng during the Civil War parallels his promotions in the Party's propaganda and research institutions. Deng entered the Civil War as a proven, and tested, leader in the CCP's propaganda establishment.

Conclusion

Deng Tuo's life and work in Jin Cha Ji provides a useful perspective on the birth and initial operation of the 'propaganda state' in China, particularly on how the CCP in north China made successful use of metropolitan intellectuals in the service of a key revolutionary function: propaganda. The Jin Cha Ji administration managed to survive Japanese attacks and economic blockade and its major propaganda organ, the *Jin Cha Ji Daily*, also survived these threats. They did this by good organization and flexible responses to changing conditions. Thus, they had institutions which could make use of metropolitan intellectuals. They made use of a range of motivating appeals, which in the case of intellectuals included opportunities to be 'culture bearers' in the establishment of a new and just society—that propaganda work was an honourable vocation. The 'institutional culture' of *Jin Cha Ji Daily* reflects a mix of habitual literati attitudes of the metropolitan elite toward society (educating it and transforming it for the good) and voluntary compliance (personal acceptance of the correctness of Marxism-Leninism) in the institutional framework of a classic 'basic-level work unit' that would characterize the PRC.

'Institutional culture' is a useful framework for organizing data on CCP propaganda work because it makes this story comparable to the study of political culture in the CCP at other times and places, such as Gilmartin's study of CCP 'sub-culture' in the 1920s.[177] It also allows fruitful comparison with later times, such as with Andrew Walder's study of the institutional culture of authority in PRC factories (and by extension, society in contemporary China).[178] While the objects of study are quite different (and therefore data in this chapter do not address several issues raised by Walder), the questions of *consent* ('voluntary and habitual compliance') and the *personalization of authority* (through personal dependence on direct superiors, incarnation of authority in a person, and service to the revolution conflated with loyalty to a superior) bear directly on the roles of metropolitan intellectuals in Jin Cha Ji propaganda organs. All this amounts to looking at how an institution actually runs and what motivates its members. Deng Tuo's case shows that the major constituents of the institutional culture which Walder argues makes up 'Communist Neo-Traditionalism' in China today, and which he suggests are barriers to the achievement of Party goals or to reform of the system, *were extant by 1944* in Jin Cha Ji propaganda institutions. Moreover, this institutional culture did not impede Party goals then, it promoted them; it did not delay reforms, it advanced them. In short, this political culture worked—then. We must look to changing context over the next forty years to explain how such an institutional culture could shift from promoting Party goals to inhibiting them.

In the following chapters we shall see that tensions within this culture helped contribute to the political instability of 1955–75 (in particular an increasingly erratic personalization of Party authority in Mao) and, in turn, this institutional culture responded to repeated assaults on Party intellectuals and their key institutions by developing counter-productive defence strategies that look more like what Walder has observed. Thus, what Walder identifies as a Weberian 'type'—Communist *Neo-Traditionalism*—I see as one stage of a complex and changing social system, a 'political culture', namely parts of Chinese culture as it digests Western influences, from John Dewey, Darwin, and Adam Smith, as well as Marx, Engels, Lenin, and Stalin. If there is a neo-traditionalism involved here, it is a *Chinese* rather than a 'Communist' one, or rather, the political culture that developed in the PRC and which we see in Deng Tuo's life was none other than the complex mix of traditional and socialist concerns and habits we have seen in Jin Cha Ji as they crashed up against the new challenges of ruling the larger part of a continent.[179]

NOTES

1. This literature is critically reviewed in Hartford and Goldstein (1989: introd.).
2. This term is used by Walder (1986). I will return to the implications of the present study for Walder's thesis on 'Communist Neo-Traditionalism' in the concluding section.
3. This approach follows the general definition of political generations—based on the formative political experiences of individuals between age 17 and 25—as used by Yahuda (1979) and by Li Zehou and Schwarcz (1983–4).
4. The best overview of this history is Grieder (1981), particularly chs. 6 and 7.
5. Kenez (1985), esp. 12–13 and ch. 10. Lenin's views on propaganda and intellectuals come from 'What is to be Done?' (Lenin 1988 edn.); see Kenez (1985: 5–6).
6. As suggested by Apter and Saich (1994) in the 'exegetical bonding' of Yan'an rectification in 1942–4.

7. On the amalgam of Yan'an ideology and organization and its demise in the PRC, see Cheek and Hamrin (1986: 17–19).
8. Jowitt (1978): this seminal essay is reprinted as 'The Leninist Phenomenon' in Jowitt (1992: 1–49). See my discussion of this model in the Introduction.
9. On the importance of ideology in Republican student movements, see Wasserstrom (1991).
10. Zuo Lu (1984b: 27).
11. Hartford (1989: 94).
12. These three stages are identified by Hartford (1980). General studies of this period covering Jin Cha Ji include: Johnson (1962), particularly 101 ff.; Kataoka (1974), particularly 92–3 and 267–74; Dorris (1976); Gatu (1983).
13. Nie Rongzhen (1939). Mao wrote the calligraphy for the book (a copy is in the Hoover Institute Library, Stanford, Calif.) and supported it in other ways; see Kataoka (1974: 92). A similar book with identical title was issued in Chongqing in Mar. 1939 in the form of notes from a journalist; see Chen Kehan (1939). See also Dorris (1976).
14. Zuo Lu (1984b: 27); Nie Rongzhen (1979: 1).
15. Nie Rongzhen (1984: ii. 372 and 380–1). (An English translation has since appeared; see Nie [1988].) Most accounts draw from Nie Rongzhen (1939). The Jin Cha Ji Military District, like others operated by the CCP's armies, was a military administrative area whose institutions were a part of and staffed by the military. The Jin Cha Ji Border Region was a separate civil administration recognized by the Nationalist government of the KMT and intended to be staffed by elected officials. For most of this period, Nie Rongzhen was leader of the Military District, Song Shaowen of the Border Region.
16. Sha had previously been a reporter for the All People's News Agency (*Quan min she*); see Chen Kehan (1939: 59). He was no longer editor in Mar. 1938. Sha's career continued in Hebei as a journalist specializing in news photography. From early 1938 to 1942 he edited, along with Qiu Lan (i.e. Qiu Xiying), *Resistance Supplement* (*Kangdi fukan*), which became *Resistance Tri-Weekly* (*Kangdi sanri kan*). From 1942 Sha Fei was director of the *Jin Cha Ji Pictorial* (*Jin Cha Ji huabao*). See *Press Yearbook 1984*: 623 and 627. I do not know who Hong Shui (pen-name?) is.
17. *Jin Cha Ji ribao dashiji* (1986: 19–20); 1938a, repr. in DTWJ: i. 235–8. Doubt about the figures comes from Patricia Stranahan, whose detailed work on the operations of *Liberation Daily* in Yan'an in the early 1940s includes figures on their much smaller publication runs in the Communist capital. See Stranahan (1990).
18. Chen Kehan (1939: 59); Zuo Lu (1984b: 28). Originals are unavailable, and these articles are not reprinted in DTWJ.
19. *Jin Cha Ji ribao dashiji* (1986: 6); a detailed map of the movements of both *Kangdi bao* and *Jin Cha Ji ribao* offices appears at the end of the book. 1938a: 9. Zuo Lu (1984b: 28) exaggerates the paper's regularity.
20. Nie Rongzhen (1984: ii. 380–1).
21. *Jin Cha Ji ribao dashiji* (1986: 7); Zuo Lu (1984b: 28); Chen Chunsen (YDT: 29); *Press Yearbook* 1984: 623. In the history of CCP journalism two leading positions are distinguished: the director, or *shezhang*, and the editor-in-chief, or *zong bianji*. The former is responsible for the whole press society including staff and administration; the latter is responsible for daily publication. The editor seems to be less important than in American newspapers, often limited to handling layout, while 'editorial policy' is often set by the director or resident Party secretary of the society.

Nonetheless, the powers of each position are sufficiently vague so that either position may hold the real power in a newspaper. When both positions are held by one person, naturally, there is no confusion.

22. A Party Branch Committee for the paper (*baoshe dang zhibu weiyuanhui*) was established under Hou Xin (later Liu Ping). The committee also included Deng Tuo, Zhou Ming, You Qi, and others. See *Jin Cha Ji ribao dashiji* (1986: 20).

23. Chen Kehan (1939: 58–9); 1938a: *Jin Cha Ji ribao dashiji* (1986: 6); the temple's name was Haihuiyan and its photo from the time appears in *Jin Cha Ji ribao dashiji*. Chen Kehan had joined the CCP in 1934 and was working at this time in the Party underground in Chongqing. Chen later became a leader in the Xinhua she (New China News Agency), the central propaganda department, and, with Deng Tuo, in the secretariat of the Beijing municipal CCP. Chen died in 1980. See Bartke (1981) and *Press Yearbook 1984*: 695–6.

24. See Nie Rongzhen's review of Party work in the border area covering 1937 and 1938 (Nie Rongzhen 1939b).

25. This is the picture given in the series of reminiscences by Deng's colleagues collected in YDT: 29–88 and *Renmin xinwenjia Deng Tuo* (1987). An indication of their rosy nature is that *Kangdi bao* did not set up a 'Readers' Letterbox' column as they claim until 10 Jan. 1939; see *Jin Cha Ji ribao dashiji* (1986: 23). In general, the reminiscences are less reliable on chronology, often misleadingly lumping events together with 'soon thereafter' or 'after that'. Almanacs, chronologies, and handbooks tend to be more precise. See Fogel (1997).

26. Wang Bisheng (1983b: 2) and Zhang Fan (YDT: 53); Potter (1986). Hartford (1980: 41–50) describes the complex 'power management' the CCP developed to achieve this end in Jin Cha Ji.

27. *Jin Cha Ji ribao dashiji*: 15; Zuo Lu (1984b: 29–30); see also Hartford (1980: 100). '*Waibao*' could be translated as 'supplementary' or 'extraordinary' edition. One of the last editorials Deng wrote before taking to the hills was an orthodox proclamation of the importance of defending Wuhan against the Japanese. Wuhan was the linchpin of Wang Ming's more urban line of Party policy in contrast to Mao's rural line. But at the time, Sept. 1938—a month before Wuhan's fall—Wang Ming's line was Party policy. This editorial indicates that Deng churned out editorials loyally according to current policy and was not censured when change came. See 'Baowei xibei, baowei da Wuhan' (Protect the Northwest, Protect Great Wuhan), *Kangdi bao* (n.d.), cited in Wang Bisheng (1983e: 2). Not included in DTWJ. For a sense of the competition between Mao and Wang Ming see Wylie (1980: 65–75) and Stranahan (1992).

28. *Jin Cha Ji ribao dashiji* (1986: 27). This was the source of Deng's famous pen-name for his *Evening Chats at Yanshan* in the 1960s; see Nie Rongzhen (1980: 3 or YDT: 6). Zhang Shuzheng's biography (1985: 25–6) provides a list of 17 localities and the dates during which Deng Tuo's paper was in them between Dec. 1937 and June 1948. A fine map of these peregrinations appears at the end of *Jin Cha Ji ribao dashiji* (1986).

29. Nie (1939b: 1). Nie was reporting to the first meeting of the newly constituted Northern Branch of the CC (*Zhonggong zhongyang beifang fenju*). Peng Zhen (Secretary), Guan Xiangying, Cheng Zihua, and Nie were its members. Its job was to represent the Party Centre and Northern Bureau in Border Region affairs. It had been established as the Jin Cha Ji Branch of the CC Politburo (*Jin Cha Ji fenju*—Nie is unclear as to what this was a 'branch' of, though he states it was set up at the order of the CC Politburo following the Sixth Plenum) on 9 Nov. 1938, but kept its

new name until Peng Zhen returned to Yan'an in the first half of 1941, at which time it reverted to its old form, Jin Cha Ji Branch of the CC Politburo, with Nie as Secretary and Liu Lantao as Vice-Secretary until its dissolution at the end of the anti-Japanese War. See Nie Rongzhen (1984: ii. 381).
30. Nie Rongzhen (1939b: 22–3).
31. Nie's 'Report' also reflects the contents of an inner-party directive. Most of Nie's key policy points—on clearing away traitors and undesirables, avoiding leftist mistakes, and enforcing organizational discipline—come word for word out of a 20 Apr. 1938 directive issued in Yan'an under the name of Mao and five other leaders, including Nie himself. See 'Guanyu gonggu yu kuoda Jin Cha Ji genjudi zhishi' (Directive on the Consolidation and Expansion of the Jin Cha Ji Base Area), in *Liuda yilai* (1981: ii. 306).
32. Nie Rongzhen (1939b: 12). *Jin Cha Ji ribao dashiji* (1986) gives a list of titles (310–19) with 1938 periodicals specially listed (314–16).
33. *Kangdi bao zengkan* became *Kangdi zhoubao* probably in 1940 when Li Xiaobai took over from Deng Tuo and the journal became a separate entity from the *Resistance News* press. See *Press Yearbook 1984*: 623. The position, 'responsible person', seems to be an informal title for editors of small publications.
34. *Xin chang cheng* was founded on 31 July 1939 in Fuping, where it was printed and distributed by *Resistance News*. See *Press Yearbook 1984*: 627. Hu Xikui later replaced Deng as director of *Jin Cha Ji Daily* for most of 1944–5. Yao Yilin, later a top Party leader, was General Secretary of the North China Bureau and the CCP's Jin Cha Ji sub-bureau between 1937–45. He was in the Ministry of Commerce in the PRC until 1967. He was close to Peng Zhen and purged with him in the Cultural Revolution. See Bartke (1981: 472).
35. All of this is in the Taihang mountain range in western Hebei—a desolate, deforested region of exceptional poverty and inaccessibility. Langyashan itself is a peak of some 3,400 feet about 100 miles south-west of Beijing. Description by Lou Ningxian (YDT: 41).
36. Nie Rongzhen (YDT: 5) and Nie Rongzhen (1984: ii. 481); Lu Dingyi in *Renmin xinwenjia Deng Tuo* (1987: pref.).
37. To be fair, Zhu Ziqiang, the editor, and his staff were much more vulnerable on the north China plain, lacking the treacherous mountainous terrain in western Hebei (the Beiyue region) which shielded *Jin Cha Ji Daily*'s operations. See Song Wenqing (1987: 330 and 332).
38. Zuo Lu (1984c: 28–9). Since this article and the whole series were written for a journalism trade journal, there is a great deal of technical detail about presses, type, and the mechanics of publishing.
39. See YDT: 30, 49, and 53.
40. For more details of this survival see Cheek (1986: ch. 2).
41. See n. 17 above and Stranahan (1990).
42. *Jin Cha Ji ribao dashiji* (1986: 309–19). Publication data by year is almost non-existent for these other publications. Also, based on the experience of *Central Hebei Guide* mentioned above, we may extend a healthy scepticism as to the regularity, number of issues, and distribution of each.
43. *Press Yearbook 1984*: 623–7. It also gives more complete (though partial) details of editors, responsible publishing unit, where published, and how often.
44. This inaugural issue is among the complete set of both papers in the Journalism Department library, Chinese People's University, Beijing. *Jin Cha Ji ribao dashiji*: 56; Chen Chunsen (YDT: 30); *Press Yearbook 1984*: 623.
45. Charts are given in *Jin Cha Ji ribao dashiji* (1986: 60–1 and 111). The organization

The Revolutionary Propagandist

is quite similar to the chart for the previous year for *Resistance News* (the key difference being the absorption of the 'Correspondence Department' [*tongxun bu*] into the editorial department).

46. *Jin Cha Ji ribao dashiji* (1986: 20). In May 1940 the CCP CC Northern Bureau under Peng Zhen set up its own Periodicals Committee with Deng Tuo as Secretary, and Liu Lantao, Yao Yilin, Li Changqing, and Hu Xikui on the committee; see *Jin Cha Ji ribao dashiji* (1986: 46).
47. Dittmer (1974: 53).
48. Zhang Fan (YDT: 46), says the paper in 1943 was forced to cross the Taihang mountains back to the far eastern border of Shanxi's Wutai district. On Morse code radio contact between the *Daily*'s dispersed teams, see Zuo Lu (1984c: 29). For precise details see Zhang Shuzheng (1985: 25–7) and *Jin Cha Ji ribao dashiji* (1986), especially the detailed map at the end of the book.
49. *Jin Cha Ji ribao dashiji* (1986: 45, 71, and 73).
50. A good initial overview of the Radio Department of Xinhua she during the war years is given by Liu Yunlai (1988: 39–42).
51. *Jin Cha Ji ribao dashiji* (1986: 48).
52. *Jin Cha Ji ribao dashiji* (1986: 75).
53. *Shi hua bao*; Chen Chunsen (YDT: 34); and Lou Ningxian (YDT: 38). The other 'temple god' (*hengha erjiang*) named was Shu Tong. A photo of Shu and Nie Rongzhen in Aug. 1940 appears at the front of vol. 2 of Nie Rongzhen (1984). Shu Tong later served as First Party Secretary in Jiangsu (1953–5) and was elected to the 8th Party Congress in 1956. He was purged in 1967 and rehabilitated in 1977.

    Although these reminiscences state that Deng Tuo was in charge of the journal, a recent bibliography of Jin Cha Ji journals gives Chen Chunsen and Qiang Yi as the editors of *Straight Talk*. See *Press Yearbook 1984*: 623. This is more a matter of greater detail than of contradiction, since the bibliography notes that *Straight Talk* was published by the *Jin Cha Ji Daily* News Society, of which Deng was the director. Qiang Yi was a noted protégé of Deng Tuo's. Nevertheless, this instance serves as a warning of the sort of generalizations common to the reminiscence literature.
54. *Jin Cha Ji ribao dashiji* (1986: 45).
55. *Jin Cha Ji ribao dashiji* (1986: 126).
56. *Jin Cha Ji ribao dashiji* (1986: 55). Other standing committee members named are: Chang Qing, Sha Kefu, Zhou Weizhi, and Tian Jian.
57. *Jin Cha Ji ribao dashiji* (1986: 74).
58. *Jin Cha Ji ribao dashiji* (1986: 51–2). Nie was forced to transfer a dozen cadres (named, p. 51) under Luo Jun, who headed the Jin Cha Ji Branch of the Xinhua Bookstore (which was also an organ of the Jin Cha Ji Branch of the CC; see pp. 51 and 77).
59. 'Zhonggong zhongyang guanyu dang bao wenti gei difang dang de zhishi' (CCP CC Directive to Local Party Branches Concerning the Question of Party Periodicals), in *Zhongguo gongchandong xinwen*: i. 86.
60. 1938b, repr. in DTWJ: i. 242–6; discussed in Wang Bisheng (1983c: 60). Since I have not seen the original I do not know under what pen-name it was published. *Zhanxian* was founded on 17 Feb. 1938 and published in Fuping. See *Press Yearbook 1984*: 627.
61. Lenin's metaphor comes from his classic statement on press and propaganda, 'What is to be Done?' (1902). Lenin's image is that of the guide line used by bricklayers to keep a wall straight. See Lenin (1988 edn.: 221–3). Deng Tuo was drawing from a tradition of CCP press and propaganda work. See van de Ven (1995).
62. DTWJ: i. 245.

114   *The Revolutionary Propagandist*

63. As Nie Rongzhen complained about this in Jan. 1939 (Nie Rongzhen 1936b: 12). A comparison of this piece of 'internal propaganda' and the internal Party directive also shows the strengths and weaknesses of different levels of documents in the CCP as historical sources. We may assume the directive is accurate, but it is brief and telegraphic. Deng's elaboration of it adds considerable local information but maintains a positive spin that must be interpreted to mean the problem still exists (in this case distribution and a local network of correspondents and reading group leaders).
64. *Jin Cha Ji ribao dashi* (1986: 71–2). Included among the editorials was 'Nawo Makesizhuyi de lilun wuqi' (Grasp the Theoretical Weapon of Marxism), reprinted in DTWJ: i. 38–41. Wang Bisheng (1983e: 3 and 1983c: 60).
65. Quotation from Deng and analysis in Wang Bisheng (1983e: 3). Wang makes clear that this approach was both the source of the paper's later successes and a model worth deep consideration today.
66. Nie Rongzhen (1984: ii. 584–5). The Central CCP had declared a period of such reform and study at the Sixth Plenum in 1938. Kathleen Hartford shares this impression based on her study of Jin Cha Ji (1980).
67. See Hartford (1980).
68. *Jin Cha Ji ribao dashiji* (1986: 90–105). The Beiyue Party Committee (around Fuping, the capital) did make some efforts at organized rectification study, organizing a Rectification Committee in July 1942 under Liu Lantao and Hu Xikui (p. 101).
69. *Jizhong daobao*, *Tingjin bao*; Zhang Fan (YDT: 52–4).
70. He said he still felt guilty three decades later (YDT: 53–4).
71. Zuo Lu (1984c: 28).
72. See Lin Maike [Michael Lindsay] (1944) and Lindsay (1975: postscript).
73. Nie Rongzhen (1939b: 16), Nie Rongzhen (1984: ii. 484 ff.); and Zhi Liangjun (YDT: 55). A photo identifying Deng with Lindsay, Song Shaowen, and Pan Zili taken in Fuping appears in Wang Bisheng (1983e: 6) and in the front of *Renmin xinwenjia Deng Tuo* (1987); the original is in Lindsay (1975: no pagination), but without identification.
74. Lou Ningxian (YDT: 38); Yu Li later became Vice-Chairman of the Jin Cha Ji Consultative Congress in January 1943. He and Deng Tuo organized the Yan-Zhao Poetry Society for other classical-style poets: see Zuo Lu (1984c: 30–1); 1979c: 23–4; DTWJ: iv. 38–9; Wang Bisheng (1981: 77), and discussion later in this chapter.
75. One of Ding Yilan's most lyrical accounts is in Ding Yilan (1984b: 10–11). The Hutuo River rises in the Wutai region of Shanxi and runs through south-central Hebei and then north to Tianjin and the Bohai. Pingshan county town is near the Hutuo some 35 miles north-west of Shijiazhuang.
76. 'Xin meng' appears in 1979c: 16 and DTWJ: iv. 28. Ding Yilan recounts further details on her courtship and life with Deng in Bo Sheng (1981).
77. Zhang Fan (YDT: 49); Jian Qing (YDT: 64).
78. Nie Rongzhen (1984: ii. 584–5).
79. Peng Zhen had been similarly called in 1941. One of the best accounts of Mao's factional and ideological struggles up to and throughout the 1942–4 rectification movement is in Wylie (1980: 130–94). Recent research argues that the leadership struggle in Yan'an was not nearly so harsh or lengthy, since Mao had essentially sidelined Wang Ming and had received Comintern's imprimatur well before the onset of rectification. See Teiwes and Sun (1995).

    It is unlikely that there was no similar manoeuvring and infighting among Party

The Revolutionary Propagandist

leaders in Jin Cha Ji. Rather, the active fighting with the Japanese, and perhaps a less volatile leadership, discouraged at least open signs of competition. Certainly there are indications of 'ideological problems' for Deng Tuo around 1944–6 that bring to mind the example of ideological struggle in Yan'an. This happened for Deng when the military situation in Jin Cha Ji had settled sufficiently to allow time for such problems.

80. 1942a, commemorating the 21st anniversary of the founding of the CCP; repr. in DTWJ: i. 42–7, quotation from pp. 42 and 47. See Wang Bisheng (1983c: 59 and 1981: 77). In this text, Deng Tuo is clearly following the lead of Zhang Ruxin's Feb. 1942 praise of Mao in the Yan'an *Liberation Daily*. Deng follows Zhang's term 'Mao Zedongism' (*Mao Zedong zhuyi*) and borrows from his title: 'Study and Grasp the Theory and Strategy of Mao Zedong'. Both men were following an authoritative *Liberation Daily* editorial of 21 Jan. 1942 which designated Mao's writings as the most important study material in the upcoming rectification campaign. See Wylie (1980: 171–3).
81. Published in Yan'an in 1942, these seminal study texts of the rectification movement have been translated and analysed in Compton (1952).
82. The linguistic and conceptual parallel of this remembered remark to the famous saying by Deng Xiaoping on 'black cat/white cat' is, frankly, suspicious.
83. Zhao Qingxue (YDT: 80–2); quote by Deng from 81–2.
84. Kuhn (1975: 261) and Mair (1985: 325–59).
85. Quoted in Zuckerman (1985: 34). These points strike me as accurate, but I have yet to locate Mao saying them in so many words. Nonetheless, the gist is included in a 16 Mar. 1942 *Liberation Daily* editorial, repr. in *Mao Zedong xinwen gongzuo wenxuan* (1983: 91–2). These functions are *precisely* those achieved by the Soviets in the 1920s. See Kenez (1985: 224 ff.).
86. 1938a: 8; also in DTWJ: i. 235–8, quote from 235–6.
87. See 1938b, repr. in DTWJ: i. 42–6.
88. Zuo Lu (1984b: 30). Deng's editorial appeared in the temporary *Kangdi waibao*, which was published on the run during the late-1938 Japanese 'mopping up' campaign in Jin Cha Ji under one of his pen-names, Wen Zhou (1938d); not in DTWJ.
89. Dittmer (1987: 4). See also Kenez (1985).
90. Here I explicitly follow the analysis of Clifford Geertz, 'Ideology as a Cultural System', in Geertz (1973), particularly 230–1. Thus, my subjects, much like their Bolshevik predecessors as described by Kenez, viewed propaganda (*xuanchuan*) as a good and necessary thing.
91. See Gramsci (1971) and Femia (1981). Propaganda organs, and especially government newspapers, were also used for less noble purposes, such as factional infighting. See Kenez (1985: 231 and *passim*), and on the vicious fights between Mao and Wang Ming for control of the press in Yan'an, Stranahan (1990).
92. And this is precisely the personalization of authority which Andrew Walder sees as a key characteristic of 'Communist Neo-Traditionalism'. See discussion at the end of this chapter.
93. Nie Rongzhen (1984: ii. 482). Sha Fei, the former editor of *Resistance News*, was the editor of this pictorial and its predecessor, *Kangdi huabao*. *Jin Cha Ji Pictorial* was set up in Fuping on 7 July 1942, the fifth anniversary of the start of war with Japan, and this is the date carried on the first issue. However, that issue was not published until Sept. 1942. The pictorial stopped publication in June 1948. In Oct. 1948 the pictorial became *Hebei huabao*, again under Sha Fei, and it published until 1953. See *Press Yearbook 1984*: 627.

94. 1942*b* (there is no pagination; page citations to this article count from the first page). Issues no. 1 and 3–10 of *Jin Cha Ji huabao* from 1942–5 are in the Harvard Yenching library.
95. In a restricted-circulation academic journal, Wang Bisheng (1983*e*: 6) accurately cites the original title without comment. Deng's article is misleadingly reprinted in its most significantly edited form as 'Nie Rongzhen zai Jin Cha Ji' in 1980*c*: 158–79. The revised version is 20% shorter than the original and all of the laudatory phrases lavished on Nie in the 1942 edition have been excised. For instance, what I have translated as 'helmsman' (*duoshi*—literally 'helmsman' and 'teacher', not the usual *duoshou* used for Mao) has been deleted from the revised title. The editing is a classic example in Chinese official historiography of making texts conform to current policy—here the post-Mao avoidance of the near-deification of any leader. In the process it obscures the past.

None the less, the bulk of the detail from the original text, including names, dates, and places, are retained faithfully (though information on the 'Double Ten' policy and Nie's defense of its permanence in pp. 10 and 12 of the original are omitted). The revised 1980 text is thus still a useful source of information about Jin Cha Ji; it is simply not useful as a source for the study of CCP journalism without reference to the original. A particularly interesting omission is the removal of a reference to 'Trotskyist traitors' along with Wang Jingwei on p. 174 of the reprint (see original, p. 9). This downplaying of the Trotskyite question is common in post-Mao materials and seems to presage a reversal for more than Chen Duxiu.

The editing of this text is archetypal of the modifications we may expect in the post-Mao reprints of individual writers' texts: editors are likely to omit currently sensitive material without notice but are equally likely to maintain a concern for historical accuracy and authenticity where such urges do not come into conflict with the current Party line, in this case the post-Cultural Revolution line of the Third Plenum of the Eleventh Central Committee of Dec. 1978, which was later enshrined in the 1981 *Resolution on Party History*. Therefore, when the original is not available, an appropriate rule of thumb in assessing such reprints is to assume similar principles apply. Thus, it is impossible to obtain a reasonably accurate reading of such reprint texts without a thorough knowledge of the current Party line at the time the reprint was compiled and sent to the printers (often up to a year before the publication date, and easily located in the dating of prefaces or postfaces). For further considerations of textual transmission in Party history, see Cheek (1989*b*).

Post-Mao historiography of the revolution is, happily, not monolithic. Diligent efforts of younger scholars in particular help guide the foreign researcher. Wang Bisheng, who noted the original title of Deng's Nie piece (and who has written the most satisfying Chinese biography of Deng, in my opinion), also saved from oblivion Deng's 1939 references to Sun Yat-sen's 'Three People's Principles'. See 1939*b*, based on a speech given to the 'Forum on Problems in Literary and Artistic Creation' called by the JCJ Border Region, 26 Feb. 1939; analysed in Wang Bisheng (1983*b*: 218–20). Deng's speech is once again reprinted with unannounced alterations in DTWJ: i. 363–75 as 'Zai bianqu wenyi zuozhe chuangzuo wenti zuotanhui de baogao' (Report to the Border Region Forum on the Question of Writers' and Artists' Creations), dated as 2 Mar. 1939. For a sound analysis of the motivations and limitations of Party historians in the PRC, see Weigelin-Schriedrzik (1993).

The various versions of Deng's essay on Nie, however, point to a significant issue for the 1940s. Deng re-edited his essay for the magazine *Qunzhong* (The Masses), where it was published in 1946 (vol. 9, nos. 23 and 24) as 'Nie Rongzhen jiangjun zenyang chuangzao Jin Cha Ji jiefang qu' (How General Nie Rongzhen Created

The Revolutionary Propagandist

the Jin Cha Ji Liberated Area). No biographies mention the reasons for the revision, but personal information from a few of his colleagues reveals that Deng was criticized in 1944 for his excessive praise of Nie, among other ideological errors Deng was supposed to have made. Thus, the 1946 version, lacking the 'helmsman' term and related hero-worship sections of the 1942 version, reflects a modification in Party policy on such hero worship then—it shall be limited to Mao. In line with slightly improved historiographical standards, DTWJ: iv. 266–89 reprints a third version with a note indicating that this is the 1946 text with (unidentified) additions from the 1942 version. Sadly, 1986a: 121–42, published the same year as DTWJ, retains the tampered version from 1980c.

96. It would be worth seeing if leaders of other base areas were similarly lionized.
97. This tone permeates the very detailed and useful series, *Zhonggong dang shi renwuzhuan* (Personalities in CCP History). A glaring example of this modern *lie zhuan* (exemplary biography) style is Zuo Lu (1984c).
98. It is, as Wang Bisheng (1983e: 7) notes, a fine example of reportage (*baogao wenxue*).
99. 1942b: 3; cut from 1980c: 162–3.
100. 1942b: 4.
101. 1942b: 6–9; some of this has been edited out of the 1980 edition, but not the names of his associates.
102. 1942b: 5 and 10.
103. 1942b: 11.
104. *Lie zhuan* are exemplary biographies with moral lessons central to traditional Chinese historiography and immortalized in Sima Qian's Han Dynasty *Historical Records*. See Ssu-ma Ch'ien (1961) and Pritchard (1968), esp. 189.
105. 1942b: 12. None of this appears in the 1980 reprint, and one may wonder why the editors would pass up the chance to show, from an original document of the 1940s, Nie's use and Deng's praise of 'seek truth from facts', which is today's slogan.
106. 1942b: 12.
107. Various authors in YDT: 56–9, 40.
108. In Zuo Lu's article on Deng's life in Shanghai and Kaifeng (1984a: 27).
109. An excellent rebuttal of the two-line struggle thesis is given in Teiwes (1984: 10–42).
110. Peng was recalled to Yan'an in 1941 to join the top leadership and his administrative policies from Jin Cha Ji became those of the famous 'Yan'an Way' in 1942–4. On the amalgam of charismatic and bureaucratic authority in Maoism and its destructive disassociation in the late 1950s and 1960s, see Cheek and Hamrin (1986: 18–19).
111. Nie Rongzhen (1984: ii. 550–1).
112. These were duly reported in the *Jin Cha Ji Daily* in February; see *Jin Cha Ji ribao dashiji* (1986: 114–16). For examples, see *Zhongguo xin minzhuzhuyi* (1984: iv) on rent (247–59) and on marriage (826–8) and the follow-ups later in 1943 by the administrative council on rent (260 ff.) and on marriage and inheritance (829 ff.). For laws in vols. 1–3, see Potter, below.
113. See the analysis of the Jin Cha Ji legal code in Potter (1986: 25–9). Peng's role in developing these programmes is made clear in his 1940 'Double Ten Programme' and 1941 'Report' (Peng Zhen 1981). Extracts of this important report are translated in Saich (1996: 1011–38).
114. Later, when Mao turned on Deng Tuo in the late 1950s, Peng Zhen (then Mayor of Beijing) would give Deng a home in Beijing's municipal administration.
115. Potter (1986: 26–8) shows how this was the intent of the 1940 programme and the 1943 legal code. This amounts to the 'power management' which Hartford (1980) has documented for the Jin Cha Ji administration over the whole period.

116. Potter (1986: 27 and 28–9).
117. Potter (1986: 28).
118. See Hartford (1980).
119. *Jin Cha Ji ribao dashiji* (1986: 115).
120. This, of course, came to characterize PRC politics in general; see Townsend (1969), esp. chs. 4 and 5.
121. This role was not limited to literary intellectuals. Writings on and by scientific specialists in Yan'an reflect similar 'honourable vocation' service to the Party. See Williams (1994: ch. 2).
122. Haraszti (1987) and Konrád and Szelényi (1979).
123. DTWJ: i. 373. The original article (1939b) is based on a speech given to the 'Forum on Problems in Literary and Artistic Creation' called by the JCJ Border Region, 26 Feb. 1939; analysed in Wang Bisheng (1983b). Deng's original article was not available to me, so I must rely on the edited reprint in DTWJ: i. 363–75. 'Zai bianqu wenyi zuozhe chuangzuo wenti zuotanhui de baogao' (Report to the Border Region Forum on the Question of Writers' and Artists' Creations), dated as 2 Mar. 1939. See discussion of text in note 95, above.
124. Chen's texts and ideas are carefully analysed in Wylie (1980: 28–37).
125. See Lee (1973); Schwarcz (1986); Goldman (1967); and Cheek (1984b).
126. This group is empathetically portrayed in Holm (1991: ch. 2); the uni-track policy is outlined on pp. 55–9 and early examples shown on pp. 66–70. Holm identifies this group, which includes Chen Boda himself and Ai Siqi and their later writing in Yan'an, as the 'New Enlightenment ideologues' (p. 58). The other group, according to Holm, were the inheritors of the May Fourth movement's individualism and cosmopolitan tastes, as represented in Zhou Yang and He Qifang.

Deng's example reflects the diversity of Party intellectuals beyond Yan'an, since, according to Holm's categorization of actors in this important debate (1991: 54–5), Deng fully conforms to the letter and spirit of Chen Boda's dialectical synthesis of old and new forms of literature (indeed, Deng's quote above nearly paraphrases Chen's own quoted in Holm [1991: 53]) yet Deng's activities, particularly his two-track policy of art for the elite and the common folk in which dialectical unity is promoted by gradually elevating the artistic quality of popular culture clearly parallels the policies of Chen's competitors, Zhou Yang and He Qifang (see Holm [1991: 64–5]). The reason for Deng's combination of what would become the two competing Yan'an models of literature is to be found in the content of 'elevating' literature: for Zhou Yang, and soon the heretic, Wang Shiwei, it was *foreign* elite literature; for Deng Tuo, 'elevated' was traditional Chinese literati arts. These, as we shall see in the Yan-Zhao Poetry Society later in this chapter, posed little threat to CCP leaders, at least in Jin Cha Ji.
127. DTWJ: i. 373, emphasis added. For 'Maoist' views, see Holm (1980).
128. See Zhang Fan (YDT: 49); Chen Chunsen (YDT: 35); and Wang Bisheng (1981: 78). His 'After Reading the Memorial Article on Comrade Zuo Quan', who died in a Japanese surprise attack on the 8th Route Army headquarters in the Taihang district in May 1942, is remembered as one of Deng's better efforts. Wang Bisheng (1983e: 7) calls it an exemplary piece of reportage (*baogao wenxue*), but it has not been reprinted. Zuo Quan had been a leading general in the Red Army; for details of his life and death, see Kataoka (1974: 274). Deng also wrote 'Tong Lei Ye' (Grieving for Lei Ye) in May 1943 (DTWJ: iv. 257–60). Lei was a reporter for the 8th Route Army political office who died in the 1942 'mopping up'. On Lei Ye and his poetry, see Wei Wei (1959: 300).

The Revolutionary Propagandist 119

129. DTWJ: i. 372. He describes it as a dialectical process.
130. Mao's sanction of such a two-track cultural policy, as implied in his Jan. 1940 speech which became 'On New Democracy', is sensitively analysed in Holm (1991: 74–6).
131. Mao's comments on this point from the 1943 text of his 'Talks' are worth quoting, since most of them were excised from the 1953 text in his *Selected Works*. Mao says, 'Cadres are the advanced element among the masses, who have generally already completed the kind of education currently offered to the masses; their ability to absorb things is higher than the masses, so that material intended for wider audiences among the masses at their present level, such as "The Little Cowherd", cannot satisfy them. Literature and art on a higher level are absolutely essential for them ... but it should not become the total or the central goal today.' Translated in McDougall (1980: 72).
132. Mao's 'Yan'an Talks' of May 1942, of course, is the *locus classicus* for his literary policies. The text of Mao's famous speech with which Deng Tuo and others worked in the 1940s has been translated by McDougall (1980). The positive side to Mao's cultural policies, mass literature, has been covered in Selden (1971) and in more detail in Holm's (1991) study of the *yang'ge* popular drama movement. The negative side has been covered by Goldman (1967: 18–50), Fabre (1990), and Dai Qing (1994).
133. Wang Bisheng (1981: 77); Deng's reply poem to the group's leader, the old poet Hao Qing, and Deng's account of the society are in 1979c: 22–4; quote from p. 24 and DTWJ: iv. 38–9. 'Yan' is the ancient name for the north-west Hebei region and 'Zhao' the name for western Hebei and eastern Shanxi, the same areas occupied by Jin Cha Ji.
134. Lou Ningxian (YDT: 39).
135. 1979c: 23–4. Deng had a similar evening of wine and poetry with Nie and General Chen Yi in 1947; see Wang Bisheng (1981: 77) and 1979c: 35.
136. This is what I argue in Cheek (1984b: 40).
137. On the docile socialist realist literature and its ideological proponents, see Birch (1960); Ragvald (1978).
138. Various authors in YDT: 33, 37–9, 49, 56–7.
139. *Bian zheng daobao*, *Jiu guo bao*, Chen Chunsen (YDT: 34), and Lou Ningxian (YDT: 41). As noted above, these reminiscences can be imprecise. *Bian zheng daobao* is listed as a publication of the Administrative Council of Jin Cha Ji, not of the *Daily*, though the *Daily* may well have staffed and printed it. See *Press Yearbook 1984*: 627. *Jiu guo bao* similarly was published by another organ, the Jin Cha Ji Border Region Government (*Press Yearbook 1984*: 623). Further details of other periodicals published in Jin Cha Ji are given in *Jin Cha Ji ribao dashiji* (1986: 309–19).
140. Chen Chunsen (YDT: 35).
141. The most famous Ming example is that of Wang Yangming's 'Nangang xiangyue', tr. in Wing-tsit Chan (1963) and discussed in Cheek (1984a). Lü Kun provided an influential and practical late Ming example, among several scholars interested in *xiangyue*. See Handlin (1983), esp. pp. 197–9. Qing *xuanjiang* lectures evolved from earlier Neo-Confucian *xiangyue* propaganda efforts.
142. For example, Lü Weiqi (1587–1641) advocated study in Confucian academies to rectify the faults of scholars, but excluded commoners, whom he directed to study at monthly *xiangyue* meetings. See Handlin (1983: 203–4). In the Qing, Salt Commissioner Li Laizhang's *Explanations of the Sacred Edict Lectures* of 1705 divided his audience between commoners and meetings for local scholars. See

Li Shanyuan quanji, 'Shengyu xuanjiang xiang-bao tiaoyue' (Regulations for Community Security (Xiang and Bao) Sacred Edict Lectures). Marvellous illustrations for the set-up of these lectures appear in this collection, reprinted and discussed in Cheek (1984a).

143. 1941: 4. The remaining seven parts appeared on the same page periodically through 12 June 1941. They are reprinted without bibliographic details in DTWJ: i. 17–37. Full runs of *Jin Cha Ji ribao* are not available in the United States. I viewed the bound photographic reproductions of the *Daily* at the Journalism Department Library, People's University, Beijing.

144. The summary given by Wang Bisheng (1983e: 4–5) stresses how Deng's views in these essays correspond to Mao's, but this is putting the cart before the horse. Deng was basing himself on the Stalinist interpretation of Marxism-Leninism, as popularized in China by Li Da and Ai Siqi, common to Party theory books in the late 1930s. These were precisely the works Mao relied upon to produce his lectures/essays on dialectical materialism, *Dialectical Materialism (Lecture Notes)*—what became 'On Practice' and 'On Contradiction'. This complex textual and intellectual history is covered (empathetically, cynically, and scathingly, respectively) in: Nick Knight's extensive introduction to Knight (1990), Fogel (1987), and Meissner (1990).

145. The form of Mao's writings was likely mimeographed versions of *Dialectical Materialism (Lecture Notes)*. See Knight (1990: 3), and a wicked bibliographical essay, 'Critical Questions on Sources', in Meissner (1990: 149–60). Both confirm my point: no *official* version of Mao's views and no certification that they represented the Party existed by spring 1941 when Deng Tuo wrote his essays for the readers of *Jin Cha Ji Daily*.

146. This leaves aside the question of how much the Jin Cha Ji leaders, of which Deng Tuo was not one, contributed to Mao's ideas as they were officially publicized. The 'collective' nature of Mao Zedong Thought and the contributions to it by other leaders, such as Liu Shaoqi, Zhu De, and Deng Xiaoping, have been stressed in the post-Mao period. See *Guangming ribao*, 18 Dec. 1985, p. 3; (tr. in FBIS-CHI, 2 Jan. 1986, p. K13) and Fang Daming, 'Mao Zedong sixiang kexue hanyi' (The Scientific Significance of Mao Zedong Thought), in Liao Gailong (1985: 46–8).

147. See Deng Tuo (1942b).

148. Mao's essay now appears in edited form as 'On New Democracy' in his *Selected Works* (Mao 1969), but originally was published in the Yan'an journal, *Chinese Culture*, edited by Ai Siqi, because the Central Committee would not approve it for official Party publication. The original title was: 'Xin minzhu de zhengzhi yu xin minzhu de wenhua' (The New Democratic Politics and New Democratic Culture) (Mao Zedong 1941); the *Selected Works* version makes several changes, including excising most of the last three pages of the original to do with cultural issues. See Cheek (1984b). On the context in Yan'an, see Holm (1991: 74–81), Guillermaz (1968: 349–51), and a good analysis in Kataoka (1974: 183 ff.). Deng's other reprinted poems echo the same support for Mao. See DTWJ: iv. 39–61 and 1979c: 5–37. Reproductions of several poems of the period in Deng's own hand (including the one under discussion here) appear in 1988: 6–45, including his 1940 paean to 'On New Democracy' (p. 15) and in honour of the 1945 publication of Mao's poem, 'Snow' (p. 43). Discussed in Wang Bisheng (1981: 77).

149. The calligraphic original is untitled, but the poem appears in 1979c: 10 and 1988: 15 as 'Du Mao Zhuxi "Xin minzhuzhuyi lun"' (Reading Chairman Mao's "On New

Democracy") which for both the essays and Mao's titles are anachronistic; clearly the title has been added by the editors.

150. *Chendu* refers to the eight battle formations used by Zhuge Liang in the popular novel, *Romance of the Three Kingdoms*, when he defeated the state of Wei.
151. *Bandang* is the title of a poem in the Book of Songs and alludes, in part, to the turmoil of the resistance war.
152. *Yunchou weiwo*, literally, 'devising plans in the army tent', is a four-character phrase which calls to mind the military genius of Zhuge Liang, who was said to win battles by playing chess in his tent.
153. The character *tun* has two readings: *tun* as an army camp, and *zhun* as one of the more inauspicious hexagram titles in the *Book of Changes*. Thus, in a pleasing pun we can read Mao rising above *tunjian*, the 'troubles of the camp' or *zhunjian*, the rather more cosmic 'great difficulties'. The impression is that Mao keeps calm while those around him are distraught.
154. This couplet is copied almost directly from Mao's poem written to the tune 'Qingping yue', no doubt in homage.
155. I am grateful to Mr Wu Tong of the Boston Museum of Fine Arts for his advice concerning calligraphic styles. Ding Yilan kindly gave me copies of a dozen unpublished pieces from 1929–65. Many of these became available in 1988.
156. On the Taiping case, see Kuhn (1977), esp. p. 366.
157. Note comments by Xu Zhucheng and Wang Ruoshui in 1957 (Ch. 4 of this volume) about Deng Tuo's high status among general intellectuals.
158. This is what He Baogang sees as 'intellectual legitimation' still operating in Chinese political culture in the post-Mao period; see He Baogang (1991) and Kelly and He Baogang (1992).
159. *Mao Zedong xuanji*. It appears in two versions: a single-volume hardback, which I viewed at Ding Yilan's, and five separate volumes in blue mimeograph ink, which I viewed at the Toyo Bunko, Tokyo and the Fairbank Center Library, Harvard. On this and other editions of Mao's collected works, see Cheek (1989*b*: 84–90).
160. Liu Lantao *et al.* (1984). This piece consists of a report on the 1944 edition with a brief introduction by Liu Lantao dated 9 Apr.
161. Wylie (1980: 171 and 174–5). For the 'Yan'an Talks', see McDougall (1980); Andrew Watson has made the standard translation of 'Economic and Financial Problems', in Watson (1980).
162. *Mao Zedong zhuyi*. Deng does not use the term 'Mao Zedong Thought' (*Mao Zedong sixiang*) in his preface, though he is nearly there in the last line of this quote with 'Mao Zedong de sixiang.' The term did not come into use until 1943 and, as in this case, was not in universal usage until a few years later, particularly after the seminal Seventh Party Congress in 1945. See Wylie (1980: 6) and Teiwes and Sun (1995). Wylie, however, is clearly mistaken, if only in a minor fashion, in his assessment that Zhang Ruxin's coinage, 'Mao Zedong zhuyi', fell out of use after Zhang's own Feb. 1942 articles on Mao's thought. See Wylie (1980: 173).
163. 1944*b*, quote from p. 1.
164. 1946; repr. in DTWJ: i. 261–8. Wang Bisheng (1983*e*: 4) describes the circumstances and the content of the speech, but strangely does not give its title.
165. 1946: 57.
166. 1946: 54; emphasis added.
167. 1946: 50–1 and 53–4.
168. *Press Yearbook 1984*: 623 and 626.
169. Wang Bisheng (1986: 242).

170. *Beifang wenhua*. An ad on p. 4 of the 8 Mar. 1946 *Jin Cha Ji Daily* gives this information. Others on the editorial board named are: Xiao San, Sha Kefu, Ai Qing, and Feng Suhai, etc. The tables of contents of early issues appear in the *Daily*, and none shows articles by Deng Tuo or his known pen-names. See further discussion in Ch. 3. Rittenberg says all the editors of *Northern Culture* were in Kalgan in the summer of 1946 (Rittenberg and Bennett 1993).
171. See also Rittenberg's memoirs (Rittenberg and Bennett 1993).
172. Personal communication. Sidney Rittenberg (interview with author, 4 Mar. 1985).
173. For stunning details of the 'rescue campaign' see Chen Yung-fa (1991 and 1996).
174. Fu Xiu (1980), esp. pp. 126–30. This article is fully in the style of 'denounce the Gang of Four' and includes a great deal of scurrilous, but unsubstantiated, information about Zhang Chunqiao (one of the 'Gang').
175. A witch-hunt it clearly had become in Yan'an, but by 1944 Mao authoritatively put a lid on the inquisitional excesses of the cadre-screening programme without curing the urge to demonize that lay at the root of the rectification system. See Teiwes and Sun (1995) and Apter and Cheek (1994: xxiv–xxv).
176. Liu Binyan (interview with author, Jan. 1989, Harvard). Someone with handwriting very similar to Liu's had written an inflammatory letter to the authorities and Liu was investigated as the possible author of the sacrilege. While this may bring to mind the irony in Milan Kundera's novel, *The Joke*, for Liu it does not.
177. Gilmartin (1995).
178. Walder (1986).
179. I rather prefer Tom Gold's analysis of related social patterns among post-Mao youth which occurred unintentionally in response to political abuses over the past 20 years. See Gold (1985).

3

Life in the Establishment (1946–1956)

Although the CCP's national success was by no means apparent in 1946, the end of the Japanese threat and years of organizational work had transformed the Jin Cha Ji administration into an establishment in north China. By 1948 the tide had turned in the Civil War with the KMT, and by early 1949 it was clear that the CCP would rule all or most of China.

3.1 Deng Tuo's official portrait, 1956

Deng Tuo served this administration as a top propagandist. His life in the new PRC establishment reveals the propaganda and education system (*xuanjiao xitong*) of the new Party-State and the role of establishment intellectuals within it. Deng's case in particular shows us the social experience of a 'transformational bureaucrat' which promoted the solidification of his bureaucratic Maoist approach to Party work. This approach came into increasing conflict with Mao, the charismatic leader. In Deng's writings on ideology and journalism we shall see the fault lines of what became a split and then a war between Mao and his bureaucrats. In order to understand Deng's service to the Party and the growing tensions that plagued both, it is necessary to have a picture of the world in which Deng moved. What role, for instance, did Deng's art collection or essays on eighteenth-century history play in his intellectual service and its problems?

The years of military attack and partisan resistance now ended for Deng and his colleagues. They settled down to the task of establishing the new revolutionary order, beginning with land reform and then a renewed bid for national leadership through United Front calls to urban Chinese. Deng Tuo was deeply involved with the rural policies not as a propagandist but as a policy research adviser. Deng joined Peng Zhen's staff as the CCP took over Beiping in early 1949. There he served as director of the new municipal government's Propaganda Department and drafted numerous Central Party administrative documents as well as speeches for the new mayor, Peng Zhen.

Deng was appointed editor-in-chief of the new Central Party paper, the *People's Daily*, in the autumn of 1949. This was his home until he was effectively fired by Mao in 1957. Deng enjoyed a comfortable traditional-style Pekinese courtyard home where he steadily developed his private aesthetic pursuits, collecting antiques and enjoying his growing art collection with fellow connoisseurs. Meanwhile Deng loyally propagandized the policies of the day both in the press and in public talks he gave at universities and meetings all around town.

The first years of the People's Republic were also the time of greatest Soviet influence.[1] Deng assiduously studied the Soviet model, going to Moscow in 1954 to view the workings of his paper's counterpart, *Pravda*. The Soviet model brought problems. It was too centralized a system with far too much focus on heavy industry for Chinese conditions. Soviet arrogance came to rankle Chinese leaders, especially Mao. By 1956 the Soviets brought a new problem: de-Stalinization. The critique of the supreme leader in Khrushchev's secret speech and the social unrest in Eastern Europe were deeply troubling to the Chinese. The success of the CCP in consolidating its rule and the impact of the Soviet 'thaw' produced the first cracks in the new edifice. Mao's response to these new challenges was to speed up agricultural collectivization. The Party bureaucracy in Beijing obliquely criticized this, and Deng Tuo swung in with the key editorial in the *People's Daily* criticizing such 'adventurism'. For that, the collective leadership, and their servants such as Deng Tuo, received their first slap on the wrist from Mao.

The distinction between rational and emotive versions of Maoism will help us understand not only the tribulations in Deng Tuo's service to the Party, but also the growing split within the entire Party that would explode in the 1960s. Deng Tuo was no more free of ideological commitments than any other actor in politics, and he subscribed to Marxism-Leninism Mao Zedong Thought. Indeed, Deng insisted that ideology and ideological remoulding (*sixiang gaizao*), tenets from the Yan'an rectification movement, were *primary* in public work. What emerges from Deng's theoretical writings in the mid-1950s is that ideological remoulding is a real but complicated process that must be handled in a nuanced and humane manner. It was for Deng a product of rational reflection, not emotional conversion.

Before 1956 this version of Maoism was in basic harmony with that of the Party leadership. Toward the end of these years the underlying tensions in the Party's orthodoxy came to the surface. Deng supported his Beijing patron, Peng Zhen, and his administrative approach to continuing the Party's social revolution.[2] Deng ultimately did not support Mao's use of his charisma as the great leader to push for dangerously ambitious mass campaigns. Deng would grow in his conviction of his role as a culture bearer propagating the new orthodoxy through a predictable system (the Party) and keeping alive China's great cultural heritage through his own artistic interests. Mao, on the other hand, would grow to doubt the loyalty of intellectuals, even Party stalwarts like Deng, and to insist that they acknowledge their role as cog and screw in *his* revolutionary machine.

What propaganda service meant to Deng Tuo, as well as the roots and the mechanisms of the emerging split in the PRC Party-State, can be seen in the details of his social life and work. Deng Tuo's activities during these first years of the PRC provide a map of the social world of an establishment intellectual. Like many of his colleagues, Deng Tuo enjoyed a busy schedule and was active in numerous fields of endeavour. Figure 3.1 gives a simplified picture of the social circles in which Deng Tuo was active in the PRC before his death. Four areas of activity are indicated by the circles: Politics and Administration, Journalism, Scholarship, and Arts and Culture. Inside each circle a few

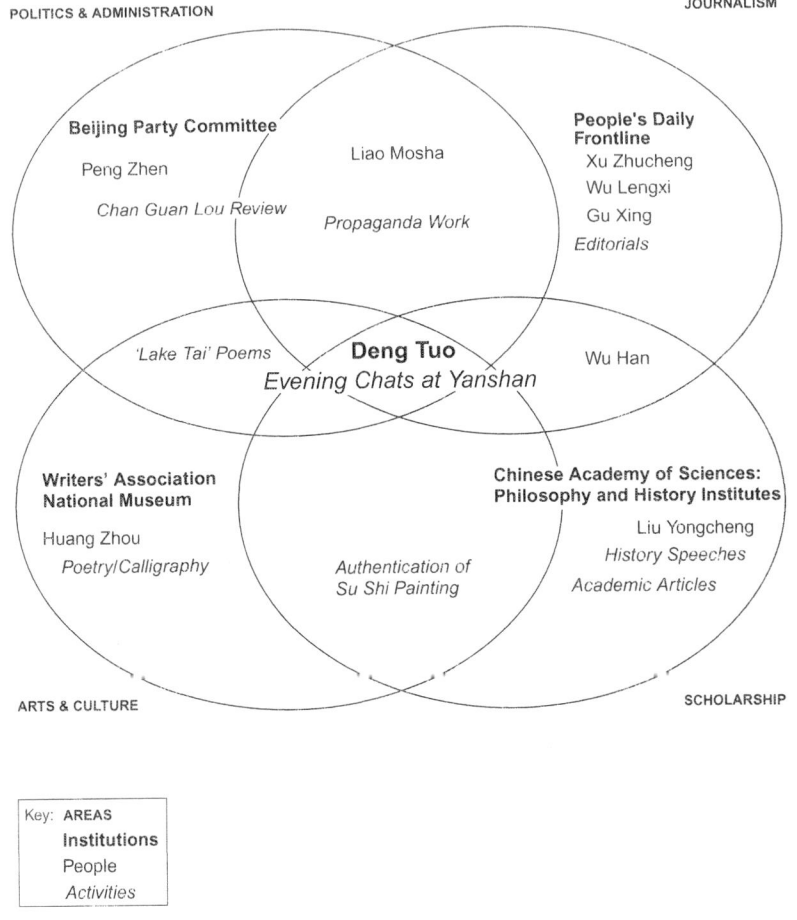

FIG. 3.1. A simplified map of Deng Tuo's social circles

representative institutions, people, and activities are listed. The circles overlap to indicate institutions, people, or activities with which Deng was involved that crossed the boundaries of the four highlighted areas of activity. This picture of Deng Tuo's circles is incomplete—it does not consider other circles of his life such as family concerns or shared activities with fellow provincials from Fujian.[3] The map is also somewhat static, including activities from the early 1950s through the early 1960s. It is clear from a first glance, however, that Deng Tuo spent a great deal of time engaged in activities other than politics. Taking Deng's propaganda writings at face value, one can only conclude that he saw this elite cultural lifestyle as compatible with the socialist society he was helping to build. Indeed, in *Evening Chats at Yanshan*, written in the early 1960s, he makes the link explicit—the current generation is to develop, not discard, China's cultural heritage. It is in the light of his busy cultural life that Deng's propaganda activities from the early years of the PRC should be read.

Politics and Administration

Deng worked in a range of institutions and positions between 1946 and 1956, but all were within the emerging propaganda *xitong* (system) of the CCP's administration. As with the Soviet propaganda state, from which the CCP drew inspiration and practical suggestions, the Chinese propaganda system was much more than the Party's media outlet for political agitation.[4] The official system included the daily administration of all media outlets, as well as editorial control. In addition, the system included policy research organs (and ultimately the Chinese Academy of Sciences). In all, the system reflected the institutional realization of Mao's famous work methods—from the people, to the people. Information was gathered from 'the people' for use by the Party and government. This data was analysed and re-presented to the public in a fashion designed to serve their best interests according to Party ideology. This communication loop between state and society was, of course, *directed* and controlled by the various propaganda organs of the CCP. All of Deng's various jobs fell within the web of this mighty net.

Deng emerged from his cadre investigation to work on the editorial board of *Northern Literature* (*Beifang wenhua*), which published its inaugural issue on 1 March 1946 in Kalgan.[5] This journal is one example of the joining together of the propaganda forces from Yan'an and Jin Cha Ji. Thus, Deng's lower status in its organization may well reflect the higher prestige of the members from Yan'an as much as Deng's recent ideological testing. The journal covered literature, history, and some Party theory (predominantly Zhang Ruxin writing on Mao). A Japanese scholar, Kikuchi Saburo, who had access to this journal (which I have not), lists the fourteen members of the editorial committee—an interesting mix of party stalwarts and recently disgraced left-wing writers: Zhang Ruxin and Zhou Yang as well as Ding Ling, Ai Qing, and Xiao Jun—and concludes that this demonstrates that *Northern Literature* was the mouthpiece of the highest leadership of the CCP.[6] It published a wide range of articles beyond fiction and poetry, such as He Ganzhi's on Liu Bang and Xiang Yü's on the founding of the Han Dynasty and on land reform and the development of capitalism.[7]

Northern Literature is an example of the divergent policy and work styles submerged beneath the unity of rectification rhetoric. The mix of actors in Kalgan and *Northern Literature* is quite amazing, if one considers previous and future CCP debates. This indicates that under the heady conditions of the Civil War and increasing national success the varying strains of Maoism worked together, but this sowed the seeds for discord in the future. For instance, among the Yan'an staff alone, Zhou Yang had just finished attacking Ding Ling. As we have seen in Chapter 2, the experience of the Jin Cha Ji press corps and that of Yan'an's was powerfully different. These differences would return to haunt China a decade later.

Kalgan, too, became the centre of Party cultural activities, as the Yan'an Lu Xun Academy was moved there in April 1946 and the Kalgan Branch of the All-China Writers and Artists Association was established on 24 April.[8] In January 1946 Deng Tuo joined 46 individual signatories and a dozen institutional signatures on a telegram from the north China literary circles in Kalgan to the Political Consultative Congress being held by the KMT. The telegram urged intellectual freedom in KMT reoccupied areas and demanded the 'elimination of fascist elements' and of spies in universities as well as the right of 'democratic personages in the cultural arena' to participate in political consultative congresses.[9] The telegram is signed on behalf of numerous large organizations, such as *Jin Cha Ji Daily*, the Lu Xun Academy, and the Jin Cha Ji Branch of the All-China Literature and Arts Federation, so Deng Tuo must have been seen as a reliable and prestigious person to be included in the limited list of individual signatories.[10]

By December 1945 Deng was back to his role as a Party spokesman, giving the standard line on Lu Xun, which was followed by 'The Mass Lu Xun and Lu Xun's Popularizations!' in August 1946. It was not Deng alone, of course, who was subject to re-education along the lines of the new Yan'an policies.[11] Beginning in the summer of 1945 the CCP began preparing its cadres for the new policies of the Civil War by instituting yet another study campaign based on the powerful consensus reached at the CCP's Seventh Party Congress. The Congress had put to rest decades of inner-Party squabbling and produced an inspirational ideology backed up by a cohesive leadership, the leadership that would steer the CCP to national power.[12] Key to this study was the unequivocal dominance of Mao Zedong Thought and the need for high cadres to maintain their friendly links with the local population. Deng had also given his rectified views on journalism in December 1945, echoing the *Liberation Daily*'s slogan, 'rise a step.' Deng lauded Mao's report to the Seventh Congress, which emphasized the need to link theory with practice and to maintain a self-critical attitude while deepening personal links with the common people. Characteristically, Deng devoted much space to the practical logistics this policy entailed.[13] On the emerging urban front, Deng produced a public statement of Seventh Congress policies as a summary of the experiences of the rectification 'study committee' of the Jin Cha Ji Branch of the Central Committee in September 1946.[14] Stressing the new version of the United Front which the CCP was crafting for the Civil War contest with the KMT, Deng provides another public gloss of CCP documents, this time Mao's long report of April 1945 to the Seventh Congress, which was known as the essay 'On Coalition Government'. Deng, using the 'nationalistic' vocabulary of Sun Yat-sen's 'Three People's Principles', stresses the themes of the United Front of 1946—national independence, peace, and democracy. Thus by 1947, with perhaps probation during 1946, Deng was clearly back in the Party's good graces. When the Communists had to quit Kalgan under KMT pressure in October 1946 Deng took charge of organizing the paper's retreat to its old haunts in western Hebei.[15] For a short period military concerns in the Civil War dominated the Jin Cha Ji press corps.

Deng was also active in the editing of the second official volume of Mao's *Selected Works*, which was published in March 1947 in Kalgan by the Jin Cha Ji Central Committee Branch. Unlike his position in *Northern Literature*, Deng 'assumed complete responsibility' for the project when Hu Xikui, the originally designated leader, was transferred.[16] In September 1945, when the *Jin Cha Ji Daily* moved to Kalgan, Deng had been appointed vice-director of the Jin Cha Ji Propaganda Department and continued to work with the paper.

In the fall of 1947 Deng was appointed to the Policy Research Office of the Party's North China Bureau and director of its Economic Group, maintaining both jobs into the early 1950s.[17] These positions reflect Deng's lesser-known role as a back-room adviser to the Party on policy matters, which was likely as important to the Party as his publicity work. In fact, research, as well as publicity, is part of the propaganda *xitong*— the integrated system of education and mobilization in the propaganda state.[18] Deng's appointment in the Policy Research Office coincided exactly with a critical reassessment of the Party's 'key revolutionary effort of the Civil War period'—land reform.[19] During the winter of 1947–8 Deng took part in a work team carrying out land reform in villages in Laiping county, Hebei, under team leader Li Baohu (also known as Zhao Zhensheng at the time). There he took part in mobilizing local peasants to carry out land reform, much in the manner described in William Hinton's *Fanshen*.[20] These months were the time when the Party reversed course from radical expropriation to moderate redistribution in its land reform efforts. The September 1947 National Land Conference and its draft 'Agricultural Law' had wrestled with 'right' and 'left' errors in land reform. The research of fall 1947, which was centred in Jin Cha Ji (largely because Yan'an had been retaken by KMT forces), produced the material for the moderate resolution enunciated in February 1948. The *Jin Cha Ji Daily* in January broached the key shift which put leftist errors at the forefront under current conditions. The Central Committee's February Directive confirmed that excessive expropriation and attacks on middle peasants must stop.[21] Deng was in the thick of this key policy change, most probably as a specialist adviser inside the Party. The lessons of the 1948 'synthesis' of radical and conservative land reform policies echoes Deng's previous experience in Jin Cha Ji. The directive enshrined the 'law of mass movements'—which required peasants to struggle with landlords in order to *fanshen*, or ideologically 'turn themselves around', but stipulated that such struggle must be preceded by lengthy and careful social investigation and organizational preparation by Party representatives.[22] This was land reform in the style of Peng Zhen and bureaucratic Maoism.

Deng's work undoubtedly had a component of reform through 'going deeply among the masses', since the 1944 criticism of him had dealt, in part, with his 'scholarly airs'. However, Deng's village work was by no means simply punitive, nor was it simply experiential. As a central policy adviser he had collected reams of data and compiled lengthy inner-Party reports on land reform. His models, of course, were Mao's own rural surveys from the 1930s. A portion of this statistical material formed the basis of Deng's lectures at Beijing University in 1950, which have since been published as a valuable sixty-page study on the history and development of CCP land reform efforts since the 1930s.[23] Deng's Economic Research Group also focused on urban and national-level economic questions. Under Peng Zhen's direction, the group met several times to prepare materials on the role of agricultural and rural handicrafts production in the national economy, and how to secure an orderly takeover of urban enterprises as the CCP's armies began to enter the cities.

In late 1948 the officials of the north China administration followed the CCP armies to Xishan county, near Beiping. By this time Deng was clearly linked as an adviser to Peng Zhen and Liu Lantao. By March 1949 the Communists had peacefully entered Beiping and Deng Tuo joined the new Municipal Party Committee as director of its Propaganda Department. He also became director of the Municipal Policy Research Office. Deng's earlier ties with Peng Zhen clearly put him in the new municipal leaders' trust. Deng Tuo was Peng Zhen's speechwriter.[24] With these posts would come the usual formal governmental responsibilities as delegate to the first three National People's Congresses and the first Chinese People's Political Consultative Conference. Although plagued with illness such as migraines and kidney problems, Deng Tuo was understandably caught up in the euphoria of victory.

In the early days of the new national regime Deng put his skills in the service of the Party organization. He drafted reports and speeches for other Central Party leaders as well as Peng Zhen. He also drafted major administrative documents, such as the 1949 'CCP Beiping Municipal Committee Resolution on Strengthening Urban Management and Construction for Production'. He had a particular flair for correcting 'phraseology' (*tifa*), part of an important public relations exercise which softened the CCP's revolutionary rhetoric.[25] After the declaration of the People's Republic of China in October 1949 the city became the capital, Beijing. Deng then made the rounds, giving speeches to the city's many universities and government organizations (of necessity still staffed by bureaucrats from the KMT regime). Deng's job was to explain what life was going to be like for the city's wary professional elites. June 1950 was a particularly busy month on the stump: Deng spoke at Yenching University (soon to be amalgamated with Beijing University) on 'Scientific Attitudes and Methods', to a group of Political Consultative Congress delegates (largely non-Party people) on 'The Future of the Chinese Revolution', and at Qinghua University (China's premier technical university) on 'Party Leadership and Reconstruction in the New Revolution'. Such speaking engagements continued into 1953.[26] As with his efforts to organize the distribution of the CCP's newspapers in 1938, Deng's stumping reflects the considerable effort that went into the CCP's largely successful efforts to win the population's support in the early 1950s.

Journalism

Deng Tuo's most prestigious and important Party position and the peak of his official career was as editor-in-chief of the *People's Daily*, China's largest newspaper and the official paper of the Central Committee. Deng took up his post in the autumn of 1949.[27] He helped found the All-China Journalists' Association in 1949, and served as its president until March 1960. During the first years, Deng more or less lived at work, while his wife, Ding Yilan, lived across town in the dormitories of her work unit, the Central Broadcasting Institute. In 1952 they moved in together in a comfortable traditional-style house in central Beijing not far from the Beijing railway station. His father, the aged former Qing dynasty district magistrate, then moved from Fujian to be with him.[28] Here Deng Tuo enjoyed a wide range of cultural activities, regularly hosting private gatherings and individual visits with some of the leading artists, poets, and cultural aesthetes of China.

Deng is credited with building the *People's Daily* and constantly working through the 1950s to improve its content, style, and layout. Nonetheless, Deng fought a losing battle with the growing bureaucratism of the Party and the imperiousness of several leaders. The actual results of Deng's efforts were mixed at best, as any reader of this profoundly boring paper can attest. Yet he tried, and ultimately would be fired for trying to carry out the spirit, if not the actual practices, of Party rule.[29] Shortly after the establishment of the *People's Daily* Deng Tuo changed the organization of the editorial board and the format of the paper from that which prevailed in the base areas during the 1940s. Party periodicals then had been organized functionally according to activity: editing, interviewing, reporting, research, etc. Deng changed to a topical organization: agriculture, industry, Party life, literature, etc., in order better to focus the paper's reporting efforts. From the start he set the policy that every letter from a reader had to be answered, and he instituted a regular newsletter to the employees of the paper, who grew from about 200 in 1950 to over 1,000 in early 1951.[30]

During the 1950s while the paper modelled itself on *Pravda*, Deng Tuo increasingly expressed vexation over the content of the *People's Daily*, particularly the dull editorials and lengthy official reports. Deng Tuo shared his frustrations with Liu Binyan, a junior editor in the 1950s who served as Deng's translator in the Soviet Union. 'Then why not improve it?' asked Liu. Deng replied:

The editor-in-chief of *Pravda*—first Bukharin, now [Dimitri] Shepilov—has always been a member of the Politburo. As for me, I am not even a member of the Central Committee. Many ministers of the government, on the other hand, are members of the Central Committee and can sign orders for *People's Daily* to publish their speeches, articles, or reports of meetings. I know better than anybody else that readers don't even look at that stuff, but even so, I can't refuse to publish it.[31]

This lack of status in the official hierarchy was the likely source of Deng's notorious pliability as editor.[32] While favouring professional standards, Deng was clearly not in a position to put his standards freely into practice at the paper. In any event, his first task was to propagandize the new government's policies.

Propaganda and Ideology: 1949–1955

For the period up to 1955, the unremarkable orthodoxy of what Deng published in public on behalf of the Party and the anonymity of the man are the key impressions left by his public writings. He blended in perfectly. However, his internal writings (in *neibu* publications), particularly on his speciality of journalism, give us a sense of what motivated the man and provide the code for deciphering signals in his open (*gongkai*) propaganda publications. From the early rectification movements and Korean war effort through the 1954 attack on the left-wing writer Hu Feng and 1955 criticism of Hu Shi's historical writings, Deng joined in with other establishment intellectuals in supporting the Party line. He may well have had doubts, consistent with his later published opinions in the 1960s, but it is unlikely.[33] Many of Deng's colleagues reflect that they did not 'see the writing on the wall' concerning Party intolerance of intellectuals in the early 1950s, though they can see it with hindsight. There is no reason to expect Deng Tuo to have been more prescient than his colleagues. As a loyal Party member, Deng could hardly have done otherwise. Additionally, inner-Party channels of dissent and feedback worked reasonably well in the early 1950s, and for all we know Deng may have made good, if discreet, use of them. For he is equally well remembered for his forthright opinions 'behind closed doors' in Party committee meetings. Deng Tuo's writing and Party work until 1956 are thus representative of the work of a satisfied man.

During the first years of the People's Republic Deng Tuo, like many other intellectuals, found solidarity in the cause of national construction. One of his early pieces, '*China Youth* and Yun Daiying', published in October 1949, was a contribution to the new commemoration literature of the victorious CCP honouring its martyrs. In this case it was the founding editor of the Communist journal, *China Youth*, in the 1920s who was executed in the KMT prison complex in Suzhou shortly before Deng Tuo was incarcerated there in the early 1930s.[34] Deng Tuo participated in the nationwide campaigns of the period, particularly the rectification movement that promoted ideological reformation among intellectuals in the early 1950s. His first article in the prestigious Party theory journal, *Study*, appeared in August 1950 and is a fair example of his work in that campaign. Entitled 'The Importance of the Rectification Movement in National Construction Work', it quotes Mao Zedong on

3.2 Deng Tuo and wife, Ding Yilan, Beihai Park, Beiping, 1949

national construction and Lenin's writings on the Soviet Union's New Economic Policy programme.[35]

During the early 1950s Deng wrote a number of other 'Party' articles, taking particular interest in youth literature. In February 1951 he published a joint pamphlet for the Youth League, *Discussions with Members of the Youth Corps on Mass Line Problems*, writing the title article and another, 'Thoroughly Criticize Fatalism'.[36] He chimed in with a contribution to the appropriation of the May Fourth Movement by the CCP on its twenty-third anniversary, echoing themes of Party stalwart, Zhou Yang.[37] Deng continued to write on journalism, penning the fortieth anniversary article for the Soviet Union's *Pravda* in the internal circulation newsletter of the *People's Daily* in August 1952.[38] Deng continued publishing as an authoritative commentator with 'China's General Line of Transition to Socialism' on New Year's Day 1954.[39] All echo standard Party views about each issue.

These articles appear hackneyed, with their constant reiteration of Party policy and ideal role models, but they were part of a concerted effort by the Party to consolidate its rule and avoid the bureaucratic corruption which had brought down its adversary, the Nationalist Party (KMT). A look at the inner-Party documents for the 1950 rectification demonstrates this urge and its continuity with the populist goals of the wartime cadre study movements, such as Deng had summarized in 1946. More significantly, these documents reveal the underlying faith in moral-ideological rectification as not only the legitimating device of the CCP in the eyes of its public but also the institutional means for a government that sought the functions of public scrutiny and feedback through moral transformation of leaders and led alike rather than through secret-ballot public elections. Here we see the key questions left unresolved in the new deal for China, as well as for its establishment intellectuals. The mechanisms for checks and balances on abuse of power are shockingly vague; the faith that honest self-criticism under the guidance of the new ideology and its trained priesthood will provide good government is inspiring. The failure of rectification in practice to do this by the 1960s is well-known, but in 1950 it had brought the best government China had seen for over a century to power and promised a proud future.

The Party's rectification programme to consolidate its power and preempt any return to the corrupt bureaucratic practices of the previous regime began in May 1950.[40] As part of its preparations for the movement, the Central Committee passed a resolution on 19 April on how to handle its key component, public self- and mutual criticism, in Party newspapers such as the *People's Daily*. Its chief concern was the danger of arrogance among leaders and the growing habit of suppressing public criticism of the regime. This, the resolution stated, would harm the people because errors would not be corrected. The danger was bureaucratism and the only way to root it out was public self- and mutual criticism. Thus, education was needed. Party members must learn to accept criticism because it is good for the Party, and journalists and editors must learn to distinguish 'good' criticism, which aided the Party's goals, from the 'bad', which questioned Party dominance. These ideals were backed up by stiff organizational rules: the Party Centre decreed that no longer could Party leaders vet criticisms before their publication and in the event that such leaders sought reprisals against their critics, they were to be handed over to the Party's Discipline Inspection Committee. Furthermore, administrative authority for selecting, investigating, and publishing 'criticisms from the masses' was now vested in the editorial boards of Party periodicals. They needed no other approval before publication. Finally, objects of criticism were ordered to reply to criticisms, acknowledging their faults and defending themselves only in the case of factual errors in the original criticism. Editorial boards, for their part, were assigned a long list of 'study materials' on the role of journalism from Lenin, Stalin, and Mao.[41]

The rectification, however, was not a sure success, because the Party immediately turned around and renewed the campaign in 1951, leading to the well-known 'Three Antis' and 'Five Antis' campaigns against corruption and bureaucratism and promoting 'reform' among businessmen and intellectuals that lasted through 1953.[42] Part of the problem was excess attacks on suspected 'enemies' prompted by the pressures of the Korean War and the presence of the American military, which passionately supported the regime's enemies, on the Asian mainland. Part of the problem was the ability of local Party leaders to subvert the goals of rectification by deflecting criticism away from themselves and onto the politically suspect and vulnerable business and intellectual communities. The Party would turn its organizational discipline upon its functionaries in 1954 in the wake of Gao Gang's failed attempt to take power, but first the attacks on intellectuals—who were so necessary for economic reconstruction—had to be moderated.

Deng Tuo, now a leading ideological and propaganda expert, reflected on these issues during 1951 in the Party theory journal, *Study*. In August, Deng criticized shortcomings among Party members in carrying out the rectification.[43] Our ideological work is weak, he complains; we must 'develop ideological struggle'. There have been 'leftist' excesses such as repudiating all of China's tradition and rightist errors of identifying things Chinese (as opposed to foreign) as equalling Marxism-Leninism. Mostly, he criticizes the vulgarization of ideology. Ideology is Marxism-Leninism and Mao Zedong Thought and it only makes sense in concrete situations. Thus, Deng concludes, the unity of theory and practice does not mean do what the local Party leader says; it means continuous research, analysis, and open discussion.

Deng turned to the role of intellectuals in the December issue of *Study*.[44] His point is to justify the necessity for ideological remoulding among intellectuals while guaranteeing a realm of free choice and variety within that requirement. This gets to the heart of Deng's ideological commitments, echoing his writings from the 1930s and 1940s. It is because ideological remoulding is so fundamental to the success of the revolution, in Deng's eyes, and because it is, ultimately, an individual 'revolution in consciousness' that it cannot be forced. Involuntary compliance, ritualism, and self-delusion are the enemies of this world-historical transformation now happening in China. Deng castigates each. Once again citing Lenin, Stalin, and 'Chairman Mao', Deng shows how individual ideological remoulding reflects the unprecedented changes wrought in the material world by proletarian revolution. But the process is complex, and there are different 'levels of consciousness' among individuals corresponding to their class background and recent social activities. Intellectuals are particularly complicated. Thus, Deng argues for latitude and variation in methods and speed of reform, while upholding the one truth to which all self-consciousness must inevitably lead. 'Whether or not people join the ideological remoulding movement can be a matter of free choice.' But, any 'consciousness' which does not recognize the responsibility of rejecting feudal and reactionary habits is literally illegal, as such habits contravene the General Programme of the PRC. Yet, the thinking person couldn't possibly stop at compliance, Deng announces. Science, the history of human societies, and the recent military revolution all demonstrate the truth and value of the proletarian revolution. Perhaps echoing his own experience in the 1930s, Deng says, 'Our country has many intellectuals who have taken the revolutionary road. They first recognized it from theory, recognizing the road which human history must travel [i.e., Marxist stages] and adopting the scientific cosmology and revolutionary outlook on life. Only after that did they gradually join the revolutionary movement.'[45] Even in this moderate articulation of ideological remoulding we can see the central pillars of Deng's positive and exclusive ideology—his metaphysics (in which 'scientific cosmology' equals dialectical materialism) and his ethics (in which 'revolutionary outlook' equals an historical materialist analysis of China's stage of historical development that determines the right action to take). Deng's moderation is instrumental, not fundamental. He counsels patience but not an openness to alternatives.[46]

Deng's focus on the primacy of ideological work and use of terms such as 'ideological struggle' bring to mind the policies of the Cultural Revolution, which began by destroying Deng. This dissonance for Western readers today is important. We must remember that the fanatical idealism of the Cultural Revolution was not dominant in 1951. Ideological reform as the basis of good government was the basis of the Yan'an rectification in 1942 and the land reform and cadre education movements in the late 1940s. Despite abuse of 'ideological struggle' in both these cases, the dominant mode of ideological remoulding was one of salvation rather than inquisition.[47] This was embraced by the entire Party leadership, as well as reflected in Deng's journalism speeches of 1954 and 1955. Deng spoke for the transformational bureaucrats of new China, serving a very orderly, indeed rather bureaucratic, administration. His approach to ideological struggle and reform was rational rather than emotive. He sought to regularize and tame the powerful forces the rectification process unleashed both within the individual and in society. Mao Zedong Thought, propaganda, ideological remoulding, and Party dictatorship were not problems for Deng Tuo; they were the tools of his trade.

Deng's faith that self- and mutual criticism and rectification guaranteed the future ability of the Party to fulfil the needs of the masses, however, left several questions unanswered (not the least of which was how did he know the masses want his particular Party?). Rectification provides no administrative protection from or correction of the abuse of power separate from the goodwill of one or another 'rectified' leader or committee. Although considerably more 'rational-bureaucratic' and supportive of science and economic modernization than the imperial dynasties, the CCP at root maintained the Chinese preference in politics for the 'rule of man' over the 'rule of law'. Nowhere in his writings does Deng address the possibility of a fundamental failure by rectification to generate sufficient quantities of such 'good men' or suggest the need for impersonal mechanisms to act as a check on human failings. No free elections, no independent courts, no free press. These are bourgeois. Correct thinking, carefully elaborated on the basis of past experience, painfully nurtured by cautious elder pilgrims on the road to salvation, and personally integrated by the reflective individual: this is the real revolution.

It is a noble vision, one that offered to reintegrate China's educated elite with the country's masses, healing the divorce which had alienated intellectuals from the common folk since the turn of the century. Increasing foreign contact among Chinese intellectuals and the end of the imperial system (which had employed the educated to administer the lives of the common people) drew the educated away from contact with China's peasant majority. Now, Deng saw himself as a culture bearer bringing the good news to his compatriots. By careful study of new classics, application of advanced knowledge, and honest introspection, the educated could once again be integrated with their native culture and return from the marginal existence of May Fourth intelligentsia.[48] Scholars could once again be true officials. But this faith included a fatal flaw. Along with his belief in the new classics and detailed explanation of the collective and incremental nature of its application, Deng believed in the charismatic genius of the supreme leader, Chairman Mao. In his 1951 talk with Youth League leaders Deng said, 'The reason why Chairman Mao has become the great revolutionary leader is because he was able to combine his personal genius and wisdom with that of the broad masses.'[49] When the genius came to disagree with the organization, the new ideology offered no way to resolve the conflict.

On Journalism

Deng had lesser problems to confront in the early 1950s. Most of his time was engaged in operating the *People's Daily*. By October 1953 the first phase of consolidation was over. On National Day (1 October) the Party declared a new sub-stage in history, the transition to socialism, and the new stage's goals and responsibilities were outlined in the General Line. This summing up and moving on provided the occasion for Deng Tuo to reflect on the progress of socialist journalism over the first four years of the PRC. This was the pinnacle of Deng's official career and he spoke not just as a representative of the Party but as a leading authority on Party journalism. He spoke on issues of professionalism, the role of the press in society, and the importance of editorials as the most efficient guide for the masses. What he said beginning in late 1953 was picked up and adopted by official Party pronouncements in 1954.

In October of 1953 Deng spoke to his staff at the *People's Daily* on issues of professionalism.[50] Professionalism in journalism, says Deng, is comprehensive. We are society's educators. 'Of course we certainly do not want just to be technical specialists. We must lead the advance in ideology and politics. . . . The responsibility of journalists is through the practice of struggle to help the Party and the State solve problems.' Such a heavy responsibility demands conscientious effort. He repeats his concrete version of 'ideological character' (*sixiang xing*) which unites theory with the details of the work at hand. He then turns to the division and organization of labour among editors, problems in writing style, the need to strengthen mutual help among journalists, and how to carry out self- and mutual criticism correctly. If the Party paper is going to fulfil its role as orthodox speaker *and* public ombudsman, all these areas must be improved. Deng particularly lambastes empty, boring, and formulaic editorials and articles. He recommends model essays, from political essays by Chairman Mao to light essays on Eastern Europe by Feng Zhi to revolutionary essays by Alexander Herzen (a personal favourite of Karl Marx).[51] Particularly important is the *People's Daily*'s role as investigator. Deng reminds his reporters of the rules: criticism must have solid evidence. If one uncovers a problem when in the field, go talk directly to the responsible cadre and do not go public. If the local officials disagree, write to the paper or to the Party Centre. On the other hand, should one uncover a serious problem, avoid the topic with local leaders and report it directly to the paper and central authorities.

At this point the staff of the *People's Daily* made an extended visit to the Soviet Union 'to learn from *Pravda*'. This was a time of strong Soviet influence in China and *Pravda* was the model for the Chinese Party press. The delegation included Deng Tuo, Hu Jiwei, Zhang Rengbei (an economist), Zhang Chunqiao, and Fang Ji (from *Beijing Daily*) among others. The trip lasted nearly two months centring on February 1954. It included an intensive 'hands on' seminar at *Pravda* where the Chinese studied how it worked. Deng resumed his friendship there with Lev Deliusin, who had been *Pravda*'s correspondent in Beijing from 1951–3. The two men grew to be good friends in the years to come.[52] According to Deliusin, Deng was an assiduous student, wanting to know every aspect of Soviet journalism, its organization and its favoured writing styles. Deng pressed Shepilov, the general editor, for everything from his experiences as a socialist journalist to how *Pravda* decided what was to be published openly and what was to be limited to 'internal' circulation publications. The *People's Daily* delegation took its mission seriously, stopping in Harbin and Shenyang in Manchuria for two weeks to write up their report before returning to Beijing. Among the immediate results of the visit, says Deliusin, the Chinese decided to shorten their newspaper articles, which previously had been long-winded and packed with details. Also, they started adding other sorts of writings— short stories and light essays (*sanwen*) to brighten up their papers. Deng also reinforced his belief in the leading role of Party journalism in public affairs, and especially the role of editorials.

As part of the new General Line the Party set about summing up past experience in its press and propaganda and 'advancing' (*gaijin*) their work. Additionally, it set about strengthening Party norms and discipline in the wake of the failed attempt in December 1953 by Gao Gang (leading Party figure in Manchuria) to manoeuvre factional support to supplant Liu Shaoqi as Mao's chosen successor.[53] These issues were stressed by the Fourth Plenum of the Seventh Central Committee in February 1954. Back from Moscow, Deng Tuo gave a keynote address on how this reform applied to journalism, probably at the Second National Propaganda Work Conference of the CCP in May.[54] It is a comprehensive statement of the achievements, problems, and future tasks of Party journalism in which Deng outlines the role of socialist journalism for the new period. It can be taken as the representative CCP policy statement from this period.[55] Deng builds upon the issues he raised in his October 1953 talk to *People's Daily* reporters and in the

Life in the Establishment 141

process gives a vivid picture of the role of the press and propaganda in the early years of the PRC.

Journalism, according to Deng, is an educative process. It educates the masses and it educates the journalists and local Party leaders. In short, journalism is an integral part of the ideological remoulding of rectification. Deng begins, 'Newspapers are the most potent weapon used by the Party to educate and lead the broad masses of the people in the revolutionary struggle and the construction of the new life.' This is educational journalism.[56] It proceeds on three levels: ideological reform of one's 'attitude' (*taidu*), organizational discipline and investigation by reporters, and public relations. No matter whether it is a national-level or local paper, Deng insists, the most important task of each paper's editors is to 'strengthen their ideological leadership' and their 'political study' (editorial boards are to 'study' and discuss regularly all Party resolutions and directives). This is inseparable from keeping in touch with 'the ideological condition of the masses' and going down to their workshops and fields to see how their life really is. Deng reiterates his themes on uniting theory and practice from his earlier theory articles—sloganmongering won't do; only a sincere effort to gather the facts and analyse them according to Marxism-Leninism and 'the works of Mao' on a case-by-case basis will do. To promote this study, selected editors from provincial-level papers will be sent to the Marxism-Leninism Institute beginning in the second half of the year.[57]

Although the proper attitude is the prerequisite for successful reform of journalism work, it is but the prelude to much labour. This labour, however, is also educational. It is how journalists concretely carry out Mao's call to keep close links with the masses. In brief, Deng makes it clear that the propaganda tasks of journalism require that articles be factual, well reasoned, and interestingly written. Nothing less will do; indeed a failure on any of these counts reflects 'ideological weakness'. Of course, the desire to be concrete should protect 'state secrets'. There are still class enemies at home and abroad. Thus, the precise number of enterprises, productive capacity, sources of raw materials, etc. should not be mentioned.[58] The way to guarantee this is through public self- and mutual criticism. Newspapers are to print much more of it. Deng laboriously lays out the ideals, methods, and departmental procedures for self- and mutual criticism in newspapers. Once again the major origin of criticisms should be letters and manuscripts from the public. All letters must be answered (a department should be set up with its director on the editorial board) and important criticisms should be investigated and, if accurate, published. The object of criticism must accept it and make a self-criticism because such criticism is good for the Party.

Serious cases go to the Discipline Inspection Committee. On the preventative side, Deng informs his listeners, all Party papers will henceforth set up a special regular column on 'Party Life'. He cites such columns in *Shanxi Daily* and *Hebei Daily* as good examples. These columns are must reading for Party members and should stress the function of Party members as role models in society.[59]

The participation of the public is central to socialist journalism; however, it is a highly controlled and directed role. 'We need the supervision of the masses,' Deng exclaims; 'no matter how highly placed or hard-working the cadre, if we do not have the supervision of the masses we will lose vigilance.' Such criticism must be under the 'leadership' of the Party cadres within the editorial committee. Deng has several purposes in mind with public participation. First is to inform the public of the Party's current work goals in general and in their line of work and to motivate individuals to work hard for them. Equally, the public will provide feedback for the Party on how its policies have been received. Finally, public participation will serve as a legitimation of the Party's right to rule. 'This is how we show our responsibility to the people.'[60] Being able to criticize leaders turns citizens into activists, says Deng. Furthermore, the editorial board serves as an organizational censor on the local Party committee and individual Party leaders. They are closely linked, but administratively separate. This holds out the threat of public attack backed up by the Discipline Inspection Committee. The Party's press is to be a check on the Party.

The picture Deng paints of press and propaganda work is reminiscent of a practical religious organization, where goodwill, study of the scripture, and 'prayer' (study sessions and mutual criticism) are backed up by organizational muscle to promote and protect group goals. Deng's problem was that in order to strengthen Central Party control over local Party committees and local leaders (a key concern after the Gao Gang affair), it was necessary to 'strengthen Party leadership of the papers'.[61] Thus the general editor must be appointed by the local Party Committee, indeed sit in on its meetings, and the local Party secretary was to 'instruct' the paper on important questions. Additionally, the general editor had to be approved by the next two higher levels of the Party. The task was also to be distributed over different organizational lines, limiting the possibility of connivance. 'The work of self- and mutual criticism in the papers should be intimately linked with the Discipline Inspection Committees of various Party Committees and the People's Police Committee at various government levels.'[62] The integrity of this assertion of Central Party norms relied, as well, on the correct choice of Party secretary by the Centre. Most fundamentally, however, it relied on the success of ideological reform through self- and mutual criticism. This was its fatal flaw. Deng finds it necessary to refer, yet again, to the 1950 Central Committee resolution on 'Self- and Mutual Criticism in Newspapers', noting that it has not been well carried out.[63] It required, for instance, the Party secretary or the general editor approved by the secretary to report on themselves in the event that they were engaged in activities that were illegal or contrary to Central Party interests. With hindsight we can wonder at the idealism of this arrangement, but if we are to understand the world of Deng Tuo's associates in the Beijing propaganda and press circles of the 1950s we must try to recall the sense of optimism and faith in Party norms that dominated the public arena—the 'symbolic capital' of Yan'an was still the currency of the day.[64]

Deng's speech gives us a good picture of socialist journalism in the new Republic. As usual, he begins with statistics. As of January 1954 there are 258 newspapers published at or above the prefectural level which daily produce over eight million copies: 151 Party papers, 17 by unions (*gonghui*), 23 for peasants, 17 for youth and children, 15 by Democratic or other parties, 14 trade or professional papers, 21 in minority languages, and 2 in Russian. Deng gives a detailed outline of the diverse tasks and responsibilities for each category of newspaper. National papers, naturally, reflect the Party's national and international policies. Regional papers should take their themes from the national ones, but must no longer reprint large sections from *People's Daily*. Instead they must link these issues with concrete examples of regional concerns and explain how these problems are to be solved. Union papers, peasant papers, and 'wall newspapers' or black-board papers (in most factories and offices) must stress the transmission of practical knowledge and promote the struggle against rich peasants, loan sharks, and profiteers. They must also promote the glory, etc. of the Worker-Peasant Alliance.[65] While Deng's admonitions clearly reflect that these goals were not being met by 1954, what is more striking is the pervasive presence of Party-controlled media around China and the powerful organizational and normative incentives in place to promote Party goals through those channels.

Deng returned to the linchpin of Party voice in the press, editorials, in a speech given a year and a half later. This was Deng's premier speciality and he makes it clear that nothing is more important than the editorial of a paper. It is the flag, the guiding thought of the remaining articles in each issue. It is the voice to which the people look for their marching orders, so daily editorials are a necessity. Deng gave the talk in the fall of 1955, perhaps in meetings surrounding the Sixth Enlarged

Plenum of the Seventh Central Committee in early October.[66] Deng repeats his orthodox themes about the ideological nature of journalism, Party supervision, and interaction with the public. This talk, however, is a roll-up-your-sleeves technical exercise in assigning, outlining, and constructing editorials. It gives a picture of Deng's working habits and the considerable effort and professional skill he put into his propaganda work.

Once again, Deng begins with statistics: the average number of *People's Daily* editorials per month since 1949. From an average of eight then the number crept up through the teens to 22 in 1954. Since 1955 they have been daily. The provincial-level papers average four to seven a month, but as of August 1955, *Liaoning Daily* has increased to an average of thirteen.[67] These are good signs, Deng says. Party leaders should write more editorials, too. The last word on the issue is the 1955 *Soviet Encyclopedia*, which lays down the law: editorials are the voice of the Party and a beacon to the people.[68] The Soviet model held for Deng, as it did for most of his compatriots in 1955.

Deng launches into a detailed outline of how to organize and write good editorials. He gives the four basic requirements for good editorials (mass audience, strong ideological stance, consistency with current policy, and clear language) and five sources for selecting topics (Central Party resolutions, regional Party resolutions and opinions, topics from work with local authorities, reporters' notes, letters from readers). Then Deng gets down to particulars. Everything must be planned a month in advance. Editorial committees must produce a detailed schedule for 35 editorials per month (just to be safe) including topic, author, length, due date for drafts, and an outline of points. He expects the outline to be a detailed précis and he shows the value of such detail in the example of his own 500-word outline for the 1 October 1952 'National Day' editorial in *People's Daily*. Because he outlined the terminology he intended to use, the Party superior who vetted it nipped a terminological blunder in the bud. Deng's draft read: 'proving the invincible strength of Marxism-Leninism, Mao Zedong Thought.' The Party leader crossed out 'Mao Zedong Thought' and added a cautionary note: 'Do not use the term "Mao Zedong Thought" together with "Marxism-Leninism". As much as possible, do not use this term in propaganda.' Later in his example, 'Mao Zedong Thought has . . .' is also revised to become 'the CCP and its leader Comrade Mao Zedong have . . .' Deng reminds his audience: imagine what might have happened if the outline had been vague.[69]

Deng gives good advice on how to write. Use more concrete words, avoid vague generalizations. Have a clear point to make, and back it up with *believable* detail. Read more, to see how to write better. He then walks his audience through the stages of writing an individual editorial and gives examples of good and poor prose. Deng's goal for this writing is clear: to convince readers to carry out Party policy with verve. Thus, he hates formulaic and dull editorials. As one who must have seen a great many such editorials, Deng is able to paint a colourful picture:

> The most common structure for a formulaic editorial cannot but begin with a discourse on current conditions, followed by a presentation of good examples and a criticism of a few bad examples. And then, the subjective causes of each. Toss up a few lessons from experience, and repeat a few generalities on advancing our work, which everyone already knows anyway. Finish up with a few sentences on how under the leadership of the Party this task will be completely achieved. Frankly, this kind of formula makes people vomit.[70]

Deng Tuo's concerns were passed on to younger journalists. In his daily routines at *People's Daily* Deng oversaw editorial writing tasks among the young editors, such as Hu Jiwei, Li Zhuang, and later Wang Ruoshui, urging upon them his professional standards as well as orthodox ideas. Hu and Wang have become famous in the post-Mao period for their unorthodox attitudes, but during the Mao years they served the Party obediently, like Deng. More importantly, Deng trained numerous less famous editors such as Li Zhuang (briefly editor of *People's Daily* in the late 1970s), and the system of editorial or commentary drafting continues at the *People's Daily* into the 1990s.[71] Deng's old superior, Nie Rongzhen, who was until 1985 a member of the Politburo, praises Deng for 'the great number of propaganda cadres he nurtured and trained'.[72]

The Soviet Thaw and Reform at People's Daily

Important changes in China and the Soviet Union in 1956 put new pressures on Deng Tuo and his *People's Daily*. These changes began with great confidence and hope and led into the first confrontations both within the CCP and between the CCP and the Soviet Union that would lead first to a split between the socialist giants and ultimately a split within the CCP. The changes were of national scope, but they caught up Deng Tuo personally in his second visit to Moscow in early 1956 and then in Warsaw, where he witnessed the heady reforms of the Soviet Thaw. This influenced the direction of his 'reform' (*gaiban*) of the *People's Daily* that summer. He believed that these were positive changes, promising a revitalization of state socialism and cultural life under socialism.

The Party decided that a new stage had been reached by late 1955. Its leaders were feeling confident. The eventual completion of the socialization of industry and agriculture looked certain. Additionally, Mao's call for a 'high tide' in the co-operativization of rural farming was proceeding ahead of schedule. Thus, the Party's previous concern with internal enemies could shift to the new enemy: a backward economy. 1956 was to become a 'leap' year in which China would jump ahead in economic growth. Central to this task were intellectuals, whose expertise would be necessary for rapid economic development.[73] Zhou Enlai chaired a national conference in January 1956 addressing the needs and concerns of intellectuals. Pay rises, improved working conditions, and less pressure from Party supervisors were on the agenda. A more colourful cultural life was encouraged. The implications of these changes for the Party press were clear. Not only should it brighten itself up a bit, but it should reflect the Party's renewed confidence to tolerate diverse opinions in the name of enlivening the nation's intellectual life.

This urge to reform was soon followed by a shocking and negative impetus, de-Stalinization. Khrushchev's 'Secret Speech' to the Soviet Party's 20th Congress in late February 1956 denounced Stalin. The Chinese were shocked. Party leaders did not agree with such a harsh assessment and did not like the implications for their own supreme leader. But it drove home the need to loosen up intellectual life inside and outside the CCP, in order to avoid the errors of Stalin and the repercussions after his death that so destabilized the Communist bloc (in Chinese eyes). Mao led the crusade. In April and May he pushed for a new policy of 'letting a hundred flowers bloom'. His goal was to solicit opinions from intellectuals and others outside the Party in order to correct mistakes.[74] While national writers and professionals were slow to respond to the call, having witnessed the ideological crucifixion of the writer Hu Feng in 1954, the Party bureaucracy set about liberalizing the press. By summer it would bring the reorganization and expansion of the *People's Daily*.

At precisely this time Deng Tuo visited Moscow and Eastern Europe. He was extremely ill and spent a month in Bazvicha sanatorium for high cadres outside Moscow. His old friend, Lev Deliusin, was in attendance. Then, in March 1956, Deng led the Chinese Journalists' Association delegation to a meeting of the Communist International Organization of Journalists held in Warsaw and was elected a vice-chairman.[75] Liu Binyan would join Deng later as his interpreter, but in the hospital Deng was on his own (with Deliusin acting as interpreter). The Moscow doctors were appalled. Too many complications, they said—stomach, lungs, kidneys, migraines. Still, the treatment worked, and as Deng recuperated in late February and early March the two journalists discussed the heady events of the day. Deng found Khrushchev's ideas on peaceful co-existence between the socialist and capitalist worlds dubious; he felt the attack on Stalin was scurrilous. He stuck to what became the Chinese position: Stalin was 70 per cent correct, 30 per cent in error. Deng did not like such criticism of the supreme leader, even within secret Party meetings; he would like it even less in public in the 1957 Hundred Flowers. Still, Deliusin found Deng open-minded and willing to consider other points of view. And their views were closer on literary matters. Deng supported Mao's policies on most topics, but he had become critical of the literary policy enshrined in Mao's 'Yan'an Talks' from 1942. Mao's worker-peasant-soldier theory of literature was, according to Deng, 'not completely correct'. It was not right to put such stringent limitations upon an artist's personality and style, he felt. In short, the 'Yan'an Talks' were appropriate for war conditions, but not for 1956. Deng spoke approvingly of the emerging 'Hundred Flowers' policy in literature.

When Deng travelled down to Poland, he was given a full dose of liberalization. Liu Binyan, his interpreter, recalls what a shock Warsaw in March 1956 was for the men.[76] The press was full of information and stories from the West and anyone could walk down to the public library and read Western European newspapers. This particularly struck Deng Tuo. He bemoaned the lack of access to such papers in China, even for senior officials such as himself, and noted this was also the case in Moscow. Impressed by the liberalization going on in Poland, Deng returned to Beijing to hear Mao's 'Hundred Flowers' speeches in April and May.

The reform of the *People's Daily* came on 1 July 1956, when it expanded its length from four to eight pages to provide space for new voices. As usual, Deng had preceded the change by soliciting detailed suggestions from Party leaders, intellectuals, and readers. With over 350 responses, the paper held a series of public forums and then made its report to the Central Committee.[77] The note to readers on 1 July was penned by Hu Qiaomu, and it explained the need to publish new ideas,

whether they come from the socialist camp or from the capitalist countries; whether they occur in the large metropolises or in the remote villages; whether they directly concern [socialist] construction or not; and whether they make pleasant reading or not.[78]

The paper set about publishing such views, but the results were lukewarm. In two months some 95 *zawen* (topical essays) and 60 pieces from readers were published, and some notable writers such as Zheng Zhendou, Mao Dun, and Xu Maoyong contributed. But the hoped-for variety did not appear. The Central Committee notice approving the change was probably too cautious an approval for the increasingly experienced intellectuals of the PRC. It stated the broad goals of the reform: 'to develop the discussion of different opinions in the press.' It recognized that the articles and letters published in the *People's Daily* and other Party papers could not convincingly be 'always completely correct'. But it carefully qualified the freedoms it was granting. 'From now on the articles published by the *People's Daily* ... in general may not represent the views of the Party Centre, and moreover may permit a few writers to publish articles opposed to the understanding of we Communists.' In fact, much of the notice berates local papers for mindlessly repeating what the *People's Daily* prints—a sure sign that Deng Tuo's pronouncements on local content from 1954 had not been heeded.[79]

Deng took his own editors to task in mid-August. He berated them for a lack of 'independent thinking' (*duli sikao*), for formulaic writing, and for over-copying Soviet papers. Ideological leaders such as themselves must exercise independence of thought in concrete matters while adhering to Party guidance and avoiding the pitfalls of 'liberalism'. In this way the full activism of each individual can be engaged. 'No doubt', says one Chinese biographer, 'this is Deng Tuo's application of the "Hundred Flowers" in journalism.'[80] Deng was as bland and cautious as the Central Party notice. His best suggestion was to revive the spirit, and more importantly the argumentative writing style, of Chinese journalists of the 1930s and 1940s, such as Zou Taofen. One may wonder if Deng felt frustration at his editors' reluctance to enter the fray with such internally contradictory marching orders. This stalled reform at *People's Daily* by late 1956 represents the beginning of the crisis that would engulf the CCP and China for the next decade.

Scholarship

At this point it may be difficult to recall the wide range of social circles in Deng Tuo's life depicted at the start of this chapter. Despite his heavy duties in journalism, Deng Tuo was also active in academic circles, particularly in historical studies. This activity reflects the rich cultural and professional life enjoyed by establishment intellectuals in the early years of the PRC. These pleasures were as much a part of the propaganda state as ideological remoulding or socialist journalism. In Deng Tuo's case this academic work was intimately linked with his political commitments. Based on his work from the late 1940s in the Policy Research Office, Deng gave a series of bi-weekly lectures at Beijing University in the spring of 1950. He was a visiting professor and his course was on the economics of land reform.[81] It was an advanced course and Deng Tuo did not deal with his personal experiences in land reform. His announced goal was to provide the academic knowledge necessary to help address the practical problems of land reform underway around China at that very time and in which his listeners would likely participate. Interestingly, Deng quotes heavily from the statistical findings of Mao Zedong's rural surveys from the early 1930s, which were not openly published until the post-Mao period, as well as limited survey data by the KMT.[82] He gives a fairly detailed study of traditional class structure, labour organization, and land rent. Deng once again demonstrates his scholastic abilities by making admirable comparisons with the Junkers, the plantations of the American South, and the system of fixed harvest division between tenant and landlord (*métayage*), as well as other European examples of labour organization and rent systems. Deng's conclusions were historically significant as well as politically correct: the degree of monetization of land rent cannot determine historical stages, such as feudalism or capitalism, since a system of land rent is not equivalent to a mode of production. Both the organization of his lectures (facts, theories, and government policies over time) and their concern with rural economics parallel Deng's 1937 book, *A History of Famine Relief*.

Deng was fully engaged in his propaganda and administrative duties in the first years of the PRC, and his historical and poetic work suffered accordingly. However, in 1955 he was invited by the Chinese Academy of Science to become a member of its Chinese History Research Institute, and Deng was among 61 scholars appointed to its Department of Philosophy and Social Sciences in May 1955. Though much less active in historical research than establishment scholars such as Wu Han or Jian Bozan, Deng did publish a few detailed historical articles after 1949 and carried out original research on Ming-Qing social-economic history, which has been published since 1979.[83]

Deng Tuo's historical publications in the 1950s conformed to the conventional picture of politically motivated historiography in the PRC.[84] When historical circles were organized in 1955 to criticize the 'thought' of the famous liberal scholar, Hu Shi, Deng Tuo wrote a long article in the *People's Daily* on the social background of the *Dream of the Red Chamber* and the 'bourgeois' errors of Hu Shi's interpretation of this Qing dynasty novel.[85] Though clearly in the service of Mao's call to criticize Hu Shi, Deng's essay was part of his continued professional interest as an historian in studying the origins and development of the urban classes in the eighteenth century. This approach to the *Dream* was continued by Deng's history student, Liu Yongcheng, in the 1980s.[86]

Deng Tuo's major new historical publication in the 1950s was 'A Demonstration of the Initial Stages of Chinese Capitalism from the Wanli to the Qianlong Periods' [1573–1796], published in *Historical Research* in October 1956 as a contribution to the debates on the theory of the 'sprouts of capitalism' (*zibenzhuyi mengya*), a popular issue in the academic press between 1956 and 1958.[87] The long article was a detailed analysis of a coal mine in old Zhili province (near Beijing) and used several reproductions of commercial contracts that Deng had uncovered there as well as on-site inspections that one Western historian has noted 'would have made Marc Bloch proud.' On the basis of these new documents, Deng rather unsurprisingly concurred with Chairman Mao's thesis that there were indeed 'sprouts' in traditional China and that they were 'blocked' by the feudal system. Deng was, however, inclined to see the emergence of these sprouts as somewhat later than other historians argued and he saw the hand of the government, however self-servingly, as behind the stimulation of commercial activity in the early Qing.[88]

Though politically correct, this history essay is a good example of Deng Tuo's work as a professional historian. It sparked a friendly critique from a trio of other historians over academic and methodological issues, contesting in particular Deng's broad conclusions reached from a single mining company's records.[89] Within academia Deng Tuo, as in the 1930s, was not afraid to take controversial stands. Deng's history essay was of sufficient professional significance not only to have been drawn from heavily in a recent Western study of urban history, but also to be translated into French and published in *Annales* in 1967.[90] The professional significance and limitations of Deng Tuo's work as an historian are reflected, as well, in the use Western historians in the past twenty years have made of it. Deng's historical work is used somewhat grudgingly by James P. Harrison in his study of peasant rebellions, and by A. F. P. Hulsewé more explicitly on the origins of the Chinese Empire as the best of a bad lot, that is, the best that can be achieved under political constraints placed on historians by the CCP.[91] Other scholars have drawn from the data Deng collected, particularly in *Famine Relief* and his 'sprouts of capitalism' articles.[92]

Deng's documentary approach, more than his specific findings, is a significant influence on historiography in China today.[93] This is not surprising as he was a meticulous and empirically minded researcher. In the case of the study of the Mentougou coal mine near Beijing, Deng visited the site several times and organized meetings with locals, particularly old-timers, to gather documents from the proverbial attic as well as local archives. This was Deng's usual procedure, according to his only history student, Liu Yongcheng, now a prominent historian of the Qing period in the Chinese Academy of Social Sciences. According to Liu, Deng Tuo had at least four other similar documentary collection projects in the works during the 1960s, which the Cultural Revolution kept from publication. They have been edited and analysed by others and published in specialist history journals since 1979.[94]

Liu Yongcheng was Deng Tuo's graduate student, or assistant [*zhushou*], in the Chinese History Department of the Academy of Sciences (as it was known then). After graduating from university in Sichuan in 1957, Liu was assigned to Deng. Liu worked in Deng's office/study across the courtyard from the family's living quarters in the family compound in central Beijing. He and Deng rarely went to the offices of the Academy of Sciences, because Deng was too busy. So Liu worked with Deng's materials, which were kept in his house. From this Liu viewed Deng's home activities, which, as we shall see below, involved frequent visits from artists, poets, and antique collectors. Liu was more of a research assistant, helping the busy public servant to make the most of his limited time to do historical research. This is, of course, a traditional Chinese teaching method—to train the student through assistance to the teacher. Deng also personally corrected Liu's first article in 1958 in *Historical Studies* (and, we may presume, supported its publication in the prestigious journal). What Liu remembers most is Deng's fiercely empirical approach and his desire to unify Marxist theory with Chinese historical data in an undogmatic way, which, Liu adds, is precisely the approach of Jian Bozan.[95] Deng may have been empirical and fair-minded, but he was not thoroughly grounded enough in the history of the Qing to suit professional academics. A Swiss scholar, Hans Vogel, who uses the contracts from the coal mine which Deng unearthed, shares the complaint of Tang Mingsui (one of the trio who criticized Deng in the 1950s) and Cartier (who translated them into French) that Deng does not do justice to the materials he collected and that the article, in fact, looks hastily written.[96]

Deng's work in historical studies reflects a sort of 'amateur ideal'. His work has stood the test of time mostly for the important materials and occasional insight he provides. His theoretical work in history, beyond a common-sense faith in concrete evidence, was minimal. In a sense he was pre-professional, as the scholarly criticism laid against him by Tang

Mingsui and Vogel suggests. Deng had apparently long since forgotten the rules of historiography which he read in Seignobos's work in the 1930s. For Deng, history still contained the *dao*, or the moral lessons, for which Confucian historians had searched. But the content had changed: Marxist teleology and economic forces had replaced stable harmony and good or evil rulers. Here, too, we see in detail how Marxist thought 'fit' literati scholarship, thus grafting the German-Russian ideology onto the Chinese intellectual world. In Deng Tuo's hands, Marxist scholarship seems something less than a disjunctive break or revolution. It is more of an extension or adaptation of literati service in new circumstances.

Arts and Culture

Deng was equally active in his aesthetic interests, which were traditional, but he leaves us few traces of them for this period. His art was private, an enjoyment among friends and a relief from the tensions of work. The relative weight of Deng's activities in his social circles would change dramatically after 1957. Then, his work in the Central Party almost ceased and he was limited to editing a local theory journal and publishing light essays under various pen-names. Deng's artistic and aesthetic endeavours would expand, imbued with a new political significance in those years. But for the early 1950s, Deng's ambitions were more than satisfied by direct political work. He simply carved a space for himself, which the Party also allowed, in which he enjoyed poetry, calligraphy, and classical art. From the early 1950s Deng had started a serious collection of calligraphy and traditional Chinese paintings. His love was ancient paintings, and he haunted the antique shops and curio dealers in the back alleys of Beijing in search of them. In his spacious traditional courtyard home he entertained some of the finest traditional artists and connoisseurs of China, as well as aspiring literati painters. Wu Zuoren, Zhou Huaimin, Huang Zhou, and Xu Linlu counted amongst his colleagues. Xie Yaliao and Tang Yun from Shanghai and Yang Renkai from Liaoning (now director of the National Museum) visited to share in the refined activities. Deng would appear in print or on scroll with many of these gentlemen after 1957.[97]

Yang Renkai and Zhou Huaimin appeared in print in 1984 to honour their old cultural partner with the preface to a privately published colour catalogue, 'A Selection of Deng Tuo's Painting Collection'.[98] This beautiful collection, including Deng's erudite authentication of a Su Shi painting, serves as a testimony to his scholarly status and aesthetic refinement. The collection is a reminder of the collecting Deng did during the 1950s. This artistic connoisseurship has meanings both public and private beyond art itself. For the public the art collection contributes to Party goals of national pride and confirms Deng's status as a member of China's cultural elite. Amongst his fellow devotees of *siwen*—what Confucius called 'this culture of ours'—Deng's particular selection of art, his chops and his colophons, provide an esoteric commentary on the preservation and transmission of China's cultural heart and Deng Tuo's personality in relation to it. To the broader 'public' among China's elite, Deng's cognoscenti collection was his certification of elite cultural status; as for gentry collectors of art objects in the late imperial period, it served 'to mark off the truly cultivated and deserving from the aspiring but less-elevated.'[99]

Like the Yan-Zhao Poetry Society in the 1940s, Deng's connoisseurship in the 1950s supported regime goals. Deng Tuo wrote numerous lyrical essays (*sanwen*) and general essays on art history of only indirect political relevance after 1957 which reflect the themes raised by personal reminiscences of the early 1950s. His concern in these essays, some of which were translated and published in the English-language journal, *Chinese Literature*, included a political concern for the future of Chinese traditional landscape painting in socialist society, the proper role of the calligraphic arts, and the proper class analysis of poetry and paintings of natural scenery in socialist society.[100] In each his love for the art rests comfortably with his socialist themes.

A glimpse into this world is given by Sidney Rittenberg, who worked in Radio Peking in the 1950s and early 1960s under Mei Yi (also a family friend of the Deng household) and became a friend of the Deng family in his own right.[101] Rittenberg recalls delightful evenings with small groups of literati friends in Deng's traditional-style living room talking history and art, slowly unrolling beautiful scrolls, as Deng's learned and contented commentary moved the viewers along the scenes. Deng was a short man, lean, and somewhat frail from his tuberculosis and migraines. Yet, after hours of connoisseurship Deng Tuo would stand up from the scrolls and announce (perhaps for the benefit of his foreign friend) 'This is China's greatness, but I would throw it all away if the Party required it!' Such a posture struck Rittenberg less as a pose than a sign of true belief, particularly since Deng was otherwise a very proud man.[102] By the 1960s, Deng's personal art collection was well known among the Beijing elite. He donated a fair portion of it to the National Gallery in 1964 and the remainder was confiscated by Kang Sheng early in the Cultural Revolution (discussed in Chapters 4 and 5).

The relative neutrality of Deng's private artistic interests during these

3.3 Deng Tuo, 1956 (informal photo)

years is highlighted by the politically charged significance of his public art after 1958. These interests were a continuation of the model established in the Yan-Zhao Poetry Society in the 1940s. Deng perceived no conflict between his elite arts and proletarian culture. The elite could enjoy the high arts while the State popularized folk and proletarian art. This, too, was the 'two-track policy' Deng had enunciated for the arts in the 1940s. During the next decade Deng churned out his share of Party theory articles on politically correct literature. He wrote a series of three articles from 1945 to 1952 extolling the regime's version of Lu Xun, particularly as applied to the policy of popularizing literature among the masses.[103]

Deng Tuo's activities as a poet and calligrapher were, in traditional literati fashion, far less formal than the modern professional activities that marked his history work. His artistic work is characteristic of what Joseph Levenson described for scholar-painters in late imperial China as 'the amateur ideal'.[104] The parallel is significant in judging the nature of such traditional interests among establishment intellectuals in China. Deng Tuo clearly shared the eclecticism and connoisseurship of the

Ming dynasty literati, but his aesthetic delight did not extend to their formalism and in no way impeded his commitment to modern values of science and rational bureaucratic organization, not to mention Communist revolution.[105] Equally, Deng's high cultural pursuits did not interfere with his commitment to help the great majority of the Chinese people achieve a better economic and cultural life. Deng's approach was more like that of a Jesuit—culturally urbane, paternalistic, and humane but also orthodox and tireless in his efforts to serve the institution that he believed served the people.

Bureaucratic Maoism Before the Great Leap

Deng's decade of service to the CCP from 1946–56 gives a picture of the social experience and establishment values among transformational bureaucrats in the CCP before the traumatic events of the latter 1950s. These values and their associated style of administration characterize bureaucratic Maoism. While by no means the 'halcyon days' pictured in the historiography of China's post-Mao leadership, these years were a time of relative leadership harmony. Deng Tuo's approach to the public and private life of the intellectual combined traditional Chinese humanism and Confucian literati aspirations, May Fourth ideals about the role of science and the elite status of intellectuals, and Marxist-Leninist faith in the rule of the Party. This uneasy combination came from Deng's childhood, university, and base area experiences. Deng's work up to 1956 represents a further consolidation of that approach and may now be generalized as how Deng Tuo liked to live and work before being forced to cross Chairman Mao in 1957.[106] Bureaucratic Maoism of the mid-1950s also reveals the fault lines along which Maoism would split by the time of the Cultural Revolution. Deng's values would swing wildly to the 'left' in the Great Leap Forward, but he returned, chastened, to his earlier views by the early 1960s. He would then search for a new or renewed Party line, following the failure of the Leap. The difference after 1960 was that he was goaded into print by the radical policies of the Great Leap which he himself had supported. Before 1956 Deng did not comment openly very much on his values because they were largely standard operating procedure of the regime.[107]

Deng Tuo accepted Mao Zedong Thought as the orthodoxy of the CCP, although he took a rather more cautious, institutional, and restrained approach to the orthodoxy than the Chairman and his personal retinue. Deng Tuo viewed this adherence to Mao's writings as no obstacle to maintaining personal integrity or interests. He believed in ideological remoulding and ideological struggle, though for Deng these were cool and predictable transformations that would not fundamentally shake China's culture. This commitment failed to address the conflict between the two authorities *within* the Party on which Deng Tuo relied: the rationality of the 'managerial' Party committee system, with ideology as *method*, and the charisma of Mao's 'genius and wisdom', which made ideology a faith. Deng Tuo's approach did not admit to the possibility of differences between Party committees and Party leader. Nor did he see any threat to the individual from the Party. Thus, he saw no need for political institutions independent of the Party and never suggested them.

Deng Tuo saw himself as a culture bearer rather than a cog and screw in the revolution. Journalism for Deng Tuo was an honourable vocation and a form of public education under Party auspices. He taught his bureaucratic Maoist vision of a scientific, rational, and ordered social revolution based on a complex ideology best ministered by elites such as himself. Later, Deng would turn to popular discussions of Chinese art and culture, but his didactic tone would remain the same. Deng Tuo accepted Mao's cultural populism but did not accept Mao's inherent anti-intellectualism. It was one thing to have a common touch, but altogether another to denigrate learning. He was always a scholar (for which he had been taken to task in 1944 and would be again in 1957) and he was proud.

His work in journalism appears laudably professional, but professional skill was instrumental for Deng. His goal was political *education*. Propaganda was ill-served, Deng would repeat time and again, by poor research, shallow thinking, and sloppy writing. On the other hand, colleagues from *People's Daily* in the 1950s (such as Liu Binyan and Wang Ruoshui) do not recall Deng as a technical specialist—they would turn to others for hands-on work. Deng was a generalist and a motivating leader and the moral example to them.

Deng Tuo saved time and energy for cultural pursuits, and later publications, that strongly resemble the pastimes of the traditional scholar elite. He was proud of China's heritage of high culture including painting, poetry, and artifacts, and he encouraged others to enjoy them. Privately, such aesthetic pursuits were part of Deng's self-cultivation as a morally active scholar, as well as a self-defining act of elite status. Publicly, Deng's cultural output was an affirmation of Chinese nationalism and a further act of public education. Deng lived his two-track cultural policy under socialism and made no attempt to produce a monistic proletarian culture for all classes.

Deng Tuo's values and approach to public life, his bureaucratic

Life in the Establishment 157

Maoism, were to be sorely tested in the next few years. The wide range of activities described by Deng Tuo's social circles were not, however, violently shaken. The social system for establishment intellectuals would endure the Hundred Flowers rectification, the anti-Rightist purges, and even the Great Leap famine. Deng would be squeezed out of political and journalistic influence after 1962, but 'space' remained in his aesthetic activities, to which his energies shifted. Deng Tuo's political life became increasingly oppressive, but his affluent social life and elite pastimes remained untouched. His children went to the most exclusive schools.[108] His art collection grew.

Lest one think that such scholars were ever anti-Maoist or at least not very interested in Mao, we need to remember that Deng Tuo and his colleagues lionized the Chairman. Disillusionment among establishment ranks certainly set in, but later, at least well into the Cultural Revolution and in some cases not until the fall of the second heir-apparent, Lin Biao, in 1971. For China's Deng Tuos Mao was the paternalistic sage-leader who justified their own status as mandarins. Mao was, in Deng's idealized version, himself (and all socialist scholar-officials) writ large, just as Deng had painted Nie Rongzhen in 1942. All the more reason for Deng Tuo and his colleagues not to anticipate conflict between the elite and their leader. As the Confucian literati of the Qing had idealized the Kangxi Emperor as the embodiment of Confucian virtues, so Deng Tuo idealized Mao Zedong. Deng Tuo and the establishment did not anticipate that the charismatic leader they had helped create might turn on them.

The power of Deng Tuo's social world of the CCP establishment is important to remember. It was the social machine that reproduced CCP cadres who would after the Great Leap no longer so innocently or immediately obey Mao's will. Its members had the social prestige to reinterpret the supreme leader and the literati staff to run things their way. Their preferences led toward the managerial model of bureaucratic Maoism. This social system was the root of what Mao attacked when he attacked 'capitalism' inside the Party in the Cultural Revolution. Intellectuals in the PRC establishment had the cultural capital to resist Mao's policies. Like the Qianlong Emperor in the eighteenth century, Mao feared his cultivated bureaucrats were thwarting his wishes and lying to his face.[109] The example of Deng Tuo shows that, like their Qing literati forebears, establishment intellectuals under Mao sought to serve their anointed leader loyally but were pulled by the realities of their social experience in the state bureaucracy away from the charismatic authority of their leader to routine measures of administration. Worse than infidels, they would become to Mao heretics.

NOTES

1. This was particularly true in press and propaganda, though the full version of the propaganda *xitong* in China was more extensive than the Soviet model. See Chang (1997).
2. Unfortunately I have been unable to obtain information on Deng's personal relationship with Peng Zhen. Deng's client status under Peng Zhen is confirmed both by Peng's veritable rescue of Deng in 1958 from Mao's wrath and by personal comments by Deng's surviving colleagues (personal communication with author). Deng supported Peng's organizational approach to Party government from the Jin Cha Ji days. My impression, however, is that Peng Zhen was no intellectual and was not personally close to Deng Tuo. As Frederick Teiwes (1988) has noted, the top CCP elite kept their distance from their subordinates. Deng Tuo was most certainly not in the top elite or its inner circle of household aides. That is, Deng was of the outer court, not the inner court.
3. For instance Deng planned to publish a collection of anecdotes on Fujian literati; see YDT: 208.
4. This does not mean that the Chinese propaganda system was identical to the Soviets'. For a careful comparison and contrast for the 1950s, see Chang (1997) and the discussion in the Introduction above.
5. An ad on p. 1 of the 1 Mar. 1946 *Jin Cha Ji Daily* announces the inaugural issue and an ad on p. 4 of the 8 Mar. issue gives this information.
6. It was published by its own publishing society and distributed by the Jin Cha Ji Branch of Xinhua shudian. See Kikuchi Saburo (1973: 264–6). Kikuchi gives a photograph of the vol. 1, no. 2 issue of 16 Mar. 1946, which indicates he at least had a copy of it and which may account for the two discrepancies in the listing of the editors between his account and my information. Based on the ad for vol. 1, no. 1 (1 Mar. 1946) advertised in the 1 Mar. 1946 *Jin Cha Ji Daily*, the editorial board included Cheng Fangwu and Zhang Ruxin as editors-in-chief with 13 members of the editorial board (in the order given in the original): Zhou Yang, Zhang Ruxin, Cheng Fangwu, Deng Tuo, Xiao Jun, Xiao San, He Ganzhi, Sha Kefu, Ding Ling, Ai Qing, Liu Aifeng, Lü Ji, and Feng Suhai (alt. pronunciation: Feng Xiuhai). Kikuchi Saburo (1973: 265) does not list Zhang Ruxin as an editor, lists the board in a different order (by proper stroke order), and adds the name Yang Xianzhen. It is possible the board changed to one chief editor and 'alphabetical' listing of its members and that Yang Xianzhen arrived in town in the intervening weeks between issues 1 and 2, but it raises some questions.

   The *Press Yearbook 1984* (p. 627) lists *Beifang wenhua* among the publications of Jin Cha Ji, but lists no chief editor and lists only six members of the editorial board with no indication that other editors, as primary source material reveals, ever participated: Cheng Fangwu, Deng Tuo, Zhou Yang, Ding Ling, Sha Kefu, and Xiao Jun. This stands as yet another reminder of the limitations of current historical materials published in the PRC: they are unlikely to lie, to fabricate, or wildly to distort historical data, but they are likely to omit relevant information. They are likely to be strategically incomplete, that is, to omit inconvenient data, as in this case, the Maoist Zhang Ruxin, among others.
7. Advertised in the 22 Apr. 1946 *Jin Cha Ji Daily*, p. 1. The tables of contents of early issues appear in the *Daily*, and none show articles by Deng Tuo or his known pennames.

Life in the Establishment

8. Kikuchi Saburo (1973: 266).
9. Deng is listed with most of the other editors of *Northern Literature* and with many more names, including Zhang Chunqiao, later of 'Gang of Four' infamy. 'Huabei jiefang qu wenhua jie zhi zhengzhi xieshang huiyi dian' (Telegram from the Literary Circles of the North China Liberated Area to the Political Consultative Congress), printed in Chongqing's *Xinhua ribao*, 24 Jan. 1946, and signed in Kalgan; repr. in Zhang Jinglu (1954–9: iii. 130–1).
10. Deng Tuo reappeared in print cautiously. His first major article since his disappearance from the *Daily* in the spring of 1944 was a 'rectified' paean in Feb. 1945 to a Jin Cha Ji labour hero, Nie Rongfu. See DTWJ: iv. 290–8.
11. Deng's experience here parallels the Yan'an experience. For the reappearance of Party literary speakers after thought reform in the 1942–4 Yan'an rectification, see Goldman (1967: ch. 2); Cheek (1984b: 48–50).
12. This cohesive leadership was really a sort of 'united front' among inner-Party factions under the total but restrained control of the newly dominant 'Chairman Mao'. See Teiwes and Sun (1995) and Wylie (1980: 270 ff.).
13. 'Lun ruhe tigao yibu' (On How to Rise a Step), repr. in DTWJ: i. 269–71. Deng developed these ideas for journalism in two further essays in July and Aug. 1948; see DTWJ: i. 272–9.
14. 'Xian jieduan geming jiben renwu: tongyi zhanxian yu heping minzhuyi xin jieduan' (Basic Revolutionary Tasks in the Current Stage: The New Stage of the United Front and Peaceful Democracy), repr. in DTWJ: i. 194–209. I have not located the original version or determined if it indeed was openly published, but the content (as in long citations of 'On Coalition Government', use of Sun Yat-sen's 'minzhu' and 'minsheng' vocabulary, and the nationalistic line of argument which stresses opposition to 'imperialism' from abroad and 'feudalism' at home) leads me to believe it was intended for urban audiences or at least for the training of cadres for working with urban constituencies. Mao's 'On Coalition Government' appears in Mao Zedong (1977: iii. 205–70) and is well analysed in Wylie (1980: 270–1). For the great importance of a revised United Front for the CCP, see Mazur (1997).
15. This chronology appears at the end of Wang Bisheng (1986: 242), but Wang does not discuss these events in the text. Deng's Lu Xun writings are reprinted in DTWJ: i. 392–6. In June 1948, Deng bid farewell to his old paper in the last issue of *Jin Cha Ji Daily* (14 June 1948, p. 1), which was combined with other base areas papers to form the North China *People's Daily*. See *Jin Cha Ji ribao*: 277–8; DTWJ: i. 280–1.
16. Liu Lantao *et al.* (1984). Hu Xikui was one of the CCP cadres released from Caolanzi Prison in Beiping in 1936 along with Bo Yibo, An Ziwen, Yang Xianzhen, *et al.* through 'false confessions' repudiating the CCP. This practice was approved by the CC at the time and by the 1945 7th Party Congress and many of these '61 Prisoners' (later denounced in the Cultural Revolution) took up high Party posts in the 1936–45 period. See Yang Xianzhen and Guan Shan (1980: 19) and Tai Huaiji (1982).

The dating here of Deng Tuo's probable return to favour is as speculative as the guess that he might have fallen out of favour based on his apparent demotions. Two things are interesting about the list Liu Lantao gives of those involved in editing the 1947 edition of Mao's *Selected Works*: Deng Tuo, chief, and Yang Xianzhen, Xiao San, Yao Yilin, Ding Ling, Sha Kefu, and others (not listed). First, there were others, such as Yang and Yao, who could have edited the edition, so we may guess Deng was not appointed due to a lack of an alternative. Second, there is a large overlap

160   *Life in the Establishment*

with the board of *Northern Literature*, suggesting both the importance of the literary journal and the prominent position of the intellectuals listed on both.

17. Information on Deng Tuo's appointments comes from 'Deng Tuo tongzhi zhuidao hui zai Jing longzhong juxing' (A Memorial Meeting for Comrade Deng Tuo Solemnly Held in Beijing), YDT: 1–4, tr. in FBIS-CHI, 6 Sept. 1979, pp. L1–L3; *Zhongguo wenxuejia cidian* (1982: ii. 111); Zhang Shuzheng (1985: 51–3); and Wang Bisheng (1986: 127 and 242).
18. A useful chart of the range of activities covered in the propaganda *xitong* in the 1950s appears in Chang (1997: 81). See also Liu (1975: 36–8).
19. This is the assessment of Suzanne Pepper in her detailed study (1978: 229–30, quote from p. 277). A broader overview echoing her findings is given by Lyman Van Slyke in Fairbank and Feuerwerker (1986: vol. 13, pt. 2, pp. 751–7).
20. Hinton (1966).
21. Pepper (1978: 316–20).
22. An important part of the 1947–8 adjustment of land reform, in which the *Jin Cha Ji Daily*'s editorial voice was prominent, was the practice of reaching outside the Party to local peasants to contribute to the rectification of Party cadres. See Pepper (1978: 314). This case is interesting because it is one instance of a practice from Jin Cha Ji which Deng Tuo would *not* support later in the PRC. When Mao reached outside the Party to intellectuals to help rectify Party cadres in 1957 Deng Tuo would resist. We do not know if Deng opposed the 1947 policy, but it was directed at cadres below his own level while the 1957 rectification was directed squarely at higher Party bureaucrats such as himself.
23. 1950*a*, repr. in DTWJ: i. 409–68. See discussion later in this chapter of the contents of his 1950 lectures.
24. Wang Bisheng (1986: 130). This continues his earlier ghost-writing for General Nie Rongzhen before 1944.
25. On the importance of *tifa* in CCP propaganda and politics, see Schoenhals (1992).
26. Wang Bisheng (1986: 130).
27. 'Memorial Meeting' (YDT: 2); Zhang Shuzheng (1985: 53), and Wang Bisheng (1986: 128 ff.). Previous sources give a slightly different chronology, with Deng serving as deputy director (*fu shezhang*) from 1949 to 1952 under veteran CCP journalist from Jin Cha Ji, Fan Changjiang, and Yang Fangzhi. See Klein and Clark (1971); *Zhongguo wenxuejia cidian* (1982: 110–11); *Press Yearbook 1984*: 626. Ding Yilan and more recent sources insist Deng was editor-in-chief in 1949. However, Deng's move from a dormitory to his fine home in 1952 may indicate a promotion. See Ding Yilan (1984*b*: 11).
28. Ding Yilan (1984*b*: 11). Liu Yongcheng, Deng's history student in the 1950s, says Deng moved into this house sometime before 1954 (personal communication, Mar. 1985). In 1957 Deng moved to a similar traditional-style house in Suian hutong, just north of Dongdan market in central Beijing. I visited the latter home, now belonging to *People's Daily* and housing three families, in May 1986 with Ding Yilan and officials from the paper.
29. This is exactly the tension Frederick Teiwes has described for Central Committee leaders between 'normative' and 'prudential' rules of behaviour. See Teiwes (1984: 96).
30. Yan Ling (1980: 111–13); staffing figures given on p. 111.
31. Liu Binyan (1990: 55).
32. See also Liu Binyan (1983*a*) and interview with author (Jan. 1989). Mao lampooned

Life in the Establishment 161

Deng's compliance with the wishes of various leaders in his Feb. 1957 talk with journalists; see translation in MacFarquhar, Cheek, and Wu (1989: 199).

33. The early years of the PRC are now considered its 'golden years' of leadership unanimity by the Party. See Teiwes (1993: introd.). For the underlying tensions, see Sullivan (1986–7: 622–3 ff.).
34. 'Zhongguo qingnian he Yun Daiying' (1949). On the historical Yun Daiying in the early CCP, see van de Ven (1991: ch. 1). In the confident spirit of open debate on such constrained topics of the day, Wen Jize, a journalist active in the Yan'an *Jiefang ribao* in the 1940s, contributed a long critical letter correcting dates and issues in Deng's article; Wen Jize (1949: 23). Deng's essay was reprinted in 1980c: 18–183; not included in DTWJ.
35. 1950b. A year later he published another endorsement (1951c). In between he published yet another piece (1951b).
36. 1951a. Deng's title essay appears on pp. 8–18, and his 'Chedi pipan mingling zhuyi' appears on pp. 38–51. The essay on fatalism had first appeared in *Xuexi* on 1 Oct. 1950, pp. 14–18. Among the other contributors to the 1951 pamphlet are: Yang Wen on the youth corps' relations with youth in general, Yang Xianzhen on Mass Line problems, Wu Jiang on revolutionizing cadre work style, Zhao Tingxin on summarizing the study of Mass Line questions, Liu Qing on Mass Line in land reform, and Li Shiyue on his personal experiences in Mass Line work.
37. DTWJ: i. 86–100. See Schwarcz (1986: 262–6). Other standard articles from the early 1950s by Deng appear in DTWJ: i.
38. 1952; extract printed in Zhang Jinglu (1954–9: iv. 126–9).
39. DTWJ: i. 225–32; tr. in *CB*, 285 (13 May 1954), 13–18. Throughout this time Deng appeared frequently in the press as one of China's leading journalists—hosting foreign guests, chairing meetings of the Journalists' Association, travelling to Moscow and Warsaw, and attending numerous ceremonial meetings such as being noted at a film screening. See Union Research Institute (Hong Kong), biographical card file, 1950–6. This service is based on cuttings from *Xinhua* (New China) *News* releases from Beijing.
40. Teiwes (1979: 106 ff.); *Zhonghua renmin gongheguo dashiji* (1983: 11).
41. 'Zhonggong zhongyang guanyu zai baozhi'.
42. Teiwes (1979: 106 ff.). A description of these campaigns appears in Barnett (1964: 125–71).
43. 1951c. This essay is discussed in Wang Bisheng (1986: 136–8), but has not been included in DTWJ. The editors presumably wished to avoid any association with the 'ideological struggle' favoured by leaders in the Cultural Revolution.
44. 1951c; repr. in DTWJ: i. 111–21.
45. 1951c: 8 or DTWJ: i. 120–1.
46. This same 'soft' version of ideological remoulding to which intellectuals must ultimately submit was delivered to scientists by Chen Boda in a speech on 18 July 1952, published as a pamphlet (Chen Boda 1953). The centrality of dialectical materialism and historical materialism in Deng's thinking is clear from his essays in 1933 and 1941, discussed in Chs. 1 and 2, and his 1950s essays discussed in this chapter. Here Deng is representative of broader ideological trends in the CCP, particularly the identification of dialectical materialism with positive science. See James Williams's (1994) discussion of Chen Boda's speech.
47. Teiwes and Sun (1995) provide a balanced assessment of the excesses of the 'rescue campaign' purges and Mao's repudiation of such inquisitions by 1944.

48. This solves one of the constituent problems of 'national dependency' as modelled by Jowitt (1978), i.e. the alienation of local elites from local culture.
49. 1951a; cited in Wang Bisheng (1986: 140).
50. 'Zai *Renmin ribao* jizhe huiyi shangde tanhua zhaiyao' (Extracts from a Talk at a Meeting of *People's Daily* Reporters), dated 21 Oct. 1953; DTWJ: i. 282–4. I have not located a contemporary edition of this text, but one may assume the extracts have been selected by the editors of his *Works* to conform to the impression of Deng they wish to present. Nonetheless, the extracts are consistent with Deng's earlier and later published views, from his 1944 journalism speech to *Evening Chats* in the early 1960s.
51. DTWJ: i. 284. Deng's complaints about unnecessary technical errors and formulaic articles were repeated for the New China News Agency in Feb. 1954, 'Xinhua she dangzu guanyu Xinhua she disanci quanguo shewu huiyi de baogao' (The NCNA's Party Group Concerning the Report of the NCNA's Third National Conference), in *Zhongguo gongchandong xinwen*: ii. 268–70.

    Feng Zhi, born in Hebei in 1905, was a poet active in the New Culture Movement at Peking University, where he studied from 1921–7. After studying in Germany in the 1930s he taught at South-West United University in Kunming and stayed on to teach in Beida's Foreign Language Department after 1949. *Dong Ou zaji* (Random Notes on Eastern Europe) was published in Beijing by People's Literature Press in 1951. See Ding Guocheng, Yu Congyang, and Yu Sheng (1986: i. 111–13). Alexander Herzen (1812–1870) is one of the famous pre-Marxian Russian revolutionaries. Herzen was active in the 1848 Paris Commune, but is best known as a publicist and essayist, particularly for his magazine *The Bell*, published in London but influential among the intelligentsia back in Russia in the 1850s. Herzen's essays have been described as 'romantic' and 'with a streak of moderation'. See Chamberlin (1973 edn.: i. 22–3).
52. Deliusin (b. 1923) had graduated from Moscow University in 1949, having studied Chinese. In fact, he had been a translator for a Soviet military delegation in Harbin from Dec. 1948 to Aug. 1949. He arrived in Beijing at the end of Dec. 1950 to take up his work for *Pravda*. He was back in Moscow by Feb. 1954 to greet Deng Tuo. Deliusin would visit China several more times over the next decade and Deng Tuo would pay him an extended visit in Moscow (while seeking medical treatment) in early 1956. Deliusin became an academic specialist on the early period of the CCP, focusing on land reform in the 1920s and 1930s. His work follows orthodox Soviet standards. His teacher was Voitinsky. Deliusin material based on interview with author, 3 Feb. 1988, and his talk at the Fairbank Center, Harvard, 8 Feb. 1988.
53. For an excellent analysis of these events using newly available materials, see Teiwes (1990).
54. 1954; repr. in DTWJ: i. 285–302. Citations here from the first version, published in *Zhongguo gongchan*. Deng's speech is dated simply 1954 and DTWJ: i. 285 adds 'Speech given at a national newspaper work conference.' Internal evidence indicates the speech must be after March and before 'the second half of the year' (1954: 327 and 343). *Zhongguo gongchan* also provides a speech from May 1954 to this Propaganda Work Conference concerning '*gaijin*' and other issues similar to Deng's speech (ii. 302–18). Finally, no other likely meeting between April and June is on record according to Lieberthal and Dickson (1989: 21).
55. As editor of *People's Daily* it was appropriate for Deng to play such a role. The official Central Committee resolution, which did not come out until 17 July 1954, exactly echoes Deng's points. See *Zhongguo gongchan* (ii: 319–29). Deng's speech

Life in the Establishment 163

is also the only policy speech by a leader selected by *Zhongguo gongchan*, vol. 3 on journalism for 1954.
56. Note the parallel to Deng's summary of journalism work in 1938, mentioned in Ch. 2. On the distinction between 'educational journalism' and the 'informational journalism' more common to Western societies, see Cheek (1989a: 48–9).
57. 1954: 339 and 343.
58. 1954: 342 and 329.
59. 1954: 329.
60. 1954: 332–3.
61. This is the subject of the final section of his speech (1954: 342–4).
62. 1954: 337.
63. 1954: 332. The resolution is reprinted in *Zhongguo gongchan*: ii. 5–7 (discussed above).
64. A good example of such idealism in the early 1950s, following the success of the CCP in gaining national power, and in 'thwarting American imperialist ambitions in Korea', is given in the early chapters of Yue Daiyun's autobiography (Yue Daiyun and Wakeman 1985); on the origins of this powerful community of belief in Yan'an, see Apter and Saich (1994).
65. 1954: 323–4 and 337–9.
66. 1955b; repr. in DTWJ: i. 308–30. I use the People's University edition, which dates it as 1955. DTWJ, which makes an unannounced revision of the text, dates it 1956. Wang Bisheng (1986: 155) erroneously dates it to 1954. Internal evidence shows the talk must be after Aug. 1955 (1955b: 329).
67. 1955b: 328. Deng's colleagues in the post-Mao period recall his distaste for daily editorials, quoting him as saying they were unnecessary. One presumes Deng changed his mind after 1955. See Hu Jiwei, quoted in Lu Keng (1985).
68. 1955b: 331. This has been cut from the reprint in DTWJ: i. 310–11 without notice.
69. 1955b: 338–9. Ding Yilan has identified the 1 Oct. 1952 editorial as written by Deng Tuo. He does not identify himself in this speech. This is a most interesting example, since it touches on the delicate question of Mao's title. The text I use was printed in 1964, hardly a time to add this to the text! Deng's use of the example in 1955 probably reflects Party policy to tone down the worship of Mao. See Sullivan (1986–7: 617–22) and Teiwes (1986).

The party leader who vetted the editorial could have been Mao or propaganda department chief Lu Dingyi. I suspect it was Mao's sometime secretary and propaganda terminology (*tifa*) specialist, Hu Qiaomu. A number of similar *tifa* corrections from the 1950s are included in *Tantan baozhi gongzuo*: 174–88. Michael Schoenhals (1992) convincingly attributes these anonymous tips to Hu Qiaomu (and gives further information on *Tantan*).

70. 1955b: 343. There are certainly more such reflections by Deng which have not yet become available, such as various internal talks at *People's Daily* from this period. See Wang Bisheng (1986: 158–9).
71. See Wu Guoguang (1994).
72. YDT: 6.
73. These conditions are covered in detail in MacFarquhar (1974: 15–38). New views in Teiwes and Sun (1995) and Kuang (1994: ch. 3).
74. MacFarquhar (1974: 39–56).
75. Deliusin (interview with author, 1988); Union Research Service (Hong Kong), Biographical Service, No. 777, 28 May 1963.
76. Liu Binyan (1990: 56–7) and interview with author (28 Oct. 1988, Harvard). The

contrasting impact of this trip on Deng and Liu Binyan, a generation younger, is instructive. Unlike Deng, Liu could not accept the 70/30 assessment of Mao, and rather than the cautious Deliusin it was the muckraking reportage writer Valentin Ovechkin whose exposé, *Everyday Life in the District*, served as the model for Liu's own notorious Hundred Flowers story, 'The Inside News of the Newspaper'. See Liu Binyan (1990: 57–9) and Nieh (1981: 411–71).

77. The only available documentation from the Central Committee on this is, in fact, dated Aug. 1956, a month after the change. See 'Zhonggong zhongyang pizhuan'. One must presume that prior approval was made and that this document (discussed below) is a document circulated at the 7th Plenum of the 7th Central Committee on 22 Aug., since it begins with 'we have given you a copy of the *People's Daily* editorial committee's report for reference' (p. 483).
78. MacFarquhar (1974: 77); Wang Bisheng (1986: 144–6).
79. 'Zhonggong zhongyang pizhuan': 483–4.
80. Wang Bisheng (1986: 149).
81. The remaining text is based on a student's lecture notes from Mar. through June 1950. Deng made corrections on these. See 1982, repr. in DTWJ: i. 409–68. Zhang Youren, a professor at Beijing University, edited this posthumous publication.
82. Mao's rural surveys had been available in internal (*neibu*) editions for cadre study since at least 1941. One survey, which shows the pattern Deng Tuo was copying, has now been translated with commentary; see Mao Zedong (1990) and Thompson (1989).
83. See sections on Deng's historical work in reminiscences in YDT: 158–83; Cheek (1981: 480–1).
84. Feuerwerker (1968a).
85. 1955a; repr. in *Hu Shi sixiang* (1955: 349–63). It was also included in Deng's 1959 *Jige wenti* collection (1959: 158–80) and its 1979 edn. (167–88). It was also included in the famous 3-vol. set on 'sprouts of capitalism', *Zhongguo zibenzhuyi* (1957: i. 69–90); see DTWJ: ii. 522–44.
86. Deng Tuo, 'Hong lou meng' (1979 edn. of *Jige wenti*: 182–4). On p. 183 Deng summarizes the significance of the 1678 code of the Hankow Rice Guild: 'This kind of guild (*hanghui*) solution obviously carried a new colour.' Deng is referring to the lack of native-origin requirements in the guild and is specifically arguing the development of an urban class (*shi min*). William T. Rowe, who has made a careful reading of Deng Tuo's history essays, uses this, perhaps a little enthusiastically (1984: 268), to defend his thesis of changes in 'personal identity' producing an urban class before Western contact. See also Liu Yongcheng (YDT: 144–50, esp. p. 147). Liu has published articles continuing Deng's themes (Liu Yongcheng 1979, 1981).
87. 1956b. It was reprinted, along with the critique by Tang Mingsui and others (below), in the 'sprouts collection'. It was also reprinted, with some corrections, in *Jige wenti* (1959: 181–231 and 1979: 189–234) and DTWJ: ii. 545–96.
88. 1956b: 30–1. William Rowe (1982: 79) makes the comparison to Marc Bloch's techniques. Rowe's review emphasizes the continuing impact of Deng's historiographical views today, especially on the role of mining as a leader in the economic changes of the period, in the recent writings of Peng Zeyi and Wei Qingyuan as well as the field in general (pp. 76 and 79–80). Rowe notes Deng Tuo's independent stand on periodization of 'sprouts', saying, 'Almost alone during the debates of the fifties, Teng T'o refused to acknowledge a date for the sprouting of capitalism in China earlier than about 1580, and he clearly was more comfortable speaking of its development in the eighteenth century' (p. 76).

Life in the Establishment 165

89. Tang Mingsui, Li Longqian *et al.* (1958). Both articles, along with Deng's earlier one on the *Dream of the Red Chamber*, were republished in the influential series on 'sprouts', *Zhongguo zibenzhuyi* (1957: i. 69–90; iii. 250–303).
    Zhang Lei, vice-director of the Guangdong Provincial Chinese Academy of Social Sciences, told me in early 1986 that Tang now teaches at Zhongshan University in Guangzhou and that Tang was friendly with Deng Tuo in the past and still respects his views. Thus the critique was 'academic', not political.
90. Rowe (1984); Cartier (1967). Cartier is now a researcher at the Centre Chine in the Maisons des Sciences de l'Homme, Paris.
91. Harrison (1969: 95); Hulsewé (1986: 105).
92. Chi Wen-shun (1965: 37 and 52–3), who cites Deng's study of famine relief (under the name Deng Yunte); Pierre-Etienne Will (1990: 252 and 261), who cites him as Deng Yunte and draws mostly from the third section of *Famine Relief* on government policy; and Rowe (1984: 73, 178–80, 267–8, 341–42). See also 1967.
93. Rowe (1982: 76). See also a 1983 Chinese review of historical trends which includes Deng's approach (Song Yuanqiang 1983).
94. Liu Yongcheng (YDT: 158–63). For instance, contracts, sales slips, and other records of the Qing period from the famous Wan Quan Tang medicine shop in Beijing which Deng collected were published by Liu in *Qingshi ziliao*, No. 1 (1980), 158–77.
95. Liu Yongcheng (interview with author, Chinese Academy of Social Sciences, Beijing, 1 Apr. 1983); Liu (YDT: 150–1); and Liu (interview with author, Cambridge, Mass., Feb. 1986). Liu worked with Deng through to Deng's death in 1966 and is now responsible for the publication of what is left of his teacher's historical research.
96. Hans Ulrich Vogel (personal communication, Apr. 1986); Cartier (1967: 50–2).
97. Ding Yilan (interview with author, Aug. 1981). Wang Bisheng (1986: 203 ff.) explores Deng's artistic activities in some detail.
98. *Deng Tuo zang hua xuanji*. My copy was given to me by Ding Yilan in 1986.
99. Naturally, the status certification of such 'traditional' artistic esoterica was contested by faith Maoists. Yet the pull of traditional certification through the arts is strong too in the PRC, as seen in the 1986 Deng Tuo poetry convocation discussed in the Preface above. The concept of 'gentry culture' and the quote about 'the truly cultivated' comes from Brook (1993: 14). See also Clunas (1991) and Bol (1992).
100. See 1961*d*; 1963*a*/1979*a*: 375–8; 1964*a*; *Chinese Literature* (Peking Foreign Languages Press), 1963 (nos. 8 and 9), 1964 (nos. 1 and 3). Several of the above are included in 1980*c*.
101. See Rittenberg and Bennett (1993).
102. Sidney Rittenberg, interviews with author (Cambridge, Mass., spring 1986 and Washington, DC, 21 Nov. 1991).
103. He also wrote in 1945 on the 'mass culture movement'; see DTWJ: i. 384–400.
104. Levenson (1968: i. 15–43).
105. See Deng's criticism of such formalism in the study and practice of calligraphy in 'Jiangdian shufa' (A Few Points on Calligraphy), YSYH/79: 376.
106. Deng Tuo's approach falls within the shared outlook of the establishment intellectuals considered in Cheek and Hamrin (1986: 7–11).
107. Thus, the description below will supplement an assessment of his pre-1956 activities with selections from later writings which elaborate Deng's values and assumptions.
108. E.g. Beijing No. 101 Middle School, attached to Peking University.

109. The concerns of the Qianlong Emperor and his bureaucratic servants are vividly documented and analysed in Kuhn (1990). Mao's anger at plodding bureaucrats (which his ideological term, 'bureaucratism', increasingly came to refer to) and especially Deng Tuo as 'pedant editor' of *People's Daily* are reflected in Mao's comments in MacFarquhar, Cheek and Wu (1989), esp. pp. 393–6, and his 'speaking note' to the famous 'On the Correct Handling of Contradictions Among the People' (pp. 131 ff.).

4

Maoism in Crisis: The Price of Engagement (1956–1960)

From 1956 Deng Tuo began to pay the price of his political engagement. By the summer of 1957 he was in serious trouble. The tensions embedded in his service to the CCP and the socialist revolution came to a head. The charismatic and managerial authority styles within the Party began to split and Deng found it increasingly difficult to balance the cog-and-screw side of his service with his role as culture bearer. Deng Tuo and his colleagues tried to resolve these increasingly acute tensions. Ultimately, however, they would fail. In 1956 the Party felt it was at the peak of its success. A decade later it would turn on itself in a disastrous fight.[1] What went wrong?

Maoism confronted its first crisis during the late 1950s and Deng Tuo was swept up in the middle of it. The CCP proved unable to cope with the challenges of the Soviet Thaw, rebellion in Eastern Europe, and domestic pressures resulting from the First Five Year Plan. The Yan'an composite of charisma and routine came apart and the constituent parts—the faith and bureaucratic orientations within Maoism—lost their mutually moderating roles within the CCP. Mao himself veered toward mass campaigns to solve the economic and bureaucratic problems of the day; the Party bureaucracy turned to hierarchy and routine. Deng Tuo swung back and forth between these emerging extremes, as did many in the revolutionary elite, opposing rash collectivization and public criticism of the Party but supporting the Party's brutal attack on liberals and Mao's utopian Great Leap Forward. By 1960 the worst had happened. The Party, with Deng Tuo as guilty as the rest, had led the country into disaster—famine, political persecution, and international isolation.

It was Mao who upset the delicate balance of policy goals, authority styles, and roles for the educated elite. As Mao veered wildly from shocking openness to ruthless repression to wild utopianism the Party was left to cope. This was not simply a matter of other Party leaders and officials resisting Mao. Indeed, the tragedy of this time is that for the most part leaders wanted to please Mao—from Liu Shaoqi to Central

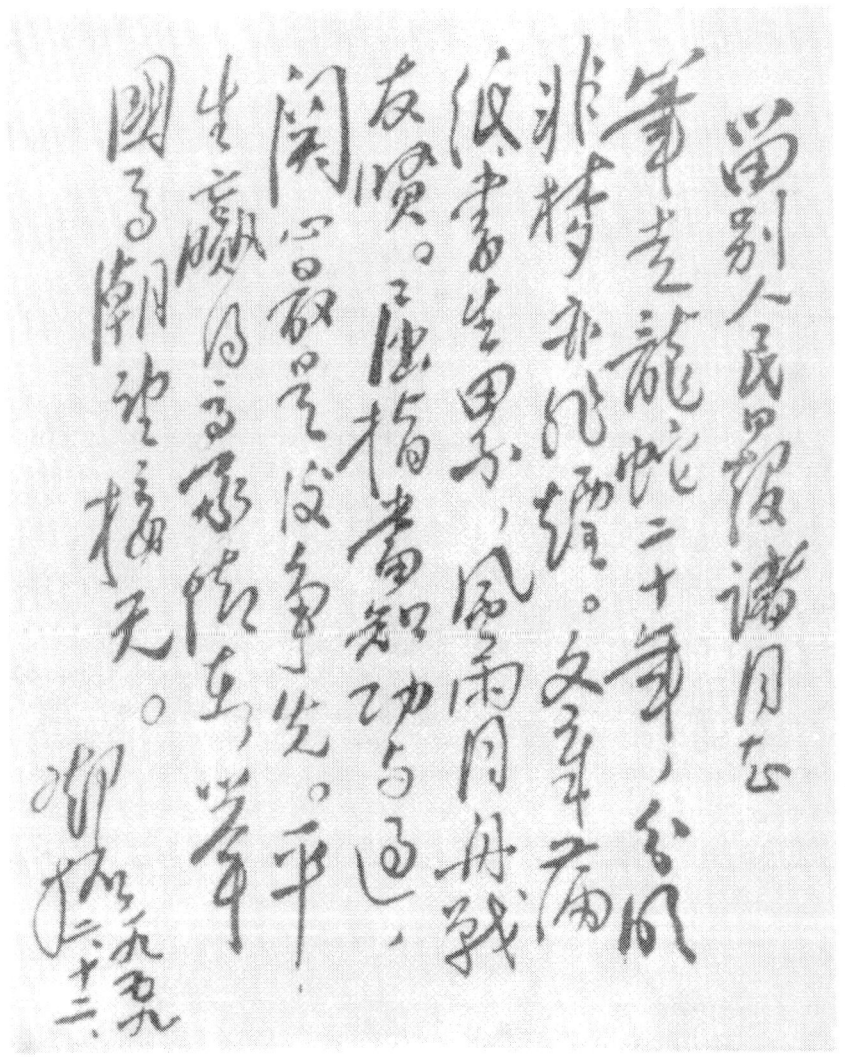

4.1 Deng Tuo's calligraphy for 'Taking Leave of Friends at *People's Daily*', February 1959

Party School director Yang Xianzhen to Deng Tuo and all down the line to local cadres. The profound charismatic legitimacy of Mao in their eyes is clearly reflected in the case of Deng Tuo, who strove to be loyal to his Chairman even in the face of the utter failure of the Chairman's radical policies and their contravention of so much that Deng Tuo held dear.

The Chairman's feelings, on the other hand, were not similarly constrained. He came to dislike Deng Tuo, with the predictable dire consequences. By spring 1957 he was incensed by the insubordination of *People's Daily* and decided to rid himself of his pesky 'pedant editor'. However, the Chairman, like many an emperor before him,[2] found that he could not simply make Deng Tuo disappear. Others protected Deng and made use of his talents.

For Deng Tuo these were miserable years. By attracting Mao's wrath he put his entire career under a cloud. While Deng had patrons to protect him, Mao, too, had minions who pestered Deng and finally brought him down. In Deng's writings these conflicts are pictured as social trends and behaviour patterns, what he would dub in 1957 as 'the politics of simpletons'. In his last days he would name individuals, such as Yao Wenyuan and Qi Benyu, but his tendency to criticize behaviours and 'work styles' was not simply prudent circumlocution. He was a Party theorist and felt it his duty to point out and rectify erroneous policies and especially the mindsets (what he called the 'ideological tendencies') behind them. He is an example, on the level of the senior theorist Ai Siqi, of what Joshua Fogel has identified as 'the second level of discourse in the world of Chinese Marxism-Leninism'. Deng Tuo likely disagreed with much of Ai's approach, but they were sociologically brothers, members of the scholar-cadre elite.[3]

Deng's troubles with Mao were part of the troubles which vexed the revolutionary elite of the PRC as Mao tried to revolutionize this elite according to his own more populist and egalitarian ideas. Party intellectuals like Deng Tuo, rather than ones like the writers Ding Ling or the younger Wang Meng, were high in the central Party propaganda apparatus and supported by Mao's colleagues. Deng Tuo sided consistently with those Party leaders who stressed collective leadership and the sanctity of Party rules. Thus, Deng Tuo's experiences parallel much of the experience of the Party as a whole.[4] Deng clearly supported the criticism of economic 'adventurism' in 1956, he had a complicated role in the Hundred Flowers campaign, he 'sat out' the anti-Rightist campaigns of 1957 and 1959 (at home working on his histories), and he supported the Great Leap.

Through these troubled years Deng Tuo maintained his role as a culture bearer who interprets the orthodoxy to the public and brings it to life among them. However, he was hampered by his commitment to two contrary roles for intellectuals. Deng's cog-and-screw role was his job as loyal Party propagandist; his culture bearer role was his status as Party theorist and cultural savant. Over the years following 1956 he continued to try to harmonize the two roles, but was unable to integrate them as he had in the 1940s. Deng Tuo had deeply felt opinions about the proper role of the Party and Party intellectuals which went beyond opportunistic obedience to this or that policy line. When confronted by an irrational Mao, Deng would attempt to interpret the Chairman in a managerial light, but his loyalty to the cog-and-screw role led him to support the disastrous Leap in 1958 and muted his criticism of it later. This reflected, of course, Leninist norms: unity in public and debate behind closed doors.[5] However, by 1958 and certainly by the now-infamous Lushan Plenum of August 1959, this deal no longer worked. 'Inner-Party democracy', the right to criticize policy inside Party channels, became impossible. Mao burned that lesson into the public mind with his purge of Peng Dehuai. He made the point to Deng Tuo by firing him from *People's Daily*.

Whatever encroachments Mao had made on Deng's political circles, his social circles (and comfortable elite daily life) were not diminished throughout these years. Deng's collection of paintings, calligraphy, and seals grew; he earned handsome royalties from his publications; and he gave more time to visits with artistic colleagues and travel to famous cultural and natural sights around China. This time, wealth, and collegial association was the social basis of his ideological 'space'.

As Deng's own energies were frustrated in the political arena, he shifted his efforts to this 'space'—his cultural activities. He began by seeking solace in his scholarly and artistic circles following his dismissal from *People's Daily* in summer 1957. By the next year there was an explosion of Deng's scholarly and literary work. More strikingly, he began to adopt a strongly traditional-looking scholarly style in public. While still loyalist in spirit and socialist in tone, the weight of Deng's artistic activities shifted to aesthetic interests and more public displays of his cultural prowess. By 1960 Deng would travel to the heartland of Neo-Confucian gentry culture, the Wuxi area in the lower Yangzi region, famous for its Ming dynasty scholar-critics. There he would consult his literati oracles, pen loyalist poems, and prepare to shift from troubled introspection to renewed public activism. In 1961 Deng Tuo would use this revived scholarly style as a vantage point from which to press a critique of 'ultra-Leftism'. The prerequisite for this cultural critique of the Great Leap in the early 1960s was both the *need*—political failure and demotion—and the *cultural space*—the cadre as culture bearer endowed with a political legitimacy at least partially independent of Party certification. These two developments were the product of Deng Tuo's participation in the crisis of Maoism.

The 1956 Oppose Adventurism Debate

The first indication of Deng Tuo's association with policies within the CCP that did not fully enjoy Mao's support came in June 1956 when Finance Minister Li Xiannian outlined the economic problems facing the nation as a result of Mao's agricultural and industrial 'leap', the mini-Leap of 1955–6. The 16 June *People's Daily*, under Deng Tuo's editorship, reported the speech and emphasized Li's new slogan, 'Oppose impetuosity and adventurism [*maojin*].' Since March, the *People's Daily* had been warning cadres 'to work according to circumstances', and in May the Central Committee had devised the new slogan, which added 'oppose adventurism', in an effort to cool down local Party cadres.[6] Li Xiannian had simply taken this new Party slogan to the public. On 20 June the *People's Daily* devoted a front-page editorial to the question: 'One Must Oppose Conservatism and Oppose Impetuosity.'[7] This editorial was drafted by Deng as editor, revised by Lu Dingyi, director of the CC's Propaganda Department, and others, and finally vetted and passed by Liu Shaoqi. Mao, when given a copy, simply wrote *bukanle*, 'did not read.'[8] One can easily see why Mao may not have wished to read the editorial.[9]

The editorial blamed the gravity of the impetuosity problem on high-level cadres who pushed for things to be done overnight with disregard of that catchword of Leninism, *objective conditions*. 'What is rightist conservatism and what is impetuosity? These questions have an objective standard. It is what is possible in objective practice.' The editorial, which bears the mark of Deng Tuo's well-known frank style, says that the mini-Leap's slogan, 'more, better, faster, and more economically' would be maintained, but that

in our actual work we should carefully and on the basis of facts consider what can be done more and fast, what cannot be done more and fast; what can be done more and fast now, what can be done more and fast in the future; how to economize appropriately, and how to achieve good quality while ensuring quantity, speed, and economy.[10]

Two themes which Deng Tuo was to press in the 1960s appear in the editorial—that a lack of 'penetrating investigation' leads to uninformed policy and that the ideological tendency toward over-hasty advances is deep-set 'and must be regularly watched by us hereafter.'[11] Deng Tuo's editorial, according to the rules he laid out in 1955, spoke for the collective leadership and its distaste for 'adventurism'. The retreat prevailed through the rest of the year under Zhou Enlai and Chen Yun, and even featured in one of the provincial mini-rectifications under way in the summer of 1956.[12]

Mao later took personal offence at the 'oppose adventurism' policy and the *People's Daily*'s role in promoting it. He criticized the policy in all but name in his speech to the Third (Enlarged) Plenum of the Eighth Central Committee on 9 October 1957, claiming that the ideal of 'more, better, faster, and more economical results' was swept away in 1956 by comrades who felt such heroic efforts were 'rash'.[13] He may have lectured the *People's Daily* staff as early as 1956, but by January 1958 at the Nanning Conference he was forthright in his anger, saying 'Why should I read what curses me?'[14] Mao singled out Deng Tuo for criticism, saying, 'Comrade [Deng Tuo] need not have come to this meeting, the ice in the Arctic cannot be broken. [Deng Tuo] is a good man, he's just incapable. I say he is a professor running the newspaper, a pedant running the paper, and [I] have said in the past that he is a dead man running the paper.'[15] Mao expanded those comments in a talk to the *People's Daily* staff in January 1958, complaining that the editorial quoted him out of context, and really opposed 'Leftism' while pretending to oppose 'Rightism'. Mao asked, ominously, 'Have you opposed Rightism or not?' and concluded, 'In the future do not raise "oppose adventurism", absolutely do not raise [it].'[16]

Deng Tuo's fall from grace occurred over the year between the summers of 1956 and 1957. Deng was nominated to the Eighth Central Committee, but withdrew his name before voting. It appears that in the increasingly tense political atmosphere, Deng's old 'errors' from the 1930s and 1940s returned to haunt him.[17] Something was going wrong for Deng; as the successful editor of *People's Daily* he was due a promotion. Whether some still-hidden competitor set Deng back or some leader decided to keep him down, we do not know. However, no evidence has come to light that Mao had a hand in Deng's exclusion from the Central Committee. Mao's personal interest in punishing Deng would come later.

The Hundred Flowers Campaign

The Party began the Hundred Flowers policy in early 1956 but by the end of the year, all the blandishments, the promises, the reformatting of the *People's Daily* to include more *zawen* and commentaries, the forums and the pay rises, failed to entice China's chastened intelligentsia to speak up. They had seen critical intellectuals pilloried by the Party from Wang Shiwei in 1942 to Yu Pingbo in 1951 to Hu Feng in 1955. At the

Maoism in Crisis

same time, local Party leaders quickly realized that *they* would be the object of such criticisms, not the top leadership, and thus did all they could do to keep the intellectuals' fears alive (for example, Ke Qingshi in Shanghai shut down the remaining non-Party press). The Eighth Party Congress in September 1956 focused the Party's attention on the shift from class struggle to economic development and the Hungarian uprising in October revitalized the lessons of the spring: the educated elite of the country must be brought on board. Mao chose one way to do this; the majority of the Party apparatus chose another.

The Party's approach to the Hundred Flowers in 1956 and early 1957 amounted to a Chinese socialist version of Vatican II—an end to the 'Latin Mass' and an introduction of lively trappings from contemporary society, but no fundamental change in dogma or authority. Deng Tuo's own contributions are typical of this 'academic Hundred Flowers'. In the summer of 1956, Deng wrote an engaging piece of reportage on a handicraft workshop in Beijing, 'Putao Chang'.[18] Here the senior editor hit the streets as a common reporter, talking with everyday folk and writing a homey 'human interest' piece on the Chang family, who make such lovely handicrafts. One goal of the establishment version of Hundred Flowers, then, was to lessen bureaucratic elitism by making senior cadres do some basic-level work *in their specialities*—in factories, offices, or farms. In October Deng published a long historical essay on the labour contracts and other commercial agreements used at the Mengtougou coal mines outside Beijing in the eighteenth century. It was detailed, scholarly, and refreshingly open about the Party line on periodization.[19] Intellectuals, then, were to explore more freely their professional interests within the broadening confines of Party forbearance.

Deng's ideas on the role of journalism under the Hundred Flowers are most clearly recorded in his advice to Xu Zhucheng, the veteran non-Party editor of Shanghai's intellectual paper, *Wen Hui Bao*. The paper had been 'voluntarily' shut down in May 1956 for a mix of national goals (reduction of excess newspapers) and local interests (Shanghai Party chief Ke Qingshi did not like the liberal paper). Xu and his staff had been reassigned *en masse* to a new publication, *Teacher News*, in Beijing.[20] However, just a few months later the Central Party decided to revive *Wen Hui Bao* and Xu was called in to run the new paper. As part of his preparations, Xu turned to Deng Tuo, whom he had not only admired as an educated and reasonable Party leader in journalism but who had only a month earlier expressed his regrets on the shutdown of the paper. Around mid-July 1956 Deng Tuo invited Xu and his colleagues to his new home in Jinyu Alley off Wangfujing Street and gave them a surprisingly frank and detailed brief on what the new *Wen Hui Bao*'s mission under the Hundred Flowers should be.²¹ Deng saw the paper, which was ostensibly an independent publication, as a useful tool in wooing intellectuals to the Party and its Hundred Flowers goals. He said the *People's Daily* had tried in a hundred ways to encourage intellectuals to become more active, but the intellectuals still distrusted the Party paper's motives.²² *Wen Hui Bao*, on the other hand, had long enjoyed the trust of intellectuals (it had been a truly independent, if Leftist, paper in the 1930s and 1940s). Thus, the paper's pre-eminent role should be 'to persuade intellectuals to put aside their doubts, to say what they think.' Intellectual passivity had to be overcome if their talents were to be mobilized for socialist construction.

Deng had several concrete suggestions about how *Wen Hui Bao* could achieve these goals. First, since China was subject to blockade by the imperialist nations and had, indeed, shut itself off from the world in the past, the paper should introduce new trends in foreign science and technology which intellectuals could use in their work. Second, the paper should concern itself with the problems and concerns of the daily life of intellectuals. Publicize their problems, be their advocate. Third, outside their work intellectuals had avocations. They 'like to grow flowers and raise birds.' So, the paper should cater to these interests with cultural and informative literary supplements. Fourth, the paper should address itself to those intellectuals in the countryside, and therefore should send reporters to rural areas and publish articles on rural topics. Finally, Deng noted that unlike *People's Daily* and the New China News Agency, papers like *Wen Hui Bao* and *Da Gong Bao* had considerable prestige overseas. They could serve the country by using that influence to promote New China in Japan, South-East Asia, and Western Europe. By early August Xu was back in Shanghai finalizing the staffing for the revived paper. The first issue of the new *Wen Hui Bao* appeared on National Day 1956.²³ Under Deng's plan the intellectuals were wooed, entertained, and co-opted to Party needs, but they were not offered political freedoms or protections. It was socialism with a cultured face, not liberalism.²⁴

This version of the Hundred Flowers did not go well in the fall of 1956. One of the few publications to respond to Mao's calls to criticize bureaucratism was roundly criticized almost immediately. Wang Meng's short story, 'Young Newcomer to the Organization Department', became a *cause célèbre* for its description of cynicism and demoralization in a central Party organization and for the fears the criticisms of this story raised among intellectuals.²⁵ In fact, the criticism of it by Chen Qitong and others in the *People's Daily* in January 1957 goaded Mao back into action in defence of the Hundred Flowers.[26] The Party was not only trying to limit the Hundred Flowers to technical or artistic topics; in Mao's view, it was trying to shut it down altogether.

Mao, on the other hand, had other ideas. He wanted the Hundred Flowers to be a *political* movement, not merely an academic one. He was far more concerned with bureaucratism in the Party and the growing alienation of the Party's power elite from the population. He found the Party's 'academic' efforts to be lacking in the desired reform effect. In early January 1957 he began a four-month campaign to kick the Party into action.[27] His two most important speeches were 'On the Correct Handling of Contradictions among the People', given on 27 February, and his speech to the National Propaganda Work Conference on 12 March. In addition, in late March and early April Mao went to the provinces, speaking in Tianjin, Ji'nan, Shanghai, and Nanjing, to rally support for his version of the Hundred Flowers—a full-blown Party rectification campaign which would for the first time include participation by non-Party intellectuals. He particularly singled out the Chen Qitong article, and the *People's Daily*'s handling of it, for criticism, and he tried to support at least the right of Wang Meng to write stories such as 'Young Newcomer'.

What Mao had to say was heady stuff. He acknowledged two kinds of contradictions, antagonistic ones between 'us and the enemy' and non-antagonistic ones 'among the people'. This gave a first theoretical justification for public criticism of the Party. Mao emphasized that the CCP and the small 'democratic parties' would co-exist and mutually check up on each other for a long time to come. He implied that the CPPCC and NPC might actually 'oversee' Party reform.[28] The Party apparatus was aghast. Liu Shaoqi and Peng Zhen clearly did not share Mao's enthusiasm for public criticism of the CCP by non-Party members, and they may well have strongly resisted it.[29] In any event, Deng Tuo and the *People's Daily* were clearly not on Mao's side. The touchstone for the Party's resistance became a 7 January 1957 *People's Daily* article by Chen Qitong and three other senior cadres from the PLA's Cultural Bureau, which attacked the Hundred Flowers policy as promoting disloyalty to the Party. In a January meeting, Mao specifically criticized this article, but the Party's propaganda services killed the story, choosing only to reprint Mao's positive comments about Chen and his colleagues, 'they are loyal, for the Party and for the people,' and ignoring the rest of Mao's comments, 'but they are dogmatists and I do not agree with their views.'[30] Most tellingly, by early April *nothing* of import had appeared in the Party's propaganda organs concerning Mao's special efforts to broaden the Hundred Flowers movement.[31]

For intellectuals, however, Mao's talks were exciting. Xu Zhucheng was recalled to Beijing in early March 1957 along with a large delegation from Shanghai's leadership to hear tapes of Mao's 27 February talk and to hear the 12 March talk. Xu and his colleagues were moved by Mao's entreaties. Xu recalls his excitement at the time when Mao led them to believe that harsh class struggle was over, that non-Party people could help in rectification and that rectification—of intellectuals as well as Party cadres—should be as gentle as spring rain. They shared few of the worries of higher Party cadres; they thought a new day was dawning.[32]

If it seemed a good time for intellectuals, these months were not for Deng Tuo and the *People's Daily*. Mao's mood shifted from his grudging acceptance of 16 February to increasing hostility toward the editor and his paper for supporting Chen Qitong.[33] Mao publicly tongue-lashed Deng and the paper several times, most notably in the 27 February 'Correct Handling of Contradictions' talk and the 10 March meeting of press and publishing circles (which Xu Zhucheng is on record as attending). During the 'Contradictions' talk, which was recorded and played around the country throughout the spring, Mao turned on the paper:

> At the meeting of provincial and municipal secretaries in late January, I had this four-man declaration [i.e. by Chen Qitong *et al.*] distributed to everyone. There were comrades from the *People's Daily* there at the time. What did they say? They expressed no attitude. Now a month has passed, more or less. What should be done? Did you publish that thing to approve or oppose it? Is there anyone from the *People's Daily* here today?[34] Sooner or later you're going to deal with this matter! . . . I will now express my attitude: I do not approve of that article, that article is wrong.[35]

Although Mao seems to have acknowledged Deng Tuo in passing as an 'expert' in journalism at a 6 March meeting of regional propaganda and education officials, he quickly turned nasty.[36] During the 10 March talk with representatives of press and publishing circles (at which Deng Tuo and Xu Zhucheng were present)[37] Mao ominously linked Deng's paper with troublesome intellectuals: 'The *People's Daily* is an example; the intellectuals there are grouped together; therefore troubles build up.' He then turned to its editor: '[I've] heard that this Chen Qitong is not a bad guy, but Ma Hanbing is very overbearing. He ran with this article to the *People's Daily*, [and] with one shout of "The Imperial Edict has come", Deng Tuo grovelled on his knees.'[38] This was not only an unkind criticism, but unfair. Deng was organizationally bound to defer to Ma Hanbing, a senior general, because Deng was his bureaucratic subordinate.[39]

Later in the meeting, Deng Tuo raised his concerns about the ease with which articles published in the *People's Daily* can spawn excessive 'winds'. He gave the topic of birth control and late marriage. As soon as the paper publicized it, couples raced off to get married. This elicited a sympathetic 'This indeed makes it hard to run a newspaper' from the Chairman. Having set the tone, Deng pressed home his point: 'For example, on the problem of letting a hundred schools contend, some take it that contention is mainly limited to academic thought, and it is inappropriate to apply this to actual work. [But] the relationship between the two is easily confused. . . . Perhaps [we'd] better delimit the scope [of these policies].'[40] Deng was stressing the danger of losing control of the planned public criticism (which, in fact, is just what happened two months later), no doubt with the example in mind of the excessively quick 'socialization' of industry in Beijing and other areas the year before, when local cadres had responded over-enthusiastically to Mao's calls. In fact, Mao had just mentioned this issue a moment before Deng Tuo raised his question.[41] Deng Tuo's ploy to get Mao to see the danger of his Hundred Flowers plans, rather glaring in the text we read today, did not work. Mao did not make the connection between the tendency of local leaders to carry out cues from the Centre in a hasty manner in winter 1955–6 with his planned expansion of the Hundred Flowers. Instead, Mao remembered the frustration of his will by the *People's Daily*.[42]

The Bedroom Showdown

Mao finally lost all patience with what he felt was the bureaucracy's obstructions. He chose to vent his anger on Deng Tuo, who as editor of the Party's mouthpiece, the *People's Daily*, could plausibly be held responsible. Mao chose to ignore the Byzantine approval network that operated within the Party for such important propaganda topics. Clearly Deng would not have delayed the story if his superiors in the Propaganda Department and the Central Committee had not wished it. Deng, however, was high enough up to ensure that Mao's point would be taken by his CC colleagues but low enough to be powerless to resist. The result was an appalling four-hour bedroom conference in Mao's personal quarters on the afternoon of 10 April 1957.

As the Party had done in the past to prepare for rectification, a high-level committee was formed at the Politburo level on 1 April to take charge of the Party's key paper.[43] On 10 April, the *People's Daily* had, after much pressuring from Mao, published an editorial on the Hundred Flowers movement and belatedly criticized the fears of Chen Qitong and Party 'conservatives'. No mention was made of Mao's provincial tour promoting the rectification. Not only was the editorial late and incomplete in propagandizing Mao's recent speeches, it was also not as fulsome an endorsement as the Chairman had apparently expected. According to Ding Yilan, Deng's widow, the delay of publicity for the speeches was neither Deng Tuo's fault nor within his power to effect. The Central Committee did not ask for them to be published. Usually draft speeches like Mao's had to go through several revisions before official publication.[44] Indeed, another source involved in that consultation process noted that the February 'Contradictions' speech was the most contradictory speech he had ever seen—it took three full circuits of revision to get it into a passable form.[45]

Wang Ruoshui, a junior editor not formally on the paper's editorial board, had written the 10 April editorial under the usual guidance of Deng Tuo and the board. After lunch that day, Wang, Deng Tuo, and the entire board received an urgent summons: 'Chairman Mao has called you to go see him.'[46] Naturally Wang was concerned that Mao was unhappy with the editorial, but 'whatever it was, just to be able to see the Chairman was exciting.' Deng Tuo gathered the editorial committee together, after mentioning to Wang 'I think I will take advantage of this opportunity to resign and have an end to it.' Indeed, Deng had already offered his resignation a number of times since the fall of 1956.[47]

The full editorial board, plus Wang and minus one latecomer, were joined by Hu Qiaomu and drove to Zhongnanhai in two cars.[48] The cars entered through the New China Gate, under the 'Serve the People' sign, and wound along Southern Lake to the Fengze Garden Pavilion. There they walked through another gate, passing through several courtyards, until they reached Mao Zedong's residence. Hu Qiaomu went in first to announce them. The editors then filed into a smallish room which had originally been the Chairman's bedroom.

One need not be a psychologist to appreciate the shocking disrespect Mao showed his propagandists and his crude display of power. The editors, who were soon joined by Chen Boda and Zhou Yang (and their one missing editor, Yuan Shuibo), were formally dressed and sat politely in a semi-circle. A semi-circle around the Chairman's bed. Although it was already afternoon, the Chairman was in his pyjamas. In fact, he had on only a pyjama top and a towel wrapped around his waist. He lounged on the bed (a large wooden affair piled with string-bound traditional Chinese books) and smoked continually.[49] About the only thing he did not do was bare his buttocks to the aghast editors. It wasn't necessary, for they got the point: he was the dominant ape in this political jungle and he was furious. His first order of business was to humiliate Deng Tuo.

Maoism in Crisis

Deng Tuo introduced each editor (Mao was reclining on the bed during the introductions like a later Roman Emperor). Deng Tuo was no stranger to personal meetings with Mao; he had enjoyed the Chairman's confidence in the early 1950s and had frequently gone to see Mao in Zhongnanhai to consult on various campaigns, such as those against Yu Pingbo and Hu Shi. This time, however, he had fallen from favour. Mao sat up, lit another cigarette, and eyed his very much cowed audience. He began with menacing informality: 'I couldn't sleep. Decided to call you in for a chat. Looked at today's editorial. Even though it's a bit late, it finally shows your stand on the article by the four men including Chen Qitong.[50] It's already been over a month since the SSC [the Supreme State Conference] and Propaganda Work Conference, but there hasn't been a peep out of the Party papers. It's been left to the non-Party papers to raise that banner....'

Deng Tuo tried to explain, offering a self-criticism of his own actions, but he was repeatedly interrupted by Mao's petulant criticisms:

— 'I think you purposely sang a different tune, purposely praised Chen Qitong and the others.'
— 'You people are not the Party paper, you're a factional paper.'
— 'In the past I said you people were pedants running the paper. Wrong, I should say you're dead men running the paper.'

Deng Tuo: In the past the Party Centre has had a regulation: no press releases on Party meetings and no quotations from a speech by the Chairman before the text has been published...

Mao: When did the Party Centre have such a regulation? News of the SSC has been published, so why not write an editorial? Why make a secret of Party policy? Not publishing news on the Propaganda Conference is an error. Non-Party people were at that meeting, so why hasn't news of it been published? Party papers should give timely propaganda of Party policies. After the SSC *People's Daily* didn't make a sound. Non-Party papers picked up the leadership function. If Party papers are passive, Party leadership also becomes passive. There is a ghost in this. Where is the ghost?

Deng Tuo: I did not pay sufficient attention to this problem...
Mao: Not insufficient attention. No attention at all![51]

The atmosphere was quite tense, recalls Wang Ruoshui, like sitting on a bed of nails. Mao was clearly furious. He said that at the January meeting of provincial Party secretaries[52] he had copies of the article by Chen Qitong and the others distributed. He then repeated his complaint of being misquoted and squarely blamed Deng Tuo (among others) for the inaccurate report which claimed the Chairman had praised Chen Qitong and the others.[53] 'That's just choosing what you want to hear,' Mao said. 'How could you have heard wrongly? The *People's Daily* merely published an abstract of an article criticizing Chen Qitong, but that was just objectivism which did not make clear what the views of the editorial board were.'

Mao next went out of his way to praise the junior editor, Wang Ruoshui, in order to humiliate Deng Tuo. Mao praised Wang for writing the editorial (ignoring the obvious fact that he had been assigned to do so by Deng). Wang deferred to his superior (while cautiously suggesting that responsibility extended beyond the paper): 'Comrade Hu Qiaomu made many corrections.' But Mao insisted: 'There must have been something good there to begin with.' He went on, 'You have all participated in many Central meetings. To go home and write no articles is to sit there uselessly, doing nothing more than wearing out our furniture.' As a dig to Deng Tuo, he added, 'In the future let whoever writes the articles run the meetings.'

Mao then turned to the assistant general editors: 'You people are really strange. Can it really be that you all agree with him [pointing to Deng Tuo]? Is it because Deng Tuo is so good at uniting people that all your opinions are so uniform?' The editors were silent, unwilling to desert their chief editor. Mao continued: 'If you have an opinion, you can debate! If you want to raise criticisms with Deng Tuo, the most he can do is fire you. How come not even a breeze got through, how come not one of you wrote a letter to the Party Centre reporting the situation? So long as you don't go making a ruckus in the street, you can discuss any opinion. No doubt Deng Tuo has his virtues and you haven't the heart to oppose him. [To Deng Tuo] I think you very much resemble Emperor Yuandi of the Han, peaceable and easygoing but lacking the strength to make quick decisions (*yourou guaduan*). With you in the Emperor's seat, the nation would be lost!'

The menace of the last sentence shocked everyone. Wang Ruoshui couldn't help eyeing nervously the small mountain of history books on the Chairman's bed. Deng Tuo, too, had obviously also felt the force of the last sentence and probably felt the time had come for him to offer his resignation. He said, 'I myself do not know if I am Han Yuandi or not; nonetheless I feel my abilities are insufficient. It is hard to feel adequate for the job. I hope the Chairman will consider relieving me of my duties. Several times I have sincerely and in good faith raised this request . . .'

Mao was incensed, finding Deng's explanation both patronizing and

Maoism in Crisis 181

insubordinate: 'I don't believe that sincerity and good faith of yours! You only know the comings and goings of limousines, you live in luxury. Now, shit or get off the pot!' Every time the masses report new larger harvests, Mao went on, Deng Tuo insisted on lowering the figures. Deng's attitude and his delay reflected just the sort of bureaucratic obstruction which Mao was trying to root out with his Hundred Flowers campaign.[54] As for the resignation, Mao retorted: 'Are you a Party member or not?'[55] Thus reminded of his duty, Deng Tuo continued on as editor for a few months, but Mao was through with him. He merely wanted to fire him, not receive his resignation.[56]

Hu Qiaomu finally spoke. By way of explanation he said the *People's Daily* had already drawn up a plan to propagandize Mao's speeches and they had already organized people to draft several articles. However, because he was unsure how to handle these articles, he had temporarily put them on the back burner. Thus, this affair could not be laid completely at the newspaper's door; he too had responsibility.[57] After hearing this, Mao made no comment.

The meeting, which lasted four hours, then degenerated into a long harangue by the Chairman on his views concerning the Hundred Flowers policy and the role of intellectuals. Ominously, he stressed that 'the hundred schools contending' was merely competition between the proletarian and bourgeois classes for the services of wavering intellectuals. In short, he said, we buy them, just as we have bought the national capitalists. However, we mustn't be open about it.[58] Mao then rambled along, announcing his views on editorial work, which papers he liked, and the proper role of Marxism. He made it clear that 'dogmatism' equalled the use of classical citation from the Marxist canon to oppose his current opinions. He even offered to write a few articles for the paper after his resignation from the State Chairmanship became effective (but stressed, in response to Deng's offer of a special column for Mao's *zawen*, that he would have to write under a truly anonymous penname).[59] Mao repeatedly criticized the *People's Daily* for expanding to an eight-page format. When told that the expanded format had been approved by the Party Centre, Mao said, 'Who is the Party Centre?' Someone, probably Hu Qiaomu, reminded Mao that he himself had approved the change. Mao sloughed it off: 'Well, if it was like that, I was confused. So much of what I say you people leave behind, but on this you go forward.' The editors returned to their offices, and Deng Tuo prepared a summary of the meeting's main points.[60]

Less than three weeks later on 27 April, the Chairman managed to convince his colleagues and quite abruptly, the Central Committee announced on 30 April that the Hundred Flowers would become a full-fledged Party rectification in the style of the famous 1942 Yan'an campaign. The precipitousness of the decision is indicated by the record of Mao's own talks promoting the campaign: barely a month earlier he was saying the rectification would begin in 1958.[61] By mid-May truly amazing criticisms and debates were appearing in the press.

The Politics of Simpletons

Deng did little to repair relations with the Chairman by his own essay contribution to the Hundred Flowers in May 1957. 'Discard the "Politics of Simpletons"', which Deng published in the *People's Daily* on 11 May under the pen-name Bu Wuji, criticizes busybody cadres and condemns the waste which results from an over-emphasis on radical politics. Deng's themes are consistent with his previous and later writings, but surely to the Chairman's annoyance, Deng appropriates the theme of 'quacks' (*yongyi*) from Mao's 16 February speech at Yinian Tang, where Mao used the term to berate Leftists who did not intend to 'cure the illness to save the patient' when criticizing Rightists and instead 'act like quacks killing patients.' In a display of classical scholarship, Deng quotes a Song poet to apply the term squarely to Mao's agricultural policies, albeit in the form of castigating lower-level cadres who rush around all the time 'politicizing' daily work.[62] As Deng would continue to do a number of times in the 1960s, he took Mao's words and cleverly shifted them to suit establishment ends rather than Mao's increasingly anti-establishment goals. However, Deng's Hundred Flowers commentary was a far cry from the rash of fundamental criticisms of the Communist system made in the press, particularly in Shanghai's *Wen Hui Bao*, during these same weeks.[63]

In fact, Deng Tuo's comments in 'Politics of Simpletons' are more likely to be his effort to cajole Mao, not to mention the many readers who then placed great faith in the authority of the *People's Daily*, into support of the *style* of politics Deng preferred. His essay directly echoes criticisms of 'adventurism' that continued in the summer and fall of 1956 in Deng's *People's Daily* and in other Party periodicals following the infamous 20 June 1956 editorial which criticized 'adventurism' in the economy. Deng bowed to Mao's call to attack those who resisted the rectification, but only in terms of castigating cadres who fail to acknowledge the need 'to let go' a bit, to stop mindless politicization of daily work. Deng's comments in his *zawen* are more pointedly aimed at radical Maoist bureaucratism, with its tendency to politicize every issue, rather than at the sluggish hierarchy of the collective leadership. He

Maoism in Crisis 183

clearly disapproves of the mindless 'campaign' mentality that radical exhortations in the national press can produce at the local level:

> For example, when comrades in one county received an order saying that all the cotton in the county should be picked on the same day, the cadres in the districts, villages, and agricultural co-operatives busied themselves carrying out activist and organizational work. The result was that in many fields where the cotton was not ready for picking, it was picked anyway.

In any event, Deng is no fan of mindless bureaucratic behaviour:

> We ourselves have created a bureaucratic structure. We move in batch after batch of cadres, and then we go on to transfer hordes of other people to do personnel work. We ourselves are constantly talking with these people, holding meetings, helping them write reports, looking at the reports, criticizing and transmitting the reports, and on and on. The result is that we're up to our ears in work, and a large part of the cadres are inextricably trapped in daily 'official business'. We comfort ourselves and console everyone else by saying the work we do serves the people and is all absolutely necessary 'political' work.... I think, if we really want to grace all this with the title 'politics', then we're going to have to call it the 'Politics of Simpletons'.[64]

This, in Deng's view, is what an unbalanced cog-and-screw mentality of yes-man bureaucrats produces—campaign waste and bureaucratic inaction. This passage, and the one following it criticizing 'quacks' who kill people, clearly echoes criticisms made in the *People's Daily* as early as October 1955 of dictatorial leadership by rural cadres, criticisms which returned in the summer of 1956. It also echoes Mao's own criticisms of Party bureaucratism in the early 1950s.[65] Deng's support of young critics, Lin Xiling and Liu Binyan, in May 1957 (discussed below) indicates that he could make use of the rectification to push his own views, just as Mao could. This essay is also Deng's first since his alarming falling out with the Chairman in April. Of note here is that Deng's habit of building his *zawen* essays around traditional Chinese sources, which became a trademark of his *Evening Chats* essays, begins here. In all, the essay reflects Deng's ability to shift Mao's attack on 'managerial' bureaucratism into an attack on the 'politicized' bureaucratism. Despite his political spanking in April, Deng showed no signs of opposing Mao, even obliquely, during the heady days of May 1957. Rather, he sought clarification from the Chairman on important policy matters and tried to nudge him in the direction Deng himself favoured. This was characteristic of Deng's service as *both* a functionary and a savant—to serve and advise.

Deng Tuo's experience during the May 1957 Hundred Flowers

movement itself is an example of the influence enjoyed, as well as the compromises and dangers faced, by many establishment intellectuals. Deng encouraged and protected individual critics, but was either unwilling or unable to make the *People's Daily* participate in the May 'blooming'. Lin Xiling, the well-known student activist of that period, recalls that Deng Tuo encouraged her criticisms of *bureaucratism* in the spring of 1957 when she met him as a reporter for the *China Youth News*.[66] Deng Tuo was her 'backstage support' when she made her famous criticisms of the Party for its lack of democracy, but when she was attacked by the Party that summer Deng Tuo could not defend her and shifted the blame, naming the already doomed Tan Xiwu as her secret supporter. Nonetheless, says Lin Xiling, Deng had saved her from even greater criticism by blocking the publication of an article she submitted in late May because he knew the anti-Rightist campaign was already on the way.[67]

Deng also shielded the young investigative reporter Liu Binyan. Liu had been Deng's translator on his 1956 trip to Moscow and Warsaw, when both had been struck by the impact of the Soviet 'thaw'. During the last half of May 1957, Liu was in Shanghai reporting for *China Youth*. Toward the end of the month he sent an article to Deng for publication in *People's Daily*, but Deng 'sat on it'. The article was 'The Profession of Journalism', and it bemoaned the restraints which the Party put on its journalists. Deng suppressed the article because he knew the anti-Rightist campaign was on the way and did not want the article to be used against Liu.[68] Nevertheless, Deng joined Peng Zhen during the anti-Rightist campaign of the summer of 1957 in the prosecution of liberals who had criticized the Party. Wu Han, too, joined in on the attack on 'Rightists' at this time.[69]

The *People's Daily* under Deng Tuo also restrained itself during the heyday of public criticisms of the Party in May. Whether or not Deng deliberately withheld other articles like Liu's is unclear. Xu Zhucheng recalls his conversation with Deng in mid-May 1957. Deng praised Xu's *Wen Hui Bao* for its lively articles and complained, 'Our *People's Daily* has planned to move ahead, too, but the higher levels block us. For example, I have organized a group to write and we have already written ten editorials. But no news has appeared in the paper, because most of these editorials have been suppressed. Only two have appeared and my plan is in ruins.'[70] However, by early summer, after the anti-Rightist campaign had started, Deng's tone had changed. He told Hu Jiwei, one of the paper's editorial board members, that the paper's restraint had paid off, because the lack of critical articles had protected the *People's Daily* from being designated a 'Rightist' publication and thus saved its journalists from inquisition. If it had done otherwise, said Deng, 'who knows how many more Rightists the paper would have had?' Hu believes Deng personally took the heat from Mao for the paper's foot-dragging in order to protect his subordinates.[71]

The picture left of Deng's activities in the Hundred Flowers shows he supported the 'academic' version of it and some limited 'well-intentioned' criticisms of bureaucratism. His advice to *Wen Hui Bao* reflects the sort of orthodox but richly varied cultural life he himself led and would particularly support in the post-Leap period. This was, after all, the life he himself had led since the 1940s, when the traditional-style Yan-Zhao Poetry Society co-existed with Maoist propaganda work. Furthermore, Deng did not support those who questioned Party rule. This, too, is consistent with his earlier and later work and pronouncements, from his 1944 address on journalism to his attacks on 'bourgeois journalism' made during the Great Leap (discussed below) to his final statements on life under socialism made in *Evening Chats*. Party rule was supposed to bring a rich nation, an equitable society, and a flowering culture. What Deng could not control was Mao's ability to tug at his loyalties to the Chairman and the Party when either or both strayed from these goals.

By late June, Deng Tuo had lost his job at *People's Daily*. Mao had called Wu Lengxi, who was working in NCNA, to a meeting in his Zhongnanhai residence some two months after his confrontation there with Deng Tuo. On 1 June Hu Qiaomu ushered Wu into Mao's study where Wu was offered the editorship of *People's Daily*. Wu expressed concern for his colleague, Deng Tuo, but after being given a fortnight to think it over, accepted the job. He was appointed by the Party Centre on 31 June and Deng Xiaoping presided over the public meeting installing Wu and moving Deng to the position of publisher (*shezhang*).[72] This was the end of Deng's leadership of the paper. His resignation had finally been accepted in all but name.

Deng Tuo sat out the anti-Rightist movement of 1957, withdrawing instead to lick his wounds. He was active in neither politics nor journalism (beyond the mechanics of editing page eight of the *Daily*) during the anti-Rightist campaign, which had begun on 8 June. He was tired and wanted to withdraw to his academic pursuits. When Xu Zhucheng was 'struggled' for his Rightist errors in July by the Journalists' Association, Deng Tuo (its president) did not attend. Instead he was working on revisions to his 1937 text on famine relief. By early August, Deng had recast the 500-page book into the colloquial style and simplified characters of current usage. Shortly after his 'promotion' to publisher, Deng took a walk with Hu Jiwei in the peaceful gardens of

Beijing's Tanzhe Monastery. Deng said he would just as soon resign from the publisher's position as well. Hu tried to persuade him to stay on, but Deng blew out a long, slow sigh and said, 'Too hard, too hard.' He said, 'If it were permissible, I really think I'd like to remain here in the monastery. Read a few books; write a few articles.'[73] For the next year Deng was in virtual limbo until he was transferred to the Beijing Party Committee in August 1958. During that year he travelled a fair amount, going to Sichuan on the new Chengdu rail line in the fall and touring Hubei and Jiangsu the following summer.

Although formally out of the *People's Daily* by 1960, Deng seems to have maintained good ties with the paper and the national press.[74] He left behind him a number of influential subordinates, such as his long-time assistant, Hu Jiwei, who became deputy editor-in-chief under Wu Lengxi, and the noted commentator, Wang Ruoshui.[75] Deng apparently had good relations with *Guangming Daily* through the editor of its 'East Wind' cultural supplement in the late 1950s, Huang Xianjun. Huang was a fellow provincial from Fujian and a high-school classmate of Deng's, and he published several of Deng's poems (under the pen-name Zuo Hai) in his supplement while heeding Deng's views on how to operate a supplement in a socialist newspaper. In particular, Huang recalls Deng Tuo's views on the value of publishing occasional essays for the busy scholar-cadre—it allows one to solicit preliminary opinions from other scholars on work in progress.[76]

Move to Beijing Committee

Deng's dismissal from the *People's Daily* was masked at first, when he was 'kicked upstairs' with a series of higher managerial titles, beginning in the summer of 1957 and lasting into 1960. His move to the Party offices in Peng Zhen's Beijing administration in August 1958 and the start-up of *Frontline* that fall marked the break.[77] Deng Tuo may have been dismissed from the *People's Daily* at Mao Zedong's behest, but Deng had the support of Peng Zhen and others to mitigate his fall from grace. Although Deng Tuo made the move under a cloud, significantly, it was only a partial cloud. Party general secretary Deng Xiaoping personally attended the going-away party for Deng Tuo at the paper in February 1959 and praised the editor. Since 1979, Deng's dismissal has been officially blamed on 'mistaken criticism from Party leaders'.[78] From the Beijing organization Deng pushed his brand of orthodoxy, and during 1960-1 even seems to have made forays back into central politics. It is important to note the strength and influence of Peng Zhen's

Beijing committee, which Mao would later dub an 'independent kingdom', because this institutional base *inside* the Party was a major forum for establishment intellectuals after the Great Leap and during the policy debates in the early 1960s, just as Shanghai later became for their radical brethren. Deng Tuo was a leading member of the Beijing apparatus.

Li Jun, a Jin Cha Ji colleague who worked with Deng on the journal *Frontline*, recalls that were it not for Deng Tuo it would not have had its distinctive merits. These merits are summed up in Deng's wish that the journal should continue 'on behalf of the former *Study* (*Xuexi*) magazine'.[79] *Study* had been replaced in 1958 (after a brief period of overlap) by the more radical *Red Flag*, under Chen Boda, Mao's former secretary, as the official theory journal of the Central Party. Thus Deng's journal in Beijing was intended from the very beginning as a vehicle for the alternative establishment approach. Deng's editorials, the many special columns he established—such as *Notes from a Three Family Village*—and the regular articles, such as Li Jun's on spare-time cultural activities for the masses, all reflected the approach of Deng and his patrons.[80] The journal argued for a relatively ordered, moderate, and flexible implementation of Party policies from the Great Leap to the Socialist Education Movement in the early 1960s.

Support of the Great Leap

While he may have been privately critical of Maoist impetuosity in agricultural policy or Maoist attacks on Party prestige, Deng Tuo publicly praised and supported the Great Leap Forward (1958–60). This was consistent with Chinese Leninist principles—public unity and obedience to Central Committee directives with the right to debate *inside* Party channels. Given the crumbling of these norms, particularly in 1959, Deng's continued support of the Great Leap well after others had criticized it inside the Party reflects an undetermined balance of two motivations: he actually believed in the policies as he wrote about them from 1958 to 1961 or, like Yang Xianzhen and others,[81] he was afraid or too prudent to reverse the radical line emerging out of the Central Committee under Mao's increasingly capricious pressure. His support of the Great Leap was extensive and unlikely to have been purely an act of political prudence, since he had already demonstrated enough integrity with regard to his own ideas, or at least stubbornness in the face of Mao, in 1957 to lose his job at the *People's Daily*. In fact, Deng's

Great Leap writings fall into three periods: support in 1958, caution in the spring of 1959, and renewed support thereafter. Each parallels Central Party policy shifts.

In January 1958 Mao once again tried to woo 'bourgeois intellectuals', this time in the service of his new war against Nature. He picked up on earlier Party writings on 'Red and Expert' to outline what he expected of intellectuals:

> Red is politics; expert is one's job . . . If one pursues politics so that one is only red and not expert, doesn't know one's job and doesn't understand practical matters, then the redness is a false redness and one is an empty-headed politician. . . . If we are to overtake Britain in 15 years, then we must mould millions upon millions of intellectuals whose loyalty is to the proletariat.[82]

After months of preliminary encouragement by the Party Centre, the Great Leap Forward was officially proclaimed in May 1958.

It is easy enough to see how Deng Tuo could make his peace with these sorts of sentiments. Numerous articles and speeches by Deng Tuo are available from the period 1958–61 in which he loyally defends the Party's Great Leap policy and its ideological line. Most of his pronouncements, naturally enough, deal with journalism, such as his August 1958 article, 'The Red-Expert Road of the Journalist', in which Deng requires newsworkers to be first, red and second, experts in their work, but in any event *both*.[83]

Deng Tuo gave his longest speech on journalism in March 1958 before an assembly of Party, government, military, and Beijing municipal officials. Titled 'The Socialist Revolution on the Newsfront' and published both in *Study* in April and later as a separate booklet, it continued Deng's long history as an official speaker for the Party on journalism theory and policy since his 1944 Jin Cha Ji address.[84] In tune with Party policy of 1958, Deng attacks the calls for 'freedom of the press' (*xinwen ziyou*) which, he says, are Rightist devices to give unlimited control of the press to the bourgeois class. The Rightists, according to Deng, had already used such 'freedoms' perniciously to distort Chairman Mao's theory of socialist democratic freedoms.[85] This refers, it seems, to the political 'blossoms' of the May 1957 Hundred Flowers rectification, which, despite Deng's support of Lin Xiling's criticism of bureaucratism, Deng concluded was not the best way to rectify the Party. Further on in the speech Deng emphasizes that the news industry must serve the socialist economic base; that is, 'It must actively rely on the leadership of the Communist Party.'[86]

Deng Tuo's role as a Party-liner had been more simply put two months earlier in an 8 February *People's Daily* article, 'A Great Leap

Forward in Thought and Work Style.'[87] In the article he held up a Hong'an county group of Great Leapers as a model to emulate. In Deng's words, they excelled at 'discovering amongst the masses new people, new creations, new discipline and at studying and producing the new ideology and work style of the new situation.' Throughout the piece Deng urged cadres to adapt their ideology and work style to the newly announced mass style of the water conservancy campaign that would come to characterize the Great Leap.

In the spring of 1959, however, Deng Tuo struck a more cautious note. The Seventh Plenum of the Eighth Central Committee meeting that April had made a sober assessment of the Leap and Mao sanctioned a partial retreat from its heady goals.[88] Deng took advantage of the new mood to press his traditional theme of caution. In 'Marxist Philosophy and Journalism', published on 25 May 1959, Deng hammers home the need to follow 'objective Marxist laws' that cannot be ignored. He introduces '16 elements of dialects' in Lenin's *Philosophical Notes* and points out that 'dialectics' in romance languages means 'discussion'. Journalism must use dialectical materialism as its mode of analysis and must promote open discussion; it cannot force flights of fancy on its readers.[89] In April Deng had also published his first *zawen* since the Hundred Flowers and it reiterated his cautious themes. Just four days after the closing of the Seventh Plenum, Deng published on 9 April in the *People's Daily* an essay on leadership under the pen-name Dan Wensheng.[90] As with his 1957 'Politics of Simpletons' and his later *Evening Chats*, Deng once again turns to history. This time he provides an exegesis of the good general from the ancient classic, Sun Zi's *Art of War*. Deng's version of this 'ancient wisdom' for the Leap amounts to a sensible interpretation of Party leadership with a strong emphasis on 'straightforwardness, seeking truth from facts, and . . . opposing liberalism.' He closes with a gentle patriotic shaming that would become his trade mark in *Evening Chats*: 'The ancients early on stressed leadership talents and accumulated rich experiences on the topic. How can we not stress the arts of leadership even more, nurture even more talented leaders to serve the glorious task of socialist construction?'

The Lushan Reversal

Mao pushed the Party back on a radical course following the disastrous Lushan Plenum of August 1959. The case of Peng Dehuai is worth reviewing here briefly because it is the historical turning point in the relationship between Mao and Leninist norms. At the Lushan Plenum of the Central Committee of the CCP held during July and August

1959 Marshal Peng Dehuai, the Minister of Defence, criticized the Great Leap for the sufferings it caused among the peasants he had visited that spring. He suggested a retreat from the economic policies of the Leap, which he blamed as the cause of the disaster. For this he was purged.

The precursor to Lushan was the January 1958 Nanning Conference. Mao had been capricious and moody in 1957, but it was at the Nanning meeting that he set the fateful precedent that a *policy* difference (over the ending of the mini-Leap and 'opposing adventurism' in 1956) could be treated as a *political question* (that is, as a sign of ideological error). This definition of policy debate took away the right of meaningful open dissent within the Party. It was also here that Mao first put forward his radical slogan, 'continuing the revolution'.[91] This was the very meeting at which Mao had ridiculed Deng Tuo and threatened the *People's Daily*. Nanning's radical policies and political intolerance came to fruition at Lushan. Together they put an end to the deal between establishment intellectuals and the Party-State which had provided Deng Tuo with his honourable vocation since Jin Cha Ji in the late 1930s.

The complex forces behind these events and the tragic cost the Party incurred in its decision to purge its censor have been well documented.[92] The question with which we are concerned here is: was there a significant group of CCP leaders who felt that the norms had been broken? Some authors have analysed Peng Dehuai's critique of the Leap and Mao's leadership as a part of a 'factional struggle'—that is, a political struggle for power within the CCP that incidentally paralleled differing economic policies.[93] It now appears that Peng's infamous 'Letter of Opinion' was, in fact, a face-saving call to Mao to slow down the Leap, to blame lower-level cadres for 'misunderstanding Mao', and to get the economy in order. Thus, Peng and his associates engaged in legal struggle and open debate, the proper Leninist minority duties.[94]

Mao's response to these criticisms, which were 'modest', was severe. He took Peng's criticism as a personal attack and declared that if the debate led to national collapse, he 'would go to the countryside to lead the peasants to overthrow the government.'[95] Mao handed the Party Centre a simple dictatorial choice—him or me, discipline Peng Dehuai or repudiate the Party Chairman. With misgivings (Zhu De defended Peng) the Party denounced Peng. A substantial body of the Party, even within radical sections of the leadership, felt Peng had been dealt with unfairly.[96] Many leaders felt Mao was not keeping his promise to move to 'the second line' of leadership, and that he was violating the rules of collective leadership.[97] Mao's leadership style and the Great Leap policies were two separate issues. Leading cadres dissented with one, the other, or both. But they dared not cross Mao in public and risk the fate of Peng Dehuai.

Added to these strains, a third and fatal blow was dealt to operational discipline following the Lushan Plenum—the rectification theory of 'save the patient'. The harsh 1959 rectification campaign ignored the limits and tenets of intra-Party struggle laid down in the 1940s and maintained, even though in a strained form, the 1957 anti-Rightist campaign. In 1959 with the Party Centre disunited, those in control of the rectification machinery used it to quell opposition. As Teiwes concludes, 'rectification was becoming less a method for reform and more a tool for purging.'[98]

This was the end of the open intra-Party debate which had served the CCP since 1942. The spectacle of Peng Dehuai's demise at the top for policy and not political differences with Mao and the harsh purge of cadres associated with Peng's views at the local level ended effective intra-Party channels for expressing differing opinions. The role of a loyal opposition within the Party guaranteed by Leninist protection of minority rights had been fundamentally violated.[99] Though Mao, at Lushan and into the 1960s until the Tenth Plenum in September 1962, tried to reassure cadres of their right to dissent openly, few were convinced.[100]

Given Mao's change of heart in late 1959, it is no surprise that Deng Tuo soon propagandized policies directly at odds with his advice from spring 1959. In February 1960 Deng Tuo appeared in *New Construction* (*Xin Jianshe*) praising Mao and his revived Leap policies.[101] The Great Leap, wrote Deng, was an unparalleled success, muted only by unfortunate natural disasters. Because Chairman Mao took agriculture as the foundation and industry as the 'pillar', such a wonder as the People's Communes has come to pass. In fact, Mao's idea that agriculture must be developed to keep pace with industry bridges a missing link in the Marxist-Leninist classics, and thus contributes a new, higher stage of Marxist-Leninist thought, which is 'entirely correct'.[102] The application of this unified policy in the Leap proves it, says Deng, 'to be entirely consistent with the basic law of objective economic development.' China's goal is to 'urbanize the countryside'—that is, to eliminate the differences between city and country, industry and agriculture, workers and peasants.[103] These words are also the diametrical opposite of what Deng would conclude in the internal review of Leap policies made in 1961 in the 'Chang Guan Lou' report (discussed in Chapter 5) and of what Deng argued in his *Evening Chats* column in 1961 and 1962. How can we explain this?

Praise of the Leap in 1960 and criticism of it in 1961 was entirely in line with Central Committee policy and Mao's pronouncements, so Deng's actions can be seen as loyalty to Leninist dicta on discipline. A closer reading of Deng's texts in retrospect shows, however, that Deng Tuo did not stress the 'psychological factor' (or 'subjective motivation', *zhuguan jidong*) or sheer human effort which Mao so depended upon in his Great Leap policies. Deng selectively praised the Great Leap. What he affirmed was Mao's vision of a radically unified economy and society—the synthesis of town and country. He advocated supplying the *material means* to effect that end: water projects and the mechanization of farming.[104] Contemporary observers may be forgiven for missing such fine-tuned, though significant, distinctions, which became clearer to outsiders only when the polemics of the Cultural Revolution highlighted their significance in the spring of 1966. With hindsight one can see signs of Deng Tuo's divergence from Mao's way—as in favouring technological revolution rather than Mao's continuing class revolution—even in Deng's declarations of public support for the Great Leap.

Deng's support of the Leap at that time and criticism of it shortly thereafter can be best explained by two things: first, the establishment supported the Leap under Liu Shaoqi and second, Deng Tuo, like so many others at the time, had become 'hot-headed' and overconfident. Roderick MacFarquhar has shown that Liu Shaoqi, rather than Mao, was the chief proponent of the Leap at its start in 1958 and has suggested that Liu saw this grandiose project as a wonderful way to inaugurate his ascent to top leadership. In the ranks of the establishment there is evidence that numerous officials and specialists supported the Leap as a *production drive*. Although Chen Yun in the highest ranks and Sun Yefang in the establishment ranks opposed the Leap, most of the establishment was openly committed to the Leap when in 1959 it became clear it was not working. Studies of Mao have shown his petulance and pride in reasserting the Leap after Peng Dehuai's embarrassing criticism of it. It is not unreasonable to suspect that the collective leadership also felt the need to defend and justify itself, as well, to protect the charisma of the Party.

'Yu Sui'an' Commentaries and Frontline *Editorials*

Deng Tuo's propaganda writing in *Frontline* during the Leap falls into two groups: his editorials for the journal and a series of commentaries he published under the pen-name Yu Sui'an. Deng's editorials reflect his national writings during the Leap. They support the Party line, while consistently stressing the material factors necessary for the Leap and warning against 'becoming dizzy with success'. His best effort to delimit the excesses of the heady Leap work style was to suggest that the Mass Line should serve as a check and balance on Party policy, that working closely with the common people should serve as feedback for Party cadres as to how the Leap was working.[105] In line with his own pronouncements on editorial writing, Deng endeavoured to relate Central Party policies to his locality, the Beijing municipality.

Of more interest are Deng's political commentaries published between October 1959 and 1961 under the pen-name Yu Sui'an.[106] These were published at the height of the renewed Leap. As his Chinese biographer, Wang Bisheng, notes, 'Deng couldn't avoid some words that followed the fashion of the day.' The articles are severe, long, and overbearing. They mark innocent people as Rightists and support the fancies of the Leap. For all their faults, these essays still reflect the strong points of Deng's *Frontline* editorials: the stress on Mass Line as a form of feedback to check the usefulness of a policy, the criticism of blind arrogance among cadres, and the criticism of abstract idealism along with the insistence on the need for concrete plans in carrying out policy.

These self-critical themes are precisely the ones Deng developed in his post-Leap critique of ultra-Leftism in 1961. Here we see the price of his political engagement in a Leninist regime. He could not press home the results of his careful research into the strengths and weaknesses of Party policy until *allowed* to do so by superiors. His dual role as cog and screw (propagandist) and as culture bearer (theoretician and expert adviser) too often pulled him in different directions.[107] Deng was not a mindless hack, though he wrote regrettable rubbish in the name of some Party policies and submitted to policies that he clearly did not approve of. Neither was Deng a dissident, though he wrote penetrating criticisms of the socialist system in China. He tried to be an independent-minded servant of the revolution, what he would later call 'independence within bounds'. He tried to *balance* following orders and giving advice. However, it is clear from the record that for Deng and his generation of establishment intellectuals, cog-and-screw obedience won out over culture-bearer autonomy—to the misfortune of all concerned.

Poetry and Academic Publications during the Leap

A second explanation of Deng's support of the Leap is that Deng and so many others became 'hot-headed' in 1958. The leading writer and

Party administrator, Xia Yan, recalls that during the Leap, officials such as himself were not only constrained to follow the current line, but were also 'influenced by the social conditions of the time' which led him and his colleagues to believe such extreme goals could indeed be reached.[108] Ding Yilan, Deng's widow, admits that these attitudes were, in Deng's case, contrary to his long experience in economic and especially agricultural work, and put the blame squarely on human frailty—Deng's and that of his leaders. As an example of Deng's 'hot-headedness', she cites his 1958 edition of classical poetry entitled *A New Collection of Tang Poetry*.[109]

In the collection's preface Deng raises the slogan, 'Let the old serve the new and politics first.' He states that this new compilation has been made to promote and improve the poetry of workers, peasants, and the masses and to purge the feudal-class view of the traditional (and immensely popular) *Three Hundred Poems of the Tang*.[110] Thus, writes Deng, only the progressive poems of Bo Zhuyi or Li Bo are selected and not their reactionary verses. Most especially the mysticism of Wang Wei has been marked for deletion.

Deng goes on to make two important points in his preface. First, he dismisses strict class analysis of the Tang poets because they all lived in a feudal age and thus would *a priori* be disqualified. This, he implies, is ludicrous because the poems are excellent. Second, he treats traditional elite Chinese culture with obvious pride: 'not only in the history of Chinese literature, but also in the history of world literature the songs and poems of Tang times are radiantly brilliant.'

These comments, and the selection of poems in the collection predicated on them, are problematic from two points of view. First, they continue Deng's elitist-oriented interpretation of Mao's populist theories. Deng holds these refined poems to be examples of literature in national forms which Mao had endorsed since his 'Talks at the Yan'an Forum on Literature and Art' in 1942. Yet Deng placed a heavier emphasis on the traditional elite literature in this popularization than did Mao. While Mao had acknowledged that there was something of value to be assimilated from the literary heritage of the past, he stressed the need to serve the workers and the peasants by writing works *derived* from their experience.[111] At the very time Deng was editing these Tang poems, Mao was promoting the collection of folk songs. The second problem with Deng's comments comes from the reverse angle. Deng's effort in this collection was in line with the Mao-backed 1958 'poetry campaign' to the degree that it was an effort 'to undermine the monopoly of literature still exercised by the May Fourth old guard of professionals.' Those who were to be undermined included Zhou Yang and other leaders in the literary

Maoism in Crisis 195

establishment in China at that time.[112] Here, Deng Tuo with his classicist approach to literature made a strange bedfellow with Mao in the assault on the foreignness of May Fourth intellectual traditions. Finally, it may be added that the selection is not very good. In his search for 'politically correct' verse from the Tang poets, Deng was forced to choose artistically inferior pieces, particularly anonymous poems which he rather disingenuously suggests were from the masses. Nonetheless, the collection is an admirable effort to combine scholastic rigour with political dictates. The volume is organized by style of poem (*wu yan jueju*, *qi yan jueju*, *wu yan lüshi*, *qi yan lüshi*, etc.) and not by political category such as 'Sufferings of the People', 'Resistance to Rent', or such. In good scholarly fashion each poem is extensively glossed, with explanations of difficult terms or obscure references. Finally there is a handy appendix of brief biographies of the poets included in the volume.[113]

A further factor which accounts for Deng Tuo's participation in the Great Leap is that he clearly prospered during the Leap years, despite his dismissal from the *People's Daily*. Like Wu Han and other establishment historians, Deng Tuo engaged in a flurry of reprints of his pre-1949 history works in 1958 and 1959.[114] In Wu Han's case, the increased publishing following his admission to the CCP in 1957 may reflect a 'material reward' for loyalty, since publishing in the 1950s was increasingly centralized and controlled by Party committees and since Wu had published little before 1957. However, there was a general upsurge in historical publications at this time, presaging the similar 'blooming' in 1961-2, and it may be more significant to look at the general pattern than at that of these two individuals.[115] In 1958 Deng republished his long book, *A History of Famine Relief in China*, still under an original and lesser-known name, Deng Yunte. In November 1959 he collected his 1930s essays in similar fashion into a volume including his more recent two articles, on *Hong lou meng* and coal mining, under his better-known revolutionary name, Deng Tuo.[116]

In addition, Deng maintained his privileged housing in Beijing and apparently was not 'sent down' to study in the countryside, as were Yang Xianzhen and the members of the Party School.[117] The different assignments of Deng and Yang in 1958 seem to reflect Yang's posting in a Central Party institution, the Party School, and Deng's in a local Party institution, the Beijing Committee. In fact, it is possible to argue that Deng was rewarded for his loyal support of the Leap, for he was appointed to a Central Party post, albeit only as an alternate, to the North China Bureau of the Central Committee when the Bureau was re-established in 1960.[118]

The Scholarly Style: Deng Tuo's Search for 'Space'

Deng Tuo's career in the Central Party ended in February 1959 when he officially left *People's Daily*.[119] If he had complained to Liu Binyan in 1956 of not being on the Central Committee, this dismissal laid to rest any reasonable hope of advancement. We can date the public development of Deng's scholarly style to his reversal of fortunes. He had a responsible position in the most powerful 'local' Party apparatus, the Beijing Municipal Party, but he was forty-seven years old. What was to mark his life, now that high office was certainly out of reach?

The *People's Daily* held a good-bye party for Deng Tuo in February 1959. His comments from the time and especially his valedictory poem (see Illus. 4.1) show that after two years of butting heads with the Chairman, Deng was ready to cede the field to Mao, but that he intended to carry on in a different vein. Deng chose to revive the scholarly style of his youth in Fuzhou. This was essentially a neo-traditional response to political misfortune. It also reflects the limited options available to Deng. He could not form (or join) another political party, and he could not with safety retreat to the protection of professional expertise. He wasn't a creative writer of the May Fourth sort, so he couldn't have his say in a timeless piece of literature, like Qian Zhongshu's *Walls*. He was not of Wang Meng's or Liu Binyan's generation, so he could not leave his urge to obey the Party behind in a bid for some 'second kind of loyalty'. And he certainly was not of the type or of the generation to leave the Party completely behind, such as some former Party intellectuals did in the late 1980s. His choice resembled the traditional option of Confucian scholar-officials: retreat to scholarly pastimes. This was not simply scholarship in history or some other branch of the humanities or social sciences. It was a way of life, a consciously emphasized self-image concretely expressed in poetry, calligraphy, aesthetics, art collecting, and lyric essays. This way of life existed among his colleagues in the privileged elite of socialist China who made up Deng's cultural circles. This life did not preclude taking part in current propaganda efforts or directly commenting now and again on current affairs. It was separate, an inner refuge, what Vera Schwarcz has identified as 'inner refusal' (in the midst of outer conformity).[120] It was space for personal integrity that politics could not touch. By 1959, Deng was in sore need of such space. By 1964, it was all he had left. In the Cultural Revolution even this space was denied.

Although Deng had maintained his classicist interests in the early 1950s, he was too busy in Beijing and *People's Daily* administration to

Maoism in Crisis 197

spend much time on such interests. Deng's public scholarly style began with his effective dismissal from the *People's Daily* in 1957 and developed (or at least its expression became clearer) after the Leap in the 1961–4 period. It began as solace and culminated in an effort to find a better way to be a socialist intellectual. We shall see in Chapter 5 that Deng articulated his scholarly style as a broad defence of the scholar-cadre as a culture bearer who could best maintain China's great heritage and modernization programme. Still, he often wondered if the effort was worth while.

Deng bemoaned the vicissitudes of editing the Party's newspaper in 1957 and intimated that he was ready to move on as early as the fall of 1956. He openly longed 'to withdraw to the monastery' during the anti-Rightist campaign. In April 1958 he made a public self-criticism to an expanded meeting of the *People's Daily* editorial board. 'I haven't been a good leader for the paper,' he said; 'I'm dissatisfied with myself, too. Some people say that my work over the past two years is not as good as before. I accept this criticism.' He went on that he wanted to continue to work, regardless of position or status, referring no doubt to his *de facto* demotion the year before. But he acknowledged two problems. First, 'I haven't correctly handled the relationship between the individual and the collective, and I have had some plans for academic research which I have not made clear to the editorial board and which have in the end become a millstone around my neck.'[121] This talk was most likely Deng's formal self-criticism which marks the end of the investigation of a cadre under the rectification process.[122] As such, we can read his acknowledged two errors in reverse light: Deng was unhappy with the pressures to submit to 'the collective' when that, in fact, amounted to the capricious whims of Mao and he preferred, under the circumstances, to do his academic work instead. Indeed, he had earlier considered just this course of action in April 1957 when the paper was being investigated by Hu Qiaomu's committee.[123]

Our first clear indication of what the scholarly style meant for Deng comes with his resignation and farewell to the *People's Daily*. On the afternoon of 20 February 1959, Wu Lengxi chaired the formal retirement party for Deng Tuo at the paper. Deng gave a brief farewell speech and read a poem. In his speech, Deng reiterates his faith in the tenets of bureaucratic Maoism: we must strengthen our 'Party discipline' (*dang xing*) in order to overcome liberalism and we must firmly rely on the ideological methods of Marxism—dialectical materialism. He urges his former subordinates to learn from the paper's past mistakes in order to serve the country better in the future.

Having stated his political views, Deng presented his *personal* feelings through a different 'voice'—poetry. 'Taking Leave of Friends at *People's Daily*' is a seven-character regulated verse in two quatrains in the Tang style (see Illus. 4.1). In this different voice, Deng again summarizes his twenty years of work as a leading Party journalist, but this time he expresses his individual values—his commitment to scholarly life, his friendship with colleagues, his hopes for the future:

> The pen's rolling like dragon and snake from twenty years,
> Distinguished brightness, neither dreamlike nor misty.
> Articles fill the page, the accumulation of a scholarly life,
> Companions in a storm-tossed boat, worthies among battle friends.
>
> Re-count to learn now the achievements and transgressions,
> Show concern so that finally the laggard may take the fore.
> A life's winnings in lofty sentiments reside,
> The nation's high tide reaches out to Heaven.[124]

Deng read the poem to a hushed audience. As he read each line, he paused to explain the significance of his imagery. In particular, he explained the third line, 'Articles fill the page, the accumulation of a scholarly life'. He said that only a few days earlier a friend had said of him: 'never not bookish' (*shusheng xiqi weineng wu*). This phrase, said Deng, has both its implied criticism of bookishness and pride and affirmation of self-confidence. He let the phrase stand as a description of himself.[125] Indeed, the phrase later became a private joke between Deng Tuo and his colleague at the *Beijing Evening News*, Gu Xing, a sort of badge of pride in the face of political pressure. Deng even carved a seal with this phrase on it and used it on calligraphy he gave to Gu Xing.[126] It is the wry humour of the pariah, who displays his deviant qualities like a Jew in Nazi Germany wearing his Star of David with a certain martyr's pride. It also evokes the traditional Chinese literati view of being out of synch with the reigning orthodoxy when that system strays from the Way. Self-mockery, fatalistic pride, and moral censure are compressed into this seven-character epigram. It is Deng Tuo's statement of 'inner refusal' when he cannot, or chooses not to, outwardly resist.

An insistence on scholarly airs and the expression of them through the exchange of elegant classical poetry is a time-honoured and unequivocal statement of resistance to political pressure among China's scholar-officials. The significance of Deng's scholarly airs after 1957 was not lost upon his audience. Mao acknowledged this scholarly style when he denounced Deng as the 'pedant editor' at the January 1958 Nanning Conference.[127] Here we can see Mao and Deng competing to set the interpretation that should apply to the scholarly style. Deng stressed the integrity and insight of the scholarly life, Mao its timidity and impracticality.

High Culture

In his private life, Deng Tuo had always been primarily interested in artistic and cultural matters—poetry, calligraphy, and connoisseurship. Before his dismissal from the *People's Daily* he did not publish many essays on these topics, but beginning in 1958, when he was established in the Beijing municipal committee, he began publishing a continual stream of articles on art and art history into 1964.[128] Liu Yongcheng, Deng's graduate student, recalls that of the stream of visitors to Deng's house the majority, and those Deng most enjoyed, were poets, calligraphers, and art collectors. This stream only increased after 1958.[129]

In China there is a field of study, *wenshi* or cultural history, which bridges our categories of general history and literary or art history. Deng Tuo contributed richly to this field by writing numerous essays on ancient painters, artefacts, and paintings and by being amongst Beijing's foremost antique collectors and authenticators of ancient art pieces. Deng amassed an impressive personal collection of calligraphy, paintings, and *objets d'art* which was plundered by his enemies in the Cultural Revolution. The inkings of his seal collection include ones he cut of his and other artists' poems as well as those which other seal carvers gave to him.[130] He is remembered particularly for his authentication of a Song dynasty painting that had baffled the experts. His essay on the Su Shi's landscape painting is considered the proof of its authenticity by art historians in China today.[131] A shrewd man, Deng bought the painting before he published his authentication. In 1964 he donated it, and the majority of 'his' collection now in the museum, to the National Gallery.[132] He was also director of the 'leadership small group', which included Jian Bozan, Fan Wenlan, and Wang Zhiqiu, that oversaw the construction of the National Museum from 1958 until its opening on 1 July 1961.[133]

Deng Tuo's activities as a poet and calligrapher were, in traditional Chinese fashion, informal. Equally, his calligraphy was intimately linked with poetry, and Deng is considered a good calligrapher of the 'running style' (*xingshu*). His calligraphic diversions brought Deng into contact with the world of professional artists in People's China. He would visit Wu Zuoren to discuss ancient styles and share in their connoisseurship of the ancient masters. He joined Huang Zhou and Zhou Huaimin in writing colophons on or matching poems to their paintings, particularly Zhou's noted landscape of Huangshan in Anhui province, which still hangs in the guest hall of that famous mountain resort.[134] These cultural pastimes provided a mechanism by which certain less aesthetic goals could be achieved. Gu Xing and editors of the *Beijing Evening News* used Deng's preference for cultural evenings discussing painting and poetry as a means of introducing their superior to their desire that he write a column for their paper in 1961. From these cultural evenings came *Evening Chats at Yanshan*.[135]

Deng's aesthetic pursuits produced another association that is rather surprising in light of later political history. He was apparently a friend of Kang Sheng, who today is reviled as the heinous 'adviser' to the 'Gang of Four'.[136] Two 'flower and painting' essays by Deng Tuo in the *Evening Chats* column, which are *not* included in the 1979 reprint, praise the work of the Shandong painter Lu Chishui. The *Beijing Evening News* printed one of Lu's paintings when one of these articles by Deng first appeared in the paper.[137] Lu Chishui was the pen-name of Kang Sheng. According to Deng's family, Deng and Kang were acquaintances and in light of Kang's role in Deng's death and the theft of Deng's art collection, they say only that Deng was too 'trusting' (*laoshi*).[138] This surprising association serves as a caution to historians as they seek to determine factional alliances and interest groups from the very partial data available now.

Deng's artistic interests were largely private, though he was not averse to putting his skills to patriotic service, and he was interested in commenting on the fine arts and their role in society. In 1963, his entry in the Beijing calligraphy and seal carving exhibition won first prize and was reprinted in the city's art magazine. In 1964 his calligraphy was on display at the prestigious Beijing art shop, Rongbaozhai, and in the city's chief shopping district, Wangfujing.[139] In *Evening Chats*, Deng wrote a series of three essays on calligraphy and its role in modern China. In one, 'A Few Points on Calligraphy', Deng begins by happily reflecting on the current (1962) interest in calligraphy but goes on to criticize the lifeless copying of ancient styles because it is not possible to determine which of the many dissimilar styles of former calligraphers is best. He writes:

Contemporary calligraphers, if you please, is it not sufficient to take the opinions of the various schools of calligraphy and integrate them? Patently this has not yet been done. Thus, it is only under the principle of 'Let a Hundred Flowers Bloom, Let a Hundred Schools Contend' and letting each style of calligraphy completely develop that we will achieve development in promoting this national art.[140]

Deng proceeds in the essay to draw from China's literary tradition, citing stories on or by famous ancient calligraphers directly in the classical language (*wenyan*)—the Chinese equivalent of quoting Ovid in Latin in *The Washington Post*. He always explains and comments on these passages, which anyone but the well educated would find hard to read. Deng not only treats calligraphy and his selection of classical literature as points of national pride, but he clearly regards these historical documents as legitimate authorities upon which to rest his case for the proper approach to art and its role in socialist society. He quotes from an essay of Zhao Congxuan of the Song dynasty in *The Chicken Ribs Collection* (*Ji lei ji*) to lampoon moribund copying of any master, a critique of what Levenson tagged as Ming 'formalism', and he cites the views of the noted Song polymath, Shen Gua, that Chinese characters are like beautiful women—although sharing common traits, who would want them all to be identical?[141]

Deng Tuo prospered during these years, but he was not happy. His poetry from 1960 reflects further disquiet with his role in the establishment, continuing the sentiment of his February 1959 poem written on his 'retirement' from the *People's Daily*: that the loyal intellectual must be prepared to suffer for his integrity.[142] In 1960, while recovering from his chronic illness, Deng visited the Yangzi River region in central China. Under the pen-name Zuo Hai, he published a cycle of five poems, 'South of the River Recitations', from which two quatrains in the third series, 'Singing the Praises of Lake Tai', address in powerful imagery Deng's feelings about the role of the intellectual in politics. Visiting the home of the famous Eastern Wood Academy (*Donglin yuan*) in Wuxi, just west of Shanghai, Deng praises the orthodox political critics of the early seventeenth century for their fortitude and martyrdom in the cause of reforming the government:

Passing By the Eastern Wood Academy
The Eastern Wood's discourses followed the Master of Turtle Hill,[143]
In all things showing concern between Heaven and earth.
None can say writers chatter emptily,
When blood stains where their heads rolled.

Asking Gao Zi to Still the Waters
With strength defying powerful traitors, with wills unmoved,
The Eastern Wood was a generation of such fine men!
Gao Panlong's moral fortitude,[144] all ages will know,
Each word stirs the heart from a martyr's verse.[145]

The Confucian scholar-officials of the Eastern Wood Academy, and particularly Gao Panlong, had opposed what they saw as the moral decadence and political misdirection of the Ming dynasty's Imperial Court. In this poem Deng not only records his emotions upon visiting the geographical site of the Academy, but implies that such politically active scholarship is still needed and may still have to suffer the political fate of Gao Panlong. This noble metaphor for Party intellectuals implicitly, but powerfully, raised the unpleasant matching image of Mao and his close associates as the weak late Ming emperors as well as their corrupt eunuch advisers whom the Eastern Wood scholars had battled against. Later in *Evening Chats*, Deng gives a short history of the Eastern Wood and makes clear his Marxist separation of their class limitations from their more general qualities worthy of emulation today. 'The truly learned scholar', he concludes, 'absolutely must take concern in politics. The learning of a scholar who is completely ignorant of politics, no matter what, is incomplete.'[146] Deng takes comfort from a camaraderie with previous scholar-officials who were demoted for their orthodox outspokenness in the central government. As with his 1957 critique of radical political mobilization and bureaucratism, the poems in 1960 did not parallel any break in Deng's service to the Party—he continued to propagandize current policy in *Frontline*. The poems expressed his personal view, signified by the use of pen-names. They were, however, published in the two major newspapers of China. This marks the beginning of Deng Tuo's return to public commentary but with his newly adopted scholarly style.

Conclusion

Between 1956 and 1960 Deng Tuo and his establishment colleagues paid the price for their political engagement in the CCP. Deng ran head-on into Chairman Mao when the Chairman shifted his concern from reforming non-Party intellectuals (1950–4), or using them in reforming the Party (1957), to reforming Party intellectuals themselves. This became part of a general—and radical—rectification of the Party. Deng Tuo's approach became explicitly uncongenial to the Chairman. Mao let Deng, whom he called the 'pedant editor', and other Party intellectuals know his displeasure in no uncertain terms. There was very little they could do about it, because their privileges in the system were just that, not rights. The fate of Peng Dehuai demonstrated that these were not defensible in the face of a determined Mao.

The cost of Deng's service was not simply to suffer Mao's wrath. Deng Tuo and most establishment intellectuals were complicit in the débâcle of the Great Leap Forward. This was not solely due to the person, Mao

Zedong, who, as a charismatic leader, pushed his views outside normal Party channels or by manipulating them. They let him do it. The record of Deng Tuo's writings in support of the Great Leap, both in early 1958 and after Lushan, is simply too extensive to claim that he acted under duress. The hot-headedness that drove Mao onward also blurred the vision of his bureaucrats. When they awoke to the grim reality of their folly in 1960, the country had been ravaged and the Party had been fractured.

Deng Tuo's response was to withdraw into his arts and cultural activities and to await his chance to speak again. From the base secured for him by Peng Zhen in the Beijing municipal Party administration, Deng Tuo created a scholarly space that provided him with a *status* based on his cultural expertise. This status was reminiscent of gentry culture in the Late Imperial period.[147] Deng Tuo was not replicating late Ming Confucian culture any more than he was reviving Gao Panlong's Eastern Wood Academy. He was employing these cultural symbols—of elite perception and sensitivity, integrity, and loyalty—to create a renewed public voice which he used to push his version of Maoism in the early 1960s.

Mao's actions and Deng Tuo's responses reflected the emerging breakdown of the Party orthodoxy, Marxism-Leninism-Mao Zedong Thought, under the pressures of administering a modernization programme. The two divergent leadership styles which emerged after the Leap represent a dissolution of the amalgam made in Yan'an. After the Leap, the 'managerial' and 'utopian' versions of Maoism would find increasingly distinct voices. These political orientations, which since Yan'an had been mutually limiting tendencies within Maoism, became mutually alienated versions of Maoism. 'Bureaucratic Maoism' and 'faith Maoism' finally became competitors. Once enunciated, there could only be room for one.

NOTES

1. Roderick MacFarquhar's trilogy (1974, 1983, 1997) gives a detailed history of this process inside the CCP leadership, as does Teiwes (1979 and 1988).
2. The Emperor of China as an absolute despot is one of the stereotypes put to rest by recent scholarship. See examples of frustrated Sons of Heaven in Huang (1981) and Kuhn (1990).
3. Ai was more involved in pure theory (philosophy) and Deng was an administrator (propaganda). Deng's philosophical approach tended more to the cautious materialism of Ai's rival, Yang Xianzhen, rather than Ai's more voluntaristic Marxism.

Yet there are further similarities. Fogel describes the young Ai as 'a man of extraordinary linguistic skills, a serious student of philosophy, an amazingly prolific writer, and a man committed to setting aright what he perceived as rampant injustice.' Replace 'linguistic skills' with 'historiographical skill' and you have Deng Tuo. All quotations from Fogel (1987: 86).

4. This broader pattern of intellectuals rising to prominence under the collective leadership and falling into disgrace in the Cultural Revolution is the December 9er syndrome. See Israel and Klein (1976).
5. Recent writings on and by the senior economist Sun Yefang demonstrate this pattern in more detail than is available for Deng Tuo. See Naughton (1986).
6. MacFarquhar (1974: 59–60 and 86ff.); Hu Huiqiang (1983: 748).
7. 'Yao fandui baoshouzhuyi.'
8. Wu Lengxi (1988).
9. Mao bitterly criticized the editorial and the *People's Daily* for this, but not until at least Oct. 1957 (see text below). There is no contemporary evidence from 1956 that Mao opposed any of these things. We simply do not know if his famous criticisms in January 1958 were an expression of long-nurtured grievances or one of his many changes of mood. On Mao's distressing moodiness during these years, see Schwartz (1989).
10. 'Yao fandui baoshouzhuyi', quoted in MacFarquhar (1974: 87); Hu Huiqiang (1983: 749).
11. 'Yao fandui baoshouzhuyi'. Deng continued this theme in *Evening Chats*, as in 'Chen Jiang he Wang Geng de anjian' (The Case of Chen Jiang and Wang Geng), *Beijing wanbao*, 22 June 1961 (YSYH/79: 540–2).
12. Teiwes (1979: 227); MacFarquhar (1974: 88ff.). MacFarquhar's account is essentially confirmed, and the link between this and Mao's January 1958 Nanning speech, by an article in an internal-circulation Party history journal; see Qiang Yuanjin and Chen Xuewei (1980: 41) and Hu Huiqiang (1983).
13. Mao Zedong, 'Zuo geming de zujinpai' (Be Activists in Promoting the Revolution), *Mao Zedong xuanji*: v. 474; Mao Tse-tung (1977: v. 491).
14. Mao Zedong, 'Nanning Speech', *Mao Zedong sixiang wansui* (1966–9: 152).
15. Mao Zedong, 'Nanning Speech', *Mao Zedong sixiang wansui* (1966–9: 151). Although the versions of this speech which are available use 'Comrade X X', Ding Yilan (personal communication, Sept. 1985) has confirmed that these phrases were directed at Deng Tuo. The Nanning conference became the scene of Mao's most violent attack on 'oppose adventurism'. Here, says a recent dictionary of Party history, Mao first made his slogan 'continuing the revolution' (*jixu geming*) and made his fateful claim that a *policy* (here the policy of moderate economic growth represented by 'oppose adventurism') was a *political question*. This definition of policy disagreements took away the right of meaningful open dissent within the party. See *Zhonggong dangshi shijian renwu lu* (1983: 395). The editors (p. 759) make it clear they are following the dictates of Hu Yaobang and the 12th Party Congress in their interpretations.
16. A brief paragraph in a new collection of Mao's informal works directly attacks the editorial, but the dating given there of 1956 is likely a typographical error and is not supported by other documentary evidence. See 'Criticism of the 20 June 1956 *People's Daily* Editorial' (June 1956) and 'Criticism of *People's Daily*, which Should Not "Oppose Adventurism"' (Jan. 1958), tr. in MacFarquhar, Cheek, and Wu (1989: 393–6). These texts come from a newly available collection of various Red Guard editions of Mao's writings published during the Cultural Revolution in 1967. They are referenced by their volume title as well as by the volume number assigned to

them in the critical assessment of their authenticity in MacFarquhar, Cheek, and Wu (1989: 78–81). The original Chinese texts have been reprinted by CCRM, Oakton, Va., which also maintains this volume numeration. The paragraph in question here comes from the Chinese text in *Mao Zedong sixiang wansui* (Sept. 1967: 159–61, quotation from p. 161). For variant texts of this passage see MacFarquhar, Cheek, and Wu (1989: 395, n. 2). The reader should keep in mind that though likely to be authentic texts of Mao Zedong, the titles were likely added by editors and not Mao.

17. Deng's key error, it seems, was the confession renouncing communism he signed to gain release from the KMT's Suzhou Reformatory in 1933. He had been censured but cleared by the Party organization during his 1944–5 'investigation'. According to a few of his colleagues, from whom this information comes, Deng withdrew his name from the 8th Central Committee list to avoid having these questions aired in the new atmosphere, where unquestioning loyalty took precedence over organizational decisions in the past. Ding Yilan denies this and maintains Deng gave way 'in order to give younger cadres the opportunity to serve.' Deng avers to his historical mistakes and his organizational clearance in his suicide note of 17 May 1966. See Wang Bisheng (1986: 225).
18. 1956*a*.
19. Deng upheld the orthodox picture of 'sprouts of capitalism' but argued that they should be dated a century later than was currently held to be the case. See discussion of 'Cong Wanli dao Qianlong' in Ch. 3.
20. Xu Zhucheng (1987: 19 and 21). Xu blames Ke Qingshi for his anti-intellectualism and says *Laoshi bao* was started by the Ministry of Culture in order to imitate a similar publication in the Soviet Union.
21. Xu Zhucheng (1987: 21); Xu also records his respect for Deng Tuo in Xu Zhucheng (1981: 312–18).
22. Indeed, page 8 of the *People's Daily*, where such intellectual essays were published, soon stopped publishing interesting ones, according to Hu Qiaomu. MacFarquhar, Cheek, and Wu (1989: 220).
23. According to Xu (1987: 21–2) it was a great success largely because he followed Deng Tuo's advice. Xu says Deng continued his support through the fall with three long letters discussing various aspects of the paper's work.
24. This was a revival, in essence, of the transitional United Front policies of the 'new democratic' period of 1949–52 as adapted for new conditions five years later. Xu's reminiscences are published clearly in the service of reviving that same United Front in the 1980s. For background on this line of CCP policy towards intellectuals, see Mazur (1994 and 1997).
25. Tr. in Nieh (1981: 473–511); selected criticisms of Wang's story are translated on pp. 518–63.
26. Mao said to representatives of press and publishing circles on 10 Mar. 1957 (including Xu Zhucheng and Deng Tuo), '[When I] read the article by Chen Qitong, Ma Hanbing, and others, [I] thought some people might think their article represented the opinion of the Centre, [and] therefore [I] felt it necessary to talk about it in a thoroughgoing manner.' See MacFarquhar, Cheek, and Wu (1989: 268).
27. This is covered in MacFarquhar (1974). Newly available copies of Mao's speeches and talks from this period confirm the intensity of his efforts and of Party resistance to them; see MacFarquhar, Cheek, and Wu (1989: 113–372). The 27 Feb. talk 'On Correct Handling of Contradictions' appears on pp. 131–90 and the 12 Mar. talk appears in Mao Tse-tung (1977: v. 422–35).
28. MacFarquhar, Cheek, and Wu (1989: 145–6); related comments on non-Party

participation in power on pp. 303, 358, 361, and 366–7. Mao's words invoked the same United Front policies from 1949 that Deng Tuo's addressed. However, Mao implied a greater political role for non-Party intellectuals and this was the rub for the Party establishment.

29. MacFarquhar (1974: 217); Teiwes (1979: 211 ff.) argues the difference of opinion was not so extreme.
30. It was the meeting of provincial and municipal Party secretaries. Mao's January summation speech to it appears in *Mao Zedong Wansui*: 81–90 and Mao describes these events in his 27 Feb. speech, as he criticizes the *People's Daily*; see MacFarquhar, Cheek, and Wu (1989: 168–9). Mao mentions the Chen Qitong article constantly in February and March, beginning with the 16 Feb. 'Talk at Yinian Tang' in Zhongnanhai during a Central Propaganda Conference; see MacFarquhar, Cheek, and Wu (1989: 118–19 ff.). Mao was incensed, and berated Deng Tuo and the *People's Daily* editorial board in April for this slight. See Wang Ruoshui (1989). I was able to confirm the contents of this article with Wang Ruoshui (interview with author, Harvard, Mar. 1989).
31. For details, see MacFarquhar (1974: 201–2). Although Mao at first said 'it was OK for the *People's Daily* to publish [Chen's article]', he repeatedly berates both Deng Tuo and the *People's Daily* for doing so thereafter; see MacFarquhar, Cheek, and Wu (1989: 119, 168–9, 194, 204, 210, 221–2, 264, 268, and *passim*).
32. Xu Zhucheng (1987: 23 ff.).
33. For an analysis of the significance of Mao's fickle moods during this period, see Schwartz (1989).
34. Deng Tuo was. See Wang Bisheng (1986: 244).
35. MacFarquhar, Cheek, and Wu (1989: 168–9).
36. It was part of Mao's answer that avoided responding to the question, 'how does one manage right and wrong in journalism?' (MacFarquhar, Cheek, and Wu 1989: 199). Deng also gave a talk to one of the meetings held during the National Propaganda Work Conference in Mar. 1957. See Wang Bisheng (1986: 155).
37. Xu Zhucheng's reminiscence of the meeting mentions that Deng Tuo, Jin Zhonghua, Wang Yunsheng, Shu Xincheng, and others he didn't recognize were sitting around the table in a building inside Zhongnanhai (these people's questions appear in the transcript translated in MacFarquhar, Cheek, and Wu 1989: 249–69, along with a few others). Neither Liu Shaoqi, Zhou Enlai, nor other top leaders were present nor were chief propagandists, like Lu Dingyi and Zhou Yang (according to the transcript, however, Zhu Muzhi, in charge of NCNA, was present). Mao, along with Kang Sheng, had greeted each guest at the door, saying to Xu, 'Your *Wen Hui Bao* is really well done. . . . When I get up in the afternoon, I read your paper first, then I turn to *People's Daily*.' Kang Sheng was the master of ceremonies. See Xu Zhucheng (1987: 24). There are differences between Xu's reminiscence of the meeting and the transcript of it translated in MacFarquhar, Cheek, and Wu (1989). Xu says the meeting was about two hours long; the transcript says it lasted from 3 to 7 p.m. Xu's comments to Mao and Mao's responses focus on Xu's troubles with the Shanghai authorities (especially Zhang Chunqiao, who was criticizing *Wen Hui Bao* for publishing criticisms of current movies) and Mao said he would get Zhou Yang to write a letter supporting *Wen Hui Bao*; in the transcript this is handled more generally. Xu recalls Mao mentioning Li Xifan, Wang Meng, and (positively) Yao Wenyuan; they do not appear in the transcript. Other points between the two texts are, however, similar.
38. Deng Tuo offered an explanation, that Ma had said the article reflected their

Maoism in Crisis 207

complaints and that he hoped no changes would be made in the article. See MacFarquhar, Cheek, and Wu (1989: 252).
39. Liu Binyan (1990: 55).
40. MacFarquhar, Cheek, and Wu (1989: 267–8). Mao side-stepped the question, returning to the marriage law example. In frustration, Zhu Muzhi next asked if there could be a special meeting convened to summarize the Party's conclusions on current policy. The Chairman was relentless—he refused to give specific guidelines to his propagandists.
41. MacFarquhar, Cheek, and Wu (1989: 265–6).
42. The primary significance of the 20 June 1956 editorial on 'Oppose Adventurism' to Mao becomes clear in his criticism of the paper, particularly in Jan. 1958; see MacFarquhar, Cheek, and Wu (1989: 393–6). During early Mar. 1957, Deng Tuo was also leading small-group discussions among journalists; see Xu Zhucheng (1987: 24–5).
43. Hu Qiaomu, Deng Xiaoping, Lu Dingyi, and Wang Jiaxiang were among the members of the new *baoshe weiyuanhui* (Newspaper Committee) which was led by an unnamed Politburo member. See Wang Bisheng (1986: 150). For an earlier example of this from 1942, see Wylie (1980: 179).
44. Ding Yilan (personal communication, Sept. 1985).
45. Chinese source, M1 (personal communication). See internal directives on how to handle the 'Contradictions' speech in *Xinhua Doc's*, vol. 4, from spring 1957 (via Schoenhals 1992).
46. Details of the meeting come from Wang Ruoshui (1989 and interview with author, May 1986, Fuzhou). The editorial was 'Jixu fangshou, guanche "Baihua jifang, baijia zhengming" de fangzhen' (Continue to Let Go, Grasp the Policy of 'Let a Hundred Flowers Bloom, Let a Hundred Schools Contend'); also briefly covered in Wang Bisheng (1986: 150 and 174).
47. Wang Ruoshui (1989). Later in this account Deng says to Mao that he has repeatedly offered his resignation and hoped that this time the Chairman might accept it. Mao did not. Hu Jiwei also suggests that Deng's thoughts on leaving *People's Daily* date back to the troubles he experienced over his preliminary selection to the 8th Central Committee. See Hu Jiwei (1986: 10).
48. The board members were: Deng, Hu Jiwei, Wang Ji, Huang Caoliang, Lin Tanqiu, and Yuan Shuibo (who came later directly to Mao's bedroom).
49. Further, so far unsubstantiated, reports in the post-Mao period would indicate such aggressive informality was not unusual for Mao. One is reminded of the famous 'toilet lectures' Lyndon Johnson gave his staffers when he was President.
50. This article was titled 'A Few Opinions We Have on Current Literary Work'. The authors—Chen Qitong, Ma Hanbin, Chen Yading, and Lü Le—were all in the military. The article expressed anxiety about implementation of the Hundred Flowers policy. It was published in the *People's Daily* on 7 Jan. 1957.
51. Quotations as recalled by Wang Ruoshui (1989). My thanks to Michael Schoenhals for helping me divine the Chairman's colloquial meaning. The gist of this meeting, and several of the key themes and phrases, have been reconfirmed from other sources, especially the author's interview with Hu Hua (Harvard, 21 May 1987); with Wang Ruoshui (Mar. 1989); and in a conference paper by a *People's Daily* member with access to the paper's archives, Zhou Xiuchang (1986: 11–12). Zhou's article is in three parts. The first, on Deng's approach to editorials, was published in *Xinwen Zhanxian*, 1986, no. 5, pp. 6–10; the second, on Deng's commentaries and *zawen*, in *Renmin ribao*, 11 May 1986, p. 5; but the third (pp. 11–12), on Deng's

confrontations with Mao, has not been openly published. This section includes a long summary of the meeting, drawn I assume from the memo which Deng produced for his editors after the meeting with Mao (mentioned, below, in Wang's reminiscence). The final source is Mao's own criticism of *People's Daily* in his Jan. 1958 Nanning speech (*Mao Zedong Wansui*: 151–2) and 'Criticism of *People's Daily*, which Should Not "Oppose Adventurism"'; see MacFarquhar, Cheek, and Wu (1989: 393–6). This text exists in various forms. The one used in MacFarquhar, Cheek, and Wu is dated Jan. 1958, but repeats (and expands upon) another dated 1956. Indeed, Zhou Xiuchang cites his summary of the meeting to 'Mao Zedong, April 1957 "Criticism of *People's Daily*."'

52. Actually it was a meeting of 'provincial and municipal Party secretaries'. Thus his comments later in this paragraph likely include Peng Zhen, first Party secretary of Beijing municipality.
53. Mao had also made this criticism, without mentioning specific names, in his 6 Mar. talk with regional propaganda, culture, and education officials; see MacFarquhar, Cheek, and Wu (1989: 210).
54. For Mao's agenda, see MacFarquhar (1974) and Teiwes (1979: chs. 6 and 7). The supreme leader's desire to 'rectify' his bureaucracy is not new in Chinese political history; see Kuhn (1987), which describes the Qianlong Emperor's use of 'literary inquisition' (*wenzi yu*) to keep his bureaucracy in check. This analysis is extended in Kuhn (1990).
55. Additional information in this paragraph based on author's interview with Wang Ruoshui in Fuzhou on 14 May 1986; Hu Jiwei (1986: 10–11) recalls this incident.
56. See text below and Wu Lengxi (1988).
57. Hu Qiaomu confirmed that he was at this meeting with Deng and Wang *et al.*, but did not discuss the content of the meeting (interview with Michel Oksenberg and Lawrence Sullivan, University of Michigan, 12 Apr. 1989).
58. If Wang Ruoshui's reminiscence is accurate on this point, this is troubling confirmation that Mao—in some of his moods—did not accept the legitimacy of the range of public opinions his exhortations would bring from non-Party critics *before* he pushed the Party to allow such criticisms three weeks later. On the other hand, Mao may have been playing both sides of the fence: stressing this to Party propagandists and stressing the right to speak up to non-Party meetings.
59. Mao had made this suggestion in his 10 Mar. meeting with journalists; see MacFarquhar, Cheek, and Wu (1989: 266).
60. The above material comes from Wang Ruoshui's reminiscence. The report is probably the basis of Zhou Xiuchang's quotations from Mao at this meeting (Zhou Xiuchang 1986: 12). Wang Bisheng (1986: 150–1) avers to this meeting without detail and cites yet another, attended by Lu Dingyi, Wang Jiaxiang, and Deng Xiaoping, and chaired by Hu Qiaomu, on 1 Apr. 1957. I am not aware of this meeting, and Wang cites 'Deng Tuo's handwritten notes in Ding Yilan's possession'.
61. See 'Zhonggong zhongyang guanyu zhengfeng' (1957: 575–9). For Mao's earlier comments see MacFarquhar, Cheek, and Wu (1989: 262 and 359) and MacFarquhar (1974: 177–83, 207–10).
62. 1957. This essay is reprinted in 1980c: 152–4 and DTWJ: iv. 525–7. Deng cited the famous poet and travel writer, Lu You (1125–1210), under his pen-name, Lu Fangwen. For Mao's use of 'quacks', see MacFarquhar, Cheek, and Wu (1989: 121); Mao also calls Party members 'doctors' in his 6 Mar. talk (p. 206).
63. For a summary and analysis of these, see MacFarquhar (1960) and Goldman (1967: 158–202).

64. 1957, tr. in Cheek (1983–4: 31–2).
65. Sullivan (1986–7: 622–3, 628–9). A 28 November 1956 *People's Daily* article criticized the 'elaborate organizational structure' of the co-operatives which reinforced authoritarian tendencies of cadres who were alienating the peasantry with grandiose plans produced by an excessively autocratic party machine. On Mao's criticisms of bureaucratism, see Teiwes (1979 and 1986).
66. See the selections of her views in J. Doolin (1964).
67. Interview with Lin Xiling (Harvard, Feb., 1986).
68. Liu Binyan (interview with author, 21 Oct. 1989, Harvard University). Liu remembers this as an act of kindness on Deng's part. Liu says he was particularly influenced by the Soviet writer, Valintine Oevechkin, whom Liu had escorted around China in Sept. 1956 as part of a *Pravda* delegation visit. Deng Tuo later returned the otherwise lost manuscript and it was published as 'Jizhe zhiyehang' (Liu Binyan 1988). See Liu Binyan (1990: 54–8).
69. MacFarquhar (1974: 270); Solomon (1971: 22–3). Wu attacked his colleague in the Democratic League, Luo Longji, and then took over his job. See MacFarquhar (1974: 271) and Fisher (1986: 161).
70. Xu Zhucheng (1987: 26–7). What Deng would have published, if this suppression was the case, is unknown, but I suspect it would have been along the lines of his 'Politics of Simpletons'.
71. Hu Jiwei (1986: 11). The same view is echoed by 'a *People's Daily* journalist's' account of Deng's role in the paper (1980*b*: 196).
72. Wu Lengxi (1988: 1–4). Wu notes that Deng Xiaoping stressed that Deng Tuo was still in charge, but Hu Jiwei says Deng was really 'put to one side'. See Hu Jiwei (1986: 11). Wang Bisheng (1986: 244) says Deng was appointed publisher by the Centre on 29 June.
73. Xu Zhucheng (1987: 29); Wang Bisheng (1986: 169–70); Hu Jiwei (1986: 11). Mei Yi, a radio journalist and long-time colleague and friend of Deng's, recalls seeing him in hospital during the summer of 1957 recovering from migraines (personal communication).
74. The muted 'dismissal', support by Deng Xiaoping, and Deng's 'gentlemanly relationship' with his successor are described in Wu Lengxi (1969–70).
75. Both served in the *People's Daily*. Hu Jiwei served as editor-in-chief of the paper from 1977 until he and Wang Ruoshui, who served during those years as deputy editor-in-chief, were demoted in the Campaign against Spiritual Pollution in 1983. Hu was until 1983 chairman of the Chinese Journalists' Association and Wang was in limbo, 'at the *People's Daily* but without a posting.' Wang was expelled from the Party in 1987 and Hu was dismissed from the NPC in 1990 in the wake of the 1989 Tianenmen massacre. See Hu Jiwei (1986: 4–14), and Kelly (1985: 115; 1987). Judy Polumbaum is working on Hu Jiwei's biography with his assistance.

    Hong Kong sources have been misleading on these points, quoting Wang Ruoshui as saying Deng Tuo was able to place him in the *People's Daily* in the early 1960s. This serves as a warning of the limitations of the lively though not always reliable Hong Kong press. See 'Pai Hsing's Lu Keng Meets Wang Ruoshui', from *Bai Xing* (Hong Kong), no. 103, 1 Sept. 1985, tr. in FBIS-CHI, 10 Sept. 1985, p. W8.
76. Huang Xianjun (1980 and YDT: 208–9). Deng repeats the value of testing work in progress in his *Evening Chats* article on pen-names, arguing that pen-names both save face for the author if he is criticized and encourage critics to speak freely. See, 'Do You Approve the Use of Pen-Names?' (1979*a*: 302 or Cheek 1983–4: 63).
77. Li Jun (1980: 101–2); Wang Bisheng (1983*a*: 79). MacFarquhar (1974: 282) notes

Deng's 1957 dismissal, but on p. 312 acknowledges he still 'continued to run the paper much as before.'
78. Chen Kehan and Li Jun (1979); tr. in FBIS–CHI, 15 Aug. 1979, p. L23; and 1980c: 199.
79. Li Jun (YDT: 101 and 105).
80. Li Jun (YDT: 101–10); Li Jun (1964). Full runs of the journal *Qianxian* are not available in the West. I am grateful to Lawrence Sullivan for sharing his photocopies from *Qianxian*.
81. It is already well-known from MacFarquhar (1974) that leading Party member Chen Yun 'got the 'flu' when the Great Leap policies gained CC support, that is he simply withdrew in protest. Yang Xianzhen has recently reflected on his failure to denounce Leap policies in 1959 following his own investigations of fraud and famine in Henan due to his fear of crossing leaders. See Hamrin (1986). Sun Yefang, a senior economic adviser, was more forthright in his criticisms and suffered for them (and is particularly honoured for his *unusual* behaviour today); see Naughton (1986).
82. *Mao Zedong Wansui*: 154, cited in MacFarquhar (1983: 28). Deng Tuo would take this injunction much more seriously than Mao in an *Evening Chats* essay of Oct. 1961, 'In All Things Show Concern'. See Ch. 5.
83. Deng Tuo, 'Xinwen gongzuo hong zhuan de daolu,' *Xinwen Zhanxian* (News Battlefront) (Beijing), 1958: 9, pp. 2–7 and 54.
84. 1958*d*.
85. 1958*d*: 12–13.
86. 1958*d*: 19.
87. 1958*c*. This was the page of the paper which Deng edited himself after his removal from the post of editor-in-chief in June 1957. Deng's use of '*Da yue jin*' in the *People's Daily* may deserve the dubious distinction of being the first usage of the term in the national press. Zhou Enlai unveiled the term a few days later in a 12 Feb. *People's Daily* editorial, though the term had been occasionally used in the provincial press since mid-Nov. 1957. See MacFarquhar (1983: 34 and 347).
88. MacFarquhar (1983: 119–55) describes the development of the retreat over the early months of the year.
89. 1959*f*. Tellingly, this is the *only* theory piece by Deng from the Leap period included in his *Works* (DTWJ: i. 331–58). Among Chinese studies on Deng, only Wang Bisheng (1986: 175–6) makes an honest, if mild, assessment of Deng's support of the Leap. Wang concludes that it was wrong, but that Deng was under heavy pressure to 'bend with the wind'.
90. 1959*e*; repr. in 1980*c*: 155–7; DTWJ: iii. 528–30.
91. 'Jixu geming'; see *Zhonggong dangshi shijian renwu lu* (1983: 395). For a broader consideration of these events, see MacFarquhar (1983: 24 ff.).
92. Teiwes (1979: ch. 9, pp. 384–440); MacFarquhar (1983: ch. 7, pp. 187–251).
93. Joffe (1975: 12 ff.).
94. Teiwes (1979: 408–12); MacFarquhar (1983: 212–16).
95. Quoted in Teiwes (1979: 414) from *Chinese Law and Government* (Winter 1968–9), 44.
96. Teiwes (1979: 422).
97. Teiwes (1979: 437).
98. Teiwes (1979: 439). The idea of rectification as something other than various forms of terrorism is not popular among Western scholars. Even mild 'educational' thought reform violates basic Western notions of intellectual and personal autonomy. It behoves historians to doubt such common sense and to listen to Chinese

Maoism in Crisis   211

reports, which turn out to be mixed. Some Chinese found thought reform personally liberating for a while. See, for example, Liu Binyan (1990). Their faith is supported by my personal interviews with Deng Tuo's colleagues. Taking the view of Chinese cadres into account raises more interesting questions: Why was thought reform felt to be so liberating in the 1940s and for whom? Why, when clear cases of administrative terror exist from the start (viz. the Wang Shiwei case of 1942 and the 'rescue campaign' purges of 1942–4—mentioned in Ch. 2 above) did the idealism survive for so many? Finally, how did this redemptive confessional community completely degenerate into a tool of state terror and then disintegrate into the pointless ritual it is in China today? The best beginning research on these questions are Teiwes (1979), esp. ch. 1; Whyte (1974); and Apter and Saich (1994).

99. For Lenin's views on minority rights of Party members under democratic centralism, see the discussion in Liebman (1975: 51–2). Liebman sums up Lenin's position as 'Freedom of discussion, unity of action.'
100. Teiwes (1979: 491). Teiwes cites the Chang Guan Lou review of 1961 as an example of how eroded official central Party channels for minority rights had become. This is discussed later in Ch. 5.
101. 1960b, tr. in *Extracts from China Mainland Magazines* (*ECMM*), 206, pp. 8–14.
102. *ECMM*, 206, p. 12.
103. *ECMM*, 206: 13–14. Deng's words here reflect Mao's transformational goals for China at the time; see Starr (1979), esp. ch. 9 on 'Political Development' and pp. 299–300.
104. *ECMM*, 206, pp. 12–14.
105. Deng's editorials are discussed in Wang Bisheng (1986: 179–80).
106. The pen-name reflects Deng's home address from the mid-1950s at No. 5 Yusui'an Alley. Eight essays have been identified, appearing in the journals *Shishi shouce* (Contemporary Handbook) and *Zhengzhi xuexi* (Political Study). Details on these essays come from Wang Bisheng (1986: 178–82 and 257–8).
107. Wang Bisheng (1986: 182–4) makes a sensitive analysis of this tension, contrasting Deng's role as a 'propagandist with strong Party discipline' and as a 'theorist with independent thinking (*sisuo*)'. For more discussion on this tension, see the conclusion of this chapter.
108. *Xia Yan on Creativity*, 'Preface', quoted in Wang Bisheng (1986: 182).
109. Ding Yilan (personal communication); 1958*i*: 1. A denunciation of Deng's editing of this volume from a Cultural Revolution perspective appeared in *Guangming Daily* by Gao Wen'ge on 24 May 1966. Deng's edition has been universally ignored in the rehabilitation literature in China in the 1980s.
110. 1958*i*: 1. The popular-tradition compilation, *Tang shi sanbai shou* (Three Hundred Poems of the Tang), attributed to Sun Zhu, had been most recently reprinted in Beijing in 1956.
111. Mao had stressed the literature of peasant tales and simple vernacular in this famous lecture on the role of literature in Party-run society; see Mao Tse-tung (1977: iii), esp. pp. 75–9. This, of course, is the 1953 revision. For Mao's earlier version of these comments, see the translation by McDougall (1980). On the 1958 movement to collect folk songs, see MacFarquhar (1983: 41–2).
112. McDougall (1980: 39). Since that very 'old guard' which this movement aimed to undermine returned to prominence in the 1980s, including Zhou Yang, who wrote the preface to *DTWJ*, the embarrassment of Deng's 1958 contribution to a campaign designed to undermine them is understandable.
113. 1958*i*: 155–65. Deng also returned to print as a poet in Sept. 1958 with a series of

poems and 'matched pairs' of others' paintings with his poetry that appeared in *People's Daily* into 1959. Seven examples can be found in *Renmin ribao* from 1 Sept. 1958 to 15 Mar. 1959, usually on p. 8 (1958*k, l, m, n, o;* 1959*a, d*).
114. Fisher (1986: 161 and n. 18).
115. This question needs considerably more research. The first thing that comes to mind is the increase of publications' relationship with the intellectual 'thaw' of 1956, but actually it is more correlated with the Great Leap and an effort to establish a separate identity from foreign and Soviet scholarship, a theme again in the 'antibourgeois' rhetoric surrounding the 1961–2 academic publication flurry. This particular instance, publishing, is a useful specific case to study further our developing re-assessment of policy periods in the PRC. That is, the Leap period is considered to be contrary to the 1961–2 period. However, Nina Halpern's study of the policy participation of economists around this time indicates a similar revision of interpretation—that continuities between the Leap and 'Thermidorean' periods are greater, particularly in institutional practice, than we previously thought. See Halpern (1987).
116. 1958*e* and 1959*j*. At least one article in the collection of essays is highly edited from two originals in the 1930s (on 'long-term blockage' in China's economy). Interestingly, the editing seems mostly to obscure Deng's lengthy debate with He Ganzhi in 1935–6 rather than to change Deng's conclusions. See 1959*i*: 47–60 (1979 edn.: 61–73). For details, see Ch. 1.
117. Hamrin (1986: 67–9).
118. 'Memorial Meeting' (YDT: 2); *Zhongguo wenxuejia cidian* (1982: 111). Deng's behaviour in 1958–60 and the low status of his Central Party appointment recall the rehabilitation phase of the rectification process described by Teiwes (1979). It seems to me that this was part of Peng Zhen's plan to prepare his *organizational support* as he sought to convince Mao of his policy suggestions. This was cut short by Mao's increasingly unpredictable behaviour, and from around 1964, his apparent frustration with Peng and the Beijing intellectuals.
119. Deng's appointment as an alternate to the North China Bureau in 1960 seems not to have changed this.
120. Schwarcz analyzes 'qinggao' and 'qijie' (integrity) in her 'Afterword' (Hamrin and Cheek 1986: 250–1) and Schwarcz (1984: 241–8).
121. The meeting was held on 21 Apr. 1958. Wang Bisheng (1986: 175).
122. For details of this pattern, see Teiwes (1979: 39–42).
123. Wang Bisheng (1986: 150). Wang concludes by saying that Deng, upon reflection, remembered his duty to the Party and stayed on in the *People's Daily* in spring 1957. However, other sources (see discussion above) make clear that the 'reminding' was provided by an angry Chairman Mao at the 10 Apr. 'bedroom' meeting.
124. 'Liu bie "*Renmin ribao*" zhu tongzhi', in 1988: 53; repr. in DTWJ: iv. 89. Deng's original calligraphy for this poem, which he presented to his colleagues, is often reprinted, as in the front matter of *Renmin xinwenjia Deng Tuo* (1987).
125. Reminiscence of Yuan Ying, who attended the meeting, cited in Wang Bisheng (1986: 174). Yuan Ying, a poet in his own right, wrote the appreciation at the end of *Deng Tuo shici xuan* and an article from 1986, 'Yu sui' (Broken Jade) (Yuan Ying 1986).
126. Gu Xing (interview with author, May 1986, Beijing). Gu Xing edited *Evening Chats* as it appeared in the *Beijing wanbao* in 1961; see discussion below. The piece in question on which this seal is marked is Deng's calligraphy of a letter of similar scholarly friendship during adversity from Lu Xun to Qu Qiubai. I saw this version

hanging in Gu Xing's Beijing apartment; the scroll has a colophon by Deng presenting the calligraphy to Gu. Another version of the calligraphy appears in Deng's collection of calligraphy (1988: 74 and 216-17).
127. See Mao's talks at the 11 and 12 Jan. 1958 Nanning Conference (*Mao Zedong sixiang wansui*: 151) and discussion, above, in this chapter.
128. Some two dozen are collected in 1980c and more in DTWJ: iv.
129. Liu Yongcheng (interview with author, Harvard, Feb. 1986). Tu Wei-ming discusses similar aspects of *haute culture* reflected in Deng's *Evening Chats* articles in the early 1960s, and it is fair to say, based on Liu Yongcheng's account, that these interests and activities pervaded Deng's life from at least the mid-1950s. See Tu Wei-ming (1979: 263-4).
130. The collection, which was also plundered in the Cultural Revolution, now contains several hundred items. A few photographs of his collection, and one of his seals, appears in a general discussion of Deng's art collection in Wang Bisheng (1983d).
131. 1962d; see YDT: 154-5 and Wang Bisheng (1986: 200 ff., esp. 205) for details. On his collection and the recent Beijing exhibition, see Wang Bisheng (1983d) and *China Daily*, 6 Jan. 1982, p. 5.
132. Deng's collection was shown at the National Art Gallery in Beijing in Dec. 1981 and Jan. 1982. See 'Art collection by Deng Tuo exhibited to mark his death', *China Daily*, 6 Jan. 1982, p. 5. The exhibition pamphlet distributed at the show gives the title 'Deng Tuo zangshu, shufa zhanlan' (Exhibition of Deng Tuo's Collection and Calligraphy) and lists 22 pieces in his own hand and 144 pieces from the Song through the Qing dynasty from his former collection. This collection was donated to the Gallery by Deng before the Cultural Revolution in 1964. Kang Sheng is accused of plundering the remainder of Deng's art collection during the Cultural Revolution. See Zhong Kan (1982: 263).
133. Chen Qiao and Shi Shuqing (YDT: 164). Memorial articles with detailed reminiscences of Deng's activities in poetry, art collecting, and *wenshi* are found in YDT: 152-202, which includes Yuan Ying's postface to Deng's 1980 collection of poetry (YDT: 175-89).
134. Jia Jinghong (1982); Chen Zongshun (1981).
135. YDT: 111-15; for details, see discussion in Ch. 5.
136. An internally circulated biography of Kang Sheng confirms this point, which was first made to me by Ding Yilan in 1981. Kang was an accomplished and published calligrapher, painter, and art critic. He chose the name Lu Chishui to parallel that of the famous Shandong painter, Qi Baishi (Kang was also a Shandong native). See Zhong Kan (1982: 262).
137. *Beijing wanbao*, 19 Dec. 1961 and 29 July 1962 (including photo of painting), repr. in 1963a: 259-62 and 461-4.
138. Ding Yilan (interview with author, Beijing, 6 Aug. 1981). We are left to wonder about the relationship between Deng Tuo and Kang Sheng. Is this an example of Deng's eagerness to cultivate all types among the powerful (and Kang was more powerful than J. Edgar Hoover was in America)? Or were political (and, let's be frank, moral) considerations put aside in an aesthetic friendship of elite literati artists? Kang's notoriety is celebrated in the rather purple, though thoroughly documented, history by John Byron and Robert Pack (1992).
139. *Beijing wenyi*, 1963, no. 3, inside cover, and YDT: 210.
140. 'Jiangdian shufa' (A Few Points on Calligraphy), 1979a: 376. This is one in a series of three *Evening Chats* on calligraphy, printed in 1979a: 375-86. The troublesome 'Hundred Flowers' slogan had been revived, in its more limited academic sense, by

Zhou Yang after the Leap in order to woo back intellectuals to Party service. See Goldman (1967).
141. 1979a: 377–8.
142. A selection is reprinted in 1979c: 69–156. Deng's 'retirement poem' appears on p. 53 and is discussed by Yuan Ying (YTD: 157–8).
143. Turtle Hill (*gui shan*) refers to Yang Shi (1053–1135), who first founded the Eastern Wood Academy at Wuxi in the Song dynasty.
144. Gao Panlong (1562–1626) was one of the leaders of the late Ming period Eastern Wood Academy and was famous for his loyal criticism of the corruption of the Court. He died in his struggles with the palace eunuchs.
145. Zuo Hai [Deng Tuo], 'Gechang Taihu—"Jiangnan yincao" zhi san', *Guangming ribao*, 7 Sept. 1960, stanzas 7 and 8; repr. in 1979c: 79. Note: the reprint deletes 3 of the original poem's 10 stanzas, which are reprinted in full in 1969a: 270–2. Other poems were published in the *People's Daily*.

This poem and these two stanzas are easily the most quoted and translated of Deng Tuo's poetry. The 1969 reprint features a portrait of Deng Tuo over stanza 7, symbolizing, no doubt, Deng's own martyrdom in 1966. Other translations include: Tung (1978: xxxi), which is more literal; Leys (1977: 35), which is more vibrant; and Hsu (1980: 765), which strikes a balance between fidelity to Chinese syntax and English verve.
146. Cheek (1983–4: 43), from 1979a: 158.
147. See Brook (1993), esp. pp. 14 ff.

5

Theory Worker and Culture Bearer: Beijing after the Great Leap (1960–1964)

Frozen out of top positions of authority in journalism and the central administration, Deng Tuo became a theory worker—one of the foremost exponents of the bureaucratic version of Maoism after the Great Leap. Deng Tuo expressed this vision negatively as part of the critique of ultra-Leftism and positively as a reaffirmation of Party rules and predictable ideological methods.[1] Faith Maoism and bureaucratic Maoism had finally come asunder, now competing for the single space of Party orthodoxy. However, within his service to bureaucratic Maoism Deng Tuo maintained his twin roles. His cog-and-screw role was as Party

5.1 Deng Tuo penning calligraphy for hosts in Inner Mongolia, 1964

theorist in his editorials and writings in *Frontline* and *People's Daily* and as factional researcher for Peng Zhen. His culture bearer role was also in his formal Party writings to do with ideology that defined the role of 'theory worker', but was predominantly expressed in Deng's informal personal essays. The most famous of these are *Evening Chats at Yanshan* (*Yanshan yehua*) and *Notes from a Three Family Village* (*Sanjia cun zhaji*).

Cultural Revolution attacks and previous scholarship depict these two essay columns of Deng Tuo's as in some fashion proto-democratic and certainly at odds with CCP rule.[2] It is the brunt of the present analysis to refute that view. The key points, themes, and assumptions of Deng Tuo's political and propaganda writings published under his own name in the formal Party press and his personal essays published under pennames in the general press were *the same*: a reaffirmation of traditional Party leadership and a cautious work style, as well as a search for new ways to improve it. His *method* for achieving these goals, however, was different in his informal essays (*zawen*). Chinese culture—its history, arts, and moral examples—and its interpreters, scholars, are the heroes of Deng Tuo's *zawen*, not Party committees or charismatic leaders. As theorist and savant Deng Tuo offered a loyalist critique, remonstrance to his leader and colleagues.

Deng Tuo made his most sustained articulation of the bureaucratic version of Maoism during these years, seeking to find in China's rich cultural past lessons for the present. Though he had spoken in the 1950s with confidence in the powers of the ideology and organization he had learned during the war years, in the 1960s he spoke in a more muted voice on the strengths of a *method*, historical materialism, which he had learned in the 1930s. Thus, he appealed to the legitimacy of historical example from China's past more than he ever had before. In part this was a result of a well-founded doubt that all answers could be deduced in the writings of the socialist pantheon, but it was also an effort to define *space* for himself and his peers as culture bearers, the individuals who might be able to correct the faults of the Party.[3]

Deng attempted to define himself and his role as an educated Chinese under socialism. He was approaching fifty, was chronically ill, had fallen from political grace and national influence in journalism, and had witnessed a national disaster in which he was complicit. He turned to the great civilization of his youth for solace and guidance. His art was solace, self-examination, and reaffirmation, but it also provided status and a platform from which to push his version of Maoism. He was looking for personal integrity and a sense of self in history after decades of submission to the Party's idea of the thought-remoulded cadre, the new man of socialism. Such new men had brought famine by carving ill-designed and useless canals through the hills while the crops rotted in the fields. Socialism somehow seemed prone to such errors. A *space* for rational reflection and a fulcrum on which to lever socialism back on the right track was needed. Deng had found refuge in the Beijing municipal Party as Vice-Secretary for Culture and Education. He found personal space and political authority (leverage) in a renewed faith in the cultivation of and lessons to be obtained from the elite culture of China's past. This was not a rejection of Marxism-Leninism by any means. He insisted the past had to be interpreted according to historical materialist rules, and he continued in *Frontline* loyally to propagandize each new Party policy. Deng Tuo tried to use this space as a check on the abuse of power in the face of the failures of the Leap and the diminution of inner-Party democracy after Lushan.

These efforts were hampered by Deng Tuo's residual loyalty to Mao and by Mao's flip-flop statements first supporting retrenchment and then supporting what can only be called 'ultra-Leftist' policies. The charisma of the leader and of Lenin's institution were at odds and ultimately one would have to be brought to heel under the control of the other.[4] This was the power issue behind the fight between these newly alienated strains of Maoism. Faith Maoism supported the charismatic leader. Bureaucratic Maoism buttressed the charismatic Party. In this contest Deng Tuo's 'apolitical' activities amounted to a politically motivated revival of culture as a critique of the faith Maoism of the Leap and a defence of the relative independence of elite cadres under bureaucratic Maoism. In *Evening Chats at Yanshan* and *Notes from a Three Family Village* the purely cultural is essentially political and concerned with power and authority in the public realm.

Politics: The Party's Mixed Agenda for 1960–1964

The post-Leap retrenchment period began with the adjustment policies announced at the July 1960 Beidaihe meeting of the Politburo. While Mao spent most of his energy in 1960 enlarging the Sino–Soviet split, the abrupt departure of Soviet advisers that summer and the worst agricultural disaster in a century (caused by the Leap policies, but exacerbated by terrible drought and typhoons) compelled the CCP bureaucracy to announce readjustment policies (the 'adjustment, consolidation, improvement, and filling out' slogan) which reversed key policies of the Leap—including brigade level of collective ownership on the communes and the wild industrialization drive. Mao was 'sold' this retrenchment package at the July meeting.[5] Responsible leaders, such as Li Fuchun, chair of the State Planning Commission, could and did draw on Mao's comments earlier in the year to support a more rational economic policy: in early 1960 Mao stressed technical innovation and technical revolution (precise terms Deng Tuo picked up in *Frontline* editorials),[6] and Mao had been periodically endorsing the mechanization of agriculture since 1958, including a suggestion for a Ministry of Agricultural Machinery made at the 1959 Lushan Plenum.[7] Of course, these reasonable comments came in the midst of Mao's welter of Great Leap bravado.

During these years Deng made his most sustained contribution to the critique of ultra-Leftism. His activities in the early 1960s were a combination of organizational muckraking within the Party and public pronouncements stating current Party policy in *Frontline* and personal reflections in newspaper columns such as *Evening Chats*. A look at Central Party policy, as announced by Mao and other top leaders at the key meetings of the period, reveals the Party's agenda for the 1961 rectification, the economic adjustments following the Leap, and the move to a new campaign, the SEM. That agenda highlights two salient points relevant to understanding the role of intellectuals in the Party. First, the years following Mao's devastating attack on Peng Dehuai at Lushan in August 1959 were a time of ideological confusion. Central politics remained Mao-centred, but Mao could no longer be trusted to act consistently. Roderick MacFarquhar summarizes the legacy of the Leap by its end in 1960 as 'Mao may have advocated attention to objective conditions, but it was his demonic desire for earth-shaking progress that demanded exaggerated claims of success.' Mao essentially had violated his own advice, trying to skip stages of socialism, forgetting the needs of agriculture in his haste to 'overtake' the Soviet Union and Great Britain, and cutting down Peng Dehuai at Lushan in 1959 in contravention to Mao's own 'save the patient' rule for inner-Party debate. In all of this Mao was not alone. Other top leaders 'were accessories to all that, but accessories after the fact.'[8]

Second, in this state of confusion, policy debate among the top leadership was more a case of winning Mao's approval than of opposing him. The simple 'two-line struggle' between Mao the impractical class-struggle advocate and Liu Shaoqi the plodding bureaucrat fails to capture the dynamics of the period and distorts its history. The two strains of Maoism we have identified in Deng Tuo's life were part of *one line*—Yan'an Communism and Mao Zedong Thought—as enshrined in the 1945 Party Constitution. The Leap had only recently broke that monolithic line. Before 1960 there were not 'two lines'. As of 1960 we can see trends that could be described that way. Indeed, the most compelling image that comes to mind after reading policy materials from this period is not so much that of a 'house divided' but of the dysfunctional family of an alcoholic father (drunk with supreme power) in which siblings vie for the fickle affections of the patriarch, divine his erratic desires, avoid his capricious wrath, and survive by blaming others. Activities of Party intellectuals during this period confirm this picture, which Frederick Teiwes has drawn for the top elite, at the level directly below the Central Committee.[9] The post-Lushan period was dominated by this confusing ambivalence. Thus, in the key statements of Mao from August 1960 to summer 1964 we can find messages which some Party intellectuals and other administratively minded senior cadres took as inspiration and as a cause for hope that the mistakes of the Leap would be a thing of the past. At the same time we can see messages which hearken back to Leap ideals and gave hope to a separate group of cadres—'outs' and ambitious younger activists—ready to link their fortunes to Mao's frustrated idealism.

The quintessential example of the ambivalent legacy of the Leap, which divided not only the Yan'an leadership but the Yan'an orthodoxy, is the various responses within the Party to the publication of volume 4 of Mao's *Selected Works* in autumn 1960. This volume contains Mao's writings from the Civil War period of the late 1940s, which stress Party discipline and criticize the Leftist excesses of the time. Two clear strains can be identified in the myriad of paeans written to extol and 'apply' the wisdom found therein. The 'faith Maoism' approach is typified in its most important proponent, Defence Minister Lin Biao. He used the fall 1960 meeting of the CC's Military Affairs Committee to push his version of Maoism. His approach is familiar to students of modern China since it became the dominant version of Maoism during the Cultural Revolution: politics is everything and correct politics stem from a nearly literal, and certainly ahistorical, reading of Mao's utterances. This approach is weak on method, that is, on how precisely to apply Mao to building a Model Army, and strong on faith. Lin's four key relationships of political work—between men and weapons, political and other work, ideological and other aspects of political work, and ideas from books and living ideas—offer less a method than a way of pandering to Mao's current hobby-horses. The heart of Lin's version of Maoism is 'The atom bomb of the spirit is much more powerful and more useful than the material atom bomb. Only we can possess this.' The charismatic power of the Party is thus indivisibly linked to (and therefore analytically inseparable from) Mao the person and his utterances. And Lin, by raising the term 'Mao Zedong Thought', in contravention to Party regulations agreed to at the 1956 Eighth CCP Congress, indicated that he was 'pinning his fortunes to Mao's star'.[10]

Lin's use of faith Maoism to build his career and bureaucratic base in the PLA was paralleled by efforts in the cultural and security spheres by Jiang Qing and Kang Sheng.[11] Each used a faith criterion to attract younger or 'left out' cadres eager to find advancement by attacking senior cadres for faith errors. In a system of lifetime tenure staffed by revolutionary cadres of considerable experience and expertise, changing the grounds of competition from knowledge, experience, and ability to faith, fidelity, and pluck provided a very rational career path for ambitious young cadres, such as Yao Wenyuan, Lin Jie, and older 'outs' such as Zhang Chunqiao, as well as others who rose to top positions through this faith by decade's end. Both Jiang Qing and Kang Sheng were 'outs'—Madame Mao was ostracized by consensus of the leadership and her abrasive personality and Kang Sheng by his failures by the early 1950s in security affairs, which came under criticism in the light of de-Stalinization. Kang, in particular, having gained Mao's ear as a well-trained Soviet specialist just when Mao needed expertise to attack the USSR, used faith criteria to attack, oust, and replace the orthodox Leninist, Yang Xianzhen, at the Central Party School.[12]

The bureaucratic Maoist version was enunciated by Lu Dingyi at a Central Propaganda Work Symposium in September 1960. Lu stressed that one should not use Mao's thought superficially, especially when teaching natural sciences. The Propaganda Department itself issued a warning not to vulgarize Mao's works, as in a case where they were credited with achievements in health care. Around the same time various leaders echoed this caution: Liu Shaoqi and Peng Zhen urged perspective and Lu Dingyi reminded cadres that Mao's thought could not surpass Marxism-Leninism.[13]

One major forum for this bureaucratic view was the Beijing municipal CCP organization under Peng Zhen. At its meetings and in its theory journal, *Frontline*, the Beijing Party pursued a bureaucratic Maoist interpretation not only of vol. 4, but of the developing policies of the 1960s. Deng Tuo was the author of all *Frontline* editorials (save the first by Peng Zhen in 1958). Although the 10 October 1960 issue carried Lin Biao's paean to vol. 4 of Mao's *Selected Works* as its lead article, the 25 October issue of *Frontline* carried Deng's editorial stressing the values of economization and strengthening agriculture 'for an even greater Leap forward'. Mao is not mentioned, only basic principles and the value of experience. Immediately following the editorial, however, is Deng's speech to a municipal Party meeting on Mao Zedong Thought and agriculture. Deng's was not an obscure interpretation; the text had also been carried in *People's Daily* on 24 October.[14] We should remember that while Deng was foremost a journalist and propagandist, he had an enduring interest in agricultural questions stemming from his 1937 book on famine relief and his village investigations in the 1940s.[15] Deng's article praises Mao's wisdom and the 'successes' of the Leap, but in fact continues his 'managerial' interpretation of Mao's ideas. He identifies six ways in which 'Comrade Mao Zedong has developed Marxist-Leninist theory on agriculture', including balanced development of agriculture and industry, mechanization and economy of scale, agriculture as the market for industrial products, and 'establishing and perfecting the People's Commune system by strengthening Party leadership, stressing the work of the entire Commune, grasping production and life, and being good at allocating labour power.' Mao Zedong Thought, in Deng's exegesis, becomes a method, a set of principles and general policy goals. As such, they are in need of careful and intelligent implementation in the wide range of different endeavours which make up socialist modernization. Deng does not need to mention who, or what organization, is qualified to put Mao's wisdom into practice. It was Party intellectuals, such as himself. This is a classic example of the bureaucratic Maoist version of CCP orthodoxy.

The Fighting Task of Theory Workers

Bureaucratic Maoism is not devoid of the living ideology claimed by the faith Maoists; rather the ideology of the bureaucratic Maoists stresses a method which could, with assiduous practice, become a daily regime that would guarantee, under Party guidance, success in practical matters and service to the salvation of China. Ideology was very real to Deng Tuo and his explanations of it in *Frontline* editorials, which fully parallel his points in *Evening Chats* and *Three Family Village*, outline the contours of the honourable vocation for the scholar-cadre he so valued. What we see in Deng Tuo's explanations is the rationalizing function of the scholar-cadre which takes the charismatic force of the leader and his 'thought' into the practical realm. He regularizes the relationship between doctrine and objective reality.

Deng's belief in the rationalizing function of the cadre as theorist is clear in his discussions on ideology. In the 10 July 1960 editorial for *Frontline*, Deng Tuo stressed the importance of 'grasping ideological work'. The editorial is full of the bland slogans and rah-rah rhetoric of the Leap, which it also praises. However, Deng soon comes to his point: some comrades disparage ideological work as an intrusion on necessary regular work. This, says Deng, is a false dichotomy. He buttresses his argument with Yan'an period citations to Mao and Liu on the importance of ideological work with the masses. The purpose of ideology, it soon transpires, is to provide a *method* for practical administration and *morale* for the troops, a unifying and inspiring vision of how one's particular work fits in the big picture of the salvation of China. Without ideology (which in Chinese is also a word for 'thought' or 'thinking'), 'the Party would lose its direction and its role as vanguard.' It is easy for people to lose the big picture in daily affairs, and it is the Party's role 'conscientiously to research each person's [ideological] progress, re-estimate changes in the ideology of the masses, and work on new ideological conditions.' Otherwise, bourgeois ideology will re-emerge to fill the void. The masses need to understand international affairs, particularly the evil intent of US imperialism, otherwise the masses will be 'simpletons' (*yongren*). Youth, in particular, need to be reminded of Communist goals. Deng gives concrete advice on how to achieve this ideological education—advice which parallels his organizational advice to cadres in Jin Cha Ji in 1938: basic-level work unit Party committees should organize reading and discussion groups based on key articles in the Party press.[16]

What guarantees this vanguard role for the Party and its representatives is the classical 'from the masses, to the masses' Mass Line work method articulated by Mao in Yan'an. In a 25 December editorial, Deng outlines his view of correct work methods. He repeats Mao's 1943 rules on Mass Line leadership, emphasizing the role of propaganda in completing the cycle of consultation and implementation in the Maoist work model: 'then go down among the masses and propagandize your synthesis [of their inchoate needs], transforming it into the masses' own opinions . . .' He adds that one should apply policy carefully in each specific area, not force compliance, not randomly direct production, not boast, and not claim special privileges.[17] The importance of the Mass Line as a method is repeated in *Frontline* throughout 1961, particularly in the new column, 'Party Building', which began that February. The 25 March column explains what Mass Line means. Under the 'work style' section, it says cadres should maintain the viewpoint (*guandian*) of the masses, 'be little students with a humble attitude and honestly learn from the masses. . . . Only by first being the students of the masses can you then become their teacher.'

This role becomes that of the scholar-cadre as culture bearer when ideology is a method not a faith. Deng Tuo calls such cadres 'theorists' (*lilun gongzuozhe*). His most extensive presentation of this in a

Frontline editorial followed the famous January 1962 '7,000 Cadres Conference' in the 25 February issue. The editorial is built around a commentary on the 1943 'Resolution on Strengthening Party Character' and is presented as a self-criticism of theory workers. It is, however, a desideratum for the bureaucratic Maoist approach to governing and the scholar-cadre role in it. Theorists are to study and research the achievements of the masses (defined in the previous line as 'the successes of the Great Leap', therefore really meaning the economic failures of the Leap), then propagandize the explanations derived from research among the masses, lead practical work, and under the leadership of Mao Zedong Thought help the masses to realize their own advancement of self-conscious effort. Theorists are active administrators in the realization of the Maoist leadership cycle. Indeed, Deng sounds here more like a management consultant or enterprise manager—a combination of social scientist, market analyst, manager, local legislator, and community activist. While other writers in this period, such as Wu Han or Jian Bozan, or the creative writers, were essentially just that—writers—Deng Tuo was an active administrator, or at least saw himself as one. His work, and the proper work of Party theorists, was not new directions in philosophy, it was praxis, civil service administration.

Ideology was the central methodology for carrying out that administrative function: 'if we do not practically check (*kaocha*) and research our nation's forces of production and their changes (in industry, agricultural, or other areas), as well as the relations between people and material within the forces of production; if we do not check the relationship between the forces and relations of production, then we will be unable to carry out correctly the Party's various policies or solve practical problems . . .'[18] Theorists, despite great efforts, have failed in recent years to achieve these lofty goals. The key to correcting this situation is to adopt the methods outlined by Comrade Mao Zedong twenty years ago in 'Rectify the Party's Work Style'. What makes this work style valuable is 'field research' (*diaocha yanjiu*), hands-on investigation by theorists in the factories and farms themselves. Diligence is needed to collect sufficient data and to appreciate conditions among the masses, otherwise we do not have the right to speak (Mao's famous phrase) and can only produce 'empty theory' (*konglun*). Theorists must be tough on themselves and use Mao's 1942 criticisms of failings in the Party (the three evil work styles of subjectivism, sectarianism, and dogmatism) to spur themselves on, 'to better complete the tasks the Party has given us.' The demands are great, but the job description is enticing—to implement the reordering of Chinese society.

Using Historical Studies

One of Deng's most powerful critiques of ultra-Leftism was a rebuttal to the radical historiography of the Great Leap. During the Leap radical historians had not only emphasized the role of peasant rebellions in China's history, but had grossly simplified the political standards by which historical figures and events were to be judged. The radical politicization of history writing made historians mere cog-and-screw propagandists of current policy. Finally, there was a strong tone of anti-intellectualism in the Leap that threatened establishment intellectuals like Deng and Jian Bozan, one of China's premier Marxist historians who led the critique of radical history.[19] For Deng Tuo, this was a return of the 'politics of simpletons', a vulgarization of proper Marxist-Leninist historiography. In a speech he gave to the Beijing Historical Association that was published in February 1961 in *Historical Studies*, Deng spelled out his views. Given Deng's unpleasant personal relations with the Chairman, this title, too, is a symbol of Deng's commitment to the Leninist norm of public unity: 'The Thought of Mao Zedong has Opened the Way for the Development of China's Science of History'.[20] Given the content of what Deng says in the article, the title was a prudent choice indeed. Politically, the article is significant because Deng uses Mao's writings from his more moderate Yan'an corpus to buttress Deng's own views, with which Mao, who had supported the radical histories written during the Great Leap period, was almost certainly in 1960 no longer in agreement. Professionally, the article is significant as a major policy statement of the patrons of establishment intellectuals on the standards of historical research and the role of history in contemporary Chinese society.

It is a clever and thoughtful article combining calls for Party unity, warnings to Mao and other leaders about the dangers of ignoring history, and a coherent philosophy of Marxist history writing. Deng begins, rather nationalistically, by noting that China's long recorded history goes back to the *Spring and Autumn Annals*, written some thirty-seven hundred years ago, three hundred years before Europe's Herodotus, the so-called 'father' of historical writing in 'the world'. Deng is quick, however, to get to the point: the task of history is not only to explain society correctly, but also to help people to change it.[21] This is, of course, the same faith that motivated Deng's history writing thirty years earlier. Throughout the article Deng Tuo attacks bourgeois theory abroad and poor research at home. Deng, who read and spoke English well, denounces the unsuspecting W. P. Webb, judged guilty for his bourgeois connections with Texas oil companies as revealed in his presidential address to the American Historical Association in 1959.[22] On the home front, Deng criticizes poor research—namely, formalism in which Marxist terminology and historical data are jumbled together in no real relationship to each other.[23] Deng's ideas are fully consonant with Jian Bozan's 'historicism' and Wu Han's concern for popularizing critical standards as well as empathetic impressions of the past.[24]

Deng's central thesis is that 'Historical facts and Marxist theories must be combined together into an organic unity' if one is to achieve the task of history writing. This concern for a strong grasp of the details of Chinese history is hammered home repeatedly:

Only after mastering the characteristics of Chinese history can one apply Marxism-Leninism to the solution of practical problems in the Chinese revolution, in the manner of shooting an arrow at a set target. Otherwise, though one may be full of praises for the good arrow which is Marxism-Leninism, one cannot hit the target in the Chinese revolution with it. And what is the use of that?[25]

Here Deng uses Mao's political metaphors, the 'arrow' and 'target', not to laud the Chairman's genius and to ferret out class enemies, but to refute the radical historiography of the Great Leap period and to define critical standards for professional historiography.

This speech on historical methods is one more in several examples of Deng's bureaucratic exegesis of Mao Zedong Thought which diverged from the Chairman's personal opinions since the mid-1950s. Throughout his discussion Deng repeatedly praises Mao, quoting him with admiration thirteen times, once for nearly an entire page. But the reader, on reflection, begins to feel that something is amiss. It soon becomes clear when one takes a second look at the articles and speeches by Mao which are quoted. All come from the 1938 to 1942 period, particularly Mao's address to the Sixth Plenum of the Sixth Central Committee in 1938, his 1940 'On New Democracy', and his 1942 rectification speeches attacking formalism. These were all created in a period when, for tactical reasons, Mao played down his more radical goals. They reflect Mao's pragmatism and common sense. To bring these up in 1960, after the heady policies of the Great Leap Forward, was little short of using Mao to criticize Mao.

For instance, Deng quotes 'Reform Our Study' (from May 1941), in which Mao emphasizes the need for detailed study of particulars before acting. Deng, on this authority, concludes, 'Unless we master large numbers of facts, we shall not be able to arrive at correct conclusions.' Who in China in 1960, when he gave the speech, or in 1961, when it was published, would miss the connection?—the same Mao who demanded detailed research of actual conditions in 1941 had admitted in 1959 that he did not really know much about economic particulars. Deng also quotes Engels on the dangers of using Marxist theories as credos instead of as research guides.[26] Deng Tuo's use of Mao's works here can be seen as an attempt to admonish Mao in a positive spirit, within the Leninist framework of public unity and the Chinese tradition of public respect for leaders, though the irony was probably not lost on the well-informed reader. One could say that Deng was calling on Mao, using Mao's own words, to return to the very fine model Mao himself had set up in the period from 1938 to 1942 but had since abandoned.

Huairou and Chang Guan Lou: Writing Peng Zhen's 1961 Investigations

Through most of 1961 Mao personally called for and frequently reiterated the need for detailed investigation of local conditions to assess what must now be done. Two separate speeches he gave in Beijing in January and June of 1961 emphasized the need for investigation (*diaocha*) and the correction of falsifications in economic and political reports—implying, of course, that the distortions emanated from the lower ranks of cadres.[27] Mao's views were pronounced at the January Ninth Plenum of the Central Committee and legislated in a Central Committee directive declaring 1961 a 'year of investigation.'[28] In response to Mao's calls, Peng Zhen in March organized a field investigation (*diaocha*) of conditions in counties around Beijing. That was followed up by a conclave in November at Chang Guan Lou, where the Beijing Party Committee put its final conclusions and recommendations on paper. Deng Tuo both participated in the field research and penned the major reports (continuing the ghost-writing services he had provided Nie Rongzhen in Jin Cha Ji and Peng in earlier years in Beijing). It was under these changed circumstances that Deng Tuo began his famous newspaper column, *Evening Chats at Yanshan*, in March 1961 and the joint column, *Notes from a Three Family Village*, in October 1961. In as much as they were critical of distortions and work styles reminiscent of those in the Great Leap, they can be said to be fully in line with both Mao's statements and Party policy of the day. They surely grew in part out of Deng's work in Peng Zhen's investigation and report writing teams.

Peng Zhen's investigation of local conditions following the Leap focused on three counties near Beijing—Shunyi, Huairou, and Fengtai. Between April and early June of 1961 three teams (headed, respectively, by Deng Xiaoping, Peng Zhen, and Liu Ren) carried out 'rural investigations' in the style Mao himself had established in 1930. The three investigations collectively became known in the Cultural Revolution as the 'Huairou Investigations' and were linked to Peng Zhen's alleged anti-Party crimes.[29] The groups investigated living and farming conditions in these counties as a result of Great Leap policies. There were related investigations, under Liu Ren, of industrial, commercial, and cultural conditions. Deng Tuo was the general compiler, 'personally writing the "investigation" reports himself.'[30] Even as recorded in a hostile text, we can see that the report documents the dismal conditions of the day and cites peasant testimony that the fault lay with government policy, that 'the People's Communes are the cause of poverty.' The reports promote the 'responsibility system' (of limited free farming) which was adopted by the Central Committee for a while in the early 1960s.[31] These results were combined with a review of Central Committee documents in the November meeting at Chang Guan Lou.

In November of 1961 Deng Tuo led the review of the spring's 'Huairou Investigations' along with classified documents of the Central Committee from the Leap period with the express purpose of finding out what led to the disaster. It was held under the auspices of the Beijing Party Committee and is known as the Chang Guan Lou review, from the name for the building near the Beijing Zoo in which it was carried out. Despite bitter accusations in the Red Guard press during the Cultural Revolution that this was a secret factional preparation for a 'Khrushchev-style' attack on Mao, it was in fact held according to the letter of the current Party policy and Mao's urgings. This investigation of the Leap may not have been entirely in the spirit of open discussion, but this was something few were willing to do lightly since the purge of Peng Dehuai.[32] On the other hand, a provincial-level unit such as Beijing municipality is hardly the logical choice for a general review of national policy in a Leninist system. Furthermore, this is the one major event in Deng's life which post-Mao materials have consistently neglected (presumably in consideration for the sensibilities of Peng Zhen, who is still alive and powerful). Deng Tuo outlined their mission:

Many shortcomings, mistakes, and problems have emerged in work these few years. What are the reasons? Natural calamities are not the most important. The fundamental problem was detachment from the masses and subjectivism. In short, the objective law has been contravened and mistakes in line have been made.... From where did the tendency to exaggerate things spring up?

The review group submitted a two-thousand-word report to Peng Zhen in December 1961. In conclusions that essentially confirmed the views of Peng Dehuai, the report said the mistakes of the Leap were the result of Left deviation, not Right opportunism, that the Party's decisions had been uninformed and divorced from economic law and thus led to waste, that the Leap's excessive emphasis on individual initiative amounted to subjective idealism, and that the Central Committee changed policies so frequently that mass confusion ensued, with nobody daring to tell the truth.[33]

The themes outlined in the Chang Guan Lou report were echoed in Deng's *Evening Chats*, which we will consider in detail in the next section. The January 1962 Party Work Conference immediately following this review witnessed Mao's famous self-criticism and opened up a time of more open policy debate.[34] However, even though Mao had felt the need to admit to some errors in the Leap and to call for more moderate policies, not even Liu Shaoqi was willing actually to circulate Mao's self-criticism, for fear of later repercussions. Supporting essays in the press, like Deng's *Evening Chats*, probably only exacerbated Mao's distaste for his critics and raised further his suspicions of their cautious approach. It is easy to see why Mao felt his policies had been vilified by 'academic authorities' such as Deng Tuo in this review and in the Beijing Party and popular press.

By way of summary, we can map out palpable shifts in the Party's mixed agenda of 1960–4 which find direct reflection in Deng Tuo's personal essays in *Evening Chats* and *Three Family Village*, not to mention other related essay columns in the PRC press. In broad strokes, the chronology goes like this:

- From spring 1961 through January 1962 there was substantial retreat from and criticism of the Leap, with Mao's consent. These are reflected in Mao's speeches in January, March, and June of 1961 stressing the need for reparative 'investigations' and concluded with Mao's famous 'self-criticism' at the 7,000 Cadre Conference. The continuing retrenchment from spring to September 1962 lacked Mao's strong endorsement.[35]

- The Socialist Education Movement began with Mao's famous call to 'never forget class struggle' at the September 1962 Tenth Plenum of the CCP CC. Various meetings on literature and culture during 1963 went back and forth on issues of use of traditional characters and operatic forms and need for new content, without major change.[36] In October 1963, Zhou Yang reported to the philosophy and social sciences faculties of CAS that while class struggle was important, scholars could be flexible about non-Marxist artistic and literary works, and that moderate means should be employed in correcting erroneous views among cultural workers. Zhou stressed tolerance and praised progressive ancient writers and the assimilation of good aspects of foreign culture.

These comments reflected the two-track cultural system Deng Tuo had lived in since the 1940s and echoed precisely the values Deng Tuo articulated in his 1961–2 essays.[37]

- In December 1963 Mao complained about the arts: the 'dead' still dominate in many departments, particularly in the area of Beijing Opera. Liu Shaoqi called an enlarged Politburo meeting in January 1964 to address these issues. Result: no great change. Mao returned in June 1964 with a nasty attack on officials responsible for China's cultural life. There were, he said, 'high and mighty bureaucrats . . . on the brink of revisionism.'[38]

While Mao may have complained of a lack of influence in cultural circles, his two major outbursts, at the Tenth Plenum in September 1962 and in June 1964 attacking 'high and mighty bureaucrats', brought an end to establishment intellectuals' essay projects. What then had been the project of Party intellectuals and broader establishment intellectuals in their post-Leap theory and *zawen* writings? Did the 'fighting tasks of theory workers' outlined by Deng Tuo as a Party propaganda leader apply to his and other intellectuals' essays of the 1960s?

Culture: Recovering Deng Tuo's Intellectual Project

Deng Tuo is best known for the short essays he wrote in two columns in the Beijing press between 1961 and 1964: his *Evening Chats at Yanshan* in the *Beijing Evening News* and his contributions to the multiple-author series, *Notes from a Three Family Village*,[39] in the municipal Party theory journal, *Frontline*. All commentators—from critics in the Cultural Revolution, to his colleagues in the post-Mao period, to Western scholars—agree these 'miscellaneous essays' (*zawen*) are among his most important, and certainly most personal, essays. However well written they are, Deng's *zawen* were by no means exceptional for the time. They are part of a general pattern of intellectual essays in the PRC press following the Leap, such as appeared in the column *The Long and the Short* in *People's Daily* in 1962, by various writers or groups of writers. Their content parallels the points raised in central CCP documents and official discussions of them in Party theory journals, such as *Frontline*. As such all these essays were part of an official effort at public education through normal channels to redress the lingering problems of the Leap. This response to the Leap and the emerging split among the top leadership over policy brought the underlying assumptions of the 'culture bearer' role in Deng Tuo's service to the fore. At first, when Deng published his essays, he was supported by the

Party. Later, as Mao focused on the objects of his fears, Deng's essays were denounced by the Party.

In Deng Tuo we find examples of the scholarly style among Party intellectuals and establishment intellectuals who served the Party. Deng Tuo's essays of the early 1960s are a systematic apology for the cadre as culture bearer in direct contrast with the purely cog-and-screw role revived by Mao and the Party in the Leap. Naturally, these essays were not explicitly a rejection and denunciation of the cog-and-screw role. Discipline was part of the Leninist ideal. In addition, such rejection would have been wildly imprudent, not only for fear of once again rousing the anger of Mao, but more so because such open criticism would violate Leninist norms of unity in public and especially would throw doubt on the charismatic authority (the unfailing correctness) of the Party.

Exegesis was the rhetorical tool. Deng offers a careful, and erudite, re-reading of Party theory and Chinese culture and history. It is a reading that can plausibly claim the example of Yan'an (though not the whole tradition from that period in Party history). It is an orthodox reading, based on precise references to the Yan'an corpus of Party texts from the 1940s. Its values are closer to the orthodox Marxism-Leninism Deng Tuo embraced in the 1930s and the practical Maoism he popularized in the 1940s than to the wild idealism of the Leap (against which it was a response). In these essays, Deng continues the two-track cultural policy he enjoyed since Jin Cha Ji in the 1940s: maintaining his love of elite culture while promoting popular models. He presents loyalists from the Song dynasty in *Evening Chats* while endorsing Lei Feng in *Frontline* editorials. His preferred goal for the masses, however, was not the dogged obedience of Lei Feng, but the moral integrity of the traditional poet-official. The nobility of Deng's vocation, as we see it depicted in every page of *Evening Chats*, is to bring the good news of China's arts and culture to every worker, peasant, and solider—empowering them to be their own scholar-aesthetes on a grand scale never before seen in the history of Chinese civilization. It was an historic mission shared by many Chinese intellectuals in the twentieth century—to save Chinese civilization by serving one or another master—and one which gave Deng some comfort during his political eclipse since 1957. In practice, however, we shall see that Deng comfortably defined his noble mission as writing essays to educated people like himself. He is not snooty; he welcomes newcomers, even goes out of his way to explain things for them. But they must play by his rules. This sense of cultural mission likely inhibited other, perhaps more practical, counter-measures on his part to reform Party policy in the gathering storm before 1966.[40]

Deng Tuo began his newspaper column, *Evening Chats at Yanshan*, in March 1961 and the joint column, *Notes from a Three Family Village*, in October 1961. This was just the time when Mao himself, and the Party establishment, pronounced 1961 a 'year of investigation'.[41] In as much as they were critical of distortions and work styles reminiscent of those in the Great Leap, Deng's columns can be said to be fully in line with both Mao's statements and Party policy of the day. In fact, however, his essays continued to 'misinterpret Mao', as Deng had in his history speech in early 1961, by emphasizing different aspects of the orthodoxy and shifting the target of blame, at least somewhat, from Mao's preferred targets.

Each of the themes raised in Deng's essays relate to different aspects of the post-Leap *context* and the various audiences to which Deng's essays, and similar essays by other establishment intellectuals, were addressed. First, the essays were a part of the renewed spirit of Chinese nationalism during the Sino–Soviet split. They were a confidence-building exercise in the face of the failures of Party policy—first the Hundred Flowers fiasco, then the Great Leap. Morale, both inside and outside the Party, was understandably low after the Leap's economic disasters. The essays encouraged confidence through a reaffirmation of Chinese culture and pride in its achievements in the face of previous Western dominance, recent Soviet leadership, and the current Sino–Soviet disputes. Second, they were a critique of the 'politics of simpletons', the vulgarization of state orthodoxy in ultra-Leftist policies among cadres at all levels. These included a number of barbs unmistakably directed at Mao's recent behaviour, particularly his capricious leadership. Third, they were an incomplete and partial step toward professional autonomy. The essays make authority claims based on scholarly knowledge or *xuewen* and administrative experience or *shijian* (practice). Finally, beneath all these themes runs an undercurrent: an affirmation of the role of culture bearer for the literati-cadre. This sense of autonomous privilege was based on Marxist method and Leninist discipline as much as on the Chinese humanistic tradition. It was not a claim of intellectual autonomy in the Western sense but of the latitude and respect necessary to let engaged intellectuals do their best for the state.

These essays were directed at a specific *audience*: China's tiny educated elite and particularly those intellectuals working inside or in close co-operation with the Party, those 'workers, peasants, and soldiers who have a relatively high cultural level', as Deng Tuo would opine in *Evening Chats*. Several essays were also intended as object lessons for the top leadership and lower cadres in the Beijing municipal administration. They also explicitly offered inspirations to intellectual youth.

Frederick Teiwes has pointed out that Deng Tuo's allegories could have any number of potential targets, 'the shortcomings of low level to fairly high ranking cadres, official policies of the Great Leap period, Mao's politburo associates, and the Chairman himself.'[42]

We may assume specific audiences for separate themes in the essays which reflect three functions for such writings: remonstrance, public education, and in-group affirmation and resistance. The critiques of ultra-Leftism are highly coded, in what Merle Goldman has identified as 'Aesopian language'. For example, the tale of the Great Yu's respect for natural law was not lost on educated readers as a criticism of the wild schemes of the Great Leap. Not only did Deng prudently speak through such metaphors, but his specific examples turn out to be a privileged 'code' referring to events and issues clear to the initiated top-level cadre only (such as terms or phrases from Mao's recent limited-circulation speeches). For example, we shall see that when Deng used the Ming dynasty case of 'quacks' he was appropriating a term from a recent Mao speech to high-level cadres. In this sense Deng's most pointed satires were not public at all, since his pen-name and use of code terms hid the author and his sharpest points from the public.

The 'Chinese pride' material and homilies on Marxist-Leninist rules of behaviour, however, are clearly educational efforts directed to the broadest audience: the intellectual youth and intellectuals without access to inside political information or advanced education. In 1983, Gu Xing recalled Deng Tuo's central goal in these essays: 'To overcome difficulty by *study*. To encourage youth to get interested and active again after the disillusionment of the Great Leap Forward and its waste. Youth didn't want to join in collective activities (*jiti huodong*), so we tried to get them to study on their own. That's what "One Third of Life" is all about.'[43]

The final audience is the modern-day literatus. Whether for the scholar-cadre, non-Party scholar, or the scholar-cadre currently 'out of office', the rich material on Chinese arts and history constitutes another code, a privileged language, for the culture bearer and the tradition of moral cultivation and elite certification through the practice of Chinese elite arts. In this language Deng Tuo goes on to reaffirm the role, necessity, and expected skills of the cadre as practical 'theorist'. This includes some self-criticism for his and his colleagues' previous support of the Leap.

It is at this level—the language of the culture-bearing scholar-elite—that Deng Tuo's essays demonstrate their most profound significance. His words are a window into some of the fundamental values of Chinese society and they highlight the mechanism by which Marxism-Leninism attached itself to those values and thus became grafted into Chinese thought. Deng's aesthetic interests and abilities implicitly legitimated his claim to a special status in the CCP regime, beyond the overt qualifications of experience, loyalty, and position. He celebrated the traditional role of the educated elite as the transmitters of civilization in Chinese culture (which is all Confucius ever claimed to do) in its current, socialist incarnation. And he reaffirmed the practical wisdom of this civilization. As such, Deng's aesthetic claims to authority drew from fundamental values in Chinese society, those models of sociability which parallel and support similar institutional frameworks. Deng's culture bearer claims, such as the role of calligraphy and elite art in identifying capable leaders and administrators, are not, so far as I know, mentioned as key qualifications of Marxist leadership by Lenin or Stalin. They were (and still perhaps are) Chinese values among its elite. They are part of what the social theorist Roberto Unger calls 'society's formative context' because the substitution of other values for these would change how Deng's society worked.[44]

The superficially traditional flavour of Deng Tuo's classical knowledge masked a deeper traditional authority pattern in which esoteric knowledge defines a status rather than one in which technical skill defines a profession. Deng Tuo was a priest, not a professional. His was a world of the aesthetically trained and certified elite. Through Marxist orthodoxy, classicist knowledge, and skill in calligraphy and traditional poetry Deng Tuo became a Communist revolutionary leader. If the elements seem somewhat contradictory, that is our misperception—and Mao's. Deng Tuo lived them harmoniously, and it was only the supreme leader who insisted that the elements could not co-exist. In *Evening Chats* Deng Tuo articulated his assumptions in the face of the initial faith Maoist assault on his literati-cadre role made by Mao personally in 1957 and by the Party generally during the Great Leap.[45] The traditional style of Deng Tuo's habits are important on two levels: on the unremarkable and ordinary level they reveal the shared values of Chinese society and Marxism-Leninism which made Party policy make sense to the public, and on the remarkable level (where their implied criticism of Mao or recent Party policy drew attention) they reveal the literati assumptions which overlapped with Leninist-Stalinist assumptions and thus served as the *mechanism* to allow a class of ritual specialists—the Confucian literati—to transform itself into a new, but fundamentally recognizable, type of ritual specialist—the Leninist cadre and 'theorist'.

The term Deng Tuo used that comes closest to articulating the role of culture bearer is 'theorist' (*lilunjia* or *lilun gongzuozhe*). The theorist is the person with the wherewithal to interpret, refine, and test Party policy on the basis of a sound *philosophical method* (dialectical materialism) and practical *administrative technique* (Mass Line propaganda). This wherewithal requires knowledge (ancient, scientific, and based on 'hands-on' practice), perceptiveness and discipline (reflected in proper ideology), integrity, tolerant judgement, and syncretic pan-specialist skills, not to mention the years of experience in administering the Maoist 'from the masses, to the masses' bureaucracy. In short, the theorist made policy manifest; brought the *dao* to life, here and now, in this organization, this village, or this school. Without such theorists the link between the masses and the leadership would be broken and the project, the salvationary mission of socialism and the Party, would evaporate. This was the honourable vocation Deng Tuo had accepted in Jin Cha Ji in the 1930s.[46]

This interpretation of *Evening Chats* and Deng's contributions to *Three Family Village* is not widely held. Previous writers have focused on a few of Deng's acid personal attacks on Mao's leadership style found among these essays and have focused on the related theme of criticism of Maoist policies from the Leap.[47] In fact, Deng's essays had not been noticed by the Western academic community before they were attacked in the spring of 1966. In May of 1966 the world discovered that the Chinese authorities had become deeply unhappy about these essays and that Deng Tuo was behind them. During the Cultural Revolution, Deng's essays were denounced, along with the contributions of his colleagues Wu Han and Liao Mosha and others, as against both socialism and the Party. Chinese scholars outside the PRC and Western scholars (myself included) found this interpretation plausible, at least to the degree that we could see that Deng and company appeared to be criticizing Mao, Maoist policy, and the crazed dictatorship we saw exploding out of China. Most Western textbooks, survey histories, and monographs dealing with the 1960s maintain this interpretation.[48] Post-Mao hagiography on Deng Tuo in China, on the other hand, interprets these texts as sound critiques of ultra-Leftism in line with the policies of Deng Xiaoping's reforms (as set by the Third Plenum, December 1978).[49] All these interpretations miss the deeper dynamic and conflict *within Maoist orthodoxy* between the roles of culture bearer and cog and screw for the intellectual elite, and how this tension came to play into the hands of top-level leaders involved in their own political struggles during the 1960s.

To understand what Deng Tuo himself might have intended in *Evening Chats* and *Notes from a Three Family Village*, and what Ma Tieding, Qin Mu, or other essayists of the time intended (see below), the historian must account for a telling fact: most of these essays are not critiques of Mao or of ultra-Leftism. On the contrary, several are quite in harmony with Mao's utopian ideals, government policies of the day, and the Party's claim to institutional charisma and infallibility. Most of the essays—the majority of the words—*appear* irrelevant to political concerns. These, however, are precisely the most politically relevant parts, since such cultural concerns speak directly to the problematic role of the scholar-cadre. This is significant both for understanding the origins of the Cultural Revolution *and* for understanding the limitations to intellectual participation in the post-Mao period which contributed to the tragedy of 1989.

Essay Columns of the 1960s

Deng Tuo's *Evening Chats at Yanshan* was the first of at least three similar Beijing newspaper and magazine columns of the 1961–2 period which directly addressed the retrenchment policies following the Leap. It was the model for others, in Beijing and around the nation.[50] However, *Evening Chats at Yanshan* was not the first light essay column in the *Beijing Evening News*, but Gu Xing, who edited the page of the *Evening News* in the early 1960s on which *Evening Chats* appeared, claims it was the first of its type in People's China and spawned a series of imitators. Unlike other light essay columns in the paper, Deng Tuo's centred on knowledge (*zhishi xing*).[51] The others, says Gu Xing, which appeared before and at the same time as *Evening Chats*, were on thought and ideology (*sixiang xing*) or were explicitly directed at a range of youth questions.[52]

The Long and the Short

The second series to begin in Beijing was *The Long and the Short* (*Chang duan lu*), which ran in the *People's Daily* from 4 May to 8 October 1961. It was written by a group of five noted essayists all using individual pen-names.[53] The famous author and screenplay writer, Xia Yan, served as the notable figure whose invitation would be difficult to turn down, though Liao Mosha became the leading personality, providing the opening piece, 'The Theory of "Comparing the Long and the Short"'.[54] Editors from the *People's Daily* approached each of the five writers individually asking them to contribute to a new essay column. Tang Tao, a *zawen* writer since the 1930s and one of the five contributors, says that Wu Lengxi, who had replaced Deng Tuo as editor of *People's Daily*, first asked Xia Yan to gather a group of writers to write the column (in fact it was Chen Xiaoyu, leading member of the Ma Tieding writing team—see next section). The plan was to publish one essay each weekday by one of the five. There was no master plan, says Tang, only the desire to write criticisms of specific problems of the day following Mao's renewed call to 'let a Hundred Schools contend.' Tang also insisted later that it is impossible to write 'worker, peasant, and soldier *zawen*'; they are inherently meant for a more educated readership.[55] As we have seen, this was precisely the time when the Central Party was advocating realism, detailed investigations, and caution in political and economic affairs, and it was Deng Tuo's job, along with his establishment colleagues in Beijing, to support those policy initiatives by organizing and writing inspirational essay columns in the papers.[56] The contents and themes of *The Long and the Short* were almost identical to *Evening Chats* and *Three Family Village*. Liao Mosha's essays in *The Long and the Short* are so similar to Deng Tuo's that they have been mistakenly identified as Deng's own (since before 1979 the true identity of the pen-names was not clear).[57]

Three Family Village

The third *zawen* series to begin in Beijing in the post-Leap period was *Notes from a Three Family Village*, which appeared in the bi-weekly journal *Frontline*. While Deng continued to publish *Evening Chats* articles on an average of twice a week between March 1961 and September 1962, in *Three Family Village* he contributed essays on the average of once every other month (the remainder being written by others) between October 1961 and July 1964.[58] This third column was created and organized in much the same manner as *Evening Chats* (see below). In September 1961 Deng Tuo invited Wu Han and Liao Mosha to a dinner at the Sichuan Restaurant in Beijing and charmed them into contributing to an *Evening Chats*-style column in *Frontline*. Liao Mosha, the only surviving member of the trio, recalls that beyond the column's name, the joint pen-name of Wu (for Wu Han), Nan (for Deng Tuo, from his pen-name, Ma Nancun), and Xing (for Liao, from his pen-name Fan Xing), and the general length and purpose of the series ('life, education, ideology, work, and Wu Han, you can write on history', Deng Tuo is recorded as saying), each essay's topic and content was left up to the individual author.[59] Given the lack of overt co-ordination, the similarity of theme and style in the essays is striking. In fact, Liao and Deng's essays are more similar to each other than to Wu Han's, whose great historical erudition stands out.[60] The themes, where they are political, are consistent with those described for this period of his writing and activities.

Provincial Essays

Similar essay columns appeared around the nation. Three have been identified as directly linked to the model of *Evening Chats: Casual Talks from History* (*Li xia manhua*) in Shandong's *Masses' Daily*; *Rambling Talks from Yunnan Clouds* (*Dianyun mantan*) in the *Yunnan Daily*; and *Stories from History* (*Lishi gushi*) aired on National Radio.[61] Not surprisingly, Deng's influence did not rely on the impact of the written word alone. Liu Mengbei, author of *Rambling Talks From Yunnan Clouds* under the pen-name Shi Suozhen, was originally a co-worker of Gu Xing's in the Beijing press corps and knew Deng Tuo. Liu had been transferred to Kunming in 1950 in the spread of Party cadres following the CCP victory over the KMT.[62]

Other essays published around this time not directly related to *Evening Chats* serve to reinforce the image of a shared project among Party intellectuals in the post-Leap period. The Party had officially revived the 'Hundred Flowers' policy in March 1961 (though in the limited academic version Deng Tuo had supported) and a number of writers and academics responded with a similar focus on elite culture and rational studies.[63] Qin Mu, the Cantonese writer with considerable overseas experience, published a collection of artistic commentaries in the form of *sanwen* (light essays) during this time. *Appreciations of the Sea of Art* includes essays he published in Beijing, Xi'an, WuHan, Guangzhou, and some overseas papers, but most had been serialized in *Shanghai Literature*, whose press published the collection. Qin Mu shares Deng Tuo's conviction that art matters and that Marxist-Leninist ideology is the best way to grasp the significance of aesthetics. His two subsidiary themes are that aesthetics should not be a secret language, but should be accessible to the general public, just like many natural science 'interest books' he mentions, and that there is no substitute for hands-on craftsmanship in the arts.[64] Qin Mu turns to Deng's favourite Qing period role model, the painter Zheng Banqiao, to provide 'A Rule for Originality'. Qing painters can help us learn how to cultivate artistic originality, says Qin Mu. The trick is diligence and learning from more than one master. In his examples, it becomes clear that 'originality' means for Qin Mu 'authentic personal expression'—a theme dear to Deng Tuo's heart. To achieve this, 'you must study widely and on the basis of a critical inheritance [formed by diligent practice of the techniques of various masters] blend together and extend that knowledge in bold originality.'⁶⁵ Qin Mu's professed desire to make every worker an artist parallels Deng Tuo's claim to popularize, not water down, Tang poetry and Song landscape painting.

Similar propaganda *zawen* came from Ma Tieding, pen-name for Chen Xiaoyu, who also edited *The Long and the Short*. He had been writing a *zawen* column, *Miscellaneous Talks on Ideology* (*Sixiang zatan*), since the late 1940s. His November 1960 edition of the column in *New Observer* included for instance his reflections on modernization and literacy. 'There is a new slogan that is becoming common,' he says, ' "Water conservance-ization" (*-hua*), mechanization—if you don't have culture (*wenhua*) you won't be able to change (*hua*) anything."⁶⁶ Ma Tieding also produced a book of satirical essays from the late 1950s and early 1960s along with cartoons (by the noted cartoonist, Hua Junwu) on 'what Western "culture" really is like', called *Record of the Setting Sun*.⁶⁷ In fact, Ma Tieding was one of the progenitors of the 'socialist *zawen*' which Deng Tuo adopted in *Evening Chats*.

Socialist Zawen: *The Establishment's Mode of Public Debate*

A final aspect of the Beijing essay columns that is relevant to their political import is the type of public discussion they typify. Both are collections of *zawen* (miscellaneous essays). Chinese scholars generally consider *zawen* to be a sub-set of *sanwen* (light essays) and group it along with a host of *belles lettres* forms, such as *xiaopin wen* (small essays), inherited from informal literati writings over the centuries. *Zawen* in the PRC have been defined as 'social commentaries of an artistic nature'.⁶⁸

This has been an extremely important literary form in Chinese politics since Lu Xun popularized it as a mode of public political criticism in the 1920s. Critics of the CCP have used *zawen* since 1942, and particularly in the Hundred Flowers period in 1957.⁶⁹ Deng Tuo's use of this mode of public discussion represents a significant departure, a domestication of Wang Shiwei's 'wild lily', from its previous use. The tone of Deng Tuo's *zawen* should not be confused with that of Lu Xun nor should their content be confused with the *zawen* of the 'Hundred Flowers' period. Deng Tuo's essays were polemical, but they were far less hostile and supercilious in tone than Lu Xun's, and unlike some of the spring 1957 critics they never suggested any major political change to the Leninist Party.⁷⁰ They are, as the Chinese term can be interpreted to mean, 'essays of miscellaneous impressions'.⁷¹ The manner they adopted, ironically, was closer to the light essays of Lu Xun's less contentious brother, Zhou Zuoren: 'mild, patient, reticent, and fair-minded'.[72] Under Deng Tuo, Lu Xun's old blade was hammered into a ploughshare to plant knowledge among the masses, to cultivate a sense of self-confidence and pride among the intellectuals, and to root out specific excesses of the leadership.

Chen Xiaoyu, whose pen-name Ma Tieding has already come up in this story, was one of the creators of this domesticated 'socialist *zawen*'. A writer for *Liberation Daily* and the New China News Agency in Yan'an, Chen served in central China during the later stages of the Civil War. There he and two other comrades (Guo Xiaochuan and Zhang Tiefu) created a joint pen-name, Ma Tieding, for a column called 'Miscellaneous Talks on Ideology' which they published in the Communist paper, *Changjiang Daily*. The series continued throughout the 1950s and into the early 1960s, resulting in several collected volumes of the essays. However, fairly early on, Zhang and Guo dropped out, so that Ma Tieding became the sole pen-name of Chen.[73] He produced hundreds of such domesticated *zawen*, which popularized the policies of the day from 'resist America' in the Korean War to condemning Hu Feng in 1955.[74] Both by his example of politically orthodox but stylistically sharp, crafted, and entertaining essays and by statement, Chen Xiaoyu set the standard for socialist *zawen*. In 1954 he wrote his reflections on essay writing.[75] His definitions and recommendations remind one of Deng Tuo's similar efforts from the mid-1950s aimed at explaining how to write editorials.[76] Chen starts with Lu Xun, noting that the master often lumped *xiaopin wen*, *zawen*, and 'random thoughts' (*zagan*) together as one form. As the old master says, these essays are for combating the forces of evil so they should use humour and satire. However, as that other master, Mao Zedong, has noted, the times have changed (i.e. one should not continue Lu Xun's anti-government stance from the KMT period). 'Although our contemporary *xiaopin wen* are directly pointed at the enemy, most of our criticism is of incorrect thinking among the People,' says Chen, and so we must temper our satire with the policy of 'cure the illness to save the patient.' In addition, there is no reason such essays cannot also praise what is good in society, since criticism and praise are dialectically indivisible.[77] Chen runs down a list of practical questions of interest to the aspiring 'miscellaneous essay' writer: what topics are appropriate? can large themes be addressed from small examples? can fictitious events and persons be used? (yes! exclaims Chen, let's not limit ourselves to the moribund Soviet examples); daily life should be the source of essay content, and finally and most fundamentally, nothing can replace craftsmanship based on assiduous practice. The one topic Chen does not emphasize is introducing knowledge in an independent fashion—the aspect identified as Deng Tuo's contribution to the genre.[78]

Miscellaneous essays were invariably written under a pen-name. In joint essay projects, pen-names could be made up of pen-names (as in the case of 'Wu Nanxing', the joint author of *Three Family Village*). Both the content of these articles and the use of the pen-names reflected an important part of Deng Tuo's approach to socialist journalism. It is impossible to hide the identity of an author from the authorities by use of a pen-name; there is always a Party propaganda official on any legitimate editorial board in China. Rather, the use of a pen-name can preserve the image of Party unity and allow a dissenting member to air his or her opinions without violating Leninist dicta. It also indicates at what level of authority an article is to be understood by the reader. That is, Deng Tuo, as editor of the *People's Daily*, wrote or spoke with the authority of the Party, and thus was compelled not to deviate from the letter of current policy. 'Ma Nancun' (Deng's pen-name for *Evening Chats*) as a citizen, however, could speak more freely and was understood to be less than authoritative. Finally, use of a pen-name often reflected the personal aesthetic style of the author or was simply a small joke or remembrance. It was one more thread of individual expression in the tight web of official service.[79]

Deng Tuo's Socialist Zawen

Beginning in March 1961, on Thursday and Sunday afternoons the readers of the *Beijing Evening News* enjoyed the wit and erudition of *Evening Chats at Yanshan* (*Yanshan yehua*), a new column on page three of the four-page daily paper. In a welcome diversion from the economic trials of daily life following the Great Leap, students, bus drivers, and office workers found in these quarter-page light essays a reminder of China's great cultural heritage with examples of hard work and success in overcoming difficulties by Chinese through the ages. Every now and again the column included clever spoofs of the reckless rhetoric of the Leap and sober admonitions to self-study as the answer to problems, both personal and political. The author, a certain Ma Nancun, was an unknown; it probably was a pen-name. But this hardly mattered. Anything published in the press had to have some sort of approval by the Party. In any event, the essays were as a rule elegantly written, fun, and inspirational. If one felt strongly about one of the topics—methods of studying art or economics or whether Beijing municipality ought to allow pet dogs—one could write in and Mr Ma would answer the next week.

On Wednesday and Saturday evenings, and sometimes the following morning, Gu Xing, the editor of page three of the *Beijing Evening News*, would receive the next instalment for *Evening Chats at Yanshan* from Deng Tuo. Gu Xing did little or no editing on each article. Stylistically, there was no need. Since Deng Tuo was his superior and effectively chief censor in Beijing's journalism and propaganda circles, Gu Xing had no need to worry about the political content of the articles. This was no hardship for Gu, not only because Deng Tuo was fifteen years his senior, an accomplished scholar and experienced journalist and editor for CCP publications, but also because Gu Xing looked up to him as a mentor and generally agreed with his opinions. Gu Xing simply passed on the bi-weekly articles to the printer and vetted the numerous letters that came in, sending the interesting ones on to 'Ma Nancun'. Finally, it was Gu Xing's job to protect the pen-name and the anonymity of the author.[80] By September 1962, when they stopped, over 150 *Evening Chats* had appeared in the *Beijing Evening News*. They were popular, and in 1963 they were collected in a handsome volume with woodblock prints and an elegant one-page introduction in Mr Ma Nancun's own flowing calligraphy.[81] In all, *Evening Chats* was a good high-school graduation present in 1964.

A Taste of Evening Chats

The first article in the new column *Evening Chats at Yanshan* appeared on 19 March 1961. It was entitled 'One Third of Life'. Its first three paragraphs read as follows:

One person's life ultimately has great significance. By what criteria can we judge it? Of course, it is difficult to suggest an absolute standard, but on the whole, by looking at whether or not a person's attitude toward life is serious and conscientious and at their attitude toward labour and work, etc. it is not hard to make a fair estimate of that person's actual worth.

Since ancient times, those who achieved something were those who took their lives seriously. Every day such people did their utmost to labour more, work more, study more—unwilling to waste their years, refusing to let time slip away. In our nation's history the working people and great statesmen, major thinkers, etc. were invariably like this.

In the 'Monograph on Financial Administration' in the *Standard History of the Han* by Ban Gu [CE 32–92], the following is recorded: '*Winter, the common people go inside; the women gather together in the alleys and help each other twist hemp thread through the night. An artisan woman gets forty-five days in a month.*[82]

These lines capture the flavour of *Evening Chats* and the author's basic style: he begins with a point, in this case an unusually broad one, and presents his case through examples which almost invariably come from the classical histories, philosophical texts, or literati *belles lettres* of traditional China. To capture the impact of Deng Tuo's language, it would be necessary to put the quotation from Ban Gu in Latin or perhaps in Chaucerian English (and orthography), rather than italics. Such ancient texts, which he frequently quoted in the *Evening News*, would have been partially inscrutable to most of even his fairly well-educated readers. Not that many Chinese read classical Chinese (*wenyan*) in the 1960s or today. This led to one of 'Ma Nancun's' favorite activities in *Evening Chats*: explaining. The next paragraph begins:

Reading this sentence, it seems strange. How can a month have forty-five days? The commentary by Yan Shiqu beneath the original text says, '*In each month the evening half constitutes fifteen days; all together forty-five days.*'

This in turn leads to an explanation of the odd title, 'One Third of Life':

A month basically has only thirty days, but the ancients counted the evening hours as half a day to get fifteen more. In this sense, don't the evening hours amount to at least one-third of one's life?

His point: use those evening hours to improve yourself. Point thus made, a few more illustrative examples (with explanation) follow. In this case, Ban Gu returns with his 'just praise' of the evening calligraphy exercises of the great despot, Emperor Qinshihuangdi, and we are acquainted with the exemplary evening reading habits of Liu Sili of the Northern Zhou (7th c. CE). Finally, the point of the essay is restated:

Why did the ancients so value the evening hours and refuse to let them pass lightly? I think it was their conscientious attitude toward their own lives. We ought to learn from their example.

Examples are at the heart of *Evening Chats*. A week later 'Welcome the "Miscellaneous Scholar"' appeared.[83] This time Mr Ma defends the generalist scholar in the face of the pretensions of narrow specialists. Once again, the validating examples are historical. But, all that is old is not necessarily good. Ban Gu returns to be criticized for his 'basically illogical' classification of 'miscellaneous scholars' (*zajia*) in the *Standard History of the Han*. Another example serves better:

In the old days, the well-known scholars were each in their own way miscellaneous scholars. Their collected works contain everything. One such book can be used by social scientists and by natural scientists. Take a random example: the Qing period scholar, Hong Liangji [1746–1809, a noted geographer and poet]. His collected works, much like those of other scholars throughout history, appear to contain everything, including his theory on population, which predated Darwin's by half a century. Nearly all the collected works of the scholars of our nation's past can be considered encyclopedic collections. They are a literary heritage worth cherishing.

There is a virulent strain of Chinese pride in these essays which is meant to be inspirational. For those who might not aspire to a life of literary production, there are other models. On 13 April 1961 'To Channel is Better than to Dam' recounted China's version of the Flood Myth, the story of the Great Yu who drained the marshes.[84] According to the most common version of the myth, Yu's father Gun had failed to end the floods and was executed. Shun, the Sage King, then turned to Yu, the son of his recently departed minister:

Yu was not angry; rather, he took the deliverance of humanity as his personal responsibility. We can see that the personal style of the characters in the ancient legends of our country was lofty indeed. In view of the lesson mirrored in his father's failure, Yu decided to change his father's methods. Rather than dam up the flood waters, he channelled them to flow freely into the sea. As this method accorded with natural law, the outcome, naturally, was successful.

The lessons in other *Evening Chats* are more or less pointed in their implications for government policy of the day (Yu's lessons could easily be applied to the post-Leap retrenchment policies), but the style of *Evening Chats* remains fairly constant. Not all examples Deng presents his readers are of the ancients and his points are not limited to common sense and national pride. *Evening Chats* address the 'how' as well as the 'what' of self-cultivation and public service. In mid-May 1961, Mr Ma addresses the question of 'criticism' (*pipan*). In 'The Correct Understanding of "Criticism"' he proceeds in the classic fashion of the *zawen* genre—from a casual conversation or observation to a pointed thesis.[85] 'Not long ago,' Ma Nancun begins, 'a few old friends, all high-level intellectuals, came to visit me.' The old friends chatted and debated the night away. But something from the evening still troubles Mr Ma:

Friends, why do you so dislike to hear the word 'criticism'? Can it be that you really think once 'criticism' is mentioned you will be attacked, everything will be refuted, and all will be done for? I think this is a terrible misunderstanding of 'criticism'.

Actually, regardless of whether it is ideological criticism or academic criticism, the purpose is certainly not to 'attack' or 'negate', rather it is to separate the wheat from the chaff, to eliminate the false and retain the true, to accept better our heritage and to develop our culture and our socialist cause.

Ma then reminds his readers that Marxism itself obtains its validity from its careful critical analysis of history. After all,

One of Marx's earliest works is called *A Critique of Political Economy*. Why did Marx call this theoretical work on researching political economy a criticism? Didn't Marx write that book in order to establish a scientific system for political-economic studies?

The problem is obvious: criticism is the only correct method of research. Research *is* criticism, and without critical research there can be no true research.

This is followed by a long quote from Lenin which credits Marx's proof that society must develop from capitalism toward communism to his 'critical attitude which overlooked nothing in its investigations'. Ma Nancun then takes pains to distinguish good Marxist critical research from the bogus idealist critical doctrine of Kant. Criticism is a method and its correct usage corresponds, Ma reminds us, in philosophical language to *aufheben* (sublation)—though of course in its materialist Marxist form, not Hegel's idealist version. The Marxist critical method is the only one that can avoid subjective, arbitrary conclusions which 'are the enemy of science'. Whatever one may make of Ma Nancun's arguments in this *Chat* it is clear that Marxist philosophical categories and methods are integral to his thinking. He believes they are science.

Evening Chats was not always so serious. Topics ranged from ancient cartoons to literati excursions on the common origins of calligraphy and painting, how to take notes, the value of the humble soybean, and a plain interest in 'strange things' (also a literati interest over the ages). On 7 June 1962 Mr Ma reported the fascinating story from various Tang period texts that eggplants can be made to grow into trees.[86] Though he valiantly tries to draw a practical lesson from this foray (what else can be grown to serve society?), the essay is really just a pleasant curio.

The range of topics and interests in *Evening Chats* raises the question of its audience and what Mr Ma hoped to achieve through his essays. Ma Nancun himself refers to his readers in July 1961 in the preface to the first booklet of *Evening Chats* in terms powerfully reminiscent of Mao's acceptance of a two-track cultural policy in his 1943 version of the 'Yan'an Talks':

自序

《燕山夜话》合集问世,奔秋重行修改,代云工程颇大,远非零篇写作那么容易。所以至今别地方署加修订付印,由此增一任务,无形又须在多时间。抓紧,再设法想没变成很难了。

有人说,零篇写作也很费工夫,你难道不怕就误了工作吗?讲一句老实话,我觉得同写难文章差不多,只要有准备,顺手写来就是了,有一点要说得好,时间的都能抢出。这又证明,一般的文章毫无越经越好,写写难就不至于因为忙而不动笔。

我们生活这样伟大的时代,活动在祖先亚评说遍的艺术地位,我们一时一刻也不应该放松努力,力学日更好,做得更好,以期无愧于先人,永无愧于后人!

一九六三年三月 邓南郡

5.2 Calligraphic frontispiece to *Evening Chats at Yanshan*, 1963
Note: Full translation in Cheek (1983–4: 34–5).

Naturally, I know that among the readers there are party, government, and army cadres, and also many teachers and students, technicians, artists, and writers. The requirements of these friends and those of the masses of workers, peasants, and soldiers naturally enough are somewhat different. The purpose of *Evening Chats at Yanshan*, of course, is to serve the workers, peasants, and soldiers. Since the important cadres in our party, government, and army are all cadres of worker, peasant, and soldier background and represent their interests, to serve them is to serve the workers, peasants, and soldiers. Since this is the case, I will continue to work in various areas to satisfy properly the needs of the masses of workers, peasants, and soldiers who have a relatively high cultural level.[87]

This, then, is a handbook for the literati-cadre. Such unofficial guides to cultured service of the state were common among the literati of dynastic China, but *Evening Chats* is one of the first from socialist China.[88] In it we will find not only tips for the aspiring cadre but a defence of Deng Tuo's approach to service in Mao's China, an apology for the cadre as culture bearer.

How Evening Chats at Yanshan *and Other Essay Columns Came to be Written*

Gu Xing and Liu Menghong, another editor of the *Beijing Evening News*, spent the spring of 1961 'volunteering' their organizational superior for the task of writing a bi-weekly newspaper column that would cheer up Beijing's intellectuals and educated youth. In classic Chinese style, they 'attacked' obliquely. Deng Tuo had published poems in the *People's Daily* and elsewhere since 1957 under the pen-name Zuo Hai, and he was one of Beijing's most noted art collectors and connoisseurs. So they organized casual dinners for Deng with the painter Wu Zuoren and others, which led to 'Matched Painting and Poem' publications, with poems by Zuo Hai. With a little more 'polishing' they wore down the resistance of their busy leader, and Deng Tuo finally agreed to write a column, which he chose to call *Evening Chats at Yanshan* (Yanshan being an old name for the Beijing region). The pen-name he chose was 'Ma Nancun,' in honour of the village he had often lived in as editor of *Jin Cha Ji Daily* during the Anti-Japanese War in rural Hebei-Malancun. A native of Fujian, Deng played on the pun in the southern Chinese pronunciation of Mandarin: 'nan' and 'lan' are both pronounced 'lan'.[89] Rather than the makings of a secret cabal, as accusations in the Cultural Revolution claimed, this was simply the efforts of junior editors to draft a famous writer to enhance their newspaper and tackle the delicate task of airing public criticisms of 'social problems'.

Evening Chats at Yanshan appeared each Thursday and Sunday afternoon beginning with 'One Third of Life' on Sunday, 19 March 1961. As mentioned at the beginning of this chapter, Deng Tuo would generally send the next instalment to Gu Xing the night before. In all, 152 essays appeared in the 'Multicoloured Land' (*Wuse di*) supplement on page three of the *Beijing Evening News* through 2 September 1962, of which 149 began appearing in small booklets of 30 from October 1961 and finally in a combined volume in August 1963.[90] Deng Tuo was paid 15 yuan (approximately $7.50) for each article, a rate higher than most according to Gu Xing, and he received a total of over 20,000 yuan (some $10,000), including the royalties for the 1963 book version.[91] The *Beijing Evening News* was widely available outside the city in the early 1960s, and *Evening Chats* had a substantial impact on readers and writers in other parts of China. According to Gu Xing, the newspaper published 300,000 issues daily in 1961, of which half, or 150,000, were distributed through the mail around the country. He says it was also available for subscription outside China. Of the four major evening newspapers published in China at the time the *Beijing Evening News* had by far the greatest circulation.[92] In addition, on an occasional basis individual *Chats* were reprinted in a number of newspapers around the country at the time—including *Sichuan Daily* and *Yangcheng Evening News* of Guangzhou.[93] Thus, *Evening Chats* reached a widely dispersed, if limited, audience of intellectuals.

Since *Evening Chats* and *Three Family Village* became the object of such virulent political attack in 1966, the question of authorship and authorial intent has become particularly important. For the moment, it seems safe to assume that Deng Tuo's 18 contributions to *Notes from a Three Family Village* reflect his personal opinions, since he was editor of both the column itself and the journal in which it was published.[94] In the case of *Evening Chats*, Gu Xing insists that Deng Tuo alone wrote the essays, with no editorial control by Gu or anyone else. This is hardly surprising, he adds, considering Deng Tuo's position. The content and argument of *Evening Chats* were Deng Tuo's own, but approximately a fifth (thirty articles) were direct responses to letters from readers and another third (fifty articles) were specifically directed to youth.[95] Some CCP old-timers, such as Xie Juecai, wrote in with comments, too, and not always on the most sensitive of political issues: Xie was concerned about pet dogs in the city. Deng's article on that topic spurred one of the livelier debates, prompting several letters that were published in the paper.

Within Beijing municipal Party circles, led by Peng Zhen, the First Party Secretary, and among some other CCP leaders, *Evening Chats* apparently raised no eyebrows and was considered to be doing a good and necessary job in 1962.[96] There is no available record of any comment made by high leaders on either column at the time. This should not be seen as complete approval, since Mao clearly supported Yao Wenyuan's attack on Deng Tuo in 1966, yet there is no record of critical comments by Mao on the columns. Support by the majority of relevant high leaders is implied by the official praise Deng and *Evening Chats*, as well as similar essay projects, have received since 1979.[97] In 1961, few outside the newspaper's editorial committee and a few close friends knew the true name of Ma Nancun, though clearly any top official could have found out by asking Peng Zhen. This conforms to Deng Tuo's own justification for pen-names.[98] Gu Xing recalls that Lao She, the noted author, asked him in 1961 who Ma Nancun really was and was surprised and pleased to hear it was Deng Tuo.[99]

Chronology of Evening Chats *and* Three Family Village

From the political context outlined above, we can see that Deng Tuo wrote *Evening Chats* and *Three Family Village* as part of the effort by the CCP at public education to correct the ideological errors of the Great Leap, to reduce its lingering malaise, and to prohibit the return of its worst policies. We have also seen that micro-chronology is important in assessing each article. What Mao may have supported in June 1961 he would likely not in May 1962.

What patterns emerge from looking at the 152 articles in *Evening Chats* and the 18 articles by Deng Tuo in *Three Family Village* when they are viewed by the date and order of their publication? In light of the political chronology for 1961–4 given above what correlations in themes emerge? The collected volume of *Evening Chats* (both the 1963 and 1979 editions) does not reprint Deng's essays in chronological order. I have tabulated all Deng's articles from these two series and have also assigned each article a number reflecting its political significance (see Appendix). Thus we may trace the pattern of Deng's political commentaries between 1961 and 1964.[100]

I chose a five-point scale to reflect a simple three-level assessment: (1) apolitical, (3) politically safe, and (5) politically contentious. Numbers 2 and 4 provide some leeway, but in the comments below I treat each as a member of its respective extreme (1 and 5) in an effort to mitigate my errors of judgement. This is not, however, a simple continuum. Rather it is a measure of how much Deng's articles stayed with current policy (level 3) or veered off to explicitly bureaucratic Maoist themes or criticisms of faith Maoism (4–5) or dropped off the explicitly

Theory Worker and Culture Bearer

TABLE 5.1 Political nature of Deng Tuo's essays

	Political level	Quantity	Per Cent of total
'Cultural'	$\begin{cases} 1 \\ 2 \end{cases}$	74 21	$\left.\begin{matrix} 42 \\ 12 \end{matrix}\right\} 54$
'Current line'	3	34	19
'Critical'	$\begin{cases} 4 \\ 5 \end{cases}$	21 27	$\left.\begin{matrix} 12 \\ 15 \end{matrix}\right\} 27$

political range to address cultural issues that, in fact, raise issues of aesthetic legitimation for cadres as culture-bearing administrators of the realm (1–2).

Thus, apolitical *is* political, but in the complex and ambivalent context of the post-Lushan period where faith and bureaucratic versions of Maoism were vying for final approval from an indecisive supreme leader. This means that Deng's views did not become unequivocally 'dissent' until they were declared to be so *ex post facto* in 1966. Thus, essays rated 4 or 5 depart from Mao's personal vision of good politics and those rated 1 or 2 articulate Deng's personal values for the scholar-cadre, which while they echo themes from the Beijing Party's official journal do not necessarily accord with the wishes of Peng Zhen or other top leaders of the bureaucratic stripe. Meanwhile, essays rated 3 largely push the current Party line.

When Deng Tuo was explicitly political in these essays, he was *not* necessarily 'anti-Maoist'. In fact, a good number (34 or 19 per cent) seem to be quite in line with commonly known Maoist interests: respect for manual labour, disgust with bourgeois culture, faith in the wisdom of the masses. However, slightly fewer (27 or 15 per cent) are extremely critical of ideas and practices with which Mao is associated while more articles (21 or 12 per cent at level 4) fall somewhere in between. On top of this over half of the essays in *Evening Chats* and *Three Family Village* (21 at level 2 + 74 at level 1 = 54 per cent) are predominantly cultural in focus and tone.

This count, which should be taken as no more than a rough estimate of relative proportions, reflects Deng Tuo's life and interests over the previous two decades, bringing to mind the circles of Deng Tuo's social activities (Chapter 3). In the political focus presented to us in the attacks of the Cultural Revolution, nearly half of Deng Tuo's life and interests, and certainly over half of *Evening Chats* and *Three Family Village*, have been largely ignored.[101] As well, half of his political opinions, those which overlap with some of Mao's socialist ideas, have not been analysed seriously. The two uncomfortable political categories (3 = current line; 5 = critical of radical policy) reflect the uneasy overlap of Deng Tuo's approach to politics with that of the ageing Chairman's, as well as the confusion of the time. This tension is rooted in the problematic twin imperatives of Marxism-Leninism: loyalty to the Party (method) and loyalty to the leader (faith).

This count supports the general impression we might obtain from a reading of the essays simply in the light of Deng Tuo's career. However, what specific chronological patterns emerge from this long list of articles? Looking at clusters of level 4 and 5 (outright critiques of Maoist policy or strident statements of bureaucratic Maoist values), there are a series of political highs and lows from March 1961 to March 1962, followed by a continuous low from then until the end of each essay column. This pattern confirms Deng Tuo's reputation as a thoroughly political man and savvy reader of political wind. Throughout the dynasties, sensible Chinese scholar-officials have known that remonstrance is at best useless and probably personally fatal if given at inopportune moments. Deng's most critical essays came during the single year of massive retreat from the Leap when Mao supported the retreat, between spring 1961 and January/February 1962. The pattern is summarized in Table 5.2.

The first series of highly political articles, ones which criticize the Great Leap, ran in March and April of 1961. All of these articles, including the apolitical advice to youth to study more in 'One Third of Life', deal with issues of the Great Leap: do not give superstitious faith to leaders, rely on trained intellectuals, use scientific methods to carry out famine relief and prevent future famine, do not twist history with vulgar Marxism, learn from foreign friends (pointing to the recently departed Soviet advisers), and respect natural laws in economic planning. This was precisely the time that Mao and the Central Committee (at the January 1961 Ninth Plenum) were calling for 'investigation' of Leap problems, and this was the height of the 1961 rectification movement. March also saw Mao's comments at the 'Canton Conference', again calling for 'investigative research'.[102] In words Deng Tuo would quote almost word for word, Mao said, 'The attitude of investigative research cannot be "I'm the boss, I'm right, I'm the official." [It] must be discussion-oriented, comradely, consultative. Don't be afraid to hear differing opinions. If previous decisions and resolutions, after going through the test of practice, prove to be wrong, then don't fear overturning them.'[103] This was also the time of Peng Zhen's 'Huairou Investigations' of counties near Beijing, which directly followed Mao's

TABLE 5.2 Pattern of Deng Tuo's 'contentious' essays

Month(s)	Titles/Topics	Mao speeches/ Related meetings	Topics
Mar.–Apr. 1961	Criticism of GLF agr. & cult. policies	Mao: Jan. 1961; Mar. 1961: Canton; Jan. 1961: 9th Plenum	Investigation; rectification
June 1961	'Stories About Bragging'; modesty; field research	Mao: June 1961; June 1961: Prop. Conf.; May–June 1961: Central Work Conf.	Investigation; cadre education
Aug. 1961	'Study More, Criticize Less'; focus on truth	Aug–Sept. 1961: 2nd Lushan Conf.	Adjusting communes; cadre education
Nov. 1961	'Great Empty Talk'; actual conditions; integrity	Chang Guan Lou Meeting	Peng Zhen review of GLF policies
Feb. 1962	'Kingly Way'; criticism of 'genius'	7,000 Cadres Conf.	Mao's self-criticism; Liu's critique of GLF

advice. Deng Tuo would write up the Huairou report in June. Thus these articles can be seen as informal study materials in the recovery from the Great Leap. Yet in January, Mao had also expressed his concern about the resurgence of 'the landlord class', the need for class struggle, and the existence of bourgeois and petty bourgeois elements inside the CCP. He called for 'wave-style forward development' to overcome recent errors in socialist construction.[104] Thus faith Maoists like Kang Sheng or Lin Biao could prepare their study materials with confidence that they were 'following the Thought of Chairman Mao'.

For a month and a half in May and June the bi-weekly articles were either apolitical or quite in tune with Maoist sentiments. The next spate of politically contentious articles appeared in June 1961. This group includes one of Deng's most famous jabs at the Great Leap and Mao, 'Stories about Bragging'. It also includes stories which promote the values of cautious practicality and criticize unfair investigation work. June was the month in which Chairman Mao himself delivered his second speech of 1961 to a Central Work Conference in Beijing on the great need for 'investigation' [*diaocha*] and 'self-criticism'.[105] It was also the month Deng wrote up the Huairou report. Here Deng can be seen as responding to the call, but certainly taking it farther than the Chairman wished. The 10 June editorial in *Frontline*, unsurprisingly, was devoted to how to do detailed field investigations and the same issue included a supplementary essay by Liao Mosha on field research.

From late June, *Evening Chats* either pressed political views similar to Mao's or discussed topics of elite cultural interest. A series of more politically contentious articles appeared in August with themes similar to the previous two sets, probably spurred by the recent (July) vetting of the 'Sixty Articles on Education' and review of the communes and cadre education at the late August second Lushan Conference.[106] Mixed, but generally less contentious, articles continued into early November.

November, however, saw a return to political critique and the first of Deng's contributions to *Notes from a Three Family Village*. 'Great Empty Talk', published in the 10 November issue of *Frontline*, is probably Deng Tuo's most direct and most hilarious assault on the Chairman. In it he ridicules Mao's Great Leap slogan 'The East Wind prevails over the West Wind.' The contemporaneous pieces in *Evening Chats* provide the reasons why Deng so hated empty political rhetoric: stubborn ignorance goes before a fall in 'Let Go to Find Firm Ground', model intellectuals are praised for their conscientious work and judges admonished to do their work according to rule. Nonetheless, these are critical themes raised by Mao himself. Deng's 'dissent' is that of the autonomous adviser, taking the old man at his word, even at the risk of offending him. A telling example of Deng's lack of dissent from some of Mao's ideas and Deng's commitment to socialism over liberal values is '"Soundless Music" and Such', published on 12 November, which derides modern music of the John Cage variety (he cites a concert at the Julliard School in New York) and denounces the decadence and fraud of bourgeois culture. This theme is repeated in a scathing review of French 'Electric Musical Theatre' in *Three Family Village* on 25 November.[107]

This was just the time of the Chang Guan Lou review of Leap policies, in which Deng Tuo and a team of Beijing Party officials summarized the findings of the Huairou investigation and other research. Like Deng's independent version of popularizing Mao's desires in *Evening Chats*, the Chang Guan Lou review was Peng Zhen's loose interpretation of Mao's repeated personal calls for the First Party Secretaries to take a hand in the investigations of economic policy in their region. Peng availed himself of the opportunity to review national economic policy, and Deng Tuo's report was scathing. For Deng Tuo, Chang Guan Lou reflects his service to his political patron and the congruence between his political work (running the review) and his personal ideas (his freely published articles).

By the end of November, however, Deng was writing about botany in *Evening Chats* and nothing (until March 1962, and then on calligraphy) in *Three Family Village*. Whatever opinions Deng had about politics from the Chang Guan Lou review waited until after the famous January 1962 '7,000 Cadre Conference' in which Mao made his second and more forthright self-criticism. In late February and early March 1962 Deng published his last series of polemical *Chats*, including his most pointedly political critique, 'The Kingly Way and the Tyrannical Way', which clearly denounced through allegory Mao's contravention of intra-Party minority rights. It should be remembered, however, that the criticism of arbitrary leadership probably was directed equally at lower-level leaders. 'Three Kinds of Zhuge Liang', published in the next issue of *Chats*, considered the strengths and faults of the famous leader in ancient history and literature. It could only have been directed at the current historic leader, Mao, and the two articles printed together in the book version stand as compelling proof of Deng Tuo's disgust with the Chairman's personal leadership style since the late 1950s.

This was the end of all but a handful of Deng's contentious essays and the end of articles directly related to recovery from the Great Leap. Only a few polemical articles appear in the remaining *Evening Chats* and *Three Family Village* pieces by Deng Tuo. Ones to which I assign a relatively high political rating (4) speak on general principles of bureaucratic Maoism. After 25 July 1962 I can find no articles in either column of the contentious (5) type. Even so, Deng went out with a flair on that day with 'Special Cure for "Amnesia"', which almost certainly is addressed to Mao and 'faith Maoists'.[108] This article suggests, as Mao warmed up for his radical comeback in September 1962's Tenth Plenum, that any return to Great Leap policies was sheer madness. The bile of Deng's essay stands out in contrast to the moderate tone of essays on similar themes in *Three Family Village* by Liao Mosha and Wu Han in previous weeks—on the need for modesty, on pride before fall, on how little we really know, on the need for caution.[109] The mix of political and apolitical essays from spring 1962 through the last ones in *Three Family Village* in the summer of 1964 strike me as Deng's cautious attempt to put his interpretation on the new 'Four Clean-ups' Movement.

What this chronology tells us is that Deng Tuo heeded his own advice (nicely stated, below, in 'Eat Broth instead of Lamb') and exercised independent thinking within bounds. In particular, the tentative linkages we can see between the 1960–1 rectification, Mao's personal calls for 'investigation' in January, March, and June 1961, the Chang Guan Lou review of November 1961, Mao's self-criticisms in June 1961 and January 1962, and the concentration of politically contentious articles in *Evening Chats* and *Three Family Village* show that Deng was a politically astute creature who chose his time carefully. As with his life in general, when political pressure prevented him from speaking out, he withdrew to his scholar's garden, writing on his aesthetic and academic interests. This pattern seems only to hold for a year, March 1961 to March 1962. From then on, Deng's political pieces in the columns are more of an effort to cope with the revived radicalism and shifting currents of the 'Four Clean-ups.' Thus the first period shows Deng Tuo's contribution to the critique of ultra-Leftism, and the second period shows both failure of its 'incomplete critique' and Deng's style of accommodation.[110] One imagines he was once again biding his time, unaware that time was running out.

Furthermore, the pattern of contentious essays really reflects shifts in the current policy of the day and the contents rarely go much beyond Deng's editorials in *Frontline* or his essays from the 1950s—with an important exception: style. In terms of policy Deng was not dissenting at all in *Evening Chats* and *Three Family Village*. When he criticized a policy it was during the prescribed period for doing so (not a crime until Mao chose to forget his policy swings and judge all behaviour by one unchanging standard of loyalty to his Cultural Revolution goals). However, in terms of *style* Deng dwells on the need for personal integrity and his models do call to mind martyrs from past centuries. This image was not Party policy. What can be missed in the chronological analysis is that, in essence, *all the essays* are political (bar a very few, such as those on bees and tiles) as justifications or examples of the scholar-cadre's aesthetic licence to rule, as Maoist-populist administrator and as Leninist organizer and analyst.

Scholarly Style and Aesthetic Legitimation

Evening Chats and Deng's essays in *Three Family Village* were written in the 'dysfunctional family' of central CCP politics, where top leaders squabbled over how to recover from the Leap and continue 'socialist construction' using *real*, not 'window dressing', values (only real values have power necessary to win the fight). In the face of recent Party failures and the continuing breakdown of inner-Party norms, Deng turned to his twin faiths: the *aesthetic moral training* of Chinese elite arts and the *practical administrative methods* of a Stalinist version of Marxist-Leninist epistemology and leadership (i.e. 'praxis') as adapted in the

Yan'an 'Mass Line'. These politically relevant values are everywhere apparent in Deng's personal essays.

Take an unpromising example. What, for instance, can the essay 'Eat Broth instead of Lamb' possibly tell us about Chinese politics?[111] In the context of events outlined above, it is clear that Deng Tuo, from a position of authority in the official press, is making in this essay several important points about the causes of the failures of the Great Leap and how to solve them. His topic is essay writing in the Song dynasty. He derides formulaic conformity to 'the style of the times' and implies that only opportunists interested in personal advancement (being able to afford lamb) would do so. Instead, he holds up the ideal of *individual integrity* and independent thinking: do what you see as right even if you will only be able to afford gruel. History, he seeks to demonstrate with his classical citations, will prove you right.

Deng Tuo is speaking here of essay writing, not political platforms. None the less he is assuming political consequences stemming from writing in the style of the times or not. He is writing for scholar-officials, not E. B. White or James Fallows, who might gain or lose income and market share in a different social system. He does not advocate disobedience to Party discipline. Other essays in *Evening Chats* lay to rest any implications of liberal independence.[112] In *Evening Chats* Deng Tuo is simply trying to get scholar-cadres to improve their work style, so they will not succumb again to the heady rhetoric of policies similar to those of the Great Leap. He is not trying to change the mechanisms of a one-party state. These themes were already present in his 1957 *zawen*, 'Discard "The Politics of Simpletons"', discussed in Chapter 4. At the same time, however, Deng shows that he is not a faith Maoist in 'Eat Broth' because the assumed object of his admonitions—intellectuals, people who write essays—are directed to values in Chinese culture, not Mao's sayings, as a basis on which to make an ethical judgement. Deng's concern here presupposes the central significance of literate people and higher intellectuals in China, in parallel with the traditional social role of the Confucian literati mentioned in his essay. Mao, on the other hand, had increasingly given up on intellectuals following the 1957 Hundred Flowers experiment and had begun to reaffirm his faith in the peasantry, the cog-and-screw role for cadres, and the anti-intellectual side of the Yan'an model.[113] The key political components of Deng Tuo's thinking are apparent even in the article 'Eat Broth instead of Lamb': a reliance on scholar-cadres (academics, writers, technocrats) to exercise independent thinking *within the bounds* of CCP leadership.

In an effort to revive this agenda from the past, I will make my review of the contents of *Evening Chats* and Deng's contributions to *Three*

Family Village along the lines of the categories which seem to me to demonstrate and defend the scholarly style as they emerge from reading these texts in the light of Deng's activities as we have seen them in the first four chapters of this book. These categories derive from my study of his life in the 1950s and remain because they seem to explain his intent and the reception of his writings in the 1960s. They are not the only categories which might help clarify the meaning of these politically contentious essays,[114] and I will note examples of the issues raised earlier in this chapter as we encounter them in the texts—the contextual functions of the essays (nationalistic pride, critique of arbitrary leadership, defence of intellectual autonomy within Marxism-Leninism) and the three key audiences and related functions of education, remonstrance, and reaffirmation of an elite.

The categories which emerge as the attributes of the 'theorist' or culture-bearing cadre are: knowledge (ancient, scientific, and based on 'hands-on' practice), aesthetic perceptiveness, discipline, integrity, tolerant judgement, and generalist skills.[115] In all his essays, Deng reflected the traditional self-image of the Chinese scholar-official, the literatus (*shi* or *wenren*), with a paternalistic sense of responsibility for the good of the common people that implicitly justified the special status and privilege of establishment intellectuals in general and Party intellectuals in particular.

Knowledge

Fundamental to all Deng's essays, and similar ones of the time throughout the PRC press, is the value of knowledge. Deng constantly praises the virtues and practicality of knowledge. As H. C. Chuang has noted, *xuewen* (knowledge) is one of the most often repeated words in *Evening Chats*.[116] Consistent with Deng's artistic activities elsewhere, his calligraphic introduction to *Evening Chats* and continual references to ancient texts in both columns reflected his belief that ancient habits from the 'feudal' past, despite their limitations, remained worth while in his day. Knowledge of the statecraft of the ancients allowed Deng, for instance, to offer the following lesson after the Great Leap:

We should take inspiration from the experiences of the ancients and pay more attention to treasuring labour power (*laodong li*) in every area and thereby treasure every individual's labour and the fruits of every labour.[117]

This is from 'On Treasuring Labour Power', published in April 1961, and is, simply, a variation on the Ninth Plenum's call to correct labour allocation. Deng's point is that good husbanding of labour is an ancient

Chinese knowledge available for use today for those sensible enough to avail themselves of the information. Furthermore, Deng did not rest his arguments simply on ancient texts. He suggests that the lesson from ancient texts—that one should carefully assess one's abilities before committing oneself to act—'is something everyone has learned through experience in daily life.'[118]

Deng treats foreign knowledge on a par with traditional (or 'feudal') ideas—as a source from which to select critically. In 'Study Needs Guidance', Deng reminds his cadre readership of *Three Family Village* about the dangers of loosely interpreting the Great Leap slogan 'achieving without a teacher'. We need to consult the ancient books of China and foreign scientific texts, writes Deng, in order not to waste time re-creating the wheel as we build socialism. Since construction cannot be done in a day, 'this requires relevant newspapers and journals to select and introduce to readers in a timely fashion the quintessence of our ancient books or foreign scientific materials which they badly need today, in order to increase guidance in various areas of study.'[119] Such practical advice as this, which indicates an intended audience of subordinates to be educated, characterizes Deng's essays more than esoteric attacks on Mao.

Science and practice are Deng's two touchstones for judging knowledge, and he never tires of showing that many ancient Chinese writings contain tips that are confirmed by science and have great practical applications. For example, Deng picks up in 'Gold in Scarab Beetles' on a report from 1934 by a Czech scientist who claimed to have recovered 25 milligrams of pure gold from a kilogram of ashes from incinerated scarab beetles. Deng then reviews a half dozen 'scientists from China's ancient period' and their comments on the scarab beetle, from a certain Duan Gonglu of the Tang to citations from the famous Song scholar, Ouyang Xiu, and the Ming naturalist, Li Shizhen. But as is often the case in Deng's review of classical authors, they turn out not to know as much as contemporary folk (here that gold can be obtained from these beetles). Deng concludes with a request that the proper authorities, scientists, test the Czech's experiment and non-specialists should not attempt such experiments recklessly.[120] In a later essay, Deng finds a Tang period source on a 'floating garden' and another from the Ming. He then notes that a version of aquaculture farming is used in the south of China and ends the essay by suggesting that floating gardens are just the trick for recovering lost cropland now covered by reservoirs in north China.[121]

Knowledge is fundamentally for the correct ordering of society and is thus linked to politics. In an essay more directed to his fellow literati-cadre, 'Welcome the "Miscellaneous Scholar"', Deng makes clear that such practical knowledge is by definition 'broad knowledge' not limited to one discipline or profession: 'No matter what sort of leadership or scientific research work we do, we need to have both specialized scholarship and extensive knowledge.' And specialists, he adds, should base themselves on a well-rounded intellectual foundation.[122]

The knowledge Deng discusses usually is of interest only to intellectuals and cadres. The intellectual audience for *Evening Chats* is even more clear when Deng discusses knowledge as method, as analysis. In spring 1962 he received a letter from a reader concerned with the problem of viewpoint (or analysis) and data in writing. Deng decides there are two schools of thought on the issue: the theory over fact and the details over analysis schools. Both are one-sided and the good writer needs to synthesize theory and data. 'On this point,' Deng notes, '[our] predecessors have already had quite a few instructive experiences.' He cites a story from the notebook of a Ming scholar, Lu Ji, which uses a rope metaphor for organizing knowledge, and interprets the paragraph of difficult-to-read classical Chinese: yes, every essay should have 'an ideological red thread' linking data systematically. On the issue of collective writing 'the ancients have some examples of great achievements. Never think that it is only we moderns who are capable of collaborative writing.' Diligence and common sense will transform these models into fine writing by youth today.[123] In response to another reader, Deng offers advice on how to handle the flood of research materials—put notes on loose-leaf note paper, one point per sheet, then organize the sheets according to your research outline and you will have a well-researched essay. Deng cites Zheng Qiao from the Song, who counsels 'energetic study and bitter reading', and lists a half dozen reference works by title, such as the great eighteenth-century encyclopedia *Gujin tushu jicheng*.[124]

The data to be analysed is knowledge obtained by personal investigation, whether into classical or foreign books, or by stomping around village fields or factory floors. 'People must go through personal practice (*tiyan*) in the real world in order to know the real state of things,' says Deng in his November 1961 cautionary tale, 'Let Go to Find Firm Ground'.[125] Deng quotes a humorous story from the notebook of the Ming scholar, Liu Yuanying, about a silly blind man who slipped off a bridge but managed to hang on with his hands to the struts. A passer-by tells him there is no river below, only 'firm ground'. But the blind fool, unable to see for himself, refuses to believe. After struggling to hold on, his hands tire, and he falls. Realizing that he is safe, the blind fool says, 'Hey, if I'd known there was firm ground I wouldn't have had to suffer so long.' Deng Tuo takes this as a parable for field investigation in villages. Not only is personal observation necessary but the confidence it brings will enable the presumed cadre reader to determine which views of the masses are relevant and which are spurious. We cannot avoid this laboriously obtained knowledge, 'because we are engaged in an unprecedented enterprise. We are revolutionaries.'

Aesthetic Perceptiveness

Deng Tuo's approach in both of his columns was primarily cultural. Many of the pieces are entirely on high-culture topics—on flowers, paintings, penmanship, and ancient texts.[126] Indeed, a balanced selection of these essays would produce a small encyclopaedia on the glories of Chinese culture, as well as a handbook of tips on how to be a good scholar-cadre in the service of the Party.[127] Deng's essays on art and culture reflect the refined tastes of the aesthete he was, but he presents them with a cheerful populism, welcoming the reader to this world of intense emotion and individual expression. In 'The Allure of Art', Deng defends himself against a charge from a friend that he is an antiquarian.[128] It is not a matter of restoring the past (*fugu*), says Deng, rather 'we must earnestly study and inherit the historical tradition of our nation's arts.' He goes on to describe the rhapsody of viewing various classic paintings. Perhaps realizing he was on ideological thin ice, Deng provides a page of quotations from Marx himself on the dialectical relationship between the low productive stage of earlier societies (Marx cites the Greeks) and the high quality of their artistic output. Art, concludes Deng, should spring from practice, life as lived, but it should be varied and individual. Everyone painting like Qi Baishi would be stupefying, he says. Ancient masters, if carefully appreciated, will bring each person's creativity to the fore. These views, of course, parallel Qin Mu's on 'originality' (discussed above).

Deng assumes a link between ability in calligraphy and painting and moral excellence. This is the key 'formative social context' of Deng's scholarly style. Artistic ability in this realm is not mentioned as a qualification for leadership by Marx, Engels, Lenin, or Stalin, or for that matter *explicitly* by Mao. Such abilities were associated with the 'superior man' qualified to rule in traditional culture. Nevertheless, these skills palpably are used to claim superior authority in Chinese Marxism, from every Politburo member scribbling on book covers and school gates to Mao's calligraphy and poetry that exploded across the nation in the early 1960s.[129] Deng Tuo offers another window into this important corner of Chinese political culture.

After performing a brief piece of evidential scholarship on whether or not the calligraphy attributed to General Zhang Fei really is that of the famous general of the Three Kingdoms period, Zhang Yide, Deng concludes in *Evening Chats*, 'and wouldn't a hero like Zhang maintain the brave spirit of writing calligraphy and painting?'[130] The link between ability in the 'three arts' (poetry, painting, and calligraphy) and the moral rectitude necessary to serve the interests of the nation was made most forcefully in Deng's November 1963 essay in *Guangming Daily*, 'Zheng Banqiao and the "Banqiao Style"'. Based on a 1961 visit to the Yangzi Delta region and published under the pen-name Zuo Hai, the essay was a contribution to the Socialist Education Movement.[131] The essay harks back to the historically oriented moral lessons of *Evening Chats*. It is, however, much more politically oblique, reflecting the increasing pressure on Party intellectuals to conform to Mao's radical vision by mid-1963. It also is painfully personal, viewed in the context of Deng's life from 1957. Instead of the noble resistance and martyrdom of the Eastern Wood scholars which Deng raised in his poems in the same newspaper three years earlier, here he focuses on a retreat from office to art. In 1960 he was ready to fight, but by late 1963 he sensed the balance of forces had moved against him.

Deng introduces the Qing period scholar-painter on the occasion of the 270th anniversary of Zheng Banqiao's birth and defends the usefulness of 'concretely analysing' representatives of 'landlords and officials from the feudal period'. He decries simplistic rejection of artists like Zheng Banqiao just because they were 'feudal'. In any event, Deng presents Zheng as having a good class background (born poor, even if in a landlord family) and a Mass Line style of leadership (as a magistrate where he demonstrated real concern for the local peasants to the point that he brought the wrath of the local elite down upon himself). But Deng's real interest is Zheng's art and what it means. He introduces an unpublished painting, 'Orchards and Bamboo Deep in the Mountains', which depicts a scene of deep quiescence. Deng notes that Zheng was serving as a magistrate when he painted this and the painting, along with its colophon, shows Zheng's wariness with the strains of office and his yearning for peace away from government. Tellingly, Deng himself had painted a similarly peaceful scene on a fan using a pair of his own poems from mid-1959.[132] Deng had already copied the Banqiao style. Deng's affinity with Zheng Banqiao was strengthened by sharing favourite poets. Both men preferred and composed in the realistic and natural style of Du Fu and Lu You (Lu Fangwen).[133]

Deng Tuo turns to Zheng's calligraphy to raise the theme of individual style and independence. Zheng has left his mark, says Deng, through his distinctive calligraphic style. He was so well trained and creative that 'he has become a school to himself.' Deng is not interested in the nomenclature of calligraphic schools; the calligraphic arts stand for the independence and integrity of the man. The traces from his brush, which can be seen in the specimens of his calligraphy today, are moving shadows of this noble man. He remains with us and he is an inspiration. 'What is the spirit of the "Banqiao Style"?' asks Deng. 'I think it is in every arena of life to be your own master and not be a slave!' Deng closes by backing off from any larger political implications by recommending to his readers that they adopt the 'Banqiao Style' as their model for study, once again returning to his constant theme: improve present work by selective inspiration from earlier Chinese heroes.

Discipline

For Deng discipline was a key to success. Disciplined study, as we have seen Deng argue in his advice to student researchers and writers above, produces useful knowledge (of morally transforming art or of practical administration). Disciplined action, as in the care of labour power, produces measurable and containable results in government policy. Finally, the responsibilities and perquisites of the literati-cadre required disciplined obedience to Party rules.

Deng Tuo's elitist faith in the Party led to his demand for obedience to Party regulations in line with the approach of his patron, Peng Zhen. In the essay, 'Do Nothing Improper', Deng reinterprets this phrase from Confucius to justify a quasi-military 'need-to-know' basis for public discussion that is quite the reverse of an 'open society'. 'No matter what work we do,' he writes, 'there should be fixed rules. . . . The highest standard in our society's rules of life is to subordinate the rights of the individual to the rights of the group.' He interprets the *li* (for the core Confucian value, 'rites' or 'propriety') as 'meaning customary rules, norms, moral standards.' The whole essay revolves around state secrets and how to protect them. In a later essay he emphasizes the self-discipline necessary to be a good scholar and good Communist.[134]

A system needs not only discipline but a regular regeneration of its ranks. Two of Deng's last three essays for *Three Family Village*, published in the spring of 1964, were concerned with the proper operation and cultivation of future members of the bureaucracy—the educated youth. 'The Load can be Shouldered', an open letter to officials who make decisions on job assignments (*fenpei*), recommends that they carefully lead their young 'apprentices' in experiencing greater professional responsibility. Without such on-the-job training, Deng concludes, how will our revolutionary successors be prepared to take over from us? Later, in 'What Kind of "New" Do You Want?', Deng speaks to his peers of their responsibility to educate youth. 'What we call "new"', says Deng, 'is the new of socialism.' He derides the false bourgeois 'new' of nineteenth-century European literature and declares it inappropriate for China, even as a stepping stone away from feudal literature. We must guide the youth in their reading of new books, he continues, since we cannot really say all new books are good, and we must lead them through the best of the older books, which after all includes the Marxist-Leninist canon. Defining what this socialism is, he admits, is no easy task but is achievable through the application of a *method*: historical and dialectical analysis.[135]

Integrity

Issues of personal integrity are central to Deng's essays and are usually expressed through role models of scholar-officials from classical history. The terms he uses are 'uncompromising integrity' (*guqi*) and 'personal integrity' (*qijie*).[136] Gao Panlong and the remonstrating Confucian critics of the late Ming Eastern Woods Academy were favourite examples in Deng's poetry (see Chapter 4) and essays, forming the core of his homily, 'In All Things Show Concern'. The Older and Younger Mi of the late Ming period were '*shu hua jia*'—scholar-official calligrapher-painters—who exercised their arts, served as government officials, and resisted the evil eunuch, Wei Zhongxian. A similar pattern of artistic ability and moral fortitude is presented in the joint biographies of the painters Chen Hongshou and Cui Zizhong.[137] Indeed, as H. C. Chuang notes in his terminological study of *Evening Chats*, the entire third volume of the collection (which carries a preface dated 25 March 1962 and includes essays from November 1961 onwards) is littered with cases of *guqi*.[138]

In looking at the themes in Deng's famous commentaries, the image of a dissident is far less appropriate than that of censor. This is the image Deng himself chose in his poetry—the loyal scholar-official braving death to remonstrate with his ruler in the name of the orthodoxy and on behalf of the 'outer court' (the bureaucracy). The essays about literati-artist models address Deng's three audiences: confronting his superiors with the ideas that they are no better than eunuchs and weak emperors of the past (unless they act now); providing youth and aspiring scholar-cadres with inspiring models to follow; and sharing with Deng's fellow intellectual elite examples of their heritage and Deng's mastery of it.

Tolerant Judgement

Deng Tuo's emphasis on the immutable laws of nature reflected the influence of Engels and echoed the epistemology of Yang Xianzhen, senior Party theoretician and former director of the Central Party School. Deng's belief in the superiority of cool, rational analysis—much like Peng Zhen's—is clearly evident in his approach to Marxism-Leninism-Mao Zedong Thought. This careful gradualist approach can be seen in 'The Kingly Way and the Tyrannical Way'. Quoting at length from several Han dynasty histories, Deng makes his socialist interpretation of what they record:

That which is called the Kingly Way can be interpreted as the honest ideological work style of a Mass Line based on practical reality. And that which is called the Tyrannical Way can be interpreted as the blustering ideological work style of wilful acts based on subjective and arbitrary decisions.[139]

While making a general point of value to lower-level cadres, Deng Tuo must surely have had in mind here the 'blustering ideological work style of wilful acts' of Mao from the terrible bedroom confrontation in April 1957 and Mao's hot-headed speeches at Beidaihe promoting the Leap in August 1958, not to mention Mao's fateful tantrum at Lushan.

Deng criticizes the abuse of traditional Party leadership methods as a means of defending those methods. In 'The Correct Understanding of "Criticism"' Deng cites Marx's *A Critique of Political Economy* to argue that criticism is the same as scientific research, and he quotes Lenin on the role of criticism in developing the workers' movement. Without criticism, insists Deng, dialectical progress—sublation of thesis and antithesis (he uses the German, *aufheben*)—is impossible. A realist, Deng acknowledges his readers' concern about unprincipled criticism, which he admits has occurred in the past. 'But the inability to use critical methods,' he states confidently, 'if you look into the causes, still stems from not understanding the correct meaning of criticism.' Rightly understood the system should work.[140] Even in 'Great Empty Talk', where Deng placed the heady rhetoric of Mao's claim that 'The East Wind Prevails over the West Wind' squarely in the realm of arbitrary and subjective work style, he admitted the necessity of 'empty talk' on occasion in political life. He asked only that it not be the major legacy to later generations.[141]

In June 1963, at the start of the Socialist Education Movement, Deng admonishes that cadre error 'cannot be changed in a day. It must be resolved slowly on the ideological level, relying completely on persuasion and under no circumstance on force.' As always, when quoting Mao, Deng Tuo selects from the Yan'an corpus (here 'Get Organized!' from 1943) to undergird his demands for careful research and moderation.[142] Keys to tolerant judgement are modesty,[143] anti-individualism,[144] clear reasoning, and an aversion to extreme opinion and coercion, particularly in the application of criticism.

Generalist Skills

Deng's idea of expertise was that of the conscientious generalist, since his goal was not original creativity, but practical implementation. This is apparent in his advice on research:

Today no matter what problem we are studying, we must read through all the related materials in Chinese and foreign books, journals and newspapers, jotting down all useful information. Only after going through the mutual combination and verification of theory and practice [i.e. Mass Line testing of theory in practice] and detailed analysis and research can we, on the basis of our predecessors' research, advance with our own opinions.[145]

The reason for Deng's generalist approach by now is clear: his role was not to discover new knowledge or to create original art (not to be confused with individual expression, which he did support), it was to transmit the cultural heritage of China and keep it alive by cultivating its higher forms himself and by popularizing them among China's masses. Furthermore, his vocation was to help bring moral administration to fruition. He was a doctor to society (making diagnoses through *diaocha* and prescriptions through *xuanchuan*), a manager of its business, not an artist or an academic in the Western (and, partially, Chinese New Culture Movement) sense. Thus, from a purely artistic or academic perspective, Deng's poetry or historical essays may be found wanting (and both have been reasonably criticized by specialists). These pursuits were but the meditations and exercises of a dedicated scholar-official in the statecraft tradition of literati. These disciplines helped prepare him for his work (and they were enjoyable of themselves), but they were not his work.

Deng's general interests form a coherent whole around the two most central concerns of his vocation: ideology and propaganda. To the Western reader these two words at first seem an utter contrast to the topics just covered—knowledge, integrity, judgement. It is the burden of this analysis to argue that all these values are inseparable for Deng Tuo and many of his generation. Ideology, as we have seen, is method to Deng Tuo; it is an accurate and systematic (he says 'scientific') way to perceive and organize reality, and it motivates one to action by keeping the historical, almost cosmic, significance of one's work in mind. In September 1962, just as Mao was reviving his 'Never Forget Class Struggle' version of 'faith' ideology, Deng outlined his version of ideology in 'Use Your Head'.[146] Deng cites Mao's admonition to the editors of *Liberation Daily* in 1942, 'Think More' (*duo xiang*). He goes on to deride simple or quick answers to the difficult problems of administering society. To Deng, and in Chinese the words are related, ideology means thinking. It is a habit to develop, not a magic charm. It is a method of linking regular concrete work with the current policies, general principles, and fundamental goals of the Party.

The reason why one must be so conscientious with thought and ideology is because the task before cadres is so great. It is the great Maoist task of 'summing up the wishes of the masses', synthesizing those needs with the insights of Marxism-Maoism, and propagandizing the results back to the masses. In two summer 1963 essays for *Three Family Village*, Deng stresses that propaganda work is the key link in actualizing the results of this work, because the masses must act—change the world and thus themselves. Doing it for them will not work. Thus, the cadre's job is to understand both the objective problems at hand and subjective attitudes of his specific audience so well that he can present the truth back to his subjects in a manner they can understand, act upon, and accept as their own.[147] When that new awareness, both of practical issues and cultural sensitivity, comes alive among ordinary people, then the propagandist, the scholar-cadre, has fulfilled the ambition of sages from ages past: to bring community life into harmony with the forces of the universe.

Conclusion

Chairman Mao's call, 'Never Forget Class Struggle', at the Tenth Plenum of the CCP in September 1962 is generally regarded as the end of the 'thaw' in 1961–2. In Deng Tuo's case there is no information on his activities in Beijing to indicate a major change before 1964. Nobody saw the Cultural Revolution coming; this was just another phase in the cycle of openness and repression. The political advice which the establishment offered during these years was an incomplete critique of Mao's increasingly dictatorial behaviour and ultra-Leftism. What is clear in the 1990s—such as the need for real limits on Party power—was not clear in 1962. Not only was Mao still alive as supreme leader and the Cultural Revolution unimaginable, but Mao's charisma still moved the hearts and minds of the establishment, which also shared responsibility with Mao for the Leap. Mao may have begun to doubt his Party, but his Party (while distressed) had not given up on the Chairman. Mao was lessened—an occasional object of satire from Deng Tuo's pen—but he was still the father of the revolution. To reject Mao, to 'kill' the father, would be to kill something inside themselves. The miraculous charisma of the Leninist Party had brought them all to power, but now Deng Tuo and his associates found themselves riding the tiger.

Deng Tuo's values were not limited to the issue of cadre as culture bearer, nor were they unique to him. He was part of a loose group of Party intellectuals and others interested in retooling Yan'an communism in a manner suitable for that section of the polity which was urban and increasingly modern. His Leninist epistemology parallels Yang Xianzhen's and supported a technocratic and gradualist version of Stalinism in the Central Committee; his historicism matches Jian Bozan's and Jian's critique of the 'mass historiography' of the Leap; his concern to popularize moral lessons from history resembles Wu Han's; his commitment to popularize Party rules conforms to Liao Mosha's; his desire to permit and enjoy a measure of personal privacy echoes Feng Ding's; his faith that elite arts can help cultivate good cadres for the Party echoes Qin Mu's popular aesthetics; and his desire to protect the organizational apparatus of the Party reflects that of his long-time patron, Peng Zhen.[148] None the less, there was a tone of concern in Deng Tuo's essays not prominent in his writings from before the Leap. Several themes reappear constantly and they all point to the need for the Party and individual officials to align themselves better with reality. Like the chastened Mao, Deng assumes less faith in the inevitability of good policy emerging from Party committees, but unlike Mao he demands more effort, even personal risks, from morally autonomous but loyal scholar-cadres. These themes represent an addition to Deng's approach to public life based on his troubled experience in the years before 1961 and stand as his last sustained discussion of the role of the educated elite in socialist China.[149]

One aspect of *Evening Chats* and Deng's related essays which this analysis does not capture adequately is the pleasure of reading them. One can imagine how the themes Deng raises in them might speak to the concerns of educated readers in Beijing or other metropolises in the early 1960s, but even taken out of their context these essays are an unusual pleasure for those who make a profession of reading the PRC press. They are literate, clear, economical, breezy, informative, and most of all, intelligent. Even the somewhat paternalistic essays directed at youth strike one's 'interest' (*quwei* or *xingqu*). In this respect they bring to mind the cheerfully informative science essays of Lewis Thomas or Isaac Asimov, or the clever natural history essays of Steven Jay Gould. One feels broadened and refreshed after reading such essays, which treat one's intelligence with respect and offer a comradely sense of shared curiosity about this world and its inhabitants. This ultimately aesthetic character of the essays, one that crosses time and culture successfully, reminds us that Deng Tuo was not a scholastic grind or frustrated reformer. He enjoyed life and felt such interesting essays were part of the renewed cultural florescence of China to which he was so proud to contribute.

This gentle comparison with contemporary American essayists (and Deng's lampoons could, of course, be compared to those by Art Buchwald or satire in *Punch*) brings us back to Beijing in 1962 usefully. Deng Tuo had no reasonable expectation before 1965 that his essays would bring the wrath of a nation-wide media campaign down upon his head, any more than Steven Jay Gould might expect to be burned at the stake for his views on evolution or Art Buchwald might anticipate imprisonment for his spoofs of Washington politics. The comparison may seem strained: Buchwald and his colleagues have never been sent to labour camps for their political essays, while thousands of Chinese intellectuals were in 1957 and 1959 in the anti-Rightist campaigns. The comparison turns out, in the end, to be a helpful reminder. What is striking in Deng Tuo's essays and the reminiscences of his writing colleagues is that they did not expect severe criticism because their neo-traditional scholarly style had not been the object of attack in the suppression of intellectuals in the anti-Rightist campaigns (or in the 1940s campaigns, either). Liberals, more internationally minded intellectuals, and less disciplined Party cadres had suffered then. Deng Tuo, Wu Han, Liao Mosha, and the writers in *The Long and the Short* were loyalists. Proud, to be sure, but writing for the system. Their 'crime' in the Cultural Revolution was a lack of sycophancy and a distaste for the rituals of full-blown faith Maoism. Each drew a line beyond which cog-and-screw service would violate their identity as culture bearers, and most would not cross it in the years to come.

Deng's critique of ultra-Leftism had failed, but it had continued the developing alienation of faith and bureaucratic Maoism. The shrill assertions of faith Maoism as the only Maoism in 1966 completed the dissolution of the 'symbolic capital' of Yan'an Maoism. As we shall see in the next chapter, Deng Tuo's 'anti-Party dissent' in *Evening Chats* and *Three Family Village* was 'manufactured dissent' designated as such when part of the Party, the faith Maoists, became for a while the voice of the entire Party and purged that other part of the Party, bureaucratic Maoists. What was left was broken jade.

NOTES

1. See Joseph (1984). Joseph gives a sensitive analysis of the political debates from the late 1950s onward, but does not cover the *zawen* essays of Deng Tuo and the *Three Family Village*.
2. See the literature review in the Introduction.
3. Sun Yefang and Jian Bozan were trying to carve similar 'space' as professional specialists in economics and history, respectively. See Naughton (1986) and Edmunds (1987). Wu Han, who collaborated with Deng in *Notes from a Three Family Village*, more closely followed Deng Tuo's agenda. See Fisher (1986).
4. The idea of the Bolshevik Party as a charismatic institution comes from Kenneth Jowitt, who characterizes the Party as THE institution of 'charismatic impersonality'. See Jowitt (1992: 4 and 9–12). The newly available version of Mao's calls for public criticism of the Party in his speeches of Jan. through Apr. 1957 can be interpreted as his first effort to lessen the charisma of the Party *relative* to his own. See documents 1–14 in MacFarquhar, Cheek, and Wu (1989: 113–372). The Cultural Revolution, of course, was the extreme example of Mao's effort to bring the Party to heel. Post-Mao efforts to criticize Mao similarly lessen the charisma of the top leader. This is, however, a case of relative dominance in charisma: Mao discovered in 1969 that he could not live without the Party and in the 1980s the post-Mao leadership has found it cannot do without the old Chairman's charismatic authority completely. This competition between the supreme leader and the collective leadership would seem to be a basic fact of Leninist regimes.
5. MacFarquhar (1983: 322–4); Lieberthal and Dickson (1989: 107–8).
6. *Qianxian*, 28 June 1960, 1–2, in which Deng Tuo interprets 'uninterrupted revolution' as technological innovation and revolution.
7. MacFarquhar (1983: 312 and 298–9).
8. MacFarquhar (1983: 33).
9. Teiwes (1979: chs. 10 and 11, esp. p. 493). Teiwes maintains this view in his introduction to the 1993 2nd edition of this study (though the 'dysfunctional family' metaphor is my image). It remains the authoritative view of the field at present, with Kenneth Lieberthal echoing the same 'no showdown with Mao' thesis in ch. 7 of Lieberthal (1987), esp. p. 357. Students of this topic await with interest vol. 3 of MacFarquhar's trilogy on the origins of the Cultural Revolution, which will provide a new interpretation of this period.
10. MacFarquhar (1983: 320–1).
11. For an alternative view that argues Lin did not actively pursue such aggrandizement during the Cultural Revolution, see Frederick Teiwes' and Warren Sun's careful study (Teiwes and Sun 1996).
12. On Kang and Yang Xianzhen, see Hamrin (1986: 60 ff. and 1991). Kang had, in fact, tried this approach in the Central Party School as early as the 1957 rectification,

but was criticized by Liu Shaoqi for vulgarizing the movement. A good summary of the rise of Lin, Jiang, and Kang is given in Lieberthal (1987: 335–48).
13. MacFarquhar (1983: 319); Lieberthal and Dickson (1989: 109).
14. 1960*e*.
15. A detailed set of lectures by Deng in 1950 on land reform appears in DTWJ: i. 409–68. See discussion on this in Chs. 1 and 3, above.
16. 1960*d*.
17. 1960*f*.
18. 1962*a*. Editorials from January through March echo these themes. Deng uses the term '*lilun gongzuozhe*' in this editorial.
19. See Edmunds (1987: 69–70 and *passim*).
20. 1961*b*; tr. in *Selections from Mainland China Magazines* (*SCMM*), 264, pp. 1–13. It has been reprinted in the 1979 edn. of Deng's collection of history essays, *Lun Zhongguo lishi* (1979), 1–18. It has also been included and glossed in a language textbook; see Wan and Johnson (1973).
21. *SCMM*, 264, p. 2. On the Cultural Nationalism Movement between 1959–64, see Edmunds (1987: 71–3).
22. *SCMM*, 264, pp. 2–4. In fact, Deng criticizes a number of historians as bourgeois, Trotskyite, or plain reactionary, from Tao Xisheng to Wittfogel and Akizawa Shuji. The latter two historians are advocates of the 'Asiatic mode of production' variant of Marxist historiography, which Deng, along with the mainstream of future PRC historians, bitterly attacked in the 1930s. For a valuable account of this debate around the world, see Fogel (1988).
23. *SCMM*, 264, pp. 10–11.
24. See Edmunds (1987) and Fisher (1986).
25. *SCMM*, 264, p. 6.
26. *SCMM*, 264, pp. 10–11, quote from p. 11.
27. From the newly available Mao texts: *Xuexi wenxuan*: 264–5 and 270, and repeated in *Mao Zedong sixiang wansui* (June 1967: 323 ff. and Sept. 1967: 242–5). These three volumes are, respectively, vols. 3, 6a, and 9 in the New Mao Texts set reprinted by CCRM (USA); see MacFarquhar, Cheek, and Wu (1989: 78–9).
28. See Liu Juinian, *Liushi niandai guomin* (1982: 184), cited in Halpern (1987). See also various Central meetings related to this policy, in Lieberthal and Dickson (1989: 112–19).
29. Mao's example is his 1930 *diaocha* of Xunwu county in southern Jiangxi. This text was, according to Roger Thompson, being prepared for open publication in the early 1960s under the direction of Deng Xiaoping, perhaps to support these very investigations. See Thompson's introduction to Mao Zedong (1990). Details of the three investigations comes from one Red Guard publication, 'Peng Zhen "Huairou diaocha"' (1967), available at the Fairbank Center Library. The text includes numerous quotes from the actual investigation reports—in usual Cultural Revolution fashion denouncing Peng *et al*. My thanks to Michael Schoenhals for pointing this out to me.
30. 'Peng Zhen "Huairou diaocha"' (1967: 2 and 26).
31. 'Peng Zhen "Huairou diaocha"' (1967: 26); the Red Guard editors complain of this on p. 1 and excerpts from the report refer to *sanbao* or other locutions for the policy frequently, for example, on p. 24. This is essentially the same system Deng Xiaoping put into effect, with such prosperous results, in the 1980s.
32. 'Peng Zhen "Huairou diaocha"' (1967: 1 and 6) (which gives the classic Cultural Revolution charge that Chang Guan Lou was linked to *Evening Chats* and *Three Family Village* and was intended as preparation for denouncing Mao at the

forthcoming 7,000 Cadres Conference). Peter Moody (1973: 154) and Ellis Joffe (1975: 33–6) both follow the Cultural Revolution criticism (although praising Deng for apparently attacking Mao). For a more critical assessment, see Teiwes (1979: 491 and 384–440). Post-Mao Chinese sources are quiet on this topic. We still do not know the true nature of this meeting.

33. Taken from a Red Guard report, 'Before and After the Chang Guan Lou' (Apr. 1967), tr. in *SCMM*, 640: 23–7, quote from p. 23. See also Lieberthal and Dickson (1989: 123–4).
34. Tr. in Schram (1975: 158–87).
35. This is the periodization given by Teiwes (1979: 471 ff).
36. Lieberthal and Dickson (1989: 142–6).
37. Teiwes (1979: 578–9).
38. Teiwes (1979: 579–81); Mao quote from p. 581.
39. Wu Nanxing (1979).
40. This cultural mission is a very broad theme in Chinese intellectual history in which Deng Tuo should be seen as one example. Susanne Weigelin-Schwiedrzik (1984) has found a similar pattern among some Party historiographers—an appreciation of Mao, organization, and the opportunity to save Chinese culture by serving the CCP while disliking utopian futurism.
41. See nn. 27 and 28 above.
42. Teiwes (1979: 476).
43. Gu Xing (interview with author, Beijing offices of the *Beijing Evening News*, 5 Apr. 1983), echoing his article in YDT: 134. 'One Third of Life' is the first essay in *Evening Chats* (1979: 5–7).
44. Unger (1987). China's inability, so far, to do away with the literati-cadre role would seem to prove Unger's point—if one assumes, as do I, that sources of power in Chinese society have not changed fundamentally from Deng Tuo's time. See Richard Kraus's (1991) excellent study of the political uses of calligraphy in China.
45. Most of the *Evening Chats* essays present themes familiar from the 1950s, although specific topics and the style of presentation were clearly influenced by the establishment's critical response to the failures of the Leap. See for comparison Deng's 'Politics of Simpletons', discussed in Ch. 3, and Liao Mosha (1956); Chen Haiyun and Sima Weizhi (1986).
46. Events in the 1980s have added new perspective on the strengths, and limitations, of this identity and this role for intellectuals in modernizing societies, both socialist and not. Deng Tuo is interesting as much for what he does not raise (such as professional independence from the state, limited government, popular democracy, and an independent judiciary) as for what he does. On the similar lure of 'directed culture' in the hands of intellectuals in state socialist regimes in Eastern Europe, see Haraszti (1987) and Konrád and Szelényi (1979).
47. Merle Goldman (1969) introduced Deng Tuo to most English readers; in light of information released since the death of Mao, Goldman has modified her view of Deng Tuo as a liberal critic at odds with the Party. See Goldman (1981: 25–32). Joachim Glaubitz (1969: 35) holds Deng Tuo up as 'a journalist against the Party'. Peter Moody (1977: 176–7) calls Deng and associate Wu Han 'Marxian Confucians' whose ultimate commitment to moral norms put them in opposition with the Party. Byung-Joon Ahn's excellent study of the politics leading up to the Cultural Revolution none the less leaves the reader with the view that Deng Tuo was anything but happy with the CCP. See Ahn (1976: 69–74).

48. For example, Meisner (1986: 330). A refreshing exception is Livio Maitan (1969/1976: 198–200), who sees Deng Tuo as arguing a position congenial to Peng Zhen while not simply being his puppet.
49. A standard example is the essays in YDT.
50. I mean this only in the sense of using *zawen* in the Party press to aid the current rectification programme. *Zawen* in the press date back to the famous examples of Lu Xun in the 1920s and 1930s and they had long since been domesticated (made less critical) in the PRC press. See for example Liao Mosha's 1956 series, mentioned above. Deng himself modelled his joint *zawen* series with Liao and Wu Han on earlier models of Ma Tieding.
51. Gu Xing (interview with author, 5 Apr. 1983); repeated in Gu Xing (1985: 12).
52. Gu Xing (interview with author, 5 Apr. 1983). Thus the *Beijing Evening News* carried three light-essay columns in the early 1960s—Deng Tuo's on knowledge; *Yixi tan* (*An Evening's Talk*) by several authors including Gu Xing, begun in 1958, on thought; and *Qingchun mantan* (*Spring Chats*) by Wen Shuyang (pen-name for the noted essayist, Yang Shu) on youth questions.
53. The contributing authors (with the pen-names they used in the column) were: Liao Mosha (Wen Yijian), Meng Chao (Chen Bo), Xia Yan (Huang Ni), Tang Tao (Wan Yiyü), and Wu Han (Zhang Bai).
54. Wen Yijian [Liao Mosha], '"Chang duan xiangjiao" shuo', *Chang duan lu*: 1–3.
55. Yuan Ying and Jiang Deming (1979: 45–6, repr. in *Chang duan lu*: 93–4) emphasize that the authors did not form this writing group themselves, but only in answer to the efforts of their superiors on the editorial board.

    Tang Tao's comments based on Gregory B. Lee's notes from an interview with Tang Tao (Beijing, 4 Nov. 1982). My thanks to Gregory Lee for sharing this data.
56. Gu Xing (1985: 12) takes care to note that Deng Tuo was following this call in his political criticisms in *Evening Chats*.
57. Ding Wang includes *Chang duan lu* in his 1969 Hong Kong edn. of *Deng Tuo's Selected Works*, mistaking 'Wen Yijian' as Deng's pen-name. See 1969: 201.
58. The breakdown of contributing authors to *Notes from a Three Family Village*, all of whom published in *Frontline* under the joint pen-name Wu Nanxing, is: Deng Tuo, 18 articles; Wu Han, 21, Liao Mosha, 21. These were the three main authors. In addition, 5 other articles in the column were written by others on the *Frontline* staff or at the request of Deng Tuo: Li Guangyuan, 1; Li Jun, 2; Zhang Shiji, 1; and Li Wen, 1. Individual authors are identified in Wu Nanxing (1979: table of contents). This brings the total to the 65 essays repr. in Wu Nanxing (1979). There are, in fact, two more essays in the column as it appeared in *Frontline*, according to my review of the original journal issues, which are not reprinted. We may presume that they are by Liao Mosha, since Su Shuangbi (1979: 43), in his enumeration of the articles by the three main contributors, differs from my count only in assigning two more to Liao. Thus, Liao contributed 23 articles. See, Cheek (1983–4: 95 and 98). Once again demonstrating the accuracy and obscurity of post-Mao historical texts on this topic, Su gives the total number of articles in *Three Family Village* as 62, which while misleading, is in fact accurate, *if* one already knows that 5 of the 65 in the reprint are not by the three men Su is discussing (giving a figure of 60 total) and that two have not been reprinted (=62)!
59. Liao Mosha (1979: 243–5); Chen Haiyun and Sima Weizhi (1986: 200–1).
60. For an analysis of Wu Han's *zawen* contributions to *The Long and the Short*, as well as to *Three Family Village*, see Fisher (1986: 166–71).
61. Deng Tuo identified the first two in the preface to his 5th volume of *Evening Chats*;

see 1979a: 427. All three are discussed in Yuan Ying and Jiang Deming (1979: 47–8), repr. in *Chang duan lu*: 98.

Other titles have been suggested, such as Wu Youheng's *Rong yin zahua* (*Banyan Tree Miscellaneous Talks*). Cultural Revolution attacks identified further essay series as 'branches of the Three Family Village black gang', etc. These are summarized in Kuo (1978: 420–1). I have not been able to locate copies of most of these essays. As is usual with Cultural Revolution attacks, accurate linkages are conflated with error. The offending 'branches' include Qin Mu's *Yihai shipei* (discussed below), which pre-dates Deng's essays and is an influence on, not a follower of, *Three Family Village*. The attacks also list Yang Shu's *Qingchun mantan*, which also pre-date Deng's series in *Beijing Evening News* (see note 52 above). Others, such as *Bashan manhua* in *Chengdu Evening News* and *Bashan yehua* in the *Chongqing Daily* along with Tao Bai's *Dengxia manji*, are worth further investigation.

62. Gu Xing (1985: 12) and Gu Xing (interview with author, 5 Apr. 1983). *Dianyun mantan* has been published in book form since 1979 (Yang Lei, interview with author, Beidaihe, Aug. 1981).
63. Kam Louie (1980: 47–74) demonstrates this in the case of Confucian studies in the early 1960s and more broadly in Louie (1986), where he notes with some disapproval the enduring strength of the elitist tradition in socialist China.
64. Qin Mu (1962). Qin Mu (b. 1919) was assistant general editor of *Yangcheng Evening News* and an editor of *Works* (*Zuopin*) magazine.
65. Qin Mu (1962: 127–9).
66. The suffix for '-ization' and the second half of the word 'culture' are both *hua* in modern Chinese, making this slogan a series of puns. Ma Tieding (1960: 6–7).
67. Ma Tieding (1962). Hua Junwu's cartoons are really very funny.
68. Perhaps the best introductory collection of *zawen* from the PRC perspective, including a valuable general essay on the form and style of various forms of *sanwen*, is Bao Ji (1981), particularly his general essay (pp. 550–80); quote from p. 551.
69. See Goldman (1967); Cheek (1984b).
70. Wang Bisheng (1986: 196) makes a qualified comparison of Deng's *zawen* with Lu Xun's. On Lu Xun's *zawen*, see Pollard (1985).
71. In other words, *zagan wen*. This is Niijima Atsuyoshi's (1962: 42) interpretation of *zawen* in Yan'an.
72. Such is David E. Pollard's assessment of Deng Tuo's *Evening Chats*. See Pollard (1985: 88).
73. Chen became editor of *New Observer* in 1959 and served in the *People's Daily* in the 1960s. He died under duress in the Cultural Revolution in Aug. 1966. See introductory and concluding essays by Feng Mu and Yuan Ying in *Ma Tieding zawen xuan*.
74. See also Ma Tieding (1962), discussed above; Ma Tieding (1955; 1960).
75. Chen Xiaoyu (1955: 50–66). The postface (p. 67) notes these essays were written in 1954.
76. See Ch. 3 above.
77. Chen Xiaoyu (1955: 60 and 55).
78. Chen Xiaoyu (1955: 58). Deng's focus on knowledge in the essays may well have been a response to the utter stupidity of Leap policies and the gullibility of the populace. Pre-Leap authors can hardly be blamed for having a stronger faith in the regular educational institutions.
79. These reasons are covered by Deng Tuo himself, writing as Mr Ma Nancun, in 'Ni zancheng yong biming ma?' (Do You Approve the Use of Pen-Names?), in *Evening*

Chats, tr. in Cheek (1983–4: 61–3). For a list of further reasons and the most complete concordance of pen-names for 20th-century authors, see Chu Pao-liang (1989), esp. preface.

80. Gu Xing (interview with author, 5 Apr. 1983); more details on this are in my introduction to Cheek (1983–4: 8 ff.).
81. 1963*a*. Booklet collections of 30 *Evening Chats* had been published separately since July 1961; see preface to 1963*a*: i. 3–4. I have seen vols. 1 and 2, but have never located copies of the separate vols. 3, 4, and 5. The subtitle '*heji*' for the 1963 edn. indicates that it is a 'combined volume' of the five booklets; it maintains the five sections with prefaces.
82. 'Shenming de sanfen zhiyi', *Beijing wanbao*, 19 Mar. 1961, p. 3; repr. in 1979*a*: 5–7. The 1979 edn. is not significantly different from the 1963 edn. for the texts quoted in this section, and is more widely available in the West. Most of the texts cited in this section I have translated in Cheek (1983–4). 'One Third of Life' is tr. in Cheek (1983–4: 38–40).
83. 'Huanying "zajia"', *Beijing wanbao*, 26 Mar. 1961; 1979*a*: 11–13 and Cheek (1983–4: 51–3).
84. 'Duse buru kaidao', *Beijing wanbao*, 13 Apr. 1961; 1979*a*: 78–9 and Cheek (1983–4: 73–5).
85. '"Pipan" zhengjie', *Beijing wanbao*, 14 May 1961; 1979*a*: 92–5 and Cheek (1983–4: 58–60).
86. For a complete list of *Evening Chats* essays and Deng Tuo's contributions to *Notes from a Three Family Village*, see Appendix. The essay on eggplants is in 1979*a*: 371–4.
87. 'Liangdian shuoming' (Two Explanations), dated 10 July 1961; 1979*a*: 3–4 and Cheek (1983–4: 36–7).
88. There are of course formal handbooks for both periods, such as Huang Liu-hung (1984 edn.) and the various *Shouce* available for cadres in the PRC. I am referring to the more informal essays of literati reflecting on that service, such as Feng Guifen's essays of the late Qing.
89. Gu Xing and Liu Menghong (YDT: 111–15).
90. YDT: 115. There were a few articles from the column not included in 1963*a* or 1979*a*, but all appear in one or the other. When I checked the originals of *Evening Chats* in copies of *Beijing wanbao* at the Beijing University Library I was able to account for all but one (because some issues were missing). One article was added to vol. 5; see Deng's note (1979*a*: 427). The two unaccounted for essays are 'Blood in Yanshan Skies' (1979*a*: 535–9) and 'A Piece of Tile' (1979*a*: 446–9). One likely appeared in the 1 July 1962 issue of *Beijing wanbao* and the other, which I suspect is 'Blood in Yanshan Skies' because it is longer than the usual *Evening Chats* essay and is a commemorative piece on a fallen comrade from Jin Cha Ji, is the added essay.

Three of the 152 '*Chats*' from the paper were not included in the 1963 edn. They are reprinted in 1979*a*: 540–8. One, 'The Case of Chen Jiang and Wang Geng', is as politically sensitive as 'Stories about Bragging' (which was published), but no more so. The other two are not striking or unusual. There may be deeper reasons for their exclusion in 1963, but they are not apparent to me.

Four of the 150 '*Chats*' in the 1963*a* were deleted from 1979*a*. They are: 'The Accomplishments of Collectors' of 13 Aug. 1961 (1963*a*: 142–5), 'Talking from Lu Chishui's Ink Chrysanthemum' of 14 Dec. 1961 (1963*a*: 259–62), 'Jiang Gaisi [Chiang Kai-shek] Destined to Die' of 24 June 1962 (1963*a*: 522–5), and 'An Ink Lotus' of 29 July 1962 (1963*a*: 461–4). When I brought this to the attention of Ding

Yilan in 1981, she freely explained why each of the four had been deleted: the 'Collectors' piece praised the Soviet Union too much, and the 'Jiang Gaisi' piece criticized the Kuomintang too much. The two 'flower' pieces were excised because their topic, the painter Lu Chishui, is in reality Kang Sheng, who later took a leading role in Deng's purge. See discussion of Deng's connections with Kang Sheng in Ch. 4, above.

91. Gu Xing (interview with author, 5 Apr. 1983); YDT: 156, in which Liu Menghong and Liu Yongcheng say Deng spent his royalties on artworks which he later donated to the state.
92. The other three papers were: Canton's *Yangcheng wanbao*, Shanghai's *Xinmin wanbao*, and Tianjin's *Xin wanbao*, which became *Tianjin wanbao* in 1961. See Gu Xing (interview with author, 5 Apr. 1983); *Suibi* (Jottings) (Guangzhou), 1980: 8, p. 39.
93. According to Yang Lei, an editor at Yunnan People's Press (interview with author, Beidaihe, Aug. 1981). As Deng Tuo notes in his preface to the fourth booklet of *Evening Chats* essays, newspapers and journals in outlying areas in 1962 had already carried reprints of several *Evening Chats*, (1979a: 305, dated 23 July 1962; this was also printed in the *Beijing Evening News*, 3 Aug. 1962, p. 3). Deng also asks readers in Sichuan to look for a particular stone rubbing in 1979a: 468 (5 Aug. 1962).
94. Liao Mosha (1979: 242) also claims no direction or editing affected the three contributors' writing in *Three Family Village*.
95. Gu Xing (interview with author, 5 Apr. 1983); YDT: 134 and 128.
96. Gu Xing (interview with author, May 1983); Peng Zhen didn't read *Evening Chats* or *Three Family Village*: it was not his sort of reading material. Mao, however, did read these essays. Gu wouldn't hazard a guess as to Mao's reaction to *Evening Chats* in 1961–2, beyond noting that the Chairman was known to take offense easily.
97. The standard official praise is given in Chen Kehan and Li Jun (1979). Similar praise for Wu Han, Liao Mosha, members of the *Chang duan lu* team, and related essayists from the 1960s appear as introductions or afterwards to reprints and collections of their essays since 1979 (see Bibliography).
98. 'Ni zancheng yong biming ma?' (Do You Support the Use of Pen-Names?), *Beijing wanbao*, 28 Sept. 1961; 1979a: 299–302, tr. in Cheek (1983–4: 61–3).
99. Gu Xing (interview with author, 5 Apr. 1983). Gu added that Lao She thought the essays were very well written. Xu Zhucheng (1981: 312–18) praised the style of journalism embodied in *Evening Chats*.
100. The Appendix lists all Deng's articles and prefaces (177 in total) published in *Evening Chats at Yanshan* and *Notes from a Three Family Village* by date of original publication in the *Beijing Evening News* or *Frontline*, or in the case of those prefaces not published in the newspaper, by their signed date. An English translation of each article's title is provided along with the page numbers on which they appear in the 1979 edn. of their respective collection, which is the most widely available today. My personal assessment of the topics and the political significance of each article is given in addition. The few words given next to each article under the heading 'Topic' are based on a common-sense judgement of what is discussed in the article. Like many newspaper columns, the titles of Deng's 'Chats' catch one's attention but only make sense after one reads the article. While topics can indicate something—ceramic tiles, flowers, and pets are unlikely to be overtly political in inspiration or impact—many topics are much more varied. Education, youth, history, public policy, etc. can be political or apolitical. Therefore, each article has been assessed for its political tone.

101. My rough count of the essays by Liao Mosha and Wu Han in *Three Family Village* only strengthens the image that more than half the essays are not overtly political. Liao's are more political and tend to range in the 3–4 levels; Wu Han's are more academic, but as in his famous essays on morality, none the less hit fundamental issues at variance with faith Maoism.
102. Lieberthal and Dickson (1989: 115); indeed, Mao stresses the First Party Secretaries of provinces and key municipalities *must personally* get involved in these investigations. From the newly available Mao texts: *Xuexi wenxuan*: 266–7. See n. 27 above. For more details on these events, see *Zhonggong Zhongyang wenxian* (1985: 280 ff.).
103. *Xuexi wenxuan*: 267.
104. *Xuexi ziliao, 1957–1961*: 429. This is vol. 12b of the new Mao Texts. Mao's 9th Plenum talk also appears in *Mao Zedong sixiang wansui* (1967–9: 258–6), which has been translated in *JPRS* 61269-2, pp. 237–45. Mao's comments on 'wave-style' development come from selections from his 13 January talk in Beijing on the eve of the formal plenum, *Xuexi wenxuan*: 265.
105. See n. 27 above on Mao volumes; *Xuexi wenxuan*: 264–5 and 270, or *Mao Zedong sixiang wansui* (Sept. 1967: 242–5). Lieberthal and Dickson (1989: 118–19).
106. Lieberthal and Dickson (1989: 121–2).
107. '"Dianzi yinyueju" yuanlai ruci' (This is the Origin of 'Electric Musical Theatre'); 1979b: 16–18.
108. 'Zhuan zhi "jianwangzheng"', *Qianxian*, 25 Nov. 1961; 1979b: 60–2.
109. Wu Nanxing [Liao Mosha], 'Jiao ranhou zhikun' (Teach and Know Consternation), *Qianxian* 25 June 1962; 1979b: 55–6; [Wu Han], 'Shuo qianxu' (On modesty), *Qianxian*, 25 July 1962; 1979b: 57–9.
110. Thus, Deng Tuo's case here confirms the general picture of the 'incomplete critique of "ultra-Leftism"' given by William Joseph (1984). It is not impossible that Deng could have published even the 'contentious' essays at any time in the spring 1961–Mar. 1962 period and that the pattern merely reflects his response to recent meetings, i.e. writing essays to popularize issues raised in key Central Party meetings, as he had time to think about these issues rather than when he felt safe to express opinions on them. Even if this were the case, it in no way lessens lampoons of Mao or the culture bearer themes.
111. 'Buchi yangrou, chi caigeng', *Beijing wanbao*, 23 July 1961; 1979a: 189–91, translated in Cheek (1983–4: 54–7).
112. 'Fei li wu' (Do Nothing Improper), *Beijing wanbao*, 6 Aug. 1961; 1979a: 153–5, translated in Cheek (1983–4: 47–50). Deng is particularly critical of bourgeois art and literature: see '"Haven't Got a Thing" Art' of 4 June 1961 (1979a: 42–4); '"Soundless Music" and Such' of 12 Nov. 1961 (1979a: 295–8); 'Does Creative Work Need Inspiration?' of 15 Mar. 1962 (1979a: 387–90); and 'Is Knowledge Edible?' of 24 May 1962 (1979a: 421–4).
113. Schram (1981), esp. pp. 424–5.
114. For examples, see Moody (1977: 79 ff.); Goldman (1981: Ch. 1). In earlier publications I used different categories: Humanism and Cultural Enjoyment, Cosmopolitanism, Intellectualism, Paternalistic Authoritarianism, Rationalism, and Gradualism. See Cheek and Hamrin (1986: 110–15).
115. Scholars of traditional China will immediately note the similarity of these attributes to Confucian ideals. See Smith *et al.* (1990). The three sets of questions confronting Song literati in the 11th century oddly parallel ones that animated Deng Tuo's generation: '[What will be] a new basis that would guide men in the creation of an integrated human society, one dedicated to benefiting all?'; 'What is human

nature? Are literati primarily social actors? Bearers of cultural tradition?'; and 'by what manner of *hsüeh* (study, learning) does one obtain access to [this basis]? Can one rely on cultural traditions, as transmitted by family, schooling, or government service? ... Can the mind apprehend values directly by contemplating the things of the world? Or does the mind itself contain primordial wisdom that can be tapped by the proper practices?' (Smith *et al.* 1990: 5).

116. Chuang (1970: 16).
117. 'Aihu laodongli de xueshuo' (On Treasuring Labour Power), *Beijing wanbao*, 30 Apr. 1961; 1979*a*: 62, tr. in Cheek (1983–4: 46).
118. 1979*a*: 60–2, tr. in Cheek (1983–4: 44–6).
119. 'Xuexi xuyao zhidao', *Qianxian*, 25 April 1961; 1979*b*: 45.
120. 'Jinguizi shengshang you huangjin' (Gold in Scarab Beetles), *Beijing wanbao*, 17 Dec. 1961; 1979*a*: 268–70.
121. 'Shuishang caiyuan' (Vegetable Gardens on Water), *Beijing wanbao*, 8 Feb. 1962; 1979*a*: 264–7.
122. 'Huangying zajia', *Beijing wanbao*, 26 Mar. 1961; 1979*a*: 11, tr. in Cheek (1983–4: 51).
123. 'Guandian he cailiao' (Viewpoint and Materials), *Beijing wanbao*, 3 May 1962; 1979*a*: 409–12.
124. 'Yiba xiao yaoshi' (A Small Key), *Beijing wanbao*, 30 July 1961; 1979*a*: 192–4. A fortnight earlier Deng had explained how to write clearly, based on the example of the Song scholar Ouyang Xiu; see 'Xinde "sanshang wenzhang"' (The New 'Three On's Essay'), *Beijing wanbao*, 16 July 1961; 1979*a*: 195–7.
125. 'Fangxia ji shidi', *Beijing wanbao*, 5 Nov. 1961; 1979*a*: 206–8.
126. Tu Wei-ming (1979: 263–4) discusses these *haute culture* aspects of *Evening Chats* with numerous citations; he cites the 1963 edn. (calling it 1965), so the page numbers differ slightly from the more available 1979 edn.
127. Indeed, Gu Xing calls *Evening Chats* a 'small encyclopaedia' (*xiao baike quanshu*) (YDT: 115; 1985: 11).
128. 'Yishu de meili', *Beijing wanbao*, 10 Aug. 1961; 1979*a*: 165–8.
129. Richard Kraus (1991) has made an exploration of this role of calligraphy in political power.
130. 'You Zhang Fei de shu hua tanqi' (Taking Up from Zhang Fei's Calligraphy and Painting), *Beijing wanbao*, 5 Aug. 1962; 1979*a*: 466–9.
131. 1963*a*. Zheng Banqiao (original name: Zheng Xie, b. 1693), from Xinghua county in Jiangsu, was a painter and poet of some note. He passed the *jinshi* exam in 1736 = Qianlong 1 and served as a magistrate in Shandong for over a decade. For selections of Deng's essay on Zheng Banqiao, see the long quotations given by Deng's detractors in the Cultural Revolution (Ch. 6 below).
132. The poems appear in 1979*c*: 57. Ding Yilan provided me with the colour photograph of the fan (front and obverse sides). It is unclear when Deng actually painted the fans, though it was obviously sometime after June 1959.
133. 1963*a*: 110 and Wang Bisheng (1986: 215).
134. 'Fei li wu' (Do Nothing Improper), *Beijing wanbao*, 6 Aug. 1961; 1979*a*: 153–5, tr. in Cheek (1983–4: 47–9), and 'Hanyang' (Self Cultivation), *Beijing wanbao*, 3 Dec. 1961; 1979*a*: 212–14.
135. 'Jiantou shi nengtiao danzi', *Qianxian*, 10 Feb. 1964; 1979*b*: 171–3; and 'Yao shenma yang de "xin"', *Qianxian*, 25 Mar. 1964; 1979*b*: 180–2, quote from p. 180.
136. See for example, 'Poor But with Lofty Ideals', *Beijing wanbao*, 19 Nov. 1961; 1979*a*: 203–5; and Chuang (1970: 29).

137. 1979a: 241–3, 237–40.
138. Chuang (1970: 29). The Beijing native son, Kunlun shan ren (Zhang Shi), comes in as another example of a filial student, excellent scholar, and unique calligrapher, trained by Lü Nan, a model of integrity. Thus, 'Zhang's personal integrity and knowledge had an excellent training.' See 1979a: 247–9. Deng also cites the case of Li Sancai, who was also persecuted by Wei Zhongxian (1979a: 523–5).
139. 'Wangdao he badao', *Beijing wanbao*, 25 Feb. 1962; 1979a: 321, tr. in Cheek (1983–4: 67).
140. '"Pipan" zhengjie', *Beijing wanbao*, 14 May 1961; 1979a: 92–5, tr. in Cheek (1983–4: 58–60), quote from p. 60.
141. 'Weida de kong hua', *Qianxian*, 10 Nov. 1961; 1979b: 8. In fact, Deng's derision of 'The East Wind over the West Wind' must also be part self-criticism. Deng Tuo had used the East and West Winds in precisely Mao's 'blustering' style in a 10 July 1960 poem published under his own name, 'Song for the Anti-American Demonstrations', in *Qianxian*, 10 July 1960, p. 25. This was the 10th anniversary of the Korean War. Deng wrote, 'The grand momentum of the East Wind, | Observes the daily weakening of the West Wind.'
142. 'Zongshi qunzhong de jingyan' (Pay Attention to the Experiences of the Masses), *Qianxian*, 10 June 1963; 1979b: 120–2, quote from p. 120.
143. 'Zhuguan he xuxin' (Subjectivity and Modesty), *Beijing wanbao*, 5 Apr. 1962; 1979a: 311–14.
144. '"Tuishi" zhongzhong' ('Judges' Etcetera), *Beijing wanbao*, 16 Nov. 1961; 1979a: 209–11.
145. 'Yiba xiao yaoshi' (A Small Key), *Beijing wanbao*, 30 July 1961; 1979a: 192–4. Chuang (1970: 17).
146. 'Duo yongxin', *Qianxian*, 10 Sept. 1962; 1979b: 69–71.
147. 'Zhongshi chunzhong de jingyan' (Pay Attention to the Experience of the Masses), *Qianxian*, 10 June 1963; 1979b: 120–2; 'Daochu you zhexue' (Philosophy Is Everywhere), *Qianxian*, 25 July 1963; 1979b: 129–31.
148. On Yang Xianzhen, Wu Han, and Peng Zhen, see chapters in Hamrin and Cheek (1986) by Hamrin, Fisher, and Potter; on Jian Bozan, see Edmunds (1987); on Feng Ding see Goldman (1981: 107–14); on Liao Mosha see YDT: 1–6 and Liao Mosha (1979: 237–44); and on Qin Mu, see discussion above in this chapter.
149. Gu Xing, the editor in charge of publishing *Evening Chats* in the *Beijing Evening News* at the time, says, '*Evening Chats at Yanshan* is a great accomplishment among Deng Tuo's life's work, an important work best able to reflect the style of his thought [*sixiang fengmao*]' (Gu Xing 1985: 12).

6.1 Deng Tuo's memorial portrait, 1982

6

Death and Afterlife as Villain and Hero

Through the mid-1960s Deng and his patron, Peng Zhen, had to contend with the growing power base of the faith Maoists—in particular Jiang Qing. Jiang Qing began her rise to power in 1963 with the issue of opera reform. Shanghai was for her what Beijing was for the establishment intellectuals—a local haven from which to promote ideas for the central government. She came to Beijing and tried to enlist Deng Tuo in her efforts to popularize her 'Revolutionary Operas'. He declined not only to write for her but to see her. Peng Zhen delegated the onerous task of rebutting the artistic theories of Madame Mao to Li Qi, deputy director of the city's Propaganda Department. The memorial article on Deng Tuo in the *People's Daily* in 1979 remarks that this non-encounter with the 'empress' was 'not unrelated to his subsequent death.'[1]

Things did become more difficult for Deng in 1964. Trouble visited Deng Tuo and Peng Zhen in the form of a work committee, apparently under the control of Kang Sheng, despatched by the Central Committee to conduct an investigation of Beijing University, which was formally in Deng Tuo's portfolio as Secretary for Culture and Education in the Municipal Party Committee. The work team, according to Yue Daiyun, who was teaching at Beida at the time, capitalized on the demotion of worker and peasant students in the previous year to attack the university as 'pro-bourgeois'. In line with Party policy to improve standards, the university had expelled students who failed two exams. The work team's findings, made in the winter of 1964, were not published due to the efforts of Peng Zhen and Deng Tuo, who Yue clearly presents as Peng's man on educational questions. The team's verdict, heard by word of mouth, was dire: Beida had been pronounced a 'thoroughly bourgeois institution', and a 'reactionary fortress'.[2]

The response of Deng Tuo and Peng Zhen to this assault on their own backyard shows the degree to which they were forced to rely on 'politicking' in the absence of more normal Party mechanisms for debate.[3] In flat contravention of Party norms (indicating once again that by 1964 such norms were often inoperative) 'Peng Zhen and Deng Tuo', says Yue Daiyun, 'rejected the findings of the Central Committee's work team and prevented it from publishing its findings, probably with the tacit support of Liu Shaoqi.'[4] Next, they convened a conference on education at the International Hotel in Beijing in the summer of 1965, the main purpose of which was to support Beida's president, Lu Ping, who had been attacked by the work team. At this meeting Deng Tuo buttonholed Tang Yijie, a politically influential faculty member of the Department of Philosophy (and Yue's husband), and several times urged him to support Lu Ping. Reflecting Peng Zhen's notorious no-nonsense approach to organizational power, the Beijing Committee stacked the meeting with some two hundred supporters of Lu Ping and only eighty opponents.[5] Indeed, Tang Yijie continued to follow Deng Tuo's orders well into 1966 until Nie Yuanzi, who argued the radical position, prevailed in May and June 1966.[6] Here we see the transmission of political orders down three levels of patronage: from Peng Zhen on the second level of national leadership (Mao being the only incumbent of the top level), to Deng Tuo, Peng's establishment aide, to a leader at a local institution, Tang Yijie at Beida.[7]

The *Three Family Village* series continued to publish articles into 1964, but they were hardly critical of the Party's right to rule and were directed at the limited cadre readership of the theory journal of the Beijing Party. The series did, however, reflect the confidence of the leadership around Peng Zhen to publish their views throughout the Socialist Education Movement. That confidence, based prosaically on Peng Zhen's political clout, faded in the summer of 1964. *Three Family Village* ceased publication that June, precisely at the time when Mao supported the attacks begun on Yang Xianzhen and Feng Ding in philosophy and on the historiography of the Taiping hero, Li Xiucheng.[8] This was the beginning of the end for the establishment intellectuals and their political patrons. The very month that *Three Family Village* stopped, the Central Committee issued a central directive to academic circles to begin the criticism campaign against Yang Xianzhen and others—that is, identifying their views as 'serious political questions'.[9] Yang, Feng, and the writer Zhao Shuli were criticized in the Beijing press, as well as in the national press, perhaps in an effort to satisfy the petulant helmsman and forestall further, more radical criticism of the establishment approach.

There was a stalemate, as reflected in the work team's struggles at Beida in 1964–5. Yet the establishment carried on in defiance of radical assaults well into 1964, because the bureaucratic Maoist approach, despite the need to please a fickle Mao, was still the established practice of the Party. Deng Tuo, along with a considerable group of leading intellectuals, was able to publish his political and literary views with impunity during this time. Though Deng's associates served Peng Zhen, their views were much more than mere advertisements for Peng's policies. None the less, by late 1965 Peng Zhen and Deng Tuo, and so many of the establishment, had been outmanoeuvred by Mao. The broader social and political reasons why this was the case are beyond the scope of this study.[10] What can be said on the basis of Deng Tuo's political life between 1956 and 1965 is that the members of the establishment were not united and lacked a method to deflect Mao's attacks on them. They were, as Kuang Rongrong has ably shown, constrained by their Leninist ideology, which gave credence to Mao's radical plans despite their irrationality.[11] The 'Way' had been too closely identified with the Ruler, and Deng's associates naturally found it difficult to remove Mao the man from Mao Zedong Thought.[12] Deng's loyal support of Central Committee policies through a 180-degree turnabout in the Leap and through the 1961 retrenchment shows that he was willing to go along with the Party line. Yet this loyalty did not give him and his organizations security from political attacks by more radical intellectuals and politicians. When such attacks came in earnest in 1966 the establishment was completely unable to protect itself. It fell like a house of cards.[13]

Deng Tuo died early in the two decades covered in this chapter. The copious materials published to discredit or rehabilitate him often tell us more about their authors than about Deng Tuo. He lives on in these debates as an example of one kind of Party cadre and the style of service and political life he preferred. There were literally thousands upon thousands of pages of materials printed on Deng Tuo, the *Three Family Village*, and the 'Peng Zhen Clique' in both periods. An exhaustive bibliography or historiography of them is not attempted here. Rather, our focus is on key themes and activities in the social circles in which Deng Tuo was active. What emerges is a stark picture of the nearly complete reversal of Deng Tuo's approach to politics, journalism, history, and the arts, as well as the purge of all his associates (however distantly associated) in the Cultural Revolution. This is followed by the return to power and influence of the surviving associates of Deng Tuo since 1978, along with the praise of Deng and his ideas. In all, these materials show the continuing power of the bureaucratic Maoist model which Deng served, along with the attractive opportunities and political vulnerabilities of the scholar-cadre role for establishment-minded intellectuals in China today.[14]

Purge of the Establishment (1965–1969)

Along with other establishment intellectuals and their political patrons, Deng Tuo was purged in 1966 and his ideas were castigated as 'anti-socialist' and 'anti-Party'. There was a radical redistribution of status and power away from these establishment intellectuals to a previously left-out group of their same generation and others from a rising generation of 'revolutionary successors'. The attacks on Deng in the Cultural Revolution, when they were more than mere name-calling, sought to discredit the authority of Party intellectuals. They were called 'academic authorities' (*xueshu quanwei*), and those far less culpable than Deng suffered more for who they were than for what they had done. What is astounding in this story is that the majority of the revolutionary elite failed to defend themselves from the onslaughts of the radicals. Deng Tuo tried, but by early 1966 he became one of the first victims of the Cultural Revolution.

The Cultural Revolution for Deng Tuo started in the autumn of 1965. Deng Tuo's activities from this time as he came under attack have been covered in several earlier studies.[15] With the information now available, the context and consequences of these activities can be better appreciated. Deng Tuo was part of the enlarged meeting of the 'Five-Man Cultural Revolution Group' headed by Peng Zhen that convened on 13 July 1965; this group (including Kang Sheng, who later claimed to have supported the radical line) tried to co-opt the radicals' forum for public criticism: opera reform. This effort, however, was unsuccessful, and in November Deng attended the meeting convened by Zhou Enlai that arranged for the belated publication in the *Beijing Daily* of Yao Wenyuan's notorious attack on Wu Han. In the fall of 1965, Yao Wenyuan had attacked Wu Han for his historical drama, 'Hai Rui Dismissed from Office', and claimed that Wu Han's play was part of a plot against Mao and the Party. That December Peng Zhen, in an accompanying editorial, tried to limit the scope of criticism to academic rather than political issues. Three weeks later Deng was given the task of convening several public meetings to discuss Wu Han's play.[16]

Deng organized a group of seven people to work on defending Wu Han in December 1965, as well as publishing his own 'criticism' of Wu in a 12 December *Beijing Daily* article written under the pen-name Xiang Yangsheng.[17] Their articles argued that Wu Han's errors were academic, not political. According to Su Shuangbi, one of the seven, Deng was deeply disturbed that Wu Han's play was being unfairly criticized. Su himself published a defence of Wu Han's portrayal of landlords in the *Beijing Daily* in late December. But it was no use. By February it was clear that they themselves were in trouble. Su recalls that Deng stood by them and did not disassociate himself from them when they were under criticism. Of the seven men Deng had assembled, most were university professors or graduates.[18] Thus, while Deng was a member of Central Party meetings organized to defend establishment interests, he was also the organizer of lower-level efforts in Beijing. It was to be his last effort in that line of command from the top elite to the intellectual leadership.

By March 1966 Deng Tuo had been relieved of his editorship of *Frontline*; Li Jun edited what was to be the last issue of that journal. In early April Deng was under investigation, and the last time Li Jun saw him was at one such scrutiny session on 6 April.[19] On 16 April 1966, the *Beijing Daily* printed its 'criticism' of Deng Tuo, for the first time exposing his pen-names and confirming in public that he was the author of *Evening Chats* and a contributor to *Three Family Village*. On 8 May 'Gao Ju' (Jiang Qing) began the barrage of criticisms against Deng Tuo in the national press, starting predictably in Shanghai's *Liberation Daily*.

The end was at hand, and Deng Tuo knew it. As an experienced editor, he understood that his impending purge was a *fait accompli* by the time criticisms of him had been approved to appear in the *People's Daily*. That fateful step came between the 8 May publication of attacks on Deng and the 11 May denunciation by Yao Wenyuan which set the particulars of the case against him. Within the week, Deng Tuo was dead. His suicide on the evening of 17 May 1966 by overdose of sleeping tablets was a poignant and tragic final statement of a loyal servant made in protest to what he considered to be unjust charges. He was faced with an impossible choice: repudiate Mao or turn his back on the rules of Party life and rational methods of leadership he so valued and had popularized in *Evening Chats*. His flexibility at an end, Deng made the most of his death, which clearly recalls the archetypal political suicide in Chinese history, that of the loyal minister Qu Yuan in the third century BCE. He wrote two last messages, one to family and one to his work unit, the Beijing Municipal CCP. In the second, addressed to Peng Zhen and second secretary Liu Ren, Deng declared his loyalty to the Party and Chairman Mao, denounced his detractors, and said good-bye.[20] In May 1966 this great embarrassment to the Cultural Revolution elite was hidden, though rumours were already rife in Shanghai the next month.[21] In 1966, however, most of the world only knew that Deng Tuo, like so many others, had simply disappeared.

Villain in the National Press

At least one hundred and ten major articles were published in the national press specifically attacking Deng Tuo and his 'organizational plot', the *Three Family Village*, against Chairman Mao and socialism. They began with Gao Ju's (Jiang Qing's) 8 May 1966 'Open Fire on the Anti-Party, Anti-Socialist Black Line' in *Liberation Daily* and extended through Zheng Xuan's 'A Great Exposé of the Secret Plot to Seize the Party and Nation—Criticizing the Chang Guan Lou Counter-Revolutionary Affair in Peng Zhen's Plot' in the *Guangming Daily* on 9 August 1967.[22] The criticisms are examples of Stalinist-style 'manufactured dissent'.[23] Those in control of political authority and propaganda outlets largely shape the deviance they claim to want to suppress. What Deng Tuo had said had not changed from 1962 to 1966; only the rules of the game had changed.

What, in the end, were the specific complaints and criticisms which the Cultural Revolution Group hurled at Deng, while they so successfully engineered his political and physical demise? Common to all these articles is an unrelenting and unforgiving hostility toward Deng Tuo, the 'inveterate capitalist roader'. Gone is any sign of the rectification tenet, 'cure the illness to save the patient.' H. C. Chuang has made a thorough and perceptive analysis of the language used in Cultural Revolution critiques. Deng and the other objects of criticism—Wu Han, Liao Mosha, and later Peng Zhen, Deng Xiaoping, and finally Liu Shaoqi—are dehumanized. They are cursed as animals: *chailang* (voracious wolves), *dushe* (poisonous snakes), *jisheng chong* (parasitic worms), and *hairen chong* (injurious vermin). Chuang concludes, 'All this indicates, at least on the semantic level, the Chinese Communists refuse to accept their enemies as human beings.'[24] Lowell Dittmer has found in his analysis of the mass criticism of the Cultural Revolution, particularly as applied to Liu Shaoqi, that forgiveness was not an option—mass criticism moved beyond 'classic' rectification by removing the educational element and retaining only the purge option. Dittmer suggests that this is, in part, an element of crowd behaviour in which the empathy which can be felt in a small group, the traditional scene of rectification, is lost. Teiwes has argued, as well, that rectification has historically been more coercive in times of leadership division or threat, and this was a time of severe division.[25]

The excesses of the Cultural Revolution lay embedded in rectification practice, which was a central tool of all versions of Maoism. At times rectification had worked impressively, as William Hinton recounts in *Fanshen* for a village in north China in the 1940s. In 1947, ironically under Liu Shaoqi's management, the 'wash your face' version of cadre rectification in north China got out of hand until Mao Zedong criticized it as 'Leftist'. This happened in part because of pent-up anger in peasant communities, but the more orchestrated original version, in Yan'an in 1942, was not without its abusiveness.[26] The errors and excesses of the Cultural Revolution were a difference of degree, not kind, from the archetypal rectification in Yan'an. The scapegoat for the 1942 rectification was an obstreperous in-house critic, Wang Shiwei. His purge led directly to the now-notorious 'rescue campaign' purges of 1942–4. A 'Five-Person Anti-Party Clique' was 'discovered' around Wang in the summer of 1942 and prosecuted that fall under Kang Sheng (who was in the rectification leadership small group) and Yang Shangkun. Significantly, the Party discovered that Wang Shiwei's 'Clique' was an *organized conspiracy* against the Party. This justified his purge and imprisonment.[27] The 'rescue campaign' was an inquisition that got out of hand. Mao soon realized its counter-productiveness and called the witch-hunt to an end before major damage was done, and the campaign has been criticized as an error in the post-Mao period.[28] None the less, the urge toward *inquisition* remains the shadow-self of rectification's tremendous ability to promise *salvation*. In the Cultural Revolution the dark side of the Yan'an Way came to the fore.

In one of the core documents of rectification theory, the 'Yan'an Talks', Mao Zedong had denied the existence of 'human nature' separate from its class nature. Kindness was not to be extended to class enemies.[29] Yao Wenyuan, who had cut his teeth on the 're-criticism' of Wang Shiwei and the Yan'an left-wing writers in 1958, predictably made the same point in his May 1966 attack on Deng Tuo.[30] In doing so Yao legitimately carries on one part of the 'glorious tradition of Yan'an'— the inquisitional side. Yao denounces the suggestion made by Deng Tuo in *Evening Chats* that leaders 'study more and criticize less' as bourgeois restorations: 'In class society, there is no such thing as supra-class equality, and equality between the proletariat and the bourgeoisie simply does not exist. The only question is who will win . . .'[31]

This comes from the single most influential attack on Deng Tuo, Yao Wenyuan's 'Criticizing *The Three Family Village*—The Reactionary Nature of *Evening Chats at Yanshan* and *Notes from a Three Family Village*', published on 10 May 1966 in Shanghai and the next day in the *People's Daily*. Later Cultural Revolution attacks largely build upon Yao's analysis. He begins this lengthy article by attacking the 'fake criticisms' of Deng Tuo and *Three Family Village* made on 16 April by the *Beijing Daily* and *Frontline*. They had claimed that to have printed the two columns by Deng Tuo, though regrettable, was only a matter of a 'loss of vigilance' and 'publication without timely criticism'. Yao retorts that this is only a smoke-screen for what was really a political problem: Deng Tuo is a capitalist roader. The *Notes from a Three Family Village*, Yao asserts, was a direct continuation of Wu Han's 1961 historical drama, 'Hai Rui Dismissed from Office'. In league with *Evening Chats*, they 'formed a deliberate, planned, and organized major attack on the Party and socialism, masterminded in detail by the "Three Family Village"—of whom Deng Tuo was the "commanding general".'[32]

In this long and rambling textual analysis of Deng Tuo's essays, Yao sets out to demonstrate that Deng was the antithesis of everything socialist and Chinese. Yao's logic is so fallacious that it is not interesting to refute his assertions on the grounds of logic, though Chinese writers after 1979 have attempted this.[33] In general, Yao indulges in quotations out of context and anachronistic value judgements—i.e. castigating Deng Tuo for advancing opinions with which Mao disagreed in 1966 but which were Party policy and embraced by Mao in 1961. Yet Yao Wenyuan's attack reflects values which were not only repeated *ad nauseam* in the other attacks on Deng Tuo but were central to the Cultural Revolution. Were there underlying values that rang true to Yao's readers embedded in his absurd verbiage?

Yao's closed-door definition of truth, which he limits to a single proletarian class within modern society, is contrary to Deng Tuo's commonsense rationality. Yao equates interest in foreign culture or praise of any past figure with the desire to 'restore capitalism'. He implies the latter is superstitious ancestor worship of 'great Bodhisattvas', 'feudal diehards', and 'geomancers'. Yao concludes his criticism of Deng's 'To Channel is Better than to Dam' by saying, 'Isn't this clearly demanding that we practice bourgeois liberalization?' In analysing 'On Treasuring Labour Power', Yao rejects Deng Tuo's faith that the ancients of the 'feudal period' could teach socialists some objective laws about society and concludes that such class enemies were incapable of comprehending any objective laws. He sums up Deng's essay by asking, 'Was this not clearly co-ordinated with the venomous attacks of US imperialism and modern revisionism [the Soviet Union]?'[34] To doubt is to sin. Yao thus draws on underlying values of the day which were critical of 'feudal' tradition in China and meddling from the Soviet Union and the US.

Yao was clearly a revolutionary romantic; the need for a monolithic unity of views meant that criticism in public or private of the Party or of Mao's habits was never right.[35] Yao fervently believed in the power of positive thinking, and in this he reflected much of the Chairman's philosophical approach in the 1960s. In 1964, Yao had criticized the novelist Zhao Shuli for his admittedly accurate description of the range of peasant characters in his fiction. Yao denounces this as counter-revolutionary because it required 'a fundamental exclusion and suppression of new things which are germinating or developing, and an extension of protection to old things which superficially still exist extensively.'[36]

Yao was stridently anti-intellectual, equating academic knowledge with capitalism. He claims that Deng Tuo, Wu Han, and Liao Mosha used '"history", "learning", and "things of interest" to dull the people's revolutionary vigilance, dupe yet more readers, and expand their influence . . .'[37] Here, Yao is trying to redefine the basis for the *legitimate* exercise of power in the public arena. In powerful metaphors, if not reasoning, Yao dubs academic skill as 'landlord' in nature because it continued the hegemony of the literati in Chinese society *similar* to that enjoyed by the scholar-officials in 'landlord' times. He lauds the models of Dazhai and Daqing in which peasants and workers espousing Mao's inspiration took control of their lives. This was the rationale for his own claim to legitimate authority—as interpreter of Mao's views and voice of the labouring masses. The denial of the knowledge so necessary to the scholar-cadre role of culture bearer was repeated in nearly every attack on Deng Tuo and his colleagues in the spring of 1966. For example, a certain Gu Bingfu in *Athletic News* declares:

Deng Tuo and his anti-Party black gang bogusly took on the style of 'scholars', 'teachers of the youth', 'historians', and 'miscellaneous scholars' and with the excuse of introducing 'knowledge' and 'history' sold their anti-Party anti-socialist black goods in a big way, spreading poison among the youth and masses. When the youth and masses wanted energetically to study the works of Chairman Mao, Deng Tuo and his black gang bellowed out a different tune, drawing people away from the needs of actual struggle to go read completely useless ancient books and writings.[38]

Yao and most other radicals could not compete with Deng Tuo, Wu Han, or other establishment intellectuals in the field of historical knowledge or organizational ability, so they changed the grounds of the debate. Anti-intellectualism served both Mao's utopian goals and their own professional ambitions.

A later critique, by Xu Rende, also commits the sin of omission, or distorted context. Xu presents 'proof' that the title, '*Three Family Village*' (*sanjiacun*), itself was politically significant, saying that Deng Tuo, Wu Han, and Liao Mosha chose the title from a poem by Lu You written in 1196 CE which included the lines:

> With a fief of ten thousand households accidentally lost,
> I am now getting old in a *sanjiacun*.

Lu You had been dismissed from office and thus Xu claims Deng and company were expressing 'Their own bitterness over the deprivation of their official ranks and their wishful thoughts of usurping political power and restoring capitalism.'[39] Deng, he hastens to remind readers, was dismissed from the *People's Daily* in the years before *Three Family Village*. H. C. Chuang has convincingly demonstrated that *sanjiacun* is, in fact, a common literary phrase as innocuous as 'one-horse town' and that the purpose of the title cannot be interpreted to be more than a gentle self-mockery and play on the number of authors—Deng, Wu, and Liao. Chuang notes that *sanjiacun* appears, innocently, in the popular classical novel, *Water Margin*, in an essay by Lu Xun and, significantly, in at least six other spots in Lu You's writings—all in the generally accepted non-political sense.[40]

Textual Analyses: The Faith Maoist's Mode of Debate

Despite his hostile approach and fallacious logic Yao Wenyuan quoted large amounts of Deng's writings. The Cultural Revolution attacks on Deng and the *Three Family Village* regularly did so, and it is clear that they felt such copious quotations from the objects of their criticism lent validity to their arguments. Some attacks were extreme versions of this, being *mostly* quotes of several paragraphs in length from Deng Tuo followed by brief commentaries. For internal Party study whole texts were collected together into small volumes, such as *Three Family Village* and *The Long and the Short*, as 'criticism materials'.[41] Such 'textual analyses' were not new but, rather, were another integral part of Maoism. They had made a noisy appearance in the first literary rectification of 1942 and had been used again against Hu Feng in 1955 and against Hundred Flowers proponents (such as Lin Xiling) in 1957.[42] This same model was repeated by a group headed by Lin Jie. 'Deng Tuo's *Evening Chats at Yanshan* is Anti-Party and Anti-Socialist Black Talk' is a long textual analysis from the 9 May 1966 *People's Daily* and comes to some thirty pages in English translation.[43] It begins with an editorial note repeating the gist of Yao's critique (which actually came out shortly afterward). There follow lengthy quotations from *Evening Chats* and *Three Family Village* followed by brief comments under five topical headings borrowed from Yao—Deng's attacks on the Party, his opposition to the Great Leap, his support for Rightists, his suggestions that the Party retire and take a rest, and his attacks on socialism under the guise of imparting knowledge.[44]

Lin Jie's compilation seeks to delegitimize Deng Tuo's claim to political authority on the basis of elite cultural abilities. This was the Cultural

Revolution rejection of the culture-bearing role of Party intellectuals. If we look at an example from Lin Jie's textual analysis, we can see both the attack on elite culture as political authority and the mechanisms of this mode of debate. One of Deng's essays which Lin Jie singles out for criticism is his 1963 'Zheng Banqiao and the "Banqiao Style"'. Lin Jie places it in section three of his attack, directly after the example of 'In Defence of Li Sancai'. The headings and use of boldface in Lin Jie's original are reproduced in the translated selection below:[45]

III. COMPLAINING ABOUT INJUSTICE TO THE RIGHT OPPORTUNISTS WHO WERE DISMISSED FROM OFFICE, PRAISING THEIR ANTI-PARTY 'BACKBONE' AND ENCOURAGING THEM TO STAGE A COMEBACK

......

Acclaiming the 'Resolute Backbone' of Zheng Banqiao who, after being Dismissed from Office on 'False Charges', Nursed Bitter Hatred; Calling on People to Imitate his Example of 'Being Your Own Master' and 'Refusing to Act as a Slave'

......

[*quotation from Deng's essay*] 'As far as I know, there are still earnest students following the "Banqiao Style". But the most important point, I think, is to grasp the spirit of the "Banqiao Style". What is this spirit of the "Banqiao Style"? I think it is **to be one's own master in all respects and refuse to be a slave!**

'Banqiao said, "Those who write should write essays of masters, not essays of slaves." This is a very important remark. As a constant reminder to himself to carry this out, he specially carved a seal with "Zheng is Master of the House." His meaning was, in everything he did, he always was his own master and blazed his own trails.'

('Zheng Banqiao and the "Banqiao Style"', *Guangming Daily*, 21 November 1963)

COMMENT: ... DENG TUO POINTS OUT AS A CROWNING TOUCH THAT THE SPIRIT OF THE 'BANQIAO STYLE' CONSISTS IN 'BEING ONE'S OWN MASTER AND REFUSING TO BE A SLAVE.' AND HE CALLS ON PEOPLE TO GRASP THIS SPIRIT AND SERIOUSLY LEARN FROM IT SO AS TO 'BLAZE A TRAIL FOR THEMSELVES'. HOW CUNNING AND VENOMOUS! ISN'T DENG TUO CALLING ON PEOPLE TO OPPOSE THE LEADERSHIP OF THE PARTY? THE WIDE ROAD OF SOCIALISM LIES BRIGHT BEFORE US, AND YET DENG TUO CALLS ON PEOPLE TO 'BLAZE TRAILS FOR THEMSELVES'. WHAT IS THIS TRAIL IF NOT THE DARK PATH LEADING TO THE RESTORATION OF CAPITALISM?

Lin Jie, and his colleagues, provided their readers with considerably more of Deng Tuo's original words to support their 'reading' of his essay than I did in Chapter 4. Deng Tuo's words outweigh Lin's by a ratio of five to one. What is of significance here is that the Cultural Revolution elite did not have to quote large sections of the writings of their 'objects of struggle'; they chose to. Western readers may well see, even in this distorted selection and bizarre presentation, signs of Deng Tuo's aesthetic sensibilities and his connection between poetry and calligraphy and the moral rectitude that legitimates the scholar-cadres' role in politics. Nonetheless, Lin Jie and his colleagues felt they were refuting that scholarly claim to authority and exposing it as a plot against the Party and socialism.

Both Yao Wenyuan's and Lin Jie's articles are textual analyses. Unlike the *zawen* (miscellaneous essays) employed by Deng Tuo in *Evening Chats*, this style of essay is implacably hostile in tone and not particularly rigorous in its argumentation. Given their stated intention of totally discrediting their object, these essays (particularly Lin Jie's) quote so much of their victim's writings that textual analyses can be and have been used as fairly reliable sources of what the victims said.[46] In most cases from Wang Shiwei to Deng Tuo to Fang Lizhi in the late 1980s, the quotes from victims in these textual analyses have been accurate even if placed out of context with a hostile commentary. The authors of such textual analyses see the reprinting of the original as part of the legitimacy of the rebuttal—contributing to their 'facticity'. This conforms to some later ideas of Mao's. John Starr discusses why Mao let so much of Confucius's original writings be quoted in the anti-Confucius campaign of the mid-1970s, thus introducing Confucius directly to a generation of Chinese who had not read him before: 'It was not enough [for Mao] that these ideas simply pass out of circulation, for their negative residue would be likely to linger on after them. Rather, they needed to be revived in order to be actively struggled against, and thus transformed and superseded dialectically.'[47] Thus, whatever their logical faults, these essays against Deng Tuo adhered to a part of the Yan'an Way of public debate.

All textual analyses that I have seen, including these, use three major rhetorical devices.[48] First, they establish a black and white dichotomy: here Deng Tuo is invariably a capitalist restorationist; he has no redeeming feature. Second, they proceed by plausible but erroneous lines of argument, usually based on citation out of context. Lin Jie highlights certain passages in his selection of *Evening Chats* and draws them together while *shifting the object of reference* to conclude that Deng favoured landlord views. In particular, he cites a portion of 'Study More, Criticize Less' to make it look as if Deng Tuo is completely denouncing Mao and the CCP's arrogance in the Great Leap, while failing to quote the beginning of that essay where Deng implicitly defends the Party by noting that 'it is always easy to be an uninvolved spectator and to criticize' and directs his readers humbly to study the practical experience of leaders in history in order to find practical solutions.[49] Third, textual analyses indulge in cheap shots, slurs, and crude puns, as in the name-calling analysed by H. C. Chuang, discussed above. The purpose is to mark the victim as a suitable object of attack, as no longer 'one of us'.

The Yan'an Orthodoxy Breaks Apart

Lin Jie, like Yao, had simply adopted the very effective rhetorical ploy of defining his own (and Mao's) group as *the* Party and faith Maoism as the true and only version of the orthodoxy. However, Deng Tuo and Peng Zhen, as we have seen from the Chang Guan Lou review, considered themselves loyal Party members. Of these two groups, which was the Party? In what relation to the CCP of 1955, which most analysts conclude was a fairly unified Party, do these groups stand? Who is orthodox, who is heterodox? Both? Neither?

Both groups, at least in part, demonstrate continuity with previous Party practice—Deng by uninterrupted service as an obedient *apparatchik*, by consistent use of Leninist epistemology to define practical Party-administered solutions to the problems of socialist transformation, and by a near-perfect disciplinary track record. Yao Wenyuan *et al.* show their Party credentials by their 'creative' application of CCP rectification methods, their emphasis on peasant culture, and their faith in the authoritative statements of Mao Zedong and use of textual analyses. These models of political behaviour and public debate reflected the rule-based application of Central Committee decisions of bureaucratic Maoism or the charismatic power of Mao Zedong of faith Maoism. Both existed in the CCP in 1955. But they maintained a 'unity of opposites' within a moderately harmonious whole. The whole broke in the wake of tensions produced by the Great Leap Forward. The pressures of modernization were too much for the Leninist response, which is more effective for revolutionary accession to power than administration of a state.[50] As several scholars have suggested, Mao the supreme leader was the one person who could destroy the Leninist organization which he had led in unifying the Party and China. I would add that it was not just the personality of Mao, but the very nature of the system, of Chinese Leninism, to present such an irreconcilable conflict of political styles which would fall out of harmony under pressures of administering a modernization programme. Yao Wenyuan and the Cultural Revolution Group travelled with Mao, the personal Party, to the extreme left of the orthodoxy—where ideological purity battled human nature—and Deng Tuo remained with the organizational Party, trying to administer economic strategies in the transition to socialism.

The two strains, and they should not be confused with simple factions or 'two lines', conflicted during the early 1960s and brought out the worst of both. Deng, frustrated that *normal* avenues of consultation within the Party were ignored by Mao, was reduced to actions bordering on factional intrigue in the Chang Guan Lou review and the rigged summer 1965 meetings, and to public satirical abuse of his nemesis. Mao, on the other hand, because he so feared bureaucratism, inflated beyond all reason the prestige of his thought and, tragically, expanded rectification from a controlled small-group intra-Party correction and education process to a frenzied, ultimately uncontrollable public blood-bath of extra-Party mass criticism and purging which only the army, under Bonapartist Lin Biao, could stop. In the end, neither half of Yan'an Maoism proved capable of 'continuing the revolution'.

As the basis for legitimacy was turned upside down, the circles of Deng Tuo's life (which we mapped in Chapter 3) were torn apart and ransacked. The intellectual and Party establishment in Beijing was crushed. In the political sphere Peng Zhen, Liu Ren, and the whole Party committee were removed. In the journalistic world, Gu Xing, the whole editorial board of the *Beijing Evening News*, and everybody associated with *Frontline* were subjected to 'mass criticism' in 1966. 'Branches' of the *Three Family Village* were 'discovered' in propaganda departments and Party editorial boards all around China.[51] The publications themselves were suspended; the circle collapsed to little more than the *People's Daily*, and even Deng's successor there, Wu Lengxi, was purged. The May 1966 issues of *Cultural Artifacts* (*Wenwu*) and *Economic Research* (*Jingji yanjiu*) both featured Yao Wenyuan's critique and extended it into their respective disciplines, detailing the 'evil exploits' of Deng Tuo and his associates in the National Museum and economic policy.[52] The effect in the artistic realm was even more personal and reached into Deng's home. The emerging Cultural Revolution elite, despite their public outcry against the 'four olds', helped themselves to Deng Tuo's art collection and calligraphy. Kang Sheng in particular selected the finest pieces of his former associate.[53]

When Deng Tuo finally committed suicide on the evening of 17 May 1966, after writing his last testimony, his children were expelled from school, his wife was paraded through the streets of Beijing, and 'revolutionary successors' occupied his traditional-style home.[54] Judging from the further sufferings of his associates, such as Wu Han and Jian Bozan, one can see why the 54-year-old scholar-cadre, already in ill health, made his choice. He left the stage with his dignity.

Rehabilitation and Role Model

It was not until January 1979 that Deng Tuo's name appeared in the official press in other than his Cultural Revolution persona as a negative role model. As the forces around Deng Xiaoping gathered strength in the fall of 1978, preparing for the now famous Third Plenum of the Eleventh Central Committee held that December, articles calling for the rehabilitation of similar establishment intellectuals, such as Wu Han and Jian Bozan, appeared in the national press.[55] After the December Plenum, a broad range of cadres purged in the Cultural Revolution, including Deng Tuo, Wu Han, and Liao Mosha, were rehabilitated by the CC. In February 1979 the Beijing Party Committee decided to reverse the verdict on the *Three Family Village*, but it was not until August that the Central Committee approved this publicly.[56] As with other well-known Party loyalists from the 1960s, the current regime has used Deng Tuo posthumously to promote its model for intellectual participation in public life. In addition, each of the professional spheres in which Deng was active has used his good political reputation as well as his professional standards to advance their own interests. Finally, literature on Deng Tuo since 1979 has reflected true personal grief over the loss of a friend and teacher that serves to express feelings of fellow intellectuals and to honour their comrade in the eyes of history and to reaffirm the dignity and prestige of intellectuals. In all of this, Deng Tuo and his ideas and methods have been held up as a model for youth in China. While these have presented Deng Tuo in a more reasonable light than the criticisms of the Cultural Revolution, the use of Deng Tuo since 1979 has not been without distortions.

These rehabilitations coincided with the consolidation of a new leadership under Deng Xiaoping in the CC and the revival of people and policies associated with the aborted reforms of the early 1960s.[57] This process continued into the 1980s and was largely complete by 1986. Peng Zhen, Deng Tuo's old patron, returned to the Politburo engineering China's rationalist legal code; Yang Xianzhen, a comrade from the north China bases in World War II, became an adviser to his old work unit, the Central Party School, and Liao Mosha, the sole survivor of the *Three Family Village*, returned to publish widely on behalf of his fallen comrades (Liao died in 1990). Bureaucratic Maoism once again mounted the saddle, after a thirteen-year hiatus. However, it is not at all clear which of the coalitions that exist in the Chinese leadership today and benefit from propaganda around Deng Tuo's rehabilitation might actually have been supported by Deng himself.[58]

The national newspaper for intellectuals, *Guangming Daily*, produced the first major rehabilitation article on Deng Tuo, as it did for many others. On 26 January 1979 Zhang Yide's 'It is No Crime to Criticize Idealism, it is Meritorious to Propagandize Materialism—Refuting Yao Wenyuan's False Charges in "Criticizing *Evening Chats at Yanshan* and *Notes from a Three Family Village*"' lived up to its title and praised Deng Tuo for his 'clear-cut views, resourceful knowledge, vivid examples, and fine literary style.' But Zhang also was out to use Deng Tuo's past to serve Deng Xiaoping's present. He acclaimed Deng Tuo as a serious model for 'integrat[ing] our revolutionary spirit with our scientific approach.'[59] This was a welcome to the return of the establishment intellectuals and their administrative expertise.

Su Shuangbi wrote a paean to the *Three Family Village* and denunciation of Yao Wenyuan and the 'gang of four' in *Guangming Daily* on 28 January. It was more or less repeated in the authoritative Central Party theory journal, *Red Flag*, in February 1979. Su has emerged as a major spokesman for the rehabilitated cadre, particularly his old teacher Wu Han, and as a propagandist for current Party intellectual policy.[60] Su's major concern was to remind his readers that Deng Tuo was attacking ultra-Leftism, not the Party itself. This analysis stands up to a close reading of the original texts in *Evening Chats*, but Su side-stepped the issue of Deng's lampoons of Chairman Mao. He did not deny the possibility, but it has not been politic for a Party loyalist to broach that topic. More generally, all the rehabilitation hagiographies of Deng Tuo have avoided key 'errors' in his career—his prison confession in the 1930s, his demotion in the mid-1940s, his role in the Chang Guan Lou review of 1961. These are not useful details for an 'exemplary biography'.

The Establishment's Mixed Mode of Debate

As Su's disinclination to deal with Deng's jibes at Mao indicates, these rehabilitation articles are not dispassionate reassessments of history. Like Yao's 1966 attacks, Su's and Zhang's and several other pro-Deng Tuo articles in the national press are written in the textual analysis mode similar in format to Yao Wenyuan's and the long tradition of rectification essays. They are propaganda for their political patrons. In Su's essay, Yao Wenyuan is implacably evil, out to 'usurp Party and state power', and a slanderous 'literary rascal'. Su frequently cites Yao's original essay for examples of his turpitude. In similar fashion, the republication of the essays in *Notes from a Three Family Village* in book form in 1979 also includes Yao's denunciation *in full* in an appendix.[61] Unlike Yao, Su is not guilty of gross misrepresentation, and from an outside perspective Yao appears to be a very unsavoury character. Yet there is nothing redeeming about the Yao we meet in Su's analysis, which is hard to believe as the complete picture. In his disinclination to follow the logic of his own analysis through to the end (Mao Zedong let Yao do these horrible things), Su falls short of objective analysis. Finally, in line with the classic textual analysis style, Su tars his subject with a set of dirty names and the accusation that Yao was part of 'an organized plot to seize state power'—that noted fiction, 'the gang of four'. Su's essay, which serves as an example of many, demonstrates that the groups within the CCP which controlled *Red Flag* and *Guangming Daily* in 1979 and 1980 felt that the textual analysis mode of public debate *and* the domesticated *zawen* of Deng Tuo and the *Three Family Village* could both be used. It seems that these two styles of public discussion are to be directed against different objects: *zawen* for contradictions among the people, textual analyses for officially designated class enemies.

Evening Chats at Yanshan was republished with official approval in April 1979, but it was not until 3 August 1979 that the *People's Daily* reported the official notice of the rehabilitation of the *Three Family Village*, its three central members and all those purged in conjunction with it. Three days later the official memorial article by Chen Kehan and Li Jun appeared in the paper, and on 5 September Deng's memorial service was held at Baobashan Cemetery of Fallen Revolutionaries outside Beijing. The establishment was present in force: Peng Zhen, Hu Yaobang, Liu Lantao, Li Xiannian, Bo Yibo, and others from the Eleventh Central Committee were present, and most of China's top leaders, including Ye Jianying, Deng Xiaoping, and Chen Yun, sent memorial wreaths. Lin Hujia, First Secretary of Deng Tuo's last home, the Beijing Municipal Party Committee, gave the laudatory address.[62] That it took six months for the CC to confirm this political shift indicates that some conflict still existed between those who favoured policies to which Deng Tuo subscribed and those who did not.[63] It is well to remember that Wang Dongxing, a powerful military figure who had prospered in the Cultural Revolution era even though he helped bring down the 'gang of four', was still in power in late 1979 and active in Beijing political life.

Evening Chats at Yanshan sold very well in the 1980s. The fourth printing of the 1979 edition, dated September 1982, brought that edition up to well over half a million copies (as listed on the standard bibliography page). Deng's widow, Ding Yilan, maintains that over a million copies have been printed nationwide on four different provincial presses.[64] Individual essays from *Evening Chats* have been reprinted in textbooks and literary collections since 1979.[65] Significantly, 'One Third of Life', the first essay in *Evening Chats*, is almost always included. Deng's emphasis in that essay on studying at home, or 'self-study' (*zixue*), as a way to reinvigorate China's troubled intellectuals after a period of political excess is mirrored in the front-page campaign in *Guangming Daily* in April and May 1983 popularizing the journal, *Self-Cultivation University* (*Zixiu daxue*).[66] In the Party's policy on journalism, Deng Tuo's approach was echoed by Deng Liqun, then director of the CC's Propaganda Department, in May 1983, and Gu Xing writes what amounts to 'the sayings of editor Deng' in his reminiscence articles on Deng Tuo's guidance of the *Beijing Evening News*.[67]

Post-Mao Model for Scholar-Cadres

Deng Tuo has also served as a model for the individual establishment intellectual. Nearly every article on him stresses his personal habits—his diligence, scholarly achievement, and his Party loyalty. Within all this Deng's cultural interests and abilities, particularly his poetry and calligraphy, have been depicted in a way which suggests that the pattern of his life in the 1950s is being presented as an encouragement and inducement to intellectuals to heed the Party's call to rejoin its revolution. In particular, photographs of Deng Tuo penning calligraphy for respectful audiences (see Illus. 5.1) and the analyses of his erudition in *Evening Chats* reflect a renewed respect for intellectual traits normally associated with traditional mandarins.[68] This stands in sharp contrast to the anti-intellectualism of the Cultural Revolution.

The last florescence of Deng Tuo reminiscences in the national press came in the spring of 1986, the twenty-year anniversary of his death. The fourth and final volume of *Deng Tuo's Works* (*Deng Tuo wenji*) appeared that April and a large 'Academic Symposium' honouring Deng was held in his home town of Fuzhou from 11 to 13 May.[69] Yuan Ying's major article on Deng, focusing on his unjust death, captured the spirit of that spring. Yuan's essay is a long piece of reportage entitled 'Broken Jade'.[70] He explicitly draws from the old Chinese saying, 'Better a piece of broken jade, than a whole tile.'[71] It is an elitist image, in tone with the Party's efforts in 1986 to revive the Hundred Flowers policy for intellectuals, yet again.

The appreciation raises the question: has anything of the scholarly values Deng Tuo pegged his identity upon survived the Cultural Revolution and the opening to the West in the 1980s? For the majority

6.2 Poetry meeting commemorating Deng Tuo, Fuzhou, May 1986
Note: Banner reads 'Poetry meeting to commemorate and study Comrade Deng Tuo'.

of China's tiny intellectual class, the answer is unclear and certainly not a matter of simple continuation. There is no Mao, contact with the world is more open, socialism has fallen apart in Europe and the former Soviet Union. On the other hand, for those who knew and worked with Deng Tuo, ranging from Peng Zhen in the Politburo to Liu Yongcheng, his research assistant in historical studies in the 1950s and now a senior researcher at CASS, the scholar-cadre values are stunningly resilient.

The core expression of these values, the 'simulacrum' of the scholar-cadre in Deng Tuo's style, was the 14 May 1986 poetry meeting held at the ancestral home at No. 4, Number 1 Hill, Fuzhou. Here Deng Tuo's peers, associates, family, and friends gathered for the literary canonization of their martyred comrade. Hu Jiwei, the former reformist editor of *People's Daily*, intoned his Tang-style poem while others chanted theirs in local dialect. The traditional courtyard of the home was festooned with hundreds of poems and epistles in flowing calligraphy. But for the cameras, tape recorder, and Mao suits, this could have been the eighteenth century. The themes of the poems are familiar: loyalty, personal integrity, long-suffering service to the nation, and cultivation of

China's arts. I attended this meeting and found myself completely out of my depth. Later I discussed the significance of poetry and calligraphy among scholar-cadres with Wang Bisheng, Deng Tuo's young biographer.[72] We identified three spheres of knowledge in the realm of traditional literature and poetry. At the centre are those, like Deng Tuo, who can compose elegant, correct, but lively original poems in any variety of classical forms filled with apt and moving imagery. At the second level are those who can recite an appropriate verse from the canon to suit the mood of the moment. At the third level are those who, at the least, can recognize the implications of a literary reference or an 'original' classical-style poem. Those who can do none of these things? They are outsiders, regardless of their skin or birth. Such aesthetic training still defines this social group among China's socialist-literati. Status in that group has not prevented Wang Bisheng from writing the most critical and independently minded biography of Deng Tuo in the PRC and it did not inhibit Hu Jiwei's drive for press freedoms in the National People's Congress. Each man, I suspect, would argue that the moral cultivation from practising the art of poetry only contributed to these 'modern' activities. However, without Mao's awful charisma, Deng Tuo's highly charged scholarly style has receded from national debate to the level of a sub-culture within China's ruling elite. The current leaders in Beijing include Deng Tuo's old patron, Peng Zhen; they are not threatened by the scholarly style and have always found uses for it. Once the refuge of integrity and 'inner refusal', the scholarly style is now little more than the sign of membership in a select club.

Local Uses of Deng Tuo

In this process of official political rehabilitation, journalism circles have relied most heavily on Deng Tuo as a model. His widow Ding Yilan's 'In Memory of Deng Tuo' appeared in *News Battlefront*, the major journalism journal, in February 1979.[73] *Guangming Daily* published a book review of the new edition of *Evening Chats* that February which strongly defended the critical commentary on current social issues embodied in Deng's 1960s *zawen* essays.[74] Over two hundred articles during the next seven years spelled out in meticulous detail just what standards and practices Comrade Editor Deng Tuo had advocated and explicitly linked these with how newspapers and journals should be run today.[75]

The *Beijing Evening News*, too, has returned from the dead. After being shut down in late May 1966 as a 'stooge of Deng Tuo', the paper started publishing again on 15 February 1980, and by 1983 had a daily circulation of 1.1 million copies, of which 40,000 were distributed nationwide.[76] A column similar to *Evening Chats*, 'A Hundred Schools Speak' (*Bai jia yan*), with its masthead written by Liao Mosha, now appears on page three in the identical spot to the old column. It is not as good as *Evening Chats*, says Gu Xing, who became editor-in-chief of the paper in June 1983, because he could locate no writer of Deng Tuo's talents (and, we may presume, who also possessed Deng's political reliability). Now it is a discussion column with different writers contributing each time.[77]

A series on Deng Tuo appeared in the Shanghai magazine, *The Journalist* (*Xinwen jizhe*). Between August 1984 and February 1985 seven articles reviewing his entire life and focusing on his work in journalism appeared once a month.[78] While this series provides some fascinating details of his life, particularly before 1945, its tone is entirely hagiographical, presenting Deng as the loyal Party journalist. In it Deng is a role model for the bureaucratic Maoist approach to journalism, propaganda, and ideology. A great deal of detail is given about the presses and editorial organization of the *Jin Cha Ji Daily*, which he edited during World War II, and Deng's long hours of work on behalf of Party journalism. In all, the picture provided is of a politically loyal and technically proficient cadre-editor. This journal is clearly aimed at young journalists and the streamlined version of Deng's life presented in it is much less complex than others in specialist journals or restricted-circulation publications.[79]

Deng Tuo's career in journalism has been recorded in the fifth volume of *Personalities in Journalism* (*Xinwenjie renwu*) published in February 1985.[80] It is a more scholarly and lengthy work, though not up to Wang Bisheng's standard. The biography focuses on Deng Tuo's work in journalism, but has particularly detailed information on his early years. It makes limited, but none the less helpful, use of footnotes. My impression, however, is that the scholarly attributes of the book are purely tactical. Properly cited documentation is introduced only enough to set up Deng Tuo as a figure worth emulating and the book as an authoritative interpretation of what in Deng is worth emulating. The book does, however, provide the first openly published critique of Deng's 'hot-headed' errors of the Great Leap period.[81] Deng is also included in the pantheon of Party 'socialist exemplars' (what we might call 'socialist *liezhuan*'—modelled on Sima Qian's 'exemplary biographies' in the ancient *Records of the Historian*) in Hu Hua's *Personalities of Chinese Communism*.[82]

There is one study of Deng Tuo's life published in China that approaches Western scholarly conventions and eschews the 'exemplary biography' style to some degree. Wang Bisheng's *Evaluative Biography of Deng Tuo* appeared in June 1986.[83] Wang is a graduate of CASS's Journalism Department and works in *People's Daily*'s cultural section. Both his agenda and his research trappings (footnotes, extensive bibliography, and a brief chronology of key events) are scholarly. Wang clearly has great respect for Deng Tuo, but as a member of a younger generation, Wang seeks to discover an acceptable role for an educated Chinese in the CCP through the life of this top propagandist and journalist. Wang side-steps some delicate questions, in large measure out of respect for a problem any literary biographer will recognize—the family and surviving spouse. The great strength of Wang's study is his literate understanding and lucid presentation of Deng Tuo's poetry and aesthetic interests.[84]

Historical circles embraced their useful martyr as well. His associates, such as his student, Liu Yongcheng, were reinstated with jobs in the new Academy of Social Sciences. Deng's works in history have been republished with praise, and he was enshrined in the first of the new *History Almanac*s in 1979 along with Fan Wenlan, Guo Moruo, Wu Yuzhang, Jian Bozan, and Wu Han.[85] He is now generally considered in Chinese historical circles as a representative historian of the old school who approached history writing in the manner of Jian Bozan's 'historicism'. A 1983 review of Chinese historiography edited by *Historical Research* places Deng, without any reference to political questions, in the midst of senior historians debating the development of 'sprouts of capitalism' in Chinese history.[86]

Artistic circles remember Deng Tuo in a similar fashion: rehonoured and republished. *A Selection of Deng Tuo's Poetry* was published in December 1979 with a laudatory preface by Nie Rongzhen, and *A Selection of Deng Tuo's Calligraphy* came out in February 1980, followed by a volume of *Deng Tuo's Lyrical Essays*. In 1986 there was another flurry. *Selected Poetry and Prose of Deng Tuo* came out in January and a catalogue of ancient paintings and calligraphy Deng donated to the National Museum was privately printed. The next year a second collection of Deng's own calligraphy appeared. These were largely consolidated in Deng's four-volume posthumous *Works* published between 1983 and 1986.[87] Finally in 1988 a large collection of photographic reprints and annotations to his calligraphy was produced by Fujian People's Press.[88] Deng Tuo can now take his place on the shelf with the scholar-officials of yore, confident that the key to his spirit as well as his political career has been preserved for later scholars to pick up.

Each of these post-Mao publications stresses the relevance of Deng Tuo as a model of culturally rich but politically orthodox intellectual and professional life. Since 1986, national press stories on Deng Tuo, as on other rehabilitated establishment intellectuals, have tapered off. But there is a lively cottage industry in specialized journals and local publications that reflect further 'local' uses of Deng within the broad rubric of what he is allowed to 'mean' as set at the national level. Of particular interest has been the response of youth—China's future establishment intellectuals. Letters by 'youth' now well into their thirties have declared Deng's beneficial influence on them in the 1960s or have apologized for wrongfully criticizing him during the Cultural Revolution.[89] The success of efforts by writers and editors to popularize Deng Tuo's essays and ideas as models of inspiration for the youth of today are hard to judge now, but based on the picture of recent studies of youth opinion in *China Youth* magazine, it would appear that many would find both his scholarship hard to match and his orthodoxy difficult to embrace.[90] John Israel has eloquently captured the likely fate of Deng Tuo's model of intellectual service in contemporary China:

> The generation now in its forties and fifties will move into power before the end of the century. Products of the narrowly specialized Soviet-style curriculum that replaced liberal education during the 1950s, these middle-aged experts may share Deng Tuo's orthodoxy but they lack his breadth. The generation in its thirties, molded by the Cultural Revolution, is tough, skeptical, and experienced in the ways of the world but may fall short on grounds of both political orthodoxy and cultural sophistication. Few of the generation in its twenties, survivors of the current Darwinian process of educational advancement, are likely to duplicate Deng's virtuosity. Perhaps Deng Tuo is both the first and last of a breed—a 'Mozartian commissar'.[91]

NOTES

1. Chen Kehan and Li Jun (1979); repr. in YDT: 14.
2. Yue and Wakeman (1985: 119–23). The critical loyalty Yue extends to the CCP in this book—she is quite frank and critical, but she professes faith that the Party can make things work and she was a Party member (at least until 1989)—places her squarely in the social group I mean to describe in Deng Tuo's life. Thus Yue's opinion of Deng is not surprising: '[He was] a man I had long admired as a skilful writer, an exemplary leader' (p. 146).
3. As Potter (1986: 38) concludes, Peng 'was not above engaging in factional conflict when his political power and position were threatened.'
4. Yue and Wakeman (1985: 123).
5. Yue and Wakeman (1985: 123 and 146).
6. Yue and Wakeman (1985: 146–8).

7. Tang's case, as presented in Yue Daiyun's autobiography, is a painful example of the price of political loyalty: a few years later Tang was trotting out the views of the radical left as part of a Beida writing group under the 'gang of four' in direct opposition to Deng Tuo's approach. Tang, as one may have expected, greeted the 'fall of the gang of four' in 1976 with decidedly mixed emotions; he was imprisoned for a while by Deng Tuo's colleagues.
8. Hamrin (1986: 80–3); for the broader context, see Goldman (1981: 95–110).
9. Su Shuangbi and Wang Hongzhi (1983: 288–9). They blame Kang Sheng, though they do not detail how he had the power to issue a central directive or dictate its contents. As far as I know, only Mao or the majority of the Politburo could do so.
10. For broader considerations, see Teiwes (1979), Lee (1978), and MacFarquhar (1997).
11. Kuang (1994).
12. It has been difficult enough with Mao dead. See the tortured reasoning in the CCP's own *Historical Resolution* (1981). An annotated version of the *Resolution* is given in *Zhonggong zhongyang wenxian* (1985).
13. Frederick Teiwes explores, on the level of the Central Committee, why such Party members allowed Mao to attack them. See Teiwes (1984: ch. 2). His conclusion, that leading Party members identified with Mao and *in extremis* deferred to Mao, is largely confirmed for the next level below the CC in the case of Deng Tuo.
14. For a recent investigation of these issues among post-Mao intellectuals, see Hua Shiping (1995).
15. Ahn Byung-joon (1976: 177); Lee (1978: 1–25); Goldman (1981: 118–33).
16. Lieberthal and Dickson (1989: 167, 173); Ahn Byung-joon (1976: 177).
17. Wang Bisheng (1986: 221–2). See accusations in 12 May 1966 *Renmin ribao* that this was Deng Tuo, repr. in 1969a: 443. Chinese biographical dictionaries in the 1980s list 'Xiang Yangsheng' as one of Deng's pen-names.
18. Su Shuangbi (interview with author, offices of the *Guangming Daily*, Beijing, 7 June 1983), and Li Jun in YDT: 108–9.
19. YDT: 109.
20. Selections from Deng's last letters are quoted in Wang Bisheng (1986: 225–6). Personal details are given by his eldest son, Deng Yun, in YDT: 244–5; also YDT: 36. It has been one of my grave frustrations, and a reminder of the limitations of my relationship with Deng Tuo's family, that I have not been able to see these surviving letters.
21. Reported by Sophia Knight (1967: 236).
22. Indexed in 1969a: 575–80, not including the first two mildly critical articles published by Deng Tuo's own editorial staff in Apr. 1966 and which Yao Wenyuan denounced as cover-ups. Ding Wang reprints 21 of these critical articles and *CB*, 792 renders five into English and indexes translations of 20 more. Others appear in *Chinese Studies in History* (1967–9). An enormous collection of Cultural Revolution attacks on Deng Tuo and the *Three Family Village* from the provincial as well as national press appears in a 7-volume cuttings file by the Union Research Institute, Hong Kong, stored at Universities Service Centre, Chinese University of Hong Kong under the title: 'Wenge: Zheng She bumen' (Cultural Revolution: Political and Cultural Section), vols. 3–9. The repetitious nature of these articles is numbing.
23. Conner (1972: 403–13). See Tom Fisher's application of this analysis to the case of Wu Han in Fisher (1986: 173–4).
24. Chuang (1967: 24). Another valuable study is Dittmer and Chen Ruoxi (1981).
25. Dittmer (1974); Teiwes (1979: 42–50).

26. Harrison (1972: 414–16); Teiwes (1976: 36–8).
27. For details on this case, including documentary and interview material, see Dai Qing (1994). See in particular Yang Shangkun, 'Activities of the Trotskyite Wang Shiwei and Liberalism in the Party, October 31, 1942' (Yang 1942, in Dai 1994: 136).
28. He Jin (1980); Seybolt (1986); Frederick Teiwes and Warren Sun (1995) analyse Mao's reaction to the rescue campaign; and Chen Yung-fa (1991).
29. Mao, 'Yan'an Talks (1943)', in McDougall (1980: 79) and Mao Zedong (1977: iii. 90).
30. Ding Wang (1979: 44–5). See *Mengya* (Shanghai), 1958, no. 6. See also Yao Wenyuan (1958).
31. Yao Wenyuan (1966), repr. in 1969a: 408–31, tr. in full in *CB*, 792 and in part in Cheek (1983–4: 79–85). Quotation from 1969a: 425 or *CB*, 792: 39.
32. *CB*, 792: 22–4. This is the *model* of sin—conscious, planned, and organized—embedded in the inquisitorial aspect of rectification. We can see it in the archetype—the 1942 literary rectification, which used Wang Shiwei as the negative model. See Dai Qing (1994). Ridiculous ideological charges and kangaroo courts, of course, were not created in rectification, but are the heritage of Stalin's fight with Trotsky in the 1920s. These techniques had been used against the CCP's first leader, Chen Duxiu, in 1927. See van de Ven (1992: ch. 5). The significance of rectification is that purging and ideological inquisition were tied to a hopeful and functional internal reform system that carried real legitimacy among cadres—for a time. This, at least, is the core of Teiwes's research and the point of Chs. 3–5 of the present study. See, for example, Deng Tuo's own defence of rectification-style criticism in the *Evening Chats* essay 'The Correct Understanding of "Criticism"', discussed in some detail in Ch. 5.
33. YDT: 284–8.
34. Cheek (1983–4: 82–3).
35. See Yao Wenyuan (1958) and Lars Ragvald's excellent study (Ragvald 1978).
36. Goldman (1981: 102), quoting *Guangming Daily*, 20 Dec. 1964.
37. Cheek (1983–4: 84). Mao had made similar charges, but against the 'Rightists' of the Hundred Flowers in May 1957; see Mao Zedong (1977: 442): 'The Rightists are trying to seize first a part and then the whole. To begin with, they are out to gain leadership in the press, education, literature and art, and science and technology. They know that in these fields the Communists are not as strong as they are, which is actually the case. They are "national treasures", not to be rubbed the wrong way. . . . Rightists in press circles are instigating the workers and peasant masses to oppose the government.'
38. Gu Bingfu (1966: 3), in the Union Research Institute cuttings file at Universities Service Centre, Chinese University of Hong Kong.
39. Xu Rende (1966).
40. Chuang (1967: 20–1).
41. Tang Tao (1980: 9) uses the term '*fanmian cailiao*' (Liao Mosha, interview with author, Beijing, 28 May 1983). Such '*fanmian jiaocai*' booklets created the justification for publishing public versions of *Three Family Village* and *Evening Chats* in the post-Mao period (in order to counter Cultural Revolution period study-material volumes).
42. One of the first was an attack on one of the left-wing writers in Yan'an (Zhou Wen 1942). On 'textual analyses' in the Yan'an rectification, see Cheek (1984b: 44–6); Dai Qing (1994).
43. Lin Jie *et al.* (1966). It first appeared in *Guangming Daily* on 8 May. An elegant translation of the whole compilation appears in Tung (1978: xix–xlvii). A rougher version is in *CB*, 792: 1–21.

44. Although Yao's major analysis appeared two days after this collection, one presumes from Yao's high rank in the Cultural Revolution Group, and later in the 'gang of four', that he masterminded the critique with Jiang Qing and that other, lesser figures, such as Lin Jie, followed their lead.
45. This translation modified (based on my reading of the *People's Daily* text) from Tung (1978: xix–xlvii), esp. sect. III (pp. xxxii, xxxiv–xxxvii) and sect. V (pp. xxxxi, xxxxiii–xxxxiv). See discussion of Deng Tuo's essay on Zheng Banqiao in Ch. 4.
46. The textual analyses of 1942 were the only sources available to Merle Goldman for Wang Shiwei's essay, 'Statesmen-Artists', or to any other Western scholar before that essay's republication in 1976. See Goldman (1967: 26–7). The textual analysis collection of materials on Lin Xiling in 1957 called *"Look" What Kind of Talk is This?* was translated by Dennis Doolin as a source of Lin's own liberal views. See Doolin (1964: 13–14, 17). This practice continues in the 1980s. Similar 'negative materials' (*fanmian jiaocai*) were prepared and distributed in 1987 on Liu Binyan and on Fang Lizhi when they were expelled from the Party. Copies at the Fairbank Center Library.
47. Starr (1979: 297). Jeffrey Wasserstrom (1992) uses the term 'facticity' to describe similar propaganda coming from the hard-line leadership in Beijing as it sought to interpret the events of spring 1989—and the massacre of 4 June—to an uneasy public. Paul Cohen notes that such extensive (and accurate) quotations of one's opponents extend at least back to the propaganda surrounding the Boxer movement at the turn of the century. See Cohen (1992: 82–113).
48. Cheek (1984*b*: 44–6).
49. 1979*a*: 178–81; see Pierre Ryckman's translation of 'Duo xue, shao ping' in Hsü Kai-yu (1980: 763–4). Lin Jie's extract is translated in Cheek (1983–4: 87–9).
50. For a theoretical perspective on this question, see Jowitt (1978, 1992: 1–50).
51. Warren Kuo (1978).
52. *Wenwu*, 1966, no. 5, pp. 1–32; *Jingji yanjiu*, 1966, no. 5, whole issue.
53. YDT: 157–8; Zhong Kan (1982: 263).
54. See Deng Yun (YDT: 241–6). Further details on the attacks made on Ding Yilan and the family were provided by their family friends. Ding Yilan was marched through the streets with 'Yin Yang tou'—a half-shaved head—and a placard confessing her 'counter-revolutionary crimes'. Personal humiliation and psychological torment seem to have been the goals of their Cultural Revolution assailants. See Thurston (1988) and Rittenberg and Bennett (1993).
55. Su Shuangbi's article on Wu Han (Su Shuangbi 1983), which first appeared in *Guangming Daily* on 15 Nov. 1978, is discussed below; see also Li Linhong (1978).
56. *People's Daily*, 22 Feb. 1979, p. 1, and *Guangming Daily*, p. 1, the next day. The official rehabilitation article appeared six months later; see Chen Kehan and Li Jun (1979). A convenient review of the rehabilitation in English is 'Reversal of Earlier Verdicts' (1979).
57. Dittmer (1981), esp. pp. 464–5, 468, and 479.
58. Pitman Potter (1986); Yang Xianzhen (1980); Liao Mosha (YDT: 1–6; 1980). On contemporary coalitions among the leadership, see Hamrin (1984 and 1989).
59. Zhang Yide (1979).
60. Su became an editor at *Guangming Daily*. He had been a student of Jian Bozan's and an ardent admirer of Wu Han. In the early 1980s he was in his fifties (interview with author, offices of *Guangming ribao*, Beijing, 7 June 1983); Su Shuangbi (1979*a, b*). See Su's essays attacking radical historiography (Su Shuangbi 1982) and the interview with Su, Ru Xin, and Xing Fensi, 'Continuing the Policy of Letting a Hundred

Flowers Bloom and a Hundred Schools Contend', in *Guangming Daily*, 20 June 1990, translated in *FBIS-CHI* 90-134, 12 July 1990, pp. 25-9.
61. Wu Nanxing (1979: 213-35). Liao Mosha (Wu Nanxing 1979: 243) says he suggested Yao's essay be included in the reprint so that readers 'could see for themselves.'
62. 'Deng Tuo tongzhi zhuidaohui zai Beijing juxing' (Memorial Meeting for Comrade Deng Tuo Held in Beijing), YDT: 1-4. The 5 Sept. 1979 Xinhua radio broadcast of this report is translated in *FBIS-CHI*, 6 Sept. 1979, pp. L1-L3. The YDT text, p. 4, says that it is 'A composite of reports in the *People's Daily* and *Beijing Daily*.' It is used here largely because it gives a more detailed list of participants, some 103 names, which are not in the *FBIS* text. It is reprinted in the memorial pamphlet published internally in Oct. 1979, *Daonian Deng Tuo tongzhi* (Mourning Comrade Deng Tuo), pp. 5-6. This is a 38-page pamphlet with many photos of the service, given to me by Ding Yilan.
63. This is the view of the Taibei review, 'Reversal of Earlier Verdicts' (1979: 9); Ding Yilan confirmed Wang Dongxing's interference with the rehabilitation.
64. Ding Yilan (interview with author). Bennet Lee reported in the *Far Eastern Economic Review* on 5 Oct. 1979, p. 59 that reprints of Deng Tuo's *Evening Chats* were getting 'snapped up quickly'.
65. Such as Bao Ji (1981: 523-31); Zhu Jinshun and Liu Xiqing (1982: 371-2—here 'One Third of Life' in a section of *zawen* by Lu Xun, Tang Tao, Xia Yan, Ma Tieding, Ye Shengtao, and Zhu Yilin, pp. 363-82); and *Zhongguo baogaowenxue congshu* (1982: 14-20) (this is Deng's 28 July 1956 'Interview of "Putao chang"' from *People's Daily*.
66. See 6 Apr. and 8 May 1983 issues of *Guangming Daily*.
67. Gu Xing (1980-1).
68. This is clearly the impression given in the photos of Deng's calligraphy and art collection, as well as of him sitting with teacups beneath his poetry and a delicate banzai tree, printed with Wang Bisheng (1983d: 36-7 and inside cover). The Mongolian writer Malaqinfu (1980) provides a similar assessment of Deng's obvious ability to lead policy on national minorities based on 18 poems Deng wrote in Huhehaote in Feb. 1964. Ding Yilan gave me a photograph of Deng penning these pieces which shows a crowd of respectful onlookers.
69. On the Deng Tuo symposium, see reports in the *Fuzhou Daily* and *Fuzhou Evening News* on 11 and 14 May 1986. I delivered a paper at the symposium, 'Deng Tuo Viewed from the West', but it was not published (though later it appeared in Japanese). Most of the papers appeared in edited form in *Renmin xinwenjia Deng Tuo*. A number of related articles appeared in the national press in May 1986, including *People's Daily* and *Xinwen zhanxian*.
70. Yuan Ying (1986).
71. Yuan Ying (1986: 18-19).
72. In Fuzhou following the poetry meeting. Wang was then in his mid-30s. He works in the *People's Daily* and is an aspiring poet of the traditional variety.
73. Ding Yilan (1979), repr. in YDT: 17-28.
74. Wang Zhen [NB *not* the late former vice president] (1979); excerpts tr. in *FBIS-CHI*, 27 Feb. 1979, pp. E19-E20.
75. I have collected approximately 100 articles on Deng Tuo published since 1979; for collections and book titles, see Bibliography.
76. Gu Xing (interview with author); Takashi Oka (1980).
77. Gu Xing (interview with author).
78. 'Huiyi Deng Tuo'.

79. Wang Bisheng, a recent graduate of the Journalism School at the Chinese Academy of Social Sciences, Beijing, who has become a major biographer of Deng Tuo, provides an example of the range of detail available in the articles on Deng Tuo. The article in the 'Huiyi Deng Tuo' series is by Bisheng (whom I presume is Wang Bisheng). In 1981 Wang produced a biographical article on Deng which provides more detail (Wang Bisheng 1981), and in 1983, Wang published part of his thesis on Deng Tuo in the journal of the graduate school of CASS (Wang Bisheng 1983c). This last article, which is not generally available, more directly addresses the political problems in Deng's life and cites *neibu* (restricted) speeches by Deng.
80. Zhang Shuzheng (1985). *Xinwenjie renwu* is a collectanea series of biographies of leading journalists. The general editor is Dai Bang; the author of the volume on Deng Tuo is Zhang Shuzheng, who in his 'Afterward' gives the impression that he did not himself know Deng Tuo as he thanks Ding Yilan and Deng's former colleagues for their assistance. The author dates the original manuscript as 'April 1981, Beijing', and the revised manuscripts as 'July 1984, Beidaihe'. It is worth noting the limitations of interviewing in China here: Ding Yilan never told me about this biography, even when I saw her in May 1985; one may guess that she has reservations about its quality. My thanks to Roderick MacFarquhar for lending me his copy.
81. Zhang Shuzheng (1985: 81–2).
82. Zhonggong dangshi renwuzhuan (1981–).
83. Wang Bisheng (1986).
84. Although Wang does not adopt the 'culture bearer' analysis I present, his distinction on the role of the 'theorist' (Wang Bisheng 1986: 182–3 especially) and his conversations with me about Deng Tuo's place in the great tradition of Chinese literati certainly led my thoughts in that direction.
85. Jin Chengji (1979).
86. Song Yuanqiang (1983: 137, 141, and 148).
87. 1979c; 1980c; 1984; DTWJ; and 1988.
88. See 1988.
89. YDT: 213–15, and 'Yanshan leiluo, yehua qianqiu'.
90. Ownby (1986), with his translations from *Zhongguo qingnian* in Ownby (1985).
91. Israel in Hamrin and Cheek (1986: xvii).

Conclusion
Broken Jade

> Better to be broken jade than unbroken crockery.
> (Yuan Ying, writing on Deng Tuo,
> *People's Daily*, 6 May 1986[1])

Deng's colleagues remember him, as the epigram above suggests, in terms of 'broken jade'. Jade is one of the ancient talismans of political power in China. Educated counsellors to the ruler, whom we today would generally consider intellectuals, have long been referred to as jade in China. When loyal ministers are unjustly dismissed or executed, then jade is broken. Like Qu Yuan, Deng Tuo was a loyal minister; he was driven to ritual suicide by those he served. In honouring Deng Tuo his colleagues refer to him as broken jade. The metaphor can serve us further. Not only the man but his career as a scholar-cadre in the CCP is 'broken jade'. Deng Tuo's charismatic role in the public arena was struck down in the Cultural Revolution and with it the priestly vocation of the Maoist cadre. Finally, the ideological system Deng Tuo served, Maoism, has shattered. Maoism is broken jade and not even Deng Xiaoping can put it back together again. While referring to Maoism—the cause of massive famine and personal brutality in the 1960s—as jade may seem a sickening absurdity, in truth Maoism was as precious as jade to Deng Tuo, and to many who served with him. It is with the pieces of Deng Tuo's life, vocation, and beliefs that his successors must fashion their future and China's.

This story is first and foremost about the life and death of a man. We set three broad questions about Deng Tuo's life and his service to Maoism in the introduction: why was such service attractive? what was it like? and, what went wrong?

A Life

Marxism-Leninism and later, Maoism were attractive to this son of the Confucian literati. As the child of an imperial official, Deng Tuo's early life and education were markedly Confucian. From this Deng imbibed the traditional ethos of Chinese intellectuals for state service. Furthermore, his father was not averse to new trends coming out of the New Culture Movement. Deng Tuo was able to read radical journals such as *New Youth* at home. Revolutionary solutions to China's problems did not require of Deng a break with or rejection of his family or his inherited values. He thus found Marxism-Leninism a novel solution to old problems. It did not pose for him what Joseph Levenson depicted as the tension between 'history and value' which plagued Liang Qichao and many earlier revolutionaries. The CCP, despite its disarray in the early 1930s, provided an adequate organizational form for participation in state administration for this young literatus. Deng had live alternatives which other members of his family took. He could have joined the KMT, become an apolitical scientist, or withdrawn from politics into the religious life. That Deng Tuo chose the CCP under these circumstances means he thought it was the best of several alternatives for fulfilling his vocation as a Chinese intellectual. Although Deng joined the Party in 1930, his own arrest and the decimation of the Shanghai Party limited his participation. When the Party was not functional, Deng Tuo stayed away. When the Party regained organizational and policy coherence after 1936, Deng returned to the fold.

Intellectual service to Maoism was for Deng Tuo an honourable vocation. Particularly during the Anti-Japanese War years (1937–45), it was exciting and deeply satisfying work. Deng felt it put noble ideas into practice. The system Deng worked in was the emerging propaganda system (*xitong*) of the CCP Party-State. It included the all-inclusive work unit, such as the *Jin Cha Ji Daily*, and came to include all aspects of public information and political feedback in the PRC. Deng's research in the Policy Research Office, as well as his work in journalism, served this system in the decade after 1946. This was a 'directed public sphere' in which the Party set the terms and selected the context of public discourse in order to educate and mobilize the public. In Deng Tuo's eyes, propaganda work was a wonderful and serious responsibility. He laboured to perfect and develop the propaganda system. We have seen in particular what this service meant to him in his detailed essays from the 1950s on how to run a socialist newspaper and especially how to compose leading editorials for *People's Daily*.

Deng Tuo saw his role in the propaganda *xitong* as a savant and culture-bearing cadre. He saw no inherent contradiction between scholarly integrity and political service. When he experienced such contradictions, they were a violation of the norms. When senior officials forced him to publish their articles in the *People's Daily* or when Mao hauled him in for his cautious editorial policies, Deng Tuo was outraged. He was, however, a prudent man. As he wrote in 'The Politics of Simpletons', bureaucratism was unavoidable but 'we should strive to minimize it.' Culture for Deng Tuo was comfortably both centuries-old Chinese and socialist. He lived a two-track cultural policy in which the masses received socialist culture and elite cadres such as himself enjoyed and continued China's elite arts. He professed the desire to share that beautiful traditional culture, to 'critically inherit it' in socialist terms for the masses. In practice, however, Deng maintained the paternalistic attitude of his Confucian forebears. He recognized that only a few of the common people would reach his level. His job in practice was to transform the masses through education (*jiaohua*). And he did it in nearly one hundred essays not only on ideological and political topics but also on art history, local culture, lessons from China's history, practical reflections on daily life, and on and on. He wrote beautifully in a clear and vigorous prose that equally eschewed Party jargon and aesthetic trills. He loved his job.

What went wrong? Deng Tuo was effectively fired by Mao in June 1957 and formally left the *People's Daily* in February 1959. His demotion reveals how Maoism divided under the pressures of state administration and economic development. Deng thought he was doing a good job; Mao thought he was a 'pedant editor'. In the years that followed, Deng wrestled with what to do. He supported the Great Leap avidly, but was horrified at the results and deeply self-critical of the Party's role in the disaster. Yet he could not, even in his most caustic *Evening Chats*, fundamentally criticize Mao. Deng's response to the Leap clarifies the genesis and characteristics of the fight that squandered the symbolic capital of Yan'an Maoism. By 1965 he was helping Peng Zhen stack meetings against equally conniving Leftists. There was precious little idealism in the organization of the 'Hai Rui Dismissed' debate, either among Deng Tuo's colleagues or Yao Wenyuan's.

What made it impossible for Deng Tuo to maintain his two-track organizational life as both Party functionary and political savant was Mao. And Mao could do it because of his position. However, the divided loyalties in Leninism, as Jowitt has articulated, ultimately undid Maoism. The previously incompatible authority styles of charisma and routine in Maoism were reflected in social reality in the example of two roles for intellectuals and Party cadres: as cogs and screws in the revolutionary machine and as culture-bearing cadres claiming an amount of independent action in the name of revolutionary goals. The ultimate leader was, of course, Mao. The organizational strength of the Party was, naturally, its established institutions. The social experience of Mao the supreme leader inevitably came to clash with that of the bureaucracy. The ideology of the day was crucial to the outcome of this structural tension between leader and administration. Unlike Confucian bureaucrats, Deng Tuo did not have an identity separate from the regime. He tried to create one in his scholarly style after 1959 in which his literati identity became a basis for loyal criticism, but his own loyalty betrayed him. He could not stop Mao without killing Maoism. And that was literally unthinkable to Deng Tuo and most of his generation. It is thinkable in China today. For that reason Deng Tuo's rehabilitation is highly problematic. We shall turn to such legacies in the last section of this conclusion.

A System

Deng Tuo became 'broken jade'. The Party repaid his loyal service as scholar-cadre by turning the propaganda machine he had helped develop against him. His death was a tragedy. His Chinese colleagues see this as a Chinese tragedy, with overtones of inevitability and moral righteousness. I see it as a Greek tragedy, with the hero's tragic flaw contributing to his own destruction. His flaw was hubris, the presumption that he could determine—through the ideological science of dialectical materialism and aesthetic training in painting, calligraphy, and poetry—what was best for China's masses. It was the hubris of 'directed culture' throughout the socialist world.[2]

The key agent of Deng's presumption and destruction was Mao. Mao was the ultimate patron, the guarantor of Deng Tuo's privileged status as social engineer. Mao was the symbol of the political style of the culture-bearing cadre. Mao was Deng Tuo, and a thousand other establishment intellectuals, writ large. Deng and the entire establishment that rose under Mao's leadership from the 1945 Seventh Party Congress contributed to Mao's apotheosis, but their quasi-imperial legitimator proved impossible to domesticate, or control. Unlike a Qing dynasty Emperor, Mao's charisma and ideology were something new. In particular, they partook of modern society by directly connecting the masses to political participation. With the volatile general public at his beck and call, Mao became a terrible Frankenstein monster who turned upon his bureaucratic supporters. Mao rejected the ideological method Deng Tuo and his colleagues intended to use for themselves and replaced it with faith in his own intuition to be applied by the faithful masses using his Little Red Book.

Deng Tuo's intellectual service, the role of the scholar-cadre as transformational bureaucrat, thus became broken jade. When Mao attacked the establishment, its members discovered they had provided themselves with no protection, not even a safe exit. Deng Tuo was but one of thousands thrown into the flames of the Cultural Revolution. What is stunning is that neither he nor his colleagues effectively resisted their demise. In his final actions in May 1966 Deng Tuo seemed resigned to his fate. With all that cultural capital—from scholarly prestige to administrative experience and bureaucratic connections—why did he not try to oppose the emerging craziness of the Cultural Revolution? Deng Tuo's inaction directly parallels the acquiescence of the Central Committee to Mao's new revolution. Frederick Teiwes has thoughtfully illuminated the senior Party officials' tragic complicity in their own demise.[3] What he found for top leaders applies to Deng Tuo: they identified with Mao too strongly to oppose him so fundamentally. Their personal hubris as transformational bureaucrats was justified by the infallible Mao. When push came to shove, Deng Tuo's generation deferred to their charismatic leader. Even in the face of certain destruction. Such was their faith. This was the fatal flaw in the jade for Deng Tuo, for intellectual service to the Party, and for Maoism.

Maoism, the numinous jade-like gift that had brought order to the realm, also shattered during Deng Tuo's life. From the days in Jin Cha Ji we have seen the twin tendencies inside Maoism of faith in the charisma of the leader and reliance on the predictable functioning of ideology as a bureaucratic method. In the Yan'an period they existed, as Jowitt has suggested for Leninism in general, in a dynamic tension. In the context of brutal war and national dependency this amalgam created, as Apter and Saich have shown, the 'symbolic capital' of Yan'an Maoism. It worked. Then. The changed social circumstances of the new Party-State blew that amalgam apart. For those in the administration, the needs of bureaucratic predictability contributed to a refinement and extension of the bureaucratic side of Maoism. They sought to strengthen the institutional charisma of the Party—its committees, its rules, its cadres. They found much to appreciate in the Soviet model. For the supreme leader, now lionized by all, the need to maintain authority over a recalcitrant bureaucracy drove Mao to ever more daring applications of faith Maoism. He found much to emulate from Stalin's leadership. The two sides rehearsed this fight from the 1955 mini-Leap until Mao delivered the knock-out blow in 1966. While the founding generation of establishment intellectuals debated the proper balance of 'red and expert', youth found in the Party something less unified. Educated Chinese eager to enjoy stable careers serving the nation were drawn to bureaucratic Maoism, not a few without cynicism or pro forma attitudes.

Those on the out—from elders who lost out on top positions to youth with less education or bureaucratic connections—were drawn to faith Maoism, again not a few without opportunism or self-aggrandizing attitudes.

Deng Tuo first articulated the bureaucratic side of Maoism in Jin Cha Ji and developed it in the 1946–56 decade. Yet, because Deng's Maoism was full Maoism—including his faith in Mao—bureaucratic Maoism proved unequal to the tasks that faced it. It could not prevent the Great Leap Forward. After the shock of the Leap it became virtually its own form of Maoism, Bureaucratic Maoism. Yet, Bureaucratic Maoism could not halt its own immolation in the Cultural Revolution. Faith Maoism proved equally insufficient to China's needs. Its developmental model in the Great Leap killed some thirty million citizens. Mao explicitly set his Maoism up against the Party's in the Cultural Revolution. The revived millenarianism of Faith Maoism in the Cultural Revolution betrayed its noble goals to factionalism and murder. The obtuse polemics and harsh dictatorship of the mid-1970s were a sad conclusion to Mao's Republic.

Deng Tuo's life has enabled us to see the genesis of this great divorce. In particular, it has shown that the split between the two tendencies in Maoism came during the aftermath of the Great Leap. It began as an attempt to win Mao to each side. This we saw in Lin Biao's and Deng Tuo's competing exegeses of volume 4 of Mao's *Selected Works*. Although less attention has been given here to the Faith Maoist writers in the early 1960s, their ideas show, as do the actions of their patrons, a fraternal competition with Bureaucratic Maoist proponents for the Revolutionary Father's ear. It did not become a murderous fight until Mao let it be so. The actors and issues at the heart of Maoism remain today, with the crucial absence of Mao himself. So far, however, the current leadership has been unable to put the ideological pieces back together again.

Intellectuals: Types, Roles, and Spheres of Activity

Deng Tuo's story suggests we change the way we look at China's intelligentsia in the twentieth century and particularly intellectual participation in the Chinese Communist movement. The dominant model in Western studies, based on Party attacks on left-wing writers in Yan'an and on an almost biennial basis throughout the PRC, posits a fundamental divergence of interests between intellectuals and the Party-State. This picture is incomplete. Neither is it a false picture. Contented

Conclusion: Broken Jade

service, troubled compliance, craven servitude, loyal criticism, passive resistance, defiant opposition—all these characterize the experience of different groups of intellectuals under the CCP. Thus, we need to disaggregate our picture of Chinese intellectuals. Further case studies of different intellectuals are needed to complement the present study. Much as local studies in anthropology and history have enriched our study of Chinese society in north, south, coastal, and interior China, we need thoughtful full biographies of leftist Party intellectuals, such as Zhang Chunqiao, and Marxian economists, like Sun Yefang. One model for intellectual–state relations and for the role of intellectuals in the PRC will no longer do.

What image of intellectual activity in the public arena might help us understand better the role of intellectuals and their relationship with the state in China? Over the past twenty years there has been a cottage industry devoted to typologies of Chinese intellectuals—Radicals (Maoists) vs. Liberals (and later Reform Radicals), Marxian-Confucians vs. Establishment Radicals, Establishment Intellectuals vs. Maoists, and more broadly, typologies such as inquisitors, technocrats, critical intellectuals, and dissidents.[4] Our inability as a field to comprehend fully the role of China's intellectuals in the popular movement of 1989, much less to predict events before, during, and since, highlights the weaknesses in our current understanding of intellectual activity in China today. It may be more fruitful to think of various Chinese intellectuals not in terms of types, but in terms of their *roles*, and furthermore in terms of *spheres of activity*.

Many of the intellectual types identified by scholars can more usefully be seen as roles individual intellectuals may occupy serially or concurrently. In 1987 Merle Goldman and I suggested three such roles: as ideological speakers for the State, a role which dominated the career of the Party theoretician Ai Siqi, for example; as academic and professional elites, roles a number of Chinese intellectuals have endeavoured (with mixed success) to separate from political life in the PRC; and as critical intellectuals, that dangerous modern role of Confucian censor and May Fourth iconoclast.[5] The focus on roles was an improvement over static 'types', but our categories only focused on the overtly political activities of Chinese intellectuals.

As we have seen in Deng Tuo's life, the previous concern of Western scholars with his political views and activities blots out large sections of his life. In addition to seeing such politically active intellectuals in terms of their political roles, it is necessary to attempt to account for *all* their activities, not just their overtly political ones.[6] A focus on key realms or spheres of intellectual activity—such as the circles of Deng Tuo's activities pictured in Chapter 3—may help us to understand the various roles intellectuals play in Chinese politics. This focus produces a more inductive study of intellectual behaviour, demanding that a researcher gather information on all domains of public activity (and private, if possible) in order to frame the significance of the political portion of an intellectual's career. Colleagues researching other Party intellectuals, such as Mary Mazur on Wu Han, are doing just this.[7]

We are a long way from a complete picture of these circles of activities in the lives of leading intellectuals, not to mention statistical data on the intelligentsia. Nevertheless, we can still identify important areas of public activity generally undertaken in greater or lesser degree by all Chinese intellectuals.[8] Like Deng Tuo, China's establishment intellectuals were and continue to be more than purely 'professional'. They have sought to speak to public issues directly, most often through advice or service to the State. However, from the perspective of Deng Tuo's life and death we can see that the social experience of the Cultural Revolution has changed both the system and the intellectuals in it. The Propaganda State has not so much dissolved as it has—to borrow David Kelly's term for post-Mao ideology—become dismembered.[9] Functioning bits of the system are floating about in the public arena, no longer held in systematic relation. The intellectuals' experiences of the Cultural Revolution have produced doubt and anxiety and the new conditions of 'market socialism' since the early 1980s have brought a broader range of possible responses for intellectuals than was available to Deng Tuo, as well as a greater alienation from bureaucratic and ideological influence.

Intellectual Identity: From Priests to Professionals

In a broader perspective Deng Tuo's life presents us with a transitional role for China's intellectuals in mid-century, between the priestly vocation of the Confucian scholar-official and the politically independent professional of bourgeois society. In the modernization of China, Deng Tuo gives an example of the changing role of the educated elite in public affairs. Part of Deng Tuo's life does not seem revolutionary in terms of China's culture and its traditional social structure. It seems obvious that revolutions must build on what is. Deng Tuo was a scholar-official. He was conscious of the parallels with Confucian literati in the dynasties and wrote about this. Deng Tuo saw no essential contradiction between his role as *cadre* and as *literatus*. He was a revolutionary, no longer maintaining the precepts of Confucian state ideology. Yet, he felt one could 'critically inherit' most of the elite, as well as popular or folk, cultural products of Chinese civilization. Indeed, like his colleagues, such as Wu Han with whom he wrote in *Notes from a Three Family Village*, he felt there was no other way 'to build the new'.

I have coined the term 'culture bearer' as a tag to describe one key aspect of Deng Tuo's service in Mao's China. The closest term used by a Chinese is Deng's own 'theoretical worker' (*lilun gongzuozhe*) or his biographer Wang Bisheng's 'theoretician' (*sixiangjia*).[10] My term and Deng Tuo's traditional scholarly style might seem contradictory to the revolutionary social engineering expected of Party leaders. The point of Deng Tuo's career is that they were not. Culture, since Dong Zhongshu articulated its political role for Emperor Han Wudi in the second century BCE, was meant to engineer society on behalf of the 'science' (my term, but equivalent to its Chinese Marxist usage) of Han cosmology—the State was to manipulate culture to bring everyone in harmony with the *dao*. To say the State and its intellectual servants in the 1950s share fundamental elements of political culture with their predecessors two thousand years ago is not to argue that China is unchanging any more than a recognition of the centrality of law, a personal God, and Platonic ideal types in current Western politics and society means that the contemporary West has not changed from Roman times. The point of dwelling on Deng Tuo's culture-bearing role is just the reverse: to understand *change* in Chinese culture. It is to identify specifically some of the 'forms' of political culture in Chinese civilization which have allowed Marxism-Leninism to 'fit' under the conditions of the early and mid-twentieth century. Because fit it did. 'Fit', however, does not mean repetition without development. It simply describes the mechanism of cross-cultural influence as Chinese actors used foreign ideas to answer (and, sadly, to create) indigenous problems.[11]

Deng Tuo used Marxist economic analysis and Leninist political organization in just this transitional manner. Maoism and the role of Party intellectual provided Deng and a generation of Chinese intellectuals with a role recognizable to the Confucian literati but more able to deal with the realities of the twentieth century. Still an elite ministering to 'the people', Party intellectuals had the benefit of an ideology committed to economic development, a coherent organization, a strong leadership, a powerful military, and an influential international patron. This transitional role fell apart with the general divorce within Maoism. For establishment intellectuals in particular, their lack of protection from arbitrary power, their inability to exit the public stage (having no family property to which to return and no legitimate excuse for resigning office), and their disinclination to form horizontal alliances all contributed to their fall from grace.

The demise of Deng Tuo and his cohort represents the shattering of that neo-traditional role for the educated as functionally diffuse 'priests' staffing the totalistic social 'church'. This is the shift from 'vocation' to 'profession' as the fundamental self-image and public role of intellectuals. Intellectuals in China today are grappling with an emerging social structure—made up of institutions, behaviour patterns, and beliefs—which might offer them roles as *specialists* in *professions*. From such a social position they could contend in a less 'directed' public sphere.[12] That would be a profound revolution in the public life of China's educated elite and would spell the end of ideologists, such as Deng Tuo.

Legacies

What light does Deng Tuo's story throw on the likely future of Chinese intellectuals and the State? Perhaps the 'blood and tears' of Deng Tuo's life and death which Hu Jiwei honoured in his memorial poem have, as Merle Goldman hopes, 'watered the seeds of democracy'. Certainly, Deng's surviving colleagues, former subordinates, and others draw lessons from his career. Elders in the CCP, such as Deng's old patron, Peng Zhen, see the man as a fallen hero. He was smart and he was loyal. For them, Deng Tuo is best used as a sort of intellectual Lei Feng, a role model to encourage today's intellectuals to do the same. It is fairly clear that no one is listening to that story.

Deng's former subordinates present a range of responses. These are 'the generation of propagandists Deng Tuo trained' for which Nie Rongzhen is so grateful. Three are relatively well-known: Hu Jiwei, Liu Binyan, and Wang Ruoshui. Hu Jiwei, the only one of the three who remained in China continuously, appears the most similar to Deng Tuo. He has little interest in foreigners. He's cautious with current Party leaders. But he has been indefatigable in his campaign for press reform and propaganda liberalization. Hu works within the system, but he pushes it as far as it can be made to go.[13] He has spoken on Deng Tuo: *xianshi*, my late teacher. Liu Binyan carries on Deng's idealism and hopes for the role of socialist journalism in the political process. Rudolf Wagner has described Liu's reporting as 'being a scout for the Party'.[14] Liu's post-Mao exposés, particularly 'Between People and Monsters', electrified China in the late 1970s. Through the 1980s his pursuit of a 'second kind of loyalty' paralleled Deng Tuo's turn to the scholarly style: an attempt to find a point from which to deal with the CCP in order to improve it. Liu tried to build a sort of 'public' within the propaganda state that would attend to his muckraking. His efforts at creating a preliminary public sphere faltered with the orthodox backlash of 1987 (in which Liu lost his Party membership) and collapsed with the general crisis of 1989. Yet, even in exile in the early 1990s Liu did not immediately reject the Party.[15] Wang Ruoshui, Deng's junior editor who caught Mao's eye in the late 1950s, speaks to the moral issues that animated Deng Tuo. Wang, however, greatly extends the explicit examination of Marxian humanism beyond Deng's faith that Maoism would not only make life better but make individuals better. Wang took most to heart the lesson of Deng Tuo's death: a system that can do that is not a good system. He has tried to argue loyally in Marxian discourse from first principles—Marx's lost goal of ending human alienation—in order to find the sort of Marxist government suitable to China.[16] John Israel rightly suggested that Deng Tuo himself was a 'Mozartian commissar'. However, *parts* of his vocation live vibrantly in the contested world of Chinese intellectuals today.

The system is nearly as dead as the man. The comments of legal expert and publisher Yu Haocheng (1927–) capture the crisis now engulfing the 'propaganda state' in China. The lesson he draws from Deng Tuo's life is the insufficiency of traditional Party methods of rule. 'How many masterful article writers like Deng Tuo and Wu Han... have died miserably under the sword of the executioner?' Yu's solution: an independent press and judicial guarantee of the current PRC constitution. 'Why must newspaper offices and publishing houses be run only by Party committees and government organs,' Yu asks, '... and why can they not be managed independently in compliance with pertinent laws and regulations?'[17] That question never occurred to Deng Tuo, because the answer is the end of the propaganda state. For Yu Haocheng, Deng's life and death are precisely what raise that paradigm-shifting question for China.

Nothing certain has come to replace Deng Tuo's shattered role for China's intellectuals. Deng Tuo's life serves as a reminder, however, that problems for China's intellectuals do not stem only from the very real abuses of the CCP. The approach to public life and the priestly presumptions to minister to the public which China's educated elite have inherited and which enlivened Deng Tuo's career actually support the authority patterns which maintain the now-troubled CCP in power. Indeed, as David Kelly notes, the tragedy of China's intellectuals in the PRC today is that they 'remain, as a stratum, an artifact of the system they oppose.'[18] To rid themselves of Party dictatorship, China's intellectuals will likely have to renounce the priestly vocation of their ancestors and of scholar-cadres of the Mao period. Perhaps they will secularize their talents as specialists in various professions and help guide the development of an open society in China as advocates in a free public arena. Changes in Chinese society brought on by the reform period make any other choice appear impractical. The lesson of this history is clear, however: any effort to renew the scholar-cadre vocation under the CCP in China today will carry the risk of Deng Tuo's fate once again.

NOTES

1. Yuan Ying (1986).
2. See Haraszti (1987: introd.).
3. Teiwes (1984: ch. 2), and MacFarquhar (1983).
4. In order, types put forward by: Goldman (1981); Moody (1977); Hamrin and Cheek (1986); and a thoughtful paper by Frederic Wakeman, Jr. (1993).
5. Goldman, Cheek, and Hamrin (1987: 3–10).
6. This has been the case in several fine studies of non-CCP intellectuals. See Alitto (1979) and Hayford (1990).
7. Mary Mazur's study of Wu Han's life can be found in her University of Chicago Ph.D. thesis (Mazur 1994). See also Mazur (1990).
8. I explore this in terms of the three realms of intellectual activity suggested by Tu Wei-ming in Cheek (1992: 135–9)—*zheng* (politics), *xue* (learning or study), and *dao* (normally translated as 'way', but here meaning the search for transcendence).
9. Kelly (1991).
10. See 1960f and Wang Bisheng (1986: 182).
11. This view is suggested in Kuhn's (1977) seminal study, esp. the last three pages, and is elaborated in Kuhn (1991).
12. These issues are addressed in Brugger and Kelly (1990), which follows Marxist humanists; Goldman (1994), which explores a 'democratic elite'; and Ding (1994), which analyses four categories of 'counterelite'.
13. Polumbaum (1994).
14. Wagner (1987: 202).
15. Liu Binyan (1990).
16. Kelly (1987).
17. Cited in Goldman (1994: 71–2), drawing from Yu Haocheng (1981).
18. Kelly (1990: 46–7).

Appendix: Evening Chats *and* Three Family Village *Essays by Date*

This appendix lists all Deng Tuo's articles and prefaces (177 in total) published in *Evening Chats at Yanshan* and *Notes from a Three Family Village* by date of original publication in the *Beijing Evening News* or *Frontline*, or in the case of those prefaces not published in the newspaper, by their signed date. Information is presented in five columns:

- The date of original publication in the Beijing press;
- An English translation of each article's title;
- An assessment of the political tone of the article. A five-point scale was chosen to reflect a simple three-level assessment: (1) apolitical, (3) politically safe, and (5) politically contentious. Numbers 2 and 4 provide some leeway, but should be treated as members of their respective extremes (1 and 5);
- Topics covered in the article;
- Page numbers in which the article appears in the 1979 edition of the respective published collection.

Titles given in capital letters I have translated in Cheek (1983–4). In all, 14 titles from *Evening Chats* are translated there. Four titles do not have page numbers under the column '1979' because they were not printed in that edition. The Chinese titles and page numbers in the 1963 edition (1963*a*) are given in Chapter 5. *Three Family Village* articles are given page numbers for Wu Nanxing (1979); they are indicated in the rightmost column by 'SJC' to avoid confusion.

Date	Title	Pol.	Topic	1979
19 Mar. 1961	ONE THIRD OF LIFE	1	GLF recovery, education, youth	5–7
23 Mar. 1961	Do Not Fear Heaven	4	GLF recovery, anti-superstition, self-reliance book review	8–10
26 Mar. 1961	WELCOME 'THE MISCELLANEOUS SCHOLAR'	4	scholarship, role models for intellectuals	11–13
30 Mar. 1961	Can Grain Grow on Trees?	3	agriculture, science, famine relief	66–8
2 Apr. 1961	The Most Modern Thought	5	historical drama, professional historicism	89–91
6 Apr. 1961	The Way to Treat Guests	5	foreign relations, courtesy	54–6
9 Apr. 1961	Critique of 'Thirty-Three *Zhenshen*'	5	foreign relations, problems in international competition	57–9
13 Apr. 1961	TO CHANNEL IS BETTER THAN TO DAM	5	agricultural policy	78–9
16 Apr. 1961	The Earliest Tradition on Outer Space Navigation	3	history of science, general interest, China pride	63–5
20 Apr. 1961	Iron in Plants	3	construction, botany	69–71
23 Apr. 1961	A New Interpretation of the Story of Lake Mountain	3	myths and science	72–4
27 Apr. 1961	Yang Dayan's Aural Reading Method	1	scholarship, reading	26–8
30 Apr. 1961	ON TREASURING LABOUR POWER	5	economics, history, GLF	60–2
4 May 1961	'The Newborn Calf Fears Not the Tiger'	3	youth, revolutionary successors	45–7
7 May 1961	The Secret is No Secret	2	scholarship, study aids	29–32
11 May 1961	Seven-Part Reading of Three-Part Poems	1	poetry, poetry reading	23–5
14 May 1961	THE CORRECT UNDERSTANDING OF 'CRITICISM'	5	theory, political norms	92–5
18 May 1961	The Rise and Fall of Two Temples	2	historical preservation	83–5
21 May 1961	[title unclear]	1	writing style, clarity	33–5

Date	Title	Pol.	Topic	1979
25 May 1961	Resurrection	2	medicine	75–7
28 May 1961	On Ambition	4	youth, rustication, public–private	51–3
1 June 1961	Cherish the Childish Heart	1	youth, child development stages	48–50
4 June 1961	'Haven't Got a Thing' Art	1	art, anti-bourgeois	42–4
6 June 1961	STORIES ABOUT BRAGGING	5	politics, negative examples, work style	513–15
8 June 1961	From Three to Ten Thousand	4	study habits, culture, gradualism	36–8
15 June 1961	A House with One Egg	5	agricultural policy	80–2
18 June 1961	The Creative Attitude of Jia Dao	3	art, poetry	20–2
22 June 1961	The Case of Chen Jiang and Wang Geng	5	political work, historical analogy, corruption	540–2 (not in 1963a)
25 June 1961	Bold Practice Writing Characters	1	calligraphy	39–41
29 June 1961	The Gold and Swords Fraud	3	moral object lesson, perils of greed	215–17
2 July 1961	The Earliest Demonstration of Beijing's Labouring Masses	3	labour history	17–19
6 July 1961	Changing the Three Don't Knows to the Three Knows	3	investigation, cadre training	14–16
9 July 1961	The Polished Gold Coin	5	theory, Marxist philosophy, vulgarization of philosophy	86–8
10 July 1961	TWO EXPLANATIONS	3	explanation of vol. 1, call to serve educated readers	3–4
13 July 1961	Just Call a Pigeon a Pigeon	1	language, proper naming of things, criticism of loose terminology	543–5 (not in 1963a)
16 July 1961	The New 'Three On's Essay'	1	education, writing methods, academics	195–7
20 July 1961	It'll Pay/Ginger Seed-Root	2	agriculture, history of agriculture	124–6
23 July 1961	EAT BROTH INSTEAD OF LAMB	4	politics, role models for intellectuals, how to write essays	189–91

Date	Title	Pol.	Topic	1979
27 July 1961	On the Topic 'Nonsense'	2	youth, science	159–61
30 July 1961	A Small Key	1	education, research methods, academics	192–4
3 Aug. 1961	Don't Seek Profound Understanding	4	education, reading habits,	186–8
6 Aug. 1961	DO NOTHING IMPROPER	3	social rules, reinterpreting texts	153–5
10 Aug. 1961	The Allure of Art	4	art, art theory, defence of beauty	165–8
13 Aug. 1961	The Contributions of Collectors	1	*haute culture*, art collecting	1963*a*: 150–2
17 Aug. 1961	Women's Day in Ancient China	1	history, women	
20 Aug. 1961	Did Wu Han Ever Kill the Concubine?	4	historical drama	114–16
24 Aug. 1961	STUDY MORE, CRITICIZE LESS	5	politics, work style	178–81
27 Aug. 1961	'Yan [Hui] was Troubled by Confucius' Lofty Wisdom'	5	politics, role models, commitment to truth	182–5
31 Aug. 1961	Do you Know what '*Dan qi*' is?	1	*haute culture*	117–20
3 Sept. 1961	The Guangyang School	2	history, inheritance, role models	111–13
7 Sept. 1961	'*Ping Long Ren*'	2	history of science, chemistry of 8th c. CE	142–4
10 Sept. 1961	On 'The Study of Maintaining Health'	2	medicine, history of science	121–3
14 Sept. 1961	Create New Poetry Tunes	3	poetry, national forms of literature	162–4
17 Sept. 1961	Who First Discovered America	1	academic history	101–3
21 Sept. 1961	A Short Examination of 'Fusang'	1	academic history	104–7
24 Sept. 1961	Speaking from Hui Shen's Citizenship	1	academic history	108–10
28 Sept. 1961	DO YOU APPROVE THE USE OF PEN-NAMES?	4	writing, editorial policy, rules of public debate	299–302
1 Oct. 1961	The Three Good Wishes of Huafeng	3	history, reinterpreting texts	146–9
5 Oct. 1961	IN ALL THINGS SHOW CONCERN	5	intellectuals, role in politics/integrity	156–8

Appendix

Date	Title	Pol.	Topic	1979
8 Oct. 1961	Navigation and Ship Construction	2	history of ship construction	138–41
12 Oct. 1961	The Season for Planting Late Cabbage	1	agriculture, history of cabbage	127–9
15 Oct. 1961	Don't Just Talk about Reading Books	4	education, study habits	175–7
19 Oct. 1961	Metaphysics Has Not Faded	3	philosophy, history of	169–71
22 Oct. 1961	The Remnant Evils of Eight-Legged Essays	5	work style, political writing	172–4
26 Oct. 1961	The Many Virtues of Raising Cattle	1	agriculture, history of cow herding	134–7
29 Oct. 1961	The History of the Sweet Potato	1	agricultural history	130–3
30 Oct. 1961	A Word on the Volume	1	introduction to vol. 2	99–100
2 Nov. 1961	Ancient Cartoons	3	cartoons, Chinese origins of satire	253–5
5 Nov. 1961	'Let Go to Find Firm Ground'	5	politics, work style, investigation work	206–8
9 Nov. 1961	The Older and Younger Mi of Wanping	5	politics, model intellectuals, moral courage	241–3
10 Nov. 1961	The Great Empty Talk	5	dangers of exaggeration, satire, public speaking	SJC: 7–9
12 Nov. 1961	'Soundless Music' and Such	3	music, anti-bourgeois	295–8
16 Nov. 1961	'Judges' Etcetera	3	political, attack on individualism and bureaucratic irresponsibility	209–11
19 Nov. 1961	Poor but with Lofty Ideals	3	youth, value of past, personal integrity	203–5
23 Nov. 1961	Beijing's Ancient Harbour	3	history of science, construction	233–6
26 Nov. 1961	Two Foreign Fables	5	ideology, historical analogy, Ernst Mach, anti-psychological factor	516–18
30 Nov. 1961	The Verdant Hills Never Change	3	nature conservation, ecology, public education in botany, forestry	271–4
3 Dec. 1961	Self-Cultivation	4	intellectual roles, inheritance from past	212–14

324   *Appendix*

Date	Title	Pol.	Topic	1979
7 Dec. 1961	Preserve Artefacts	2	art conservation, public education, local history of Beijing	250–2
10 Dec. 1961	Three Gardens of the Mi Clan	1	local history of Beijing	244–6
14 Dec. 1961	Talking from Lu Chishui's Ink Chrysanthemum	1	painting, modern *guohua*, Lu Chishui (Kang Sheng), Wu Junjing	1963*a*: 268–70
17 Dec. 1961	Gold in Scarab Beetles	1	science, history of science	
21 Dec. 1961	Chen in the South and Cui in the North	2	art history, biography of Cui Zizhong, integrity	237–40
24 Dec. 1961	Does the Fault Lie with the 'Ignoramus'?	1	education, culture, youth	226–9
25 Dec. 1961	The Origin of 'Electric Musical Theatre'	2	attack on bourgeois culture and theatre as decadent, Chinese national pride	SJC: 16–18
28 Dec. 1961	Self-Set without Free Time	1	etymology, culture	230–2
31 Dec. 1961	See in the New Year by Drinking *Tu-su* [Wine]	1	popular customs, medicine	281–3
4 Jan. 1962	Snowflake Crystals	3	history of science, China did it first	278–80
7 Jan. 1962	Kunlun Mountain Man	5	politics, model intellectual, moral courage	247–9
11 Jan. 1962	Poinsettia	1	flowers	275–7
14 Jan. 1962	Wen Tianxiang on Study	4	education, defence of scholar activism	218–21
18 Jan. 1962	Selecting Poems and Selecting Essays	1	academic, bibliography	222–5
25 Jan. 1962	The Theory of 'Internal Heat' in Chinese Medicine	1	medicine, popularization of	288–91
28 Jan. 1962	An Example of the Common Origins of Calligraphy and Painting	5	Intellectual Model, politics and art, art history	257–60
1 Feb. 1962	Corrections for 'Precious Island Travel Notes'	1	historical methods, art history, Su Dongbo	261–3

Date	Title	Pol.	Topic	1979
4 Feb. 1962	This Year's Spring Festival	3	social customs, critical inheritance of old, respect for labour, agricultural reserves	546–8 (not in 1963a)
8 Feb. 1962	Vegetable Gardens on Water	1	agriculture, science	264–7
11 Feb. 1962	'The Jade Emperor's' Birthday	1	superstition, historical inheritance	284–7
15 Feb. 1962	Sanqi, Shanqi, and Tianqi	2	medicine, Chinese medicine, taxonomy	292–4
18 Feb. 1962	A Universal Key	4	education, study methods, intellectual independence	307–10
22 Feb. 1962	Is Resourcefulness Reliable?	5	ideology, criticism of 'genius'	323–6
25 Feb. 1962	THE KINGLY WAY AND THE TYRANNICAL WAY	5	historical analogy criticizing Mao, political commentary	319–22
1 Mar. 1962	Three Kinds of Zhuge Liang	5	historical analogy criticizing Mao, political commentary	315–18
4 Mar. 1962	A Few Points on Calligraphy	1	art, study habits, calligraphy	375–9
8 Mar. 1962	Selecting Models and Diligent Practice	1	art, children's education, calligraphy	379–83
10 Mar. 1962	By the Rules and Not	1	Calligraphy; aesthetics, classical examples of; artistic freedom	SJC: 35–7
11 Mar. 1962	Handshake and Double-Hand Salute	1	Public education, customs	327–30
15 Mar. 1962	Does Creative Work Need Inspiration?	5	literature and art theory, Materialist v. Idealist approaches	387–90
18 Mar. 1962	Keep Raising Silkworms	1	agriculture, natural history, trivia	355–8
22 Mar. 1962	Start Writing in a Tracing Book	1	art, children's education, calligraphy	383–6
25 Mar. 1962	Is This a Good Phenomenon?	1	public education, bookshops	391–3
	A Word from the Author	1	preface to vol. 3, how *Evening Chats* is written	201–2
29 Mar. 1962	In Defence of Li Sancai	4	historical figures, local history, Beijing, historical	

Appendix

Date	Title	Pol.	Topic	1979
			analysis, model intellectual	
1 Apr. 1962	Stuttering, Runny Eyes, and such	1	public education, school texts, manners	335–8
5 Apr. 1962	Subjectivity and Modesty	4	ideology, caution, Party work	311–14
8 Apr. 1962	To Change or Not to Change	2	art theory, painting, academics, public education	394–6
12 Apr. 1962	The Soybean is a Treasure	1	agriculture, natural history, national pride	351–4
15 Apr. 1962	Underground and Surface Water	1	agriculture, water conservancy, public education	347–50
19 Apr. 1962	'Posture' is Important in Reading, too	1	youth, reading habits, education	405–8
22 Apr. 1962	Learn from Xu Guangqi	3	agriculture, model intellectual, history	339–42
25 Apr. 1962	Study Needs Guidance	2	education, science	SJC: 44–5
26 Apr. 1962	After Finding a 'Fire Well'	1	agriculture, natural science	367–70
29 Apr. 1962	Interesting News about Rain	1	agriculture, history of science in China, meteorology	363–6
3 May 1962	Viewpoint and Materials	4	collective writing, analytical methods, political work	409–12
6 May 1962	The Lessons of Reclaimed Land	3	agriculture, proper experimental method	343–6
10 May 1962	If You Have a Book Read it Right Away	1	youth, reading habits, academics, education	397–400
13 May 1962	Life and Humour	1	Sino–foreign comparison, social habits, on, humour and satire	498–500
17 May 1962	Don't Use Numbers Indiscriminately	1	public education, customs	331–4
20 May 1962	'Half an Analects'	5	political study, dangers of vulgarization of classics by Marx, Mao	401–4
24 May 1962	Is Knowledge Edible?	3	ideology, science, anti-bourgeois	421–4
27 May 1962	Ode to Bees and Raising Bees	1	agriculture, poetry	359–62
31 May 1962	Unlimited Length Essays	2	writing, prose style, advice to cadres	413–16

Date	Title	Pol.	Topic	1979
3 June 1962	Compile a 'Tricks of the Trade' Collectanea	1	popular culture and history, public education, techniques and technology	417–20
7 June 1962	Can an Eggplant Become a Tree?	1	natural history, trivia	371–4
10 June 1962	Learning Cannot Exaggerate	5	youth, intellectuals, ideology, *shishi qiushi*, anti-radical	435–7
10 June 1962	Civilian and Martial Clowns	1	theatre, stage, Beijing Opera characters, clowns; training of actors	SJC: 52–4
14 June 1962	Can Eagles Represent Heroes?	1	art, history of symbols, reinterpretation	470–3
17 June 1962	Zhaojun without Resentment	2	Sino–Mongolian relations, interracial marriage, historical figure reassessed	530–4
21 June 1962	An Investigation of 'Roast'	2	language reform, etymology, Qi Baishi as a model, local history of Beijing	458–61
24 June 1962	Jiang Gaisi [Chiang Kai-shek] Destined to Die	3	attack on Chiang Kai-shek, evils of KMT rule in Taiwan, American imperialism	1963*a*: 454–7
28 June 1962	Educational Methods of 'Opera School'	1	education, teaching methods, opera	
1 July 1962	A Piece of Tile	1	historical analysis, trivia	446–9
5 July 1962	Be the Best in Whatever Occupation	3	youth, education, rustication policy	442–5
8 July 1962	Private Study and Family Traditions	1	education, youth, family	438–41
12 July 1962	Be Discriminate with Historical Sites	1	historical methodology, national history, caution	519–22
15 July 1962	Plain Boiled Water is the Best to Drink	1	water, public health, trivia	486–9
19 July 1962	On Raising Dogs	1	pets, public attitudes on	474–7
22 July 1962	Raising Cats to Catch Mice	1	pets, public attitudes on	478–81
25 July 1962	Special Cure for 'Amnesia'	5	political cautionary tale, satire of 'forgetfulness', likely lampoons of Mao	SJC: 60–2

Date	Title	Pol.	Topic	1979
26 July 1962	One Stream in Ten Days, One Stone in Five	3	youth, art theory and work, manual labour	462–5
29 July 1962	An Ink Lotus	1	painting, flowers, Lu Chishui [Kang Sheng], Qi Baishi, social significance of painting	1963a: 501–4
2 Aug. 1962	Is He Mocking You?	4	defence of satire, public commentary defended, on Hua Junwu's cartoons	
3 Aug. 1962	A Note after Editing	4	preface to vol. 4	305–6
5 Aug. 1962	Taking Up from Zhang Fei's [Zhang Yide's] Calligraphy and Painting	1	art history, forgeries, verification, Yue Fei	466–9
9 Aug. 1962	Who was the Earliest to Study Scientific Theory	1	science: history of, Chinese and foreign, nuclear energy, national pride, youth	430–4
12 Aug. 1962	A Few Points on Teaching	1	education, teaching methods, universities	450–3
16 Aug. 1962	The Wonders of Long Hair	1	hair, popular science, health	490–3
19 Aug. 1962	The Uses of the Paper Mulberry Tree	1	agriculture, forestry, medicine	482–5
23 Aug. 1962	Why do we Quarrel?	2	social problems, public manners	494–7
26 Aug. 1962	The Death of Lin Baishui	2	journalism, historical figures, nationalist hero, Fujian native	526–9
30 Aug. 1962	Knight behind Castle [Belated Action]	1	language, etymology, chess	505–8
2 Sept. 1962	Thirty-Six Strategems	2	book review, textual criticism of ancient text, moral lessons	509–12
10 Sept. 1962	Use Your Head	3	advice to students, youth, study methods, proper ideology/thinking, *sixiang*	SJC: 69–71
15 Oct. 1962	Blood in the Skies of Yanshan	1	CCP history, reminiscence of Jin Cha Ji, biography	535–9
Mid-Oct. 1962	FOR THE READER'S INFORMATION	1	preface to vol. 5, reasons for stopping series	427–9

Appendix

Date	Title	Pol.	Topic	1979
25 Oct. 1962	Vegetarian Pork	1	mushrooms, lore and trivia of, nutrition, science	SJC: 75–6
10 Mar. 1963	Are these Characters Simplified or Miswritten?	1	'spelling', language reform, proper writing	SJC: 101–2
15 Mar. 1963	AUTHOR'S PREFACE	1	introduction to combined volume	front page
25 Apr. 1963	Is Seeing the Doctor Uneconomical?	1	public health, public education, economization	SJC: 111–13
10 June 1963	Pay Attention to the Experiences of the Masses	4	Socialist Education Movement, cadre education, *guwei jinyong* explained	SJC: 120–2
25 July 1963	Philosophy is Everywhere	4	Socialist Education Movement, dialectics in daily life, ideology, *sixiang*	SJC: 129–31
10 Sept. 1963	Up to the Mountains, Down to the Villages, Under the Water	3	youth; rustification movement, support	SJC: 138–40
10 Nov. 1963	Environment is Not the Problem	3	criticism of Western environmental determinism	SJC: 151–3
25 Dec. 1963	Send More Singing Materials to the Village	3	youth, rustification movement support, art, village culture	SJC: 160–2
10 Feb. 1964	The Load Can Be Shouldered	3	job allocation/*fenpei*, youth, succession issue	SJC: 171–3
25 Mar. 1964	What Kind of 'New' do you Want?	4	youth, education, arts policy	SJC: 180–2
25 June 1964	Advance in the Face of Adversity	3	Beijing Opera, CCP leadership	SJC: 198–200

Bibliography

I. Works by Deng Tuo
(by date with original pen–names)

Works published during Deng Tuo's lifetime:
1931 [Xiao Jing], 'Zi jin shan xia' (Beneath Violet Gold Mountain), *Nanhua ribao*, during spring 1931. (See Li Tuozhi 1979: 243, or YDT: 226.)
1933 [Deng Yunte], 'Xingshi luoji haishi weiwu bianzhengfa?' (Formal Logic or Dialectical Materialism?), *Xin Zhonghua*, I:23 (10 Dec.), 52–8.
1935a [Deng Junte, tr.], Ge–la–bu [Amadeus W. Grabau], 'Renlei shifo qiyuan yu yazhou?' (Did Humans Originate in Asia?), *Shishi leibian*, 3:10 (10 Jun.), 81–90. (Translation of Grabau's article in *Asia* [New York], 35:1.)
1935b [Deng Yunte], 'Zhongguo shehui jingji "changqi tingzhi" de kaocha' (A Study of the Protracted Stagnation of China's Social Economy), *Zhongshan wenhua jiaoyu guan jikan*, 2:4 (Oct.), 1111–29.
1936a [– –], 'Zhongguo lishishang shougongye fazhan de tezhi' (Characteristics of the Development of the Handicraft Industry in Chinese History), *Zhongshan wenhua jiaoyu guan jikan*, 3:2 (Apr.), 427–46.
1936b [– –], 'Lun Zhongguo fengjian zhidu de tingzhi wenti' (On the Question of the Stoppage in China's Feudal System), *Shidai luntan*, 1:8 (Jul.), 378–85.
1936c [– –], 'Zhongguo fengjian zhi tingzhi de lishi genyuan' (The Historical Roots of the Stoppage in China's Feudal System), *Shidai luntan*, 1:11 (1 Sept.), 535–9.
1937a [– –], 'Zhongguo jindai zibenzhuyi fazhan de guocheng ji qi texing' (The Process and Characteristics of the Development of China's Modern Capitalism), *Zhongshan wenhua jiaoyu guan jikan*, 4:1 (Jan.), 103–7.
1937b [– –], 'Zhongguo fengjian shehui qianqi nongye shengchan guanxi de fenzhi' (An Analysis of the Agricultural Production Relations in the Early Stages of Chinese Feudalism), *Zhongshan wenhua jiaoyu guan jikan*, 4:3 (Jul.), 993–1012.
1937c [– –], *Zhongguo jiuhuang shi* (A History of Famine Relief in China). Shanghai: Shangwu yinshu guan.
1938a [Yin Zhou], '*Kangdi bao* wushiqi de huigu yu zhanwang' (Review and Prospects of *Resistance News* Upon Its 50th Issue), *Kangdi bao*, 27 Jun., 1. (Reprinted in: *Xinwen shiliao*, 5: 8–9.)
1938b [unsigned], 'Lun dangbao he dangde gongzuo' (On Party Papers and Party Work), *Zhanxian*. (Unseen; cited in Wang Bisheng, 1983c: 60.)
1938c [– –], 'Weida haozhuang de qiqi jinian da zhandou' (The Grand and Heroic Great Struggle of July 7th Remembered), *Kangdi bao*, 7 Jul. (Unseen; cited in Wang Bisheng, 1983c: 60 and 1983e: 7.)

1938*d* [Wen Zhou], 'Zhanshi xuanchuan gudong gongzuo' (Propaganda and Agitation In a Time of War), *Kangdi waibao*. (Unseen; cited in Zuo Lu, 1984*b*: 30.)

1939*a* [Deng Yunte], *Shina kyuke shi* (A History of Famine Relief in China), trans. Kawasaki Masao. Tokyo: Seikatsu sha. (Translation of 1937*c*.)

1939*b* [pen–name unknown], 'Sanminzhuyi de xianshizhuyi yu wenyi chuangzuo zhu wenti' (The Realism of the Three People's Principles and Various Problems in Literary and Artistic Creation), *Bianqu wenhua*, 1. (Text of speech given by Deng Tuo on 26 Feb. 1939. Unseen; discussed in Wang Bisheng, 1983*b*.)

1939*c* [unsigned], 'KangRi juexin shabudiao' (The Spirit of Resisting Japan Cannot Be Burned), *Kangdi bao*, 13 Dec. (Unseen; cited in Zuo Lu, 1984*c*: 28.)

1940*a* [- -], 'Jinian Zhonggong weida dansheng de shijiu zhounian' (Commemorating the 19th Anniversary of the Great Birth of the Chinese Communist Party), *Kangdi bao*, 1 Jul. (Unseen; cited in Wang Bisheng, 1983*e*: 2–3.)

1940*b* [Wen Zhou], 'Yidang zhuanzheng haishi minzhu xianzheng?' (Single Party Dictatorship or a Democratic Constitution?), *Kangdi bao*, 6 Oct., 1.

1941 [Di Mangong], 'Weiwu bianzhengfa jianbian: 1. Lilun yu shijian de kaiduan' (A Short Course in Dialectical Materialism: 1. Beginning with Theory and Practice), *Jin Cha Ji ribao*, 2 Mar., 4. (The remaining seven parts appear on the same page periodically through 12 Jun. 1941. They are reprinted without bibliographic detail in DTWJ, I: 17–37.)

1942*a* [unsigned], 'Jinian qiyi, quan dang xuexi zhangwo Mao Zedongzhuyi' (Commemorating July 1st, The Whole Party Studies and Grasps Mao Zedong–ism), *Jin Cha Ji ribao*, 1 Jul., 1. (Unseen; cited in Wang Bisheng, 1983*e*: 5 and YDT: 32, 50–1.)

1942*b* [Xiao Si], 'Jin Cha Ji duoshi Nie Rongzhen—Dihou motan kangRi genjudi ji qi chuangzaozhe de shengping' (Jin Cha Ji's Helmsman Nie Rongzhen—A Model Anti-Japanese Base Area Behind the Lines and the Life of its Creator), *Jin Cha Ji huabao*, 1 (7 Jul.): 1–13. (Note: there is no pagination; the first page is counted here as 1. A highly edited version of this is reprinted in 1980*c*: 158–79.)

1944*a* [unsigned], 'Benbao liunian laide gongzuo de huigu he jiantao' (A Review and Self–Criticism of This Paper's Work Over the Past Six Years), *Jin Cha Ji ribao*, 1 Jan., 1. (Unseen; cited by Zuo Lu, 1984*c*: 3.)

1944*b* [- -], 'Bianzhe de hua' (A Word from the Editor), *Mao Zedong xuanji* (Selected Works of Mao Zedong). N.p.: Jin Cha Ji xinhua shudian: 1–3.

1946 [Deng Tuo], 'Gaizao women de tongxun yu baodao fangfa' (Reform our News and Reporting Methods), *Xinwen gongzuo zhinan* (Kalgan), 1: 49–56. (Published version of a May 1944 speech.)

1949 [- -], '*Zhongguo qingnian* he Hui Daiying' (*China Youth* and Hui Daiying), *Zhongguo qingnian*, 23: 7–8.

1950*a* [- -], 'Jiu Zhongguo nongcun de jieji guanxi yu tudi zhidu' (Village Class Relations and the Land System in Old China). (Lecture notes from Beijing University; selections printed in *Shehui kexue zhanxian*, 1982:3, 72–7.)

1950*b* [- -], 'Zhengfeng yundong zai guojia jianshe gongzuo zhongde zhongyaoxing' (The Importance of the Rectification Movement in the Work of National Construction), *Xuexi*, 2:11 (16 Aug.), 3–5. (Reprinted in a booklet with the same title in the series, *Xinhua huoye wenxuan* [Loose–Leaf Selections from New China], 16. N.p.: Xinhua shudian, Central–South Division.)

1950c [– –], 'Chedi pipan minglingzhuyi' (Thoroughly Criticize Fatalism), *Xuexi*, 3 (1 Oct.), 14–8. (Reprinted in 1951a: 38–51.)

1951a [Deng Tuo *et al.*], *He qingnian tuanyuanmen tantan qunzhong luxian wenti* (Discussions with Members of the Youth Corps on Mass Line Problems). Beijing: Qingnian chubanshe, 5th printing, Jan. 1952. (Title essay by DengTuo, 8–18.)

1951b [Deng Tuo], 'Guanyu dangde zhengzhi luxian he zuzhi luxian' (On the Party's PoliticalLine and Organizational Line), *Xuexi*, 3:11 (1 Feb.), 11–12, 26.

1951c [– –], 'Jiaqiang sixiang gongzuo, zhankai sixiang douzheng' (Strengthen Ideological Work, Open Ideological Struggle), *Xuexi*, 4:9 (16 Aug.), 16–19.

1951d [– –], 'Sixiang gaizao bixu shi zijuede yundong' (Thought Reform Should Be a Self–Consciousness Movement), *Xuexi*, 5: 4 (30 Dec.), 5–8.

1952 [– –], 'Wei xin shenghuo er douzheng de youli wuqi' (A PowerfulWeapon in the Struggle for the New Life), *Renmin ribao tongxun* (People's Daily Newsletter), 25 (16 Aug.). (Abstracted in Zhang Jinglu, 4: 126–9.)

1954 [– –], 'Zenyang gaijin baozhi gongzuo' (How to Advance Newspaper Work), *Zhongguo gongchandang xinwen gongzuo wenjian huibian*, 2: 323–44. (Reprinted in DTWJ, I: 285–302.)

1955a [– –], 'Lun *HongLou Meng* de shehui beijing he lishi yiyi' (On the Social Background and Historical Significance of the *Dream of the Red Chamber*), *Renmin ribao*, 9 Jan., 3. (Reprinted in *Hu Shi sixiang pipan ziliao jikan*, 1955: 349–55, *Zhongguo zibenzhuyi mengya wenti taolunji*, 1: 69–90, and in 1959j.)

1955b [– –], 'Guanyu baozhi shelun' (On Newspaper Editorials), in *Zhongguo baokan gongzuo wenji* (Collection of Articles on Chinese PressWork). Beijing: Renmin daxue xinwenxi (1964), 1: 329–47. (Reprinted in DTWJ, I: 308–30.)

1956a [– –], 'Fang "Putaochang"' (Interviewing "Putaochang"), *Renmin ribao*. (Reprinted in 1980c: 9–13.)

1956b [– –], 'Cong Wanli dao Qianlong—Guanyu Zhongguo zibenzhuyi mengya shiqide yige lunzheng' (From Wanli to Qianlong—A Demonstration of the Initial Stages of Chinese Capitalism), *Lishi yanjiu*, 10: 1–31. (Revised and republished in 1959j: 181–233 and in *Zhongguo zibenzhuyi mengya wenti taolunji*, Supplement, 1960.)

1957 [Bu Wuji], 'Feiqi "yongen zhengzhi"' (Discard "The Politics of Simpletons"), *Renmin ribao*, 11 May, 8. (Reprinted in 1980c: 152–4; translated in Cheek, 1983–4: 31–3.)

1958a [Deng Tuo], 'Yingxiong de lu—Bao–Cheng tielu zhengshi tongche yougan' (Hero's Road—Thoughts on Riding the Baoji–Chengdu Railroad), *Renmin ribao*, 17 Jan. (Reprinted in 1980c: 4–8.)

1958b [– –], 'Deng Tuo tongzhi de tici' (A Poem in Deng Tuo's Hand). (Written on Deng's visit to Zigong, Sichuan, 13 Jan. 1958. Photograph of original, transcription, and details in Dian Niu, 1982.)

1958c [Deng Tuo], 'Sixiang zuofeng de dayuejin' (A Great Leap Forward in Ideological Workstyle), *Renmin ribao*, 8 Feb., 4.

1958d [- -], 'Xinwen zhanxian shangde shehuizhuyi geming' (The Socialist Revolution on the News Front), *Xuexi*, 8: 2–17, 26. Subtitled: 'Zai Zhongyang zhishu jiguan julebu de baogao 1958.3.4' (Report to the Association of Organs Directly Under the Central Committee, 4 Mar. 1958). (Reprinted as a booklet with the same title, in the series, *Shehuizhuyi jiaoyu hui baogao*, No. 4. Beijing: Zhongguo qingnian chubanshe, 1958.)

1958e [Deng Yunte], *Zhongguo jiuhuang shi*. Beijing: Sanlian shudian. (Revised version of 1937c text in simplified characters.)

1958f [pen–name uncertain], 'Chencang dao shang' (On the Chencang [i.e., Baoji] Road), *Luxingjia*, 7. (Reprinted in 1980c: 18–21.)

1958g [- -], 'Lao huajia de xin chuangzuo' (New Creations From a Veteran Artist), *Meishu*, 7. (On the Shandong painter, Wang Youshi. Reprinted in 1980c: 14–17.)

1958h [Deng Tuo], 'Xinwen gongzuozhe hong–zhuan de daolu' (The Red–Expert Road of the Journalist), *Xinwen zhanxian*, 8 (25 Aug.): 2–7, 54.

1958i [- -, ed.], *Xinbian Tang shi sanbaishou* (Newly Edited Three Hundred Poems of the Tang). Beijing: Zhonghua shuju. (Two editions: one dated September 1958 with 90,000 words which does not have Deng's name on it and another dated December 1958 with 109,000 words which does. The introduction to the second volume, bearing Deng's name, is longer.)

1958j [- -], 'Cong Tiananmen dao quan Zhongguo' (From Tiananmen to All China), *Xin guancha*, 19. (Reprinted in 1980c: 1–3.)

1958k [Zuo Hai], [untitled poem accompanying a painting], *Renmin ribao*, 1 Sept., 8.

1958l [- -] [untitled poem accompanying a painting], *Renmin ribao*, 4 Sept., 8.

1958m [- -], [untitled poem accompanying a drawing], *Renmin ribao*, 10 Sept., 8.

1958n [- -], [untitled poem accompanying a painting], *Renmin ribao*, 27 Sept., 8.

1958o [- -], [untitled poem accompanying a painting], *Renmin ribao*, 6 Nov., 8. (In praise of the People's Communes.)

1959a [Deng Tuo], 'Qingchun ze—Yingjie 1959 nian yuandan' (In Celebration of the Beneficence of Spring—Greeting New Year's Day 1959), *Renmin ribao*, 1 Jan., 8.

1959b [- -], 'Ren yue yuan' (Man Moon Garden), *Renmin ribao*, 4 Jan., 8.

1959c [- -], '"Liangtiao tui zoulu" de lilun yiyi' (The Theoretical Significance of "Walking on Two Legs"), *Xin jianshe*, 3 (7 Mar.): 1–3.

1959d [- -], 'Cheng Yanqiu tongzhi shishi zhounian jinian yanchu guan hou' (After Seeing the Memorial Performance Commemorating the Anniversary of Comrade Cheng Yanqiu's Death), *Renmin ribao*, 15 Mar., 8.

1959e [Dan Wenshang], 'Tan "Jiang cai"' (On "Talent as a Field Commander"), *Renmin ribao*, 9 Apr. (Reprinted in 1980c: 155–7 and DTWJ, III: 528–30.)

1959f [Deng Tuo], 'Makesizhuyi zhexue he xinwen gongzuo' (Marxist Philosophy and Journalism), *Xinwen zhanxian*, 9 (25 May): 1–10.

1959g [pen–name uncertain], 'Ertong hua de fengge' (The Style of Children's Paintings), *Renmin ribao*, Jun. (Reprinted in 1980c: 22–5.)

1959h [Deng Tuo], 'Jin yibu jiaqiang he gonggu gongnong lianmeng' (Advance a Step in Strengthening and Stabilizing the Worker–Peasant Alliance), *Hongqi*, 12 (16 Jun.): 30–

7. (Translated in JPRS–D, Readex Card: 1959–1480. The translated text misprints his name as 'Teng Chih'.)

1959*i* [pen–name uncertain], 'Tantan Zhou Wenju de "Taizhen shang ma tu"' (Talking About Zhou Wenju's "Taizhen shang ma tu"), *Zhongguo huabao*, 9. (Zhou's painting is reproduced in the original journal. Reprinted in 1980*c*: 26–32.)

1959*j* [Deng Tuo], *Lun Zhongguo lishi de jige wenti* (A Few Questions in Chinese History). Beijing: Sanlian shudian, Nov. 1959, Feb. 1963, and expanded edition with an extra essay, Apr. 1979. (The 1959 version of this book has been included in DTWJ, 2: 365–596.)

1960*a* [pen–name uncertain], 'Xinnian tan Yang Liuqing nianhua' (New Year's Chat on Yang Liuqing's New Year's Painting), *Guangming ribao*, Jan. (Reprinted in 1980*c*: 33–6.)

1960*b* [Deng Tuo], 'Nongye shi woguo guomin jingji fazhan de jichu' (Agriculture is the Foundation for Our Country's National Economic Development), *Xin jianshe*, 137 (7 Feb.): 1–5. (Translated in SCMM, 206: 8–14.)

1960*c* [unsigned], 'Shangye he fuwuye yuejin zhi hua' (The Flowering of the Leap Forward in Commerce and Service Industries), *Qianxian*, 4 (25 Feb.): 1–2.

1960*d* [– –], 'Bixu jingchang gua sixiang gongzuo' (The Necessity to Grasp Regularly Ideological Work), *Qianxian*, 13 (10 Jul.): 1–2.

1960*e* [Deng Tuo], 'Zai nongye shengchan diyi xian shang guanche shixian Mao Zedong sixiang' (Carry Out the Realization of Mao Zedong Thought on the Front Line of Agricultural Production), *Renmin ribao*, 24 Oct., 7. (Also *Qianxian*, 20 [25 Oct.]: 3–10.)

1960*f* [unsigned], 'Jiangjiu zhengquede gongzuo fangfa he gongzuo zuofeng' [Stress correct work methods and correct work style], *Qianxian*, 24 (25 Dec.): 1–3.

1961*a* [pen–name uncertain], 'Jianshang Xin Luoshan ren zuopin de ganshou' (An Appreciation of Xin Luoshan's Works), *Meishu*, 1 (Jan.). (Reprinted in 1980*c*:46–52. Second article on this early Qing painter, also named Hua Yan, is 1961*e*.)

1961*b* [Deng Tuo], 'Mao Zedong sixiang kaipile Zhongguo lishi kexue fazhan de daolu' (The Thought of Mao Zedong Has Opened the Way for the Development of China's Science of History),*Lishi yanjiu*, 1: 1–12. Subtitled: 'Gei Beijing shi lishi xuehui huiyuan de baogao' (Report Given to the Members of the Beijing Municipal Historical Society). (Reprinted in 1979*d*: 1–18. Translated in SCMM, 264: 1–13.)

1961*c* [pen–name uncertain], 'Jinian woguo gudai shi da huajia' (Commemorating Ten of Our Nation's Great Ancient Painters), *Renmin ribao*. (Reprinted in 1980*c*:37–9.)

1961*d* [Zuo Hai], 'Ni kan shanshui fengjing meibumei?' (Do You Think the Natural Scenery is Pretty or Not?), *Qianxian*, 6: 12–13. (Reprinted in 1980*c*: 40–3, which cites *Guangming ribao*, Apr. 1961.)

1961*e* [pen–name uncertain], 'Xin Luoshan ren de hua' (The Paintings of Xin Luoshan), *Meishu*, 4 (Reprinted in 1980*c*: 44–5.)

1961*f* [Deng Tuo], 'Gei biye tongxue de yidian zengyan' (A Few Words of Advice to Senior Middle School Graduates), *Zhongguo qingnian*, 9: 5–6 (Translated in SCMM, 264: 21–3.)

1961g [pen–name uncertain], 'Zhongguo gudai huihua de guanghui yishu chengjiu' (The Radiant Artistic Accomplishments of China's Ancient Painters), *Zhongguo huabao*, 6. (Reprinted in 1980c: 53–7.)

1961h [Zuo Hai], 'Xiao qi' (A Rest), *Qianxian*, 17: back cover. (Poem by Zuo Hai; matching painting by Shao Yusu.)

1961i [– –], 'Xiu pu hong' (Xiu pu hong), *Qianxian*, 22: back cover. (Poem by Zuo Hai; matching painting by Huang Zhou.)

1962–4 [pen–names uncertain], several articles on art and art history. (Reprinted in 1980c: 74–140 and 1969a: 223–63.)

1962a [unsigned], 'Lilun zhanxian shangde zhongyao renwu' (Important Tasks on the Ideological Front), *Qianxian*, 4: 1.

1962b [pen–name uncertain], 'Yige faxiande shenhua shijie—Guilin Ludiyan canguan ji' (A Mythical World Discovered—Record of a Visit to Guilin's Reed Flute Grotto), *Renmin ribao*. (Reprinted in 1980c: 58–64.)

1962c [Zuo Hai], 'Su Dongbo "Xiao–Xiang zhu shi tu tiba"' (Su Dongbo's Annotations on "Bamboo and Rocks of the Xiao and Xiang Rivers"), *Renmin huabao*, 6: 22–3, plus color foldout. (Reprinted in 1980c: 65–9 without painting and with first paragraph expanded.)

1963a [Ma Nancun], *Yanshan yehua (heji)* (Evening Chats at Yanshan [Collected Volume]). Beijing: Beijing chubanshe. (Revised and reprinted as 1979a.) (Detailed listing of the 153 articles from *Beijing wanbao* between 19 Mar. 1961 and 2 Sept. 1962 and the six related prefaces for this newspaper column given in Appendix I.)

1963b [Tso Hai], 'Huang Chou's "Gathering Water Chestnuts"', *Chinese Literature*, 8: 106–12.

1963c [– –], 'Chou Hsun's "Waiting for a Ferry"', *Chinese Literature*, 9: 101–4.

1963d [Zuo Hai], 'Cao Xueqin he "Hong Lou Meng"' (Cao Xueqin and the *Dream of the Red Chamber*), *Renmin huabao*, 10. (Reprinted in 1980c: 101–6.)

1963e [Deng Tuo], 'Zheng Banqiao he "Banqiao ti"' (Zheng Banqiao and the "Banqiao Style"), *Guangming ribao*, 21 Nov. (Reprinted in 1980c: 107–12 and 1969a: 245–50.)

1964a [Tso Hai], 'Ladies on a Spring Outing', *Chinese Literature*, 1: 119-23.

1964b [– –], 'Chinese Painting and Calligraphy', *Chinese Literature*, 3: 89–98.

1964c [Zuo Hai], 'Zhongguo shanshui hua chuang xinde daolu' (Chinese Landscape Painting Creates a New Road), *Qianxian*, 7: 9–11.

1966a [pen–name uncertain], 'Wu Zuoren de yishu shengya' (The Artistic Life of Wu Zuoren). (Unpublished manuscript, 1966; reprinted in 1980c: 141–9.)

Posthumous publications & collections of Deng Tuo's works:

1966b, *Deng Tuo shiwen xuan* (Selected Poetry and Prose of Deng Tuo). Hong Kong: Zunzheng yinshu guan.

1966c, To Taku, De Gan, Ryo Umatsusa, *Enzan yawa: fu—Sankason sakki* (Evening Chats at Yanshan: Appendix—Notes From a Three Family Village). Tokyo: Mainichi shinbunsha. (Revised edition, Sept. 1979.)

1967, Cartier, Michel (tr. and ed. with introductory remarks), 'En Chine du XVIe au XVIIIe siècle: Les Mines de Charbon de Men–t'ou–k'o' (by Teng T'o), *Annales: economies, societies, civilizations*, 22:1, 50–87. (Translation of 1956b.)

1969a, Ding Wang (ed.), *Deng Tuo xuanji* (Selected Works of Deng Tuo). Vol. 2 of Ding Wang (1969).

1969b, Glaubitz, Joachim (ed.), *Opposition gegen Mao: Abendgespräche am Yenshan und andere politische Dokumente*. Freiburg: Breisgau. (Translation into German of essays from *Evening Chats* and *Three Family Village* by Deng Tuo, and other essays.)

1979a [Ma Nancun], *Yanshan yehua (heji)*. Beijing: Beijing chubanshe. (Revised reprint of 1963a.)

1979b [Wu Nanxing], *Sanjiacun zhaji* (Notes From a Three Family Village). Beijing: Renmin wenxue chubanshe. (First publication in book form of the 1961–4 column. Wu Nanxing is the joint pen–name for Deng Tuo, Wu Han, and Liao Mosha. Individual essay authors identified in table of contents.)

1979c, *Deng Tuo shici xuan* (Selected Poetry of Deng Tuo). Beijing: Renmin wenxue chubanshe.

1979d [Deng Tuo], *Lun Zhongguo lishi de jige wenti* (A Few Questions in Chinese History). Beijing: Sanlian shudian. (Reprint of 1959j with additional essays.)

1980a, *Deng Tuo shufa xuan* (Selected Calligraphy of Deng Tuo). Beijing: Renmin meishu chubanshe.

1980b, Deng Tuo and Liu Yongcheng, 'Chongwenmenwai Wanquan Tang yaopu ziliao jilu' (A Compilation of Materials on the Wanquan Tang Medicine Shop at Chongwenmenwai [Beijing]), *Qingshi ziliao*, I: 158–77. (Deng's research materials compiled and introduced by his former student, Liu.)

1980c, *Deng Tuo sanwen* (Lyrical Essays by Deng Tuo). Beijing: Renmin ribao chubanshe.

1981, Deng Tuo and Liu Yongcheng, '"Liu Bi Ju" de cailiao zhengmingle shenmo?' (What Do the Materials on 'Liu Bi Ju' Demonstrate?), *Zhongguo gudai shi luncong* (Fujian), 2: 11–29. (Deng's research materials compiled and introduced by his former student, Liu.)

1982, Deng Tuo (posthumous), 'Jiu Zhongguo nongcun de jieji guanxi yu tudi zhidu' (Village Class Relations and the Land System in Old China), *Shehui kexue zhanxian*, 3: 72–7.

1983, Liu Yongcheng and He Zhiqing, 'Wanquan Tang de youlai yu fazhan' (The Origins and Development of Wanquan Tang), *Zhongguo shehui jingji shi yanjiu*, 1: 1–16. (Article by Deng's former student, Liu, based on Deng's collection of documents.)

1983–4, Cheek, Timothy, 'The Politics of Cultural Reform: Deng Tuo and the Retooling of Chinese Marxism', *Chinese Law and Government*, 16:4 (Winter 1983–84). (Translations from *Evening Chats* and other essays by Deng Tuo and related material.)

1983–6, *Deng Tuo wenji* (Deng Tuo's Works). Beijing: Beijing chubanshe, 4 vols.

1984, *Deng Tuo zanghua xuanji* (Selected Paintings from the Collection of Deng Tuo). N.p.: n. p., preface dated 27 Jun. (Given to me by Ding Yilan in May 1986; a partial reproduction, some plates in color, of Deng Tuo's art collection which was exhibited in Beijing in Dec. 1981.)

1986a, *Deng Tuo shi wenxuan* (Selected Poetry and Prose of Deng Tuo). Beijing: Renmin ribao chubanshe.

1986b, *Deng Tuo shici moji* (Deng Tuo's Poetry in His Own Hand). Beijing: Rongbaozhai. (A packet of 12 photolithographic reproductions of Deng's calligraphy; preface notes by Ding Yilan dated Spring 1986.)

1988, Ding Yilan (ed.), *Deng Tuo shici moji xuan* (Selection of Deng Tuo's Poetry in His Own Hand). Fuzhou: Fujian renmin chubanshe.

1993, Ding Yilan (ed.) and Cheng Mei (annotations), *Deng Tuo shi ji* (Poems of Deng Tuo). Beijing: Zhongguo shehui kexue chubanshe.

1996, Wang Bisheng (ed.), *Deng Tuo sanwen xuanji* (Selected Lyric Essays by Deng Tuo). Tianjin: Baihua wenyi chubanshe.

II. Books and Articles

Ahn, Byung-joon (1973), 'Adjustments in the Great Leap Forward and Their Ideological Legacy, 1959–62', in Johnson (1973: 257–300).

— — (1976), *Chinese Politics and the Cultural Revolution*. Seattle: University of Washington Press.

Alitto, Guy S. (1979), *The Last Confucian: Liang Shu–ming and the Chinese Dilemma of Modernity*. Berkeley: University of California Press.

Ansley, Clive (1971), *The Heresy of Wu Han: His Play 'Hai Jui's Dismissal' and Its Role in China's Cultural Revolution*. Toronto: University of Toronto Press.

Apter, David, and Cheek, Timothy (1994), 'The Trial', in Dai Qing (1994: xvii–xxxi).

Apter, David, and Saich, Tony (1994), *Revolutionary Discourse in Mao's Republic*. Cambridge: Harvard University Press.

'Art Collection by Deng Tuo Exhibited to Mark his Death', *China Daily*, 6 Jan. (1982), 5.

Averill, Steven (1991), 'Moral Economy and the Chinese Revolution', *Peasant Studies*, 18:2, 65–96.

Bao Ji (ed.) (1981), *Xiandai sanwen baibian changzhe* (A Hundred Modern Essays with Commentary). Tianjin: Renmin chubanshe.

Barnett, A. Doak (1964), *Communist China: The Early Years, 1949–55*. New York: Praeger.

Bartke, Wolfgang (1981), *Who's Who in the People's Republic of China*. Armonk, NY: M.E. Sharpe.

'Before and After the Chang Guan Lou Counter–Revolutionary Incident' (Apr. 1967), trans. in SCMM, 640: 23–7.

'Beijing shiwei jueding wei "Sanjiacun" yuan'an chedi pingfan' (The Beijing Municipal Party Committee Decides to Reverse Completely the Unjust Case of 'The Three Family Village'), *Renmin ribao*, 3 Aug. 1979, 1.

Beijing tushuguan guanzang geming lishi wenxian jianmu (A Brief Catalogue of Documentary Holdings in the Beijing Library of Revolutionary History). Beijing: Shumu wenxian chubanshe, 1984.

Bi Sheng: pen-name for Wang Bisheng.

Birch, Cyril (1960), 'Fiction of the Yenan Period', *The China Quarterly*, No. 4: 1–11.

Bo Sheng (1981), 'Xie zai juanpa shangde shi' (A Poem Written on a Silk Handkerchief), *Xin guancha*, 6: 22–3.

Bol, Peter (1992), *'This Culture of Ours': Intellectual Transitions in T'ang and Sung China*. Stanford: Stanford University Press.

Brook, Timothy (ed.) (1989), *The Asiatic Mode of Production in China*. Armonk, NY: M.E. Sharpe.

– – (1993), *Praying for Power: Buddhism in the Formation of Gentry Society in Late-Ming China*. Cambridge: Harvard Council on East Asian Studies.

– – (forthcoming), 'Capitalism and the Writing of Modern History in China', in Immanuel Wallerstein *et al.* (eds.), *China and Capitalism: Geneologies of Historical Knowledge*.

Brugger, Bill, and Kelly, David (1990), *Chinese Marxism in the Post-Mao Era*. Stanford: Stanford University Press.

Byron, John, and Pack, Robert (1992), *The Claws of the Dragon: Kang Sheng, The Evil Genius Behind Mao and His Legacy of Terror in People's China*. New York: Simon and Schuster.

Carry the Great Revolution on the Journalistic Front Through to the End. Peking: Foreign Languages Press, 1969.

Cartier, Michel (tr. and ed. with introductory remarks) (1967), 'En Chine du XVIe au XVIIIe siècle: Les Mines de Charbon de Men–t'ou–k'o' (by Teng T'o), *Annales: economies, societies, civilizations*, 22:1, 50–87. (Translation of Deng Tuo, 1956*b*.)

CCRM: Center for Chinese Research Materials. See 'Mao zhu weikan gao–*Mao Zedong sixiang wansui bieji ji qita*' (1988), below.

Chai Fei, and Li Jingmin (1981), 'Fang Deng Tuo furen Ding Yilan' (Interview with Deng Tuo's Wife, Ding Yilan), *Changcheng wenyi*, 6: 32–4.

Chamberlin, William Henry (1973), *The Russian Revolution* (original edition 1935). New York: Grosset & Dunlap.

Chan, Anita, Madsen, Richard, and Unger, Jonathan (1984), *Chen Village: The Recent History of a Peasant Community in Mao's China*. Berkeley: University of California Press.

Chan, Wing-tsit (trans. and ed.) (1963), *Instructions for Practical Living, and other Neo-Confucian Writing by Wang Yang-ming*. New York: Columbia University Press.

Chang duan lu (The Long and the Short). Beijing: Renmin ribao chubanshe, 1980.

'Chang Guan Lou fangeming shijian de qianqian houhou' (Before and After the Counter-Revolutionary Chang Guan Lou Incident), *Dongfang hong* [Beijing Mining Institute], 20 Apr. 1967. (Reprinted in Ding Wang, 1969: 548–66; translated as part of 'Counter-Revolutionary Revisionist P'eng Chen's Towering Crimes', in SCMM, 640.]

Chang, Julian (1997), 'The Mechanics of State Propaganda: The People's Republic of China and the Soviet Union in the 1950s', in Cheek and Saich (1997: 76–124).

Chang Shuhong (1980), 'Huainian Deng Tuo tongzhi' (Mourning Comrade Deng Tuo), YDT: 168–72.

Chao Xun (1980), '"Xi Weng" Cao Yu moji buji' (Supplementary Notes on "Xi Weng" in Cao Yu's Hand), *Guangming ribao*, 24 Feb. (Discussion of a painting in Deng Tuo's art collection. See Jing Dang, 3 Feb., also in the 'Dong Feng' or 'East Wind' column, for more on this.)

Cheek, Timothy (1981), 'Deng Tuo: Culture, Leninism and Alternative Marxism in the Chinese Communist Party', *The China Quarterly*, No. 87: 470–91.

– – (1984*a*), 'Contracts and Ideological Control in Village Administration: Tensions within the "Village Covenant" System in Late Imperial China', paper delivered at the 36th Annual Meeting of the Association for Asian Studies, Washington, DC.

– – (1984*b*), 'The Fading of Wild Lilies: Wang Shiwei and Mao Zedong's *Yan'an Talks* in the First CPC Rectification Movement', *The Australian Journal of Chinese Affairs*, No. 11: 25–58.

– – (1983–4), 'The Politics of Cultural Reform: Deng Tuo and the Retooling of Chinese Marxism—Editor's Introduction', *Chinese Law and Government*, 16:4 (Winter 1983–4), 3–30.

– – (1986), 'Orthodoxy and Dissent in People's China: The Life and Death of Deng Tuo (1912–1966)'. Harvard, Ph.d. thesis.

– – (1989*a*), 'Redefining Propaganda: Debates on the Role of Journalism in Post Mao China', *Issues and Studies*, 25:2, 25–50.

– – (1989*b*), 'Textually Speaking: An Assessment of Newly Available Mao Texts', in MacFarquhar, Cheek, and Wu (1989: 75–103).

– – (1990), 'Studying Deng Tuo: The Academic Politician', *Republican China*, 15:2, 1–15.

– – (1992), 'From Priests to Professionals: Intellectuals and the State under the CCP', in Wasserstrom and Perry (1992: 124–45).

– – (forthcoming), 'From Markets to Democracy in China: Gaps in the Civil Society Model', in Lindau and Cheek (forthcoming).

– –, and Hamrin, Carol Lee (1986), 'Introduction: Collaboration and Conflict in the Search for a New Order', in Hamrin and Cheek (1986: 3–20).

– –, and Saich, Tony (eds.) (1997), *New Perspectives on State Socialism in China*. Armonk, NY: M.E. Sharpe.

Chen Boda (1953), *Speech Before the Study Group of Research Members of Academia Sinica*. Peking: Foreign Languages Press.

Chen Chunsen (1980), 'Maozhen shizai xie zongheng' (Writing with Ease for Ten Years), YDT: 29–36.

Chen Haiyun, and Sima Weizhi (1986), 'Liao Mosha de fengyu suiyue' (Liao Mosha's Years of Tribulation), *Xin wenxue shiliao*, 1.

Chen Haosu (1980), 'Jiang Qing de chou'e biaoyan' (Jiang Qing's Disgusting Performance), *Renmin ribao*, 23 Dec.

Ch'en, Jerome (1969), 'Resolutions of the Tsunyi Conference', *The China Quarterly*, No. 40: 1–38.

Chen Kehan (1939), *KangRi mofan genjudi–Jin Cha Ji bianqu* (A Model Anti–Japanese Base Area:The Jin Cha Ji Border Region). Chongqing: Xinhua ribao she.

– –, and Li Jun (1979), 'Zhandou zai sixiang lilun zhanxian de zui qianxian—Dao Deng Tuo tongzhi' (Battling at the Front Line of Ideology and Theory—Mourning Comrade Deng Tuo), *Renmin ribao*, 6 Aug., 3, and YDT: 8–16. (Excerpts translated in FBIS–CHI, 15 Aug. 1979, L22–L26.)

Chen Qiao, and Shi Shuqing (1980), 'Deng Tuo tongzhi he Zhongguo lishi bowuguan' (Comrade Deng Tuo and the National History Museum), YDT: 164–7.

Chen Qingchuan *et al.* (eds.) (1985), *Zhongguo shixuejia pingzhuan* (Evaluative Biographies of Chinese Historians). Kaifeng: Zhongzhou guji chubanshe.

Chen Wenyuan (1981), 'Shouci tichu Mao Zedong sixiang de shijian gaiwei 1943 nian' (The First Use of Mao Zedong Thought Was In 1943), *Hongqi*, 8: inside back cover.

Chen Xiaoyu (1955), 'Guangyu xiaopin wen' (On Small Essays), in Ma Tieding (1955*b*: 50-66).

Chen Yung-fa (1991), *Yan'an zhi yin* (Yan'an's Shadow). Taipei: Academia Sinica, Institute for Modern History.

– – (1996), 'Suspecting History and the Mass Line: Another "Yan'an Way"', in Hershatter, Honig, Lipman, and Stross (1996: 242-57).

Chen Zongshun (1981), 'Hong mei qing' (Feelings on Red Plum), *Nanjing ribao*, 20 Mar. (On poetry–painting collaboration between Deng Tuo and Zhou Huaimin.)

Cheng Mei, and Gu Xing (1980), 'He renmin tong xiuqi, gong mingyun—Cong *Yanshan yehua* xuexi Deng Tuo tongzhi de banbao sixiang' (Sharing Weal and Woe, A Common Destiny, With the People—Study Comrade Deng Tuo's Thoughts on Running Newspapers from his *Evening Chats at Yanshan*), *Tianjin ribao tongxun*, 12: 10–25.

Chi, Wen-shun (1965), 'Water Conservancy in Communist China', *The China Quarterly*, No. 23: 37–54.

Chronology: see *Jin Cha Ji ribao dashiji* (Chronology of *Jin Cha Ji Daily*).

Chu, Pao-liang (1989), *Twentieth Century Writers and Their Pen Names*. Taipei: Han-hsüeh yen-chiu chung-hsin, rev. edn., 2 vols.

Chuang, H.C. (1967), 'The Great Proletarian Cultural Revolution—A Terminological Study', *Studies in Chinese Communist Terminology*, No. 12. Berkeley: University of California, Center for Chinese Studies.

– – (1970), '*Evening Chats at Yenshan*, or the Case of Teng T'o', *Studies in Chinese Communist Terminology*, No. 14. Berkeley: University of California, Center for Chinese Studies.

Clunas, Craig (1991), *Superfluous Things: Material Culture and Social Status in Early Modern China*. Urbana, Ill.: University of Illinois Press.

Coble, Parks (1991), *Facing Japan: Chinese Politics and Japanese Imperialism, 1931–1937*. Cambridge: Harvard Council on East Asian Studies.

Cohen, Paul A. (1974), *Between Tradition and Modernity: Wang T'ao and Reform in Late Ch'ing China*. Cambridge: Harvard University Press.

– – (1984), *Discovering History in China: American Historical Writing on the Recent Chinese Past*. New York: Columbia University Press.

– – (1992), 'The Contested Past: The Boxers as History and Myth', *Journal of Asian Studies*, 51: 82-113.
Compton, Boyd (1952), *Mao's China: Party Reform Documents 1942–44*. Seattle: University of Washington Press.
Conner, Walter D. (1972), 'The Manufacture of Deviance: The Case of the Soviet Purge, 1936–1938', *American Sociological Review*, 37: 403–13.
'Counter–Revolutionary Revisionist P'eng Chen's Towering Crimes of Opposing the Party, Socialism, and the Thought of Mao Zedong', published by the Liaison Center for Thorough Criticism of Liu–Teng–T'ao, Tungfang Commune, translated in SCMM. 639 and 640 (1969).
Dai, Qing (1994), *Wang Shiwei and 'Wild Lilies': Rectification and Purges in the Chinese Communist Party, 1942–1944*. Armonk, NY: M.E. Sharpe.
Daonian Deng Tuo tongzhi (Mourning Comrade Deng Tuo). Beijing: no publication data. (A list of contributors on p. 8 dated Oct. 1979. This is the booklet from the funeral on 5 Sept. 1979.)
deBary, Wm. Theodore, (comp.) (1960), *Sources of Chinese Tradition*. New York: Columbia University Press.
Deng Guozhi (1980), 'Deng Tuo de shufa' (Deng Tuo's Calligraphy), YDT: 201–2.
– – (1982), 'Zai Zhongguo meishuguan kan "Deng Tuo zanghua, shufa zhan"' (Viewing "Deng Tuo's Collection of Paintings and Calligraphy" at the National Gallery of Art), *Wenhui bao* (Hong Kong), 19 Jan.
Deng Hua (1980), 'Huainian Tuo shu' (Mourning Uncle Tuo), YDT: 247–52.
Deng Tuo, works by: see Bibliography, part I.
'Deng Tuo he *Renmin ribao*' (Deng Tuo and *People's Daily*), by 'a *People's Daily* reporter' (1980), in YDT: 89–100, and Deng Tuo (1980c: 188–92).
[Deng Tuo] (1981), Notice on Exhibition of Deng Tuo's Art Collection, opening 20 Dec. 1981, Xinhua News Release, 20 Dec. and *Beijing wanbao*, 19 Dec.
'Deng Tuo shufa' (Deng Tuo's Calligraphy), *Xinwen zhanxian* (1982) 2: photo and note on inside cover.
'Deng Tuo tongzhi zhuidaohui zai Beijing juxing' (Memorial Meeting for Comrade Deng Tuo Held in Beijing). Xinhua Radio broadcast, 5 Sept. 1979; trans. FBIS, 6 Sept. 1979; reprinted in YDT: 1-4.
Deng Yun (1980), 'Huiyi wode baba Deng Tuo' (Commemorating My Father Deng Tuo), YDT: 238–46.
Dian Niu (1982), 'Deng Tuo tongzhi de tici (A Poem in Deng Tuo's Hand), *Jingyan shi tongxun* (Sichuan), 2: inside cover. (Photograph of Deng's poem written during his visit to the Zigong Saltworks, 13 Jan. 1958.)
Ding Guocheng, Yu Congyang, and Yu Sheng (1986), *Zhongguo zuojia biming tanyuan* (Studies on the Origins of Chinese Writers' Pen–names). Changchun: Shidai wenyi chubanshe.
Ding Wang (1969), *Zhonggong wenhua da geming ziliao huibian* (Sourcebooks of the Chinese Communist Cultural Revolution). Hong Kong: Mingbao Monthly Press. (*Deng Tuo xuanji* [Selected Works of Deng Tuo] is Vol. 2 of this series.)

– – (1979), *Yao Wenyuan, Mao Yuanxin pingzhuan* (A Critical Biography of Yao Wenyuan and Mao Yuanxin). Hong Kong: Mingbao Monthly Press.

Ding, X.L. (1994), *The Decline of Communism in China: Legitimacy Crisis, 1977–1989*. Cambridge: Cambridge University Press.

Ding Yilan (1979), 'Yi Deng Tuo' (Commemorating Deng Tuo), *Xinwen zhanxian*, 1: 25–31, or YDT: 17–28.

– – (1980), 'Shuo jiju hua: "Shengming de sanfen zhiyi" wei chongxin fabiao Deng Tuo de zawen' (A Few Words on 'One Third of Life' and the Republication of Deng Tuo's *zawen*), *Ye du* (Taiyuan), 1: 5.

– – (1982*a*), 'Deng Tuo huai xiang shi qishou' (Seven Poems by Deng Tuo in Memory of His Home County), *Fuzhou wanbao*, 1 Jan.

– – (1982*b*), 'Deng Tuo tongzhi douzheng he xuexi de lishi pianduan—Ding Yilan tongzhi jianghua jilu gao' (A Fragment from Comrade Deng Tuo's History of Struggle and Study—Comrade Ding Yilan's Lecture Notes), *Xiaoyou zhiyin*, 1–7.

– – (1982*c*), 'Jinxiu caihua di houxian—Ding Yilan tongzhi tan Deng Tuo de yeyu xuexi' (Beautiful Literary Talent Guides Later Worthies—Comrade Ding Yilan on Deng Tuo's Sparetime Studies), *Zhongguo qingnian bao*, 1 Jul.

– – (1984*a*), 'Huiyi Deng Tuo shenghuo, gongzuo pianduan: yinyan 1. Guxiang yu qing shaonian shiqi shenghuo' (Fragments of Deng Tuo's Life and Works Recalled: Foreword [and] 1. Home Town and Early Life), *Xinwen jizhe*, 8: 11–14.

– – (1984*b*), 'Huiyi Deng Tuo shenghuo, gongzuo pianduan: 5. Hutuo hebian ding xinmeng' (Fragments of Deng Tuo's Life and Works Recalled: 5. An Alliance of the Heart Sworn by the Banks of the Hutuo River), *Xinwen jizhe*, 12: 10–11.

– – (1985), 'KangRi zhanzheng zhong yige zai diren houfang de zhanchang—Jin Cha Ji bianqu (zai Ha–fo daxue de yanjiang)' (A Battlefield Behind Enemy Lines During the Anti-Japanese War—The Jin Cha Ji Border Region [Lecture Given at Harvard University]), 1 May.

Ding Yilan, interviews:
    'Interview with the Wife of Deng Tuo, Ding Yilan', see Zhang Sheng (1979).
    interview with Ding Yilan, see Huang Weijing (1980).
    'A Meeting With Ding Yilan', see He Yun (1980).
    on Deng Tuo's poetry, see Si Wei (1980).
    letters about Deng Tuo from youth, see 'Yanshan leiluo, yehua qianqiu' (1980).
    interview with Ding Yilan, see Chai Fei, and Li Jingmin (1981).
    on personal life with Deng Tuo, see Bo Sheng (1981).
    conversations on radio broadcasting, see Xiao Yang, and Du Zhang (1981).
    interview, see Lin Yinxuan (1982*a*).

Dirlik, Arif (1974), 'Mirror to Revolution: Early Marxist Images of Chinese History', *Journal of Asian Studies*, 32:2, 193–224.

– – (1977), 'The Problem of Class View Point Versus Historicism in Chinese Historiography', *Modern China*, 3:4, 465–88.

– – (1978), *Revolution and History: Origins of Marxist Historiography in China, 1919–1937*. Berkeley: University of California Press.

Dittmer, Lowell (1974), *Liu Shao-ch'i and the Chinese Cultural Revolution: The Politics of Mass Criticism*. Berkeley: University of California Press.
— — (1981), 'Death and Transfiguration: Liu Shaoqi's Rehabilitation and Contemporary Chinese Politics', *Journal of Asian Studies*, 40:3, 455–80.
— — (1987), *China's Continuous Revolution: The Post-Liberation Epoch, 1949-1981*. Berkeley: University of California Press.
Dittmer, Lowell, and Chen Ruoxi (1981), 'Ethics and Rhetoric of the Chinese Cultural Revolution', *Studies in Chinese Terminology*, No. 19. Berkeley: University of California, Center for Chinese Studies.
Djilas, Milovan (1957), *The New Class: An Analysis of the Communist System*. New York: Praeger.
Domenach, Jean–Luc (1982), *Aux Origines du Grand Bond en Avant: Le cas d'une province Chinoisie, 1956–1958*. Paris: Editions de l'Ecole des Hautes Etudes en Sciences Sociales, Presses de la Fondation Nationale des Sciences Politiques.
Doolin, Dennis J. (1964), *Communist China: The Politics of Student Opposition*. Stanford: Hoover Institution Press.
Dorrill, William F. (1969), 'The Fukien Rebellion and the CCP: A Case of Maoist Revisionism', *The China Quarterly*, No. 37: 31–53.
Dorris, Carl E. (1976), 'Peasant Mobilization in North China and the Origins of Yenan Communism', *The China Quarterly*, No. 68: 697–719.
Du Yu (1982), 'Deng Tuo tongzhi yishou yi shi' (A Lost Poem by Deng Tuo), *Chongqing ribao*, 28 Apr.
Durkheim, Emile (1982 edn.), *The Rules of Sociological Method*, trans. W. D. Halls. New York: Free Press.
Eastman, Lloyd E. (1972), 'Fascism in Kuomintang China: The Blue Shirts', *The China Quarterly*, No. 49: 1-31.
— — (1974), *The Abortive Revolution*. Cambridge: Harvard University Press.
Edmunds, Clifford G. (1987), 'The Politics of Historiography: Jian Bozan's Historicism', in Goldman, Cheek, and Hamrin (1987: 65–106).
Elmquist, Paul O. (1951), 'The Sino–Japanese Undeclared War of 1932 at Shanghai', *Papers on China*, Vol. 5. Harvard: Committee on International and Regional Studies, 38–74.
Esherick, Joseph W., and Rankin, Mary B. (eds.) (1990), *Chinese Local Elites and Patterns of Dominance*. Berkeley: University of California Press.
Fabre, Guilhem (1990), *Gènese du Pouvoir et de L'opposition en China: Le Printemps de Yan'an, 1942*. Paris: Éditions L'Harmattan.
Fairbank, John King, and Liu, Kwang-ching (1950), *Modern China: A Bibliographic Guide*. Cambridge: Harvard University Press.
— —, and Feuerwerker, Albert (eds.) (1986), *The Cambridge History of China*, Vol. 13, Part 2. Cambridge: Cambridge University Press.
Fan Changjiang (1981), *Tongxun yu lunwen* (News Reports and Essays). Chongqing: Xinhua chubanshe.
Fan Jin (1941), 'Ji zhong de xinwen' (Journalism in Central Hebei), *Xinhua ribao* (Chongqing), 1 Sept. (Reprinted in Zhang Jinglu, 1959: 229–37.)

FBIS. Foreign Broadcast Information Service. (US government translation service.)
Fei Shaokang (1982), 'Lianxi qunzhong ben zhongxin—Yi DengTuo tongzhi 1958 nianchu Zigong zhixing' (A BasicLoyalty to Uniting with the Masses—In Memory of Deng Tuo's Visit to Zigong in Early 1958), *Xinwen zhanxian*, 2: 34–5.
Feigon, Lee (1983), *Chen Duxiu: Founder of the Chinese Communist Party*.Princeton: Princeton University Press.
Femia, Joseph V. (1981), *Gramsci's PoliticalThought: Hegemony, Consciousness, and the RevolutionaryProcess*. Oxford: Clarendon Press.
Feng Zhi (1951), *Dong Ou zaji* (Random Notes on Eastern Europe). Beijing: Renmin wenxue chubanshe.
Feuerwerker, Albert (ed.) (1968a), *History in Communist China*. Cambridge: MITPress.
– – (1968b), 'China's History in Marxian Dress', in Feuerwerker (1968: 14–44).
Feuerwerker, Albert, and Cheng, S. (1967), *Chinese Communist Studies of Modern Chinese History*. Cambridge: Harvard East Asian Monographs.
Fischer, David Hackett (1970), *Historians' Fallacies:Toward aLogic of Historical Thought*. New York: Harper and Row.
Fisher, Tom (1982), 'The Play'sTheThing: Wu Han and Hai Rui Revisited', *The Australian Journal of Chinese Affairs*, No. 7: 1–36.
– – (1986), 'Wu Han:The 'Upright Official' as a Model in the Humanities', in Hamrin and Cheek (1986: 155–84).
Fogel, Joshua A. (1984),*Politics and Sinology: The Case of Naito Konan (1866–1934)*. Cambridge: Harvard Council on EastAsian Studies.
– – (1987), *Ai Ssu–ch'i's Contribution to the Development of Chinese Marxism*. Cambridge: Harvard Council on EastAsian Studies.
– – (1988), 'TheAsiatic Mode of Production in Soviet Russia, China, and Japan', *The American Historical Review*, 93:1, 56–79.
– – (1997), 'Mendacity and Veracity in the Recent Chinese Communist Memoir Literature', in Cheek and Saich (1997: 354-8).
Fokkema, D.W. (1965), *Literary Doctrine in China and Soviet Influence, 1956–1960*. The Hague: Mouton & Co.
Franke,Wolfgang (1968), *An Introduction to the Sources of Ming History*. Kuala Lumpur: University of Malaya Press.
Fu Jialin [FuYiling] (1980), 'Qingnian shidai de Deng Tuo' (The Young Deng Tuo), YDT: 220–3.
Fu Ke (1980), 'Sisheng jiwang ji kailai—Huainian Deng Tuo tongzhi' (A Fallen Comrade Carried Forward into the Future—Mourning Comrade DengTuo), YDT: 218–19.
Fu Xiu (1980), 'Wo zai Jin Cha Ji jiefang qu gongzuo de yiduan huiyi' (A Recollection of MyWork in the Jin Cha Ji Liberated Area), *Wenxue ziliao xuanbian*, 3: 121–35.
Furth, Charlotte (1970),*Ting Wen–chiang: Science and China's New Culture*. Cambridge: Harvard University Press.
Gao Ju [Jiang Qing] (1966), *Xiang fandang fanshehuizhuyi de heixian kaihuo* (Open Fire on theAnti–Party, Anti–Socialist Black Line). Beijing: Beijing chubanshe.

Gao Qixiang (1982), 'Zawen yinxiang' (The Impact of *Zawen*), in *Beijing wenyi nianjian 1982* (Beijing Literature and Arts Almanac 1982). Beijing: Gongen chubanshe, 50–8.

Garavente, Anthony (1965), 'The Long March', *The China Quarterly*, No. 22: 89–124.

Gardner, Charles S. (1970), *Chinese Traditional Historiography*. Cambridge: Harvard University Press. (Third printing with corrections.)

Gatu, Dagfinn (1983), *Toward Revolution: War, Social Change, and The Chinese Communist Party in North China, 1937–45*. Stockholm: Institute of Oriental Studies.

Ge Gongzhen (1964), *Zhongguo baoxue shi* (A History of Chinese Journalism).Taipei.

Geertz, Clifford (1973), *The Interpretation of Cultures*. NewYork: Basic Books.

Geisert, Bradley (1986), 'From Conflict to Quiescence: The Kuomintang, Party Factionalism and Local Elites in Jiangsu, 1927–31'.*The China Quarterly*, No. 108: 680–703.

Gilmartin, Christina (1995), 'The Politics of Gender in the Making of the Party', in Saich and van de Ven (1995: 33-55).

Glaubitz, Joachim (ed.) (1969), *Opposition gegen Mao: Abendgespräche am Yenshan und andere politische Dokumente*. Freiburg: Breisgau.

Gold, Tom (1985), 'After Comradeship: Personal Relations in China Since the Cultural Revolution',*The China Quarterly*, No. 104: 657-75.

– – (1988), 'Guerrilla Interviewing among the *Getihu*', in Link, Madsen, and Pickowicz (1988).

Goldman, Merle (1967*a*), 'The Fall of Chou Yang', *The China Quarterly*, No. 27: 132-48.

– – (1967*b*), *Literary Dissent In Communist China*. Cambridge: Harvard University Press.

– – (1969), 'The Unique "Blooming and Contending" of 1961–62',*The China Quarterly*, No. 37: 54–83.

– – (1981), *China's Intellectuals: Advise and Dissent*. Cambridge: Harvard University Press.

– – (1994), *Sowing the Seeds of Democracy in China: Political Reform in the Deng Xiaoping Era*. Cambridge: Harvard University Press.

– – , with Cheek, Timothy, and Hamrin, Carol Lee (1987), *Intellectuals and the State: In Search of a New Relationship*. Cambridge: Harvard Council on East Asian Studies.

Goodman, David S.G., and Segal, Gerald (eds.) (1991), *China in the Nineties: Crisis Management and Beyond*. Oxford: Clarendon Press.

Gramsci, Antonio (1971), *Selections from the Prison Notebooks, 1929-1936*, ed. Quintin Hoare and Geoffrey Nowell Smith. London: Lawrence and Wishard.

The Great Socialist Cultural Revolution. Peking: Foreign Languages Press, 1966.

Grieder, Jerome B. (1981), *Intellectuals and the State in Modern China*. New York: Free Press.

Gu Bingfu (1966), 'Deng Tuo shi xiong'e de chailang' (Deng Tuo is a Fiendish Wolf), *Tiyu bao*, 13, 3.

Gu Xing (1980–81), 'Deng Tuo tongzhi zhidao women ban wanbao' (Comrade Deng Tuo Guided Us In Running the Evening News), *Beijing wanbao tongxunyuan zhiyou* (Newsletter of the *Beijing Evening News* Correspondents), 1 (May), 7–10; 2 (Oct.), 4–

8; and (1981), 1 (Jan.), 4–7. (Revised version of same in *Xinwen yanjiu ziliao* (1980) 4: 87–9, and 5: 17–20.)
– – (1985), 'Huiyi DengTuo shenghuo, gongzuo pianduan: 7. Yanshan bixue wo honghua' (Fragmemts of DengTuo's Life andWorks Recalled: 7. Blood in Yanshan Skies is a Fertile Red Flower), *Xinwen jizhe*, 2: 11–13.
– –, and Liu Menghong (1979), 'DengTuo tongzhi he tade "Yanshan yehua"' (Comrade Deng Tuo and his "Evening Chats atYanshan"), *Xinwen yanjiu ziliao*, 1: 111–16, or YDT: 111–36.
– –, and Cheng Mei (1991), *Deng Tuo zhuan* (Biography of DengTuo). Taiyuan: Shanxi jiaoyu chubanshe.
Guan Zhichang (1982), '"Sanjiacun" heidian zhushuai Deng Tuo qiren' (The Man Deng Tuo—Leader of the 'Three Family Village' Black Shop), *Zhuanji wenxue*, 4: 5, 37–9.
Guillermaz, Jacques (1968), *A History of the Chinese Communist Party: 1921–1949*. London: Methuen & Co.
Habermas, Jürgen (1989), *The Structural Transformation of the Public Sphere: An Inquiry into a Category of Bourgeois Society*. Cambridge: MIT Press.
Halpern, Nina (1987), 'The Economists', in Goldman, Cheek, and Hamrin (1987: 45–64).
Hamrin, CarolLee (1975), 'AlternativesWithin Chinese Marxism: 1955–65: Yang Hsien-chien'sTheory of Dialectics', University ofWisconsin, Ph.d. thesis.
– – (1984), 'Competing "PolicyPackages" and Chinese ForeignPolicy', *Asian Survey*, 24:5, 487–518.
– – (1986), 'Yang Xianzhen: Upholding OrthodoxyLeninist Theory', in Hamrin and Cheek (1986: 51–91).
– – (1990), *China and the Challenge of the Future*. Boulder, CO:WestviewPress.
– – (1991), 'Yang Xianzhen's *Philosophic "Criminal Case"'*, *Chinese Law and Government*, 24: 1-2.
– –, and Cheek,Timothy (eds.) (1986), *China's Establishment Intellectuals*. Armonk, NY: M.E. Sharpe.
– –, and Zhao, Suisheng (eds.) (1995), *Decision-making in Deng's China*. Armonk, NY: M.E. Sharpe.
Handlin, Joanna B. (1983), *Action in Late Ming Thought: The Reorientation of Lü K'un and Other Scholar Officials*. Berkeley: University of California Press.
Haraszti, Miklós (1987), *The Velvet Prison:Artists Under State Socialism*. New York: Basic Books.
Harding, Harry (1993), 'The Evolution ofAmerican Scholarship on Contemporary China', in Shambaugh (1993: 14–40).
Harrison, James,P. (1969), *The Communists and Chinese Peasant Rebellions*. New York: Atheneum.
– – (1972), *The Long March To Power: A History of the Chinese Communist Party, 1921–1972*. New York: Praeger.
Hartford, Kathleen J. (1980), 'Step By Step: Reform, Resistance, and Revolution in Chin–Ch'a–Chi Border Region 1937–1945'. Stanford University, Ph.d. thesis.
– – (1989), 'Repression and Communist Success: The Case of Jin-Cha-Ji, 1938-1943', in Hartford and Goldstein (1989: 92-127).

– – (1995), 'Fits and Starts: The Chinese Communist Party in Rural Hebei 1921–1936', in Saich and van de Ven (1995: 144–74).

– –, and Goldstein, Steven M. (eds.) (1989), *Single Sparks: China's Rural Revolutions*. Armonk, NY: M.E. Sharpe.

Hayford, Charles (1990), *To the People: James Yen and Village China*. New York: Columbia University Press.

He, Baogang (1991), 'Legitimacy in the Deng Era in China: A Critical Appraisal', *The Journal of Communist Studies*, 7:1.

He Ganzhi (1936a), 'Zhongguo fengjian zhidu changqi tingzhi de fenzhe' (An Analysis of the Long–Term Blockages in Feudal China), *Shidai luntan*, 1: 5, 238–43.

– – (1936b), 'Yaxiya shengchan fangfa wenti zai Riben' (The AMP Issue in Japan), *Shidai luntan*, 1: 8, 386–92.

– – (1989), *He Ganzhi wenji* (Works of He Ganzhi). Beijing: Renmin daxue chubanshe.

He Jin (1980), 'Dui Yan'an qiangjiu yundong de chubu tantao' (A Preliminary Inquiry into the Yan'an Rescue Movement), *Dangshi yanjiu*, 6: 61–5.

He Yun (1980), 'Huijianle Ding Yilan' (A Visit with Ding Yilan), *Taiguo Zhonghua ribao*, Jul. (From Ding Yilan's clipping file.)

Hearst, Nancy, and Saich, Tony (1997), "Newly Available Sources on CCP History from the People's Republic of China', in Cheek and Saich (1997: 323-38).

Hershatter, Gail, Honig, Emily, Lipman, Jonathan N., and Stross, Randall (eds.) (1996), *Remapping China: Fissures in Historical Terrain*. Stanford: Stanford University Press.

Hexter, J.H. (1971), *Doing History*. Bloomington: Indiana University Press.

Hicks, George (ed.) (1990), *The Broken Mirror: China After Tiananmen*. London: Longman.

Hinton, William (1966), *Fanshen: A Documentary of Revolution in a Chinese Village*. New York: Vintage Books.

Holm, David (1980), 'National Form and the Popularization of Literature in Yenan', in *La littérature Chinoise au temps de la guerre de résistance contre le Japon (de 1937 à 1945)*. Paris: Éditions de la Fondation Singer–Polignac, 215–35.

– – (1991), *Art and Ideology in Revolutionary China*. Oxford: Clarendon Press.

Hong weibing ziliao. Reprints of Red Guard publications by Center for Chinese Research Materials, Association of Research Libraries, Washington, DC, 1975 (20 vols.; #20 is a table of contents.)

Hsia, Tsi–an (1968), 'Twenty Years After the Yenan Forum', in T. A. Hsia, *The Gates of Darkness*. Seattle: University of Washington Press.

Hsiao, Ching–cheng, and Cheek, Timothy, 'Open and Closed Media: External and Internal Newspapers in the Propaganda System', in Hamrin and Zhao (1995: 76–90).

Hsiao, Kung–ch'üan (1960), *Rural China: Imperial Control in the 19th Century*. Seattle: University of Washington Press.

Hsu, Kai–yu (1980), *Literature of the People's Republic of China*. Bloomington: Indiana University Press.

Hu Guocheng (1981), 'Shei shi diyige dao Moxige de luxingjia?' (Who Was the First Traveller to Mexico?), *Beijing ribao*, 21 Jan., 3. (See Luo Rongqu in *China Reconstructs*, Apr. 1983: 39–40.)

Hu Huiqiang (1983), 'Cong pi fan maojin dao da yuejin' (From the Criticism of Oppose Adventurism to the Great Leap Forward), *Dangshi yanjiu ziliao*, 4: 748.

Hu Jiwei (1986), 'Pingsheng yingde haoqing zai–Jinian Deng Tuo tongzhi shishi ershi zhounian' (The Lofty Sentiments Earned Throughout a Lifetime Remain–Commemorating the 20th Anniversary of Comrade Deng Tuo's Death), in Deng Tuo (1986a: 4–14).

Hu Shi sixiang pipan ziliao jikan (Materials on the Criticism of Hu Shi's Ideology). Shanghai: Xin wenyi chubanshe, 1955.

Hua, Shiping (1994), 'One Servant, Two Masters: The Dilemma of Chinese Establishment Intellectuals', *Modern China*, 26:1, 92–114.

'Huabei jiefang qu wenhuajie zhi zhengzhi xieshang huiyi dian' (Telegram from the Literary Circles of the North China Liberated Districts to the Political Consultative Congress), *Xinhua ribao*, 24 Jan. 1946. (Reprinted in Zhang Jinglu, 1959: 4, 130–1.)

Huang, Liu-hung (1984 edn.), *A Complete Book Concerning Happiness and Benevolence: A Manual for Local Magistrates in Seventeenth-Century China*. Tucson: University of Arizona Press.

Huang, Philip (1972), *Liang Ch'i-ch'ao and Modern Chinese Liberalism*. Seattle: University of Washington Press.

Huang, Ray (1981), *1587, A Year of No Significance: The Ming Dynasty in Decline*. New Haven: Yale University Press.

– – (1991), 'The Paradigmatic Crisis in Chinese Studies', *Modern China*, 17:3, 299–341.

Huang Weijing (1980), 'Yanshan leiluo qianqiu hua–Deng Tuo furen Ding Yilan fangwen ji' (Open and Upright Yanshan, Evening Chats for a Thousand Years–Notes of an Interview with Deng Tuo's Wife, Ding Yilan), *Changcheng* (Hebei edition), 2: 195–9 and 205.

Huang Xianjun (1979), 'Wenzhang manzhi shusheng lei–Huiyi Deng Tuo tongzhi' (Accumulated Literary Works Abound from the Scholar–Remembering Comrade Deng Tuo), *Rongshu wenxue congkan* (Fuzhou), 1: 233–9. Reprinted in YDT: 207–12.

– – (1980), 'Deng Tuo tongzhi tan fukan' (Comrade Deng Tuo on Newspaper Supplements), *Xinwen zhanxian*, 5: 38–9.

Huang Zhou, second author of art article, see Yang Renkai (1982).

Hulsewé, A.FP. (1986), 'Chinese Communist Treatment of the Origins and Foundation of the Chinese Empire', in Feuerwerker (1968: 96–123).

Israel, John (1966), *Student Nationalism in China, 1927–1937*. Stanford: Stanford University Press.

– – (forthcoming), *Southwest United University*.

– –, and Klein, Donald W. (1976), *Rebels and Bureaucrats: China's December 9ers*. Berkeley: University of California Press.

Jia Jinghong (1982), 'Jiang shan ming mei bi you shen–Fang lao huajia Zhou Huaimin' (Radiant and Enchanting Rivers and Mountains Penned with Spirit–An Interview with the Veteran Painter, Zhou Huaimin), *Beijing wanbao*, 15 Jan., 3.

Jian Bozan. See Zhang Chuanxi (1980).

Jian Qing (1980), 'Kong gu huiyin–Huiyi Deng Tuo tongzhi' (Echoes in the Empty Valleys–Commemorating Comrade Deng Tuo), in YDT: 62–8.

Jiang Guangci xuanji (Selected Works of Jiang Guangci). Hong Kong: Gangqing chubanshe, 1979.

Jin Cha Ji ribao dashiji (Chronology of *Jin Cha Ji Daily*). Beijing: Dazhong chubanshe, 1986.

Jin Chengji (1979), 'Jianchi lishi kexue geming chendi de douzheng jilu–Du DengTuo tongzhi de *Lun Zhongguo lishi de jige wenti*' (A Record of Upholding the Revolution in Historical Science–On Reading Comrade Deng Tuo's *A Few Questions in Chinese History*), *Guangming ribao*, 30 Jan., 4. (Reprinted in *1979 Zhongguo lishixue nianjian*, 315–18.)

Jing Dang (1982), 'Faxian 'Xi Weng' Cao Yuan moji' (Discovering Cao Yuan's Writing of 'Xi Weng'), *Guangming ribao*, 3 Feb.

Joffe, Ellis (1975), *Between Two Plenums: China's Intraleadership Conflict, 1959–62*. Ann Arbor: Center for Chinese Studies, University of Michigan. (MichiganPapers in Chinese Studies, No. 22.)

Johnson, Chalmers (1962), *Peasant Nationalism and CommunistPower*. Stanford: Stanford UniversityPress.

– – (ed.) (1973), *Ideology and Politics in Contemporary China*. Seattle: University of Washington Press.

Johnson, David, Nathan, Andrew, and Rawski, Evelyn S. (eds.) (1985), *Popular Culture in Late Imperial China*. Berkeley: University of CaliforniaPress.

Joseph, William (1984), *The Critique of Ultra–Leftism in China, 1958–1981*. Stanford: Stanford UniversityPress.

Jowitt, Kenneth (1978), *The Leninist Response to National Dependency*. Berkeley: Institute of International Studies, University of California. (Research Series, No. 37.)

– – (1992), *New World Disorder: The Leninist Extinction*. Berkeley: University of California Press.

KangRi zhanzheng shiqi jiefang qu gaikuang (An Outline ofLiberated Areas During the Anti–Japanese War). Beijing: Renmin chubanshe, 1953. (Revision of the 1944 text; this is a 4th printing dated 1981.)

Kataoka,Tetsuya (1974), *Resistance and Revolution in China:The Communists and the Second United Front*. Berkeley: University of CaliforniaPress.

Kelly, David A. (1985), 'Wang Ruoshui: Writings on Humanism, Alienation, and Philosophy', *Chinese Studies in Philosophy*, 16:3. (Annotated translations with commentary.)

– – (1987), 'The Emergence of Humanism: Wang Ruoshui and the Critique of Socialist Alienation', in Goldman, Cheek, and Hamrin (1987: 159–82).

– – (1990), 'Chinese Intellectuals in the 1989 Democracy Movement', in Hicks (1990: 24-51).

– – (1991), 'Chinese Marxism since Tiananmen: Between Evaporation and Dismemberment', in Goodman and Segal (1991: 19-34).

– –, and He Baogang (1992), 'Emergent Civil Society and the Intellectuals in China', in Miller (1992: 24-39).

Kenez,Peter (1985),*The Birth of the Propaganda State: Soviet Methods of Mass Mobilization, 1917–1929*. Cambridge: Cambridge University Press.

Kikuchi, Saburo (1973 edn.), *Chugoku kakumei bungaku undo shi* (A History of the Chinese Revolutionary Literary Movement). Tokyo: Kazama. (Reprint of 1953 original.)

Klein, Donald W., and Clark, Anne B. (1971), *Biographic Dictionary of Chinese Communism*. Cambridge: Harvard University Press.

Knight, Nick (1990), *Mao Zedong on Dialectical Materialism: Writings on Philosophy 1937*. Armonk, NY: M.E. Sharpe.

Knight, Sophia (1967), *Window on Shanghai: Letters from China, 1965–67*. London: André Deutsch.

Konrád, George, and Szelényi, Ivan (1979), *Intellectuals on the Road to Class Power*. New York: Harcourt, Brace, Jovanovich.

Kroll, Paul (forthcoming), 'The Poetry of Liu Yong'.

Kuang, Rongrong (1994), 'Institutional Change and Agricultura Performance in the People's Republic of China, 1949-1989'. University of Denver, Ph.d. thesis.

Kraus, Richard (1991), *Brushes with Power: Modern Politics and the Chinese Art of Calligraphy*. Berkeley: University of California Press.

Kuhn, Philip A. (1975), 'Local Self Government Under The Republic: Problems of Control, Autonomy, and Mobilization', in Wakeman and Grant (1975: 257–98).

– – (1977), 'Origins of the Taiping Vision: Cross–Cultural Dimensions of a Chinese Rebellion', *Comparative Studies in Society and History*, 19:3, 350-66.

– – (1987), 'Political Crime and Bureaucratic Monarchy: A Chinese Case of 1768', *Late Imperial China*, 8:1, 80–104.

– – (1990), *Soulstealers: The Chinese Sorcery Scare of 1768*. Cambridge: Harvard University Press.

– – (1991), 'Talk at the annual meeting of the Association for Asian Studies'.

Kuo, Warren (ed.) (1978), *A Comprehensive Glossary of Chinese Communist Terminology*. Taipei: Institute of International Relations.

Kuriyama, Kurt Y. (1979), *Humanists and Technocrats: Political Conflict in Contemporary China*. Lanham, MD: University Press of America.

Leclerc de Sablon, Jean, and Ba San (1983), 'Chine: souvenirs d'une idealiste incorrigible', *L'express* (Paris), 10 Nov., 143–58.

Lee, Gregory (1989), *Dai Wangshu*. Hong Kong: The Chinese University of Hong Kong Press.

Lee, Hong Yung (1975), 'Utility and Limitation of the Red Guard Publications as Source Publications: A Bibliographical Survey', *Journal of Asian Studies*, 24:3, 779–93.

– – (1978), *The Politics of the Chinese Cultural Revolution: A Case Study*. Berkeley: University of California Press.

Lee, Leo Ou–fan (1973), *The Romantic Generation of Modern Chinese Writers*. Cambridge: Harvard University Press.

Lenin, N.V. (1988 edn.), *What Is To Be Done?*, trans. Joe Fineberg and G. Hanna. Harmondsworth: Penguin Books.

Levenson, Joseph R. (1953), *Liang Ch'i–ch'ao and the Mind of Modern China*. Cambridge: Harvard University Press.

– – (1968 edn.), *Confucian China and Its Modern Fate: A Trilogy*. Berkeley: University of California Press.

Leys, Simon (1977a), *The Chairman's New Clothes: Mao and the Cultural Revolution*, trans. Carol Appleyard and Patrick Goode. New York: St. Martin's Press. (Original French edition, 1971.)

– – (1977b), *Chinese Shadows*. New York: Viking Press. (French edition, 1974.)

– – (1986), *The Burning Forest: Essays on Chinese Culture and Politics*. New York: Holt, Rinehart and Winston.

Li Jun (1964), 'Lun qunzhong yeyu wenhua huodong de chedi geminghua' (On the Complete Revolutionization of the Spare-Time Activities of the Masses), *Qianxian*, 3: 9–11.

– – (1980), 'Deng Tuo tongzhi yu *Qianxian* zazhi' (Comrade Deng Tuo and *Frontline* Magazine), YDT: 101–110.

Li, Linhong (1978), 'A Decennial Memorial to Comrade Jian Bozan: A Refutation of Qi Benyu's Frameup', *Lishi yanjiu*, 9: 27–37. (Extract translation in FBIS–CHI, 20 Sept. 1978, E19–E20.)

Li Shanyuan quanji. (preface dated 1705; edited by Wei Xiang.)

Li Suinian (ed.) (1982), *Liushi niandai guomin jingji tiaozhengde huigu* (Reminiscences on the National Economic Adjustments of the 1960s). Beijing: Zhongguo caizheng jingji chubanshe.

Li Tuozhi (1979), 'Daonian wangyou Deng Tuo' (Mouming Our Lost Friend Deng Tuo), *Rongshu wenxue congkan*, 1: 240–50. (Reprinted in YDT: 224–33.)

– – (1982), 'Di Deng Tuo' (Mourning Deng Tuo), *Mingbao yuekan* (Hong Kong), 3. (A long poem.)

Li Weiyi (1981), 'Shei zui xian dadao Meizhou?' (Who was the First to Reach America?), *Beijing wanbao*, 22 Dec., 3.

Li Yimeng (1980), 'Xu' (Introduction), in Deng Tuo (1980a: 1–3).

Li Zehou (1979), *Zhongguo jindai sixiang shi lun* (Historical Discussions on Chinese Modern Thought). Beijing: Renmin chubanshe.

– –, and Schwarcz, Vera (1983–84), 'Six Generations of Modern Chinese Intellectuals', *Chinese Studies in History*, 17:2, 42–56.

Li Zhi *et al*. (1980), 'Gensui Deng Tuo tongzhi ban bao' (Following Comrade Deng Tuo Publishing the Newspaper), in YDT: 84–8. (A joint piece by thirteen named authors who worked at *Jin Cha Ji Daily*.)

Li Zhu (1980), 'Huainian Deng Tuo jiujiu' (Mourning Uncle Deng Tuo), in YDT: 253–5.

Liang Huiru (1980), 'Deng Tuo chang shi zan Zhao Dan' (Deng Tuo's Extended Poem in Praise of Zhao Dan), *Dagong bao* (Hong Kong), 2 Nov. Poem reprinted in Deng Tuo (1979c: 134–5).

Liao Gailong (ed.) (1985), *Zhongguo dangshi wenzhai niankan: 1982* (Annual Selection of Abstracted Articles on CCP History: 1982). Hangzhou: Zhejiang renmin chubanshe.

Liao Mosha [Wen Bi] (1956), 'Luantan zaji' (Report What Comes Handy), *Xin jianshe* (Beijing), vols. 18–24 (one in each issue).

– – (1979), 'Houji' (Afterword), in Wu Nanxing (1979: 237–44). (Reprinted in YDT: 137–43.)

– – (1980*a* edn.), 'Wo you xuedao yidian bianzhengfa' (Once Again I Study a Point of Dialectics), in *Chang duan lu*, 1–6.
– – (1980*b*), 'Dai xu' (In Lieu of a Preface), in YDT: 1–6. (Pagination separate from rest of volume. First published in *Xinwen zhanxian*, 1980:10.)
– – *et al.* (1980*c*), *Yi Deng Tuo* (Commemorating Deng Tuo). Fuzhou: Fujian renmin chubanshe.
Lieberthal, Kenneth G. (1987), 'The Great Leap Forward and the Split in the Yenan Leadership', in MacFarquhar and Fairbank (1987: 293-359).
– – (1995), *Governing China: From Revolution Through Reform*. New York: W.W. Norton.
– –, and Dickson, Bruce J. (1989), *A Research Guide to Central Party and Government Meetings in China, 1949–1986*. Armonk, NY: M.E. Sharpe.
Liebman, Marcel (1975), *Lenin Under Leninism*. London: Jonathan Cape.
Lin Jie *et al.* (1966), 'Deng Tuo de 'Yanshan yehua' shi fandang fanshehuizhuyi de hei hua' (Deng Tuo's *Evening Chats at Yanshan* Is Anti–Party, Anti–Socialist Double Talk), *Guangming ribao*, 8 May. (Best translated in Tung, 1978: xix–xxxxvii.)
Lin Maike [Michael Lindsay] (1944), 'Jin Cha Ji yinxiang ji' (Impressions of Jin Cha Ji), *Jiefang ribao* (Yan'an), 5 Jun., 3.
Lin, Man-houng (1991), 'Two Social Theories Revealed in Statecraft Controversies Over China's Monetary Crisis, 1808–1854', *Late Imperial China*, 12:2, 1-35.
Lin Xiling (1984), interview 3 Feb., Harvard University. See also, Jean Leclerc de Sablon, and Ba San (1983).
Lin Yinxuan (1982*a*), 'Fang Deng Tuo furen Ding Yilan' (An Interview with Deng Tuo's Wife, Ding Yilan), *Fuzhou wanbao*, 1 Jan.
– – (1982*b*), 'Yiban xinxiang xianying gui' (A Sincere Offering To a Noble Spirit), *Fuzhou wanbao*, 4 Apr.
Lindau, Juan, and Cheek, Timothy (eds.) (forthcoming), *Market Reform and Democratization: Comparing China and Mexico*. Boulder, CO: Rowman and Littlefield.
Lindsay, Michael (1975), *The Unknown War: North China 1937–45*. London: Bergström and Boyle Books.
Link, Perry, Madsen, Richard, and Pickowicz, Paul G. (eds.) (1989), *Unofficial China: Popular Culture and Thought in the People's Republic of China*. Boulder, CO: Westview Press.
Liu, Alan L. (1975), *Communications and National Integration in Communist China*. Berkeley: University of California Press.
Liu Binyan (1983), interview on AFP Newswire (Paris), 21 Apr.
– – (1983), *People or Monsters? And Other Stories and Reportage from China After Mao*. Bloomington: Indiana University Press.
– – (1988), 'Jizhe zheyihang' (The Profession of Journalism), in *Liu Binyan yanlun ji* (Liu Binyan on Public Affairs). Hong Kong: Xiangjiang chubanshe, 1: 243–5.
– – (1990), *A Higher Kind of Loyalty*. New York: Pantheon.
Liu Boqin (1980), 'Wo wei Deng Tuo zhiyin' (I Cut Seals for Deng Tuo), *Beijing wanbao*, 6 Jul.

Liu, Chun-jo (1964), *Controversies In Modern Chinese Intellectual History*. Cambridge: Harvard East Asia Monographs.

'Liu-Deng shi Peng-Liu fangeming jituan de hei houtai' (Liu-Deng Are the Black Backstage Supporters of Peng-Liu's Counter-Revolutionary Clique), *Dongfang hong*, 31:4 (Beijing: Association of Representatives of the Capital University and College Red Guards at the Beijing Mining Institute, 19 May 1967). (Reproduced in *Hong weibing ziliao*, ARL, Washington, DC, 1975, Vol. 13, 4084.)

Liu Fulin (1980), 'Zuishi xuxin liu jingjie-Huiyi he Deng Tuo tongzhi de yici huijian' (A Most Humble and Indomitable Person-Recalling a Meeting with Comrade Deng Tuo), in YDT: 213-5.

Liu Guangzhi (1982), 'Chizi zhi xin-Huainian Deng Tuo tongzhi' (A Loyal Heart-Thinking of Comrade Deng Tuo), *Renmin ribao*, 20 Sept.

Liu Lantao *et al.* (1984), 'Sishi nianqian de yibu *Mao Zedong xuanji*' (An Edition of the *Selected Works of Mao Zedong* from Forty Years Ago), *Liaowang zhoukan*, 17: 11.

Liu Menghong, and Liu Yongcheng (1979), 'Jiechu de gongji, wusi de fengxian-Yi Deng Tuo tongzhi dui woguo gudai shu hua he wenxian de yanjiu ji shouzang' (Outstanding Contribution, Selfless Offering-Commemorating Comrade Deng Tuo's Research on Our Country's Ancient Calligraphy, Painting, and Documents as well as His Collections), in YDT: 152-63. (Originally published in *Wenxian*, 1979:2 without the ten character supra-title and with Ding Yilan as first author.)

Liu Shaoqi (1937), 'Guanyu guoqu baiqu gongzuo gei zhongyang de yifeng xin' (A Letter to the Central Committee on the Past Work in the White Areas-4 Mar. 1937), in *Liuda yilai*, 1: 803-12.

-- (1939), 'Lun gongkai yu mimi gongzuo' (On Open and Secret Work-20 Oct. 1939) in *Zhonggong zhongyang wenjian*, 11: 184-203.

Liu Yongcheng (1979), '*Hong lou meng* shidai de jieji guanxi' (Class Relations Around the Time of *Dream of the Red Chamber*), *Hong lou meng xuekan*. Tianjin: Baihua wenyi chubanshe, No. 2: 269-93.

-- (1980*a*), 'Deng Tuo', in *1979 Zhongguo lishixue nianjian* (1980), 315-18.

-- (1980*b*), 'Huainian Makesizhuyi shixuejia Deng Tuo tongzhi' (Cherishing the Memory of the Marxist Historian Comrade Deng Tuo), in YDT: 144-51.

-- (1981), 'Lun *Hong lou meng* de sixiang qingxiang' (On the Ideological Tendency in *Dream of the Red Chamber*), *Hong lou meng yanjiu jikan*. Shanghai: Shanghai guji chubanshe, No. 7: 37-62.

Liu Yunlai (1988), *Xinhuashe shihua* (Historical Chats on the New China News Agency). Beijing: Xinhuashe chubanshe.

Liuda yilai: Dangnei mimi wenjian (Since the Sixth Party Congress: Secret Inner Party Documents), Secretariat of the CCP CC, ed. Beijing: Renmin chubanshe, 2 vols.

Lou Ningxian (1980), 'Feng yu tongzhou zhanyou xian' (A Worthy Battle Companion in the Same Boat Through Winds and Storms), in YDT: 37-43.

Louie, Kam (1980), *Critiques of Confucius in Contemporary China*. New York: St. Martin's Press.

-- (1986), *Inheriting Tradition: Interpretations of the Classical Philosophers in Communist China, 1949-1966*. Hong Kong: Oxford University Press.

Lu, Keng (1985), '*Pai Hsing's* Lu Keng Meets Wang Ruoshui', *Baixing*, 103. (Trans. in FBIS-CHI, 10 Sept., W4–W8.)

'Lun 'Sanjiacun'' yuan'an' (On the 'Three Family Village' Unjust Case), by 'A former member of the *Frontline* editorial board' (1980), in YDT: 267–79.

Ma Nancun [Deng Tuo] (1963 and 1979), *Yanshan yehua (heji)*. Beijing: Beijing chubanshe.

Ma Tieding (ed.) (1955a), *Cong Hu Feng fangeming shijian zhong xiqu jieji douzheng de jiaoxun* (Lessons for Class Struggle Drawn from the Hu Feng Counterrevolutionary Affair). Beijing: Tongsu duwu chubanshe.

– – (1955b), 'Guanyu xiaopin wen' (On Small Essays), in Ma Tieding, *Zawen ji: di'er ben* (Miscellaneous Essays: Vol. 2). Beijing: Tongsu duwu chubanshe, 50–66.

– – (1960), 'Sixiang za tan' (Random Talks on Ideology), *Xin guancha*, 11 Nov.: 6–7.

– – (1962), *Canzhao lu* (Record of the Setting Sun). Beijing: Zuojia chubanshe.

Ma Tieding zawen xuan (Selected Miscellaneous Essays of Ma Tieding). Beijing: Renmin ribao chubanshe, 1981.

MacFarquhar, Roderick (1960), *The Hundred Flowers Campaign and the Chinese Intellectuals*. New York: Praeger.

– – (1974), *The Origins of the Cultural Revolution, 1: Contradictions Among the People 1956–1957*. New York: Columbia University Press.

– – (1983), *The Origins of the Cultural Revolution, 2: The Great Leap Forward 1958–1960*. New York: Columbia University Press.

– – (1997), *The Origins of the Cultural Revolution, 3: The Coming of the Cataclysm 1961-1966*. New York: Columbia University Press.

MacFarquhar, Roderick, and Fairbank, John King (eds.) (1987), *The Cambridge History of China*. Cambridge: Cambridge University Press, vol. 14.

MacFarquhar, Roderick, Cheek, Timothy, and Wu, Eugene (eds.) (1989), *The Secret Speeches of Chairman Mao: From the Hundred Flowers to the Great Leap Forward*. Cambridge: Harvard Council on East Asian Studies.

Mair, Victor (1985), 'Language and Ideology in the Written Popularizations of the *Sacred Edicts*', in Johnson, Nathan, and Rawski (1985: 325–59).

Maitan, Livio (1976), *Party, Army and Masses in China: A Marxist Interpretation of the Cultural Revolution and Its Aftermath*, trans. Gregor Benton and Marie Collitti. London: New Left Books. (Originally published in Rome in 1969.)

Malaqinfu (1980), 'Zhan chi jinying buzhu: Chongdu Deng Tuo tongzhi de "Neimeng yincao"' (The Golden Eagle Spreading Its Wings Cannot Be Held Down: Rereading Comrade Deng Tuo's 'Mongolian Recitations'), *Hong yan*, 1: 3–6.

Mao Zedong (1941), 'Xin minzhu de zhengzhi yu xin minzhu de wenhua' (The New Democratic Politics and New Democratic Culture), *Zhongguo wenhua* (Yan'an), 1:1, 1–24. (This is the original version of 'On New Democracy' in the official *Selected Works*.)

– – (1960 & 1977 edn.), *Mao Zedong xuanji* (Selected Works of Mao Zedong), Vols. 1–5. Beijing: Renmin chubanshe.

– – (1966–1969 edn.), *Mao Zedong sixiang wansui* (Long Live Mao Zedong Thought). No publication data, 1967, 1969. 3 volumes. (Reprinted by Institute of International Relations, Taipei.)
– – (1967a edn.), *Mao Zedong sixiang wansui* (Long Live Mao Zedong Thought) (N.p.: n.p., Jun. 1967), *shang*, 1–216. (CCRM 'Mao zhu weikan gao', vol. 6A. See MacFarquhar, Cheek, and Wu, 1989: 78.)
– – (1967b edn.), *Mao Zedong sixiang wansui* (Long Live Mao Zedong Thought) (N.p.: n.p., Sept. 1967). (CCRM 'Mao zhu weikan gao', vol. 9, 336 pp. See MacFarquhar, Cheek, and Wu, 1989: 79.)
– – (1971 edn.), *Mo Takuto syu* (Collected Writings of Mao Zedong), ed. Takeuchi Minoru. Tokyo: Hokubo sha.
– – (1977 edn.), *Selected Works of Mao Tsetung*, Vols. 1–5. Beijing: Foreign Languages Press.
– –. See also collections of Mao works under: *Xuexi wenxuan* and *Xuexi ziliao*, below.
– – (1983), *Mao Zedong xinwen gongzuo wenxuan* (Selected Writings by Mao Zedong on Journalism). Beijing: Xinhua chubanshe.
– – (1990 edn.), *Report from Xunwu*, trans. Roger Thompson. Stanford: Stanford University Press.
'Mao zhu weikan gao–*Mao Zedong sixiang wansui bieji ji qita*' (Unofficially Published Works of Mao Zedong–Additional Volumes of *Long Live Mao Zedong Thought* and Other Secret Speeches of Mao). Oakton, VA: Center for Chinese Research Materials, 1988, 23 vols. (See MacFarquhar, Cheek, and Wu, 1989:78–81.)
Mazur, Mary (1990), 'Studying Wu Han: The Political Academic', *Republican China*, 15:2, 17–39.
– – (1994), 'Wu Han: A Man of His Times'. University of Chicago, Ph.d. thesis.
– – (1997), 'The United Front Redefined for the Party-State', in Cheek and Saich (1997: 51-75).
McCormick, Barrett L., and Kelly, David (1994), 'The Limits of Anti–Liberalism', *Journal of Asian Studies*, 53:3, 804–31.
McDougall, Bonnie S. (1980), *Mao Zedong's 'Talks at the Yan'an Conference on Literature and Art': A Translation of the 1943 Text with Commentary*. Ann Arbor: Center for Chinese Studies, Michigan Papers in Chinese Studies, No. 39.
– – (1984), 'Writers and Performers, Their Work, and Their Audiences in the First Three Decades', in McDougall (ed.), *Popular Chinese Literature and Performing Arts in the People's Republic of China, 1949–1979*. Berkeley: University of California Press, 269–304.
McNeil, Gordon H. (1970), 'Seignobos', in S. William Halperin, *Essays in Modern European Historiography*. Chicago: University of Chicago Press, 352–69.
Meisner, Maurice (1967), *Li Ta–chao and the Origins of Chinese Marxism*. Cambridge: Harvard University Press.
– – (1986), *Mao's China and After*. New York: Free Press.
Meissner, Werner (1990), *Philosophy and Politics in China: The Controversy over Dialectical Materialism in the 1930s*. Stanford: Stanford University Press.

Bibliography

Miller, Robert F. (ed.) (1992), *The Developments of Civil Society in Communist Systems*. Sydney: Allen & Unwin.

Milton, David, and Milton, Nancy Dall (1976), *The Wind Will Not Subside: Years in Revolutionary China, 1964–1969*. New York: Pantheon Books.

Moody, Peter R. (1973), *The Politics of the Eighth Central Committee of the Communist Party of China*. Hamden: Shoe String Press.

– – (1977), *Opposition and Dissent in Contemporary China*. Stanford: Hoover Institution Press.

Mote, Frederick W. (1960), 'Confucian Eremetism in the Yüan Period', in Arthur F. Wright (ed.), *The Confucian Persuasion*. Stanford: Stanford University Press, 202–40.

Munro, Donald (1977), *The Concept of Man in Contemporary China*. Ann Arbor: University of Michigan Press.

Naughton, Barry J. (1986), 'Sun Yefang: Toward a Reconstruction of Socialist Economics', in Hamrin and Cheek (1986: 124–54).

Nieh, Hualing (1981), *Literature of the Hundred Flowers*, vol. 2. New York: Columbia University Press.

Nie Rongzhen (1939a), *KangRi mofan genjudi–Jin Cha Ji bianqu* (A Model Anti-Japanese Base Area–The Jin Cha Ji Border Region). N.p.: Balujun junzheng zazhi she.

– – (1939b), 'Zai Zhonggong zhongyang beifang fenju dang daibiao dahui shangde baogao' (Report to the CCP CC Northern Bureau Party Congress), in *Zhonggong dangshi ziliao* (Materials on CCP History), 20:12.

– – (1979), 'Xu' (Introduction), in Deng Tuo (1979c): 1–5, and YDT: 5–7.

– – (1984), *Nie Rongzhen huiyi lu* (Reminiscences of Nie Rongzhen). Beijing: Zhanshi chubanshe.

– – (1988), *Inside the Red Star: The Memoirs of Marshal Nie Rongzhen*. Beijing: New World Press.

Niijima, Atsuyoshi (1962), 'En'an seifu undo–Sono katei, riron, igi' (The Rectification Movement in Yan'an–Its Process, Theory and Significance), *Toyo bunka*, 32: 27–73.

Ownby, David (trans. and ed.) (1985), 'Changing Attitudes Among Chinese Youths: Letters to *Zhongguo qingnian*', *Chinese Sociology and Anthropology*, 17:4.

– – (1986), 'The Audience: Growing Alienation Among Chinese Youths', in Hamrin and Cheek (1986: 212–45).

Panofsky, Erwin (1976), *Gothic Architecture and Scholasticism*. New York: New American Library.

Peng, Dehuai (1984), *Memoirs of a Chinese Marshal–The Autobiographical Notes of Peng Dehuai (1898–1974)*. Beijing: Foreign Languages Press.

Peng Zhen (1940), '*Jin Cha Ji ribao* san zhounian zhici' (Speech on the Third Anniversary of the *Jin Cha Ji Daily*), *Jin Cha Ji ribao*, 7 Nov.

– – (1981 edn.), *Guanyu Jin Cha Ji bianqu dangde gongzuo he juti zhengce baogao* (Report on the Party Work and Concrete Policies in the Jin Cha Ji Border Region). Beijing: Zhonggong zhongyang dangxiao chubanshe.

'Peng Zhen "Huairou diaocha" shi Liu, Deng hei silingbu yinmo fanpi zibenzhuyide yanzhong buji' (Peng Zhen's 'Huairou Investigations' are a Serious Step in Liu Shaoqi's and Deng Xiaoping's Black Headquarters' Secret Plot to Restore Capitalism),

Published on 1 August 1967 by the *Red Flag* Criticize Peng Alliance General Station of the Capital Red Congress and the Hebei Beijing Normal School. (Copy at the Fairbank Center Library, Harvard.)

Pepper, Suzanne (1973), 'Socialism, Democracy, and Chinese Communism: A Problem of Choice for the Intelligentsia, 1945–49', in Johnson (1973: 161–219).

– – (1978), *Civil War in China: The Political Struggle, 1945–1949.* Berkeley: University of California Press.

Perry, Elizabeth J. (1992), 'Chinese Political Culture Revisited', in Wasserstrom and Perry (1992: 1-11).

Pollard, David (1985), 'Lu Xun's *Zawen*', in Lee Ou–fan Lee (ed.), *Lu Xun and His Legacy*. Berkeley: University of California Press.

Polumbaum, Judy (1994), 'To Protect or Restrict? Points of Contention in China's Draft Press Law', in Potter (1994: 247–69).

Potter, Pitman B. (1986), 'Peng Zhen: Evolving Views on Party Organization and Law', in Hamrin and Cheek (1986: 21–50).

– – (ed.) (1994), *Domestic Law Reforms in Post–Mao China*. Armonk, NY: M.E. Sharpe.

Press Yearbook 1984. See *Zhongguo xinwen nianjian 1984*, below.

Pritchard, Earl H. (1968), 'Traditional Chinese Historiography and Local History', in Hayden White, *The Uses of History: Essays in Intellectual and Social History*. Detroit: Wayne State University Press, 187-219.

Pusey, James R. (1969), *Wu Han: Attacking the Present Through the Past*. Cambridge: Harvard East Asia Monographs, No. 33.

– – (1983), *China and Charles Darwin*. Cambridge: Harvard Council on East Asian Studies.

Qi Gong (1980), 'Du Deng Tuo tongzhi de shufa' (On Comrade Deng Tuo's Calligraphy), YDT: 196–200.

Qiang Yuanjin and Chen Xuewei (1980), 'Chongping 1956 nian de "fan maojin"' (A Reassessment of the 1956 'Oppose Adventurism'), *Dangshi yanjiu*, 6.

Qin Mu (1962), *Yi hai shibei* (Appreciations of the Sea of Art). Shanghai: Shanghai wenyi chubanshe.

Ragvald, Lars (1978), *Yao Wen–yuan as a Literary Critic and Theorist: Chinese Zhdanovism*. Stockholm: University of Stockholm.

Ren Wenping (1979), 'Yizhuang chumu jingxin de wenziyu–Wei "Sanjiacun zhaji" "Yanshan yehua" huifu mingju' (A Blood–curdling Literary Inquisition–On Behalf of the Rehabilitation of 'Notes from a Three Family Village' and 'Evening Chats at Yanshan'), *Renmin ribao*, 22 Feb. Reprinted in Wu Nanxing (1979: 201–12) and YDT: 280–89.

Renmin xinwenjia Deng Tuo (Deng Tuo: The People's Journalist). Beijing: Renmin chubanshe, 1987.

'Reversal of Earlier Verdicts on the "Three Family Village" Case', *Issues and Studies* (Taipei), Sept. 1979, 9–12.

Rittenberg, Sidney, and Bennett, Amanda (1993), *The Man Who Stayed Behind*. New York: Simon and Schuster.

Rowe, William T. (1982), 'Review Article: Recent Writings in the People's Republic of China on Early Ch'ing Economic History', *Ch'ing-shih wen-t'i*, 4:7, 73–90.
— — (1984), *Hankow: Commerce and Society in a Chinese City*. Stanford: Stanford University Press.
— — (1990), 'The Public Sphere in Modern China', *Modern China*, 16:3, 309–29.
Safarov, G.I. (1928), *Klassyi I Klassovaya Borba v. Kitaiskii Istorii* (Class and Class Struggle in Chinese History). Moscow: Gos. Izdat.
Saich, Tony (trans. and ed.) (1992-93), 'Luo Zhanglong's *Bloodshed of the Peking–Hankow Workers*', *Chinese Sociology and Anthropology*, 5:2.
— — (1996), *The Rise to Power of the Chinese Communist Party: Documents and Analysis*. Armonk, NY: M.E. Sharpe.
— —, and van de Ven, Hans J. (1995), *New Perspectives on the Chinese Communist Revolution*. Armonk, NY: M.E. Sharpe.
San Ding (1980), 'Deng Tuo tongzhi yu Rongbaozhai' (Comrade Deng Tuo and Rongbaozhai), YDT: 173–4.
Schneider, Laurence A. (1980), *A Madman of Ch'u: The Chinese Myth of Loyalty and Dissent*. Berkeley: University of California Press.
Schoenhals, Michael (1992), *Doing Things with Words in Chinese Politics*. Berkeley: University of California, Center for Chinese Studies.
Schram, Stuart (1967), *Mao Tse-tung*. Harmondsworth: Penguin Books.
— — (1974), *Mao Tse-tung Unrehearsed: Talks and Letters 1956–71*. London: Penguin.
— — (1975), *Chairman Mao Talks to the People*. New York: Pantheon.
— — (1981), 'To Utopia and Back: A Cycle in the History of the Chinese Communist Party', *The China Quarterly*, No. 87: 407–39.
Schurmann, Franz (1968), *Ideology and Organization in Communist China*, revised edition. Berkeley: University of California Press.
Schwarcz, Vera (1984), *Long Road Home: A China Journal*. New Haven: Yale University Press.
— — (1986), *The Chinese Enlightenment: Intellectuals and the Legacy of the May Fourth Movement of 1919*. Berkeley: University of California Press.
Schwartz, Benjamin I. (1972), 'The Limits of "Tradition Versus Modernity" as Categories of Explanation: The Case of the Chinese Intellectuals', *Daedalus*, 101:2, 71–88.
— — (1973), 'A Personal View of Some Thoughts of Mao Tse-tung', in Johnson (1973: 352–72).
— — (1989), 'Thoughts and the Late Mao: Between Total Redemption and Utter Frustration', in MacFarquhar, Cheek, and Wu (1989: 19–38).
SCMM. *Survey of China Mainland Magazines*. U.S. Government translation service.
Seidman, Steven (ed.) (1989), *Jürgen Habermas on Society and Politics: A Reader*. Boston: Beacon Press.
Selden, Mark (1971), *The Yenan Way In Revolutionary China*. Cambridge: Harvard University Press.
Seybolt, Peter J. (1986), 'Terror and Conformity: Counterespionage Campaigns, Rectification, and Mass Movements, 1942–1943', *Modern China*, 12:1, 39-74.

Sha Ying (1981a), 'DengTuo tongzhi zai ba xiaoshi yiwai' (Comrade Deng Tuo Outside of Office Hours), *Ba xiaoshi yiwai* (Tianjin), 1: 11–12.

– – (1981b), 'Chongdu "Yanshan yehua" zagan' (Random Thoughts on Rereading 'Evening Chats at Yanshan'), *Renwen zazhi* (Taiyuan), 1: 63–7.

Sha–fa–lou–fu (1932), *Zhongguo shehui fazhan shi* (A History of Chinese Social Development), trans. LiLiren. Shanghai: Xinsheng shuju. (Translation of Safarov, 1928).

Shambaugh, David (ed.) (1993), *American Studies of Contemporary China*. Armonk, NY: M.E. Sharpe.

Shanghai Municipal Party Committee Organization Department *et al*. (eds.) (1991), *Zhongguo gongchandang Shanghai shi zuzhi ziliao: 1920.8–1987.10* (Historical Materials on the Organization of the Shanghai CCP: August 1920–October 1987). Shanghai: Shanghai renmin chubanshe.

Sheel, Kamal (1989), *Peasant Society and Marxist Intellectuals in China: Fang Zhimin and the Origin of a Revolutionary Movement in the Xinjiang Region*. Princeton: Princeton University Press.

Shu Shen (1980a), 'Xiang DengTuo xuexi' (Study Deng Tuo), *Xin wanbao* (Hong Kong), 30 Mar.

– – (1980b), 'Tan "Sanjiacun zhaji"' (On 'Notes From a Three Family Village'), *Xin wanbao*, 11 and 18 May.

Si Wei (1980), 'Ding Yilan tan DengTuo shi' (Ding Yilan On DengTuo's Poetry), *Da–gong bao*, 3 Aug.

Situ Hao (1980), 'DengTuo do *Xinbian Tang shi sanbai shou*' (Deng Tuo's *New Edition of Three Hundred Poems from the Tang*), *Dagong bao*, 5 Aug.

Smith, Kidder *et al*. (1990), *Sung Dynasty Uses of the I Ching*. Princeton: Princeton University Press.

Solomon, Richard (1971), *Mao's Revolution and the Chinese Political Culture*. Berkeley: University of California Press.

Song Wenqing (1987), 'KangRi zhanzheng shiqi de *Jizhong daobao*' (The *Central Hebei Guide* During the Anti-Japanese War), in *KangRi zhanzheng shiqi de Zhongguo xinwenjie* (Chinese Journalism During the Anti-Japanese War). Chongqing: Chongqing chubanshe.

Song Yuanqiang (1983), 'Zhongguo zibenzhuyi mengya taolun de liangge jieduan' (Two Periods in the Debate on the Sprouts of Capitalism in China), in *Jianguo yilai shixue lilun wenti taolun zhuyao* (Summary of Discussions on Questions in Historical Thinking Since Liberation). Ji'nan: Ji-Lu shushe, 130–65.

Ssu-ma Ch'ien (1961 edn.), *Records of the Grand Historian of China,* trans. Burton Watson. 2 vols. New York: Columbia University Press.

Starr, John Bryan (1979), *Continuing The Revolution: The Political Thought of Mao*. Princeton: Princeton University Press.

Stranahan, Patricia (1990), *Molding the Medium: The Chinese Communist Party and the Liberation Daily*. Armonk, NY: M.E. Sharpe.

– – (1992), 'Strange Bedfellows: The Communist Party and Shanghai's Elite in the National Salvation Movement', *The China Quarterly,* No. 129: 26-51.

– – (1994), 'The Last Battle: Mao and Internationalists' Fight for the *Liberation Daily*', *The China Quarterly*, No. 123: 521-37.
– – (forthcoming), *UNDERGROUND: The Shanghai Communist Party and the Politics of Survival (1927–1937)*. Boulder, CO: Rowman & Littlefield.
Su Shuangbi (1963), 'Shi lishi xuehui dierju nianhui zuori bimu' (The Second Annual Meeting of the Municipal Historical Association Closed Yesterday), *Beijing ribao*, 24 Feb.
– – (1978), 'Ping Yao Wenyuan "Ping xinbian lishi ju *Hai Rui baguan*"' (Criticizing Yao Wenyuan's 'Criticizing the New Historical Play, "Hai Rui Dismissed From Office"'), *Guangming ribao*, 15 Nov. (Reprinted as a pamphlet with the same title by Shanghai renmin chubanshe in Feb. 1979.)
– – (1979*a*), 'Two Good Books That Pinpoint the Defects of the Era–Refuting Yao Wenyuan's False Charges against *Evening Chats at Yanshan* and *Notes from a Three Family Village*', *Guangming ribao*, 28 Jan., 3, (Translated in FBIS–CHI, 9 Feb. 1979, E8–E11.)
– – (1979*b*), 'Ping Yao Wenyuan de "Ping *Sanjiacun*"' (Criticizing Yao Wenyuan's "Criticizing The *Three Family Village*"), *Hongqi*, 2: 41–8.
– – (1982), *Jieji douzheng yu lishi kexue* (Class Struggle and the Science of History). Shanghai: Shanghai renmin chubanshe.
– – (1986*a*), 'Xueshu jie de pengyou he zhanshi–Wei jinian Deng Tuo shishi ershi zhounian erxie' (A Fighter and a Friend in Academic Circles–Writing on the 20th Anniversary of the Death of Deng Tuo), *Fujian luntan*, 1: 8–12 and 18.
– – (1986*b*), 'Guanyu kaizhan "baijia zhengming" zhongde jige wenti' (A Few Questions Concerning the Development of 'A Hundred Schools Contending'), *Guangming ribao*, 30 Apr., 3 (Translated in FBIS–CHI, 19 May 1986, K4–K12; abstracted in *China Daily*, 21 May, 4.)
– – and Wang Hongzhi (1983), 'Wu Han', in *Zhonggong dangshi renwuzhuan*.
– – (1984) *Wu Han zhuan* (Biography of Wu Han). Beijing: Beijing chubanshe.
– –, Ru Xin, and Xing Fensi (1990), 'Continuing the Policy of Letting a Hundred Flowers Bloom and a Hundred Schools Contend', *Guangming ribao*, 29 Jun. as trans. in FBIS-CHI 90-134 (12 Jul.), 25-9.
Sui Zhi (1959), 'Huabei dihou xinwen shiye huiyi' (Reminiscences of News Work Behind the Enemy Lines in North China), in Zhang Jinglu, Vol. 3 (1959), 225–9.
Sullivan, Lawrence R. (1986-87), 'Leadership and Authority in the Chinese Communist Party: Perspectives from the 1950s', *Pacific Affairs*, 59: 4, 622–48.
Sun Zhenhua (1980), 'Dushu yu jianfen' (Reading Books and Collecting Manure), *Xingtai ribao*, 24 Jul.
Tai Huaiji (1982), *Tiandi you zhengqi: Caolanzi jianyu douzheng yu 'liushiyi ren an'* (Heaven and Earth Have Upright Spirit: The Struggle in Caolanzi Prison and the '61' Man Case). Beijing: Beijing chubanshe.
Takashi, Oka (1980), 'Peking Evening News: Scourge of Bureaucrats, Advisor of Lovelorn', *The Christian Science Monitor*, 14 Aug., 1.

Tang Mingsui *et al* (1958), 'Dui Deng Tuo tongzhi 'CongWanli dao Qianlong' yiwen de shangque buchong' (A Discussion and Supplement to Comrade DengTuo's 'From Wanli to Qianlong'), *Lishi yanjiu*,1: 41–63.

Tang Tao (1980), 'Shishi qiushi–Women de wei ren de daode' (Seek Truth From Facts– Our Morality for Man), in *Chang duan lu* (1980: 7–12).

Tang Zhuguo (1966),*Yanjing jiuyu* (Old Words from Yanjing). Taipei: Shuangshizi chubanshe. (Tang was a student at Beida in the early 1960s.)

Tantan baozhi gongzuo (Talks on NewspaperWork). Beijing: Xinwen yanjiusuo, 1978.

Tao Bai (1980), 'Huai Deng Tuo tongzhi' (Thinking of Comrade DengTuo), YDT: 234– 7.

Tawney, R. H. (1939),*Agrarian China: Selected Source Materials From Chinese Authors*. Chicago: University of ChicagoPress.

Teiwes, Frederick C. (1976), 'The Origins of Rectification: Inner PartyPurges and Education BeforeLiberation', *The China Quarterly*, No. 65: 15–53.

– – (1979), *Politics andPurges in China: Rectification and the Decline of Party Norms, 1950–1965*. Armonk, NY: M.E. Sharpe.

– – (1984), *Leadership,Legitimacy and Conflict in China: From a Charismatic Mao to the Politics of Succession*. Armonk, NY: M.E. Sharpe.

– – (1986), 'Peng Dehuai and Mao Zedong',*The Australian Journal of Chinese Affairs*, No. 16

– – (1988), 'Mao and His Lieutenants',*The Australian Journal of Chinese Affairs*, Nos. 19–20.

(1990), *Politics at Mao's Court. Gao Gang andParty Factionalism in the Early 1950s*. Armonk, NY: M.E. Sharpe.

– – (1993), *Politics andPurges in China,* 2nd. edn. Armonk, NY: M.E. Sharpe.

– –, and Sun,Warren (1995), 'From a Leninist to a Charismatic Party: The CCP's ChangingLeadership, 1937–1945', in Saich and van deVen (1995: 339–87).

– – (1996), *The Tragedy of Lin Biao: Riding the Tiger During the Cultural Revolution* London: C. Hurst & Co.

Teng, Ssu–yü, and Biggerstaff, Knight (comps.) (1971 edn.), *AnAnnotated Bibliography of Selected Chinese Reference Works*, 3rd edn. Cambridge: Harvard University Press.

Thompson, Roger (1989), 'The "Discovery" of Mao Zedong's *Report from Xunwu*: Deng Xiaoping Writes a New Chapter in EarlyParty History', *CCP Research Newsletter*, No. 3: 8–17.

Thurston, Anne (1988), *Enemies of thePeople*. Cambridge: Harvard UniversityPress.

ToTaku, De Gan, and Ryo Umatsusa (1966), *Enzan yawa: fu–Sankason sakki* (Evening Chats atYanshan: Appendix–Notes From AThree Family Village). Tokyo: Mainichi shinbunsha. (Revised edn., Sept. 1979.)

Townsend, James. R. (1969),*Political Participation in Communist China*. Berkeley: University of California Press.

Tsou,Tang (1968), 'Revolution, Reintegration, and Crisis in Communist China: A Framework ForAnalysis', in Ping–ti Ho and Tang Tsou, eds., *China in Crisis: China's Cultural Heritage and the Communist Political System*, Vol. 1, Book 1. Chicago: University of ChicagoPress, 277–347.

Tu Wei–ming (1979), *Humanity and Self Cultivation*. Berkeley: Asian Humanities Press.

Tung, Robert (1978 edn.), *Proscribed Chinese Writing*. London: Curzon Press, rev. edn.

Übelhör, Monika (1989), 'The Community Compact (*Hsiang-yüeh*) of the Sung and Its Educational Significance', in Wm. Theodore de Bary and John W. Chafee, (eds.), *Neo–Confucian Education: The Formative Stage.* Berkeley: University of California Press, 371–88.

Uhalley, Stephen, Jr. (1966), 'The Cultural Revolution and the Attack on the "Three Family Village"', *The China Quarterly*, No. 27: 149–61.

Unger, Jonathan (ed.) (1993), *Using the Past to Serve the Present: Historiography and Politics in Contemporary China*. Armonk, NY: M.E. Sharpe.

Unger, Roberto M. (1987), *Social Theory: Its Situation and Its Task*. Cambridge: Cambridge University Press.

Union Research Institute, clipping file from the Chinese press. (Held at the Universities Service Centre, The Chinese University of Hong Kong.)

van de Ven, Hans (1991), *From Friend to Comrade: The Chinese Communist Party, 1920–1927*. Berkeley: University of California Press.

– – (1995), 'The Power of Words: Party Periodicals, Ideology, and Organization in the Early CCP', in Saich and van de Ven (1995: 5-32).

Van Slyke, Lyman P. (1967), *Enemies and Friends: The United Front in Chinese Communist History*. Stanford: Stanford University Press.

Wagner, Rudolf (1987), 'The Chinese Writer in His Own Mirror: Writer, State, and Society–the Literary Evidence', in Goldman *et. al* (1987: 183–232).

Wakeman, Frederic, Jr. (1972), 'The Price of Autonomy: Intellectuals in Ming and Ch'ing Politics', *Daedalus*, 2: 35–70.

– – (1983), 'Chinese Intellectuals Since the Cultural Revolution', New England China Seminar, Harvard University.

– – (1993), 'The Civil Society and Public Sphere Debate: Western Reflections on Chinese Political Culture', *Modern China*, 19:2, 108–38.

– –, and Grant, Carolyn (eds.) (1975), *Conflict and Control in Late Imperial China*. Berkeley: University of California Press.

Walder, Andrew (1986), *Communist Neo–Traditionalism: Work and Authority in Chinese Industry*. Berkeley: University of California Press.

Wan, Grace, and Johnson, Wallace (1973), *An Advanced Reader in Chinese History*. Lawrence: University of Kansas Publications.

Wang Bisheng (1981), 'Deng Tuo tongzhi de shengping he wenxue huodong' (Comrade Deng Tuo's Life and Literary Activities), *Xin wenxue shiliao*, 4: 71–81.

– – (1983*a*), 'Deng Tuo de shengping he sixiang chutan' (A Preliminary Exploration of Deng Tuo's Life and Thought). Chinese Academy of Social Sciences, Journalism Department, M.A. thesis.

– – (1983*b*), 'Deng Tuo zai kangzhan chuqi yipian guanyu lilun de zhongyao wenzhang– "San min zhuyi de xianshizhuyi yu wenyi chuangzuo zhu wenti"' (An Important Article by Deng Tuo on Literary and Artistic Theory from the Early Period of the Resistance War–'The Realism of the Three People's Principles and a Few Questions in Literary and Artistic Creation'), *Xin wenxue shiliao*, 1: 218–20.

– – (1983c), 'Deng Tuo–Yidai xinwen gongzuozhe de mofan' (Deng Tuo–The Model of a Generation of Journalists), *Xuexi yu sikao*, 2: 58–62 and 49. (Published by the Graduate School of the Chinese Academy of Social Sciences.)

– – (1983d), 'Deng Tuo he wenwu' (Deng Tuo and Cultural Artifacts), *Wenwu tiandi*, 3: 36–7.

– – (1983e), 'Fenghuo shinian xie zongheng–Deng Tuo tongzhi zai Jin Cha Ji bianqu xinwen xuanchuan huodong jishu' (Writing with Ease Through Ten Years of War–An Account of Comrade Deng Tuo's Journalism and Propaganda Activities in the Jin Cha Ji Border Region), *Xinwen shiliao*, 5: 1–7. (Note on p. 7 says this is ch. 3 of Wang's M.A. thesis.)

Bisheng (Wang Bisheng) (1985), 'Deng Tuo shenghuo, gongzuo pianduan: 6. Zhandou zai xin Zhongguo xinwen gangwei shang' (Fragments of Deng Tuo's Life and Work: 6. Struggle at the Journalism Post in New China), *Xinwen jizhe*, 1: 14–15.

– – (1986), *Deng Tuo pingzhuan* (A Critical Biography of Deng Tuo). Beijing: Qunzhong chubanshe.

Wang, Ching-wei (1933), 'The Crisis in Fukien and the Policy of the Government', *The Far Eastern Review*, 29:12, 533-4.

Wang Ruoshui (1989), 'Wenzhang manzhi shusheng lei–Ji 1957 nian Mao Zedong de jianjie' (Articles Filling Pages, Accumulations of a Scholarly Life–Record of a Meeting with Mao Zedong in 1957), *Lianhe bao* (Taipei), 10 Mar., 4.

Wang Wei (1980), 'Wangshi yi dangnian–Huainian Deng Tuo tongzhi' (Recollections of Those Years–Mourning Comrade Deng Tuo), YDT: 69–72.

Wang Xiaobo (1981), 'Zuo Quan', in *Buqu de gongchang dangren* (Beijing) 2, 259–83.

Wang Zhangling (1967), *Zhonggong de wenyi zhengfeng* (Chinese Communist Literary Rectification). Taipei: Guoji guanxi yanjiu suo.

Wang Zhen (1979), 'Dui pipan Lin Biao, "siren bang" zuoqing jihuizhuyi xian you zhongyao yiyi' (Of Great Significance in the Criticism of the Opportunist Line of Lin Biao and the 'Gang of Four'), *Guangming ribao*, 10 Feb., 2. (Excerpts trans. in FBIS–CHI, 27 Feb. 1979, E19–E20.)

Wasserstrom, Jefferey (1991a), *Student Protests in Twentieth–Century China: The View from Shanghai*. Stanford: Stanford University Press.

– – (1991b), 'Tiananmen: More Lessons for Scholars', *CCP Research Newsletter*, No. 8: 66-79.

– – (1992a), 'Towards a Social History of the Chinese Revolution: A Review–Part I: The Evolution of a Field', in *Social History*, 17:1, 1–21 and 'Part II: The State of the Field', ibid, 17: 2, 289–317.

– – (1992b), 'Afterword', in Wasserstrom and Perry (1992: 244-80).

– –, and Perry, Elizabeth (1992), *Popular Protest and Political Culture in China: Learning from 1989*. Boulder, CO: Westview Press.

Watson, Andrew (1980), *Mao Zedong and the Political Economy of the Border Region*. Cambridge: Cambridge University Press.

Wei Wei (1959), *Jin cha ji shi chao* (Poems Copied from Jin Cha Ji). Beijing: Zhongguo qingnian chubanshe.

Wei Yi (1979), 'DengTuo yong zhan siren bang huo zanyang' (DengTuo's Brave Struggle Against the Gang of FourWinsPraise), *Mingbao* (Hong Kong), 30Aug., 12.

Weigelin–Schwiedrzik, Susanne (1984), *Parteigeschichtsschreibung in der R China: Typen, Methoden, Themen und Funktionen*. Weisbaden: Harrassowitz.

– – (1993), 'Party Historiography', in Unger (1993: 151-73).

Wen Bi. SeeLiao Mosha

Wen Jize (1949), 'Guanyu Hui Daiying tongzhi de si' (On the Death of Comrade Hui Daiying), *Zhongguo qingnian*, 26: 23.

Wenge: Zheng she bumen (The Cultural Revolution: Political and Social Division), 7 vols. Hong Kong: Union Research Institute. (Clippings of Red Guard material and national publications, including Deng Tuo and the 'Three FamilyVillage' now stored at the Universities Services Centre, The Chinese University of Hong Kong.)

Wenxue yundong shiliao xuan: Di wu ce (Selected Materials on the Literary Movement: Vol. 5). Shanghai: Shanghai jiaoyu chubanshe, 1979.

Whyte, Martin King (1974), *Small Groups and Political Rituals in China*. Berkeley: University of California Press.

Will, Pierre–Etienne (1990), *Bureaucracy and Famine in Eighteenth–Century China*. Trans. from French by Elborg Forster. Stanford: Stanford University Press.

Williams, James (1990), 'FangLizhi's Expanding Universe', *The China Quarterly*, No. 123: 458-83.

– – (1994), 'FangLizhi's Big Bang: Science and Politics in Mao's China'. University of California at Berkeley, Ph.d. thesis.

Williams, Philip (1993), *Village Echoes: The Fiction of Wu Zuxiang*. Boulder, CO: WestviewPress.

Wong, Siu–lun (1979), *Sociology and Socialism in Contemporary China*. London: Routledge and KeganPaul.

Wu, Guoguang (1994), 'Command Communication: The Politics of Editorial Formulation in the *People's Daily*', *The China Quarterly*, No. 137: 194-211.

Wu Han (1963), 'Tan xingqu' (On Interests), *Qianxian*, 25 Sept. Reprinted inWu Nanxing (1979: 141-3).

Wu Jilu (1982), 'Deng Tuo tongzhi yu xiezuo' (Comrade DengTuo and Writing), *Xiezuo*, 3: 27-9.

Wu, Lengxi (1969-70 edn.), 'The Confessions of WuLeng–hsi', *ChineseLaw and Government*,. II :4.

– – (1988), '"Wu bupa" ji qita: huiyi Mao zhuxi de jici tanhua' ('The Five Don't Fears' and Other Things: Recalling a Few Talks with Chairman Mao), *Renmin ribao huiyilu* (Reminiscences on the *People's Daily*). Beijing: Renmin ribao chubanshe, 1–10.

Wu Nanxing (1979), *Sanjiacun zhaji* (Notes from aThree Family Village). Beijing: Renmin wenxue chubanshe.

Wylie, Raymond F. (1980), *The Emergence of Maoism: Mao Tse–tung, Ch'en Po–ta and the Search for Chinese Theory 1935–1945*. Stanford: Stanford University Press.

Xiao Yang, and Du Zhang (1981), 'Dangde guangrong zhao wo xin–Ji lao boyinyuan DingYilan de yici tanhua' (The Glory of the Party Reflects My Heart–A Record of a Conversation with Veteran Broadcaster DingYilan), *Wenhui bao*, 17 May.

Xiaoyou zhi sheng (Voice of the Alumnae). Fuzhou No. 1 Middle School, 1982.
'Xinhuashe dangzu guanyu Xinhuashe disanci quanguo shewu huiyi de baogao' (The NCNAParty Group Concerning the Report of the NCNA's Third National Conference) (Feb. 1954), in *Zhongguo gongchandang xinwen gongzuo wenjian huibian*, Vol. 2, 362–70.
Xing Xianting (1980), 'Huiyi Deng Tuo tongzhi' (Commemorating Comrade Deng Tuo), YDT: 73–6.
Xu Rende (1966), 'Kan Deng Tuo hei bang de langzi yexin cong "Sanjiacun" hei zhaopai de laili' (See the Wild Ambition of Deng Tuo's Black Gang from the History of the Black Signboard 'Three Family Village'), *Renmin ribao*, 3 Jun., 4.
Xu Zhucheng (1981), *Baohai jiu wen* (Old Stories about Journalism). Shanghai: Shanghai renmin chubanshe.
– – (1987), 'Yangmo qinli ji' (A Personal Diary of an Open Plot), *Zhongguo zhichun* (China Spring), 55.
Xuexi wenxuan (Study Selections). N.p.: n.p., n.d. CCRM 'Mao zhu weikan gao', vol. 3, 348 pp. (See MacFarquhar, Cheek, and Wu, 1989: 78.)
Xuexi ziliao, 1957–1961 (Study Materials, 1957–1961). N.p.: n.p., n.d. CCRM 'Mao zhu weikan gao', vol. 12B, 518 pp. (See MacFarquhar, Cheek, and Wu, 1989: 80.)
YDT. See Liao Mosha *et al.* (1980).
YSYH/79. See Ma Nancun (1979 edn.).
Yahuda, Michael (1979), 'Political Generations in China', *The China Quarterly*, No. 80: 796–805.
Yan, Huai (1995), 'Organizational Hierarchy and the Cadre Management System', in Hamrin and Zhao (1995: 39–50).
Yan Ling (1980), 'Fenming feimeng yi feiyan–Huiyi Deng Tuo tongzhi zai *Renmin ribao*' (Clear and Not Dreamy or Foggy–Remembering Comrade Deng Tuo at the *People's Daily*), *Xinwen yanjiu ziliao*, 5: 110–16.
'Yanshan leiluo, yehua qianqiu–Deng Tuo furen Ding Yilan gei duzhe de xin he bafeng gei ta de xin' (Open and Upright Yanshan, Evening Chats for a Thousand Years–A Letter to Readers from Deng Tuo's Wife Ding Yilan and Eight Letters Sent to Her), *Suibi* (Guangzhou), 1980: 8, 34–45.
Yang Dehua (1981), 'Yipian bingxin wangu qing–Ding Yilan tongzhi tan Deng Tuo zang hua' (A Chaste and Everlasting Sentiment–Comrade Ding Yilan Talks About Deng Tuo's Collection of Paintings), *Beijing wanbao*, 19 Dec.
Yang Renkai (1980), 'Yi Deng Tuo tongzhi ersan shi' (Remembering Two or Three Things About Comrade Deng Tuo), YDT: 216–17.
– –, Huang Zhou, and Zhou Huaimin (1982), 'Renjian yi mo rou nan jin–Ji Deng Tuo yuanzang Su Shi "Xiao Xiang zhu shi tu"' (Calligraphy Among Us From the Past Like Southern Gold–Remembering Su Shi's Painting, 'Stones and Bamboo of the Xiao and Xiang Rivers'), *Guangming ribao*, 3 Jan.
Yang, Shangkun (1942), 'Activities of the Trotskyite Wang Shiwei and Liberalism in the Party, Oct. 31, 1942', in Dai Qing (1994: 135-45).
Yang Shu (1980), 'Jianbi zhong zai tiandi jian–Huainian Deng Tuo tongzhi' (A Talented Pen Forever With Us–Mourning Comrade Deng Tuo), YDT: 203–6.

Yang Xianzhen (1980a), 'One Who Inspired and Guided the Building of the Party School: In Memory of Comrade Liu Shaoqi', *Hongqi*, 7. Trans. in JPRS 75739 (21 May), 35-43.

– – (1980b), 'Ru Caolanzi jianyu qianhou' (Before and After Entering Caolanzi Prison), *Geming shi ziliao*, 10: 6–22.

– – (1983), 'Cong Taihang wenhua ren zuotanhui dao Zhao Shuli de "Xiao Erhei jiehun" chuban' (From the Taihang Cultured Men's Forum to the Publication of Zhao Shuli's 'The Marriage of Xiao Erhei'), *Xin wenxue shiliao*, 2: 28–35.

– –, and Guan Shan (1980), 'Ru Caolanzi jianyou qianhou' (Before and After Entering Caolanzi Prison), *Geming shi ziliao* (Oct.), I:17-28.

'Yao fandui baoshouzhuyi, yeyao fandui jizao qingxu' (One Must Oppose Conservatism and Oppose Impetuosity), *Renmin ribao*, 20 Jun. 1956, 1. Trans. SCMP, 1327: 11–14.

Yao Wenyuan (1958), *Lun wenxue shangde xiuzhengzhuyi sichao* (On the Revisionist Tide in Literature). Shanghai: Xin wenyi chubanshe.

– – (1966), 'Ping "Sanjiacun"–"Yanshan yehua" "Sanjiacun zhaji" de fandong benzhi' (Criticizing the *Three Family Village*–The Reactionary Nature of *Evening Chats at Yanshan* and *Notes From a Three Family Village*, *Wenhui bao*, 10 May and *Renmin ribao*, 11 May.

Yeh, Wen–hsin (1990), *The Alienated Academy*. Cambridge: Harvard Council on East Asian Studies.

Yu Guokun (1980), 'He ru bomo xie yunyan–Du Deng Tuo tongzhi yizuo "Guilin za shi"' (Writing of Cloudy Mists Like an Impressionist Painter–Reading Comrade Deng Tuo's Posthumous Poem, 'Random Poems on Guilin'), YDT: 190–4.

Yu Haocheng (1981), 'Achieving Freedom of the Press Is an Important Problem', *Dushu*, 1:26–9. (Trans. in JPRS-PSMA, no. 77495, 3 Mar. 1991, 20.)

Yu Hong (1983), 'Deng Tuo zhuanlüe' (A Biographical Sketch of Deng Tuo), *Zhongguo xiandai shehui kexuejia zhuanlüe*, 3: 67–77.

Yuan Ying (1979), 'Bumie de shihun–Huai Deng Tuo tongzhi he tade shi' (The Inextinguishable Poetic Spirit–Cherishing Comrade Deng Tuo and His Poetry), Deng Tuo (1979c: 157–89), and YDT: 175–89.

– – (1986), 'Yu sui' (Broken Jade), *Baogao wenxue*, 5: 11–19. (A shorter version appears in *Renmin ribao*, 6 May, 7.)

– –, and Jiang Deming (1979), '*Chang duan lu* de shimo yu gong "zui"' (The Origins and End and Accomplishments and 'Crimes' of *The Long and the Short*), *Xinwen zhanxian*, 5: 44–8. Reprinted in *Chang duan lu* (1980: 91–100).

Yue, Daiyun, and Wakeman, Carolyn (1985), *To The Storm: The Odyessy of a Revolutionary Chinese Woman*. Berkeley: University of California Press.

Zeng Bairong (1981), 'Zajia zheliu' (The Miscellaneous Scholar), *Beijing wanbao*, 19 May, 3.

Zhang Chuanxi (1980), 'Lilun, shiliao, wenzhang' (Theory, Historical Materials, Essays), *Renmin ribao*, 22 Feb., 5.

Zhang Dongsun (1933), 'Dongde luoji shi kenengde ma?' (Is a Logic of Motion Possible?), *Xin Zhonghua*, 1:18, 1-4.

Zhang Fan (1980), 'Wenqi sui zhangu: Huiyi Deng Tuo tongzhi zai *Jin Cha Ji ribao* bianji de peiyang' (The Flag of Literature Follows the Drum of Battle: Reminiscences of Comrade Deng Tuo's Cultivation of Editors at *Jin Cha Ji Daily*), *Xinwen yanjiu ziliao*, 2: 16–21, and YDT: 44–54.

Zhang Jinglu (1954-59), *Zhongguo xiandai chuban shiliao* (Historical Materials on Contemporary Chinese Publishing). Beijing: Zhonghua shuju, multiple volumes.

Zhang Ruxin (1942), 'Chedi fenzui Wang Shiwei de Tuopai lilun ji qi fandang huodong' (Completely Demolish Wang Shiwei's Trotskyite Theories and his Anti–Party Movement), *Jiefang ribao*, 17 Jun., 4.

Zhang Sheng (1979), 'Fang Deng Tuo furen Ding Yilan' (An Interview with Deng Tuo's Wife, Ding Yilan), *Dagong bao*, 12 Feb., 1.

Zhang Shuzheng (1985), 'Deng Tuo', *Xinwenjie renwu (5)* (Personalities in Journalism: 5). Beijing: Xinhua chubanshe.

Zhang Yide (1979), 'Pipan weixinlun wuzui, xuanchuan weiwulun yougong–Tuidao Yao Wenyuan "Ping Sanjiacun" dui "Yanshan yehua" "Sanjiacun zhaji" de wuxian' (It Is No Crime To Criticize Idealism, It Is Meritorious To Propagate Materialism–Refuting Yao Wenyuan's False Charges in His Article 'Criticizing the Three Family Village': Against 'Evening Chats at Yanshan' and 'Notes From A Three Family Village'), *Guangming ribao*, 26 Jan., 3. (Translated in FBIS–CHI, 9 Feb. 1979, E2–E8.)

Zhang Zhimin (1980), 'Xiegei "Sanjiacun"' (Written for the 'Three Family Village'), *Beijing ribao*, 3 Aug.

Zhang Zhuhong (1987), *Zhongguo xiandai geming shi shiliuoxue* (Historiography of China's Modern Revolutionary History). Beijing: Zhonggong dangshi ziliao chubanshe.

Zhao Qingxue (1980), 'Deng Tuo jiao wo xie gao' (Deng Tuo Taught Me to Write for Newspapers), YDT: 77–83.

Zhelokhovtsev, A. (1984), 'Deng Tuo's Posthumous Fate', *Far Eastern Affairs* (Moscow), 4, 82–91.

Zhi Liangjun (1980), 'Huainian Deng Tuo tongzhi' (Mourning Comrade Deng Tuo), YDT: 55–61.

Zhonggong dangshi renwuzhuan (Biographies of Chinese Communist Party History Personalities). Xi'an: Shaanxi renmin chubanshe. (Serial volumes beginning in 1980.)

Zhonggong dangshi shijian renwu lu (A Record of People and Events in Party History). Shanghai: Shanghai renmin chubanshe, 1983.

Zhonggong renming lu (Biographies of Chinese Communists). Taipei: Guoji guanxi yanjiusuo yinxing, 1967.

'Zhonggong zhongyang guanyu zai baozhi kanwushang zhankai piping and ziwo piping de jueding' (Resolution of the Party Central Committee on Developing Criticism and Self–Criticism in Newspapers and Periodicals) (19 Apr. 1950), *Zhongguo gongchandang xinwen gongzuo wenjian huibian*, 2: 5–8.

'Zhonggong zhongyang guanyu zhengfeng yundong de zhishi' (Central Committee Directive on the Rectification Campaign). (Dated 27 Apr. 1957.) Reprinted in *Zhonggong dangshi cankao ziliao* (Beijing: Renmin chubanshe, 1980), 8: 575–9.

'Zhonggong zhongyang pizhuan *Renmin ribao* bianji weiyuanhui xiang zhongyang de baogao' (The Central Committee Approves and Transmits the Report of the Editorial Board of the *People's Daily* Presented to the Central Committee') (Aug. 1956), *Zhongguo gongchandang xinwen gongzuo wenjian huibian*, 2: 483–4.

Zhonggong zhongyang wenjian xuanji (Selected Central Documents of the CCP). Beijing: Zhonggong zhongyang dangxiao chubanshe, (14 volumes), 1982-1987.

Zhonggong zhongyang wenxian yanjiushi (ed.) (1985), *Guanyu jianguoyilai dangde ruogan lishi wenti de jueyi zhushiben (xiuding)* (Annotations for the revised edition of the *Resolution on Certain Historical Questions of the Party Since the Founding of the Nation*). Beijing: Renmin chubanshe.

Zhongguo baogao wenxue congshu–Di 3 ji, di 5 fence (Chinese Reportage—Vol. 3, No. 5). Hubei: Changjiang wenyi chubanshe, 1982.

Zhongguo dangdai shehui kexuejia (zhuanji congshu) (Contemporary Chinese Social Scientists [Biographical Series]). Beijing: Shumu wenxian chubanshe, 1983-86.

Zhongguo dangdai wenxue shi (Contemporary Chinese Literary History). Fuzhou: Fujian renmin chubanshe, Vol. 1: May 1980, Vol. 2: Dec. 1981.

Zhongguo gongchandang xinwen gongzuo wenjian huibian (Collection of Documents on CCP Journalism Work). Beijing: Xinhua chubanshe, 1980, 3 vols.

Zhongguo lishixue nianjian 1979 (Chinese History Almanac 1979). Beijing: Sanlian shudian, 1980.

Zhongguo wenxuejia cidian: Xiandai dier fence (A Dictionary of Chinese Writers: Modern Period, Vol. 2). Chengdu: Sichuan renmin chubanshe, 1982.

Zhongguo xiandai shehui kexuejia zhuanlüe (Biographical Sketches of Contemporary Chinese Social Scientists). Taiyuan: Shanxi renmin chubanshe, 1980 –.

Zhongguo xin minzhuzhuyi geming shiqi genjudi de fazhi wenxian xuanbian (Selected Base Area Documents on the Legal System from the Period of the New Democratic Revolution), Vol. 4. Beijing: Zhongguo shehui kexue chubanshe, 1984.

Zhongguo xinwen nianjian 1984 (Press Yearbook 1984). Beijing: Renmin ribao chubanshe, 1984. (English title on cover.)

Zhongguo zibenzhuyi mengya wenti taolun ji (Essays on the Sprouts of Capitalism in China). Beijing: Zhongguo renmin daxue, Zhongguo lishi yanjiushi, Vols. 1–2: 1957; supplement: 1960.

Zhonghua renmin gongheguo dashiji, 1949–1980 (Chronology of the People's Republic of China, 1949–1980). Beijing: Xinhua chubanshe, 1983 edn.

'Zhonghua renmin gongheguo zuigao renmin jianchayuan tebie jiancha ting qi songshu' (Indictment from the Special Prosecutor's Office of the Highest People's Procuratorate of the PRC), Xinhuashe telegram dated 20 November 1980, hard copy dated next day, dateline: Beijing. (Indictment of Jiang Qing *et al.* mentioning Deng Tuo. From Ding Yilan's clipping file.)

Zhong Kan (1982), *Kang Sheng pingzhuan* (A Critical Biography of Kang Sheng). Beijing: Hongqi chubanshe.

Zhou Huaimin. See Yang Renkai *et al.* (1982).

Zhou Libo (1939), *Jin Cha Ji bianqu yinxiang ji* (A Diary of Impressions of the Jin Cha Ji Border Region). Chongqing: Dushu shenghuo chubanshe.

Zhou Wen (1942), 'Cong Lu Xun de zawen tandao Shiwei' (From Lu Xun's *Zawen* to [Wang] Shiwei), *Jiefang ribao*, 16 Jun., 4.

Zhou Xiuchang (1986), 'Jiechude pinglunjia Deng Tuo' (The Outstanding Commentator, Deng Tuo), paper presented at 'Symposium on Deng Tuo', Fuzhou, May 1986, 1-12. (Expurgated portions reprinted in *Xinwen zhanxian*, 5 (1986), 6-10 and *Renmin ribao* 11 May 1986, 5.)

Zhou Yang (1983), *'Deng Tuo wenji* xu' (Preface to *Collected Works of Deng Tuo*), *Renmin ribao*, 22 Dec., 8. (Translated in JPRS–China Report:Political, Sociological, and Military, No. 6, 16 Jan. 1984, 71–2.)

Zhu Jinshun, and Liu Xiqing (1982), *Fanwen duben* (A Reader of Model Essays). Beijing: Beijing chubanshe.

Zhu Shuxin (1979), 'Suowei "Sanjiacun fandang jituan" wanquan shi Lin Biao, "Siren bang" zhizao de da yuan'an' (The So-Called 'Three Family Village Anti-Party Clique' Was a Complete Fabrication of Lin Biao and the 'Gang of Four'), *Guangming ribao*, 23 Feb., 3.

— — (1981), 'Deng Tuo zanghua, shufa zhanlan zai Beijing juxing' (Exhibition of Deng Tuo's Collection of Paintings and Calligraphy Held in Beijing), Xinhua news release, Beijing, 20 Dec.

Zuckerman, Laurence (1985), 'Letter From China', *Columbia Journalism Review*, 34.

Zun Dang (1982), 'Budu pingsheng wei jian shu' (Reading All My Life There Are Books I Have Not Seen), *Beijing wanbao*, 26 Apr.

Zuo Lu (1984*a*), 'Huiyi Deng Tuo shenghuo, gongzuo pianduan: 2. Xuesheng, zhanshi, xuezhe (Fragments of Deng Tuo's Life and Work Recalled: 2. Student, Fighter, Scholar), *Xinwen jizhe*, 9: 26–9.

— — (1984*b*), 'Huiyi Deng Tuo shenghuo, gongzuo pianduan: 3. Shi wenchang you shi zhanchang' (Fragments of Deng Tuo's Life and Work Recalled: A Literary and Battle Field), *Xinwen jizhe*, 10: 27–30.

— — (1984*c*), 'Huiyi Deng Tuo shenghuo, gongzuo pianduan: 4. Xinwen shi shang qiji' (Fragments of Deng Tuo's Life and Work Recalled: 4. A Miracle in the History of Journalism), *Xinwen jizhe*, 11: 28–31.

Glossary

Glossary I: Deng Tuo's Pen-Names

The names listed below are the known pen-names, sobriquets, and literary aliases for Deng Tuo. The best summary of names and description of the time and place of their use can be found in Zhang Shuzheng (1985: 123-4), and for Deng's childhood names, Wang Bisheng (1981: 71).

* Indicates joint pen-names of writing groups of which Deng Tuo was a member.
** Indicates pen-names Deng Tuo selected but did not use in published work.

Bu Wuji 卜無忌
Dan Wensheng 單文生
Deng Junte 鄧君特
Deng Tuo 鄧拓
Deng Tuozhou 鄧拓洲
Deng Yunte 鄧雲特
Deng Zijian 鄧子健
Di Mangong 狄曼公
Ding Binggen 丁丙根
Ding Luo'an 丁蘿庵
Ding Mangong 丁曼公
Gao Mi 高密
Guan Bai 關白
Jin Shiwei** 金世偉
Ma Nancun 馬南村
Man Gong 曼公

Ou Zi 鷗子
Shi Siping* 石思平
Tuo Ping 拓平
Wen Zhou 溫洲
Wu Nanxing* 無南星
Xiang Yangsheng 向陽生
Xiao Jing 曉晶
Xiao Si 簫斯
Xuchu 旭初
Yin Zhou 殷洲
You Ren 右任
Yu Suian 于遂安
Zhao Kai** 趙凱
Zuo Hai 左海

Glossary II: Newspapers & Periodicals

[with holding library for hard to find items]
* Indicates periodicals unseen; as cited in secondary sources or in reprints

Ba xiaoshi yiwai 八小時以外
Baogao wenxue 報告文學
Beifang wenhua* 北方文化
Beijing ribao 北京日報
Beijing wanbao 北京晚報
Beijing wanbao tongxunyuan zhiyou
    北京晚報通訊員之友
    [copy held by Ding Yilan]
Bianqu wenhua* 邊區文化

Buqu de gongchandang ren
    不屈的共產黨人
Changcheng (Hebei)* 長城
Changcheng wenyi 長城文藝
Chongqing ribao* 重慶日報
Dagong bao 大公報
Dangshi yanjiu 黨史研究
Fujian luntan 福建論壇
Fuzhou wanbao 福州晚報
Geming shiliao 革命史料

Guangming ribao 光明日報
Hong lou meng xuekan 紅樓夢學刊
Hong lou meng yanjiu jikan
　紅樓夢研究季刊
Hongqi 紅旗
Hong yan 鴻
Jianshe bao 建設報
Jiefang ribao (Yan'an) 解放日報
Jin Cha Ji huabao 晉察冀畫報
　[Harvard-Yenching Library]
Jin Cha Ji ribao 晉察冀日報
　[Hoover Institution, Stanford and
　People's University, Beijing]
Jingyan shi tongxun* 井鹽史通訊
Jiuguo bao 救國報
Kangdi bao 抗敵報
Kangdi bao zengkan* 抗敵報增刊
Kangdi waibao* 抗敵外報
Kangdi zhoubao* 抗敵周報
Liaowang zhoukan 瞭望周刊
Lishi yanjiu 歷史研究
Luxingjia* 旅行家
Meishu* 美術
Mingbao (Hong Kong) 明報
Nanhua ribao* 南華日報
Nanjing ribao 南京日報
Qianxian 前線
Qingshi ziliao 清史資料
Renmin huabao 人民畫報
Renmin ribao 人民日報
Renmin ribao tongxun*
　人民日報通訊
Renwu zazhi* 人物雜志
Rongshu wenxue congkan
　榕樹文學叢刊
Shehui kexue zhanxian 社會科學戰線
Shehuizhuyi jiaoyu hui baogao
　社會主義教育會報告
Shidai luntan 時代論壇
　[Beijing University Library]
Shishi leibian 時事類編
Shiwu bao 時務報
Suibi 隨筆

Tianjin ribao tongxun*
　天津日報通訊
Toyo bunka 東亞文化
Wenhui bao 文匯報
Wenwu tiandi 文物天地
Wenxian 文獻
Wenxue ziliao xuanbian
　文學資料選編
Xiaoyou zhiyin 校友之音
　[copy held by Ding Yilan]
Xiezuo 寫作
Xin guancha 新觀察
Xin jianshe 新建設
Xin wanbao (Hong Kong) 新晚報
Xin wenxue shiliao 新文學史料
Xin Zhonghua 新中華
Xinhua huoye wenxuan
　新華活葉文選
Xinhua ribao 新華日報
Xinwen gongzuo zhinan
　新聞工作指南
Xinwen jizhe 新聞記者
Xinwen shiliao 新聞史料
Xinwen yanjiu ziliao 新聞研究資料
Xinwen zhanxian 新聞戰線
Xingtai ribao* 邢台日報
Xuexi 學習
Xuexi yu sikao 學習與思考
Ye du 夜讀
Zhanxian* 戰線
Zhongguo gudai shi luncong
　中國古代史論叢
Zhongguo hua 中國畫
Zhongguo huabao 中國畫報
Zhongguo qingnian 中國青年
Zhongguo shehui jingji shi yanjiu
　中國社會經濟史研究
Zhongguo wenhua 中國文化
Zhonghua ribao (Thailand) 中華日報
Zhongshan wenhua jiaoyuguan jikan
　中山文化教育館季刊
Zhuanji wenxue 傳記文學

Glossary III: General Names & Terms

Ai Qing 艾青
Ai Siqi 艾思奇
An Ziwen 安子文
Bai jia yan 百家言
bandang 板蕩
Beigoukou (Pingshan) 北沟口
（平山）
beiju 悲劇
bian cai heyi 編采合一
Bianqu canyi hui 邊區參議會
Bianzheng daobao 邊政導報
Bo Yibo 薄一波
Cai Tingkai 蔡廷鍇
chailang 豺狼
Chang Guan Lou 暢觀樓
Chanping wang 鏟平王
Chen Erkang 陳兒康
Chen Hanseng 陳翰笙
Chen Mingshu 陳銘舒
Cheng Fangwu 成仿吾
Cheng Zihua 程子華
Chenjiayuan (Hebei) 陳家院
Chenzhuanghoushan (Lingshou county)
陳庄候山
Chi Wen-shun 紀文順
Chu Lucai 楚麓材
Chuang Hsin-cheng 床信正
da shoubi 大手筆
Dagan River (Wutai area) 大甘河
Dai Li 戴笠
dang xing 黨性
dao 道
dao dihou zhi dihou qu
到敵候之敵候去
Dazhuang (Hebei) 大庄
Deng Boyu 鄧伯禹
Deng Cuiying 鄧萃英
Deng Mengwei 鄧孟偉
Deng Mouqi 鄧茂七
Deng Ouyu 鄧鷗予
Deng Shubin 鄧淑彬
Deng Shuqun 鄧叔群
Deng Su 鄧肅

Deng Yizhong (aka Deng Ouyu)
鄧儀中
Deng Zhongzhou 鄧仲輖
Dianyun mantan 滇雲漫譚
diaocha 調查
Ding Wenjiang 丁文江
Diyi shan 第一山
Dong Lin shuyuan 東林書院
Dong Lu'an [aka Yu Li] 董魯安
Doucunbeigou (in Wutai) 豆村北沟
Du Guoxiang 杜國庠
duli sikao 獨立思考
dushe 毒蛇
Duan ku tang 短褲堂
Erzhuang (Pingshan) 二庄
fanmian cailiao 反面教材
Fan Wenlan 范文瀾
Fang Changjiang 方長江
Fang Shengtao 方聲濤
fanxing 反省
Feng Ding 馮定
Feng Shuhai 馮宿海
Feng Wenbin 馮文彬
Fu Yiling [aka Fu Jialin] 傅衣凌
Fuping xian (Hebei) 阜平縣
ganshi 干事
Gao Panlong 高攀龍
gaoji ganbu 高級干部
gaoji zhishifenzi 高級知識份子
gong fei 共匪
gongkai 公開
Gongli de xuangao 公理的宣告
gongtong de 共同的
Gu Xiancheng 顧賢成
Guan Xiangying 關向應
guihua 規劃
Guishan, see Yang Guishan
Gunlonggou (Hebei) 滾龍沟
guwen 顧問
Haihuiyan (Shanxi) 海會奄
hairen chong 害人蟲
hanghui 行會
Hao Qing 皓青

He Ganzhi 何幹之
He Long 賀龍
He Qifang 何其芳
hengha erjiang 哼哈二將
Hong Shui 洪水
hong wuyue tuji 紅五月突擊
Hu Kaiming 胡開明
Hu Qiaomu 胡喬木
Hu Renkui 胡仁奎
Hu Xikui 胡錫奎
Hu Yaobang 胡耀邦
Huang Jing 黃敬
Huang Qixiang 黃琪翔
Huang Zhanyun 黃展雲
Huang Zhou 黃胄
huodong 活動
Hutuo River 滹沱河
Ji Bufei 季步飛
Ji Lei Ji 雞肋集
jia 家
Jian Bozan 剪伯贊
Jiang Guangchi 蔣光赤
Jiang Guangnai 蔣光鼐
jiang yuan 醬園
Jiaodianzhuang (in Manshan) 蛟滇庄
jiaohua 教化
jie she lu qi 結社綠起
Jin Cha Ji bianqu 晉察冀邊區
jingshi 經實
jisheng chong 寄生蟲
jiti huodong 集體活動
jixu geming 繼續革命
juan 卷
jueju 絕句
junzi 君子
Kang Sheng 康生
Langyashan (Hebei) 狼牙山
laoshi (trusting) 老實
Li Changqing 李長青
Li Da 李達
Li Guangyuan 李光遠
Li Jishen 李濟深
Li Qi 李琪
Li Shiyue 李十月
Li Wen 李文

Li Xiaobai 李肖白
Li Xuefeng 李雪峰
Li Zehou 李澤厚
lilungongzuozhe 理論工作者
Lin Hujia 林乎加
Lin Xiling 林希翎
Lingshou xian (Hebei) 靈壽縣
Lishi gushi 歷史故事
Liu Aifeng 劉璦風
Liu Binyan 劉賓雁
Liu Bocheng 劉伯承
Liu Dianji 劉奠基
Liu Mengbei 劉孟北
Liu Qing 劉青
Liu Ren 劉仁
Liu Xiangwen 劉湘紋
Liu Yong 劉永
Liu Zhiming 劉芝明
Lixia manhua 歷下漫話
Lu Chishui [aka Kang Sheng] 魯赤水
Lu You 陸游
Lü Ji 呂驥
Lü Zhengcao 呂正操
Luo Gengmo 駱耕漠
Ma Dungu 馬沌古
Ma Tieding 馬鐵丁
Malancun (Hebei) 馬闌村
Manshan (Hebei-Shanxi) 漫山
Mao Zedong-zhuyi 毛澤東主義
maojin 冒進
Meng Chao 孟超
minzu 民族
minzuhua 民族化
mishu 秘書
nainai 奶奶
Nan Guan Cao 南冠草
neibu 內部
Pan Zili 潘自力
peihe 配合
Peng Dehuai 彭德懷
Peng Zeyi 彭澤益
Pingshan xian (Hebei) 平山縣
Qi Jiguang 戚繼光
qilü 七律
Qingchun manyu 青春漫語

Glossary

Qiu Lan [aka Qiu Xiying] 丘嵐（丘希映）
Qu Yuan 屈原
Qu Yunbai 瞿雲白
quan dang ban bao 全黨辦報
Quyang xian (Hebei) 曲陽縣
re nao 熱鬧
Ruan Muhan 阮慕韓
sanwen 散文
Sha Fei 沙飛
Sha Kefu 沙可夫
Sha River 沙河
Sha xian (Fujian) 沙縣
Shaan Gan Ning 陝甘寧
Shang Zhen 尚晨
Shanghai fandi da tongmeng 上海反帝大同盟
Shanghai fazheng xueyuan 上海法政學院
shehui jingji xi 社會經濟系
shelun 社論
shezhang 社長
Shi hua bao 實話報
shi min 市民
Shi Suozhen [aka Liu Mengbei] 史索真
shishi qiushi 實事求是
Shu Tong 舒同
shuji 書記
shusheng qi 書生氣
shuyuan 書院
siqing yundong 四青運動
siwei 思維
si wen 思文
sixiang 思想
sixiang fengmao 思想風貌
sixiangjia 思想家
Song Shaowen 宋劭文
Su Manshu 蘇曼殊
Sun Chuanfang 孫傳芳
Sun Yefang 孫冶方
Tang Tao 唐弢
Tang Yanjie 唐延杰
Tao Xisheng 陶希聖
tongxun fenshe 通訊分社

Tsou Tang 鄒讜
tun 屯
Wang Dongxing 王東興
Wang Kangzhi 王亢之
Wang Lixi 王禮錫
Wang Meng 王蒙
Wang Ruoshui 王若水
Wang Ruowang 王若望
Wang Zhiqiu 王治秋
Wei Qingyuan 韋慶原
Wen Shuyang (aka Yang Shu) 文淑陽
Wen Tianxiang 文天祥
wenhua sixiang 文化思想
wenren 文人
wenshi 文史
wenyan 文言
Wu Han 吳晗
Wu Jiang 吳江
Wu Lengxi 吳冷西
Wu Tong 吳同
Wu Yuzhang 吳玉章
Wu Zuoren 吳作人
wuse di 五色地
Wutai xian (Shanxi) 五台縣
Xia Yan 夏衍
xiandao 先導
xiangyue 鄉約
xiao baike quanshu 小百科全書
Xiao San 簫三
xiaobao 小報
xiaoren 小人
Xie Diannan 謝甸男
Xie Juecai 謝覺哉
Xin Changcheng 新長城
Xin kangdi bao 新抗敵報
xin wenyanwen 新文言文
xingshu 行書
xinwen ziyou 新聞自由
Xu Dixin 許滌新
xuanchuan 宣傳
xuanjiao xitong 宣教系統
xuanwan 樧腕
Xue Muqiao 薛暮橋
xuewen 學文
xuexi xiaozu 學習小組

Yan Lingfeng 嚴靈峰
yanshan yehua 燕山夜話
Yan-Zhao shi she 燕趙詩社
Yang Guishan 楊龜山
Yang Shangkun 楊尚昆
Yang Shu 楊述
Yang Wen 楊文
yangban 洋板
yang'ge 秧歌
Yao Wenyuan 姚文元
Yao Yilin 姚依林
Ye Shengtao 葉聖陶
Ye Shuiyi 葉水意
yecao she 野草社
yi li jiaomin 以禮教民
yi qi shi you 以啟詩友
yinxian 引線
Yixi tan 一夕談
yizhi 意志
yongyi 庸醫
Yu Li [aka Dong Lu'an] 丁力
Yuan Ying (1897-1953) 圓瑛
yunchou weiwo 運籌帷幄
zagan wen 雜感文
zawen 雜文
Zhang Bojun 張伯鈞
Zhang Chunqiao 張春橋
Zhang Dongsun 張東孫
Zhang Jiliang 張際亮
Zhang Junmai (Carson Chang) 張君勱
Zhang Lei 張磊
Zhang Ruihua 張瑞華
Zhang Shiji 張世績
Zhao Shuli 趙樹理
zhentu 陣圖
zhengdun 整頓
Zhengfeng wenxian 整風文獻
zhengguihua 正規化
zhibu 支部
zhishi xing 知識性
zhongdian baodao 重點報道
Zhongguo shehui kexuejia lianmeng
    中國社會科學家聯盟
Zhongguo zuoyi zong tongmeng
    中國左翼文化總同盟
Zhonghua minzu kangRi xianfeng dui
    中華民族抗日先鋒隊
zhongyang fenju 中央分局
Zhou Huaimin 周懷民
Zhou Xinmin 周新民
Zhou Yinren 周蔭人
Zhu Jingwo 朱鏡我
Zhu Yilin 朱毅麟
zhuguan jidong 主觀激動
zhun 屯
zhuren 主人
zhushou 助手
Zhuyu (Fujian) 竹嶼
zibenzhuyi mengya 資本主義萌芽
zixue 自學
zong bianji 總編輯
zongdui zhang 總隊長
zonghe 總合
zuohai wenren 左海文人

Index

aesthetic legitimation, *see* culture, as political tool
Ai Qing 121, 127, 169
Ai Siqi 6, 35, 40, 100, 118, 120, 169, 203-4, 313
Allito, Guy 6
All-China Journalists' Association 131, 146, 185, 209
Alliance of Chinese Social Scientists (*Zhongguo shehui kexuejia lianmeng*) 34
An Gang 79
An Ziwen 38
Apter, David 13, 311
art, *see* culture
Asiatic Mode of Production, *see* historiography
Asimov, Isaac 267
aufheben (sublation) 40, 244

Ba Jin 56
Band, William 88
Battlefront (*Zhanxian*) 80-1, 113
Beifang wenhua, see *Northern Culture*
Beijing Evening News (*Beijing wanbao*) 198, 200, 235, 240, 246-8, 271, 292, 298-9, 319
Beijing Party Committee, *see* Chinese Communist Party
Beijing University 149, 279-80
Beiping 78, 124, 130
Beiyu Party Committee, *see* Chinese Communist Party
Bethune, Norman 83, 88, 90

Blue Shirts 43, 52
  see also Dai Li
Bo Yibo 38, 295
Border Region, *see* Jin-Cha-Ji
Brook, Timothy 47
Bu Wuji (Deng Tuo) 182
Buchwald, Art 267
Buddhism 4, 31
bureaucracy 1, 3
bureaucratic authority 2, 11-13, 69, 86, 98, 155-7, 167, 203, 221, 291-2, 309-10
  see also charismatic authority

Cai Tingkai 42
Cai Yuanpei 46
calligraphy 3, 9, 30, 168, 233, 244, 259-60
  see also Deng Tuo, calligraphy
Caolanzi Prison 38, 159
Carlson, Evans 83
Central Committee, of CCP, *see* Chinese Communist Party
Central Hebei Guide (*Jizhong daobao*) 74, 82, 91, 112
Chang Guan Lou 191, 226-8, 251-3, 292
Chang duan lu, see *Long and the Short, The*
charismatic authority 2, 11-13, 69, 86, 98, 156-7, 167, 203, 219, 268, 291-2, 307, 309-10
  see also bureaucratic authority
Chen Boda 6, 94, 118, 161, 178
Chen Chunsen 78, 98, 113

Chen Duxiu 6, 116
Chen Hanseng 44
Chen Kehan 72, 111, 295
Chen Mingshu 42
Chen Qitong 175-7, 179, 207
Chen Xiaoyu 236, 239-40, 272
  see also Ma Tieding
Chen Yi 10
Chen Yun 171, 192, 210
Chen Yung-fa 13
Cheng Fangwu 79, 106
Cheng Zihua 103, 111
Chenjiayuan (Hebei) 84
Chiang Kaishek 32, 40
China Youth (*Zhongquo qingnian*) 133, 184
Chinese Academy of Science(s) 15, 149, 151
Chinese Communist Party (CCP) 10
  and intellectuals 7-10
  Beidaihe Politburo meeting (1960) 217
  Beijing Party Committee 91, 186-7, 203, 217, 220, 226-7, 231
  Beiyue Party Committee 114
  Beiping organization 52
  directives 112, 114, 135-6
  Discipline Inspection Committee 135, 142
  disaggregation of 20
  Eighth Party Congress 172-3, 189
    Ninth Plenum (1961) 226, 250-1, 256
    Tenth Plenum (1962) 229, 253
  General Line 139, 140
  inner-party democracy 170, 217
  literary policy 93-6
  Lushan plenum (1959) 189-91, 218

  mass line 66, 68-70, 82, 86-99, 105, 161, 193, 234, 255, 260, 263-4
  Military Affairs Committee 219
  Nanning Conference (1958) 190
  National Land Conference (1947) 130
  Northern Bureau of CC 72, 111, 113, 195
    Policy Research Office 129-30, 149, 308
  propaganda department 37, 124, 129, 130, 177, 220
  Seventh Party Congress 128, 310
  7,000 Cadres Conference (1962) 223, 228, 251, 253
  'two-line struggle' 218-19
  underground party 38
  work teams 279-80
Chinese Culture (*Zhongguo wenhua*) 120
Chinese Nationalist Party, see Kuomintang
Chinese People's Vanguard in Resisting Japan (*Zhonghua minzu kangRi xianfeng dui*) 51-2
Chinese Rural Economy Research Society (*Zhongguo nongcun jingji yanjiuhui*) 44-5
Christianity 4, 31
Chu Lucai 28
Chuang Hsin-cheng (H.C. Chuang) 20, 63, 256, 284
civil society 16
Cohen, Paul 5
Comintern 44, 48
Communist Manifesto 29
community compacts (*xiangyue*) 17, 86, 99, 119
Confucianism 3, 261, 275, 307-8

Cultural Revolution 2, 20, 137, 192, 234, 281, 284-91, 296, 307, 311
culture
  and intellectuals 18, 152-5, 309
  and propaganda vi, 86
  as elite arts 10, 18, 97, 152-5, 165, 199-202, 216-17, 233, 254-64, 300
  as identity 4, 152-5, 194, 232
  as political tool 4, 93-96, 216-17, 229-35, 231, 233-5, 237, 254-64, 310
  as symbol 4, 165
  Chinese culture 3, 126-7, 165, 194, 216, 259-61, 309
  defined 7
  institutional culture 67, 80-5, 108-9
  organizational culture 18
  political culture 67, 109, 259, 310
  two-track policy 95-8, 99-100, 103, 154, 156, 230-1, 244-6, 309

Dagan River (Wutai area)
Dai Li 38, 43
Dai Qing 13
Dan Wensheng (Deng Tuo) 189
danwei, see work unit
dang xing, see party character
Darwinism 4
December 9th Movement 51
Deliusin, Lev 140, 146-7, 162
democratic parties 175
Deng Boyu 27, 46, 52
Deng Chumin 46
Deng Mouqi 27
Deng Ouyu (Deng Yizhong) 27-9, 55, 56, 132

Deng Shuqun (1902-70) 27, 33-4, 56
Deng Su 27
Deng Tuo
  and Kuomintang 46
  and Mao Zedong 90, 100, 138, 147, 155, 157, 172, 176-81, 190, 198-9, 202, 309-10
    criticisms of Mao 225-6, 233, 253, 266, 277
    poem on Mao 101-3, 121
    Mao's *Selected Works* 101, 103-4, 129, 159
  and the Party 2, 66, 113, 129, 223
  and Policy Research Office 129-30, 149, 308
  and social history debates 32
  as administrator 125, 127-31, 129-30, 223, 226-8
  as aesthete 10, 18, 125, 152-5, 152-6, 165, 170, 199-202, 213, 254, 259-61, 290, 292, 300
  as doctor 14, 264
  as priest vi, 55
  as role model 296-301
  as theorist 3, 86, 93-6, 100, 130, 136-7, 169, 211, 220-3, 233-4, 254-65, 315
  as *wenren* (literatus) 53, 99, 138, 151, 216, 297, 310, 314
  biographies and reminiscences 6, 38, 44, 47, 52, 59, 70, 82, 107-8, 116-7, 110, 119, 234, 294, 296-301, 306, 313
  calligraphy 3, 9, 28, 102-3, 120, 168, 198, 199-202, 215, 245, 259-61, 292, 296, 300, 305
  commemorations of v, 21, 31, 295, 296-7

cultural policy as two tracks 95-8, 99-100, 103, 154, 156, 230-1, 244-6, 308-9
death 281, 283, 292-3, 307, 317
English ability 46, 83, 224
essays (*sanwen, zawen*) 87-91, 153, 169, 173, 182-4, 189, 200-1, 216, 226, 231-2, 238-46, 248-54
  see also *Evening Chats and Yanshan; Notes from a Three Family Village*
friends and family 21, 31
Fuzhou years 25-7, 29, 35-6, 38-9,
ghostwriting for leaders 131, 226
historical writing 32, 36-7, 46-51, 148-52, 195, 224-6, 300
illnesses 37, 91, 146-7, 153, 216, 293
journalism 68, 74, 86, 105, 125, 131-45, 128-9, 139-42, 173-4, 188-9, 248-54, 298-9
  on editorials 139, 143-5
  journalism policy 80-1, 139-45
Kaifeng years 44-6, 51-2
on dialectical materialism 39-42, 100-1, 137
on literature and *Yan'an Talks* 93-4
painting 31, 259-60, 292
poetry 9, 28, 30-1, 37-8, 51, 54, 68, 85, 89, 95, 96-8, 101-3, 114, 120, 186, 193-5, 198-202, 246, 296, 297-8, 300
prison 37-8, 52, 107, 205
propaganda work 1, 2, 3, 37, 51, 66, 85, 86-7, 88, 89-91, 113, 125, 127-31, 133-45, 191-3, 254-65, 308
rehabilitation 5, 293-4, 310

scholarly style 53, 98-9, 125, 148-52, 156-7, 170, 195, 196-202, 230-1, 254-65, 267, 298
Shanghai years 33-5, 37, 44-5
social circles 124-7, 157, 170, 292, 313-14
Soviet Union trips 140, 145-8
Deng Tuozhou (Deng Tuo) 25, 43
Deng Xiaoping 185, 186, 207, 226, 293
Deng Yun 56, 302
Deng Yunte (Deng Tuo) 46, 55-6, 195
Deng Yizhong, *see* Deng Ouyu
Deng Zhongzhou 27-8
Deng Zijian (Deng Tuo) 45, 55
dialectical materialism, *see* ideology
Ding Binggen (Deng Tuo) 35, 37
Ding Ling 10, 97, 127, 128, 159, 194
Ding Wenjiang 6, 32
Ding Yilan 55, 84, 114, 131, 160, 163, 178, 194, 295, 298, 304
Dittmer, Lowell 284
Donglin dang, *see* Eastern Wood Party
Dong Lu'an, *see* Yu Li
Du Fu 29, 260

Eastern Wood Party (*Donglin dang*) vii, 201-2, 262
Edmunds, Clifford 6
Eighth Route Army 71
  115th division 72
Engels, Friedrich 39, 100, 226, 263
essays, *see* Deng Tuo, essays;
  see also *sanwen, zawen*
establishment intellectuals, *see* intellectuals
Evening Chats at Yanshan (*Yanshan yehua*) 2, 20, 41, 111,

126, 183, 189, 191, 200, 202,
216-17, 218, 221, 226, 229-35,
238, 240-54, 256-65, 293, 285,
288-91, 295-6, 298
   audience 231-2, 240, 244-5,
   247, 257-8, 262
   chronology of essays 248-54,
   274, 319-29
   see also *Notes From a Three
   Family Village*

Fan Jin 91
Fan Wenlan 46, 199
Fan Xing, *see* Liao Mosha
Fang Ji 140
Fang Lizhi 290
Feng Ding 266, 280
Feng Suhai 122
Feng Wenbin 107
Feng Zhi 139, 162
Fisher, Tom 6
Fogel, Joshua 6, 111, 169
Four Clean-Ups movement, *see*
   rectification movements,
   Socialist Education Movement
Frontline (*Qianxian*) 186-7, 192,
   216-17, 218, 220-2, 229-30, 252,
   271, 283, 292, 319
Fu Jialin, *see* Fu Yiling
Fu Weiping 49
Fu Yiling (Fu Jialin) 29-30, 31,
   35-6, 39, 51, 53
Fujian rebellion 38-9, 42-5, 54
Fuping (Hebei) 72 , 89, 113, 115
Furth, Charlotte 6
Fuzhou (Fujian) v, 21, 25-7, 29,
   31, 35, 38-9, 44, 96, 126, 246

Gao Gang 136, 140, 142, 262
Gao Panlong vii, 201-2, 214, 262
Geertz, Clifford 19, 115

getihu (entrepreneuers) 5
Gilmartin, Christina 108
Goldman, Merle 232, 313, 316
Gould, Steven Jay 267
Great Leap Forward 2, 11, 155,
   187-93, 210, 223, 225, 226-9,
   232, 248, 250-1, 255, 309
Great Proletarian Cultural
   Revolution, *see* Cultural
   Revolution
Grieder, Jerome 19
Gu Hill (Fuzhou) 28
Gu Xing 198, 200, 212-13, 232,
   235, 241, 246-8, 271, 292, 296,
   299
Guan Xiangying 111
Guanghua University 34
Guangming Daily 186, 294, 298
Guishan, *see* Yang Guishan
Gunlonggou (Hebei) 84
Guo Moruo 30
Guo Xiaochuan 239
Guomindang (Chinese Nationalist
   Party), see Kuomintang

Habermas, Jürgen 15-16, 23
Hamrin, Carol 6, 11
Hao Qing 67, 96-7, 119
Haraszti, Miklós 16, 94
Harding, Harry 7
Harrison, James P. 150
Hartford, Kathleen 71, 93
Hayford, Charles 6
He Baogang 121
He Ganzhi 48-50, 63, 79, 127, 212
He Qifang 118
hegemony 87, 103
Henan University 27, 44-5
Herzen, Alexander 139, 162
historical materialism, *see*
   ideology

historiography
  Asiatic Mode of Production 49, 63
  biographies and reminiscences (Chinese) 38, 39-40, 44, 47, 52, 59, 70, 82, 89, 107-8, 116-17, 209, 210, 294, 299-300, 306
  biographies (Western) 5-6, 216, 234, 313
  Chinese Marxist 50-1, 116-17, 149-51, 224-6, 269, 299
  Confucian 50-1, 90, 117
  new sources on CCP history 20-1
  reminiscence literature (*huiyilu*) 31, 81-2, 91, 111, 115, 119, 234, 294, 296-301
  PRC reprints 49, 88-9, 116-17, 120, 162, 163, 210, 271, 295, 296-300, 303
  social history 5, 7
  social history debates in China 32, 46-50, 164-5
Holm, David 118, 119
Hong Shui 72, 110
Hou Xin 77, 111
Hu Feng 146, 172, 288
Hu Hua 207, 299
Hu Jiwei v-vii, 4, 140, 145, 163, 184, 185-6, 207, 209, 297-8, 316
Hu Kaiming 106
Hu Qiaomu 35, 147, 163, 178, 180-1, 185, 207
Hu Shi 149-50, 179
Hu Xikui 74, 106, 112, 113, 114, 129
Hu Yaobang 204, 295
Hua Junwu 238
Huairou Investigations 226-8, 250-2
Huang Jing 53
Huang Xianjun 186

Huang Zhou 152, 199
huiyilu, see historiography, reminiscence literature
Hulsewé A.F.P. 150
Hundred Flowers Movement, see rectification movements and Deng Tuo
Hundred Regiments Campaign 74

ideological remolding, see rectification
ideological struggle 114-15, 136, 156, 161
ideology 7, 20
  and culture 18-19,
  and propaganda 133-9
  and intellectuals 20, 125, 244
  and the party 7
  as method 19, 99-106, 125, 137, 156, 216, 221-3, 233-4, 244, 262, 264-5
  as motivator 87
  Chinese humanism 155
  historical materialsm 50
  see also Mao Zedong Thought
intellectuals vi, 6-7, 312-16
  and the party 2, 4, 7-10, 66-7, 86, 118, 136-9, 219, 261-2, 308, 314-16, 317-19
  and tradition 118, 230-1, 254-65, 307-8
  as cog & screw cadre 3, 69, 95, 97-8, 107, 125, 167, 169-70, 183, 193, 215-16, 230-1, 234, 267, 309-10
  as culture-bearing cadre 3, 20, 54, 69, 94, 97-8, 107, 125, 138, 167, 169-70, 183, 193, 197, 216, 222, 230-1, 234, 246, 256-65, 267, 287, 289, 308, 309-10, 315
  as Leninist cadre 4, 10, 54
  as priests vi, 55, 233

Index

autonomy 231-2
establishment intellectuals 8, 35, 68, 97, 123, 133, 135, 148, 157, 165, 184, 187, 190, 193, 224, 229, 279-80, 287, 293, 296, 300, 310-11, 314
  integrity 4, 196, 198, 216, 255, 261-2
  metropolitan intellectuals 67, 70, 84, 87, 91, 93-4, 108, 243
  political generations 54
  scholar-officials v, 10, 26, 216, 258, 264, 266, 297, 307, 310, 319
  wenren 2, 3-4, 53, 216, 230-1, 255-6, 314
intelligentsia, *see* intellectuals
Israel, John 301, 317

Japan 37, 76, 78, 84
Jesuits 23, 155
Ji Bufei 38, 43
Jian Bozan 6, 149, 151, 199, 223, 224-5, 266, 300
Jiang Guangchi 30
Jiang Guangnai 42
Jiang Qing 220, 279, 283, 284
Jin Cha Ji (Shanxi-Chahar-Hebei) 9, 11, 18, 65-108, 234
  Border Region government 72, 74, 92-3, 110, 114
  cultural organizations 79
  Military District 72, 74, 88, 110
  Party Committee 74, 77, 104-5, 113
Jin-Cha-Ji Daily (*Jin-Cha-Ji ribao*) 67, 77, 80-1, 92, 99, 106, 123, 299, 308
  rectification 81-2
  staffing 78, 82, 106
Jin Cha Ji Pictorial (*Jin cha ji huabao*) 88, 115

Jin Zhonghua 206
journalism 6, 14, 17-18, 316
  and propaganda 17
  socialist journalism 99, 105, 128-9, 139-45, 173-4, 188-9, 298-9
  see also Deng Tuo, journalism
Jowitt, Kenneth 10-13, 70, 162, 268, 309-10

Kaifeng 44-6, 51-2
Kalgan (Zhangjiakou) 78, 106, 127, 128, 129
Kang Cunhuai 78
Kang Sheng 10, 70, 200, 206, 213, 220, 251, 268-9, 274, 279, 282, 285, 292
Kangxi Emperor 17, 157
Ke Qingshi 173
Kelly, David 314, 317
Kenez, Peter 14, 69
Kikuchi, Saburo 127, 158
KMT, *see* Kuomintang
Knight, Nick 120
Konrád, George 94
Korean War 136
Kuang Rongrong 281
Kuomintang 4, 8, 27, 34, 37, 42, 46, 135, 308

Laiping (Hebei) 129
land reform 127, 129-30, 137, 149, 160
Langyashan (Hebei) 74, 112
Lao She 248
law 92-3
League of Left-Wing Writers 34
Lee, Gregory B. 271
legitimation 103
Lei Feng 230, 316

Lenin, V.I. 68-9, 80-1, 93, 94-5, 100, 109, 113, 134, 189, 244
Leninism 10-13, 309
  minority rights 4
Leninist response (Jowitt) 10-13, 70
Levenson, Joseph 154-5, 201, 308
Leys, Simon 1
Li Baohu (Zhao Zhensheng) 129
Li Changqing 74, 113
Li Da 36, 40, 100, 120
Li Dazhao 6
Li Fuchun 218
Li Gang 30
Li Gongchuo 51
Li Guangyuan 271
Li Jishen 43
Li Jun 187, 271, 283, 295
Li, Lillian 63
Li Qi 279
Li Shiyue 161
Li Tuozhi 31, 35, 44, 52
Li Wen 271
Li Xiannian 171, 295
Li Xiaobai 78, 112
Li Yafeng 47
Li Zehou 22, 60
Li Zhuang 145
Liang Qichao 6, 17, 29-30, 308
Liang Shuming 6
Liao Mosha 234, 235-6, 252, 253, 266, 271, 272, 287, 293, 299
liberalism 6, 20, 148, 189, 197, 286
Liberation Daily (*Jiefang ribao*) 76, 115, 239
lie zhuan (exemplary biographies) 117
Lin Biao 71, 157, 219-20, 251, 292, 312
Lin Hujia 295
Lin Jie 220, 288-90

Lin Maike, *see* Michael Lindsay
Lin Xiling 183, 188, 288
Lin Zexu 28, 54, 56
Lindsay, Michael 78, 82-3, 88, 114
literary policy, *see* Chinese Communist Party, literary policy
Literary Rectification (1942) *see* Rectification Movements
Liu Binyan 107, 122, 132, 146-7, 164, 183, 184, 196, 209, 211, 316
Liu Dianji 97
Liu Lantao 59-60, 103, 112, 113, 114, 130, 159, 295, 316-17
Liu Mengbei 237
Liu Menghong 246
Liu Ping 77, 79
Liu Qing 161
Liu Ren 91, 226-7, 283, 292
Liu Shaoqi 140, 167, 175, 192, 218, 220, 228, 280, 284
Liu Yong 31
Liu Yongcheng 150-1, 164, 165, 199, 213, 300
Liu Zihou 51
Long and the Short, The (*Chang duan lu*) 229, 235-6, 238, 271
Lu Chishui, *see* Kang Sheng
Lu Dingyi 163, 171, 207, 220
Lu Ping 280
Lu Xun 30, 56, 91, 97, 128, 154, 212, 238
Lu You 29, 260
Lü Kun 119
Lü Zhengcao 97
Luo Gengmo 44
Luo Jun 113
Luo Longji 209
Luo Zhanglong 45, 62
Lushan plenum, *see* Chinese Communist Party

Ma Hanbing 176

Index

Ma Nancun (Deng Tuo) 236, 240-1, 242, 244, 246, 248, 272
Ma Tieding 234, 238, 271-2
  see also Chen Xiaoyu
MacFarquhar, Roderick 192, 210, 218
Malancun (Hebei) 73, 246
Mao Zedong 6, 86, 110, 168, 232, 174-5, 239, 251, 274, 303
  and the CCP 3, 171, 228, 266, 291, 309-10
  Comrade Mao Zedong 74
  criticism of Deng Tuo 172, 176-81, 190, 198-9, 204
  Yan'an Talks 9, 93-4, 96, 104, 119, 147, 194, 244, 285
  see also *Selected Works of Mao Zedong*
Mao Zedong Thought (Maoism) vi-vii, 4, 6-7, 10, 66, 120, 128, 220-1, 224-5, 234, 307
  bureaucratic Maoism vi, 2, 66, 69, 98, 99-106, 124, 135-57, 167, 203, 215-17, 220-1, 249, 280-1, 291-2, 293, 311-12
  faith Maoism vi, 2, 18, 66, 69, 98, 167, 203, 215-18, 219-20, 249, 288-92, 311-12
  Yan'an 2, 218-19, 267, 291, 292, 311
Maoism, *see* Mao Zedong Thought
Mao Zedongism 85, 90, 104, 115, 121
Marxism-Leninism 3, 4, 8, 10, 26, 35, 53, 99, 141, 220, 224-5, 230, 307-8, 317
  as science 41-2, 161, 224-5, 315
  dialectical materialism 39-42, 100-1, 120, 161, 189, 197, 234, 262
  see also science

Mass Line, *see* Chinese Communist Party, mass line
masses 3, 15, 86, 94, 138, 141, 222, 310
Masses, The (*Qunzhong*) 116
May Fourth Movement (1919), *see* New Culture Movement
Mazur, Mary 6, 314
Mei Yi 153
Meissner, Werner 60
Meng Chao 271

Nakano Kenji 24
Nanhua Daily 35
Nanjing 33, 43
national forms of literature 94-5, 97, 194
  see also Chinese Communist Party, literary policy
National People's Congress (NPC) v
neo-traditionalism 3, 5, 12, 26, 54, 109, 115, 196
New China (Shanghai, 1930s) 39
New China Daily (*Xinhua ribao*) 80-1
New China News Agency (Xinhua she) 78, 174, 239
New Culture Movement 28, 32, 68, 118, 134, 194, 308
  and Deng Tuo 94-5
New Construction (*Xin jianshe*) 191
New Democracy 95, 102-3
New Great Wall (*Xin changcheng*) 74, 112
New Youth (*Xin qingnian*) 29-31
Nie Rongfu 159
Nie Rongzhen 1, 10, 87-91, 103, 111, 145, 159, 300

and Jin-Cha-Ji 9, 71-2, 73-4, 78, 92, 97
Nie Yuanzi 280
Nineteenth Route Army 42, 44
Northern Culture (Beifang wenhua) 106, 121-2, 127, 158, 160
Notes From a Three Family Village (Sanjiacun zha ji) 2, 187, 216-17, 221, 226, 229, 231-5, 236-7, 248-54, 256-65, 271-2, 280, 283, 288-91, 319-29
see also *Evening Chats at Yanshan*

Ovechkin, Valentine 164, 209

party character (*parti'nost, dang xing*) 81, 197, 223
pen-names 240, 273-4
Peng Dehuai 189-91, 202, 218
Peng Zeyi 164
Peng Zhen 9, 71, 73, 79, 89-93, 111, 112, 113, 124-5, 130, 158, 175, 184, 186-7, 203, 216, 220, 226-7, 247-8, 250, 261, 263, 266, 274, 279, 282, 283, 292, 293, 295, 309, 316
People's Daily (Renmin ribao) v, 2, 106, 124, 131-2, 135, 139, 140, 143, 144-8, 171, 184, 196, 216, 221, 229, 235, 246, 279-80, 292, 308-9
  Mao's criticism of 169, 172, 176-81, 190
People's Liberation Army (PLA) 220
poetry v, 9, 95, 127, 297-8
  see also Deng Tuo, poetry
Policy Research Office, *see* Chinese Communist Party, Northern Bureau of CC
political culture, *see* culture

Potter, Pitman 73, 92
Pravda 132, 134, 140, 209
  and Deng Tuo 132, 134, 140
  and Deliusin 140, 162
press, *see* journalism; propaganda; Deng Tuo
propaganda 13-18, 54, 133-9, 220, 254-65
  defined 7, 13-14, 89
  and culture vi, 86
  and Chinese culture 15, 86
  and journalism 14, 17, 86
  as political feedback 86, 222-3
  see also rectification
  internal propaganda 80-1, 114
  procedures 101
  system (*xuanjiao xitong*) 15-16, 23, 68, 123, 127, 129, 158, 160, 308
  tifa (phraseology) 131, 144, 160, 163
  work conferences 104-5, 140-1, 179, 206, 220, 251
  see also Chinese Communist Party, propaganda department; Deng Tuo, propaganda work
propaganda state 1, 13-14, 66, 69, 80, 86-7, 108, 148, 314
public sphere 13-18
  directed public sphere 16, 308, 316
purges 13, 70, 106-8, 282, 303
  see also rectification movements; Cultural Revolution
Pusey, James 17

Qi Benyu 169
Qi Jiguang (1528–87) 28
Qianlong Emperor 157, 208
Qiang Yi 113
Qin Mu 234, 237-8, 259, 266, 272
Qinghua University 33, 131

Qu Qiubai 94, 212
Qu Yuan (338–278 BCE) vi, 29, 283, 307
Qunzhong, see *The Masses*

radio 78, 113, 237
Ragvald, Lars 6
rational-bureaucratic authority, *see* bureaucratic authority
rectification (*zhengfeng*) 15, 137, 138, 177, 212, 284-5, 288, 294-5
   as a training system 15, 81-2, 197, 303
   as political feedback 135-6
   ideological remolding 81-2, 89, 125, 136-8, 141, 156, 161, 210-11
   managerial approach 98
Rectification Documents 85
rectification movements 8
   Yan'an 13, 70, 137, 182, 288
   Jin Cha Ji 70, 81-2, 85, 107, 114
   early PRC 133-8, 135-6
   Hundred Flowers Movement 2, 146, 160, 172-86, 238, 288, 303
   anti-Rightist campaign 184-5, 191
   Socialist Education Movement 228-9, 253-4, 260, 263-4, 280
   see also purges
remonstrance 4, 216, 232, 262
reportage (*baogao wenxue*) 117, 118, 173
Resistance News (Kangdi bao) 72, 75, 80-1, 86, 113
Resistance Weekly (Kangdi zhoukan) 74
rescue campaign, *see* purges
Resolution on Party History (1981) 116

Rittenberg, Sidney 59-60, 107, 122, 153
Rowe, William T. 164
Ruan Muhan 97

sacred editcts (*shengyu*) 17, 86, 99, 119
Safarov, Georgii Ivanovich 48, 50, 63
Saich, Tony 13, 311
Sanjiacun zhaji, see *Notes From a Three Family Village*
sanwen (lyrical essays) 140, 153, 237
   and Deng Tuo 153, 199
Schoenhals, Michael 163, 207, 269
scholar-official, *see* intellectuals
Schwarcz, Vera 196
science 137, 155, 161, 174, 257, 294
   as Marxism-Leninism 41-2, 137, 161, 244, 263, 315
Seignobos, Charles 36, 58, 59, 152
Selected Works of Mao Zedong 2, 101, 103-4, 121, 159, 219-21, 312
Serge, Victor 16
Sha Fei 72, 115
Sha Kefu 121, 159
Shang Zhen 44
Shanghai 33-4
Shanghai Academy of Law and Politics 36
Shanghai Anti-Imperialist Great Alliance (*Shanghai fandi da tongmeng*) 35
Shehui kexuejia yanjiuhui, see Social Scientist Research Association

Shanghai Academy of Law and Politics (*Shanghai fazheng xueyuan*) 36
Sheel, Kamel 6
Shi Suozhen, *see* Liu Mengbei
Shihua bao, see *Straight Talk News*
Shu Tong 113
Shu Xincheng 206
Sima Guang 50, 64
sixiang, see ideology
Social Scientist Research Association 34-5
Socialist Education Movement, *see* rectification movements
Song Shaowen 79, 97, 110
Soviet Encyclopedia 144
Soviet Union 9, 107, 132, 134, 140, 217
   de-Stalinization (thaw) 124-5, 145-8, 184
   press and propaganda of 14, 68-9, 158
Stalin, Joseph 100, 109
Starr, John 290
Straight Talk News (*Shihua bao*) 78-9, 99, 113
Stranahan, Patricia 37, 110
Study (*Xuexi*) 133, 161, 187, 188
Su Dongpo 29
Su Manshu 30
Su Shi 152
Su Shuangbi 282, 294, 304-5
Sun Fo 46
Sun Yatsen 159
Sun Yatsen Institute for Advancement of Culture and Education 46
Sun Yefang 9, 44, 192, 204, 210
Suzhou Reformatory 37-8
symbolic capital 13, 311
Szelényi, Ivan 94

Taihang region 112, 113
Taiyuan (Shanxi) 53, 71
Tan Xiwu 184
Tang Mingsui 151, 165
Tang Tao 235-6, 271
Tang Yanjie 90
Tang Yijie 280
Tang Yun 152
Tao Bai 37, 272
Tao Xisheng 47, 269
Teiwes, Frederick 15, 191, 219, 232, 268, 284, 302, 311
textual analysis 286, 288-91, 294-6, 304
Thomas, Lewis 267
Three Family Village 285-91, 292-5
   see also *Notes From a Three Family Village*
tifa, see propaganda
tradition, *see* culture
Trotskyism 47, 49
Tu Wei-ming 213

ultra-Leftism 193, 216-17, 218, 224, 231-2, 265, 267, 275, 294
United Front 6, 43-4, 73, 80, 93, 101, 124, 129, 159, 205-6
United States 27, 34, 82, 93

Vogel, Hans 151

Wagner, Rudolf 316
Walder, Andrew 108-9, 115
Wang Bisheng 116, 193, 210, 211, 298, 300, 306, 315
Wang Dongxing 295
Wang Jiaxiang 207
Wang Jingwei 116
Wang Kangzhi 106
Wang Lixi 32

Wang Meng 174, 196
Wang Ming 59, 62, 74, 85, 101, 111, 114
Wang Ruoshui 145, 178, 179-80, 186, 207, 209, 316-17
Wang Shiwei 10, 13, 98, 118, 172, 238, 285, 290
Wang Tao 6
Wang Xuewen 35
Wang Yangming 17, 119
Wang Yunsheng 206
Wang Yunwu 49
Wang Zhiqiu 199
Warsaw 145, 147
Wasserstrom, Jeffrey 6
Wei Qingyuan 164
Weigelin-Schwiedrzik, Susanne 270
Wen Hui Bao 173-4, 182, 184-5, 206
Wen Jize 161
Wen Shuyang, *see* Yang Shu
Wen Tianxiang 28, 30, 54
wenren (literatus), *see* intellectuals
work unit (*danwei*) 66, 76-9, 108
Wu Han 1, 6, 149, 184, 195, 223, 225, 234, 236, 253, 266, 271, 282, 286, 287, 293, 300, 314, 317
Wu Jiang 161
Wu Lengxi 185, 186, 197, 235, 292
Wu Nanxing (Deng Tuo *et al*) 236, 240, 271
Wu Tong 121
Wu Zuxiang 56
Wu Zuoren 152, 199, 246
Wushi Hill (Fuzhou) 26
Wutai (Shanxi) 71, 114
Wylie, Raymond 6, 104

Xia Wanshun 37-8, 59

Xia Yan 194, 235, 271
Xiang Lida 46
Xiang Yangsheng (Deng Tuo) 282
xiangyue, see community compacts
Xiao Jing (Deng Tuo) 36
Xiao Jun 10, 127
Xiao San 121, 159
xiaopin wen, *see zawen*
Xie Juecai 247
Xie Yaliao 152
Xin Jianshe, see *New Construction*
Xinhua she, *see* New China News Agency
Xu Dixin 35
Xu Linlu 152
Xu Maoyong 148
Xu Rende 287
Xu Zhucheng 173-4, 176, 184, 185, 206
xuanjiao xitong (Culture and Education system), *see* propaganda, system
Xue Muqiao 44
Xuexi, see *Study*

Yan'an 11, 96
 period (1937-47) 9
 and left-wing writers 97-8, 118
 rectification movement 13, 115, 159
Yan Fu 36
Yan Xishan 71
Yan-Zhao Poetry Society 96-8, 114, 118, 153-4, 185
Yanshan yehua, see *Evening Chats at Yanshan*
Yang Renkai 152
Yang Shangkun 285, 303
Yang Shu (also Wen Shuyang) 272
Yang Wen 161

Yang Xianzhen 6, 38, 100, 158, 159, 161, 168, 187, 195, 210, 220, 263, 266, 280, 293
yang'ge 95, 97, 119
Yao Wenyuan 6, 169, 220, 248, 282, 283, 285-8, 291-2, 294
Yao Yilin 74, 112, 113, 159
Ye Qing 60
Yen, James 6
Yenching University 82, 131
You Qi 111
youth 231-2, 246, 300
Yu Haocheng 317-18
Yu Li (Dong Lu'an) 79, 84, 97, 114
Yu Pingbo 172, 179
Yu Sui'an (Deng Tuo) 192-3
Yuan Shuibo 178
Yuan Ying (1897-1953) 31
Yuan Ying (1924–) 212, 296
Yue Daiyun 163, 279, 301
Yun Daiying 133

zawen (miscellaneous essays) 147, 181, 182-3, 189, 216, 229, 231-2, 235-46, 271-2, 290, 295-6
  xiaopin wen 238-9
Zhang Chunqiao 122, 140, 159, 220
Zhang Dongsun 39-42, 100
Zhang Fan 78, 81, 82
Zhang Jiafu 37
Zhang Junmai (Carson Chang) 32
Zhang Lei 165
Zhang Rengbei 140
Zhang Ruxin 106, 115, 121, 127
Zhang Ruihua 90
Zhang Shiji 271
Zhang Tiefu 239
Zhang Xueliang 42
Zhang Yide 294
Zhang Zhidong 17

Zhanxian, see *Battlefront*
Zhao Qingxue 85
Zhao Shuli 286
Zhao Tingxin 161
Zheng Banqiao 237, 260-1, 276, 289
Zhongguo nongcun jingji yanjiuhui, see Chinese Rural Economy Research Society
Zhongguo shehui kexuejia lianmeng, see Alliance of Chinese Social Scientists
Zhonghua minzu kangRi xianfeng dui, see Chinese People's Vanguard in Resisting Japan
Zhou Enlai 146, 171, 282
Zhou Huaimin 152, 199
Zhou Ming 111
Zhou Xinmin 36
Zhou Xiuchang 207
Zhou Yang 118, 127, 128, 134, 178, 194, 228
Zhou Zuoren 239
Zhu De 190
Zhu Muzhi 206, 207
Zhu Xi (1130-1200) 41
Zhu Ziqiang 112
Zhuge Liang 101, 103, 121
Zou Taofen 148
Zuo Hai (Deng Tuo as poet) 28, 186, 201, 246, 260
Zuo Lu 39-41

Printed in the USA/Agawam, MA
October 4, 2012

569517.045